America's Alternative Religions

SUNY Series in Religious Studies
Harold Coward, editor

America's Alternative Religions

Edited by Timothy Miller

State University of New York Press

Published by
State University of New York Press, Albany

© 1995 State University of New York

For information, address State University of New York Press,
State University Plaza, Albany, N.Y., 12246

Production by Marilyn P. Semerad
Marketing by Fran Keneston

Library of Congress Cataloging-in-Publication Data

America's alternative religions / edited by Timothy Miller.
    p.   cm. — (SUNY series in religious studies)
   Includes bibliographical references and index.
    ISBN 0-7914-2397-2 (alk. paper). — ISBN 0-7914-2398-0 (pbk. :
alk. paper).
    1. Cults—United States. 2. Sects—United States. 3. United
States—Religion—1960– I. Miller, Timothy, 1944– . II. Series.
BL2525.A55 1995
200'.973—dc20   94-16605
                                   CIP

10 9 8 7 6 5 4 3 2

In memory of William C. Shepherd

CONTENTS

INTRODUCTION

Timothy Miller

American religion has been going through a great diversification and decentralization in the waning years of the twentieth century. Some of the largest denominations have been losing members; world religions other than Christianity and Judaism have in some cases grown substantially; new and previously obscure groups have found themselves front and center in the news. Even within the large, traditional denominations, the forces of diversification are strong: witness, for example, the very substantial charismatic movement in the Catholic Church and most mainline Protestant churches.

This volume is a study of and guide to many of the most prominent alternative, or nonmainstream, religions. Most of the religions surveyed here have already been written about abundantly, in many cases by the authors of these chapters. What purpose, then, does this book purport to serve? First, it seeks to provide, at moderate length, sketches that will provide straightforward introductions to the various religions. Second, it seeks to impart a sense of the historical development of the groups in question, recognizing that no human organization is static, but that all change and mature over time. Finally, it seeks to convey objective sketches of the religions covered, free from the taint of either adulation or vituperation. A great deal of the available literature on alternative religions—in this case they are usually called

"cults"—comes from those determined to eradicate them, often in the name of another religion held to be the One True Faith. This volume, written by scholars with detailed knowledge of the groups they discuss, seeks a balance that much anticult literature lacks.

Alternative Terminology

Many terms are popularly used to describe what are here called "alternative religions." "Cult" is undoubtedly the most common; "sect," used in a variety of ways, is not far behind. In academic discourse those terms are related. "Sect" usually refers to a dissident group that has separated from another, usually mainstream, religion (often proclaiming its intent to recover principles or practices believed to have been present in earlier times but from which the denomination has drifted away), while a "cult" is a small, intense religious group whose ties to mainstream religion and culture tend to be less pronounced, one that often espouses a belief system not rooted in Christianity or Judaism and often under the personal direction of a single charismatic leader.

Despite the fact that both terms have useful definitions widely accepted by scholars of religion and society, they are largely avoided in this book, as they generally

1

have been by scholars for several years, because in popular use they have become largely pejorative. "Cult" today typically means a group that the speaker does not like, considers potentially harmful, and wants to deprecate. "Sect" is less intense, but still typically pejorative.

Scholars have used a variety of terms to avoid the negative connotations of "sect" and "cult." Some have employed "marginal," a term certainly less pejorative than "cult," but still one that tends to minimize the importance and value of the group in question. "Nonmainstream" has had some following, but it is cumbersome. "New religious movement" has been generally embraced by scholars and by adherents of the nonmainstream religions themselves, but it has at the same time been the source of confusion: does it apply only to truly "new" (at least in the United States) religions, or does it apply to all nonmainstream faiths? The prevailing tendency has been for the term to apply to a wide spectrum of religions, old and new, but it remains ambiguous.

It may be that no perfect term exists to describe nonmainstream religions succinctly, but this book adopts a usage that seems to be properly descriptive without bearing heavily pejorative connotations: alternative religions. Like other alternative cultural institutions (alternative newspapers, alternative theatre, alternative schools), alternative religions differ from their mainstream counterparts, but they are not inherently inferior to them.

Mainstream and Alternative: Finding the Dividing Line

One could not speak of alternatives without a center in relation to which the alternative groups play counterpoint. Mainstream American religion consists of the major (the most populous and socially well established) Christian and Jewish organizations and their adherents. It is comprised of the Catholic Church, the major Protestant denominations and their principal offshoots, the three nationally prominent

movements within Judaism (Orthodoxy, Conservatism, and Reform), and, by most measures, Eastern Orthodoxy.

Defining the mainstream precisely is impossible, even if its general contours are reasonably clear. Protestantism, especially, provides many borderline cases. By the broadest definition, Protestantism encompasses virtually all of Christendom not encompassed by Catholicism or Eastern Orthodoxy, even including, at the widest casting of the net, such groups as Mormons and Unificationists, groups that have incorporated important Protestant elements into their faith and practice but have also added more components that render them distinctly unorthodox. What of the Pentecostalists and faith healers, who believe devoutly in the teachings of the Christian Bible but have beliefs and practices quite alien to the majority of Christians?

Since a consensus definition of mainstream is impossible, this book imposes a defensible but arbitrary one: the Protestant mainstream consists of the various denominations of Lutherans, Episcopalians, Methodists, Disciples of Christ, Baptists, Presbyterians, and the United Church of Christ, along with the major groups with historical ties to those denominational clusters that have not veered sharply in new theological or social directions in breaking with the parent body—that is, such groups as the Churches of Christ and the non–United Church Congregationalists. We also deem mainstream many smaller groups with independent histories but social and doctrinal congeniality with the mainline denominations—the Reformed Church in America, for example, the contemporary descendant of the Dutch Reformed Church, whose mainstream standing goes back to early colonial days. Nondenominational churches also qualify in many cases. The mainstream is by no means monolithic; it includes a relatively broad spectrum of theological beliefs, from liberal to conservative, and liturgical practices, as well as a racially and culturally diverse constituency. If it has any single identifiable hallmark other than general identity with the overall Christian tradition, it is probably tolerance, a belief that the various mainstream groups, at least, are all essentially legitimate expressions of the historic Christian faith.

Similarly Judaism has a recognizable mainstream, consisting of Orthodox, Conservative, Reform, and perhaps Reconstructionist variants; as with mainstream Protestantism, all temples and synagogues are not alike, but there is a reasonably wide tolerance of diversity, both in matters of belief and in the extent to which one chooses to follow traditional Jewish law in daily life.

Unlike Protestantism and Judaism, Catholicism is still largely a single organization, one that has a remarkable history of being able to keep its dissidents within its walls. Dissidents there are, nevertheless, and while some agitate for change from within, others do leave—or are expelled, excommunicated—and start independent organizations. The situation of Eastern Orthodoxy is similar but not identical; it is composed of some dozens of independent historic churches, united by a powerful sense of history and common cause. While some of its members do leave for other spiritual venues, Orthodoxy has a good record for having sufficient latitude to satisfy the needs of a wide variety of potential sectarians.

Any proper definition of the mainstream, however, has to be flexible. Groups do come and go and experience changes in status. Two hundred years ago the Methodists were decidedly unconventional, but today they epitomize the mainstream. Quakers have been around quite a bit longer, and have moved substantially toward the mainstream, but are not, at least in all their branches, entirely there yet. Pentecostalists still have practices that distinguish them clearly from the traditional mainstream, but their growth has been so substantial that they will soon be—perhaps already should be—generally deemed a mainstream group (or, more precisely, cluster of groups) simply because the term "mainstream" ceases to make sense if huge masses of people are excluded from it.

Geography can make an impact on one's assessment of mainstreamness. Buddhism might logically be deemed mainstream in Hawaii, but in Kansas it would be decidedly unusual. For academics, discipline can make a difference: what the theologian sees as unorthodox might not seem so to the historian or the sociologist. Finally, one's own perspective makes a difference as well. Most people think of their beliefs and practices as normal, if not necessarily exactly like everyone else's, and have their own firm conclusions about what is conventional and what unusual. In any event, all analyses and boundaries must be fluid; different groups meet the needs of different people in different situations in different times, meaning that a sense of dynamism and development must be present in any analysis of the alternative religions. This book takes that dynamism as a central theme.

The Alternative Religions

Sociologists of religion have long tried to establish clear markers by which the mainstream denominations and the alternative groups may be distinguished. Categories in which such distinctions may fall have typically included the following:

1. Leadership: mainstream religions tend to have educated, paid clergy, while others tend to have charismatic and lay leadership.
2. Organization: mainstream groups tend to be highly structured and bureaucratized, while the marginal groups are less so.
3. Size: mainstream groups are big; non-mainstream groups are small.
4. Membership: mainstream groups tend to emphasize birthright membership and impose few specific standards of belief or conduct on members, while conversion and voluntary membership are the norm for alternative religions, which regard themselves as moral communities that exclude the unworthy.
5. Worship: mainstream groups tend to have orderly, calm, preplanned worship, while the marginal religions have fervent, spontaneous services.
6. Dedication to duty: mainstream bodies tend to be satisfied with once-a-week (or

less frequent) attendance, while other groups make more substantial demands on members' time, and tend to regulate members' lives more comprehensively than mainstream groups do.

7. Social status: the mainstream religions have intricate mutually supportive relationships with the wealthy and the dominant social classes, while the alternative groups often appeal to the poor, the uneducated, and the powerless.[1]

While some of those generalizations may have some basis in fact, none of them is entirely—or even, perhaps, mainly—accurate. Today, it is abundantly clear that nonmainstream religions draw members from the socially well connected as well as from less influential strata of society; in many cases they have bureaucracies and paid leaders; some of them (the Mormons are the best example here), are not tiny in size but are among the largest religious bodies in the country. A comprehensive system for distinguishing mainstream from marginal is elusive and will probably never be developed satisfactorily. Bryan Wilson, a leading contemporary sociologist of religion, contends that it is time "to recognize the impossibility—in any terms that are not unduly vague—of any *general* theory of new movements."[2] And Wilson does not regret the impossibility of the quest:

> If our study of new religions produces no unified theory to explain, under one set of theoretical propositions, all such phenomena, wherever they are found, we need not regard such a conclusion with alarm. It is a sociological bias— and an unwarranted bias—to suppose that comparative analysis should always lead to unified theory and universally valid formulations. Such a conclusion can be produced only by ignoring the importance of empirical evidence and the historical diversity of societies and their cultures, and only by subsuming factually diverse contents under highly abstract summary propositions which obscure by their abstraction as much as they illuminate about social reality. New religions throughout the world undoubtedly have some

features and functions in common, but they also manifest manifold differences, and the parts which they play in different societies are likely to differ as much as do those societies themselves.[3]

The Alternative Scene

America's alternative religions number several hundred, or perhaps a few thousand. Their members number one or two hundreds of thousands, or perhaps many millions. It all depends on how one defines "alternative," how one counts noses, and what threshold of size one uses in making up one's list (there are thousands of slightly offbeat local churches and equivalent organizations with handfuls of members; here we presume we are dealing with more substantial groups, those with at least a few hundreds of followers and more than one location). Those who decry the menace of the "cults"—whose book sales and platform invitations often depend on stoking public fears of a huge and imminently threatening network of cultic goons—tend to find more groups and members than most scholars do. Bob Larson, whose *Larson's Book of Cults* is an anticult bestseller, counts 1,500 to 3,000 "cult groups" whose "prolific growth" is "not likely to recede anytime soon."[4] A. James Rudin and Marcia R. Rudin count 1,000 to 3,000 groups with up to three million past and present members.[5] Flo Conway and Jim Siegelman in 1978 counted three million members in 1,000 groups—in addition to six million meditators.[6] Robert D. Hicks has found estimates ranging up to 3,000 groups and ten million members.[7]

While no accurate count can possibly be conducted, such figures are undoubtedly vastly inflated. Academic investigators David Bromley and Anson Shupe argue that "the claim that the new religions all have enormous memberships can only be accepted as the grossest exaggeration, and the further claim that they are spreading rapidly can be dismissed as virtual myth."[8] J. Gordon Melton, a ranking expert on alternative religions, provides substantial evidence for smaller numbers. His *Encyclopedia of American Religions*, the most exhaustive compilation of its kind, lists 1,730 bodies, including all of the mainstream groups and a fair number of defunct organizations.[9] Elsewhere, Melton concludes that some 500 to 600 groups could be considered alternative religions, and of them over 100 "are primarily ethnic bodies confined to first- and second-generation immigrant communities" that do not actively seek members from the general population. Noting that most of the groups have only a few hundred members each, he concludes that 150,000 to 200,000 is a reasonable estimate of membership in alternative religions[10]—a far cry from 3 or 10 million.

Other anticult claims tend to be similarly exaggerated. It is beyond the scope of this brief introduction to provide point-by-point analyses of all charges made by critics of alternative religions, but responsible scholars tend to agree that alternative religions are, although by definition unorthodox, not inherently evil in nature or intent; that they are not typically run by power-hungry leaders who utterly dominate zombie-like followers; that members are there voluntarily (if misguidedly, in the eyes of their detractors) and are not victims of brainwashing or mind control in any rational sense of those terms; and, importantly, that there are no reliable signs from which an outsider can accurately predict the rare case of a group's going errant.[11] A generation that has seen the nightmare of nine hundred induced suicides at Jonestown and the flaming deaths of some eighty Branch Davidians at Waco has every reason to want to protect itself against groups and leaders gone crazy, but few outsiders had any reason to fear terrible occurrences in the Peoples Temple, a congregation in good standing of the quintessentially mainline Christian Church (Disciples of Christ), or to foresee the federal assault on the Branch Davidians that touched off an inferno.

The anticult movement is composed predominantly of born-again evangelical Protestants, and much of their criticism is focused on the fact that certain religions do not teach orthodox Christianity. If one believes that only Christians of a certain stripe are right with God, then the loss of the rest of the human race is of course tragic. In a nation committed to freedom of religion, however, the non-Christian and the unorthodox have every right to espouse their beliefs and perform their own rituals. They may legitimately be targets of conversion attempts, but they should not be denied free exercise of religion.

Hostility toward alternative religions is not new. The early Mormons were persecuted literally to death in many cases; their founder was among the victims. Being a Quaker was a capital crime for a time in Massachusetts Bay Colony, and the authorities executed a handful of Quakers for their religious witness. Ferocious persecutions stud the history of Anabaptists. The Shakers, widely idealized today for their quiet charm and sublime furniture, were once accused of battery, enslavement and exploitation of members, and even murder.[12] A mob could burn a Catholic convent in Boston, and avowed anti-Catholics could be serious presidential contenders in the nineteenth century. Centuries earlier, when Christianity was new, martyrs' deaths abounded. Jews have suffered persecution unmatched in kind and scale. By comparison, the rhetoric and even the deprogrammings aimed at American alternative religions are mild.

Still, intolerance does thrive. The rise of deprogramming is a relatively recent development that uses sophisticated forms of psychological and physical coercion to separate believers from their chosen religious bodies. While the motives of those hiring professional deprogrammers for specific jobs are undoubtedly high-minded (it is hard to stand by idly if one believes that a close relative is having his or her life destroyed), deprogramming has nevertheless become a grave threat to religious liberty in the twentieth century. It does not, however, seem to be eradicating the alternative religions; although names of groups and faces of members change, nonmainstream groups are as much a part of the landscape as ever.

Any religion, indeed any group, can have a downside; many religions cause problems for some of their members. Thus religious groups should be subjected to occasional external criticism. As long as both a group and its detractors operate within the law and within the generally accepted confines of civil behavior, the result of the dialogue between supporters and opponents should be productive. Religion, like government and every other human institution, should never be above close scrutiny. But adults also deserve the freedom to choose their own spiritual paths.

Why Do People Join?

What is the underlying appeal of the alternative religions? That question has as many answers as alternative religions have members. Some join out of intellectual assent to the group's principles. Some are idealists who see particular groups as good vehicles for improving society. Some join because they like the people they have met in a group and feel at home there, just as they might join a mainstream religion for that reason. Some join communal movements for the security they offer. Many simply join experimentally, checking out life's options, which helps explain why alternative religions' attrition rates are so high. It stands to reason that most converts join for some personal gain; many point to benefits they have received from membership, ranging from improved health (often in the form of escaping drug dependency) to education and self-improvement to a sense of warm community to—not insignificantly—profound spiritual experience.[13]

Many anticult activists allege that recruits often join "cults" because they are subjected to brainwashing, to some sort of mind control. While it is true that religions of all types (especially conversion-oriented evangelical Protestantism) use psychological pressure to try to induce persons to join (what is more anxiety producing than the threat that one will suffer eternity in torment if one does not join a particular religion?), there is no evidence that most

alternative religions use, on a systematic basis, conversion techniques more intimidating than those generally accepted as legitimate in more conventional religious circles. Moreover, it is of significance that the typical former member of an alternative religion who alleges that he or she has been psychologically abused by the "cult" typically left the group via deprogramming—an admittedly intense use of sophisticated psychological tools and techniques designed to induce one to change one's mind and behavior. As Eileen Barker has put it, some of them are "*taught, while undergoing forcible deprogramming, that they were brainwashed.*"[14]

Certainly those who convert have some predisposition toward joining. Alternative religions often recruit among the young, whose lifeways are not yet firmly established and who are therefore open to new ways of thinking and behaving. Victor Turner and others have emphasized that the initiate joining a new religion or making other comparable life changes is in a state of liminality, of transition.[15] A person unsure about his or her future (one nearing completion of college and not sure what will follow, for example), or one who has gone through a major life transition (the breakup of a serious romance, for example), may be more open to a dramatic change of direction in life than one who is more settled. The fact that one is predisposed to a life change prior to conversion, however, hardly means that the conversion process itself necessarily involves ethically repugnant levels and types of psychological pressure that could be deemed mind control. James T. Richardson, after surveying a wide variety of scholarly and popular literature on the subject, has concluded that

> proponents of the brainwashing thesis . . . have not produced . . . hard evidence to support their position. From our perspective, the burden of proof is on those who proffer the brainwashing hypothesis. Until such evidence is forthcoming, we shall place confidence in the rapidly accumulating body of data which yields a more complex, if mundane explanation for the affiliation and disaffiliation processes.[16]

Many of those who allege mind control also decry the alternative religions for "totalism," for orchestrating virtually the entire lives of members. Certainly something like totalism exists in some religions, to some extent; as Bryan Wilson has written,

> New religions tend to set spontaneity, immediacy, and sincerity over against the cultivated and measured responses of conventional religion. They call for total allegiance rather than more regular and regulated religious observance. Thus they mobilize enthusiasm at a level which is not usually attained in traditional religion and which, when it does abnormally occur there, is a source of embarrassment to other believers, with their moderated expectations concerning religious performance.

Wilson goes on, however, to note that religions tend to have problems maintaining such intensity, that they soon are forced to undergo the phenomenon of routinization and emphasize stability over ecstasy.[17] In any event, it is worth noting that the most sustained example of "totalism" in the Western world has been Catholic monasticism, which demands obedience, voluntary poverty, total sexual abstinence, and lifetime commitment. The life may be intense and dedicated, but by no rational standard are most who choose to undertake such a path abused.

The brainwashing/totalism controversies aside, one can no more attribute conversion to a single cause than one can say that all married persons decided to get married for the same reasons. Humanity is more complex than that. Moreover, the world of alternative religions is a world of amazing diversity; groups differ enormously, and their appeal to specific persons varies widely. The peculiar chemistry of a particular individual and a particular group is different in each case.

to keep the volume to an acceptable length. In many cases separate but related groups are covered in single chapters, so that well over one hundred are covered in all, either explicitly or by implication. Nevertheless, hundreds had to be omitted.

Several standards were observed in the selection process. First, an attempt was made to include the groups that have received substantial publicity and are manifestly of considerable public interest. Second, smaller and shorter-lived groups were generally not included; those discussed had to have substantial constituencies, usually in the thousands, and to have been present in the United States for at least a decade or two. Third, they truly had to represent some notable departure from the religious mainstream (the Local Church movement, for example, is not a subject of a chapter because, although it is of Chinese origin and the subject of some controversy, it is essentially orthodox in its theology and practice). Fourth, they had to be essentially religious groups, not special-interest secular organizations or movements or spheres of interest (such as astrology) with spiritual overtones whose central concern is not typically considered religious; some would define the Masonic orders as religious, for example, but the Masons themselves, while admitting a substantial religious content to their practices, tend to be members of regular churches and do not define their religion principally in terms of Masonry. Fifth, an attempt was made to convey a sense of the wide variety of America's alternative religions, to include groups derived from mainstream Christianity and Judaism and from most of the other major religions of the world, along with some that do not derive directly from any established world religion, but have been created by American founders. Groups included here are from the Western hemisphere, the Near East, the Far East, white America, black America, Native America.

The Groups Covered in This Book

Since five hundred or more alternative religions were candidates for inclusion in this book, a winnowing had to be undertaken

Categories of Alternative Religions

This volume presents the religions it covers in categories. The selection and arrangement of the categories, however, proved complicated. There are many possible bases for categorization: geography (grouping religions by places of origin), major world religions (from which major tradition did an alternative religion derive?), theology, leadership and structure, and others. Some authors contributing to the book urged that we dispense with categories altogether, simply listing religious bodies alphabetically or by date of origin. Others feared that a given religion might be misunderstood if its chapter stood in a section with one or more specific other religions: who, for example, would want to be in the same category as Satanism? In some cases, accurate categorization of a given group was a perplexing task: Swedenborgianism, for example, has a historical presence tied to groups in the category of Ancient Wisdom and New Age (some regard the movement's founder, Emanuel Swedenborg, as the original source, over two centuries ago, of what is now called the New Age movement), but its denominational churches today are conservative and relatively orthodox Protestant institutions. The categories we are using emerged after much discussion, and are intended to help the reader understand where religious bodies stand in relation to other bodies, but they should not be taken as inerrant.

Whither the Alternative Religions?

Do the alternative religions embody the future direction of American religion as a whole? Will they one day pass from the scene entirely? Or will they stay as they have been, a small but enduring part of the religious landscape?

From a historical perspective, the answer seems clear. Religious dissent can be tracked as far back as religion itself. Innovators—variously known as prophets, messiahs, shamans, evangelists, seers, and the like—appear in every age. In the vast web of human society, each event has an impact, even if not necessarily a very large one. Some founders of new movements—

Jesus is an obvious example here—set in motion world-changing currents. Others have limited influence and are not long remembered, except perhaps by graduate students looking for dissertation topics.

The influence of innovative religions is limited in part because of the essential conservatism of a settled society. Most persons, finding sufficient reward (or challenge) in such mundane daily realities as job and family, are not prepared to chuck everything for a world-changing crusade. The average American is happy with blue jeans and is not terribly interested in donning saffron robes or saris. The majority would rather use their money to buy new cars than to support modern prophets. But, on the other hand, we are not all alike. There are always some who are prepared to go against the flow, persons who, their curiosity ablaze, want to check out the exotic, the new, the unusual. Some satisfy such cravings in secular ways, while others explore religious options.

That is not to say that the conservative majority displays no interest in the new and unusual. The historic emphasis on individualism, among other things, in the dominant Protestant religions has meant that innovations have not been entirely confined to the margins of American religious life. Revivalism and Pentecostalism, to name only two examples, are religious innovations popularized in America that have had profound influence on the course of American and world religion.

Changes in the larger society have encouraged American religion to travel in new directions during the last few decades. The social upheavals of the 1960s opened the eyes of many young Americans to new political and cultural options; from the idealism and search for meaning of that era came members for a number of religions newly established in the United States. The repeal of the Asian Exclusion Act in 1965 complemented the social ferment perfectly, permitting holy men (and occasionally women) from the East to teach their ways to eager young Americans.

We end where we began: Since about 1960, substantial decentralization has been taking place in the religious marketplace.

The Catholic Church and several major Protestant denominations are at best static in membership and in several cases are losing members. The exception to the pattern of membership decline in large denominations is found among the Southern Baptists, easily the most diverse and raucous of the large Protestant families. Growth is focused in small denominations, in independent churches, in non-Christian religions. In decentralization, religion is running parallel to trends in other parts of American life, as cable television, for example, undermines the mass markets of the networks and desktop publishing enables the flourishing of a myriad of tiny periodicals.

Tomorrow someone will leave a mainline religious body and join an alternative religion, perhaps even marry someone with a very different religious background. Some friends and family members of the convert will be outraged by the move, but life will go on. The great vitality of religion in the United States will be alive and well.

For Further Reading

A bibliography of other books providing reliable information on alternative religions is provided following appendix 1 at the end of this volume.

Notes

I wish to thank many of the authors whose work appears in this volume for their useful comments on earlier drafts of this introduction. I also acknowledge with gratitude support from the General Research Fund at the University of Kansas for portions of my own work published herein.

1. This kind of distinguishing between mainstream and marginal religions, traditionally known as the church-sect typology, can be found in many standard works of sociology of religion. See, for example, Ernst Troeltsch, *The Social Teaching of the Christian Churches* (New York: Harper and Brothers, 1960; first published in English in 1931), 331–43; Elmer T. Clark, *The Small Sects in America*, rev. ed. (Nashville: Abingdon, 1949), 218–31; H. Richard Niebuhr, *The Social Sources of Denominationalism* (New York: Meridian, 1957; first published in 1929), chapters 2–4; Liston Pope, *Millhands and Preachers: A Study of Gastonia* (New Haven: Yale University Press, 1942), chapter 7; J. Milton Yinger, *Religion, Society and the Individual* (New York: Macmillan, 1957), 142–55.

2. Bryan R. Wilson, *The Social Dimensions of Sectarianism: Sects and New Religious Movements in Contemporary Society* (Oxford: Clarendon Press, 1990), 204.

3. Bryan Wilson, *Religion in Sociological Perspective* (Oxford: Oxford University Press, 1982), 147.

4. Bob Larson, *Larson's Book of Cults* (Wheaton, Ill.: Tyndale House, 1982), 19, 22.

5. A. James Rudin and Marcia R. Rudin, *Prison or Paradise? The New Religious Cults* (Philadelphia: Fortress, 1980), 15–16.

6. Flo Conway and Jim Siegelman, *Snapping: America's Epidemic of Sudden Personality Change* (Philadelphia: Lippincott, 1978), 11–12.

7. Robert D. Hicks, "Police Pursuit of Satanic Crime." *Skeptical Inquirer* 14, no. 4 (Summer 1990): 378–79.

8. David G. Bromley and Anson D. Shupe, Jr., *Strange Gods: The Great American Cult Scare* (Boston: Beacon, 1981), 58.

9. J. Gordon Melton, *The Encyclopedia of American Religions*, 4th ed. (Detroit: Gale Research, 1993).

10. J. Gordon Melton, *Encyclopedic Handbook of Cults in America* (New York: Garland, 1986), 6–7.

11. See the bibliography at the end of appendix 1 for scholarly books that examine, and refute, these charges in detail.

12. For a summary of the wide array of alleged Shaker misdeeds, see Donald E. Miller, "Deprogramming in Historical Perspective," in David G. Bromley and James T. Richardson, eds., *The Brainwashing/Deprogramming Controversy: Sociological, Psychological, Legal and Historical Perspectives* (Lewiston, N.Y.: Edwin Mellen, 1983), 18–27.

13. For a discussion of benefits various group members believed they received, see Barker, *New Religious Movements: A Practical Introduction* (London: Her Majesty's Stationery Office, 1989), 25–31.

14. Ibid., 19.

15. See Victor Turner, *The Ritual Process: Structure and Anti-Structure* (Chicago: Aldine, 1969). Scholarly works that apply Turner's insights to American alternative religions include Robert Ellwood, *Alternative Altars: Unconventional and Eastern Spirituality in America* (Chicago: University of Chicago Press, 1979), 28–32; J. Gordon Melton and Robert L. Moore, *The Cult Experience: Responding to the New Religious Pluralism* (New York: Pilgrim, 1982), 47–60.

16. James T. Richardson, "The Brainwashing/Deprogramming Controversy: An Introduction," in Bromley and Richardson, *The Brainwashing/Deprogramming Controversy*, 11.

17. Wilson, *Social Dimensions of Sectarianism*, 211–12.

Part I
Established Christian Alternatives

Many American alternative religions are rooted in Christianity but have added new or unusually nuanced doctrines, scriptures, or practices to the mainstream Christian tradition. Several such movements have survived long enough to become generally accepted fixtures on the American religious scene, even if many other Christians do not regard them as entirely orthodox. In some cases their membership reaches into the millions, although in others members number only a few thousand. The groups presented in this section retain certain distinctive features but do not, by and large, any longer generate the controversy they once may have. They have become what sociologists of religion sometimes call "established sects."

That is not to say that these religions are never controversial. Christian Science, in its more than a century of existence, has been the focus of repeated disputes over its resolute aversion to most medical healing procedures, an aversion that has in some cases led to deaths of Scientists and their children. The unusual doctrines and practices of Mormonism, such as its belief that humans become Gods in the afterlife, its unorthodox prehistory of the Americas, its conduct of rituals closed to outsiders and even to some members, and its former practice of polygamy and exclusion of blacks from the priesthood, have made the Mormon Church the focus of repeated attacks, especially from evangelical Protestants. Now, Wesleyan Holiness believers are seldom accused of "sinless" perfectionism, and

neither they nor their estranged brothers and sisters of the Pentecostal movement are any longer commonly referred to as Holy Rollers. Yet the belief of Pentecostals in tongues-speech as an evidence of the baptism of the Holy Spirit and the emotional and freewheeling nature of their worship services continues to alienate many outsiders, and their advocacy of faith healing is often criticized by the majority who believe in conventional medicine. Jehovah's Witnesses are criticized for placing high demands and strict lifestyle requirements on believers. The Mennonites are, at least during wartime, calumniated for their pacifism, as are their fellow Anabaptists, the Amish and Hutterites. The Amish, moreover, are at times criticized for their aversion to modern technology and the Hutterites have been seen by some neighbors as growing too fast and pushing traditional family farmers out of the land and crop markets.

Controversy notwithstanding, however, these groups have all been present long enough and have survived controversies about their beliefs and practices well enough to become generally accepted fixtures on the American religious scene, and they promise to remain on that scene for the foreseeable future. Some, notably Pentecostalism and the Latter Day Saints, have experienced considerable growth in the twentieth century and may increase their stature in society still further. In that event they may eventually shed their alternative status and become currents within the religious mainstream.

Part 1
Established Christian Allegiances

1

THE ANABAPTISTS
Donald F. Durnbaugh

Once caricatured as the "Bolsheviks of the Reformation Era," the varied dissenters called Anabaptists by their enemies have survived persecution and infamy to become respected, if singular, religious bodies on the current scene. The most direct descendants of the Anabaptist movements are the Mennonites, the Amish, and the Hutterian Brethren. In addition, there are other denominations, such as the Baptists and Brethren as well as several communitarian bodies, who have been formatively influenced by the original sixteenth-century movement. Study of Anabaptist roots, development, and significance has become, in the past fifty years, one of the most actively pursued areas of scholarly research and publication.

Origins

January 21, 1525, is customarily cited as the birthdate of Anabaptism. On that date a small number of erstwhile followers of the reformer Ulrich Zwingli in Zurich baptized each other. They had previously concluded that infant baptism had no biblical base. Taught by their mentor Zwingli that traditions alone were insufficient grounds for churchly rites, they concluded that their own baptisms as infants were invalid.

In addition, they believed that Zwingli was compromising too much with the canton leaders, softpedalling his own religious connections for essentially political considerations. They began to doubt the entire system of church establishment, that is, the close collaboration between church and state, which had prevailed since the adoption of Christianity as the state religion from the time of Constantine and succeeding emperors in the fourth century. These "Swiss Brethren" came to believe that the church must be independent and free from political constraint, using only internal discipline to maintain its integrity and avoiding coercive constraint. Religious liberty and voluntary church membership (which came to be characterized by the baptism of adults only) became their criteria for the true church. Their goal was to be obedient and converted disciples of Jesus Christ, forsaking all other connection.

Response to the Anabaptist innovation of these Swiss Brethren came swiftly. The increasing numbers of their converts, cutting across class and economic lines, were pressed by the authorities to abjure their newfound convictions. Repressive measures ranged from fines, beatings, and expulsions to life imprisonment for those unwilling to recant. Soon authorities began to pronounce death sentences upon incorrigible Anabaptists. In 1527 Felix Manz was one of the first to die, drowned in the Limmat River, in mordant parody on his rebaptism. Persecution, however, proved for the authorities in some ways to be counterproductive. The people viewing the executions were impressed by the bravery with which the "heretics" met their fate; also those Anabaptists driven away spread the new and exciting gospel to other places. Indeed, similar dissenting views had independently surfaced in the South and North Germanies and the Low Countries.

Not surprisingly, given the feverish temper of the times, fanatics became active; they were also called Anabaptists by their opponents. In an effort to screen their movement from these enthusiasts, in February of 1527, Swiss Brethren leaders called a meeting at Schleitheim near Schaffhausen. The agreements there were concluded, called the "Brotherly Union," and were designed to distance the Swiss Brethren from the fanatics on the one side and the state churches on the other. The seven points accepted were: (1) baptism would be given to those who repented and walked "in the resurrection of Christ" manner; (2) the ban (exclusion) should be used to discipline those who fell "into error and sin," to be used for the purpose of restoration; (3) the Lord's Supper should be held in remembrance of the shed blood and bruised body of Christ; (4) Christians should separate themselves from the world; (5) conscientious pastors of good repute should lead their flocks; (6) the sword (coercion) was ordained by God but is outside the perfection of Christ; and (7) Christ's followers must not swear oaths.

Apocalyptic urgency permeated the movement, particularly in northern Germany among followers of Melchior Hoffman, an itinerant Lutheran evangelist who joined the Anabaptist movement in Strassburg where he was later imprisoned until his death. Hoffman's followers, called Melchiorites, anticipated the early return of Jesus Christ and sought to pinpoint the location of His arrival. They projected the early arrival of Christ in the city of Münster in Westphalia where Lutheran-minded reforming priests had introduced the Reformation, only to be supplanted by Anabaptist prophets of Melchiorite orientation. These prophets announced that Münster was to be the site of the New Jerusalem and soon found a fervent following. Scores flocked to Münster from the Low Countries, eager to await the imminent coming of the Lord.

The revolutionary Anabaptists seized control of the fortified city, alternating festivities and atrocities to control the population. They forced Münsterite residents of Catholic or Lutheran persuasion to leave the city. Münster was soon surrounded by a combined force of Catholics and Protestants. A long and grueling siege, ending through betrayal in 1535, resulted in the overthrow of the desperate defendants. The victors meted out bloody retribution to citizens; the tortured execution of the leaders ended the Anabaptist reign. The episode, although marginal to the essential story of Anabaptism, darkened its reputation for centuries. It seemed to confirm the authorities' worst fears about the dangers of the dissenting movement and to justify their brutal policies of repression.

The Mennonites

Scattered and disillusioned remnants of the Münsterites, along with the many Anabaptists who had never fallen into extremes, were gathered and pastored by several able second-generation leaders. Chief among these were the Frisians Menno Simons and Dirk Philips. They succeeded in leading, organizing, and shepherding congregations in the Low Countries and northern Europe. A grateful following accepted the name "Mennonites" to acknowledge the pastoral achievement of Menno Simons.

Only a small number of the Brethren in the Swiss cantons were able to persist in their faith. Most were hunted down unmercifully and expelled or killed. A few were able to hold out in the Emmental valleys near Bern. Many fled to the Palatinate in southern Germany or to the Alsace. Even more found refuge in Bohemia and Moravia, nominally under the sway of the Austro-Spanish Hapsburg emperors, but controlled in practice by the Czech nobility. The latter tended to favor the dissenters, who became known for their prowess in agriculture and crafts, their sobriety and diligence, and their humble attitude.

A considerable migration moved from the Netherlands through northern Germany to East Prussia. The Mennonites were skilled in reclaiming swampland by extensive drainage systems, thus creating new farm lands. These efforts paid off in important but not complete measures of toleration from the side of local governments. In the eighteenth century, a large migration of Mennonites ensued from Prussia to South Russia after Russian rulers extended significant and sweeping rights to attract these proficient farmers. By 1800 there were many thousands of Mennonites located there in self-governing colonies.

Mass Mennonite migration to North America began in the late seventeenth century, although there are scattered cases of Mennonites resident in the colonies before that time. The tolerant Quaker colony of Pennsylvania became the favored focus of migration following the landing of the ship *Concord* in 1683. Mennonites spread from Philadelphia into Chester, Berks, and Montgomery counties, but especially into what became Lancaster County. They later spread south into the Shenandoah Valley of Virginia and then west into the Ohio Territory. Few Mennonites until recent times settled in the Deep South because of their abhorrence of slavery. By 1900 they were found on the West Coast.

Participants in these migrations formed the (Old) Mennonite Church, which remains the largest of the Mennonite denominations. Its major centers are in Lancaster, Pennsylvania; Harrisonburg, Virginia; and Goshen, Indiana. Although Lancaster has no Mennonite college or seminary, Eastern Mennonite College and Seminary in Harrisonburg, Virginia, and Goshen College and the Associated Mennonite Biblical Seminaries in nearby Elkhart, Indiana, became intellectual centers and administrative offices followed. Herald Press in Scottdale, western Pennsylvania, is the publishing office of the Mennonite Church; annually it releases a large number of Anabaptist/Mennonite books. Goshen College sponsors the respected scholarly journal, *Mennonite Quarterly Review*. Worldwide adult membership in 1992 numbered over 160,000 in some 2,000 congregations.

There are other significant Mennonite denominations. The General Conference Mennonite Church derives primarily from later migrations, from Switzerland, the Alsace, southern Germany, and, especially, from Russia in the nineteenth century. To these elements were added in the mid-nineteenth century a reforming element from the older Mennonites. This arose from the efforts of the progressive leader John H. Oberholtzer. He was more open to American ways and urged his ministerial brethren to accept a constitution of his authorship to regularize church procedures. His opponents saw no need for this innovation and were content to follow the older, unwritten, traditional understandings (the order or *Ordnung*). A particular difficulty for Oberholtzer was the plain dress or "garb" that had become mandatory for members, in particular for church leaders. He saw no biblical imperatives for a certain prescribed form, while agreeing that all Christians should dress modestly. By 1847 disagreements over these issues led to a rupture and Oberholtzer and his followers departed.

In 1861 he made common cause with several congregations in Iowa to form a "general conference," understood as necessary to pursue church extension and evangelism. The new alignment linked recent immigrants from southern Germany and the Alsace with the progressive elements from eastern Pennsylvania. To this mix was added a large group of Russian immigrants in the 1870s and 1880s. They had left Europe because of the pressure of conscription and absorption by the Russian culture. General Conference Mennonites have been generally more open to higher education and participation in politics than have the (Old) Mennonites. They established Bethel College in Kansas and Bluffton College in Ohio; Newton, Kansas, became the center of denominational agencies. Adult membership in 1990 was about 33,000.

Among the many other Mennonite denominations in the United States and

Canada are the Mennonite Brethren and the Brethren in Christ. The former resulted from a religious revival in Russia in the mid-nineteenth century. Those who joined this movement were influenced by Pietist evangelists of Baptist persuasion. They urged a livelier and more spiritual worship experience, with greater emotional expression than had been traditional among Russian Mennonites. Their urging met with what could best be described as repression by the Mennonite leadership, precipitating a schism and the formation of a new religious organization. Mennonite Brethren also accepted through Baptist influence and their own study of the Bible the form of baptism by immersion rather than the customary Mennonite practice of baptism by pouring. They migrated largely as a body to North America beginning in the 1870s, with many settling in Canada. Hillsboro, Kansas, emerged as a Mennonite Brethren center, as did Winnipeg in Canada. Mennonite Brethren instituted several colleges in the United States and Canada and a seminary in Fresno, California. Their membership in 1990 was about 40,000.

The Brethren in Christ came from Mennonite stock in Pennsylvania in the 1770s. Here the precipitant was evangelical Christianity in the form of Wesleyan Pietism. With much of the early leadership coming from the Engel family, circles of believers began to meet to pray, sing, and edify each other. The break with the Mennonites came with the decision by members of the new movement to achieve apostolic baptism by immersion. They sought this without success among the German Baptist Brethren (Dunkers). Therefore, they proceeded to a river to baptize themselves, from which act came their nickname "River Brethren."

They grew modestly in numbers in the early national period. During the Civil War, as they sought to free their male members from military service, they found it necessary to take on a formal, legal name, Brethren in Christ, by which they are still known. Never a large movement, in 1990 their membership was about 20,000. They support two colleges, Messiah College in Grantham, Pennsylvania, near

Harrisburg, and Upland College in California. They have no separate theological seminary. Brethren in Christ are known for their ardent missionary program, and their union of Anabaptist and Wesleyan theological motifs.

Old Order Amish

The Amish represent the most conservative element of the Anabaptist movement. Because of their studied rejection of many aspects of modern culture (such as commercial electricity, motor vehicles, radio and television, high schools and colleges) and their sectarian patterns (beards and bonnets, plain dress, horse-drawn buggies and farm equipment, German speech, and strict church discipline), they attract the curious and are sometimes considered by outsiders to be the only Anabaptists.

Amish take their name from Jakob Ammann, possibly a convert from the Swiss Reformed Church. In the early 1690s, Ammann began to insist on greater rigor in church discipline, fearing that colleagues in the ministry had become too lax and lenient. They did not practice shunning (complete avoidance) of those considered to be sinners and were friendly with sympathetic members of the state church. These older ministers, led by Hans Reist, resisted Ammann's initiatives, which they felt to be presumptuous and unnecessarily harsh. Several meetings called by Ammann and his followers in 1693 failed to elicit unity, whereupon Ammann arbitrarily excommunicated all those leaders (and their followers) who did not accept his policies. Most Anabaptists in the Alsace and some in southern Germany and Switzerland followed the conservative leader in the schism.

Amish began migrating to North America in the 1720s, locating first in Berks County and then primarily in what became Lancaster County, Pennsylvania. Later migrations concentrated upon Ohio, Indiana, and Illinois, as well as Ontario, Canada. Holmes County, Ohio, today contains the largest concentration of Amish settlements. In 1992 there were about

63,000 adult Old Order Amish members in nearly 450 districts in twenty-two states and three foreign countries; if children living in Amish households are counted, the total Amish population numbers about 135,000. This size (and continual growth) is remarkable, when the predictions of social scientists in the early twentieth century are recalled: they confidently projected the early demise of the group because of its backward ways. Amish families customarily contain many children, about three-fourths of whom become members of the faith as young adults.

Despite this steady growth, over the years the Amish have lost adherents to related groups such as the Mennonites and the Church of the Brethren, and more recently to Bible churches. However, more serious loss has occurred through repeated division and consequent formation of new Amish sects. This process continues to the present. These divisions rarely come about because of divergence in doctrine. Rather, they ordinarily represent differing decisions by leaders about how the principle of nonconformity to the world is best maintained. Innovations such as the automobile, or the telephone, or rural electrification have often brought controversy. The Old Order Amish represent those who have sought most strictly to avoid intercourse with the world. It is not the case, as often presupposed, that Amish continue to live by eighteenth century patterns in the twentieth century, as a kind of fossil. Instead, as careful scholarship has demonstrated, their lifestyle demonstrates carefully considered adaptation of modern innovation. If appliances or inventions strengthen the family, church, and economic basis, they will be cautiously accepted. If they threaten the integrity of these central institutions, they are rejected. Thus, Amish may use propane lights, gas-powered stoves and refrigerators, and hydraulic-powered tools. Some Amish districts permit stationary or steel-wheeled tractors; others do not.

Although agriculturally based for centuries by conscious choice, today's Amish are increasingly entering other trades. These include cabinetmaking, construction, crafts, and other small enterprises that can be carried on in home shops. Some in Lancaster County even cater to tourists through the sale of baked goods, fruits and vegetables, and hand-sewn items. At the same time, the high price of farm land and the pressure of non-Amish population and visitors is motivating the migration of Amish to new areas of settlement, such as upstate New York or Kentucky. These areas promise cheaper land for farms, less intrusive visitation, and fewer government regulations.

The Hutterite Brethren

The beginning of the Hutterites, the longest-lasting communal movement in history, goes back to the dispersal of the Swiss Brethren movement after 1525. Many Anabaptists found refuge in Moravia, centering in Nikolsburg under the lord of Liechtenstein. Among the Anabaptists there, two principal groups emerged. One was led by Balthasar Hubmaier, an articulate theologian who had previously initiated the largest single Anabaptist congregation in Waldshut, South Germany, before being expelled by the authorities as a notorious heretic. A moderate in doctrine, he believed that Christians could be magistrates and government leaders, and that the latter were permitted to conduct defensive war. For this reason, he and his followers were nicknamed the "men of the sword." Another opposing group, inspired by the teachings of Hans Hut, contended for the strict nonresistant approach, and were nicknamed "men of the staff."

The lord of Liechtenstein, who himself had been converted by Hubmaier, asked the more radical party to leave his lands (partly in fear of his Austrian overlords). These Anabaptists, refugees once again, trudged away and made camp in a ruined village. Then, according to their chronicle, "at that time, these men spread down a cloak before the people, and every man did lay his substance down upon it, with a willing heart and without constraint, for the sustenance of those in necessity, according to the prophets and apostles." They took seriously the verses in the early chapters of the Acts of the Apostles where the first Christians are described as having all in common.

After finding shelter on the lands of other Moravian lords, the Anabaptists began to create their communal settlements; a colony or *Bruderhof* was a self-sufficient community, with clearly outlined duties and schedules for its members. Some early disunity threatened to break up the new movement, but this was resolved by the arrival of an Anabaptist leader from the Tyrol named Jakob Hutter, along with a number of other refugees. His wise guidance restored unity. Although Hutter returned to the Austrian lands where he was captured and martyred, the communal movement took his name and has since been known as the Hutterian Brethren, or, more colloquially, as the Hutterites.

By 1600 the Hutterites numbered about thirty thousand members in some one hundred colonies. The brethren were noted for their economic efficiency and prosperity, skill in crafts, universal adult literacy, successful schools, and missionary activity. This "golden period" of development was rudely interrupted by the violent Counter Reformation, pressed by the imperial forces. Catholic leaders were determined to retake territories lost to Protestantism and the Moravian lands were high on their list of priorities. Most Hutterite colonies were crushed, with great loss of life and property; some survivors were able to flee to Slovakia, and later to Transylvania, but these new colonies were again overrun by Catholic oppression, spearheaded by the Jesuits. A handful escaped to the Ukraine, where they finally found shelter on the estates of tolerant landowners. Here their numbers increased somewhat.

In the late nineteenth century, the remaining Hutterites were forced to move again when the tsars extended military conscription to their area. Some twelve hundred of the Hutterian Brethren moved to North America between 1874 and 1877, settling in the Northwest of the United States and the western provinces of Canada. About half of the emigrants chose to farm individually, while the rest took up once more the communitarian way. The first colony was at Bon Homme, South Dakota. In the course of the migration, three families of Hutterite colonies developed. They were called the *Schmiedeleut* (after their leader, a blacksmith), the *Lehrerleut* (after their leader, a teacher), and the *Dariusleut* (after their leader named Darius). Among outsiders, only experts can distinguish the three groups, who are similar in most respects in belief, teachings, and practices. To settle important matters, elders from all three groups gather on occasion.

Ironically, even the drastic and costly move to the New World with its promised religious liberties did not spare the Hutterian Brethren from serious problems. When the United States entered World War I in 1917, Hutterite men were drafted. Consistent with their age-old belief, they refused to drill and wear the uniform, bringing upon themselves the weight of military discipline. Two died after inhuman treatment in military prisons. Patriot mobs raided colonies to force the purchase of war bonds. These incidents led most colonies to decide to migrate to Canada.

Even there, Hutterites experienced discrimination. Some Canadian provinces legislated against them in the first half of the twentieth century, responding to complaints by individual farmers about unfair competition from the communal enterprises. Criticism centered upon the expansion of the colonies, as their high birth rate created the need for new land for expansion. In most cases, a *modus vivendi* was worked out, allowing the purchase of requisite land, although usually not in contiguous properties.

Although the Hutterian Brethren retain their German language and traditional lifestyle, in some ways resembling the Amish, they are up to the minute in agricultural practices. They employ the latest and largest farm machinery, often adapting commercial products to their own needs; they also have invented some of their own equipment. They use computers, radios, cellular phones, and fax machines—in fact, anything that will facilitate their economic pursuits.

Hutterite colonies maintain schools on their own grounds, with teachers supplied by local school authorities. Before and after these sessions, they have their own lessons, in which children learn by rote traditional prayers and doctrines. As in the case of the Amish, instead of dwindling, the Hutterian movement is expanding rapidly. The fecundity of its women, once among the highest on record, and the absence of birth control result in large families. Most children remain in the community, choosing to accept baptism ordinarily in the late teenage years. In 1990 there were over thirty-five thousand adult members of the Hutterian Brethren in nearly four hundred colonies.

In the 1920s, a modern communal movement patterned after the Hutterian Brethren emerged in Germany. It was led by Eberhard Arnold and his wife Emmy. After receiving his doctorate, Arnold pursued a career as an editor and evangelist, until his work was interrupted by the outbreak of World War I. His experiences in the German army, his disillusionment with the official church, and his growing conviction that only a radical Christianity could meet the challenge of the times, brought him to a complete rejection of the traditional Protestant cultural faith in which he had been raised. He and those he gathered around him were also profoundly influenced by the idealistic youth movement *(Wandervogel)* and Christian socialism.

The Arnolds began a commune near Fulda, Germany, that met with varying degrees of success over time. In his studies, Eberhard Arnold discovered the Hutterites of the sixteenth century and came to believe that they were the best example of primitive, radical Christianity. A friendly scholar informed him, to his amazement and delight, that the Hutterian Brethren still existed, alive and well in North America. In 1930 to 1931, Arnold visited all of the Hutterite colonies in the United States and Canada and was there accepted as one of them. Upon returning to Germany, he reorganized his colony along Hutterite lines.

Because of their communism, pacifism, and internationalism, the Bruderhof was suppressed by the Nazis in 1937 (some years after Arnold's death) and forced into exile. Members were enabled by the aid of sympathetic Dutch Mennonites to flee to England, where they reestablished themselves and won new converts. When World War II broke out, the generally tolerant English government informed the colonies that their German members would have to be interned. Unwilling to accept this disruption of their unity, the entire population of the Bruderhofs (German, English, and other nationalities) chose to migrate. They sought shelter in Canada and the United States without success. Paraguay was the only country willing to take them in. Between late 1940 and the spring of 1941 members braved the ocean voyage, despite the threat of submarine warfare.

The several-hundred–strong population of men, women, and children made a new beginning in the hot and unhealthy new locale, losing a number of children in the early days as they struggled to put roofs over their heads. In the 1950s, following severe internal struggles, the Paraguayan colonies were closed down and the Society of Brothers moved to the eastern United States. Its relationship with the older colonies in the West has been troubled. For a time, connections were completely broken off; they were then restored, and are currently strained. In 1992 there were nine colonies: three in New York, two in Pennsylvania, and one each in Connecticut, England, Germany, and Nigeria, with nearly two thousand adult members.

Other Anabaptist Groups

The several Mennonite groups, the Amish, and the Hutterian Brethren are the direct descendants of the Anabaptists. In addition, many other current religious denominations owe their origin in part to them. Among those that can be mentioned in this brief space are the Baptists, the Brethren, and several communitarian bodies.

The extent of the debt owed by modern Baptists to Anabaptism has occasioned vigorous debate among historians. An older school of thought considered Baptists to be the direct descendants of original Christianity, with Anabaptism an important vehicle of transmission in the centuries-long history. The predominant modern school of interpretation grounds Baptist origins squarely within Radical Puritanism in late-sixteenth- and early-seventeenth-century England, and much can be said for this perspective. However, other historians rightly point out that there were major influences by and connections with Anabaptism during the crystalization of early Baptism. This can be briefly sketched.

In 1607 John Smyth and his followers from a separatist congregation at Gainesborough sought shelter in Holland from a suppressive Anglican establishment. Their left-wing Independent (Congregational) position required that they be separate from the state. While in Amsterdam in 1608 and 1609, Smyth baptized himself and some forty of his followers after coming to the conviction of the error of infant baptism. This "se-baptism" (self-baptism) did not finally satisfy their consciences, however, and Smyth then sought affiliation with Mennonites. He died in 1612 before Mennonite acceptance was forthcoming. An associate, Thomas Helwys, led Smyth's followers back to England where they became known as the General Baptists. This group stayed in close and amicable touch with the Amsterdam Mennonites through correspondence and personal visits, although they differed on church-state issues.

Another, and eventually larger, Baptist strand of development took form in the early 1640s. Known as the Particular Baptists, they emerged from an Independent congregation at Southwark, coalescing about their conviction that immersion baptism was required of every believer. They heard that a society of Christians called Collegiants in the Netherlands practiced this rite. The Collegiants were closely linked to the Dutch Mennonites. The English dissenters sent a representative to the Netherlands to learn more about the Collegiant practice. Upon his return, the representative proceeded to baptize others, and in

this, the Particular Baptists took form. Thus, through both strands of the early Baptists, there are associations with Anabaptism. Recent discussions among Baptist and Mennonite theologians have affirmed both affinities and divergences.

Another Anabaptist-linked family of denominations is the Brethren, nicknamed for its baptismal practice of threefold immersion as "Dunkers." The Brethren emerged from Radical Pietism, a movement of reform and renewal within the German Lutheran and Reformed state churches after 1675. In some cases, Pietism became separatist and led to new religious initiatives. Those Radical Pietists who formed the Brethren movement did so in 1708 as religious refugees in Schwarzenau, Germany. Their leaders had close connections with German Mennonites, read Mennonite confessions of faith, and consciously adopted an Anabaptist concept of the church. Contemporaries called them "New Anabaptists" to link them with the "Old Anabaptists" or Mennonites.

The Brethren began to arrive in North America in 1719, and by 1735 almost all members of the movement had left Europe. In the American colonies they sustained their close connection with Mennonites, often settling in the same geographical areas across the nation. Both largely agricultural and sharing many beliefs and practices, the Brethren and the Mennonites were considered to be sister churches of "like precious faith." Frequent intermarriage strengthened these bonds.

As was the case with the Mennonites, the Brethren experienced division. The largest continuing body is the Church of the Brethren, with headquarters in Elgin, Illinois. There are six liberal arts colleges and one seminary affiliated with the Church of the Brethren; a scholarly quarterly, *Brethren Life and Thought,* is published on behalf of the church. From 1881 to 1883, a three-way split involved the mainline Brethren, a conservative wing (Old German Baptist Brethren—nicknamed the Old Orders), and a progressive wing (the Brethren Church—headquartered at Ashland, Ohio, and thus sometimes called the Ashland Brethren). In

1939 a split from the latter created the Grace Brethren Church.

Over the centuries, a number of communitarian bodies with Anabaptist connections have appeared. The earliest was an abortive settlement in Delaware created in 1663 by the Dutch Collegiant Pieter C. Plockhoy. The promising "commonwealth," which had official Dutch support, was destroyed by an English raid in 1664. More successful was the Ephrata Community of Lancaster County, a spin-off of the Brethren, established by its leader Conrad Beissel in 1732. It flourished during the colonial period, both economically and culturally. It was particularly famous for its choral singing, folk art *(Fraktur),* and publishing. The Ephrata Cloister (as it came to be known) was weakened, however, by the stresses brought on by the American Revolution and faded away in the nineteenth century. Its grounds remain today a favored site of tourist visitation.

In modern times, there are two significant communities linked with Anabaptism. One is Koinonia Farm in Americus, Georgia, founded in 1942 by a biblical scholar and social activist, the Baptist Clarence Jordan. This interracial colony suffered from bigotry and violence because of its firm but nonviolent stand for civil rights. An early program to provide decent housing for its black neighbors has flowered, under the leadership of Millard Fuller, to become the well-known Habitat for Humanity project, with ventures in many countries.

The second significant community to be linked with Anabaptism is the Reba Place Fellowship, founded in 1957 in Evanston, Illinois. Early members had been students and faculty members at Goshen College in northern Indiana, mightily influenced by the insights of scholars studying the origins of the Anabaptist movement. This "recovery of the Anabaptist vision," enunciated most vigorously by Mennonite scholar Harold S. Bender, provided the stimulus for the small group. They sought to realize this vision in urban America, hence the location in a racially mixed and run-down suburb just north of Chicago.

In the 1970s, Reba Place Fellowship was invigorated by the charismatic movement, gaining in membership and renewed vitality. In 1976 it chose to align itself formally with the Mennonite Church and the Church of the Brethren. The 1980s brought reorganization, allowing membership by individuals and families in the fellowship as well as those fully communal. It is considered to be the most successful post–World War II urban commune.

Suggestions for Further Reading

GENERAL
Durnbaugh, Donald F. *The Believers Church: The History and Character of Radical Protestantism.* Scottdale, Pa.: Herald Press, 1985.

AMISH
Hostetler, John A. *Amish Society.* 4th ed. Baltimore: Johns Hopkins Press, 1993.

ANABAPTISM
Estep, William R. *The Anabaptist Story.* Grand Rapids, Mich.: Eerdmans, 1975.

Klaassen, Walter. *Anabaptism: Neither Catholic nor Protestant.* Waterloo, Ontario: Conrad Press, 1973.

BAPTISTS
Torbet, Robert G. *A History of the Baptists.* Valley Forge, Pa.: Judson Press, 1973.

BRETHREN
Durnbaugh, Donald F., ed. *The Brethren Encyclopedia,* three vol. Oak Brook, Ill. and Philadelphia: Brethren Encyclopedia Inc., 1983–1984.

———, ed. *Church of the Brethren: Yesterday and Today.* Elgin, Ill.: Brethren Press, 1986.

COMMUNAL GROUPS
Jackson, Dave, and Neta Jackson. *Glimpses of Glory—Thirty Years of Community: The Story*

of Reba Place Fellowship. Elgin, Ill.: Brethren Press, 1987.

Lee, Dallas. *The Cotton Patch Evidence: The Story of Clarence Jordan and the Koinonia Farm Experiment.* New York: Harper and Row, 1971.

Saxby, Trevor J. *Pilgrims of a Common Life: Christian Community of Goods Through the Centuries.* Scottdale, Pa.: Herald Press, 1987.

HUTTERIAN BRETHREN

Hostetler, John A. *Hutterite Society.* Baltimore: Johns Hopkins Press, 1974.

MENNONITES

Dyck, Cornelius J., ed. *An Introduction to Mennonite History.* Scottdale, Pa.: Herald Press, 1981.

The Mennonite Encyclopedia, volumes 1–4 (1955–1959), volume 5 (1990).

2

SYMBOL AND SIGN IN METHODIST HOLINESS AND PENTECOSTAL SPIRITUALITY

Charles Edwin Jones

The Holiness and Pentecostal movements are sometimes regarded as one movement by outsiders because of their common emphasis on the present work of the Holy Spirit. Actually they are a mother and daughter estranged by mutually contradictory beliefs concerning the purpose and sign of the baptism of the Holy Spirit and by mutually incompatible modes of devotion and worship. The estrangement is rooted in differences over the uses of metaphor.

Because of its empirical bent, the twentieth-century mind is skeptical of the necessity of metaphor and wants to believe that it can be appropriated or discarded at will. In reality, whether observed or not, quite the opposite is true. In the void created by each overarching symbol lost, a new symbol inevitably appears.

Nowhere is the operation of this principle more apparent than in the spiritual history of the Holiness and Pentecostal movements in this century. Close neighbors on the ideological landscape at the beginning, both were caught up in the popular romanticism of the day. Both had roots in and stood outside the power structures of established Methodism. Both were convinced of the present activity of the Holy Spirit and were looking for the Lord's return. Both movements professed post-conversion experiences of purity and power which they identified as the baptism of the Holy Spirit. Many in each group had personal and family ties with members of the other. Sermons and testimonies of each abounded with allusions to biblical events and each sang from a repertoire reminiscent of the camp meeting and every-night mission of the recent past.

The Holiness movement is rooted in John Wesley's belief that in his death and resurrection Christ made provision for both acts of sin and the compulsion to sin. With Wesley, it maintains that Calvary purchased both forgiveness of sins (initial sanctification) and freedom from inbred sin (entire sanctification) for all who ask in faith believing. Holiness people hold that crisis experiences mark the beginning of infancy and maturity in the Christian life,[1] and that each experience will be evidenced by the witness of the Holy Spirit and by righteous conduct. A reaction to the decline in the middle years of the nineteenth century of Methodist emphasis on Christian perfection, the movement took shape under the leadership of Walter and Phoebe Palmer, John S. Inskip, William McDonald, and other eastern Methodists. Traditions and formulations developed by them were to leave a permanent imprint on thought patterns and institutions both inside and outside of episcopal Methodism.

Pentecostalism, which sprang up on the fringes of the Holiness ranks in the first years of the new century, stresses divine empowerment and supernatural intervention in the common life. It insists that the presence of the Holy Spirit will be signalled not only by an inner witness, but by charisms such as tongues, prophecy, and healing. Agnes Ozman, a student in the Topeka, Kansas, Bible school of Charles F. Parham, first spoke in tongues in the final hours of 1900. The insurgency gained widespread visibility after 1906 as a result of a protracted outbreak of charismatic phenomena at the Azusa Street Apostolic Faith Mission in Los Angeles. The leader was the black evangelist William J. Seymour, a convert of Parham.

Tongues-speaking, more than any other characteristic, set converts to Pentecostalism apart from onetime Holiness brethren. Controversy over tongues blinded both groups to fundamental differences between them in the manner in which scripture was to be appropriated. Neither side recognized the underlying cause of the impasse; neither, the basis of the confusion between them.

Pentecost could not at the same time be a lived-out metaphor and a repeatable event. This impossibility is made evident by examination of the analogies used by the two movements: the Exodus typology of Wesleyan Holiness and the latter-rain typology of the Apostolic Faith.[2]

Holiness people reclaimed the text by means of metaphor. They desired to epitomize the experience of entire sanctification, which they said freed the believer from the "bent to sinning"[3] and from fascination with worldly things. John Wesley regarded the doctrine as the "grand depositum of the people called Methodists."[4] Because, however, they also held it to be "the central idea of Christianity,"[5] Holiness teachers did not contend for exclusive use of Methodist terminology in proclaiming it.[6] Instead, they entwined vernacular idiom and doctrinal metaphor in such a manner as to make the biblical event and personal experience synonymous, and combined biblical, literary, and commonplace images in such a way as to differentiate infancy and adulthood in the Christian life. By use of symbol, they succeeded in making "second blessing" holiness comprehensible to multitudes both inside and outside the denomination.

Pioneers of the Apostolic Faith, on the other hand, sought to reclaim the text by literal reenactment. They did this by welding elements of the theology of salvation of Methodist Holiness and teachings concerning the end times of some in the Reformed[7] camp into a new amalgam: the Pentecost of the latter days. Holiness people, from Phoebe Palmer on, regarded the experience of the disciples at Pentecost as an archetype of the baptism of the Holy Spirit. To this, proponents of the Apostolic Faith added the typology of the early and latter rain. They read Peter's exposition[8] of Joel 2:28–32 on the Day of Pentecost as a prophecy of the revival of the phenomenon of Pentecost in their own times. They believed the movement in which they united to be the divinely commissioned instrument of the latter-day Pentecost. As such, it transcended every human tradition. Unlike many in the Holiness camp, few in the Apostolic Faith movement looked upon the reformation of Methodism as a worthwhile goal. They regarded themselves as the end-time counterpart of the disciples at Pentecost and considered the interval between the first and the twentieth centuries a period of spiritual drought.[9]

The Holiness movement, which had risen as an instrument of revival in the church, regarded the perfect love of God and man experienced by the entirely sanctified as the birthright of all Christians. All within it agreed with John Freeman Owen:

"Holiness is God's choice and plan for us even if John Wesley had been a horse jockey and Hester Ann Rogers had been a fortune teller."[10]

Affirmation of the universality of Methodism's "peculiar" doctrine fueled the Holiness movement's desire to establish forums for its propagation outside the church. The most influential and most copied of these were the Tuesday Meeting for the Promotion of Holiness in New York (begun in 1835) and the National Camp Meeting Association for the Promotion of Holiness (formed in 1867). By 1886, the cumulative total of National Association tabernacle and camp meetings conducted by evangelists associated with Inskip and

McDonald stood at seventy-six. That year more than two hundred cottage meetings modelled after Mrs. Palmer's were being held weekly. Through such agencies the Holiness message spread throughout the English-speaking world.

Prominent among those seeking entire sanctification in these meetings were wives of business and professional men and clergy of the established denominations on the eastern seaboard. None were recent converts. Most were first- and second-generation city dwellers far enough removed from the rigors of country life to idealize it and well enough grounded in the Scriptures and belles-lettres to internalize metaphors based on them. While other less spiritually minded members of the "leisure class" devoted themselves to club life, earnest Methodists pursued the "interior life"[11] in the parlors of like-minded city neighbors in winter and in mountain meadow and seaside encampments in summer.

Apologists made extensive use of metaphor pastorally. They dressed the quest for holiness in the cultural garments of the age. In sermon, song, and testimony they recalled the journey from sin to full salvation in a composite of images drawn from the Exodus, Isaiah's prophecy of the end of exile,[12] and Bunyan's allegory of pilgrimage.

They portrayed the entirely sanctified as modern-day Children of Israel who upon arrival in the Promised Land recounted their flight from bondage. Each stage was symbolic. The Red Sea crossing signified forgiveness of sins (justification); the forty years in the Sinai wilderness, struggle with the disposition to sin (the carnal mind); the Jordan crossing, heart cleansing (entire sanctification); and the conquest of Canaan, victory over sin (the life of holiness). The Land of Beulah, a place from which the Christian pilgrim could see over into heaven, represented the rest of faith of the sanctified. Sojourn there gave one heaven-in-the-heart even in adverse circumstances. Holiness shined in the faces and marked the actions and ethics of all who lived in Beulah. They voted for prohibition and inscribed "Holiness unto the Lord" on the walls of their chapels to remind themselves of the fact.

The Exodus typology held endless fascination for Methodist Holiness songwriters. In the course of a half century, they explored nearly every aspect of it. Stanzas which entwine several facets of the image— Scripture, doctrine, camp meeting, and natural setting—are linked by a refrain of testimony or shouting. Representative of this genre is "I've Pitched My Tent in Beulah." Written in 1908 by M. J. Harris during a camp meeting at Hollow Rock, Ohio, the text encapsulates the image:

I long ago left Egypt for the Promised
  Land,
I trusted in my Savior and to His
  guiding hand,
He led me out to victory thro' the great
  red sea.[13]

You need not look for me down in
  Egypt's sand,
For I have pitched my tent far up in
  Beulah Land.

I did not halt or tremble, for Canaan I
  was bound,
My Guide I fully trusted and He led me
  in,
I shouted, "Hallelujah, my heart is free
  from sin."

I pitched my tent near Hebron, there
  grapes of Eschol found.
With milk and honey flowing, and new
  wine so free,
I have no love for Egypt. It has no
  charms for me.

The singer is no utopian as she sets out for the eternal city. Outwardly, the way for the sanctified is the same as for others. The difference, Mrs. Harris believed, is an undivided heart symbolized by Beulah, that point of constancy in the internal terrain from which the sanctified can see over into heaven.

My heart is so enraptured as I press
  along.
Each day I find new blessings, which fill
  my heart with song.
I'm ever marching onward to that land
  on high.

Some day I'll reach my mansion that's
builded in the sky.

She is in fact remarkably like John
Bunyan's wayfarer, who late in his
"progress" passes through Vanity Fair, a
place identical in every particular to the
City of Destruction from whence he had
come. Vanity Fair and the City of Destruction are in fact the same place. It is rather
the protagonist Christian who has
changed. The entirely sanctified have
heaven-in-the-heart as they wander the wilderness of this world.

In contrast to the metaphorical understandings of the Holiness pioneers, the fathers and mothers of the Apostolic Faith
movement attempted to reclaim the biblical
text literally. They believed themselves to be
eyewitnesses to fulfillment of Joel 2. Rain,[14]
they thought, symbolized the baptism of the
Holy Spirit. The Pentecost of the first century then was the "former" or "early" rain
of autumn and winter, its twentieth-century
counterpart the "latter" rain of springtime.
Study of Acts showed that the "former" rain
had been signalled by tongues. The "latter"
rain would be also. Tongues was the sign,
they said, linking the two.

Reliance on belief in the relationship
between the two Pentecosts was characteristic. Focus on it caused D. Wesley Myland
to include in his work on the latter rain a
"Chart Showing Rainfall in Palestine from
1861 to 1907."[15] It likewise prompted B. F.
Lawrence to excuse modern "abuses of the
gift" by citing those "in the Corinthian
Church."

> There are abuses of the gift among us;
> there were in the Corinthian Church. If
> ours are therefore false, so were theirs.
>
> We are sometimes condemned as
> heretical, but we are the only body of
> Christians on earth to whom the 12th
> and 14th chapters of 1st Cor. are ap-
> plicable; we are the only body of Chris-
> tians on earth who do not forbid to
> speak with tongues.[16]

For the Apostolic Faith, tongues had become both sign and symbol of the baptism of the Holy Spirit.

Faith in the tie between the Pentecosts
of the first and twentieth centuries dominated the thinking and actions of followers of Charles F. Parham and William J.
Seymour. Workers in every-night missions
in Topeka, Houston, Los Angeles, and elsewhere expected to see the Day of Pentecost
reenacted in every service. Seekers received
the baptism of the Holy Spirit after the
manner of Acts 2. They "tarried" for the
enduement of power in an "upper" room.
They were "slain by the Spirit." They spoke
the heavenly language and sang in the
heavenly choir.

From the beginning, the primacy of
tongues, prophecy, and healing led to practical and theological problems. When pru-
dently used, these gifts endowed believers
with a sense of assurance and unity. When
abused, they spawned disillusionment and
division. Some during the Azusa Street revival in Los Angeles declared the banish-
ment by the Spirit of race discrimination
only to see its reappearance within months
in a split along racial lines. The result was
a competing fellowship formed by departing whites a few blocks away. Many believers abandoned doctors and medicine
and took the Lord alone as healer. A few
believed (until they tested it) that the
tongue they had been given was a foreign
language usable in missionary evangelism
and set out for foreign fields trusting providence alone for sustenance. Others, upon
discovering that in Acts baptism was "in
the name of Jesus," insisted on being rebaptized by that formula. Many gave up
belief in the Trinity as well.[17]

The first decades of the new century were
for inhabitants of the Beulah Land and
the Upper Room both the best and the
worst of times. For mature Holiness people,
metaphorical appropriation of Scripture
was at the height of its effectiveness. For
their children, however, the situation was
quite the opposite. Holiness parents expected children to absorb knowledge of the
tradition by osmosis. Educators appeared
to be at war with metaphor and children
taught to read by "Dick and Jane" found
the saga of Bunyan's pilgrim obscure. This
development, full of foreboding implications for the future, had little immediate
effect on the shape of the movement's
thought or the content of its worship. Holi-

ness people continued to sing with un-abated zeal of the Land of Beulah and the Altar of Sacrifice. Their out-of-fashion mind-set prevented them from becoming engulfed in the literalist tide which during these years swept over conservative Protestantism.

For the Apostolic Faith, the early decades were a time of conquest. Heralds of the new Pentecost displayed a vitality and aggressiveness both admired by and threatening to Holiness compatriots. Freed from the shackles of tradition and institution and spurred on by belief in the nearness of the Lord's return, its advocates went everywhere proclaiming this gospel of the Kingdom. Some, hearing the call to "Jerusalem," set out posthaste to lead Holiness brothers and sisters into the Apostolic Faith. Efforts toward this end met with a mixed response. Although Holiness editors had sometimes given positive assessments of the revival from a distance, firsthand contact of Holiness people with tongues-speakers nearly always elicited negative reactions. One pastor, put off by the disruptions of would-be latter-rain prophets, entitled his exposé of them *Satan in the Synagogue*.[18]

Externally, separation from parent bodies appeared to be a boon to both movements. Holiness churches were free to spread their version of Wesleyanism unhindered by the drift of the Methodist parent toward modernity. In the 1880s and 1890s, more than a dozen church bodies emerged,[19] most of whose membership was in the first decades of the new century gathered into the Church of the Nazarene and the Pilgrim Holiness Church.[20]

Holiness separatists found their most eager audience among native-born newcomers in the cities and in newly settled areas of the Southwest and West. Many recent arrivals gravitated to mission projects left behind by Methodist congregations moving from the central city. The Nazarene paterfamilias P. F. Bresee, who established a much-admired tabernacle church in downtown Los Angeles, said he desired to create an atmosphere where the poor would feel at home.[21] His focus, however, was not on the residents of skid row, but on people with families and self-direction.

For young people, who made up the bulk of the workers in the missions, marriage and children prevented every-night participation. Family responsibilities, they felt, pointed to the need for a stable environment. They moved to residential neighborhoods, often (as in Los Angeles) returning on the streetcar to the universally accessible tabernacle church downtown for worship.

When alternatives presented themselves in locations closer to home, however, pragmatic considerations prevailed. Holiness churches did not view relocation as an abandonment of the poor, but as a step necessary to conserve converts already made and to save the souls and stability of their own children. Accouterments, such as stained glass and pipe organs which at times came with Gothic and Romanesque buildings they inherited from mainline churches, seemed somehow out of keeping with a pattern of worship which had won for them epithets such as "Holy Roller" and "Noisyrene." It was in such settings, however, that they sought to reconstitute the worship of the camp meeting.

Pentecostalism found a receptive audience among displaced country folk and among ethnic and foreign-language minorities who found in its stress on power and supernaturalism a strong antidote to lack of status and helplessness. Preaching in schoolhouses, abandoned theaters, and mission halls, tongues-speaking evangelists convinced multitudes that the sights and sounds they had seen and heard were identical to those on the Day of Pentecost. This was that, they said, foretold by the Prophet Joel. If Holiness was a religion of the higher life, the Apostolic Faith was one of the common life. Pentecostals were as one in belief in the everyday presence and activity of the Holy Spirit. This expectation was at the heart of worship in the earliest days of the movement. And it continued to characterize their collective praise as they too departed the central city.

As Holiness churches began the long trek out along the streetcar lines toward the suburbs, they faced their own version of the ages-old dilemma of Christ versus culture, of investment in an out-of-fashion spirituality and of their children's and their own fascination with the present. Holiness newcomers were in fact fast being gathered into churches which found their raison d'etre in the aspirations of the faithful rather than the needs of the poor. Almost imperceptibly, a shift in priorities occurred in which conserving converts took precedence over rescuing the fallen. The salvation of their own sons and daughters replaced unknown outsiders as the aim of evangelism.

The exalted vistas of Beulah Land had been obscured by the inability of sons and daughters to apprehend their power and beauty and by attractions of the urban emporium near at hand. To gain the insulation needed for Holiness cultural and institutional survival, revivalists attempted to shore up boundaries between the church and the world. Appeals to the unconverted increasingly dwelt on worldliness and the sins of adolescence; those to the unsanctified, on surrender of desire for worldly approval and success. In order to "take the way with the Lord's despised few,"[22] seekers after entire sanctification were instructed to lay time, talents, ambitions, and the "unknown bundle" on the Altar of Sacrifice.[23] "Dying out" would bring one into union with God, the church, and God-fearing parents. The internal landscape as a metaphor of assurance of salvation had been exchanged for the alter covenant, a contract for conformity to the standards of the elders.

For many, this concerted and prolonged crusade to save Holiness children from worldliness had quite the opposite effect from that intended. Preachments concerning the illusive morality of stars of the silver screen whetted the appetites of many for forbidden fruit. Antics of adolescent rebellion in this era foreshadowed wholesale rejection of many of the convictions of the elders in the age of television which was to come.

The Holiness denomination subsumed the Holiness cause. Church standards supplanted individual convictions and promotion of programs and institutions replaced the authority of zeal and ordered aggressiveness of the early years. Entire sanctification, which faded as the central aspiration of many in the second and third generations, became instead the Holiness cultus. Christian perfection remained as the unassailable shibboleth of doctrinal affirmation long after fixation on numerical and financial prosperity had replaced personal and collective sanctity as the central agenda. The outlook and methods of the business corporation captured the collective mind; conformity superseded conviction as the mark of group identity.

The paths Pentecostals took led in unpredictable directions as well. The theology of the latter rain required continual reenactment of the Upper Room experience. In the every-night missions of its birth, what had begun as a movement for empowerment of already convinced Christians was soon transformed into a movement for primary evangelism. Appeals to the unconverted included the promise of healing for both body and soul. The administration of the gifts of healing, tongues, and prophecy required a large degree of flexibility and independence. Preparation for such ministry was ad hoc. As a result, a new kind of leadership emerged for which natural abilities and supernatural signs were the sole qualification. The charismatic leader and church rose and fell together. As in the case of the flamboyant Aimee Semple McPherson, the survival of a controversial ministry depended on the strength of the bond between the pastor and her gathered following.[24]

Radio and television upset this fragile relationship. The lack of binding discipline in the churches and the invisible tie between the radio or television preacher and his hearers was to undermine accountability. The electronic pulpit, by tailoring the message to the medium, placed the ego and finances of the preacher at the forefront. Personal and family corporations formed to shelter ministries, such as those of Oral Roberts, Kenneth Copeland, Jim and Tammy Bakker, Jimmy Swaggart, and others, relied on secular and legal expedients far removed from the rigorous behavioral standards and ethics of the pioneer generation. Babel echoed throughout the Upper Room. Gospel rock nearly drowned out the heavenly choir.

Tallies of Pentecostal church members who had never spoken in tongues stood in incongruous juxtaposition to official pronouncements on tongues-speech as the initial physical evidence of baptism in the Holy Spirit.[25] Had they been taken, polls of those in Holiness churches who had never professed entire sanctification would undoubtedly have produced similar results.

The rise in the 1960s and 1970s of Neo-Pentecostalism in the mainline churches—with its employment of a technique for receiving the gift of tongues, its belief in tongues as a special prayer language, and its perception of tongues as a sign of the "release" of the Spirit already given in baptism—posed a threat to the underpinnings of both movements. It met official resistance in both. The music developed by Roman Catholics and others in the renewal movement, however, gained wide currency in Evangelical circles. Both movements largely adopted the worship style of Neo-Pentecostalism. By the 1990s, many Holiness services were, except for tongues, toned-down versions of those of the Charismatics. Differences which remained

in self-image and shibboleth clouded recognition of their commonality.

Although each movement professed the experiences of the elders and attempted to set boundaries of fellowship on the basis of them, neither was successful in carrying the typological understandings or the creative separatism of its youth with it. Faced with the challenges posed by their own children, potential converts, and the technological revolution, they embraced much of the world their fathers and mothers had shunned.

The distance both movements had travelled was evident in the silent truce they declared in their ancient war with Hollywood and in the enthusiasm they showed for the politics and lifestyle of Ronald Reagan. The geniality and wit of the great communicator had a familiar ring to it. The metamorphosis that had occurred in Holiness and Pentecostal opinion concerning this divorced actor mirrored the transformation that had taken place in the thinking of the two movements.[26]

Pilgrim had settled down. He was now into product development and marketing.

Notes

1. The definitive statement of this teaching is William Taylor, *Infancy and Manhood in the Christian Life* (London: S. W. Partridge; New York: Carlton and Porter, 1867).

2. Apostolic Faith was the name first preferred by both proponents and opponents of glossolalic Pentecostalism. This name is used here to distinguish that group from Wesleyan Holiness people who in the first decades of this century often used Pentecostal in theological discourse and self-description.

3. From Charles Wesley's hymn, "Love Divine, All Loves Excelling" (1747).

4. Letter by John Wesley to Robert Carr Brackenbury, September 15, 1790.

5. See Jesse T. Peck's much-reprinted, often-abridged, *The Central Idea of Christianity* (Boston: Henry V. Degen, 1858).

6. Among Holiness people, the second experience of grace was variously known as entire sanctification, heart holiness, perfect love,

the baptism of the Holy Spirit, a clean heart, and the rest of faith.

7. See Edith Lydia Waldvogel (Blumhofer), "The 'Overcoming Life': A Study in the Reformed Evangelical Origins of Pentecostalism" (Ph.D. diss., Harvard University, 1977).

8. Acts 2:16–21.

9. B. F. Lawrence, *The Apostolic Faith Restored* (St. Louis, Mo.: Gospel Publishing House, 1916), 116–19.

10. John Lakin Brasher, *Glimpses* (Cincinnati: Revivalist Press, ca. 1954), 60.

11. In 1846, Bowdoin College professor Thomas C. Upham published *Principles of the Interior Life*, which by repeated reprinting and abridgment came to be regarded as a Holiness classic.

12. Isaiah 62:4 (AV): "Thou shalt no more be termed Forsaken; neither shall thy land any more be termed Desolate: but thou shalt be called Hephzibah, and thy land Beulah:

for the Lord delighteth in thee, and thy land shall be married."

13. It is possible that the lack of capitalization indicates double-entendre: the blood of Christ and the Red Sea. It is also possible that it is an indicator of careless editing.

14. Joel 2:23 (AV): "Be glad then, ye children of Zion, and rejoice in the Lord your God: for he hath given you the former rain moderately, and he will cause to come down for you the rain, the former rain, and the latter rain in the first month."

15. For rainfall chart, see D. Wesley Myland, *The Latter Rain Covenant and Pentecostal Power, with Testimony of Healings and Baptism* (Chicago: Evangel Publishing House, 1910), 178–179. For analysis, see D. William Faupel, "The Everlasting Gospel: The Significance of Eschatology in the Development of Pentecostal Thought" (Ph.D. diss., University of Birmingham, 1989), 62–70.

16. Lawrence, *The Apostolic Faith Restored*, 29.

17. W. J. Hollenweger, *The Pentecostals: The Charismatic Movement in the Churches* (Minneapolis: Augsburg Publishing House, 1972), 31–32.

18. See John Matthews, *Satan in the Synogogue: The Gift of the Spirit vs. the Tricks of the Devil; Jesus on the Pinnacle of the Temple [and] Satan at His Side; Satan in the Synagogue* (Kansas City, Mo.: [Publishing House of the Pentecostal Church of the Nazarene], 1915).

19. In 1926, the Nazarene historian J. B. Chapman speculated that "if the right men had taken the right steps at the right time, doubtless there would have been a [single] holiness church, as distinct and definite as the Church of the Nazarene, with a million members." See *A History of the Church of the Nazarene* (Kansas City, Mo.: Nazarene Publishing House, 1926), 21.

20. For time-line charts of mergers see Charles Edwin Jones, *Perfectionist Persuasion: The Holiness Movement and American Methodism, 1867–1936* (Metuchen, N.J.: Scarecrow Press, 1974), 122–23.

21. See the insightful biography by his contemporary E. A. Girvin, *Phineas F. Bresee: A Prince in Israel* (Kansas City, Mo.: Pentecostal Nazarene Publishing House, ca. 1916).

22. From Herbert Buffum's much-used altar song, "I'm Going Through" (1914), which glories in hardships ahead:

> I'd rather walk with Jesus alone,
> And have for my pillow like Jacob a stone,
> Living each moment with His face in view,
> Than stray from this pathway and fail to go through.

After World War II, singers usually substituted "anointed" for "despised."

23. Phoebe Palmer's chief contribution to Methodist-Holiness pastoral strategy was the so-called altar covenant. This analogy, based on Romans 12:1, likened the seeker after entire sanctification to an offering placed on the Altar of Sacrifice. In the Old Testament, the sacrifice was sanctified the instant it touched the altar; the self-offering of the fully consecrated believer would be also. Feeling had no part in it. The struggle which caused Mrs. Palmer to develop the altar covenant is recorded in Thomas C. Oden, ed., *Phoebe Palmer: Selected Writings* (New York: Paulist Press, 1988), 107–130.

24. Two books by Lately Thomas (i.e. Robert V. P. Steele), sometime disciple of Mrs. McPherson, make clear the power in crisis of this relationship: *The Vanishing Evangelist: The Aimee Semple McPherson Kidnapping Affair* (New York: Viking Press, 1959); and *Storming Heaven: The Lives and Turmoils of Minnie Kennedy and Aimee Semple McPherson* (New York: Morrow, 1970).

25. See Margaret M. Poloma, *The Assemblies of God at the Crossroads: Charisma and Institutional Dilemmas* (Knoxville: University of Tennessee Press, 1989), 39–40.

26. For analysis of the accommodation of a major denomination in each movement, see Ronald Paul Benefiel, "The Church of Nazarene: A Religious Organization in Change and Conflict" (Ph.d. diss., University of Southern California, 1986); and Edith L. Blumhofer, *Restoring the Faith: The Assemblies of God, Penetecostalism, and American Culture* (Urbana: University of Illinois Press, 1993).

Suggestions for Further Reading

HOLINESS

Dieter, M. E. *The Holiness Revival of the Nineteenth Century.* Metuchen, N.J.: Scarecrow Press, 1980.

Jones, C. E. *Perfectionist Persuasion.* Metuchen, N.J.: Scarecrow Press, 1974.

Peters, J. L. *Christian Perfection and American Methodism.* New York: Abingdon Press, 1956.

Smith, T. L. *Revivalism and Social Reform in Mid-Nineteenth-Century America.* New York: Abingdon Press, 1957.

————. *Called Unto Holiness.* Kansas City, Mo.: Nazarene Publishing House, 1962.

PENTECOSTAL

Anderson, R. M. *Vision of the Disinherited.* New York: Oxford University Press, 1979.

Brumback, C. *Suddenly from Heaven.* Springfield, Mo.: Gospel Publishing House, 1961.

Dayton, D. W. *Theological Roots of Pentecostalism.* Metuchen, N.J.: Scarecrow Press, 1987.

Harrell, D. E. *All Things Are Possible.* Bloomington: Indiana University Press, 1975.

Quebedeaux, R. *The New Charismatics II.* San Francisco: Harper and Row, 1983.

Synan, V. *The Holiness-Pentecostal Movement in the United States.* Grand Rapids, Mich.: Eerdmans, 1971.

3

THE ADVENTIST AND JEHOVAH'S WITNESS BRANCH OF PROTESTANTISM

Jerry Bergman

The Seventh-Day Adventists (SDAs) and the Jehovah's Witnesses (JWs) are the major surviving traditions that grew out of the Adventist Millennial movement of the middle 1800s. Although their history and many of their major doctrinal beliefs are similar, they differ radically on some issues, such as the desirability of higher education, the relationship of a Christian to secular society, and the propriety of military involvement. The differences are such that the Seventh-Day Adventists are generally respected in the larger society, while the Jehovah's Witnesses remain one of the most persecuted sects today.[1]

The major catalyst of the modern American millennial movement was Baptist lay leader William Miller. Originally a deist, Miller was challenged by friends to study the Bible alone, independent of others' interpretations. His study convinced him not only that the Bible was God's word, but that his generation would see the end of the world and the establishment of the millennial reign of Christ. He further believed that he had an obligation to preach his new insight to the world, and soon began speaking throughout the United States about his ideas. The first of such efforts was in 1831 at Dresden, New York.[2] The appeal of Miller's message grew so rapidly that within months he had to turn down speaking invitations.

Although he lacked formal theological training, a Baptist group licensed him to preach in 1833. In the same year he published a sixty-four page pamphlet, and in 1836 he published a book, *Evidences from Scripture and History of the Second Coming of Christ,* in which he predicted Christ's return about the year 1843. These publications, plus the journal *Signs of the Times,* edited by Joshua Himes, catapulted Miller's work into national prominence. The next decade found him working as a full-time itinerant evangelist, focusing on the imminent return of Jesus Christ.[3]

Millennial movements, although often at the outer edges of the formal denominations, have existed in Christianity since its start, and have played a major role in the history of the church.[4] Date-setting for Christ's second coming and speculation about whether current events prove that we are living in the end time can be found in most denominations throughout history. Movements which expect the return of Christ to bring a final end to the current evil order become especially popular in tumultuous times or in periods of great social change.[5] One of the first well-documented early millennial sects included the Montanists who spread from Phrygia, and included the church father Tertullian. A major difference between the mainline churches and Miller's movement in the 1830s was that for the latter, apocalyptic notions were a core teaching. They are still prominent today in the movement's modern offshoots.[6]

One of Miller's major conclusions was that Bible prophecy was like a treasure map; one only had to decipher the symbolism to find the secret path. Miller came to believe that a key to reading the map is the conclusion that a prophetic day is equal to a calendar year (Numbers 14:34; Ezekiel 4:6) and that, according to Daniel 8:14, after 2,300 days "the sanctuary will be cleansed," and after a period another seventy weeks, the "end of sins" would occur (Daniel 9:24–27). Putting these three seemingly unrelated pieces together, Miller concluded that the seventy weeks would last 490 years and end in 34 A.D., 3.5 years after Christ's death. Counting backward gives 457 B.C. as the start of the seventy weeks. Then, assuming that both the seventy weeks and the 2,300 "days" began at 457 B.C., he reasoned that the "cleansing of the sanctuary," which he took to mean the cleansing of the earth and the beginning of the millennial reign of Christ, would be 2,300 years later, or about 1843. Other lines of evidence also led Miller to the same date, confirming his belief that he had read the cryptic map correctly.

As the movement grew, the academic and religious community completed more careful evaluations of Miller's ideas. Many concluded that his date-setting eschatology was seriously flawed and, further, that he was preaching not just idle speculation, but definitely harmful ideas. The result was that "formerly cooperative churches closed their doors to Miller and his associates [and] numerous accounts appeared of ministers and laymen being expelled from their churches" for espousing his views.[7] Miller responded defensively and tightened up the vagaries of his pronouncements, stating, "I am fully convinced that somewhere between March 21st, 1843 and March 21st, 1844 . . . Christ will come."[8] As both the persecution and the movement grew, many of the adherents left the established churches and associated with each other in various informal networks. His estimated 100,000 sympathizers began to form loose fellowships whose leadership consisted primarily of the writers and editors of the various journals that were distributed among the movement's followers.[9]

After the March 21, 1844, deadline passed and Miller admitted that he was both disappointed and wrong, he and many of his followers remained confident that the return of Jesus was imminent. The publication of a new date, October 22, 1844, helped retain many adherents and attracted more followers. This date, now labeled "the great disappointment," was the last one published by the movement. After 1844, attempts began to organize the large number of scattered believers, requiring leaders to deal more honestly with their many date failures. Some concluded that Miller's chronology was basically correct, but in error by ten years. Some even reasoned that the millennium had already actually begun, and the saints must now wait for Christ's ceremonial return. What was to occur was believed to be a literal and visible event, but the reinterpretation taught that the major events predicted actually occurred, but could not be discerned except by signs or the evidence of faith, a response called "spiritualizing" the failure. (The *Watchtower* later taught that Christ "returned" in 1874, but only in the sense that he now turned his attention to the earth.) In the late 1850s, Adventist George Storrs began to preach and publish these ideas in his magazine *The Bible Examiner.* The writings of Storrs were to have a profound influence upon Charles T. Russell, the man who later founded the Jehovah's Witnesses.[10]

By far the two largest children of Miller's movement are the Seventh-Day Adventists, a church built mostly from the rubble of the 1844 disappointment, and the Jehovah's Witnesses. Among the other denominations that still exist today which came out of this period are the Advent Christian Church, which is doctrinally closer to Miller's views than any of the other Adventist groups, the Primitive Adventist Church and the Church of God, Abrahamic Faith. Many of the Adventist groups, including the Church of God and the Jehovah's Witnesses, denied the Trinity and taught that Jesus is the Son of God in a sense similar to that in which humans have sons, a doctrine that severely alienated them from many other Christian groups.

The movement that coalesced after the 1844 disappointment and became the Seventh-Day Adventists included Ellen G. Harmon, her husband-to-be James White, the sea captain Joseph Bates, and a small band of followers.[11] Mrs. White claimed to have visions, many of which formed the basis of her voluminous writing. She was soon accepted by many as a prophet, and under her charismatic leadership this group grew rapidly. Although the core beliefs that she espoused were inherited from her Methodist upbringing and the Baptist-Miller tradition, she was influenced by many others, including the Seventh-Day Baptists from whom she learned the concept of honoring the Sabbath on the seventh day of the week, Saturday (thus the name *Seventh-Day Adventist*, which was first used officially in 1860). They rationalized the 1844 date: It was correct, but they had expected the wrong event—Christ was not to come to the earth at this time to cleanse it, but was then to cleanse the *Heavenly* sanctuary, an event referred to as the "investigative judgment." The next step, which was expected to follow soon after 1844, was Christ's return to the Earth to take the faithful to Heaven.[12]

The many differences between the SDA and the mainline Protestant denominations include SDA's rejection of the innate immortality of the soul, the belief that all of the dead await the resurrection in an unconscious state, and a heavy emphasis on the Old Testament, especially its dietary laws which the church concludes require eating meat only from animals that chew their cud and have split hooves.[13] The SDAs accept the mainline doctrines of the Trinity, salvation by the atonement of Christ, the Bible as the fully inspired word of God, and an *ex nihilo* creation. The church has also always stressed world missions, healthful living (thus members do not use tea, coffee, alcohol, or tobacco), tithing, and responsibility for education and welfare programs, and it soon established several large publishing houses which now print voluminous literature, including numerous magazines dealing with health (*Life and Health*), theology (*Ministry*), current affairs (*Signs of the Times*), creation (*Origins*), and

religious freedom (*Liberty*). The SDA Church sent out its first missionary, John Nevins Andrews, in 1874, and has since expanded into a worldwide movement totaling more than five million members today. The primary SDA governing body headquarters has been in Battle Creek, Michigan (1863–1903), Washington, D.C. (1903–1988) and Silver Spring, Maryland (since 1988).

The founder of the Jehovah's Witnesses, Charles Taze Russell, was born in 1852 in Pittsburgh, Pennsylvania. Although relatively little is known of his early background, his parents were Scottish-Irish and he was raised a Presbyterian "indoctrinated from the Catechism."[14] As a young man, he became disillusioned with Christianity and fell prey to infidelity. Never totally losing his interest in religion, he soon attended a religious meeting in Allegheny, Pennsylvania, at which, he later stated, he first heard the views of the Adventists. The minister at these services, Jonas Wendell, caused Russell to firm up his "wavering faith in the divine inspiration of the Bible."[15] Russell soon accepted Adventist beliefs, concluding that we were now living in the time of the end, and that the world and all in it except the Adventists would be burned up in 1873 or 1874. His new associates included George Storrs, publisher of the *Bible Examiner*, H. B. Rice, the publisher of *The Last Triumph* (both of whom looked to the 1875 date), and N. H. Barbour.

Russell was introduced to Barbour in 1876 while in Philadelphia on a business trip. There he obtained a copy of Barbour's *The Herald of the Morning* and noted in its content a similarity to his own ideas, especially the conclusion that Christ actually had returned invisibly in 1874. He immediately contacted Barbour to arrange a series of meetings at Russell's expense. Major support for his conclusion that the Scriptures teach Christ's coming is invisible came from the Christadelphian Benjamin Wilson, who produced a bilingual New Testament called *The Diaglott*. In Matthew 24:27, 37, 39 it renders the Greek word παροθσια "presence" instead of "coming" as is used in almost all other English versions. From this, Russell and Barbour concluded that παρουσια actually means not a visible physical coming, but an invisible presence.

Russell's early contributions to the work were primarily financial. Following a conflict between him and Barbour, he withdrew his financial assistance from the *Herald,* which soon folded. In July of 1879 he began his own journal, *The Watchtower and Herald of Christ's Presence,* a semimonthly magazine which is still published today. The first issue had a printing of 6,000 copies, and as of 1992 it is published in 110 languages with an average printing of 15,300,000 copies.

In 1879 Russell married Maria Francis Ackley, a talented writer and an important *Watchtower* writer for almost a decade. She was listed as its associate editor for many years, and also contributed heavily to Russell's many books. The Watchtower movement actually began as a small Bible study group which included some of Russell's friends and his father, Joseph L., who died in 1897 at the age of eighty-four (his mother, Eliza Birney, had died when Russell was nine). Russell's marriage to Maria ended seventeen years later amid scandalous allegations of adultery, womanizing, cruelty, and financial mismanagement. Much was made of these charges, but little proof existed for most of them. However, judging from Russell's own testimony at the hearings relating to his divorce, he had no qualms about prevaricating if it would benefit him, and was unethical, unscrupulous, and egotistical. These traits of Russell resulted in numerous schisms, a problem which has plagued the Watchtower Society ever since. Accusations of dishonesty, immorality, and gross misuse of funds provided by members for the Watchtower's use have plagued them, and some of these have been proved. Especially during the administration of the second president, J. F. Rutherford, charges of the leader's adultery were common and occasionally rationalized by Witnesses because Rutherford's wife, Mary, who died in 1962, was an invalid. Rutherford's heavy drinking, smoking, swearing, pugnaciousness, high-style living in a California mansion, luxurious cars, and numerous long trips abroad also caused him to come under frequent attack.

The Witnesses have seen most of their prophecies proved false, and this has caused the movement major problems.[16] In 1876 Russell adopted not only the belief that the second coming had occurred in 1874, but also a teaching that the flock should prepare for the final climax which he expected in 1878. At this time, the gathered saints were also to be translated into spirit form.[17] The harvest deadline was soon extended to 1881, reflecting a prophetic failure which "precipitated a more serious crisis which required a longer period to assimilate."[18] The harvest was then eventually redefined to extend to 1914, a date which was discussed for almost twenty years.[19]

An 1877 publication, *The Three Worlds* or *Plan of Redemption,* discussed Russell's time prophesies. It predicted the end of the present system of things in 1914, a date his followers looked forward to and stressed from that point on. Russell died only two years after 1914, a disappointed man. The year 1914 was his third major prophetic failure, and it caused one of the most serious crises in the history of the movement. They had been preaching this date for decades, committing "the movement publicly to its prophesies in a firm and extensive way."[20] Attempts to explain what looked like another failure began as early as 1912.[21] The prophecies were revised, focusing first upon 1918, then 1925, and then 1975, the latter which proved to be the most disastrous of all predictions, resulting in upwards of a million adherents' becoming disillusioned and leaving the sect.

Joseph Zygmunt concludes that the believer's responses to these prophetic failures often involve an initial disappointment, then puzzlement and chagrin, and finally an adjustment involving explaining away the failure, or regressing to an attitude of watchful waiting for the yet-unfulfilled prophesies to in some way yet occur. In contrast, the SDAs, although stressing that we are in the last days and using much of the same line of reasoning as the Witnesses, have had far fewer difficulties with specifying dates in their publications.[22]

Major beliefs that differentiate the Witnesses from the mainline Protestant churches include their denial of the Trinity and the belief that God the Father has alone existed from eternity. God first created His son, Jesus Christ, who is a lesser god, inferior to the father. Their support for this position includes John 14:28, where Jesus said, "My Father is greater than I" and John 5:19 where Jesus said that he (Jesus) "can do nothing of his own accord." They teach that the Holy Spirit is not the third person of a trinity, or even a person, but simply God's active force. They cite Acts 1:8, in which Jesus says, "You shall receive power when the Holy Spirit has come upon you" and Ephesians 5:18: "Be filled with the Spirit," reasoning that only a disembodied force can come upon a person in this way.

Based on Scriptures such as Psalms 16:10, "You will not leave my soul in Hell," and Psalms 146:4, "His spirit goes out, he goes back to the ground, and in that day his thoughts do perish," they conclude that hell is only the grave and not a place or a condition where souls are punished. They also reject the immortality of the soul, using Scriptures such as Numbers 23:10, "Let my soul die the death of the upright ones" and Ezekiel 18:4, "The soul that is sinning, it itself will die." They conclude that the soul refers to life only and includes the lives of animals (Numbers 31:28; Genesis 1:21,24). Their belief that the eventual home for most righteous persons is the earth, where God's chosen will live on forever, is based on passages such as Revelation 21:1,4: "I saw a new Earth, for the former Earth had passed away and death will be no more." The earth will become a paradise (Luke 23:42, 43; 2 Peter 3:13; Acts 17:31; Isaiah 11:3–5) and even animals and humans will be at peace with one another (Isaiah 11:6–9). Conversely, heaven will be the home of only 144,000, a number which includes both Jews and Gentiles (Revelations 7:4). Those in Heaven will have the role of serving as co-rulers with God and Jesus over the earth.

The Witnesses' most controversial beliefs include their conclusion that the Watchtower Society is God's organization, and it is only through it that salvation can be achieved.[23] All of those who are not part of this "ark of salvation" will be destroyed in the Battle of Armageddon, which they still expect will come very soon. All other churches, therefore, as they are not in support of God's organization, are in opposition to it. The Witnesses are particularly hostile toward those religions with belief systems that compete directly with their own, concluding that they are being used by Satan to deliberately mislead people into everlasting destruction. All the religious ships in the water are sinking except one— and all of those that tell their members that they are safe are actually condemning them to their everlasting death. The Watchtower is adamant that Christians should have nothing to do with what they call the world, which specifically includes all political, economic, and governmental systems. In support of this they quote such Scriptures as 1 John 5:19, "We know we originate with God, but the whole world is lying in the power of the wicked one"; James 4:4, "Whoever, therefore, wants to be a friend of the world is constituting himself an enemy of God"; and 1 John 2:15, 16, "Do not be loving either the world or the things in the world. If anyone loves the world, the love of the Father is not in him." They define this separation as requiring avoidance of an extremely long list of activities which includes saluting the flag, becoming part of the armed forces, voting, running for office, any patriotic display, involvement in the sale or manufacture of weaponry, using tobacco, accepting blood transfusions, using most blood products, using pornography, celebration of birthdays, Christmas and all other holidays, membership in organizations such as civic groups, the Boy or Girl Scouts, and even participating in extracurricular school activities such as sports.[24]

Like the Witnesses, many of the SDA are conscientious objectors, although SDA can participate in a war effort in a noncombatant role as medics or health-care workers. The SDA church has always taught that the Bible forbids killing, even in a war situation, but noncombatant duties are an acceptable alternative to directly bearing arms.[25] In Germany during the twenties and thirties, the SDA central body ruled that each member could act in accord with his own conscience.[26] This was decidedly in contrast to the position of the Jehovah's Witnesses, who are total objectors and teach that the only acceptable stand is to resist becoming part of any armed force activity, including in a noncombatant capacity, by all possible means. Even working in factories which produce or sell war implements or in a hospital is forbidden. The only alternatives acceptable to Witnesses were prison, fleeing the country, or execution, and the first choice was by far the most common. Close to five thousand Jehovah's Witnesses were imprisoned in the United States during World War II, by far the largest number of any group of conscientious objectors.[27]

A Witness who violates the rules is to be expelled from membership, meaning that he or she is no longer able to have *any* association with his or her relatives, friends, or family who are still Witnesses. Those expelled are to be treated as if dead, although limited contact can be made strictly for business dealings, or, if a person's spouse is disfellowshipped, involvement in nonreligious conversations on nonreligious matters relating to the marriage is allowed. Marital sexual relations are allowed, but are often strained. In the case of disfellowshipped children who are not living with their parents, all communication is to be cut off. If it is determined that a Witness has not steadfastly complied with this rule, he or she will likely also be disfellowshipped.[28]

Seventh-Day Adventists have some latitude to try to work out local conflicts to meet the requirements of authorities without being deemed guilty of compromising their faith, but the Witnesses are not even to present *an appearance* of compromise. In Malawi, the government required all citizens to obtain identification cards, but the Watchtower hierarchy determined that the purchase of such gave the appearance of belonging to a political party, something which they deem totally unacceptable. Witnesses are to behave like ambassadors in the nations that they find themselves living in, and as such are not to involve themselves in any local political affairs.[29]

Conversely, the SDAs are at times more involved in the political affairs of their nations than the Witnesses. For example, most German SDA journals consistently expressed "support for Hitler and Nazism," even condemning Germany's enemies, including Jews, as "inspired by the spirit of Satan."[30] Identifying with nationalist Germans, they welcomed "with joy the reawakening of Germany and the fight of Hitler's government . . . for morality and order, incorruptibility and justice in government, for the attack on class consciousness and the elevation of the ethnic community. . . . The Christian is happy to know that the direction of his country is in the hands of a man like Hitler . . . a nondrinker, non-smoker and vegetarian."[31] Although much friction existed, such as over the Adventists' teaching that members should not involve themselves in work or military activities or attend school on Saturday, they believed that whatever must be done for the church to survive was necessary, even if it meant some compromising. Nonetheless, the Nazi government was by no means convinced of SDA loyalty: its roots were in America, and they regarded it as a foreign sect having the potential of causing problems. SDA services were often monitored by Gestapo officers, their literature was scrutinized, and much discrimination against Adventists existed in employment and schools. On November 26, 1933, the Gestapo dissolved the SDA Church, ordering the confiscation of all church property. Although legal intervention and rulings in the Adventists' favor by the various German courts and agencies lifted the ban, the action warned them that they were in a precarious position. The few Adventists who refused to bear arms were "sent without trial to concentration camps and mental institutions," and some were executed.[32]

The legal difficulties that Adventists experience today largely relate to their Saturday Sabbath observation. In America and other countries, many SDAs have been denied employment or fired because they refuse to work on their Sabbath.[33] The vast majority of religious discrimination cases which are brought to the courts deal with the Saturday Sabbath question.[34] In about 50 percent of these cases the courts rule that the reasonable accommodation test does not require that an employee be excused from working on Saturday, although the Saturday Sabbath groups have an advantage in working for businesses that are open on Sunday.

Another commonality of the SDA and the Witnesses is their open and active disbelief in and opposition to the teaching of biological evolution. From the beginning of the modern evolution-creation controversy after 1859, both groups have published hundreds of books and articles against evolution. The Jehovah's Witness journals today still feature a steady flow of articles that oppose evolution, and disbelief in evolution is one of the central tenets of the faith. If a person were to publicly state his or her acceptance of Darwinism and reject the creationist world view, he or she would be disfellowshipped. This issue, though, is rarely a problem, even among college-trained Witnesses, and disfellowshipping for this reason is almost unknown. Even those who leave the Witnesses generally do not accept the theory of evolution.

The Seventh-Day Adventists are not the only major American denomination that opposes Darwinism, but they were a major drive in the modern resurgence of the creation movement.[35] Henry Morris, the founder of the revived early 1960s creation movement, claims that the "most important creationist writer of the first half-century was George McCready Price, an SDA who wrote about twenty-five books, the first published in 1902, the last in 1955."[36] SDA members Frank Marsh, Clifford Burdick, and Harold Clark all published extensively in the area of conservative creationism, and their works formed the core of major early creationist writings. Morris read Professor George McCready Price's *The New Geology* in early 1943 at Rice Institute where he taught science. It was, he later acknowledged, a life-changing experience that was critical in developing his views which later culminated in the book he co-authored with John C.

Whitcomb, *The Genesis Flood,* a major catalyst in the creation revival of the 1970s and 1980s.[37] In addition, SDA institutions such as Loma Linda University have produced many creationist Ph.D.-level scientists. Further, the work by the SDA creationists has achieved more respect than that of other creation groups; the Geoscience Research Institute (GRI) of Loma Linda University, for example, which Raymond Eve and Francis Harrold note has a staff of five Ph.D. researchers, publishes a semi-annual journal *(Origins)* and serves mainly as a source of scientific advice to SDA teachers.[38] The SDA Church officially teaches a universe millions of years or so old and the recent creation of life on Earth, but many SDA scientists, including those at the GRI, accept a recent date for creation but not Darwinism.

The SDA encourage education, but to protect SDA members from secular philosophies they run a large number of colleges for a small denomination.[39] As early as 1912, the group ran eighty-six colleges and academies, and seventy-four hospitals.[40] The Witnesses, on the other hand, strongly discourage members from pursuing any higher education. The Witnesses are extremely opposed to exposing their young people to the generally secular philosophy which prevails at most colleges and universities. College attendance is also felt to constitute improper involvement with the world and to be unnecessary, since the time is so short before Armageddon. One of the church's chief concerns about members' attending universities is that they could be influenced to accept Darwinism and also have their faith shaken. In support of this view, the Watchtower points to research such as the 1991 Gallup poll which found that 65 percent of non–high school graduates are strict creationists compared to only 25 percent of all college graduates. As a result of this discouragement, and the fact that most converts are from the working classes, in most countries at most 2 or 3 percent of Witnesses have college degrees. In contrast, Booton Herndon claims that in the late 1950s, SDAs were college graduates at a rate three times that of the general public;[41] because

the overall population of college graduates has risen drastically, the current level
is about two times as high.[42]

Church-state conflicts have presented
the Witnesses with their greatest problems.
The frequency and intensity of these conflicts have made the Jehovah's Witnesses
one of the most persecuted denominations
in the United States and in the world today. In the past, the JWs fought major
court battles over their refusal to salute
the flag (they interpret all allegiance
pledges to a national emblem as idolatry)
and their refusal to participate in military
service. But today, perhaps their most important legal thicket involves child custody
cases.[43] Because the Witnesses tend to be
hostile toward society, and also because
most people have a very difficult time understanding their beliefs, studies have consistently shown that they are among the
most disliked of all established religious
groups today.[44] This, plus the perception
based partly on empirical research that it
is difficult for a child raised as a strict
Jehovah's Witness to be well adjusted to
society, has motivated many courts to
award the children to the non-Witness parent.[45] When one person in a marriage becomes a Witness, marital discord is
relatively common, and divorce not un-
commonly follows. If young children are
involved in divorce cases, custody battles
often focus on the alleged harmful effects
of the Witness religion.

In one decision, the court ruled that the
child, a first-grader born June 12, 1983,
was to be removed from the mother's home
and placed in the custody of the father
specifically because the mother was raising the child as a Witness.[46] The court
ruled, even though the domestic court services investigation recommended that the
child remain with the mother, that he
should not be raised a Witness. The reasons included the potential threat to the
child's health due to the Witnesses' prohibition of blood transfusions, their dispar-
agement of higher education, their
teaching that all non-Witnesses including
the child's father are in the bonds of Satan
and will be destroyed at Armageddon, and
the fact that "the behavior of the minor

child, Scotty, reflects that he is becoming
more and more alienated from his father
and from his extended family believing
that 'Christmas persons,' those who celebrate Christmas as opposed to . . . [the
JWs] who do not . . . are going to die . . . and
should be shunned."[47] The court also evaluated a booklet entitled *Preparing for Child
Custody Cases,* written by the Watchtower
headquarters to help JWs deal with what
is now becoming a common problem, and
concluded that this booklet "recommends
the giving of testimony under oath which
is known to be untrue." The court concluded that "because of the absolute conflict between the parents with reference to
the Jehovah's Witness religion, and for
good cause shown, sole custody of said minor child should be granted to the respon-
dent-father." Further, the wife was to be

enjoined and restrained from exposing
said minor child to any activities in
which she participates as a member of
the Jehovah's Witness religion and is
to restrain from indoctrinating or attempting to indoctrinate the minor
child in the restrictions and prohibitions
of that religion; that petitioner is specifically ordered restrained from teaching said child or exposing said child to
teachings that his father, grandmother,
or other paternal relatives are "of the
Devil" or are "of Satan," or that his
relatives including his father and
grandmother are "going to die" and
will be just be "dust. . . ."[48]

In a similar case, *Mendez v. Mendez,* the
judge ruled that it is in the best interests of
the child for custody to go to the father,
Ignacio Mendez, and that all decisions on
"critical, medical, dental health, and general welfare and rearing," and on religious
training are to be "vested solely and exclusively within the discretion of the husband." The wife "shall not expose or permit
any other person to expose the minor child
to any religious practices, attendances,
teachings or events which are in any way
inconsistent with the Catholic religion. Nor
shall the wife preclude the child from engaging in any activity which is permitted
by the Catholic religion."[49] In this case,

249 of the 485 custody transcript pages, a whopping 51 percent, contain references to religion.[50] The case was upheld on appeal, and on March 7, 1988, the U.S. Supreme Court denied Rita Mendez's appeal for *writ of certiorari.*

Walker concluded that the Watchtower attempts to prevail in these cases by advising Witnesses to paint decidedly untrue pictures in court and "to say in court *the exact opposite* of what they would normally say in a Kingdom Hall."[51] For example, the Watchtower booklet *School and Jehovah's Witnesses* and all official teachings strongly discourage Witness children from being involved in organized sports or after-school activities, hobbies and higher education, concluding that this time should be used principally to pursue Watchtower interests.[52] The booklet, though, instructs Witnesses to imply exactly the opposite in court.

Most of these cases involve fairly young couples in which the wives become Jehovah's Witnesses, resulting in divorces and child custody battles. In about 90 percent of all child custody cases the state-appointed psychologists recommend that the custody of minor children be given to the mother, but in cases involving Jehovah's Witnesses, a significantly higher proportion of awards are to the non-Witness father. On the other hand, for the SDAs to even bring religion into a custody case is rare, and in no past published case was religion a deciding factor. The SDAs have managed to almost totally avoid these kinds of confrontations, and have been accepted into the mainstream of religious society.[53]

The Witnesses tend to appeal to people who are at down-points in their lives, especially those experiencing trauma or adjustment problems. Historically, many have been recruited from the marginal and lower-class members of society, but because of their work ethic and encouragement of generally responsible economic decisions, they now tend to be in some ways more middle class.[54] JW leaders are regularly accused by their detractors of brainwashing, specifically because they attempt to rigidly control all information that the members

receive. Reading any literature critical of the Witnesses is a disfellowshipping offense, and one is to unquestioningly accept all of the teachings of the Watchtower Society without exception.[55] They are enjoined from reading *any* religious literature aside from that printed by the Watchtower Society, and are discouraged from writing in the areas of religion, philosophy, sociology, or current events except for required school papers. Even writing books in favor of the society is discouraged: the few active Witnesses that wrote books supportive of the society, including Jay Hess and Professors Anthony Wills and James Penton, were eventually disfellowshipped.[56] Conversely, although some once-prominent SDA members have been forced to leave because they produced books critical of their denomination, most are relatively free to pursue reading, research, and study that they feel is appropriate. One major issue in the 1980s was the research that indicated that Ellen White had borrowed heavily from others for her writings, at times to an extent that some feel borders on plagiarism. This was a problem because her works are considered by the church as inspired by God. The SDA encouragement of education has always put them largely in the middle-class camp, and today many more SDAs than Witnesses are upper middle class.

Of all modern religions, the group whose members have by far experienced the most persecution and have suffered the most martyrdom at the hands of citizens of their own country is the Witnesses: "no chapter in human history has been so largely written in terms of persecution and intolerance as the one dealing with religious freedom ... and the Jehovah's Witnesses are living proof of the fact that even in this nation, conceived as it was in the ideals of freedom, the right to practice religion in unconventional ways is still far from secure."[57] According to jurist Archibald Cox, the Witnesses were "the principal victims of religious persecution in the United States in the twentieth century. . . . "[58] The persecution has sometimes been of such intensity that former Attorney General Francis Biddle once made a nationwide appeal on radio, part of which said, " . . . Jehovah's Witnesses have been repeatedly set upon and beaten. They had committed no crime; but the mob adjudged they had, and meted out mob punishment."[59]

An American Civil Liberties Union summary concluded that "the record of violence against [the Jehovah's Witnesses] has been unparalleled in America since the attacks on the Mormons" and that " . . . Documents filed with the Department of Justice by attorneys . . . showed over 3,035 instances of mob violence in forty-five states during 1940 involving 1,488 men, women and children."[60] And Christine King concludes,

> many of the teachings have led the sect into bitter conflict with civil authorities all over the world, in democratic as well as in totalitarian states. . . . [The major reason was because the] Witnesses will not fight or undertake war-related work. . . . they will not undertake civil duties which they see as conflicting with their duty to Jehovah—God. Witnesses will not vote . . . , salute a national flag or recognize a national anthem, and they refuse to enlist. In peace time they are normally tolerated in democratic countries, but in war-time and in totalitarian regimes they frequently face imprisonment.[61]

Conversely, Isidore Starr argues that the Jehovah's Witnesses have done more than any other religious group in America to defend basic American freedoms before the Supreme Court.[62] Samuel Walker estimates that between 1938 and 1955, the Witnesses brought forty-five cases before the high court, and were victorious in a total of thirty-six.[63] They have by this means not only forced the clarification of many freedom and human rights issues, but in at least two instances—the more famous involved the mandatory recitation of the Pledge of Allegiance in schools—have forced the court to reverse itself. Thus, while their stand has produced a certain vindication, the persecution continues today in different forms in spite of their Supreme Court victories.[64] The Witnesses are now banned or their activities severely pro-

scribed in dozens of countries, and are severely persecuted in many more. As Judge Henry Edgerton concluded from his experience on the bench, "the principal threat to civil liberties [at this time] came not from the federal government, but from the activities of local officials and from the terrorism practiced by private persons against unpopular groups, especially the pacifistic group called Jehovah's Witnesses."[65]

A major problem was that the hostility of citizens was condoned by law enforcement officials who often violated the law themselves, or at the least condoned mob violence. Wills noted the following in the case of a black Witness:

> When he refused to salute [the American flag], the police beat him to unconsciousness. When he came to they repeated it. He was released two days later with hemorrhaging, and permanent head and brain injuries. [And in another Witness case] on December 5, 1942, August Schmidt called unintentionally on the home of Sergeant Ellis of Redondo Beach, California. Ellis returned the call, dragging him to his car, forcing him to enter at gunpoint, and beat him with a blackjack.[66]

The record of the United States justice system during this time is a poor one: out of the many thousands of assaults against the Witnesses in those years, the Department of Justice found courage to prosecute and secure a conviction in but one.[67]

Empirical studies have confirmed that the same attitude is still the norm in the United States. Seymour Martin Lipset concluded in a study of prejudice that the Witnesses were among the most disliked of all religious minorities that he studied—the group average showed that the public expressed *more dislike of them than even the most hated ethnic minorities,* a whopping 41 percent.[68] And research by Merlin Brinkerhoff and Marlene Mackie concluded that the religious groups found the least acceptable were the so-called new cults, followed by the Jehovah's Witnesses, Mormons, and conservative Christians.[69]

In 1940 the Canadian government banned the Jehovah's Witnesses, and the ban was vigorously enforced. William Kaplan noted that the result was "beatings, mob action, police persecution, as well as state persecution . . . and Witness children who refused to sing the national anthem and salute the flag during patriotic exercises in public schools were often expelled from class."[70] The newly released Canadian records reveal that official government behind-the-scenes activities caused "able bodied young Jehovah's Witnesses" to be sent to "camps," and entire families that "practiced the religion were imprisoned."[71] And in the case of several cities such as Hamilton, the children were removed from their homes and "sentenced to some kind of state care for respectfully refusing to sing the national anthem." Men refusing military service were sent to work camps throughout Canada established primarily for the Jehovah's Witnesses.[72]

In Nazi Germany, of all religions, the Witnesses and the Jews were the *only* groups to be uniformly persecuted: "The Third Reich was not willing . . . to tolerate [any] minority Christian sects who might prove a challenge . . . [but] only one group, the Jehovah's Witnesses, were the victims of total persecution."[73] James Beckford concluded that their persecution in Nazi Germany far surpassed that which even the Witnesses had previously experienced, or ever expected:

> . . . the brutality and ruthlessness of persecution in Germany must have shocked even the most hardened veterans of Watch Tower clashes with civil, military, and religious authorities. . . . In February 1933, however, Hitler formally proscribed all Watch Tower activities. . . . Nazi ideologists accused them of sympathizing with the Jews, being implicated in international communism and showing disrespect for the *Führer*.[74]

Adventist Contributions to Health

Although the Seventh-Day Adventist theology is a blend of liberal Protestantism, fundamentalism, and the unique elements added by the Millerite movement, its unique contribution is emphasizing the importance of health. Ellen G. White a century ago stressed that the body is a temple of God, and advocated a set of health practices, some of which are becoming accepted by mainline science.[75] Although they advocated many views now regarded as nostrums, some of their views have proved correct. Probably the most well known is their emphasis upon the health problems which results from a diet high in red meat, a concern that has been largely verified by research on cholesterol and saturated fats. They also shun alcohol and tobacco, and many eschew coffee and tea and eat a vegetarian diet bolstered by eggs and milk. SDA literature was discussing cholesterol for decades before it became a staple of scientific medical journals. Their reasons for a meatless diet include the conclusion that the human digestive organs are more similar to those of animals which eat grain than those of meat-eaters.[76] These beliefs were reinforced by the large number of medical missionaries of the SDA Church. For example, they noted in China that in spite of the poverty, certain diseases were rare and the people's longevity warranted an evaluation of their living and eating habits. The Chinese diet is extremely low in red meat, and high in soy beans, rice, wheat, and corn. Empirical studies of SDA hospitals and colleges constituted an important factor in the modern emphasis on diet as an important means in dealing with many major health concerns.[77] Actually, many of the early studies exploring the relationship between diet, especially a high-fat diet, and heart attacks and cancer, were on Adventists. Further, some of the early studies on cigarette smoking as a cause of lung cancer used SDAs as a control group. Dr. Ernest Wynder of the Sloan-Kettering Institute studied SDAs who lived and worked in Los Angeles, then compared the patients admitted to SDA hospitals, the majority of whom were not members of the church. Of the Adventists, 70 percent had never smoked, and the rest had some smoking history before they joined the church. The researchers concluded that lung cancer was far less common among the Adventists (actually, only one case was found, a sixty-two-year-old new SDA convert who had smoked a pack of cigarettes a day for twenty years). Further, the Adventists had far less cardiovascular disease than the control group.[78] Hundreds of studies now exist which delineate these differences.

Dr. John Kellogg, founder of Kellogg Cereal Corporation in Battle Creek, Michigan, was an early SDA physician who developed breakfast cereal (first granola, then corn flakes) to help insure that Seventh-Day Adventists were able to obtain the necessary food value in palatable forms without eating meat.[79] The Seventh-Day Adventists are also extremely active in building hospitals in countries throughout the world, and now have over 250 clinics, hospitals and dispensaries worldwide.

As to the future of the SDAs and the Witnesses, the SDAs will probably continue to grow and become more mainline and respectable. Many of their contentions relative to health (especially concerning low-fat diets and not smoking) have in recent years become American mainstream views. Conversely, the Witnesses will likely change far less, although they are now less antagonistic towards medicine, psychology, and even education than formerly. As more and more Witnesses become semi-professionals and more solidly middle class, they will likely eventually make peace with society. A critical factor is that it is becoming increasingly difficult for Witnesses to rationalize beliefs such as the one affirming that the return of Christ commenced in 1914, and that Armageddon will occur during the generation which was alive in 1914. The Watchtower now solemnly pronounces that because of the 1914 prophecy the year 2,000 is about the upper limit for the destruction of evil and God's ushering in of the new world. If the expected end does not come soon, drastic changes in both their theology and chronology will be necessary.[80]

The author sincerely thanks Professor Ronald L. Numbers of the University of Wisconsin and Warren Johns, Librarian at Andrews University, for their helpful comments on this chapter.

Notes

1. William Kaplan, *State and Salvation.* (Toronto: University of Toronto Press, 1989).

2. J. Gordon Melton, *The Encyclopedia of American Religions,* vol. 1 and 2 (Wilmington, N.C.: McGrath Publishing Company, 1978), 459.

3. Jerry Bergman, *Jehovah's Witnesses and Kindred Groups: A Historical Compendium and Bibliography* (New York: Garland, 1984).

4. Melton, *Encyclopedia of American Religions,* 453.

5. Joseph F. Zygmunt, "Prophetic Failure and Chiliastic Identity: The Case of Jehovah's Witnesses," *American Journal of Sociology* 75, no. 6 (May 1970): 926–48.

6. Ingemar Linden, *The Last Trump: An Historico-Genetical Study of Some Important Chapters in the Making and Development of the Seventh-Day Adventist Church* (Frankfurt am Main: Peter Lang, 1978).

7. Melton, *Encyclopedia of American Religions,* 460.

8. Ibid.

9. Warren Johns, letter to author, 19 April 1992.

10. Watchtower Bible and Tract Society, *Jehovah's Witnesses in the Divine Purpose* (New York: Watchtower Bible and Tract Society of New York, Inc., 1959).

11. P. Gerard Damsteegt, *Foundations of the Seventh-Day Adventist Message and Mission* (Grand Rapids: William B. Eerdmans Publishing Company, 1977).

12. S. H. Lane, *Our Paradise Home: The Earth Made New and the Restoration of All Things* (Washington, D.C.: Review and Herald Publishing Association, 1903).

13. Harold Shryock, *Happiness and Health* (Mountain View, Calif.: Pacific Press Publishing Association, 1950); Norman F. Douty, *An-*

other Look at Seventh-Day Adventism: With Special Reference to Questions on Doctrine (Grand Rapids, Mich.: Baker Book House 1962); Ronald L. Numbers, *Prophetess of Health: A Study of Ellen G. White* (New York: Harper and Row, 1976).

14. Watchtower Bible and Tract Society, *The Watchtower*, 1916, 170–71.

15. Ibid.

16. Zygmunt, "Prophetic Failure and Chiliastic Identity," 926–48.

17. Ibid., 931.

18. Ibid., 923.

19. Watchtower Bible and Tract Society, *The Watchtower*, October 1884.

20. Zygmunt, "Prophetic Failure and Chiliastic Identity," 932–33.

21. Watchtower Bible and Tract Society, *The Watchtower*, December 1, 1912.

22. E. G. White, *His Glorious Appearing: An Exposition of Matthew Twenty-Four* (Takoma Park, Washington, D.C.: Review and Herald Publishing Association, 1986); E. G. White, *Christ Our Savior* (Nashville, Tenn.: Southern Publishing Association, 1900); Carlyle B. Haynes, *Twelve Great Signs of the Return of Jesus* (Takoma Park, Washington, D.C.: Review and Herald Publishing Association, 1925).

23. Raymond Franz, *In Search of Christian Freedom* (Atlanta, Ga.: Commentary Press, 1991).

24. Rosalie Duron, "We Don't Want to See You Anymore: A Mother Explains the Painful Other Side of the Mendez Story," *Liberty* (Sept./Oct. 1991): 16–18.

25. Booton Herndon, *The Seventh Day: The Story of the Seventh-Day Adventists* (New York: McGraw-Hill Book Company, Inc., 1963), 211.

26. Christine Elizabeth King, "The Nazi State and the New Religions: Five Case Studies in Non-conformity" *Studies in Religion and Society*, vol. 4 (Lewiston, N.Y.: The Edwin Mellen Press, 1979), 90.

27. Mulford Q. Sibley, and Philip Jacob, *Conscription of Conscience: The American State and the Conscientious Objector, 1940–47* (Ithaca, N.Y.: Cornell University Press, 1952).

28. Raymond Franz, *Crisis of Conscience* (Atlanta, Ga.: Commentary Press, 1983).

29. Ibid.

30. King, "The Nazi State and the New Religions," 94.

31. Ibid., 93.

32. Ibid., 98.

33. Geoffrey J. Paxton, *The Shaking of Adventism* (Grand Rapids, Mich.: Baker Book House, 1977).

34. Elder Witt, *The Supreme Court and Individual Rights* (Washington, D.C.: Congressional Quarterly, 1988).

35. Henry M. Morris, *History of Modern Creationism* (San Diego, Calif.: Master Book Publishers, 1984).

36. Ibid., 79–80.

37. Raymond A. Eve and Francis B. Harrold, *The Creationist Movement in Modern America* (Boston, Mass.: Twayne Publishers, 1991).

38. Ibid., 130.

39. Ronald L. Numbers, letter to author, 19 February 1992.

40. Rev. D. M. Canright, *Seventh-Day Adventism Renounced: After An Experience of Twenty-Eight Years By a Prominent Minister and Writer of That Faith* (Nashville, Tenn.: B. C. Goodpasture, 1948).

41. Herndon, *The Seventh Day*, 216.

42. Johns, letter to author, 19 April 1992.

43. Mitchell A. Tyner, "Who Gets the Kid?" *Liberty* (May/June 1991): 8–11.

44. Merlin B. Brinkerhoff and Marlene M. Mackie, "The Applicability of Social Distance for Religious Research: An Exploration" *Review of Religious Research* 28, no. 2 (Dec. 1986).

45. Pamela Ward, "Mendez v. Mendez" *Liberty* (July/Aug. 1988): 20–23.

46. *Estes v. Estes*, 89C6103, the District Court of Johnson County, Kansas (5 September 1991).

47. Ibid., 18–19.

48. Ibid., 21.

49. Ward, "Mendez v. Mendez," 23.

50. Ibid., 22.

51. James K. Walker, "Deception in Court: Jehovah's Witnesses on the Witness Stand" *Watchman Expositor* 7, no. 10: 7.

52. Ibid., 23.

53. Herndon, *The Seventh Day*, 2.

54. Werner Cohn, "Jehovah's Witnesses as a Proletarian Sect" (Master's thesis, New School for Social Research, 1954); M. James Penton, *Jehovah's Witnesses in Canada: Champions of Freedom of Speech and Worship* (Toronto: MacMillan of Canada, 1976).

55. Franz, *Crisis of Conscience*.

56. Anthony Wills (published under the pseudonym Timothy White), *A People for His Name: The History of Jehovah's Witnesses and*

an Evaluation (New York: Vantage Press, 1967). (See also ref. 59.)

57. Frank J. Sorauf, "Jehovah's Witnesses," in *Guide to American Law* (St. Paul, Minn.: West Publishing Inc., 1984), 336.

58. Archibald Cox, *The Court and the Constitution*. (Boston, Mass.: Houghton Mifflin Co., 1987), 189.

59. William J. Whalen, *Armageddon Around the Corner: A Report on Jehovah's Witnesses* (New York: The John Day Company, 1962), 183.

60. American Civil Liberties Union, *The Persecution of Jehovah's Witnesses* (New York, January 1941), 1.

61. King, "The Nazi State and the New Religions," 248.

62. Isidore Starr, *Human Rights in the United States* (New York: Oxford Book Co., 1964).

63. Samuel Walker, *In Defense of American Liberties: A History of the ACLU* (New York: Oxford University Press, 1990).

64. Penton, *Jehovah's Witnesses in Canada.*

65. Henry W. Edgerton, *Freedom in the Balance: Opinions of Judge Henry W. Edgerton,* ed. Eleanor Bontecou (Westport, Conn.: Greenwood Press Publishers, 1978), 2.

66. Wills, *A People for His Name,* 330–31.

67. Haig Bosmajian, *Freedom of Expression* (New York: Neal-Schuman Pub., 1988).

68. Seymour Martin Lipset, "The Sources of the 'Radical Right'" in *The Radical Right,* ed. Daniel Bell (Garden City, N.Y.: Anchor Books, 1964), 435.

69. Brinkerhoff and Mackie, "Applicability of Social Distance."

70. Kaplan, *State and Salvation,* xii.

71. Barbara Yaffe, "Witnesses Seek Apology for Wartime Persecution," *The Globe and Mail, Canada's National Newspaper,* 9 September 1984, p. 4.

72. Jeff Sallot and Barbara Yaffe, "Secret Files Reveal Bigotry, Suppression," *The Globe and Mail, Canada's National Newspaper,* 4 September 1984.

73. King, "The Nazi State and the New Religions," 213.

74. James A. Beckford, *The Trumpet of Prophecy: A Sociological Study of Jehovah's Witnesses* (Oxford: Basil Blackwell, 1975), 33–34.

75. Numbers, *Prophetess of Health,* 39–42, 79–81, 163.

76. Herndon, *The Seventh Day,* 89.

77. Ibid., 88.

78. The N of the SDA group was 564, of the control group of non-Adventists was 8,128.

79. Numbers, *Prophetess of Health,* 188–90.

80. *The Watchtower,* 1 June 1990, p. 12, non-bound volume edition.

Suggestions for Further Reading

Beckford, James A. *The Trumpet of Prophecy: A Sociological Study of Jehovah's Witnesses.* Oxford: Basil Blackwell, 1975.

Bergman, Jerry. *Jehovah's Witnesses and Kindred Groups: A Historical Compendium and Bibliography.* New York: Garland Publishing, 1984.

Harrison, Barbara Grizzuti. *Visions of Glory: A History and Memory of Jehovah's Witnesses.* New York: Simon and Schuster, 1978.

Land, Gary, ed. *Adventism in America.* Grand Rapids: Eerdmans, 1986.

Penton, M. James. *Apocalypse Delayed: The Story of Jehovah's Witnesses.* Toronto: University of Toronto Press, 1985.

4

THE LATTER DAY SAINT CHURCHES

Steven L. Shields

Most Americans today are generally familiar with the Church of Jesus Christ of Latter-day Saints (commonly referred to as the "Mormon" or "LDS" Church), which is headquartered in Salt Lake City, Utah. If the young men and women missionaries have not knocked on their doors, many persons have seen them walking down the street or riding bicycles in pairs. Those who have not seen missionaries are at least acquainted with the famous Mormon Tabernacle Choir from its radio and television programs and its many popular trips around the world.

The Mormon Church generally receives all the credit (and most of the criticism) for the work begun by Joseph Smith, Jr., in the early 1800s, because it is the largest, most powerful, wealthiest, and most famous of the Latter Day Saint Churches. The Mormons spare no effort to present a positive and community-oriented image—and they do not provide free publicity for other Latter Day Saints whom the mainstream Mormon institution deems "apostate."

However, the Latter Day Saint movement is much more diverse than the Mormon Church would suggest. There are, in fact, numerous denominations, mostly in the United States, that base their beliefs and systems in some fashion on the principles laid down by Joseph Smith, Jr., who founded the Latter Day Saint movement and led it until his death in 1844 at the hands of an angry mob.

After his "First Vision" experience at the age of about 15,[1] Smith proceeded to receive continued angelic visitations. These revolved generally around the reported discovery of an ancient record describing some of the inhabitants of the American continents who had descended from the ancient Israelites. During a four-year period, which began in 1823, Smith met with a "personage" named Moroni. Moroni directed Smith to a hill near the Smith family home in upstate New York where, under a large stone, Smith reported that he found an ancient record engraved on plates having the appearance of gold, along with some other artifacts.[2] Given a special power from God to translate the unknown language, Smith published the Book of Mormon in March of 1830. The official organization of a church followed on April 6, 1830.

Joseph Smith, Jr., and his contemporaries saw themselves as divinely appointed "restorers." They were attempting to reconstruct the Christian Church of the New Testament as they perceived it. In this quest, the Latter Day Saint movement resembles the Campbellite movement, which most Christian historians call the "Restoration" movement. Thomas Campbell and his son Alexander, allied with Barton W. Stone and Walter Scott, were united in an effort to restore the principles of what they defined as "primitive" Christianity. Alexander Campbell and the others never perceived the Latter Day Saints as Christian in any way. In fact, Campbell published a tract early in the 1830s giving a scathing critique of The Book of Mormon. Yet, the fact remains that both the Latter Day Saints and the Campbellites were attempting to do much the same thing.

Smith's small church grew rapidly after a move to Kirtland, Ohio, in 1831 and a merger with Sidney Rigdon's Campbellite congregation in that vicinity. Continued growth occurred during the 1830s and the church branched out with colonies in Missouri, a state which was divinely appointed as a special place. Joseph Smith, Jr., wrote that God chose Independence, Missouri, as the "Center Place" and directed the building of a temple there.[3] Independence was designated as the "land of Zion" and the place for the "New Jerusalem," evoking a connection with the millennialistic ideas prevalent in the Latter Day Saint Church of the early 1830s, as well as in other Christian groups in America at that time.

Conflict with non–Latter Day Saint neighbors saw the church and its followers expelled from a succession of communities, both in Ohio and Missouri. They ended up in Quincy, Illinois, as forlorn refugees escaping the wrath of the Missouri State Militia in the winter of 1838–1839.[4]

Needing a place to settle where they could go about their own business in their own way, the Latter Day Saints located some marshy acreage about sixty miles north of Quincy, which they proceeded to purchase. The area was at first quite inhospitable, with mosquito infestations and swampy areas, but the industrious Latter Day Saints drained the land, fought off debilitating illnesses, and proceeded to build a magnificent city in which they merged government, business, and religion in a unique blend of society. They named their city Nauvoo, which Smith claimed was a Hebrew word meaning "beautiful place." There the Latter Day Saints prospered and grew numerically, with converts pouring in from all over the United States and England. Nauvoo, endowed with a powerful city charter by the Illinois Legislature, became a political entity that ultimately could have controlled the state of Illinois.

With the building of a temple in Nauvoo, and the emergence of various rituals that were believed to have a bearing on one's eternal salvation, the concept of the "land of Zion" became temporarily transplanted from Independence to the new city on the banks of the Mississippi. Significant doctrinal innovations were developed at Nauvoo—innovations which became crucial in the differences between those members of the church who followed Brigham Young west to Utah in 1846 and those who became the nucleus around which the Reorganized Church and other smaller Latter Day Saint groups became focused.[5]

Unfortunately, residents of the surrounding area felt the threat of these newcomers and trouble ensued. It resulted in the death of the Latter Day Saint leader Joseph Smith, Jr. Smith's death left a void in the church he had founded and led for fourteen years. Many of his doctrinal teachings during the Nauvoo period had never been publicly acknowledged or taught. This created irreconcilable rifts in the church as its followers sought direction for the future.

Smith left the issue of succession in the leadership of the church rather unclear. He apparently did not believe he would be killed as he left Nauvoo for the Hancock County seat on what would be his last journey, or he would have issued final instructions regarding what should happen in the event of his death. Or, possibly, but quite unlikely, Smith did not want clear-cut succession instructions to be available, leaving his followers to decide for themselves in which direction they should go. In any event, the confusion that followed Smith's death left the Latter Day Saint Church severely fragmented for the next twenty years. During that time numerous leaders emerged, claiming different segments of the original church. Finally, when the dust had settled, Brigham Young had been the most successful leader and had persuaded a significant following to make the journey to what became the state of Utah. Five other distinct church organizations that emerged from the period of fragmentation have survived to the present day, most notably the Reorganized Church of Jesus Christ of Latter

Day Saints, now headquartered in Independence, Missouri. The other churches are the Church of Jesus Christ of Latter Day Saints (Strangite), led by James J. Strang; the Church of Christ (Temple Lot), originally led by Granville Hedrick; the Church of Jesus Christ, led by Alpheus Cutler; and the Church of Jesus Christ, organized by William Bickerton and others.[6]

Almost two hundred separate and distinct church organizations or fellowships have been identified as having their roots in the Latter Day Saint movement. Of course, most of these are or were very small and have had minimal influence.[7] Societal influence is generally directly related to numerical size or wealth of a given group of people. The Mormon Church, with its more than 8 million members worldwide, commands virtually all of the national media attention given to the Latter Day Saints in practically every nation of the world. The Reorganized Church of Jesus Christ of Latter Day Saints has approximately 250,000 members worldwide, and is rarely, if ever, mentioned in the national media of any nation. Yet, in localized areas where the church has a substantial following, the organization does make a significant impact.

The four other major fragments of the original church are very small numerically.[8] Of the many other organizations that can be viewed as part of the Latter Day Saint movement, the ones which seem to have some impact and occasionally receive national and sometimes international media coverage are those that observe a fundamentalistic belief system, most notably those Latter Day Saint groups which still practice polygamy. Some elements of the Latter Day Saint movement have been noted in the media because of murders of or committed by their members in the name of religion.[9]

When Brigham Young led his followers across the vastness of the United States in 1847 and settled in Utah, the territory had barely been won from Mexico. Although disturbed briefly by the 1849 gold rush, when thousands passed through on their way to California, the Mormons in Utah were left to themselves in a rather forsaken wilderness. There they took root. They colonized the Mountain West, and shaped their religion without the pressure of hostile neighbors.

During the Civil War, the Union shifted the stage lines northward to keep them out of Confederate hands—and the new lines passed directly through Utah. The United States government adopted a policy of doing what needed to be done to assure that Utah remained in its control in order to maintain the loyalty of California and other important western areas. The transcontinental telegraph, completed in 1861, was built with the help of Mormon people in Utah, and contributed to a new era of communications in the nation. When military protection of the overland routes was required in 1862, President Abraham Lincoln bypassed the territorial governor of Utah and wired Brigham Young, Mormon Church president, directly and authorized him to "raise, arm and equip a company of cavalry for ninety days service, to protect the property of the telegraph and overland mail companies."[10]

Utah and the Mormons were in the good graces of the federal government for only a short time. When the War Between the States had ended, and reconstruction was underway, the federal officials began to go after the Mormons once again over the issue of polygamy. Anti-polygamy legislation was passed in Congress, and many Mormon leaders were arrested, left the country, or went into hiding. Finally, bowing to governmental pressure in 1890, Wilford Woodruff, then president of the Mormon Church, issued a declaration ordering the cessation of polygamy "for the temporal salvation of the church."[11]

Polygamy was an issue that might well have destroyed the Mormon Church in the United States had its leaders not finally given in to government pressure in 1890.[12] The United States press was filled with such negative reports that the Reorganized Latter Day Saints adopted the prefix "Reorganized" in the later 1860s in order to find a way to distance themselves from the Latter Day Saints in Utah. Up until that time both churches had used identical names. Overseas, polygamy still causes problems in many areas for Latter Day Saints of any brand.

Utah emerged from its troubles with the government a stronger and more determined place. Statehood was granted in 1896, and the Mormon Church was as prosperous as ever. When the Great Depression enshrouded the United States, the Mormon Church was quick to respond with a welfare system to assist its church members by providing a supplement to federally sponsored welfare programs. This church welfare system is still in place today, providing assistance to church members when and where needed, as a supplement to government aid. In areas where the church has significant concentrations of membership, the church provides farms, storehouses, factories, family counseling, and employment services.[13]

The Reorganized Church began to emerge in the early 1850s when several Latter Day Saint leaders found themselves dissatisfied with the various claimants to the prophetic office in the church. One leader, Jason W. Briggs, sought God's direction on the matter and he reported a revelation which directed him and those who would follow him to wait for a member of the Smith family to take the lead of the church. As the Reorganized Church developed, it built its own theology and practice on the foundations of the early church, but it bitterly opposed the polygamy that was the hallmark of the Mormon Church at that time.

The initial missionary thrust of the Reorganized Church centered on reclaiming those Latter Day Saints who had followed other leaders. The early "reorganizers" saw themselves in a role of redeeming the "fallen" church and preparing a people who would receive the divinely appointed leader—whom most believed should be Joseph Smith III, the son of the slain prophet.[14] The Reorganized Church's base has always been in the Midwestern United States, and was numerically small. After Joseph Smith III assumed leadership of the church in 1860, headquarters were unofficially located in his home in Nauvoo, Illinois for several years. A move in 1868 to Plano, Illinois—about sixty miles west of

Chicago—brought about the first developing Latter Day Saint community of the reorganization. A church building was constructed, a publishing house was established, and many church members located their homes in the community.

As the church continued to grow and gather strength and numbers, the headquarters moved once again to Lamoni, Iowa. This community, established in the 1870s by Reorganized Church members, was located on the Missouri-Iowa state line, about 125 miles north of the Independence–Kansas City area. Joseph Smith III moved his family to Lamoni in the early 1880s, and the church printing house and other offices were quickly relocated as well.

The years in Lamoni were remarkable growth years for the church. Printing and publishing efforts continued at an increased pace. Sunday school materials were written and published, along with various periodicals and books. Graceland College was established in Lamoni, which continues to this day as a four-year liberal arts college.

Joseph Smith III and his family moved one final time in 1905 to Independence, Missouri, marking an official recognition of the place that Independence still occupied in the theology of the church. Church headquarters was officially still in Lamoni, but increasing numbers of church officials and members "gathered" to Independence. Church legislative assemblies were alternated between Lamoni and Independence for several years before the church finally voted to officially make Independence its headquarters in 1920.

The Latter Day Saint churches are theologically diverse. Even those issues, ideas, and verbiage which seem common to most, if not all, of the groups are really fundamentally different because of differing foundational ideologies and philosophies among the various churches. While the groups may share particular structures, or a common verbiage, they actually differ widely. It would be difficult, if not impossible, to adequately address all of the differences that exist across the broader Latter Day Saint movement in the space allowed for this chapter. Therefore, most of the discussion will center on the Mormon Church in Utah, which would be generally representative of the more conservative churches in the movement, and the Reorganized Church in Missouri, which provides a more liberal expression of the Latter Day Saint ideals.

The foundation of the Latter Day Saint movement was the Book of Mormon. This book was used by the earliest missionaries who attempted to persuade persons to join the fledgling church. And, while most of the Latter Day Saint churches still consider the Book of Mormon part of the canon of Scripture, opinions and beliefs about it take a wide range of viewpoints. The Mormon Church holds fast to its belief that the Book of Mormon is an actual history of real people, while many (although not all) in the Reorganized Church no longer view it in that light. The Reorganized Church tends to be much more pluralistic in all issues of belief than does the Mormon Church, which has essentially taken a catechistic approach to all of its beliefs.

This is perhaps best illustrated by the different ways in which "intellectuals" are treated in the two churches. The Mormon Church over the past twenty years has a lengthy history of dealing with those of its members whom church officials perceive to be "liberal." This category includes historians and theologians who develop different interpretations of the church's history and beliefs than that which has commonly been accepted. Rather than deal openly with the issues, Mormon Church officials have blacklisted many members and prohibited them from working for the church or any of its institutions, including its universities and colleges. This prohibition has extended into the lowest reaches of church service where perceived liberal members are excluded from offering volunteer time in the local congregation. Some church officials have even re-recorded sermons in order to bring them into line editorially with current church policies.[15]

Mormon Church officials warn church members against listening to "alternate voices." They fear that intellectual thought may destroy the faith of the membership. Church members are counselled not to criti-cize church leaders even if the criticism is true.[16] Authors Linda King Newell and Valeen Tippetts Avery were banned for ten months from speaking on historical topics in church meetings. Church headquarters telephoned the bishops of wards (congregations) in Idaho, Utah, and Arizona to provide these instructions. At issue was the authors' best-selling biography of Emma Smith, which was published in 1985 and in which church officials felt the presentation of Joseph Smith, Jr., was less than appropriate.[17] The LDS Church issued a new policy in 1986 which required researchers to provide pre-publication copies of their writings for approval by the church before permission would be granted for the publication of quotes from archival materials.[18]

On the other hand, Reorganized Church archives are open to all legitimate researchers, with only the request that they acknowledge the sources of quoted materials. The church officially sponsors a journal, *Restoration Studies,* which is published periodically (five times in twelve years). Each journal contains several dozen scholarly and intellectual papers on a wide variety of topics, from a broad perspective of viewpoints and faith.

Most of the Latter Day Saint churches today still cling tenaciously to the early view that Joseph Smith, Jr., was in fact restoring the church (in a structural, practical, and theological sense) that had been established by Christ, and that through Divine inspiration, he was restoring to the church many things which allegedly had been lost through the ages. Recent understandings in some Latter Day Saint organizations, though, particularly the Reorganized Church, interpret "restoration" as an ongoing process of trying to bring humanity and God back into a balanced and righteous relationship. The Reorganized Church has been ardently pursuing a social gospel for at least the past thirty years, which has caused the church to become more ecumenically minded. Most of the other Latter Day Saint groups have pursued an "only true church" mentality which has rejected all others as being either of the devil, or at least less than what God would have them be.

The Mormon Church views Joseph Smith, Jr., as essential and foundational to its belief and faith. Smith's teachings are published in various formats and function as an extra-biblical source of authority. On the other hand, the Reorganized Church places a great importance on the discipleship of each believer, emphasizing Smith's historical role over his contemporary one. Issues of eternal life and the hereafter, while hardly ever discussed in a Reorganized Church setting due to its growing understanding of salvation through grace which motivates good works, are the primary focus of Mormon discipleship, because Mormon beliefs suggest that it is a person's good works that lead to a receiving of the grace of salvation.

"Zion" is a concept prominent to most Latter Day Saint churches; it describes a future place where equality and justice will reign. One Latter Day Saint historian has said,

> Until 1830 the word Zion was often used but was not necessarily well defined, nor its context made apparent. But the idea of Zion as a special city quickly grew. In 1831 Independence [Missouri] was identified as Zion and, for a while, Nauvoo [Illinois] served this function, but that died with Joseph [Smith, Jr.] and his brother in 1844.[19]

Many in the Mormon Church saw Zion transferred to Utah; many in the Reorganized Church today believe Zion can be established in the only place ever specifically designated as such by Joseph Smith, Jr., and that place is Independence, Missouri. Yet the modern-day interpretation of Zion by the Reorganized Church would stress Zion as being established in the various communities where church members live around the world, defining Zion more as a condition than as a single place.

Although the establishment of Zion was perhaps the most persistent goal of the early church that saw itself as the "usher" to bring in the second coming of Christ and the millennial reign, the members of the early Reorganization had to reevaluate this viewpoint when they began to coalesce around the leadership of Jason Briggs and Zenos H. Gurley, Sr., in the 1850s.[20]

> When young Smith [Joseph Smith III] assumed leadership over the Reorganized Church, his followers believed that he would begin the long-anticipated gathering of the Saints for the building of a zionic community. . . . [However] Smith realized that the early Mormons had tried to accomplish too much too quickly . . . [and that] non-Mormons did not understand the significance of such a society to the Mormon movement's millennialism, invariably castigated it, and in some cases sought to destroy it.[21]

The Mormon Church and the Reorganized Church are both broadly international in their membership and perspectives—even though the practical application of their beliefs and structures are handled in different ways by the two churches. In essence, the Mormon Church tends to replicate itself exactly, regardless of the cultural setting. The Reorganized Church has left much of the local practice and structure to indigenous leaders whenever possible. Thus, while the Mormon Church in Africa is similar to that in the United States, the Reorganized Church in Africa would mostly likely be hardly recognizable by a United States RLDS church member.[22]

It is difficult to typify the ordinary church member in any of the Latter Day Saint churches. The Mormon Church tends to have a Republican political outlook, but has devout believers in various political parties. Members of both the Mormon Church and the Reorganized Church are engaged in a broad range of professions, and tend to be middle-American. Both churches have had difficulty in establishing effective missions in the inner cities in large urban centers in the United States. In southern California, for example, both churches tend to be on the outer edges of the cities, in areas that are generally populated by European Americans who speak English. In recent years, the Mormon Church in the Los Angeles area was reported to have disbanded all of its African-American congregations and required its members to integrate into largely European-American groups. It has also had difficulty maintaining Spanish-speaking congregations in southern California, even though the Mormon Church has been extremely successful in Latin countries.

The Reorganized Church is not numerically large enough to have had a major national social impact. In many areas, though, the church has dramatically impacted the people amongst whom it has ministered. There are places around the world where entire villages are predominantly populated by members of the Reorganized Church.[23] In the United States, its influence is greatest in its headquarters city of Independence, Missouri—but that influence is limited, since the church does not hold a majority even there.

Joseph Smith III's successor and son, Frederick Madison Smith, brought the Reorganized Church into the twentieth century with great effort. F. M. Smith began the process of making the church a responsible part of its community and society in general. It was F. M. Smith who led the thinking in the church that Zion was more process than place. Smith proposed that Zion was a condition of love, humility, moral goodness, and unity in the cause of Christ.[24] This became the hallmark of the Reorganized Church's efforts in ministry and evangelism.

Frederick M. Smith's successor and brother, Israel A. Smith, had been trained as a lawyer. His efforts in rewriting the Missouri State Constitution in 1943, as well as various previous stints in governmental service, were indirect ways in which the Reorganized Church had an impact on society. Although the church did not direct Israel's efforts, his upbringing and morals and values certainly played a role in his efforts.

While the Mormon Church has had a profound impact on groups in other nations, none can compare with its strong influence in the United States. George Gallup, Jr., concluded in a 1983 national survey that "The Church of Jesus Christ of Latter-day Saints, while representing only about one percent of the adult population in the United States, is clearly having a profound impact on the United States as a whole."[25] The Mormon people see this not as an accident. This has been a driving force in their very existence since almost the beginning of the Latter Day Saint movement, but more especially since the beginning of the twentieth century.

Many prominent Mormons have been in high-profile jobs with the United States government. It is through their influence that the Mormon Church has been able to exert its own influence. Of course, in Utah, the Mormon Church is the local power. Practically all members of state and local governments are members of the Mormon Church. Extensive financial investments and holdings not only in Utah but elsewhere help the Mormon Church to spread its influence. Through various holding and investment companies, the Mormon Church controls some broadcast media in all major urban centers in the United States. The church owns farms, ranches, insurance companies, publishing houses, retail stores, real estate holdings, etc. throughout the country and perhaps in nations abroad. This accumulation of wealth could be seen as a negative by critics—it is the church's own theology of its destiny that has been the driving force behind its financial and business ventures. This same drive has caused the Mormon people to be noted for their financial and business success—indeed, this type of success is often rewarded with high-ranking church jobs. Missionaries are driven to success orientation by motivational speakers, the measurement of the number of copies of the Book of Mormon they place in a given period of time, and the number of persons they baptize into the church.[26]

Political power at the national level was hard fought for and hard earned. Brigham H. Roberts was elected to the House of Representatives from Utah, and later Reed Smoot was elected as a Senator. Both men were polygamists who had married their multiple wives prior to the 1890 official cut-off date. After extensive hearings, the House refused to seat Roberts. A few years later when it was Smoot's turn, he was finally seated in the Senate after unusually lengthy hearings.[27]

Recently many Mormons have served in prominent positions in the national government. Richard Richards was the head of the Republican National Committee; Terrel H. Bell was Secretary of Education; Angela Buchanan was the Treasurer of the United States during the Reagan administration; Ezra Taft Benson (the late Mormon Church prophet) was the Secretary of Agriculture in Eisenhower's cabinet; Brent Scowcroft was George Bush's national security advisor; and many ambassadors, members of Congress, and government officials served in every branch of government, including the FBI and CIA.[28]

These prominent Mormons believe that God has placed them in their positions in order to wield influence for the church. Senator Orrin Hatch, (R) Utah, maintains strong ties with his church's leadership and visits the leaders of the church in Salt Lake City, regularly reporting on his activities. He has done favors for church leaders and consulted with them on legislative issues. In the 1970s, Hatch used his influence to arrange contacts between church leaders and the Chinese government; in the 1980s he arranged contacts for the church with the Soviet government.[29]

Keith Nyborg, then United States Ambassador to Finland, and a Mormon, told a *Church News* reporter in 1982 that his diplomatic duties and his faith often overlap.

> We are here because the Lord wants us here; it is not really of our own doing and not entirely political. . . . If people ask about the Church, we can explain. But we don't want the news media to pick up on our Church membership and make it a public cause.

The reporter added, "The Finnish LDS public communications office noted that during the year the Nyborgs have been here [in Finland], the Church has been given 1,260 inches of publicity in the press; the year before, it was only 70 inches."[30]

It is plainly evident that the Latter Day Saint movement as a whole has had a profound impact on American society, and that society itself has had a profound impact on the Latter Day Saint movement, as each is part of the other. Both the Mormon Church and the Reorganized Church, as well as the several smaller and lesser-known Latter Day Saint organizations and groups, have had an impact in local areas where numbers of members have been concentrated, and where efforts in ministry have been exerted.

The societal impact of the Latter Day Saint churches on a national level in the United States has been caused mainly by the Utah Church. That body has also been the main beneficiary of the positive results of that societal impact. The Mormon Church, through its high national and international profile, has brought considerable respectability to the Latter Day Saint movement at large.

The Reorganized Church, due to its smaller size and very distinct theological differences with its larger counterpart, has had influence mainly in more localized areas. At the same time, in the areas where it has been present, the Reorganized Church, too, has gained respectability that reflects on the movement as a whole.

Race relations have been a particularly difficult issue for the Mormon Church, because it taught for many years that persons of African-American descent were less valiant than European Americans and even Asian Americans in the pre-earth life, and thus were prohibited by God from being ordained in ministry. In 1969, the church declared "Negroes [sic] are not yet to receive the priesthood, for reasons which we believe are known to God, but which He has not made fully known to man."[31] For many years those African Americans who chose to become Mormons were ministered to through various auxiliary organizations. The policy barring African Americans from ordination was rescinded in 1978, a change which church leaders stated was announced to them by revelation from God. Civil rights groups that had been unsuccessfully trying to sue the church for years suggest that the church finally had to give in to social pressure, much as it did with polygamy in 1890.

Native Americans have always been the target of Mormon proselytizing efforts. Mormon beliefs suggest that Native Americans are descendants of the Twelve Tribes of Israel, and have a favored place in the church. In her studies of the societal impact in the United States of non-Anglo groups, Jessie Embry discovered:

> During the 1960s, for example, Apostle Spencer W. Kimball was very active in organizing Indian congregations, generally called Lamanite [a uniquely Mormon term for Native Americans] branches. There were even separate Indian missions in the Southwest and North Central United States. These congregations were organized to preserve the Native American culture. During the same time, Kimball and fellow apostle LeGrand Richards organized a German-speaking ward [congregation] in the Salt Lake Valley. At that ward's initial meeting, Kimball explained that the Quorum of the Twelve [one of the church's leading bodies] favored the arrangement; as the church expanded to all nations, it was "not right" to force everyone to learn English. But the General Authorities hoped that as the immigrant members in the United States learned English, they would return to their geographical wards [Mormon congregations are assigned geographically, with identical programs in each].[32]

After a period of trying to phase out the ethnic congregations, the church in 1977 reintroduced the idea and proposed a "basic unit plan" which was an effort to provide the essential church programs for smaller groups. Embry concluded that "neither the ethnic branches nor integrated wards have met the needs of all church members. Language and cultural differences have often weakened the uniting ties of religion."[33]

The Mormon Church and its people have struggled with ethnicity for a long time. Often Native American groups shared facilities with Anglo groups, but were not treated equally. As an experience in Washington state was reported,

> Because the Bishop was concerned about saving money, he would shut off the lights while Indians, members and nonmembers, were playing basketball. Native Americans resented this, viewed it as prejudice, and stopped attending church.[34]

When a Native American branch in Omaha, Nebraska, was eliminated, the former branch president, a Native American, stated that " . . . the reason a lot of Indians quit the church was because they pushed them into a basement. For the Native Americans, this was proof that the rich white people did not want them in their meeting house."[35]

This difficulty has worsened in recent years, exacerbated by the dispute between church leaders and George P. Lee, the first Native American to serve as a General Authority[36] of the Mormon Church. He was excommunicated for his views, which were perceived by church leaders as opposing the teachings of the church. The attitudes of the church authorities have been described as symptomatic of a dramatic change in the Mormon view of the position of Native Americans in Mormon theology.

> Years passed, and ultimately George Lee's brethren [Mormon church leaders], virtually all businessmen, decided—as was related to Native Americans who then told me—that the church was not getting a "good return on its investment" in the Indian programs. For instance, some Navajo Bishops and clerks could hardly be constrained to keep all the statistics and fill out all of the paperwork required of a branch. They had other things to do. A talented institute teacher would not restrain himself or his family from taking part in powwows and other cultural activities, or even stop wearing turquoise and silver. In fact, and this was especially maddening, many Indian people began to feel that religion itself was good; they'd combine Church programs with their own native ceremonies and songs. That tendency might be understandable, to a degree, in Africa or Tonga or South America—but not in the enlightened United States. Some tribes were also beginning to resist and criticize the non-Indian

adoption, education, or assimilation of their children.

Before long, some LDS Native Americans began to feel less "special" within the Church. The "Christ in the Americas" program disappeared from the presentations on Temple Square. The Church's Indian seminary and institute program vanished, and other programs rapidly eroded . . . [37]

Several years ago, when the Equal Rights Amendment was a hot issue, the Mormon Church was oppsed to its passage and successfully campaigned through the church women's group in several key states against its ratification. The Equal Rights Amendment ultimately died because it had not been ratified by the requisite number of states.[38]

The era of the civil rights struggles in the 1950s and 1960s were a challenge to the Reorganized Church's thinking. The members of the church were divided on the issue.

The church's official position on blacks had, since 1865, been open and supportive. But the real relationship essentially formed along the same lines of division and opinions found in any cross-section of society. President W. Wallace Smith did not favor the confrontational methods of the Civil Rights movement. F. Henry Edwards—perhaps the most outspoken member of the First Presidency—considered the race question to be a social issue and thus believed it inappropriate for the First Presidency to take a stand. . . .

The 1955 beginning of the black boycott in Alabama pushed the church for a response. The resulting resolution, adopted in 1956, was weaker than many wanted, but it did affirm the church's openness to all races.[39]

Although the Reorganized Church was unprepared for the theological implications of expanded missionary efforts throughout the various elements of American society and in other nations of the world—especially non-Western nations—the church has been successful in its many endeavors. Various institutions have been established by the church and its members

to deal with education, health care, water projects, food production and distribution, energy sources, and home construction. In the United States numerous social projects have been developed by local congregations and jurisdictions of the Reorganized Church as they have endeavored to fulfill their understanding of the ministry of Jesus Christ in their communities.

The Mormon faithful see their church as the coming world power, destined to control the outcome of history. They see the church organizations and programs as aids in bringing to pass "Zion." The late Bruce R. McConkie, once a member of the Twelve Apostles of the church, wrote, "We see the Lord break down the barriers so that the world of Islam and the world of communism can hear the message of the Restoration."[40]

Faithful Mormons believe that the United States government will be eroded and weakened until the Constitution "hangs by a thread" and at that time their highly placed military and political leaders, along with church leaders, will rescue the government and usher in the millennial reign of Jesus Christ. They see world events as direct fulfillment of their interpretations of Scripture and prophecy. They see even their secular jobs and vocations as mere tools to be used to spread the influence of their church in ever-widening circles.[41]

A 1982 editorial in the LDS *Church News* stated,

Most people in this nation [the United States] do not understand the origin and destiny of the United States as the Latter-day Saints do . . . How wonderful it would be if all Americans viewed the marvelous country in which we live in the same light as the Latter-day Saints . . .

The Lord created the United States for a specific purpose. He provided freedom of speech, press, assembly and worship . . .

Here He had determined to restore the gospel. From here it would be taken abroad. From here, during the Millennium, Christ will govern the world.[42]

Over the years the Reorganized Church has worked cooperatively with other groups in the communities where it has been present; the Mormon Church has tended to do things on its own. This is due to the unique and distinct understandings each organization has developed concerning the institutional mission of the church. The two organizations, while coming from common roots and using common language, have developed deeply divergent philosophical understandings of not only the language used in the LDS tradition, but also the history of the larger movement. This has caused each organization to pursue its mission and to place values and priorities in entirely different ways from the other.

One can only view the historical trends to suggest a future. The Mormon Church is one of the most rapidly growing religious organizations in the world today, and trends suggest that this growth will continue in the foreseeable future. Because its political leanings tend to be on the conservative side, fewer Mormons are likely to be involved in the United States government while the Republican party is out of power (although there are some faithful Mormons who are Democrats).

The Reorganized Church will also grow in numbers, but the membership growth will take place in non-Western nations. With the establishment of its temple in Independence, Missouri, the Reorganized Church will continue to emphasize those things which contribute to world peace, and through doing so may well establish itself as a key player on the international scene. Just how this will take place is mostly theoretical at this writing. The Reorganized Church and its involvement in reconciliation ministries on an international level will command attention in various segments of national and worldwide community.

Other Latter Day Saints churches are not likely to command numerically large followings or to have great social impact, except in isolated localities. Many groups will pass from existence, and new ones will be organized to take their place—as has been the history of the Latter Day Saint movement from the beginning.

Notes

1. Joseph Smith, Jr., *Pearl of Great Price* (Salt Lake City: The Church of Jesus Christ of Latter-day Saints, 1982), 50–51. The "First Vision" is the Latter Day Saint moniker for Joseph Smith Jr.'s experience in which he reported, in several different versions, that sometime in the spring of 1820 he became confused about different competing churches and prayed about what his response should be. In his 1842 version, he stated that two personages appeared to him, one being God, the other Jesus Christ. Although rarely referred to in the first years of the movement, this event later became pivotal in the evangelistic efforts of the major Latter Day Saint churches.

2. Paul M. Edwards, *Our Legacy of Faith: A Brief History of the Reorganized Church of Jesus Christ of Latter Day Saints* (Independence: Herald Publishing House, 1991), 35.

3. *Book of Doctrine and Covenants* (Independence: Reorganized Church of Jesus Christ of Latter Day Saints, 1990), 74–77.

4. Leonard J. Arrington and Davis Bitton, *The Mormon Experience: A History of the Latter-day Saints* (New York: Alfred A. Knopf, 1979), 48, describe some of the experiences that the early Latter Day Saints had in their relations with their neighbors.

5. Edwards, *Our Legacy of Faith*, 95–111.

6. Steven L. Shields, "The Latter Day Saint Movement: A Study in Survival," which gives a narrative description of these six churches, appears in *When Prophets Die: The Postcharismatic Fate of New Religious Movements*, ed. Timothy Miller (Albany: State University of New York Press, 1991), 59ff.

7. For a catalog of these different groups, see Steven L. Shields, *Divergent Paths of the Restoration* (Los Angeles: Restoration Research, 1990).

8. The "original church" is the organization as it existed under Joseph Smith, Jr.'s, leadership during his lifetime.

9. Among these are the Ervil M. LeBaron stories, some of which have been reported in Ben Bradlee, Jr. and Dale Van Atta, *Prophet of Blood: The Untold Story of Ervil LeBaron and the Lambs of God* (New York: G. P. Putnam's Sons, 1981). More recently the Jeff Lundgren case at Kirtland, Ohio, was referred to in "Media and Cults," *Saints Herald* (March 1990): 1–2.

10. Arrington and Bitton, *The Mormon Experience*, 170–71.

11. Ibid., 179–84.

12. See "Official Declaration 1," in the *Doctrine and Covenants* (Salt Lake City: The Church of Jesus Christ of Latter-day Saints, 1982), 291–93. This declaration by the then-president of the Mormon Church brought an end to the public practice of polygamy and paved the way for Utah to become a state.

13. Thomas G. Alexander, *Mormonism in Transition* (Urbana and Chicago: University of Illinois Press, 1986); Arrington and Bitton, *The Mormon Experience*, 272–78; Richard O. Cowan, *The Church in the Twentieth Century* (Salt Lake City: Bookcraft, Inc., 1985), 138 ff.

14. Edwards, *Our Legacy of Faith*, 127–39.

15. Lavinia Fielding Anderson, "The LDS Intellectual Community and Church Leadership: A Contemporary Chronology," *Dialogue* 26 (Spring 1993), Salt Lake City.

16. Ibid., 29–30.

17. Ibid., 25.

18. Ibid., 29, 49, 50.

19. Edwards, *Our Legacy of Faith*, 223.

20. Roger D. Launius, *Joseph Smith III: Pragmatic Prophet* (Urbana and Chicago: University of Illinois Press, 1988), 168–69.

21. Ibid., 169.

22. Maurice L. Draper, *Isles and Continents* (Independence: Herald House, 1982). The author chronicles the development of the Reorganized Church in areas outside of North America, focusing on the rapid expansion which occurred between 1958 and 1978, when the church expanded into Africa, Asia, and South America.

23. Draper, *Isles and Continents*.

24. Edwards, *Our Legacy of Faith*, 223ff.

25. As quoted in John Heinerman and Anson Shupe, *The Mormon Corporate Empire* (Boston: Beacon Press, 1985), 128.

26. Robert Gottlieb and Peter Wiley, *America's Saints: The Rise of Mormon Power* (New York: G. P. Putnam's Sons, 1984). This book takes a comprehensive look at the extensive economic empire controlled by the Mormon Church, and how LDS politicians both locally and nationally are gaining power and influence. The book chronicles the Mormon Church's rise to power since World War II.

27. Heinerman and Shupe, *The Mormon Corporate Empire*, 132–34.

28. Ibid., 135–37. See also pp. 128–40 and 162–68 for a narrative of the CIA's aggressive recruitment of Mormon missionaries for CIA service. Several Mormons made the news in the 1980s who were either CIA or FBI agents. There is also the story of the Los Angeles FBI office and its director, Richard Bretzing, who promoted Mormon agents over Hispanic Catholic agents, who used his secretary to do church work on government time, etc. An interesting twist is that the Mormon Church security system often recruits church members away from the FBI and CIA. The security system provides bodyguard service for church leaders, as well as security for church properties.

29. Ibid., 139–40.

30. Ibid., 137–38, quoting Dorothy Stowe, "Ex-Missionary Makes Transition from 'Finlandia' to Finland," *LDS Church News,* Salt Lake City, 20 November 1982, p. 4.

31. Arrington and Bitton, *The Mormon Experience*, 321–25.

32. Jessie L. Embry, "Ethnic Groups and the LDS Church," *Dialogue* 25 (Winter 1992): 81–97.

33. Ibid.

34. Ibid., 87–88.

35. Ibid.

36. The term "General Authority" is the moniker used in the Mormon Church to describe the highest-ranking officers of the church. This includes the president of the church, his counselors in the First Presidency, the Twelve Apostles, the Presiding Bishopric, and the members of the Quorums of Seventy.

37. Linda Sillitoe, "Who We Are, Where We Come From," *Dialogue* 25 (Fall 1992): 9–18.

38. Ibid., 144–52.

39. Ibid., 261–63.

40. Richard O. Cowan, *The Church in the Twentieth Century* (Salt Lake City: Bookcraft, 1985), 425.

41. Heinerman and Shupe, *The Mormon Corporate Empire*, 128–32.

42. "Preserving Our Loyalties," *Church News,* 6 November 1982, p. 16, as quoted in *The Mormon Corporate Empire,* 129–30.

Suggestions for Further Reading

Arrington, Leonard J., and Davis Bitton. *The Mormon Experience: A History of the Latter-day Saints.* New York: Alfred A. Knopf, 1979.

Edwards, Paul M. *Our Legacy of Faith: A Brief History of the Reorganized Church of Jesus Christ of Latter Day Saints.* Independence: Herald Publishing House, 1991.

Gottlieb, Robert and Peter Wiley. *America's Saints: The Rise of Mormon Power.* New York: Putnam's, 1984.

Ludlow, Daniel H., ed. *Encyclopedia of Mormonism.* New York: Macmillan, 1992.

O'Dea, Thomas F. *The Mormons.* Chicago: University of Chicago Press, 1957.

Shields, Steven L. *Divergent Paths of the Restoration.* Los Angeles: Restoration Research, 1990.

5

CHRISTIAN SCIENCE AND AMERICAN CULTURE

John K. Simmons

Introduction

Christian Science, founded by Mary Baker Eddy (1821–1910), emerged as a unique religious phenomenon in American culture during the tumultuous latter decades of the nineteenth century. Because it is one of only a handful of Christian sects actually "born in the USA," the story of the Christian Science movement has as much to reveal about the religious imagination of Americans as it does about the complexities and nuances of American culture.[1] The opening line in Mrs. Eddy's[2] seminal work, *Science and Health with Key to the Scriptures,* provides an immediate insight into a primary religious impulse of her time. "To those leaning on the sustaining infinite, to-day is big with blessings."[3] The cultural experience of American citizens living in the late nineteenth century was anything but sustaining. In fact, day-to-day life often seemed as fractured and unstable as bedrock in California. Though all religions, to some extent, embody a spiritual search for permanence in a constantly changing world, Mrs. Eddy's delineation of a "sustaining" metaphysical reality found a ready audience in believers who had lost faith in a traditional Christian cosmology challenged by scientific and social revolutions. In this chapter we will explore the relationship between Christian Science and American culture while chronologically tracking the emergence and growth of the movement.

Philosophical/Theological Background

While members, past and present, of the Christian Science movement understandably claim Mrs. Eddy's truths to be part of a unique and final religious revelation, most outside observers place Christian Science in the metaphysical family of religious organizations with roots "both in the idealistic philosophy of the nineteenth century and in the search for alternative means of healing at a time when the healing arts were still in a primitive state."[4] The broad descriptive term "metaphysical" is not used in a manner common to the trained philosopher. Instead, it denotes the primacy of Mind as *the* controlling factor in human experience. At the heart of the metaphysical perspective is the theological/ontological affirmation that God is perfect Mind and human beings, in reality, exist in a state of eternal manifestation of that Divine Mind. The implications of this type of metaphysical perfectionism are nicely summarized in Mrs. Eddy's "Scientific Statement of Being":

> There is no life, truth, intelligence nor substance in matter. All is infinite Mind and its infinite manifestation, for God is All-in-All. Spirit is immortal truth; matter is mortal error. Spirit is the real and eternal; matter is the unreal and temporal. Spirit is God, and man is His image and likeness. Therefore man is not material; he is spiritual.[5]

If God is Mind and the substance of being is Spirit, then humans, as the perfect reflection or expression of Mind can be, must be as perfect as God. Contrary to Protestant orthodoxy, it is not original sin that causes human beings to experience suffering, insecurity, lack, illness, and death but a profound *error* in thinking. While traditional Christianity places the kingdom of heaven in a realm beyond and hereafter, Christian Science calls for the actualization or demonstration of perfection in the here and now by *knowing* the truth of being. The Christian Scientist does not pray to a whimsical, distant, "old man in the sky" for health, security, and prosperity. These are qualities of God's unchanging expression that human beings invariably will reflect, experientially, once they depart from erring, limited, mortal thinking. God, as Divine Principle, can be demonstrated, *scientifically,* by anyone who knows and affirms this principle of being. The infinite, indeed, is sustaining, as the path to salvation becomes strewn with discarded material thoughts. Though Mrs. Eddy's attackers, and there were many, scoffed at her theology, claiming it was irrational, dangerous, and impractical, she stressed the practical nature of her "science." It was in day-to-day challenges, lived experience, that Christian Scientists proved that "God's infinitude and omnipotence rule out the legitimacy, permanence, and substantiality of anything contrary to God's nature as Principle, Mind, Spirit, Soul, Life, Truth, and Love."[6] Thus, healing, both of sin and sickness, became a focus of the religion, a practical manifestation of the change in thinking from the material to the spiritual.

On the question of evil, Mrs. Eddy departed from the more benign interpretations found in other metaphysical religions of the period, subsumed under the title New Thought.[7] Probably from her strict Calvinist upbringing, Mrs. Eddy retained an intense, often suffocating awareness of evil—not as a reality in God's perfect creation, but as a definite, and dangerous, presence in mortal mind. "Mortal mind" or "malicious animal magnetism" were terms she used to describe the mental error which was the collective consciousness of all human beings who had not yet attained her realization of humanity as the perfect, ever-unfolding reflection of Divine Mind.

And, in the hands (or minds) of the devious, malicious animal magnetism could be manipulated to actually cause another harm. For instance, in 1882, she publicly claimed that her last husband, Asa Gilbert Eddy, died of "mental assassination," accusing a former student she felt betrayed her, one Edward J. Arens.[8] In another celebrated case (1878) that earned her much negative publicity, she actually sued another renegade student, Daniel H. Spofford, claiming that he was deliberately practicing malicious mesmerism on one of her unhealed patients, Lucretia Brown. Irreverently dubbed "The Second Salem Witch Trial," the suit was eventually thrown out of court.[9] In 1872, after a breakup with her first formal student, Richard Kennedy, she came to believe he was using mental malpractice to undermine her Christian Science practice, and ordered her students to stand outside her bedroom door to mentally ward off any attacks by Kennedy.[10] While no Christian Scientist would equate "mortal mind" with the devil of orthodox Christianity, it is hard not to see some parallel with the ontological dualism of Mrs. Eddy's early Congregational upbringing.

The "Christian" element in Christian Science emerges in the teaching that Jesus was the ultimate "Christian Scientist" who demonstrably overcame sin, sickness, and death through his superior perception of the allness of Spirit and the nothingness of matter. Jesus was seen not as a unique savior who atoned for human sin as traditional Christianity taught, but as the first human being to understand and fully express Divine Mind. As Stephen Gottschalk notes, Christian Science calls for a "radical reinterpretation of the meaning of the gospel."[11] The real lesson of the gospels finds Jesus as exemplar—a human being who attained Christ consciousness and was then, scientifically, able to demonstrate mastery of sin, disease, and death. While orthodoxy describes Jesus' works as "supernatural interruptions of natural process and law,"[12] Christian Science sees no miracles; rather, Jesus' short ministry proved the ontological basis of spiritual principle.

Spiritual Forbearers of Christian Science

Charismatic prophets like Mrs. Eddy are prone to claim that their revelations are unique. But a lesson learned from studying nineteenth-century sectarian religions such as Christian Science is that a successful prophet is one who profits from popular religious sentiments already existing in the spiritual imagination of the citizenry. Mid-nineteenth-century America was certainly in an experimental mood and there was no dearth of alternative religious perspectives. Without claiming that Mrs. Eddy studied or even agreed with these perspectives, one might note that a variety of worldviews prepared the psychic way for Christian Science, including Swedenborgianism, Mesmerism, Transcendentalism, and Spiritualism. Together they implanted in the American spiritual imagination the connection among physical, psychological, and spiritual health.

Emanuel Swedenborg (1688–1772), the extraordinary Swedish visionary, in voluminous writings, taught that the Divine and the natural are consubstantial in God and Man. Everything that exists visibly, in day-to-day experience, reflects patterns laid out in the spiritual world and is the end product of spiritual force.

If Swedenborgianism offered a unitive view of existence, Franz Anton Mesmer (1734–1815) provided the very principle interconnecting the human and spiritual realms: "animal magnetism," a subtle, universal substance that when properly manipulated could give vitality to the dying and the sick. Both teachings stressed that one's relationship towards nature, society, and God depended upon attunement to the harmonizing emanations from the highest realm, Spirit or Mind. In a world that preceded the great war between science and religion and amongst people who had been raised to view earthly phenomena through a practical commonsense aperture, Swedenborg and Mesmer gave scientific validity to their quest for self-understanding and religious assurance.

Emersonian Transcendentalism added to this "can do" religious vitality characteristic of alternative religions in the nineteenth century. Immanence, individual effort in self-actualization, intuition, imagination all became qualities of life designed to pierce the restricting shell of materiality and usher the initiate into direct contact with the Oversoul. At the same time, Spiritualism underscored the possibility of access to spiritual realms by creating the first toll-free connection to those who had shuffled off this mortal coil.

Again, there is no evidence that these spiritualities directly affected the revelation of Mrs. Eddy. In fact, she went out of her way to condemn Mesmerism and Spiritualism and, to a lesser degree, Transcendentalism. The point is that the combined perspectives represented by these worldviews engaged the religious imagination of the American people as popular religion outside of traditional organized religion. Thus these religious forbearers prepared the way for Mrs. Eddy's spiritual leap into the sustaining infinite.

Direct Influences/Controversies/The Founding Years

Perhaps no one had more influence on Mary Baker Eddy than Phineas Parkhurst Quimby (1802–1866). Quimby was a blacksmith's son born in Lebanon, New Hampshire, who later became a successful clockmaker in Belfast, Maine.[13] In 1838, while attending a lecture by the French mesmerist Charles Poyen, Quimby underwent his first "ecstatic" revelation and gave up his clockmaking career to become a successful mesmerist and healer. In time, however, Quimby began to suspect that the healings he produced were caused by more than a manipulation of "magnetic fluids." Animal magnetism alone could not account for his enormous healing success. In a flash of spiritual insight, he became convinced that it was not a physical process at all, but the confidence the healer inspired in his patient and the accompanying expectation of recovery—in other words, Mind over material conditions.

Quimby then launched a completely new healing ministry based on an integration of scientifically demonstrable mind healing and Christian teachings. It was Quimby who first came up with the term for God, "Divine Mind." He went on to teach that the Christ was the spirit of God in all human beings and a channel, when properly attuned, for ailing humans to connect to emanations of health, happiness, prosperity, and abundance. Limited, material thinking produced limited experience; spiritual thought generated abundance. A controversy rages to this day concerning the question of whether Quimby should rightfully be considered the "founder" of a "Christian Science" and, thus, the intellectual and spiritual source of the metaphysical movement. Many accuse Mrs. Eddy of appropriating Quimby's teachings and claiming them as her own divine revelation. Quimby, however, was not formally educated and left no comprehensive writings on his philosophy. In fact, it would fall to prolific writers such as Warren Felt Evans (1817–1889), Julius Dresser (1838–1893), and his son Horatio Dresser (1866–1954) to popularize Quimby's teachings. In chronicling the emergence of Christian Science, what is most important about Quimby is that in October of 1862, he treated and at least initially inspired an intense young woman who would eventually go on to found the First Church of Christ, Scientist—one Mary Baker Eddy.

The story of Mary Morse Baker-Glover-Patterson-Eddy's life and her extraordinary accomplishment in carving an enduring religious organization out of a male-dominated society is well documented.[14] Though it is not necessary to retell the fascinating story of her rise to metaphysical stardom in its entirety, a few key milestones in her life should be noted. Born on a farm in Bow Township, near Concord, New Hampshire, this imaginative and attractive but emotionally tormented child would grow into an adulthood that, until her meeting with Quimby, was a study in misery—sickness, bad and broken marriages, and emotional disturbances turned her life into an unceasing quest for mental and physical health. A classic "nervous American," she was both possessed and tormented by the "relentless Calvinist theology" she learned at Old North Church in Concord. In the words of Sydney Ahlstrom, "everything we know of her early years makes them an understandable prelude to an adult life of ceaseless search for health, religious certainty, and communion with God on the one hand, and for attention and fame on the other."[15]

The short respite of peace she enjoyed while studying with Quimby was shattered by his death in 1866. However, following what she believed was her own miraculous healing after a fall on ice—just a few months after Quimby's demise—she became convinced that her purpose in life was to reveal the truth of Christian Science. For the next nine years, she thought, wrote, and lived in poverty, percolating her plan and promise. 1875 was a pivotal year in the emergence of Christian Science because not only did Mrs. Eddy then establish the first "Christian Scientists Home" in Lynn, Massachusetts, but she published the first edition of her textbook, *Science and Health*.

American Culture and the Birth of Christian Science

To live in the latter decades of the nineteenth century was to live in a time of radical, and often frightening, cultural change. The Civil War left the nation in a state of grief and repentance, and the churches were called upon to provide new visions, new choices for American citizens. But what were those choices to be? The social stability of a nation just done with a soul-shaking war was rocked by hurricane-force winds generated by two equally tempestuous revolutions: an intellectual revolution and enormous socioeconomic change.

The intellectual revolution attacked the biblically oriented self-understanding of America's destiny on two fronts. First, the thinking, writings, and scholarly investigations of Charles Darwin, Sigmund Freud, and Karl Marx completely undermined the covenantal biblical notion of a transcendent, moral God who, as was commonly accepted, had chosen America and the American people for a special purpose. As if that was not enough, the Bible itself seemed to come under attack from scholars who, for the first time, were examining the book not as sacred text but as a literary-historical account that could be examined from an objective, critical standpoint. For many, this Higher Biblical Criticism, as it was called, undermined the authority of the Bible and thus called into question basic assumptions about the nature and meaning of life.

At the same time the intellectual, theological, and cultural underpinnings of the nation came under attack, society was undergoing massive changes. Industrialization, immigration, and urbanization combined to push American society into a complex sociocultural labyrinth without a map for guidance or leaders who possessed the intuitive qualities necessary for successful travel through the maze. The simplicity of agrarian/small-town values—voluntary cooperation, rugged individualism tempered by community spirit, implicitly accepted Protestant moral precepts such as thrift, sobriety, modesty, hard work, and honesty—seemed to set one at a disadvantage in the exploding urban jungles characterized by slums, crime, labor unrest, political corruption, and capitalist exploitation. Furthermore, the immigration of non-Anglo-Saxon, non-English-speaking, non-Protestant peoples into a once homogeneous society caused a severe national identity crisis. People were in genuine distress as to the nature and meaning of their own lives, not to mention the life of the nation.

Mary Baker Eddy's contemporaries, religious and civil leaders, rose to the occasion, offering a highly variegated set of cures for these cultural afflictions. Social Gospelers, Reform Darwinists, Progressives, Fundamentalists, Holiness-Pentecostals, Adventists, New Thoughters, Post-millennialists, and Pre-millennialists all answered the call led by such disparate notables as Dwight Moody, Washington Gladden, Lester Ward, Emma Curtis Hopkins, John Dewey, Billy Sunday, and Richard Ely. And, of course, Mary Baker Eddy offered the sustaining infinite of Divine Mind as a spiritual balm for cultural upheaval. If a person understood that all the social turmoil was simply the false testimony of mortal mind, an error in ontological perception, then Christian Science was, indeed, the remedy for all ills, social and otherwise. Her message was clear: change your thinking, and change your reality. Much to the chagrin of the religious and intellectual establishment, numerous nervous Americans embraced this message and joined the Christian Science movement.

Christian Science: Growth and Development

For Mary Baker Eddy, the years 1875 to the turn of the century were spent building what would become a centrally controlled religious organization without rival in the rigidity of its restraints upon branch churches and members. Although in the beginning of her movement Mrs. Eddy had not opted for a formal institution, she grew dissatisfied with this direction and reversed herself. The early church structure included the establishment of the Church of Christ, Scientist (1879), the Massachusetts Metaphysical College (1881), and the National Christian Science Association (1886). However, when the congregational pattern of church polity, characteristic of her first religious organization, proved too democratic and a catalyst for rebellion, she shocked her followers by disorganizing the National Christian Science Association. When, in 1892, she reorganized the Christian Science movement around the Mother Church in Boston, her unwavering motivation must have been to create a fixed and enduring institution that would never slip from her ecclesiastical grasp.

For example, all members were urged to join the Mother Church. Other churches were reduced to the status of "branch churches," satellites revolving around the sun she controlled. There were no ministers in the organization to vie for power. Religious services were conducted by Readers who read only from the Bible and *Science and Health* and only from set lessons issued quarterly from the Mother Church.

All rules and regulations governing the Christian Science movement are laid out in the *Manual of the Mother Church.* At Mrs. Eddy's request, the first codification was undertaken by a committee in 1895 and would go through eighty-nine editions before revisions ceased with her death on December 3, 1910. Since changes cannot be made without her approval, church structure and liturgical activity have remained the same within the movement to the present time.

The Christian Science Church has been remarkably free from schism. In the decade after Mrs. Eddy's demise, a legal battle, known within the movement as the Great Litigation, ensued over the question of who would lead the church. In 1921, the case was decided in favor of a five-person board of directors, based on a legal interpretation of *The Manual of the Mother Church.* Since the settlement, there have been power struggles within the church organization, but none that resulted in a new Christian Science organization. The only legitimate sectarian movement to develop from the original organization was begun by Annie Bill in the decade after Mrs. Eddy's death, but Bill's group, which went through various spiritual and organizational permutations, died out after a generation.[16] The tendency within the organization has been for members who for one reason or another have left the church to remain independent, if excommunicated, Christian Scientists. In fact, Stephen Gottschalk makes the rather astounding claim that of the 350,000–450,000 people who, today, might consider themselves to be Christian Scientists, the majority do not have formal ties to the denomination.[17]

Current Challenges/Concluding Remarks

Is the Christian Science movement a sect, a cult, or a denomination? From a sociological perspective, the group has, historically, moved back and forth on a cult-sect-denomination continuum. As was the case with most nineteenth-century founders of "made-in-America" Christian groups, Mrs. Eddy thought of her church in sectarian terms. She had restored, renewed, the "true Christianity." On her side were Jesus, the apostles, and the prophets. However, to one outside the movement, Christian Science has added so much "novel culture" to orthodox Christian doctrine that the group appears to meet the descriptive criteria of a cult. Certainly, the attacks on the movement from the religious, medical, and educational establishment, throughout the existence of the organization, demonstrate a level of tension with the dominant culture that is cultic in nature.[18] Yet, Christian Science has drawn a conservative, middle-class membership and, with one exception, functions, liturgically and organizationally, like any other conservative Protestant Christian denomination in American society. The notable exception is the radical reliance on spiritual healing. The eschewing of any type of medical help in the face of illness has tended to move Christian Science from denomination to sect or cult on the sociological continuum based on the oft-publicized deaths of children of Christian Science parents, especially when the illness was allegedly curable if medical help had been sought.

Since the height of membership in the 1950s, the Christian Science movement has been on a steady decline. While analysts have laid the blame for the movement's downward spiral toward organizational oblivion on everything from the invention of penicillin to the secularization of society, it is, ironically, American culture itself that has been a major cause of the group's demise. While Mrs. Eddy's *Manual* has locked the church in a crusty, late-nineteenth century Victorian time warp in terms of the language and presentation of her teachings, the essence of her message has been co-opted by leaders in mainstream Protestant churches and by American culture itself. Preachers such as California's Robert Schuller or his predecessor, Norman Vincent Peale, have taken the mind over matter, "positive thinking" message of Christian Science and adapted it to a quasi-orthodox Protestant Christian theological stance. Protestant, Catholic, and Jewish religious writers have produced books that top the charts while offering thinly disguised Christian Science ideas. The most popular title, Peale's *The Power of Positive Thinking,* sold two million copies! Others include Bishop Fulton Sheen's *Peace of Soul* and Rabbi Joshua Liebman's *Peace of Mind.* Finally, Christian Science is on the decline because the message is simply no longer extraordinary. The ideas

present in Mrs. Eddy's one-hundred-year-old "discovery" have been absorbed and reexpressed in terms that resonate with popular culture in America. For example, commercial slogans such as "Just do it!" (Nike), "Be All You Can Be" (U.S. Armed Forces), "Master the Possibilities" (Master Card), or "To Know No Boundaries" (Merrill Lynch) suggest that human beings have the capacity to create their own, "perfected," reality through control of mental attitude. Hoary metaphysical principles permeate everything from pop-psychology to New Age philosophy as we are exhorted to overcome our limitations and seek health, wealth, and happiness in the attainment of higher consciousness. If the Christian Science movement goes the way of the dinosaur, it will not be because Mrs. Eddy failed—her own intuitive insight into the American religious imagination was simply ahead of its time!

Notes

1. Other nineteenth century "made-in-America" religions include Mormonism, Spiritualism, Adventism, Jehovah's Witnesses, New Thought, and Holiness-Pentecostalism.

2. The use of "Mrs. Eddy" throughout this chapter is not meant to be sexist. This is how her devotees refer to her.

3. Mary Baker Eddy, *Science and Health with Key to the Scriptures* (Boston: Trustees under the Will of Mary Baker Eddy, 1875), vii.

4. J. Gordon Melton, *The Encyclopedia of American Religions* 3rd ed. (Detroit): Gale Research, 1989), 105.

5. Eddy, *Science and Health,* 468.

6. Stephen Gottschalk, "Christian Science," *Encyclopedia of Religion,* vol. 3 (New York: Macmillan, 1987), 444.

7. New Thought religious organizations include Unity School of Christianity, Divine Science, Religious Science.

8. Stephen Gottschalk, *The Emergence of Christian Science in American Religious Life* (Berkeley: University of California Press, 1973), 125–26.

9. Georgine Milmine, *The Life of Mary Baker Eddy and the History of Christian Science* (New York: Doubleday, 1909), 240.

10. Milmine, *Life of Mary Baker Eddy,* 231.

11. Gottschalk, "Christian Science," 443.

12. Ibid., 444.

13. Sydney E. Ahlstrom, *A Religious History of the American People* (New Haven: Yale University Press, 1974), 1020–21.

14. Please see bibliography for detailed histories of the life and teaching of Mary Baker Eddy.

15. Ahlstrom, *Religious History,* 1021.

16. John K. Simmons, "Charisma and Covenant," in *When Prophets Die,* ed. Timothy Miller (New York: State University of New York Press, 1991), 107–123.

17. Gottschalk, "Christian Science," 444.

18. Rodney Stark and William S. Bainbridge, *The Future of Religion* (Berkeley: University of California Press, 1985). This is a useful and accurate study of sects, cults, and denominations.

Suggestions for Further Reading

Ahlstrom, Sydney E. *A Religious History of the American People.* New Haven: Yale University Press, 1974.

Braden, Charles S. *Christian Science Today.* Dallas: Southern Methodist University Press, 1958.

Gottschalk, Stephen. *The Emergence of Christian Science in American Religious Life.* Berkeley: University of California Press, 1973.

Judah, J. Stillson. *The History and Philosophy of the Metaphysical Movements in America.* Philadelphia: Westminster Press.

Peel, Robert. *Christian Science.* New York: Henry Holt and Company, 1958.

———. *Mary Baker Eddy: The Years of Discovery.* New York: Holt, Rinehart, and Winston, 1966.

———. *Mary Baker Eddy: The Years of Trial.* New York: Holt, Rinehart, and Winston, 1971.

———. *Mary Baker Eddy: The Years of Authority.* New York: Holt, Rinehart, and Winston, 1977.

6

ON THE VERGE: THE EVOLUTION OF AMERICAN QUAKERISM

Margaret Hope Bacon

The Religious Society of Friends, or Quakerism, as it is popularly known, presents an intriguing case history of an alternative religion that became mainstream, yet retained some of its outsider characteristics. While large numbers of Quakers in the United States today hold their worship in a manner indistinguishable from many other Protestant denominations, entertain a conventional view of the Bible, and adhere to popular values in regard to many of the issues of the day, others retain a unique form of worship, believe the Bible can only be read under the inspiration of the Inner Light, and find themselves in opposition to popular cultural beliefs in regard to such issues as pacifism, civil liberties, affirmative action, and reproductive rights. Both groups correctly appeal to the same historical tradition, for contradictions were built into the Quaker movement at its birth in the ferment of Puritan England in the middle of the seventeenth century.[1]

At the time of its beginnings, Quakerism shared a number of views in varying degrees with other radical sects: a belief in the direct access of the human being to the Holy Spirit without the necessity of intermediaries; a belief that common people could read the Bible and interpret it for themselves; permission for women to preach and prophesy; a measure of pacifism; egalitarianism, including the use of the plain language; a refusal to swear oaths; and a lay ministry.[2] Only the Quakers, however, institutionalized these values, brought them to the New World, and managed to survive with many of the values intact into the present. While never a large group, the Quakers have had a large influence on the emergence of an American culture, despite the many schisms and diversities in their midst.

Quakerism dates its origin to 1652, when George Fox, its charismatic founder, came into the north country in England, and met a large group of Seekers who found his preaching compelling. Fox believed that the risen Christ was present and available to everyone as a teacher, and that through inner baptisms and inner communion it was possible for men and women to rid themselves of the burden of sin, and become as Adam and Eve had been before the fall. Fox was an ardent student of the Bible, and believed it to be divinely inspired, but he also believed that it must be read in the light of the Spirit, and if no biblical text could be found to justify an inspired course of action, then Spirit itself could suffice as justification. He advocated the use of the plain language (saying thee and thou rather than you in the singular), refused to take off his hat to authorities (or in fact to recognize anyone's authority over him), objected to all priests and "steeple houses," believed that the sacraments must be inward, not outward, and taught his followers to worship in silence, waiting for the inspiration of the Holy Spirit.[3]

Those in the group that gathered around him called themselves Children of the Light, but were eventually nicknamed Quakers by a hostile judge. They suffered much persecution in England over their refusal to pay tithes or obey authority. On fire with the desire to spread the good news of their new religion, they travelled up and down the British Isles preaching, and lived somewhat communally, Friends supporting both the travelling ministers and their families who remained at home, and caring for each other when they were imprisoned. Originally, Quakers were loosely organized, but with the coming of persecution it became necessary for some structure to be developed. As a result, beginning around 1660, local congregations were set up as meetings for worship throughout the country. Each meeting was responsible for the care and discipline of its own members and the supervision of smaller worship groups, called preparative meetings. Meetings occurred monthly for the conduct of business, and were called monthly meetings. Once every three months monthly meetings in a region would gather for a quarterly meeting, and once a year all the quarters for a yearly meeting. In keeping with Quaker egalitarian beliefs, each meeting was autonomous, but the whole was bound together by a common set of rules, or "book of discipline" developed by the yearly meeting. Yearly meetings kept in touch with one another through epistles prepared and read at the time of the meeting.[4]

The Quaker testimony concerning the equality of women, which has become so prominent in the life of the Society, was strengthened by the fact that separate women's meetings were set up on a monthly, quarterly, and sometimes yearly basis. Although women were not given full equality with the men in making meeting decisions, the fact that they had their own separate space caused them to learn to keep minutes and accounts, write epistles, and develop strategies on their own, and it prepared them for later activities in the public arena.[5]

When the first Quaker pioneers landed on the American continent in 1656, two women in the Massachusetts Bay Colony and one in Virginia, they were representatives of the first alternative religion to pose a threat to the established churches—Congregationalism in New England, and the Church of England in the southern colonies. The fact that these people believed in a direct relationship between God and human beings, their attitude toward the Bible, and the autonomy of their women were all regarded as heretical. The pioneers in New England were imprisoned, searched for signs of witchcraft, and shipped out. Later, when more Quakers arrived to take their place, the Puritans began to pass anti-Quaker laws. Eventually a number of Quakers were imprisoned and flogged and four were hanged. Persecution was somewhat less virulent at first in the southern colonies, but soon Virginia and Maryland were imprisoning Quaker visitors. In New York the Quakers were whipped and punished until the directors of the Dutch West India Company intervened. In all of the colonies the Quakers were regarded as dangerous heretics, their attitudes bringing into question not only religious beliefs but also established government.[6]

Persecution only deepened the commitment of the first generation of Friends to preach the Truth throughout the New World, and tightened the bonds of the Quaker movement. Additional Quaker ministers, including the founder, George Fox, came out from the British Isles to help with the establishment of Quakerism, and to protest to the British monarch the sorry treatment of his subjects. Partly as a result of this political work, partly perhaps because they ultimately wore out their persecutors, Quakers became more tolerated in some of the colonies, although the Puritans continued to be implacably opposed to them. The establishment of the Colony of West Jersey in 1675, and of Pennsylvania in 1682, in both of which William Penn played a part, constituted a response to the hostile climate against Friends and the need to establish a sanctuary for those desiring to settle in the American colonies. Other persecuted minorities, including the

Mennonites, also found a safe home in these middle colonies.[7]

As persecution began to fade, the Quakers were able to prosper in their new homeland. They were frugal and industrious, and retained many ties to Quaker merchants and bankers in England. As a result they grew prosperous, even wealthy. In North Carolina and in Rhode Island Quaker governors were elected. In Pennsylvania many members of the ruling assembly were Quakers, and in New Jersey they comprised the proprietors of the colony. They built solid, handsome meeting houses for their unique form of silent worship, and equally solid homes in which to raise their large families. Set aside by their unique dress, their use of the plain language, and their refusal to pay tithes or support the military, Friends nevertheless became well-respected citizens in many areas.[8]

But Friends also remained outsiders in some respects during this period (which covered roughly the first fifty years of the eighteenth century), their testimony against war in particular setting them aside from the rest of society. Friends in government were plagued with problems of conscience over this testimony against war. When the royal government in England demanded that the colonies levy taxes to support British troops dedicated to protecting the colonists against the Native Americans, Friends found it necessary to develop elaborate rationalizations for the taxes, and more and more voices of protest arose within the Quaker community. Eventually, beginning at the time of the French and Indian War, Friends began one by one to resign from government. Amid the growing tensions between Great Britain and the American colonies they tried to stay neutral, and became increasingly unpopular with their fellow citizens as a result. During the Revolutionary War many Friends suffered distraints for their refusal to pay military taxes, and a group of prominent Philadelphia Quakers were exiled to Virginia.[9]

During the first half of the seventeenth century, while Friends were prospering, they experienced growing difficulties in keeping their young people from adopting the ways of the majority society. Friends forbade marriage outside of the Society, but many young people so married anyway, and were disowned by their local meetings. In addition, some prosperous Quaker families began to adopt a more opulent lifestyle, and when criticized by Friends, some chose to become Anglicans or Presbyterians. This experience, combined with renewed tension at the time of the French and Indian War, led to a strong upsurge of reformation within the Society. A number of gifted ministers, both men and women, travelled throughout the colonies preaching the necessity of separating from "the world's people," as well as making religion the center of one's life.[10]

As Friends heeded this preaching and withdrew from government and other establishment activities, they became more concerned with expressing Quaker testimonies through new organizations. The second half of the eighteenth century saw the development of the Pennsylvania Abolition Society (1775), the Philadelphia Committee for Alleviating the Miseries of the Public Prisons (1787), the Female Society for the Relief and Employment of the Poor (1795), and the Indian Affairs Committee of Philadelphia Yearly Meeting (1796). Concern for the mentally ill led to the creation of the Frankford Asylum in 1813. Thus the reforms for which Quakers are known today—advocacy for African Americans, prison reform, work with the poor, and mental-health reform—all had their origin during this period of retreat from the world.[11]

At the same time, Friends began to establish academies where Quaker teachers could be trained to provide "a guarded education" to Quaker youth. The establishment of Nine Partners near Poughkeepsie in 1796 and of Westtown School in Chester County in 1799 marked the beginning of this trend, which was to help keep Friends separate from the world for generations, and came in time to provide excellent secondary education to non-Friends as well.[12]

Along with the separation from the world's people came an increased emphasis on policing members for actions which might have a negative impact on the Society as a whole. Thus members were disciplined, and in some cases disowned, not only for such sins as fornication and drunkenness but also for defaulting on debts or "departing from the truth" in public statements.

Increasingly, the theology of the individual Friend, once regarded simply as a matter of divine inspiration, came under the scrutiny of the meeting elders. When a minister in a local meeting felt called upon by God to travel in the ministry, he or she had to apply to the select committee of ministers and elders of the monthly, quarterly, or yearly meeting for a certificate or minute recommending her/him to the Christian care of other meetings. Without such a minute, the minister could not speak in a meeting other than her/his own. This permission became a powerful tool to ensure orthodoxy in preaching.[13]

Following the early evangelical period of Quakerism's birth and spread, the group had entered into a period of quietism, emphasizing the subjection of the whole self to the Holy Spirit. Both will and mind as well as personal desires were to be silenced in order that the individual might serve as a channel for that Spirit. Quietists were not passive; many of them were indeed active reformers. Many of the ministers of the Quaker period of reformation were quietists, combining a call to Friends to separate themselves from the world with increased attention to the observance of Quaker testimonies. Thus John Woolman, well known for leading the Society of Friends to give up the practice of slave-owning, was himself a quietist.[14]

Influenced by John Wesley and the evangelical movement, a number of British Friends and their American counterparts became concerned in the early nineteenth century that this concept of the Inner Light was leading Friends away from the authority of the Scriptures and belief in the atonement of Christ as the road to salvation. While George Fox had always emphasized the primacy of the direct relationship between souls and their Creator, he had never questioned that the historical Jesus was also the risen Christ to whom

men and women had direct access. Thus there had been room from the birth of Quakerism for both an evangelical and a liberal theology. Though most of the orthodox of his day had regarded Fox as a heretic because of his reliance on the Holy Spirit, every generation of Quakers following his had included both evangelical and mystic, or prophetic, Friends.[15]

At times Quakers were able to live with this ambiguity, since they did not require members to subscribe to a creed. In periods of strength and creative growth, members have felt themselves bound together by a sense of a living testimony, a spiritual unity of purpose behind apparent diversity. In less creative periods, however, when persecution has ceased and no overwhelming sense of task or mission pulls members together, tensions over doctrinal differences have come to the surface. This was the situation at the end of the eighteenth and the beginning of the nineteenth century. Although the effort to impose uniformity of belief seems to have begun with the London Yearly Meeting, it had its most visible effects in the United States.

In Philadelphia Yearly Meeting, where the problem first erupted, the wealthy and somewhat worldly urban Friends were the first to become concerned about doctrinal orthodoxy. Their apparent attempt to impose their views was resented by the rural Friends, most of whom still clung to quietism and who valued their independence, born of the Quaker belief in individual access to God of the American frontier spirit. The controversy came to a head over the preaching of Elias Hicks, an old-fashioned country quietist from Long Island, and a strong opponent of slavery and of the new evangelicalism. He insisted on the primacy of the Christ within over the Christ of the Bible, and downplayed the importance of the crucifixion and resurrection, it was feared. A travelling minister, he frequently preached these doctrines in and around the Philadelphia Yearly Meeting. Efforts of the elders of that meeting to silence him and to refuse to accept his travelling minute led to a growing controversy in which Friends from England embroiled themselves. Finally the majority party in the Yearly Meeting, under the leadership of a teacher, John Comly, withdrew from the meeting in 1827, and began to meet separately.[16]

With much pain and bitterness, the Religious Society of Friends in America now split into two factions, the Hicksite and the Orthodox. Families were divided, the ownership of meeting houses and schools contested, and lawsuits commenced. The next year, both the Hicksite and Orthodox factions prepared communications, in the form of epistles, to be sent to all the other yearly meetings. This was and is the standard form of communication between the otherwise autonomous bodies. Now however each yearly meeting had to decide which branch to recognize. The decision triggered conflict within many yearly meetings, and ultimately the schism spread to New York, Maryland, and Ohio and later to Indiana and Illinois. In broad terms, the Orthodox were generally the well-to-do establishment urban Friends, while the Hicksites were more rural. However, there were many exceptions. Hicksites were generally far more active in antislavery activities, and Hicksite women gave much of the leadership to the early women's rights movement.[17]

The separation unfortunately led to further schisms. Within the Hicksite fold a conservative and a liberal wing developed, especially in New York, where a Hicksite preacher, George White, objected to the involvement of Friends in antislavery and other reforms. As a result several Friends were disowned for antislavery activities. In northern New York State a schism developed in the Hicksite Yearly Meeting, resulting in the establishment of the Congregational Friends. Similar separations happened in Michigan, Ohio, Indiana, and Pennsylvania.

Among the Orthodox there were small schisms over slavery in Indiana in 1842 and in Iowa a few years later. Beginning in the 1840s the entire Orthodox group was wracked by a struggle between the followers of Joseph John Gurney and John Wilbur. Gurney was a wealthy British Quaker who toured the United States in 1837, preaching a progressive, evangelical

Quakerism, emphasizing Bible study, more attention to education, and an evangelical theology. His opponent, from Rhode Island, was a farmer who, like Elias Hicks, wanted to guard what he considered the older ways with more emphasis on individual inspiration. The Gurneyites were more cosmopolitan; the Wilburites, rural and conservative. A separation between the Gurneyites and the Wilburites took place in New England Yearly Meeting in 1845 and spread to Ohio and North Carolina. Philadelphia Yearly Meeting, torn between the two groups, decided to cut off all correspondence with other yearly meetings rather than face a second division. It alone therefore remained Orthodox, the others all becoming either Wilburite or Gurneyite.

By the time of the Civil War the Society of Friends in the United States was therefore divided into four bodies: the Hicksite, Orthodox, Gurneyite, and Wilburite. The war was a time of testing for those Friends who had been deeply involved with the antislavery struggle. Some continued to believe that slavery could be ended by moral force alone, and viewed the war as a tragic breakdown in that process. Others accepted the war as the inevitable outcome of the antislavery crusade. When drafted, some young Quaker men accepted the service, while women became battlefield nurses. Meetings disciplined and disowned members who thus departed from the testimony against war, but particularly among the Hicksites it was not difficult for the truant to make an apology and be reinstated after the war.

In the post–Civil War era more changes occurred. Many of the frontier meetings were strongly Gurneyite, and joined other denominations when a series of Holiness revivals swept the area. There were altar calls and mourning benches, all quite foreign to previous Quaker experience. Some participating Friends saw this as a return to the religious ecstasy of the beginnings; but others feared it was the end of traditional Quakerism.[18]

Following the revivals, meetings sought to keep alive the fervor they had experienced by hiring pastors to preach, rather than relying exclusively on the ministry of their members. They also turned to a more organized service of worship, with prayer, hymns, a sermon, and Bible reading. Aspects of older Quaker ways were retained: the monthly meeting, the travelling ministers, and the concept that all members were ministers. Nevertheless, to conservative Friends it appeared as though these Quakers had become indistinguishable from their Methodist or Baptist neighbors. As a result, a second phase of the Wilburite separation occurred as some Friends withdrew to form Conservative yearly meetings in Indiana, Iowa, Canada, Kansas, and later North Carolina.[19] Doctrinal disputes continued to disturb the Gurneyite yearly meetings, which finally united in 1902 in a five-year meeting. This group, now Friends United Meeting, comprises the largest body of American Quakers today. Dissenting yearly meetings with a more evangelical flavor organized an Evangelical Friends Alliance, embracing yearly meetings in the Far West. Both the Friends United Meeting and the Evangelical Friends Alliance have developed foreign missions, the latter with an evangelical flavor.

The Religious Society of Friends thus entered the twentieth century divided between a liberal eastern wing, the Hicksites, socially active and somewhat liberal in theology; the Orthodox in Philadelphia Yearly Meeting, Christocentric and closely tied with the business and professional establishment in that city; the Gurneyites, the largest group, with a pastoral form of worship, a biblical orientation, and a middle-class orientation; and the Wilburites, a withdrawn, primarily rural, people who kept to the older Quaker speech and costume.

These separations were painful to Friends, but may have been typical of an alternative religion adapting itself to majority culture. Of old American stock, the Quakers were looked on in many communities as examples of probity and good order. They remained separated from the community as a whole by their antiwar beliefs and their attitude toward women, who continued to serve as ministers and to be given an equal education. In the Gurneyite meetings many Quaker women

had distinguished themselves especially during the temperance campaigns, while the Hicksite women were leaders in the campaign for suffrage.[20]

World War I was a time of testing and opportunity for Friends. Many meetings and families had inherited the Quaker peace testimony but given it little thought; the war fervor which swept the United States carried many young men, believing that this war was different, into the army. Others, however, in all the branches of the Friends felt it necessary to declare themselves conscientious objectors. For their sake, the various branches of the Religious Society of Friends joined together in 1917 to create the American Friends Service Committee, charged with providing opportunities for alternative service for conscientious objectors during wartime. The program of wartime and postwar reconstruction which was developed first in France and later in Germany was so successful that the committee continues to exist, finding new challenges to meet, until the present day. Always controversial, because it did not proselytize (a restriction laid on it by the governments of the countries where it worked) because it hired non-Friends as well as Friends, and because it was often more radical in its social outlook than constituent yearly meetings, it was nevertheless a tie binding the various branches together for many years. Again at the time of World War II, all branches of Quakerism joined the other historic peace churches in negotiating with the government for the establishment of alternative service for conscientious objectors, called Civilian Public Service. More recently, all the branches of Quakerdom, along with Mennonites and Brethren, have supported a "New Call to Peacemaking." And Quaker women of all persuasions have gathered to consider the history and present status of women in the Society of Friends, most notably at Woodbrooke College in the summer of 1990.[21]

Until World War I, the peace testimony was considered an essential part of Quaker belief, and those who violated it by going to war were disowned. This however was not the case during either World War I or

World War II. In the latter period, there were more Friends in the armed services than in the Civilian Public Service. While the Society of Friends enforced the peace testimony it continued to be an alternative religion. But even this distinction has been watered down in the twentieth century.

Is the Religious Society of Friends an alternative religion today? The answer is yes and no. Many of its members have played important roles in American history. It has produced two American presidents, Herbert Hoover of Iowa and Richard Nixon of California. Friends have been noted in all the professions, in business and in banking, and are today heavily represented in universities and colleges, a number of which they founded. In *Notable American Women* and the *Dictionary of American Biography* Friends are represented in excess of their numbers. It is generally conceded that Friends gave leadership in the struggle against slavery, for the rights of women and Native Americans, and have played a prominent role in prison and mental-hospital reform.

Many young people have begun attending the silent Friends meetings in university towns or cities, attracted by the peace testimony and by social activism, believing that they have found a religion which permits them to believe whatever they wish, and to join in group meditation. They are sometimes startled when older members of the meeting insist that Quakerism has a strong Christocentric heritage and because of its worldwide fellowship with other Quaker groups it cannot be entirely bent to the wishes of a particular congregation.

The very reliance on the Inward Christ, or the Inner Light, which was the hallmark of the origins of the Society, has encouraged a degree of individualism which may be partly responsible for the wide range of modern Quaker belief. To go from a liberal, silent Friends meeting, where former Jews and Muslims are accepted into the fellowship and same-sex marriage is celebrated, to an evangelical meeting, with a conventional service and where a strongly Christocentric message of salvation is preached and homosexuality is regarded as sin, can be profoundly unsettling. It is tempting for each extreme to tell itself that it is an expression of "the real Quakerism." Yet both have roots in the original Quaker message and both express testimonies in regard to peace and equality which have made an impact on American culture, and continue today to represent aspects of the American conscience.

Notes

1. Henry J. Cadbury, *Introduction to the Journal of George Fox*, ed. Rufus M. Jones (London: Religious Society of Friends, 1963), 7–18.

2. Hugh Barbour, *The Quakers in Puritan England* (New Haven, Conn.: Yale University Press, 1964), 1–32.

3. Ibid., 33–71.

4. William Braithwaite, *Second Period of Quakerism* (New York: Macmillan, 1919), 251–89.

5. Margaret Hope Bacon, *Mothers of Feminism: The Story of Quaker Women in America* (San Francisco: Harper and Row, 1986), 54.

6. Rufus Jones, *Quakers in the American Colonies* (London: Macmillan, 1911), 26–89, 219–22, 266–79.

7. Ibid., 418.

8. Frederick Tolles, *Meeting House and Counting House* (Chapel Hill, N.C.: University of North Carolina Press, 1948), 109–143.

9. Jack Marietta, *The Reformation of American Quakerism, 1748–1783* (Philadelphia: University of Pennsylvania Press, 1984), 251–79.

10. Ibid., 58–72.

11. Margaret H. Bacon, *The Quiet Rebels: The Story of the Quakers in America* (New York, Basic Books, 1969), 122–50.

12. Howard Brinton, *Quaker Education in Theory and Practice* (Wallingford, Pa.: Pendle Hill Pamphlets, 1940), 33.

13. Marietta, *The Reformation of American Quakerism*, 38–61.

14. Ibid., 88–89.

15. Henry J. Cadbury, *Introduction to the Journal of George Fox*, 7–18.

16. H. Larry Ingle, *Quakers in Conflict: The Hicksite Reformation* (Knoxville: University of Tennessee Press, 1986), 141–59.

17. Bacon, *Mothers of Feminism*, 93.

18. Thomas Hamm, *The Transformation of American Quakerism* (Bloomington: Indiana University Press, 1988), 77–97.

19. Ibid., 77–97.

20. Bacon, *Mothers of Feminism*, 93.

21. J. William Frost, " 'Our Deeds Carry Our Message,' The Early History of the American Friends Service Committee," *Quaker History* 81, no. 1 (Spring 1992) (Haverford, Pa.: Friends Historical Association); *First International Theological Conference of Quaker Women* (Richmond, Ind.: Earlham School of Religion).

Suggestions for Further Reading

Barbour, Hugh. *The Quakers in Puritan England*. New Haven, Conn.: Yale University Press, 1964.

Brinton, Howard. *Friends for Three Hundred Years*. New York: Harper, 1952.

Brock, Peter. *The Quaker Peace Testimony, 1660–1914*. York: Sessions, 1991.

Elliott, Errol T. *Quakers on the American Frontier*. Richmond, Ind.: Friends United Press, 1969.

Frost, J. William, and Edwin Bronner. *The Quakers*. Lewiston, N.Y.: Edwin Mellen, 1990.

Jones, Rufus. *Quakers in the American Colonies*. London: Macmillan, 1911.

———. *A Service of Love in Wartime*. New York: Macmillan, 1920.

Hamm, Thomas. *The Transformation of American Quakerism*. Bloomington: Indiana University Press, 1988.

Ingle, H. Larry. *Quakers in Conflict: The Hicksite Reformation*. Knoxville: University of Tennessee Press, 1986.

Marietta, Jack D. *The Reformation of American Quakerism, 1748–1783*. Philadelphia: University of Pennsylvania Press, 1984.

Tolles, Frederick. *Meeting House and Counting House*. Chapel Hill: University of North Carolina Press, 1948.

7

SWEDENBORGIANISM

Eugene Taylor

Swedenborgianism refers to a small, upper-class, conservative Christian denomination known as the Church of the New Jerusalem, founded in England in the late eighteenth century and based on the writings of the eighteenth-century scientist and interpreter of revealed religion, Emanuel Swedenborg (1688–1772).[1] The Church of the New Jerusalem as an orthodox Christian denomination ordains ministers and oversees traditional parishes, has internal opposing organizations that govern themselves either by an episcopal or congregational form of polity, and maintains membership today in the National Council of Churches. Denominational membership has always been small, middle to upper class, conservative, and antimystical. At the same time, Swedenborgianism is the term more widely used to refer to a popular nineteenth-century philosophy of self-realization allied with New England Transcendentalism and the American Spiritualist churches.

Swedenborg was born January 29, 1688, in Stockholm, the child of Jasper Swedborg (at the height of his career a Lutheran bishop), and Sara Behm (wealthy daughter of Albert Behm, Assessor in the College of Mines).[2] Raised in an intense religious environment somewhat hostile to the ideas of the European Enlightenment, Swedenborg nevertheless became attracted to the natural sciences at an early age. By the age of twenty-one, he was graduated from the University of Upsala.

In 1709 he embarked upon the first of his many travels abroad. His intent was to study mathematics, astronomy, physics, and natural history and to send books and scientific instruments back to his university. Eventually he would grasp most of the known sciences of his day, and numerous trade skills as well. His personal quest was to use science in pursuit of ultimate questions, believing that the new objective methods could reveal the true nature of the soul. To these ends, he began his career with studies of the inorganic world and the heavens. Profoundly unsatisfied with the initial results, he turned his attention to anatomy and physiology. Again travelling abroad, he studied microscopy with Boorhave, collated a physiological encyclopedia, and made a number of recognized contributions to medical knowledge. These studies culminated in *The Economy of the Animal Kingdom* and its sequel, *The Animal Kingdom*, in 1744 and 1745. At the same time, Swedenborg had undertaken a study of the sense organs and the processes of perception, which led to his work *The Soul, or Rational Psychology*. As a counterpoint to these volumes, he also produced a Platonic-like creation myth entitled *The Worship and Love of God*, which presaged the direction of his later theological writings.[3]

The path from geology and astronomy through physiology and then sensory psychology eventually led Swedenborg to his own consciousness as an object of scientific study. To take up this work he developed a primitive but functional method of dream interpretation in which he sought to record the symbolic functions of the mind. Simultaneously, he also passed through episodes of painful religious deliberation in which the source of all knowledge and the basis of his perceptual world were continually challenged.

The combined effect of dream analysis, breath control, and intense inward concentration led to a spiritual crisis in 1744, when Swedenborg was fifty-six years old. During this crisis, which he later interpreted as an awakening to the experience of higher consciousness, Swedenborg recounted that he was visited by an angel and heard a voice speak to him, commanding him to take up his pen so that God could dictate the true internal meaning of the books of the Bible.

From then on the inward character of Swedenborg's life changed dramatically, even though outwardly he continued to be the mild, sedate bachelor who lived alone with his gardener and housekeeper, meanwhile attending to the affairs of Parliament and of Swedish science. Out of his internal explorations he produced an eight-volume Latin work entitled *The Arcana Coelestia*, a hermeneutical analysis of Genesis and Exodus which was published anonymously and distributed abroad.[4] He also composed a five-volume *Spiritual Diary* in which he described the realms of the heavens and hells revealed to him by God's angels.

However, Swedenborg's analysis of the internal sense of the Bible was disrupted in 1757 by another cataclysmic event, the experience of a completely transformed Christianity. In this vision he saw a dissolution of the denominations and foretold the emergence of a worldwide spiritual consciousness, which he called the New Jerusalem. His major works from then on described this new dispensation. They included *The Divine Love and Wisdom, Divine Providence, Conjugial Love, The Apocalypse Revealed, The Apocalypse Explained,* and *The True Christian Religion.*[5]

While these works by an anonymous author were attracting a devoted following elsewhere, Swedenborg continued to enjoy a quiet normal life at home in Sweden. But a series of dramatic clairvoyant episodes, later investigated by Immanuel Kant, led to public disclosure of his authorship.[6] This brought Swedenborg's name to the attention of the orthodox Lutheran clergy, who instituted charges against him as author of the tracts circulating in Europe. Heresy-hunters demanded his confinement and the seizure of his assets, events avoided only through intercession of the king. Soon after, Swedenborg's works were banned in Sweden and his followers persecuted. A short time later, Swedenborg died in London in 1772. His remains were buried in a small chapel on English soil. There they rested until the early part of the twentieth century, when, in due recognition of a patriarch of Swedish history, they were removed to the cathedral at Upsala.

After Swedenborg's death, instead of a transformed Christianity, a new Christian denomination, called the Church of the New Jerusalem, sprang up following his teachings. Despite onslaughts from the state Lutheran Church, a society of his followers banded together in Sweden, but this was not an organized religious body. It was a heterodox group of adherents who mixed Spiritualism and Mesmerism with the founder's original teachings. In 1772 some of Swedenborg's writings were translated into German, after which a religious movement of some note operated until 1846, when it was disrupted by a scandal involving spiritualism and mediumship. In France the new Christian denomination flourished in the shadow of Catholicism and evidently had some influence on French Freemasonry.

The main centers of Swedenborgian thought, however, became England and America. The Swedenborgians first became a registered sect in England in 1787 and the first minister was formally ordained in 1788. At first, the sect had numerous converts among the Baptists and the Methodists. Although traditionally Christian in orientation, among other innovations the English Swedenborgians denied the doctrine of the Trinity and they required the ritual of rebaptism to initiate members of the Old Church into the new dispensation.

From England, Swedenborgianism was brought to the United States by James Glen in 1784. Primarily a religion of the upper class, including doctors, schoolmasters, literary persons, and ministers, the church attracted converts largely from the Protestant denominations, including Episcopalians, Lutherans, Methodists, and Quakers. Its main centers became Philadelphia, Boston, New York, and Baltimore.

Several controversies faced the fledgling denomination. First was the problem of the separatists versus the non-separatists. Because Swedenborg had defined the transformation of Christianity as a dissolution of traditional sectarian lines, early members believed that change would come from within the already established churches. To establish a new and separate church would only add another denomination to the list that would soon dissolve. Thus, it was believed that members of the New Church should not be required to renounce their membership in the Old Church. Others believed a separate church with rebaptism and a succession of ordained New Church ministers was called for, and they eventually won the day.

A second major issue developed over the status of New Church ministers. Known as the conjugial heresy, this crisis centered on the church in Boston, which took the position that a minister was married to his congregation and could not preach elsewhere. Such an exclusivist doctrine went against a standing custom of pulpit visitation by other ministers throughout New England churches, but it did serve to draw attention to the New Church in Massachusetts and its own agenda. In the end, exclusivity was eventually given up as impractical.

A third but more divisive debate arose over the status of Swedenborg's writings. One camp, centered in the Massachusetts churches, believed that the Old and the New Testament constituted the primary spiritual documents of Christianity and that Swedenborg's writings represented the most important commentaries on the internal meaning of the Scriptures. Another camp, centered in the Philadelphia church, believed that Swedenborg's writings were divinely inspired and as infallible renderings of the word of God constituted a third testament, superseding the first two. A schism occurred in 1890 when a new body calling itself the General Church broke from the national organization, which from its beginnings in the 1820s had been called the General Convention.

The General Convention, which at the time had the greater number of members, became the more liberal body by retaining a governmental system based on delegates who represented the individual parishes and by maintaining a flexible interpretation of the writings. The General Church adopted a stricter interpretation of the texts and a more definite hierarchy of authority. At the bottom were lay persons, then an advisory council of ministers, and at the top was a bishop whose decisions were final and could not be appealed. The community of the General Church gathered a number of congregations to its cause and established a headquarters in Bryn Athyn, Pennsylvania, just north of Philadelphia. Here, members built homes, erected a church, and established their own educational system from kindergarten through graduate theological seminary.

In the 1920s, a group calling itself the Lord's New Church, Which Is Known as Nova Hierosolyma, claiming even greater orthodoxy, broke from the General Church, again over the interpretation of the Scriptures. The issue this time involved a claim that if Swedenborg's writings were, in fact, a Third Testament, then they, too, must have an internal sense and were in need of interpretation. Headquartered partly in Bryn Athyn and partly in Holland, the Lord's New Church continues its existence as a very small but international subdenomination of Swedenborgianism.

Aside from the denominational history, a distinction must also be made between churched and unchurched Swedenborgians. On the one hand there are those calling themselves Swedenborgians who have historically joined the church as a new Christian denomination. On the other are those who were not members of the New Church or even any specific Christian denomination but who read Swedenborg for confirmation of their own inner journeys toward self-realization. These nondenominational readers who have been inspired by Swedenborg's life and writings have numbered in the hundreds of thousands, if not millions.

Many readers of Swedenborg have played major roles in American cultural history.[7] As Henry Ward Beecher put it, no one in nineteenth-century America could call himself educated who had not read Swedenborg's works. Benjamin Franklin was on the subscription list for the first editions of Swedenborg's works published in America. Robert Hargrove, minister of the Baltimore New Church, received an invitation from Thomas Jefferson to preach a Swedenborgian sermon before Congress. Figures as diverse as Abraham Lincoln and Andrew Carnegie knew and read the writings. William Dean Howells's father had been a Swedenborgian minister and New Church publisher. Helen Keller counted herself a Swedenborgian when she wrote *My Religion* and composed, as well, an introduction to an edition of Swedenborg's *True Christian Religion*. It may not be stretching the point too far to say that in their day Swedenborgian ideas ranked next to Transcendentalism as a cultural force and that, because he contributed a dynamic language of inner experience to public understanding of self-realization, Swedenborg may have played a role in nineteenth-century popular culture similar to that played by Freud in the twentieth.

Reasons for the extensive Swedenborgian influence in the nineteenth century are not hard to find. One of the best-loved heros of American folklore, John Chapman, was an eminent Swedenborgian and the first to promulgate the doctrines beyond the Ohio Valley. Also known as Johnny Appleseed, "the picturesque sower of a two-fold seed," Chapman was an itinerant nurseryman who planted apple trees throughout the United States and also distributed Swedenborgian tracts.[8]

Swedenborgians were also noted for their early interest in mesmerism, or what we call today hypnosis. Traditional accounts of mesmerism date its introduction from the travels of Charles Poyen

throughout New England in the 1830s, but members of the Baltimore Swedenborg Society became involved with the practice as early as the 1790s, and the issue was volatile enough to cause a split in the congregation.[9] While the orthodox denominational position consistently repudiated the practice of mesmerism, there is much evidence to show that it attracted numerous members to the New Church teachings. The reason for this is that mesmerism was a form of parlor entertainment in the early part of the nineteenth century, but it also gave people access to altered states of consciousness that were quite unfamiliar to them. Swedenborg's descriptions of the inner states provided a map, not only to describe the experiences people had while entranced, but also to guide a heightened and suggestible attention toward higher spiritual domains. The connection became widely accepted at mid-century with the publication of *Mesmer and Swedenborg* in 1844 by the Rev. George Bush, a Professor of Theology at New York University who had, himself, been converted to the New Church through his experiments with mesmerism.

Homeopathy was another important vehicle for the influence of Swedenborg on nineteenth-century America. Founded in the late eighteenth century in Germany by Samuel Hahnemann, homeopathy was a medical system totally unlike the practices of doctors trained in European-style scientific medicine. Experiencing a resurgence today, it is a total psychophysical regime based on the doctrines of similarity and of infinitesimals. Drugs are not administered in large doses, but in extreme dilutions, and the specific drug given always mimics the symptoms of the illness. Such doctrines are entirely commensurate with Swedenborg's idea that the physiological body is derived from the spiritual, which must be affected first for healing to take place.

Historically, Hans Birch Gram, a student of Hahnemann, was the first to bring homeopathy to the United States in 1825. He settled in New York and gathered around him a number of students, most of whom were Swedenborgians. Eventually, the major homeopathic apothecaries in the United States were also the major Swedenborgian publishing houses. Two of the most noted were Boericke and Tafel in Philadelphia and Otis Clapp in Boston.

In its heyday, homeopathy was widely popular in America and constituted a serious threat to the status of scientific, or allopathic, medicine. At a time when many died in hospitals and scientific doctors engaged extensively in the questionable practices of drugging, blistering, bleeding, and purging, homeopathy was a viable religious and medicinal alternative for many. At one point the practice was so widespread that homeopathic hospitals and insane asylums flourished, and there were numerous homeopathic medical colleges as well. Two of the better known were the Hahnemann Medical College in Philadelphia and the Boston University Medical School.

The pervasive Swedenborgian influence on nineteenth-century American culture was also manifested in Spiritualism, the belief in communications between the living and the dead. As a major national movement, Spiritualism grew rapidly in the late 1840s, fueled by the alleged otherworldly communications of the Fox sisters from Hydesville, New York, who believed they could speak by way of rappings with a dead man who had once lived in their home. Inflamed by the national press in 1848, their claims brought the young girls wide attention and they toured for years throughout the country giving lectures. They were part of an extended subcultural network of lycea, occult newspapers, and travelling mediums, mental healers, and nostrum vendors who claimed millions of adherents between the 1840s and 1880s.

The father of the Spiritualist movement in the United States was an uneducated shoemaker's apprentice from Poughkeepsie, New York, named Andrew Jackson Davis. Davis, who seemed to show clairvoyant abilities when in the mesmeric trance, eventually claimed he had established communication with Swedenborg, who had showed him the cosmological system of spiritual consciousness, and Galen, who had imparted extensive medical knowledge which allowed Davis to miraculously heal others. In 1847 Davis published *The Principles of Nature, Her Divine Revelations, and a Voice to Mankind,* which purported to be a record of these trance communications. The book became an immediate success, went into numerous editions, and quickly became the bible of the Spiritualist healers.[10] According to one commentator, "The coincidences with the *Arcana Coelestia* are all but absolutely verbal."[11] The book contains the Swedenborgian doctrines of the Grand Man, the Science of Correspondences, and Swedenborg's views on the subservient relation of the natural to the spiritual world. At its heart, however, it was a Spiritualist and not a Swedenborgian text. In fact, the close connection of Spiritualism to Swedenborgian thought has always been systematically denied by orthodox adherents of the Christian denomination of the Church of the New Jerusalem.

Additional Swedenborgian influences can be found in the utopian socialist communities of the early and mid-nineteenth century. One of the most notable examples was the work of Thomas Lake Harris, Spiritualist orator, trance poet, and founder of several socialist enclaves. Harris became interested in Swedenborg through the writings of Andrew Jackson Davis and combined Swedenborg with his new-found interest in the socialist writings of Robert Dale Owen and Charles Fourier. After an unsuccessful attempt to found a utopian community based on these principles at Mountain Cove, Virginia, Harris returned to New York City, became an advocate of what came to be called Christian Spiritualism, and formed an unaffiliated congregation, the Church of the Good Shepherd, based on Spiritualist and Swedenborgian teachings. Thereafter he began to write voluminously about his spiritual experiences; his most notable works for the present discussion were *Wisdom of the Ages,* Harris's heavenly discourses with Swedenborg and Socrates, and *The Lyric of the Morning Land,* full of Swedenborgian-like doctrines.

Harris's best-known community was the Brotherhood of the New Life, built at

Wassaic, New York, and later removed to Brocton-on-Lake-Erie; it was a mixture of blue-collar converts and rich socialites from England and America, among them Sir Laurence Oliphant and his mother. This he followed with Fountain Grove Colony in Santa Rosa, California, a religious commune that was supported by extensive vineyards and a winery. Harris is recorded by historians as an eccentric but charismatic spiritual leader whose activities were widely reported by the press for almost four decades at the close of the nineteenth century. Throughout this period his alleged connections to Swedenborg were duly noted by an adoring public.

Swedenborgianism was also associated with mental healing and what came to be known as the New Thought movement, which was launched by Julius and Annetta Dresser and given its most cohesive literary form by the Reverend Warren Felt Evans. The Dressers became the foremost exponents of Phineas P. Quimby's proto–New Thought teaching and spearheaded a number of legal and literary challenges against Christian Science. Their son, Horatio W. Dresser, was also a Swedenborgian minister and the editor of *The Quimby Manuscripts*. Evans, a Methodist minister, converted to the New Church about the same time that he was miraculously healed of a longstanding nervous affliction by Quimby in 1863. His works, such as *The Mental Cure, Mental Medicine,* and *Soul and Body,* were published before Mary Baker Eddy's *Science and Health* had become widely read. Evans continued his writing and healing ministry over a twenty-year period and at the end of his career produced his best-known works, *The Divine Law of Cure* (1881) and *Esoteric Christianity and Mental Therapeutics* (1886). Especially in Evans's early works, of all writers Swedenborg was mentioned most frequently.[12]

The most visible line showing the Swedenborgian influence on nineteenth-century American culture was its fusion with New England Transcendentalism. Members of the original Transcendentalist circle made a careful study of Swedenborg's major theological works. Swedenborgian thought was readily adapted by writers such as Christopher Pearse Cranch and Margaret Fuller;[13] Lydia Marie Child had, in fact, been a member of the Boston Swedenborg Church from the early 1820s; and their most eminent inspiration, Ralph Waldo Emerson, was an expositor of Swedenborg's life and work on a number of occasions.

Emerson came to know the founders of the first Swedenborg Society in Boston when he was a student at Harvard College beginning in 1818. Indeed, Emerson was in the audience at commencement in 1821 when one of them, Sampson Reed, read his now famous "Oration on Genius," which the historian Perry Miller long maintained was the first salvo of the Transcendental movement in New England.[14] Emerson procured a copy and avidly followed Reed's elaboration of its thesis into a book, *The Growth of the Mind* (1826). Emerson, in turn, using *The Growth of the Mind* as a model for his own first book, *Nature* (1836), developed as the core of his work the Swedenborgian idea of correspondences, that every aspect of the material universe is reflected in the inner spiritual life of the soul.

In 1843, Emerson opened a new phase of his contact with Swedenborgian thought when he began a life-long friendship with Henry James, Sr., philosopher of religion, philanthropist, public lecturer, and eminent father of William James, the Harvard psychologist, and Henry James, the novelist. Emerson introduced James, Sr., to Thomas Carlyle in England and an important Swedenborgian connection soon developed.

Long before he had met James, Carlyle had been introduced to Swedenborg's writings by the English physician James John Garth Wilkinson. When Henry James, Sr., experienced a spiritual crisis of his own just outside London in 1844, he was introduced to Wilkinson, who became the equivalent of a pastoral psychiatrist to the entire James family. James, Sr., in turn, began to sponsor Wilkinson's translation of Swedenborg's scientific writings and he successfully steered Wilkinson away from the practice of allopathic medicine toward homeopathy. Eventually, Wilkinson produced a number of Swedenborgian tracts under Henry James, Sr.'s patronage. One little volume was a biography of Swedenborg that Emerson later used as the basis for his chapter "Swedenborg, the Mystic," in his widely read *Representative Men* (1859). There, Emerson characterized the Swedish seer as humanity's best embodiment of the heroic and visionary journey that culminates in self-realization. Moreover, Swedenborg showed clearly that, without recourse to the traditional denominations, the priesthood, or the ecclesiastical texts, Divinity could be known directly by looking within.

Meanwhile, Henry James, Sr., had returned to America and settled in New York City, where he resumed receiving guests into his home. These included the eminent Emerson (who had his own bedroom) and other members of the Transcendentalist circle, among them Henry David Thoreau, Margaret Fuller, and Bronson Alcott. James also began an extensive examination of Swedenborg's writings, a task that would culminate in no fewer then twelve volumes and pamphlets on Swedenborgian thought, despite the fact that he was never an official member of the New Church.

Henry James, Sr., was to inoculate the Transcendentalists with his brand of Swedenborgianism from several directions. One in particular should be noted. The Transcendentalists had by the early 1840s launched their own utopian community, Brook Farm, in West Roxbury, Massachusetts. Led by George Ripley, Brook Farm at first ran on Transcendentalist ideas. The great lights from Concord would often come to visit. Even Nathaniel Hawthorne, who shovelled manure in the morning in order to buy time to write in the afternoon, was a member. The commune became a Fourierist phalanx in 1845, but disbanded in 1847 when its main building was destroyed by fire. It then had a final Swedenborgian phase when, between 1847 and 1849, its literary publication, *The Harbinger,* removed from Boston to New York City and Henry James, Sr., became its editor.

At the same time, James Sr.'s interpretation of Swedenborg was also to have more far-reaching consequences. This particular line of influence can be found in the philosophical movement called pragmatism. To see this connection, however, one must recognize that there was a fundamental relationship between the old and the new way of thinking. To wit: As Transcendentalism was the first uniquely American literary aesthetic independent of European roots, pragmatism, its heir, was the first uniquely American philosophy to have international consequences. While some scholars have at least acknowledged the Transcendentalist line leading to pragmatism, the Swedenborgian connection has not been spelled out in detail.

Pragmatism was, first of all, a rule of logic. It required that one consider the consequences of any thought in order for that thought to be complete. In its more widely known form, it was also a standard by which belief systems could be tested by their results. It became a way to see the relationship between how we think and how we act. It was also eminently democratic in that it endeavored to argue, based on outcome, for the legitimacy of radically divergent kinds of religious belief.

First articulated by Charles Sanders Peirce in 1878 in an essay called "How to Make Our Ideas Clear," the philosophy of pragmatism did not have a national following until William James presented Peirce's work at the University of California at Berkeley in 1898. James thereafter became its foremost exponent. It became the quintessential philosophy of the Progressive Era in America and, before the onslaught of the logical positivists in the 1930s, under the name of functionalism it came to dominate then-modern theories in psychology, philosophy, education, economics, and religion.[15]

Numerous scholars have traced the origin of pragmatism to the philosophies of John Stewart Mill and Alexander Bain, and some of it can be seen in Kant. An important source was also Peirce's reading of Swedenborg.[16] Peirce had read Swedenborg's works in the 1860s. He also spent many hours discussing Swedenborgian ideas with Henry James, Sr., most certainly focusing on the Doctrine of Use and

Swedenborg's expanded definition of rationality. Peirce then explicitly incorporated the Swedenborgian influence in his cosmological essays during the 1890s and, after 1906, in his attempts to work out the metaphysical consequences of what he had by then renamed pragmaticism.[17]

As for Swedenborgianism today, there are numerous signs of life still in it. By most estimates there are at present probably about seven thousand members of the Church of the New Jerusalem in the United States and Canada and some sixty thousand worldwide, twenty thousand of whom are black South Africans. The Swedenborg Foundation, located in West Chester, Pennsylvania, exists as a nonsectarian information clearinghouse, the main purpose of which is to disseminate Swedenborg's writings. The foundation also sponsors a literary and spiritual journal called *Chrysalis*. A consortium of editors and publishers has recently convened as Swedenborg Publishers International, comprised of groups that publish on any aspect of Swedenborg's life and writings. They produce a newsletter, edited by Leon Rhodes of Bryn Athyn, Pennsylvania. The Swedenborgians also maintain a four-year undergraduate liberal arts institution of higher learning, Urbana College, in Urbana, Illinois. The Swedenborg School of Religion in Newton, Massachusetts, and the Academy of the New Church in Bryn Athyn continue to train and ordain ministers. Several theological libraries and bookrooms also exist for the benefit of the public, notably the Swedenborg Library in Boston. Recently, the Swedenborg Chapel in Cambridge, Massachusetts, has initiated a new student chaplaincy through the Harvard-Radcliffe United Ministries.

While membership in the General Convention is presently declining, it seems to be growing in the General Church. At the same time, there does seem to be some new interest in Swedenborg's ideas in the American counterculture. Wilson Van Dusen, the clinical psychologist and Buddhist meditator, has composed a number of popular books based on Swedenborg, among them *The Natural Depth in Man* and *The Presence of Other Worlds*.[18] These have initiated a line of psychological interest in Swedenborg that has developed as a serious competitor to the prevailing but more conservative theological interpretation of the writings. Recently, an article on Swedenborg has appeared in the *Journal of Transpersonal Psychology*. Plans are also now underway to produce a translation from Japanese to English of a work on Swedenborg by the Zen exponent D. T. Suzuki. Such signs indicate that, while there will likely be continued attrition in the organized church in the United States, Swedenborgian thought at present continues to have a modest but perennial influence on American folk culture.

Notes

1. "Swedenborgian" and "Swedenborgianism" are pronounced with a soft "g," while Swedenborg is pronounced with a hard "g."

2. Two biographies are George Trobridge, *Swedenborg: Life and Teaching* (New York: Swedenborg Foundation, 1968), and Cyriel Odhner Sigstedt, *The Swedenborg Epic: The Life and Works of Emanuel Swedenborg* (London: Swedenborg Society, 1981).

3. Emanuel Swedenborg, *On the Worship and Love of God* (Boston: J. Allen, 1832).

4. Five treatises, *Heaven and Hell, The White Horse Mentioned in the Revelation, The New Jerusalem and Its Heavenly Doctrine, Earth in the Universe*, and *The Last Judgement* were separate volumes that Swedenborg later extracted from the *Arcana*.

5. A concise and accessible summary of Swedenborg's theological ideas can be found in Samuel M. Warren, *A Compendium of the Theological Writings of Emanuel Swedenborg* (New York: Swedenborg Foundation, 1979).

6. For the English translation, see Immanuel Kant, *Dreams of a Spirit-Seer, Illustrated by Dreams of Metaphysics*, trans. E. F. Goerwitz (London: New Church Press, 1899).

7. See, for instance, Erland Brock, et al. (eds.), *Swedenborg and His Influence* (Bryn Athyn, Penn.: Academy of the New Church, 1988) and Robin Larsen, et al. (eds.), *Emanuel Swedenborg: A Continuing Vision* (New York: Swedenborg Foundation, 1988).

8. From Marguerite Block, *The New Church in the New World* (New York: Holt, Rinehart and Winston, 1984 ed.) 115–17.

9. Block, 88.

10. During his numerous entrancements, Davis was able to count among his auditors such notables as Edgar Allen Poe, the writer, and Albert Brisbane, foremost exponent of the doctrines of Charles Fourier.

11. Block, *The New Church,* 136.

12. Charles S. Braden, *Spirits in Rebellion: The Rise and Development of New Thought* (Dallas: Southern Methodist University Press, 1963). The effect of the New Thought movement on the American popular culture was significant and continues to this day. Presently functioning religious groups such as the Unity School of Christianity, Divine Science, and Religious Science, had their origins in New Thought. The indirect but pervasive connection of these organizations to Swedenborg's writings is one reason that the Church of the New Jerusalem, perhaps somewhat inaccurately, is often classed by scholars as a New Age religion.

This issue is a thorny one and in need of further analysis. I have maintained throughout this chapter that the Christian denomination of the New Church has consistently disavowed associating itself with mesmerism, homeopathy, and mental healing, even though there is much evidence that Swedenborgians and their ministers were heavily involved in such practices in the nine-

teenth century. Today, the situation remains much the same. Some Swedenborgians are associated with the counterculture movement, but the church as a whole in all its branches is not. In fact, an internal examination of the liturgy of the Church of the New Jerusalem and the theological training of its ministers shows it to be more aligned with the conservative practices of Lutherans and Episcopalians than with the Spiritualist churches of the last century or the New Age movement today.

13. Richard Kenneth Silver, "The Spiritual Kingdom in America: The Influence of Emanuel Swedenborg on American Society and Culture, 1815–1860" (Ph.D. diss., Stanford University, 1983), 88–89.

14. Perry Miller, *The Transcendentalists: An Anthology* (Cambridge: Harvard University Press, 1950), 50.

15. Darnell Rucker, *The Chicago Pragmatists* (Minneapolis: University of Minnesota Press, 1969); Charles Morris, *The Pragmatic Movement in American Philosophy* (New York: George Braziller, 1970).

16. The influence on William James is self-evident, but likewise not well developed.

17. C. Hartshorn and P. Weiss, eds., *The Collected Papers of Charles Sanders Peirce* (Cambridge: Harvard University Press, 1958), vol. 5, no. 402, fn 3. See also E. I. Taylor, Peirce, and Swedenborg, *Studia Swedenborgiana* vol. 6, no. 1 (1986), 25–51.

18. Wilson Van Dusen, *The Natural Depth in Man* (New York: Harper and Row, 1972) and *The Presence of Other Worlds* (New York: Swedenborg Foundation, 1974). See also Van Dusen's psychological commentary to Emanuel Swedenborg, *Journal of Dreams* (New York: Swedenborg Foundation, 1986).

Suggestions for Further Reading

Block, Marguerite. *The New Church in the New World.* New York: Holt, Rinehart and Winston, 1984.

The Collected Works of Emanuel Swedenborg. Boston: Houghton Mifflin, n.d.

Trobridge, George. *Swedenborg: Life and Teaching.* New York: Swedenborg Foundation, 1968.

Warren, Samuel M. *A Compendium of the Theological Writings of Emanuel Swedenborg.* New York: Swedenborg Foundation, 1979.

8

UNITARIAN UNIVERSALISM:
AN INTERPRETATION THROUGH ITS HISTORY

Mason Olds

Thomas Jefferson was a man of the Enlightenment, and as such he was a man of reason. He employed reason not only to criticize the tyrannical forms of government in his age and to justify his own democratic views, but also to determine the legitimacy of religious beliefs. His reasoning led him to a liberal rather than an orthodox faith.[1] In spite of the fact that he refused to write or speak publicly about his religious views, the religious issue was raised during his campaigns for the presidency. Some thought that he should not be elected because of his unorthodox beliefs; however, his critics did not prevail.

In a letter written in 1822, Jefferson said: "I rejoice that in this blessed country of free inquiry and belief, which has surrendered its conscience to neither kings nor priests, the genuine doctrine of only one God is reviving, and I trust that there is not a young man now living in the United States who will not die a Unitarian."[2] What follows is an attempt to understand the nature of Unitarian Universalism. Since the time of Jefferson it has undergone significant development. It is therefore by examining its history and evolution that we gain an understanding of its nature.

Forerunners of Unitarian Universalism

In Christian history even before the time of Jefferson there were many who held beliefs we would now call Unitarian Universalist. As early as the first century, the Ebionites held a unitarian view of God (i.e., that God was truly one and without the three manifestations specified by the doctrine of the Trinity) and an adoptionist view of Jesus (that Jesus was the adopted, not born, son of God). In the third century, Origen of Alexandria (c. 185–255) advocated among other things a doctrine of universal salvation, but his views were later condemned by a council in the sixth century. In the fourth century, Arius promoted a Christology which maintained that Jesus was less than God but greater than other humans; however, he was condemned for heresy at the Council of Nicaea (325). In the sixteenth century, Michael Servetus (1511–1553) got into a conflict with John Calvin and was burned at the stake for repudiating the doctrine of the Trinity. Later in the same century there was a strong Unitarian movement in Transylvania. King John Sigismund, influenced by Unitarian minister Francis David, embraced the Unitarian faith, and later issued an edict granting religious toleration. In the seventeenth century, the Socinians—named after the Italian Faustus Socinus (1539–1604), "the architect of modern Unitarianism," and his uncle, Laelius—were banished from Poland. They had dared promote such Unitarian beliefs as that Jesus was more man than God, and he saved people by providing an example for them to follow, rather than by his death. At about the same time John Biddle was promoting Unitarianism in England.[3]

The Unitarianism which Jefferson praised stood within this earlier tradition. It advocated the unity of God and repudiated Trinitarian views; it also denied that Jesus was a part of the Godhead, though it considered his teaching normative for faith. It sometimes advocated the doctrine that eventually all souls would be saved, and at times it promoted religious tolerance. With respect to these issues, Unitarianism was primarily a minority point of view, and usually those who supported it were condemned as heretics, banished, or even executed. Like Jefferson, Unitarian Universalists today embrace this part of the Western religious tradition.

The Rise of Unitarian Universalism in the United States

The more recent history for understanding Unitarianism begins in the latter half of the eighteenth century, especially in and around Boston and to a lesser extent in Philadelphia.[4] At this time, there were two major religious movements in the colonies. One emphasized emotionalism and found its expression in the revivals of the Great Awakening. The other emphasized reason and found its expression in "rational Christianity" and deism, both products of the American Enlightenment.[5]

The Great Awakening revivals started in the Middle Atlantic colonies, spread into New England, and finally flourished in the South. Jonathan Edwards (1703–1758) was the minister of the Congregational Church in Northampton, Massachusetts, and was one of the advocates of Revivalism, becoming best known for his sermon entitled "Sinners in the Hands of an Angry God." Most Revivalists were Calvinists, advocating a revelational theory of religious truth, a Trinitarian doctrine of God, a doctrine of original sin, a substitutionary theory of the atonement, and a doctrine of election with eternal damnation for those not among the elect. Although Edwards himself was

reserved and tried to appeal to the intellect, other Revivalists soon pandered to emotionalism in order for people to experience "saving grace." Often they attacked ministers who did not support the revivals as being unconverted—that is, as not being true Christians in their hearts.

Most liberal churches were located around Boston, and Harvard College had become the breeding ground for "Unitarian moral theology." By 1787, King's Chapel, an Anglican church, had become Unitarian, and nine years later the First Unitarian Church in Philadelphia was organized with support from Joseph Priestley (1733–1804). At about the same time, a few around Philadelphia began to promote Universalism, the belief that all would be saved and none damned; notable among them was John Murray (1741–1815), who later came to New England and founded the First Universalist Society in America at Gloucester, Massachusetts, in 1779. Elmo Robinson says about this period, "At first, there were itinerant preachers who spread the gospel of universal salvation wherever they could find an audience to listen. Then, if a group of believers accepted the message wholeheartedly, they might organize a Universalist church, or as they preferred to call it, a Universalist society."[6] However, the creation of Universalist societies went slowly; by 1800 there were only five.

Liberal religious thought, of both Unitarian and the Universalist varieties, arose as a reaction to the theological doctrines associated with Puritanism (Calvinism) and to the excesses of the Great Awakening. The liberals attacked the Trinitarian doctrine of God and the notion of God's wrath. They spoke instead of the unity of God, "the Monarch of the Universe" who sought to communicate his goodness to humanity on earth. They also repudiated the doctrine of original sin, believing that individuals were neutral, not evil, at birth. Furthermore, human reason was to be the check on claims of divine revelation; that is, revelation must be validated by reason. The liberals disdained the orthodox position of standing on faith alone and disparaging good works. As for Jesus, he was a son of God, not God the son. Although he was not divine, God in a special way dwelt in him. Instead of interpreting Jesus' death as evidence of a wrathful God seeking vengeance for human sin, the liberals were more concerned about the psychological effects of Jesus' death on human beings. For instance, by seeing how others participated in the death of an innocent Jesus, they might become cognizant of their own involvement in the innocent sufferings of others and repent. Moreover, the liberals denied the doctrine of particular election—that only a select few were saved—and maintained that any benefits from Jesus' life and death were for the whole world, not for just the elect, and that in the end all souls would be saved. Thus, rather than seeing the revivals as a great awakening, they viewed them as a time of great terror, for they were keenly aware of the negative psychological effects of such doctrines as "an angry God" and "eternal damnation" on the families of the deceased.

As the eighteenth century wore on, it was obvious that a serious theological rift had developed within the Standing Order of the Established Churches in Massachusetts. Since shortly after the founding of Plymouth Colony in 1620 and Massachusetts Bay Colony in 1630, Congregationalism, which had developed within the Puritan movement in England, had been the established religion. It maintained this privileged position until 1833. Following the revivals of the Great Awakening, it was evident that at least three different views developed in the Standing Order. There were Calvinists who were strong advocates of the revivals, and there were also "old Calvinists" who opposed them. However, there had developed a third party. Charles Chauncy (1705–1787), minister of First Church in Boston, became especially critical of Calvinist theology and of the revivals sweeping New England. He began to formulate a more liberal theology which was dubbed "Arminianism."[7] Jonathan Mayhew (1705–1766), who had become minister at West Church, also began advocating similar liberal views.

The incident which ultimately led to the schism in the Standing Order was the appointment of a liberal, Henry Ware (1764–1845), to the Hollis Chair of Divinity at Harvard.[8] Jedidiah Morse and other conservatives thought that the new appointee should be a moderate Calvinist. However, most of the committee members were liberals, so they gave the position to Ware. Morse responded by organizing the conservatives in order to do battle against the liberals. In 1808 they founded Andover Theological Seminary to ensure that young men studying for the ministry could receive an orthodox theological education.

Morse's faction kept up the attack on the liberals until William E. Channing, the liberal minister of Federal Street Church in Boston, responded. In 1819 Channing had been invited to give the installation sermon of Jared Sparks, a recent Harvard graduate, at the new Unitarian Church in Baltimore. Channing used the occasion to explain and promote the basic beliefs of "Unitarian Christianity." In many respects, his theology simply continued the liberal thought of men such as Chauncy and Mayhew. Other liberals viewed the sermon as a fair statement of their beliefs, and the conservatives saw it as a focal point for their attacks. A sustained and bitter controversy followed, the result being a rupture in the Standing Order. By 1825, the liberals decided it was time for them to form their own organization, so they created the American Unitarian Association. Charles Forman says, "on May 26, 1825, a constitution for the American Unitarian Association was adopted, defining the purposes of the new organization to 'diffuse the knowledge and promote the interests of pure Christianity.' "[9] Immediately 125 churches, all but 25 in Massachusetts, joined the new association. In Boston, only Old South Church refused to join. The members of these churches were the educators, judges, statesmen, businessmen, and leading writers of America, and many had received their educations at Harvard, which had also come under the control of the liberals.

For a brief period during their formative stage, the Unitarian churches along with the (Trinitarian) Congregational churches enjoyed the privileges and benefits of the established Standing Order. The still-separate Universalists, along with Baptists, Quakers, and Methodists were dissenters. Universalists, however, like the Unitarians, were opposed to the Calvinist doctrine of election. Since, they believed, Christ had died for the sins of the whole world, all sinners would be saved, not just the elect. They trace their denominational roots back to a group of New Englanders along with representatives from New York who met in Oxford, Massachusetts, on September 4, 1793. Of this gathering, Elmo Robinson says, "Unknowingly without formal action, without constitution or bylaws, without officers or funds, they laid the foundation of the Universalist General Convention, an organization which continued to function until its merger with the American Unitarian Association . . . "[10] Universalists had national meetings in stated sessions from 1793 through 1961, in 1833 adopting the name "The General Convention of Universalists in the United States," and in 1942 changing it to the "Universalist Church of America."[11]

In time, the dissenting groups, led by the Baptists, joined forces, and together they were able to bring about disestablishment in Massachusetts in 1833. Although the Unitarians were limited primarily to eastern Massachusetts, their worldview and values dominated that region from early in the nineteenth century until the end of the Civil War. But, of course, as changes occurred in the broader society involving immigration, industry, and pluralism, the Unitarians gradually became another denomination among the many. With this change in status, they have become staunch defenders of Thomas Jefferson's concept of "a wall of separation" between church and state.

The Merger of the Unitarians and the Universalists

On May 11, 1961, in the city of Boston, the two liberal denominations, the American Unitarian Association and the Universalist Church of America, finally merged into the Unitarian Universalist Association (UUA). As early as 1856 it had been suggested that the two denominations unite, but it took 105 years for the idea to bear fruit. Unlike the Unitarians, the Universalists, with few exceptions, appealed to New England farmers, small townspeople, and laborers. From their beginning, they were outside the religious establishment, so they had to create grassroots support. As a rule, their members were not as well educated and socially positioned as the Unitarians. In fact, when the merger occurred in 1961, it was the hope of the delegates that the strengths of one denomination would complement the weaknesses of the other.

Congregational Church Polity

One of the problems created by the Protestant Reformation in the sixteenth century was that of church polity. Quite early the church had created a hierarchical episcopal form of government. At the top was the pope, then cardinals, bishops, priests, and finally the laity. Decisions originated at the top and eventually filtered down to the laity at the bottom. Following the Reformation, questions related to religious authority and church government were raised and critically examined by the various denominations. The Anglican, the Orthodox, and the Methodist churches retained the episcopal system, although with significant alterations. The Presbyterian church offered still a different kind of government by placing much of its authority in the presbytery, a regional jurisdiction which provided certain constraints on the local church. However, in the left wing of the Puritan movement in England and in the Anabaptist movements on the continent, a congregational form of church government developed. In the congregational system, the power of the local church is in the hands of the people who make up its membership, not the bishop or presbytery or conference. The members own the church property, they hire and dismiss their minister, and they determine their own reason for being. Among the churches adopting this type of government were the Congregationalists, Baptists, and Quakers, all derived from the Puritan movement in England.

When the schism occurred in the Standing Order, both Congregationalists and Unitarians retained congregational church government, a form which the Universalist societies also had adopted. The churches which became members of the Unitarian Universalist Association continued the congregational form of government. The Unitarian Universalist Association, then, is an instrument for coordinating and carrying out the common programs of the local churches which voluntarily affiliate with it. A Unitarian Universalist church is a democratic society which takes seriously the Protestant principle of "the priesthood of believers." Unlike the more hierarchical church structures, which hand truth down from on high, Unitarian Universalist churches believe the truth may come from any member of the society, not just the professional minister, or the administrator at the Unitarian Universalist headquarters in Boston. If a local church member has a relevant idea, he or she may present it, and with rational persuasion attempt to convince the membership to adopt it. In fact, it may eventually reach the floor of the annual meetings of the denomination and become official policy. Given a highly educated laity, more and more policies are originating at the local level.

Non-creedal Religious Societies

Unitarian Universalist churches are also non-creedal societies. To one outside Unitarian Universalism, this can be confusing. Usually, if one is a member of a more traditional church, one at least nominally affirms the various doctrines expressed in the Apostles' Creed, but in Unitarian Universalism there is no creedal requirement. All members are expected to do their own study and thinking and to arrive at their own convictions about matters of religious

faith. Faith is viewed as a religious quest involving the celebration of life rather than the giving of intellectual assent to some fixed, traditional creed which originated in a bygone era. With such radical freedom about religious belief, Unitarians might well see a liberal Christian sitting in the same row with a Buddhist, an agnostic, a humanist, and perhaps even an atheist at a religious service. What unites them is that they are willing to tolerate and respect the beliefs of others, and to learn from each other as they reveal details of their private quests. If a specific creed were adopted, others would feel excluded from religious and human fellowship.

Of course, in a non-creedal church operating on democratic principles, certain implications follow. For instance, Unitarian Universalism focuses more on the character of people and their deeds than on what a person does or does not believe. In other words, it places deed before creed, or as one contemporary says, "it is by their deeds that you shall know them."[12] Thomas Jefferson said something rather similar: "It is in our lives, and not our words that our religion must be read." Also, Unitarian Universalism emphasizes living a moral, productive, happy life within the perimeters of birth and death rather than being anxious about how to get to heaven or avoid hell. Or, as one minister says: "Unitarian Universalism is cooperation with a universe that created us; it is a celebration of life; it is being in love with goodness and justice; it is a sense of humor about absolutes."[13] Unitarian Universalists of all theological persuasions can agree on these few general sentiments. Each can believe this much; others may believe more.

Types of Unitarian Universalist Theology

At the time of the merger in 1961, it was possible to identify somewhat vaguely at least six theological positions within the membership.[14] First, there was *Christian liberalism*, which of course was the position of the founders of the American Unitarian Association and the Universalist Church of America, and has been a significant part of the movement until the present.[15] It accepts Christianity as normative, and yet it seeks to interpret it in the light of modern thought in such areas as natural science, psychology, sociology, and historical criticism. It views God as the ground for the existence of the universe and for the undergirding of moral values. It also accepts Jesus as normative in terms of his life and moral teachings.

Second, there was *deism,* which also has its roots in the American Enlightenment of the eighteenth century. Since there was no Unitarian church in Charlottesville, Thomas Jefferson maintained his membership in the Episcopal Church. Yet, as we have noted, his theology was that of a Unitarian, more specifically that of a deist. For the deist, Christianity is not normative, and such doctrines as the existence of God, the freedom of the will, and the living of a moral life can be found in other world religions outside Christianity. Often the concept of God is employed to account for the existence of the universe, the rational order of nature, and the norms for moral living. Even today it is possible to extrapolate from a few Unitarian Universalists a vague kind of modern deism.

Third, there was the position of *mystical religion.* Shortly after the creation of the American Unitarian Association in 1825 there developed a conflict between the Christian liberals and the Transcendentalists. For some of the Transcendentalists such as Ralph Waldo Emerson, there was a world soul which permeated all of life. With "intuition" one could place oneself in contact with it. Hence the solitary individual walking in the autumn woods may well intuit his or her relationship to the world soul.[16] Such a view of course raised questions about the need for churches as institutions and the value of public worship. Since the early conflicts in the 1830s, the proponents of mystical religion have redefined their positions. For instance, some today have become interested in such issues as extrasensory perception and cosmic consciousness.

Fourth, there was the position of *naturalistic theism.* Following the American Civil War, Americans in general and Unitarians in particular became interested in Darwin's theory of evolution by means of natural selection. At first there were Christian liberals who repudiated the doctrine. However, there were some younger radicals who embraced it. Once again this created conflict within the membership of the association. At the same time there was a move led by Henry W. Bellows, minister of All Souls Church in New York City, to organize Unitarianism on a national basis rather than restricting the movement's primary influence to the East. In order to organize a National Conference of Unitarian Churches, he thought it necessary for Unitarians to unite behind some minimal creed.[17] The radicals would not hear of it, so in response they organized the Free Religious Association.[18] Although there were a number of theological positions in the Free Religious Association, men such as Octavius Brooks Frothingham and William J. Potter began to give articulation to naturalistic theism. They brought God down out of the heavens and placed God within the natural and historical process. In other words, God was that power within the universe which enabled it to evolve from one stage to the next and provided a teleology for values. Thus, theism and evolution were compatible. In the mid-twentieth century Unitarians such as Henry Nelson Wieman and Charles Hartshorne promoted their versions of naturalistic theism, and they have a number of followers within the UUA.

Fifth, there were those who advocated a position known as *religious humanism.* From the mid-1890s until the First World War, there were roughly two decades of theological calm. The national organizational needs of the denomination, represented by the national conference, had been incorporated into the organizational structure of the American Unitarian Association without a formal creed, and the Free Religious Association died out following the World's Columbian Exposition of 1893 in Chicago.[19] However, the calm was broken with the transfer of John H. Dietrich, who was under indictment for heresy, from the ministry of the Reformed Church to that of the American Unitarian Association. About 1915, Dietrich began promoting religious humanism, and in 1917 Curtis W. Reese and others joined him in forming the humanist movement. Thus, while the mainline denominations were fighting about modernism and fundamentalism, the Unitarians and to a lesser extent the Universalists were engaged in the humanist-theist controversy. From about 1920 until 1938, most of the energies of the denomination were devoted to the controversy, and it only began to subside as Germans diverted their attention away from theological concerns to ominous actions which led to the Second World War.[20]

The humanists repudiated three of the fundamental notions of the theists, namely that it was necessary to postulate the existence of God to account for religion, the universe, and morality. Already the naturalistic theists had repudiated the belief in the supernatural realm, but they still retained a doctrine of God to account for other things about the universe such as the evolutionary process and morality. However, the humanists interpreted the universe as being a self-contained, eternal, natural system. Since it neither came into existence nor will ever cease to be, there was no need to postulate a creator. Furthermore, humans had evolved by means of natural selection, and were creators of their moral and religious norms which had changed over time. They also viewed the universe as indifferent to the human enterprise, and thought most problems were created by humans. If these problems were to be solved, then humans must solve them. They must create a blueprint for the kind of people they wished to become and for the kind of world in which they wished to dwell, and then they must bring their aspirations into reality. The purpose of a liberal religious society was to provide a place for bringing people together for addressing personal, community, and world problems and aspirations. For the humanists, then, one could be religious even without belief in God.

As we have seen, some of the Transcendentalists in the 1830s and some of the naturalistic theists in the 1870s forced Unitarian Universalist churches to decide whether Christianity was normative; by and large, they concluded that it need not be. However, by the 1920s, the religious humanists were forcing the denomination to determine whether even liberal theism was normative. The denomination was confronted with a serious dilemma: if the churches adopted a creed affirming belief in God, they were violating one of their most strongly held principles involving the freedom of conscience in religious matters. If they remained true to the principle of freedom of belief, then they must accept members who might not believe in God. By the end of the controversy, even liberal Christians and naturalistic theists, both of whom believed in God, thought the greater danger lay in imposing a creed on the autonomous conscience. Thus, humanists were accepted as full members in the liberal religious community.

Finally, there was a sixth position which was designated *Existentialism*.[21] Today, of the three Unitarian Universalist churches in Atlanta, one is called "The First Existentialist Congregation." As we have noted, some theological positions focus on the rational component of the personality, whereas others focus on the affective component. The Existentialists believe that each in its own way distorts the components of the personality. They therefore refer to the total person with intellect, emotion, and volition, and view faith as a centered act in which the whole person is involved. Furthermore, they believe that many of our contemporaries are living life on the surface, the surface either of reason or emotion, so they try to challenge people to live life in its depths. It is only then that one can act freely and choose to live authentically, thus achieving important goals of the religious life.

Of course it is difficult to find all six theological positions in their pure forms, but at least they provide an inkling of the rich theological diversity which exists in any Unitarian Universalist congregation. The reason that such wide diversity prevails is that a Unitarian Universalist church is a non-creedal society, and all members are accorded the right to do their own theo-logical thinking. Every time there has been an attempt to curtail belief by creating and enforcing a creed the members have balked, so Unitarian Universalism has re-mained a free tradition in an ever-changing world.

The Unitarian Universalist Mission

Members of the Unitarian Universalist movement believe that it provides several important functions for American society. First, it affords a religious home for those who cannot accept the traditional faith of their parents. Often Unitarian Universal-ism is criticized for not mimicking the doc-trines of the mainline denominations, but this is to misunderstand its mission. It seeks to provide an alternative to rather than an echo of that provided by the other de-nominations and religions.

Second, it also provides a religious home for couples involved in mixed religious marriages, especially Christians and Jews, or humanists and Christians. Neither part-ner has to compromise personal religious beliefs by subscribing to a particular reli-gious creed. As long as they are willing to tolerate the beliefs of others, they will be welcomed into a local society to engage in their religious quest.

Third, although it does not relish this function, Unitarian Universalism often serves as a halfway house for a person re-belling against a traditional childhood faith. Such a person uses a local society as a support group, but once the rebellion is worked through, the person might then withdraw from religious fellowship alto-gether. Of course Unitarians would much rather the person continue the religious quest within the society, but when this does not happen, it accepts its function as a halfway house out of religion.

Fourth, if a particular injustice exists in a community, the local Unitarian Univer-salist society, a voluntary association, of-ten provides a place for addressing the issue. Once a consensus is reached, the so-ciety may become an instrument for pro-phetic criticism and change. Since the fo-cus is placed on living happy, creative, and productive lives in the world, it is natural for its members to wish to change the com-munity for the better, so that all the citi-zens, not just Unitarian Universalists, may live well. Thus, Unitarian Universalists tend to be more socially active than their coun-terparts in other denominations. Their so-cieties naturally appeal to those individuals who wish to get involved in the important social and political issues of our time.

Unrealized Goals

Through the years Unitarian Universalism has set its goals, but like all institutions it has not been entirely successful in reach-ing them. For instance:

1. It has not been successful in reaching the mythical "common person." In the main, Unitarian Universalism appeals to people who are well educated. In order to meet their needs, a minister must prepare attentively the pulpit address which in-volves careful research and cautiously ex-pressed ideas in a manuscript which is read in an interesting and entertaining man-ner. As the address is the focal point of the order of service in most societies, the ser-vice may appear excessively intellectual to one who desires a more powerful emotional tone.

However, as more women have come into the Unitarian Universalist ministry, while still maintaining the intellectual component, they have also supplemented it with a nurturing and emotional compo-nent. Although women have been ordained since Olympia Brown broke the ice in 1863, there has been only a significant influx of women into the ministry in the past twenty years. But today the feminine influence, which is widely regarded as enhancing the worship service, is being felt by both women and men and no doubt will continue.

2. Like nearly all truly democratic groups, the Unitarian Universalist Associa-tion is not the most efficient of institutions. Hierarchically governed denominations

can define issues and move on them quickly. However, in congregationally organized denominations, the democratic process must work itself out, taking into deliberate account the concerns of both the minority and the majority. Today there are many who would find the more democratic structure attractive. Yet, Unitarian Universalists have been most remiss about informing the public of their very existence. It is not so much that Unitarian Universalism has been repudiated, but that many potential members are not even aware of its existence.

3. Since Unitarian Universalism is concerned more with moral living than with metaphysical speculation, it has attempted to address the pressing social issues of our time. It opposed the war in Vietnam and has supported racial equality, a woman's right to an abortion, equal rights for gays and lesbians, universal healthcare, separation of church and state, gun control, and protection of the environment, to name just a few issues. As such issues are complex and extremely controversial, some potential members have shied away from Unitarian Universalism because they wish to remain free of controversy. Like many other liberal denominations, Unitarian Universalism has paid a price for its involvement in these issues.

4. Historically Unitarian Universalism has been more interested in influencing the broader society than in increasing its numerical size as a denomination. Its influence has certainly been felt even though it has not always been acknowledged. For example, it pioneered what became a widespread repudiation of Calvinist theology in the late eighteenth and early nineteenth centuries. There certainly is not much emphasis today on the doctrine of "double predestination" or concern about the suffering and torments experienced by those in hell, except by a few staunch fundamentalists. The Unitarian Universalists addressed these issues early, and then the mainline denominations recapitulated the issues in the modernist/fundamentalist controversy. In fact, many of the mainline denominations have promoted a Christian liberalism which was not unlike that of

the creators of the American Unitarian Association and the Universalist Church of America.

Unitarian Universalism Today

Today Unitarian Universalists are organized in a national association with its headquarters in Boston. The association is led by a president who is elected for a term of four years and may serve only two consecutive terms. The president is assisted by heads of several departments such as district services, ministry, religious education, and social justice, among others.

A General Assembly meets annually, usually in a large city in the United States, and delegates from the various local societies meet to transact the business of the association. The United States is partitioned into twenty districts which form an intermediate organizational structure between the local societies and the national headquarters. Each district has a director who facilitates constructive interaction between the local societies, the district, and the Unitarian Universalist Association and offers at the district level such services as extension programs and seminars for lay leadership.

Presently the Unitarian Universalist Association provides two denominational divinity schools, Meadville/Lombard Theological School in Chicago and Starr King School for the Ministry in Berkeley, California. It also supports the interdenominational Harvard Divinity School, due to its longstanding connection with Unitarians. Furthermore, it owns Beacon Press, a publishing company in Boston. In addition, the association maintains about fifteen camps and conference sites located throughout the United States.

Although today Unitarian Universalism is organized on a national scale, proportionately its numerical strength is still in Massachusetts where there are 153 churches, with a membership of 36,000. The state of California is the second strongest having 74 churches with 15,000 members. New York State has 64 churches with

14,000 members, Pennsylvania has 35 churches with 6,500 members, and Florida has 35 churches with 5,500 members. But at the other end North Dakota has only 2 churches with 135 members. In all, there are only 1,020 congregations with a membership of about 200,000, including about 50,000 children in church schools.[22]

Of course we now know that Jefferson's hope "that there is not a young man now living in the United States who will not die a Unitarian" was not realized. However, there are those who believe that his hope was only delayed, and that Unitarian Universalism is poised for growth as the "baby boom" generation begins to seek a base for its religious quest and for religiously educating its children. It is believed that Unitarian Universalism may yet realize its unclaimed legacy as the nation moves into the twenty-first century.

Notes

1. Perhaps the best study of the various ramifications of Jefferson's religion is Charles B. Sanford, *The Religious Life of Thomas Jefferson* (Charlottesville: University of Virginia Press, 1984). See especially 177–78.

2. Quoted in David B. Parke, *The Epic of Unitarianism* (Boston: Beacon Press, 1957), 99.

3. The basic source for understanding the history of Unitarianism is Earl Morse Wilbur, *A History of Unitarianism: Socinianism and Its Antecedents*, vol. 1 (Boston: Beacon Press, 1945) *A History of Unitariansim: In Transylvania, England, and America*, vol. 2 (Boston: Beacon Press, 1952). The most comprehensive source for understanding the history of Universalism is Russell E. Miller, *The Larger Hope: The First Century of the Universalist Church in America, 1770–1870*, vol. 1 and *The Larger Hope: The Second Century of the Universalist Church in America, 1870–1970*, vol. 2 (Boston: Unitarian Universalist Historical Society, 1985).

4. The major study of the rise of Unitarianism in the United States is Conrad Wright, *The Beginnings of Unitarianism in America* (Boston: Starr King Press; distributed by Beacon Press, 1955).

5. One of the most perceptive studies of the American Enlightenment is Henry E. May, *The Enlightenment in America* (New York: Oxford University Press, 1976). See especially his chapters on New England and Philadelphia, 177–96, 197–222.

6. Elmo Arnold Robinson, *American Universalism* (New York: Exposition Press, 1970), 39.

7. The term was derived from Jacob Arminius (1560–1609) who repudiated strict Calvinism in the Netherlands, especially the doctrine of election. He thought that humans had some choice in determining whether they would be saved or lost. His view was condemned at the Synod of Dort in 1619. Thus, a thinker who questioned Calvinism and advocated some degree of human choice in determining his or her eternal destiny was dubbed an "Arminian."

8. Of the many accounts of this story, perhaps Charles Forman's is the most complete. See his "Elected Now By Time: The Unitarian Controversy, 1805–1835," in Conrad Wright, ed., *Stream of Light* (Boston: Unitarian Universalist Association, 1975), 3–32.

9. Ibid., 31.

10. Robinson, *American Universalism*, 51–52.

11. Ibid., 52.

12. John A. Buehrens and F. Forrester Church, *Our Chosen Faith* (Boston: Beacon Press, 1989), 41–55. This is a chapter written by Church entitled "Deeds Not Creeds." See also James Luther Adams, *An Examined Faith*, ed. George K. Beach (Boston: Beacon Press, 1991), 321.

13. Buehrens and Church, *Our Chosen Faith*, 77.

14. Robert B. Tapp et al., "Theology and the Frontiers of Learning," in *The Free Church in a Changing World* (Boston: Unitarian Universalist Association, 1963), 25–26.

15. It is interesting to compare the theological positions in Unitarianism in the nineteenth century with those at the time of the merger of the Unitarians with the Universalists in 1960. For a summary outline of the earlier positions, see Mason Olds, "Varieties of Nineteenth-Century Unitarianism," in *religious humanism* 16, no. 4 (Autumn 1982): 150–60.

16. See, e.g. Gay Wilson Allen, *Waldo Emerson* (New York: Penguin Books, 1982), 376.

17. Walter Donald Kring, *Henry Whitney Bellows* (Boston: Skinner House, 1979), 305–322.

18. The story of the Free Religious Association is well told in Stow Person's, *Free Religion* (Boston: Beacon Press, 1963). See esp. 42–43.

19. There were many factors which contributed to the demise of the Free Religious Association (FRA); e.g., when the Unitarians finally decided not to require a creedal statement for church membership, many of the Unitarians actively involved in FRA returned to the Unitarian fold, and others became involved in the Ethical Culture movement. All of this was taking place at about the time of the World's Columbian Exposition. Many FRA members had great hope in the World Parliament of Religions, a component of the exposition, but were quite disappointed when the representatives of the world's faiths came as apologists, rather than to study religion objectively and scientifically. After that the FRA gradually dissolved.

20. For more detailed information about Dietrich and the controversy, see Mason Olds, *Religious Humanism in America: Dietrich, Reese, and Potter* (Washington, D.C.: University Press of America, 1977), 30–52.

21. John F. Hayward, *Existentialism and Religious Liberalism* (Boston: Beacon Press, 1962), 16–27.

22. *Unitarian Universalist Association: 1992 Directory* (Boston: Unitarian Universalist Association, 1992), 36–37.

Suggestions for Further Reading

Buehrens, John A., and F. Forrester Church. *Our Chosen Faith: An Introduction to Unitarian Universalism.* Boston: Beacon Press, 1989.

Cassara, Ernest, ed. *Universalism in America: A Documentary History of a Liberal Faith.* Boston: Skinner House, n.d. (Selected writings from 1741 to 1961, plus commentaries and introduction.)

Olds, Mason. *Religious Humanism in America: Dietrich, Reese, and Potter.* Washington, D.C.: University Press of America, 1977.

Parke, David B., ed. *The Epic of Unitarianism: Original Writings from the History of Liberal Religion.* Boston: Skinner House, 1992. (The collection provides significant materials from the sixteenth to the twentieth century.)

Wright, Conrad, ed. *A Stream of Light: A Sesquicentennial History of American Unitarianism.* Boston: Unitarian Universalist Association, 1975.

Part II
Contemporary Christian and Jewish Movements

Many American religious movements are as thoroughly rooted in mainstream Christianity or Judaism as the groups presented in the previous section, but, because their origins have been relatively recent, their numbers remain small, or they are widely regarded as embracing especially unusual ideas or practices, they are to some extent regarded as outsiders by the American religious establishment. The following seven chapters present representative examples of the many modern religious groups operating just outside the mainstream of Christianity and Judaism today.

It is a truism of sociology of religion that sectarian religious groups typically see themselves as restoring to the faith a pristine purity of doctrine and practice from which their parent bodies have deviated. Thus the majority of groups considered here deem themselves bastions of Christian or Jewish orthodoxy. Catholic Traditionalists believe they are restoring the One True Catholic Church that was gravely damaged by the reforms of the Second Vatican Council. The Boston Church of Christ contends that it alone understands the true nature of the earliest Christian church; the former Holy Order of MANS has embraced what it considers the authentic version of Eastern Orthodoxy. Hasidic Judaism is devoted to observing Jewish tradition, and in some cases the Hasidim reach out to the larger

Jewish community, urging relatively secular Jews to become more observant. The former Children of God (now the Family) consider themselves a simple confraternity of Christian missionaries, and the British-Israelites, despite the fact that their central theories of population migration are sharply rejected by most other Christians and Jews, as well as secular historians, see themselves as the true heirs of ancient Israel. The Branch Davidians, an offshoot of the Seventh-Day Adventists, similarly saw themselves as restorers of the ancient house of the biblical King David. (Incidentally, although many Branch Davidians perished in the Waco conflagration, others survive, and other wings of the larger Davidian movement survive as well.)

An orthodox self-image, however, does not mean that these groups are accepted as part of the mainstream by the established Christian and Jewish communities. Most would tolerate these unconventional perspectives on their parent traditions, and in the case of Hasidism many Jews would see these sectarians as indeed true pillars of tradition, even though most non-Hasidim have little desire to return to such a high level of traditional observance and intensive community life. On balance, these groups do not seem destined to be widely accepted as mainstream in the near future.

Part II

Contemporary Christian and Jewish Movement

9

ROMAN CATHOLIC TRADITIONALISM

William Dinges

Between 1962 and 1965, the hierarchy of the Roman Catholic Church initiated a series of reforms to realign Catholicism more positively with the modern world. This *aggiornamento* ("updating") by the Second Vatican Council brought both vitality and adaptation to the church along with conflict and fragmentation over issues of power, authority, and initiatives toward a more inculturated Catholicism.[1]

Aggiornamento also facilitated the rise of new cause-oriented interest groups and social movements within the church. Collectively, these movements give expression to increased ideological diversity and denominational dynamics among Catholics. Among the more important of these developments are the rise of Catholic Charismatic Renewal, a new Catholic left, floating or nonterritorial parishes, movements concerned with multiculturalism in a Catholic context, and initiatives toward a creative dialogue with Eastern traditions and New Age theologies. In addition, postconciliar Catholicism has also included the rise of movements of conservative and traditionalist dissent that illustrate Catholicism's "restructuring" along liberal and conservative lines following the pattern of mainline Protestantism.[2]

The Catholic Right

Postconciliar movements on the Catholic right are primarily the result of controversy surrounding the meaning and implementation of the Second Vatican Council. These movements consist of a segmented montage of groups and organizations championing in rather sectarian fashion the defense of symbols and structures of Catholic identity and ecclesiology that have lost legitimacy and/or credibility in the contemporary church. They have been variously identified as "conservative," "traditionalist," "neo-orthodox," "ultra-conservative" or "fundamentalist," although how such movements should be properly labelled and differentiated is, itself, problematic.

The traditionalist Catholic movement on which this chapter is focused represents the most radicalized segment on the Catholic right and the most representative Catholic analogue to Protestant fundamentalism. Traditionalist Catholics have denounced Vatican II as a "false" and "heretical" council. They refuse to accept its liturgical reforms and sacramental rites, repudiate its "modernist-inspired" liberal and ecumenist theology, and continue openly to defy hierarchical authority by adhering to the Tridentine liturgy and to a dogged defense of preconciliar doctrinal and disciplinary formulations. In moral and cultural orientations, traditionalists scorn any Catholic embrace of birth control, divorce, abortion, ecumenism, or "pick and choose" religiosity. Until his death at age eighty-six in 1991, French Archbishop Marcel Lefebvre (and his clerical Fraternity of St. Pius X [SSPX], founded in 1970 in Econe,

Switzerland) was the most media-visible symbol of traditionalist dissent both here and abroad.[3]

In addition to the traditionalist movement, the postconciliar Catholic right also includes organizations (some of which predate Vatican II) such as Catholics United for the Faith, *Opus Dei,* the Blue Army, the Latin Liturgy Association, and the Traditionalist Mass Society.[4] Like traditionalist Catholics, these groups (herein deemed "conservative") have also been carriers of anti-conciliarism, although their critique of the council has been more normative in character and focused primarily on the alleged "abuses" and "misinterpretations" of its decrees. Although conservative Catholics have developed their own institutional infrastructures, unlike traditionalists, they have not set up their own counter-church ones. Nor do conservative Catholics generally exemplify the counterrevolutionary mentality that characterizes many aspects of traditionalist ideology. Although often highly critical of church hierarchy, especially liberal or progressive bishops, conservative Catholics have generally opted for the ultramontanist solution—that is, one rooted in papal power, not decentralization—to the church's postconciliar malaise.

Differences over the Second Vatican Council notwithstanding, conservatives and traditionalists share many ideological affinities that distinguish them from progressive Catholics. Both espouse a cognitive (but highly selective) defiance of modernity. Both show heightened concern with internal threat and subversion. Both view liberal and progressive Catholics as "modernists" intent upon destroying the church from within. Both espouse an "authoritarian heteronomy" that treats the ecclesial magisterium of the church in much the same way that Protestant fundamentalists treat the Bible.[5] Both promote ethical rigorism, heightened supernaturalism, and a rigid sacred/profane dichotomy. Traditionalists and conservatives also espouse ideological motifs associated with a broad range of right-wing sociopolitical agenda items (e.g., condemnations of feminism, sex education, environmentalism, liberalism, and abortion). In addition, both

groups have been severely critical of the influence of bureaucratic and "new knowledge class" elites on Catholicism's postconciliar administrative infrastructure.

History and Current State of the Traditionalist Movement in the United States

Although not as large as other postconciliar phenomena such as Catholic Charismatic Renewal, the traditionalist movement in the United States has grown steadily over the last quarter century. The movement now includes a national network of churches and chapels, priories, schools, religious foundations, home-study programs, and a variety of publications dedicated to promoting the traditionalist cause. At the present time, there are approximately 224 traditionalist mass sites and/or chapel locations in the United States. Approximately 104 of these locations are served by priests of the SSPX; 30 by priests of the Society of St. Pius V; and 60 by priests (some of whom serve more than one chapel location) who consider themselves in union with Rome but who operate illicitly and independently of the local bishop. Another 30 traditionalist chapels are served by "sedevacantist" priests (see below).[6]

While the traditionalist movement arose in the context of a negative reaction to the Second Vatican Council, the reform of the church's liturgy was the precipitating factor that galvanized traditionalist discontent into an ideologically self-conscious social movement. The complex transformation that brought Catholic worship into conformity with the council's call for liturgical reform began with Pope Paul VI's approval of the Constitution on the Sacred Liturgy *(Sacrosanctum Consilium)* on 4 December 1963 and ended with the promulgation of a new rite of the mass *(Novus Ordo Missae)* on 3 April 1969. Over the next two and one-half years, the *Novus Ordo* liturgy gradually replaced the Tridentine mass in most American dioceses, although technically both liturgies were still in use until 1971. However, in November of that year, the *Novus Ordo* mass became mandatory throughout the entire church.

While the initial changes in the liturgy between 1963 and 1969 entailed modifications and adaptations of the Tridentine liturgy, the *Novus Ordo* mass constituted a new rite of worship providing for greater flexibility and ending many of the baroque accretions and archaic ceremonialisms that had characterized the Tridentine liturgy.

Although the majority of American Catholics reacted positively to liturgical reforms, pockets of resistance arose simultaneous with their implementation. Throughout the latter half of the 1960s, scattered groups of dissenters, disturbed by the "modernist" direction of the council symbolized in the alterations in the mass, engaged in public protests, letter-writing campaigns, withholding contributions, and the picketing of chancery offices. These protests, however, did not constitute at the time a traditionalist movement per se, but were part of the broader conservative Catholic anxiety over Vatican II's "tampering" with the sacred deposit of faith.

In addition to turmoil over liturgical changes, conservative Catholic fears surrounding *aggiornamento* were also exacerbated by the appearance of "recklessness" and "near anarchy" permeating other aspects of church life at the time. Much of this anti-conciliar sentiment found its earliest expression in the pages of *The Wanderer,* a lay-owned St. Paul, Minnesota, newspaper and long-time bastion of Catholic social and ecclesial conservatism.

The initial opposition to the changes in the church's liturgical practice focused on issues of aesthetics, on the "desacralizing" and "Protestant" aspects of the changes, and on their purported threat to the integrity of Roman Catholic identity. Opposition also arose in response to the perception of liturgical abuses and excesses totally unrelated to the actual intent of the conciliar decrees. The Reverend Gommar De Pauw, a professor of theology and academic dean at Saint Mary's Major Seminary in Emmitsburg, Maryland, launched the Catholic Traditionalist Movement, Inc., in 1965 as one of the first organizational efforts to mobilize Catholics against these developments and against other "misguided" initiatives of "liberal-inspired innovators" working to update the church.

Other "traditionalist" initiatives were forthcoming. The two most notable were the Orthodox Roman Catholic Movement, Inc. (ORCM), founded by Fr. Francis Fenton, in Bridgeport, Connecticut, in 1973, and Archbishop Lefebvre's SSPX.

Several of the Lefebvre's priests began their work among American Catholics between 1973 and 1974. By the early 1980s, the society had established a national network of publishing enterprises, chapels, schools, and priories, including a seminary, first located in Ridgefield, Connecticut, and moved in 1988 to Winona, Minnesota. In addition to the labors of Frs. De Pauw and Fenton and priests of the SSPX, unaffiliated traditionalist clerics scattered throughout the country also began to establish "wildcat" parishes. By the mid-1970s, these collective efforts gave distinctive organizational coherence to a campaign of "remnant faithful" Catholics committed to preserving the "True Mass" and to defending the "pure and unadulterated" doctrine and discipline of a rapidly changing church that few any longer recognized as the faith on which they had once been nurtured.

Although the particulars varied, the pattern in which traditionalist chapels were established typically involved small and beleaguered groups of Catholics gathering in homes, motels, VFW halls, or rented facilities for discussion and/or devotional practices. In some instances, traditionalists allied themselves with a local traditionalist priest or long-time pastor resisting Vatican II reforms. In others, local Catholics alarmed over *aggiornamento* contacted priests of the SSPX or the ORCM whose efforts on behalf of the traditionalist cause were gradually becoming more visible. By the mid-1970s, a circuit riding network of traditionalist chapels had been established throughout the United States. As the number of traditionalist Catholics in a specific area increased, larger and more permanent chapel locations were often secured.

The emergence of Catholic traditionalism as a distinct sectarian social movement derived not only from traditionalist perceptions of modernist betrayal of the faith by the church's theologians and hierarchy, but also from growing conflict and division within the ranks of the Catholic right itself. This split occurred largely because the initial dispute over liturgical reform rapidly became a dispute over doctrine and the legitimacy of the council itself. These issues, in turn, developed into a more schism-prone conflict over authority in the church.

By the late 1960s, the more ideologically radicalized traditionalist critics of *aggiornamento* were charging that the new mass was a "heretical" and "invalid" rite. These accusations stemmed from alleged "Protestant" participation in the formulation of the new rite and from the purported "mistranslations" of its canon, the most sacred portion of the mass. This traditionalist assault on the doctrinal integrity of the new liturgy was increasingly accompanied by strident and polemical attacks— laden with conspiracy and eschatological motifs—on the council and on the person of Pope Paul VI.

With the prohibition of the Tridentine mass after 1971, the question of the legitimacy of traditionalist dissent in the church came to a head. Traditionalist Catholics now found themselves in a painful test of obedience and loyalty that many could not resolve short of open defiance of the hierarchy. This defiance—especially in the context of a broader crisis of authority in the church following Vatican II and the widespread repudiation of Paul VI's *Humanae Vitae*—led more moderate conservatives to distance themselves from traditionalist leaders and organizations. The ecclesiastical censorship of Fr. De Pauw in the late 1960s and the suspension of Archbishop Lefebvre in 1976 (following his public defiance of a direct Vatican order prohibiting ordinations) exacerbated the deepening tension on the Catholic right. This winnowing process differentiating conservative and traditionalist Catholics was further advanced with Lefebvre's excommunication in 1988.

Opposition to Traditionalists

Liberal and progressive Catholics have generally discounted the traditionalist cause as little more than a fringe element of Catholics clinging nostalgically to the past, or as a fossilized expression of Catholicism's "integralist" proclivities. Not surprisingly, however, the primary source of opposition to traditionalist organizational initiatives (if not traditionalist ideology per se) has come from the hierarchy and, as previously noted, from conservative Catholics.

In general, the bishops in the United States have tried to blunt the traditionalist cause through a policy of firmness, enticement, and circumvention. They have avoided public debates or media-fed confrontations with traditionalist priests and apologists. Individual bishops have disciplined traditionalist priests under their authority either by early retirement, or by withdrawing their canonical faculties to celebrate mass publicly or to administer other sacraments. Individual bishops have also refused knowingly to rent or sell abandoned church property to traditionalist organizations. Following the prohibition of the Tridentine mass in 1971, the American bishops advised Catholics attending traditionalist-sponsored Tridentine liturgies that they were not "fulfilling their Sunday obligations," and that priests saying mass without permission in the dioceses in which they were practicing did not have proper canonical authority to administer sacraments. With the Vatican suspension of Archbishop Lefebvre in 1976, American Catholics were warned to avoid Lefebvre's movement because of its "schismatic" potential.

The policy of American bishops toward traditionalist Catholics has also been mitigated by Vatican initiatives. The Vatican attitude toward the traditionalist movement, especially during the pontificate of John Paul II, has been lenient, flexible, and geared toward averting schism. In October 1984, in apparent reaction to Archbishop Lefebvre's threats to consecrate a bishop, John Paul II issued a papal indult permitting limited use of the Tridentine liturgy but with narrow stipulations: Catholics desiring the old liturgy had to secure permission of the local bishop and make it "publicly clear beyond all ambiguity" that they were not connected with groups that impugned the lawfulness and doctrinal integrity of the new mass. However, while conservative Catholics welcomed the indult as an "acceptable solution" to the problem of the liturgy, most traditionalists repudiated the effort as yet another Vatican ploy to coopt their cause.

A similar reaction followed the establishment of the *Ecclesia Dei* commission in 1988. This commission grew out of a July 2, 1988, letter by John Paul II promising relaxation of the rules regarding the Tridentine liturgy. The commission was intended to mollify conservatives disaffected by liturgical changes and to integrate traditionalist Catholics back into the church following Archbishop Lefebvre's excommunication for consecrating four bishops on June 30th.

Responses by the American hierarchy to *Ecclesia Dei* have been mixed. Some bishops have allowed the Tridentine liturgy in response to petitions on an "experimental basis." In other instances, permission has been refused. Additional problems have arisen because the *Ecclesia Dei* commission initially began issuing "celebrets" to priests authorizing them to use the Tridentine liturgy without prior agreement of the local bishop. This practice was subsequently stopped.

As noted previously, the other principal source of opposition to the traditionalist cause has come from conservative Catholic quarters. Conservative Catholics have been uneasy with the traditionalist challenge to hierarchical (notably papal) authority. Conservative apologists have decried the traditionalist assault on the hierarchy both because of the "Protestant principle" such dissent portrays and because traditionalist radicalism implicitly casts aspersions on the legitimacy of their own campaign against "modernist" influence in the postconciliar church—which parallels that of traditionalists in many other respects.

Traditionalist Catholics, for their part, have assailed conservatives for their lack of courage and "false sense of obedience"

in the face of the "grave crisis" in the church. Traditionalists charge that conservative accommodation to papal authority has undercut resistance to *aggiornamento* and, thereby, only further contributed to widespread "apostasy" and the church's "auto-destruction."

Internal Fragmentation

As is typically the case with ideologically inspired social movements, Catholic traditionalism has been rife with internal tension and division. Conflicts have arisen over issues of doctrine, over the proper mode of dissent, over whether or not to respond to blandishments of the official church, and over matters of practical organizational strategy and the mobilization of resources. The question of the status of the papacy has been particularly contentious. A minority of traditionalists have espoused a "sedevacantist" position, holding that the See of Peter is currently vacant because of the "heresies" of the post-conciliar church.[7] This position has been repudiated, however, by the more mainstream elements of the traditionalist cause.

Efforts to unify traditionalist Catholics in the United States over the last three decades have met with little success. Following a failed attempt in 1967 to circumvent hierarchical authority by affiliating with what proved to be a bogus religious order, Fr. De Pauw vowed not to align himself with any other traditionalist initiative—continuing single-handedly his own organizational efforts in Westbury, Long Island. Both Frs. De Pauw and Fenton attacked Archbishop Lefebvre and his priests for taking over traditionalist strongholds in the United States in the early 1970s that had been built up by other traditionalist priests and for provoking Vatican censorship. Conflict within the ORCM (leading eventually to the organization's demise) centered on Fr. Fenton's affiliation with the John Birch Society, his autocratic authority within the organization, financial problems, and control of the ORCM board of directors. In 1979, Fenton left the ORCM and moved to

Colorado Springs, Colorado, where he established the Traditional Catholics of America, Inc. (TCA)

Nor has the Society of St. Pius X been without internal trouble. In 1983 Archbishop Lefebvre expelled nine priests from his society for assuming a sedevacantist position and for failing to "pray for the Pope." This expulsion led to the formation of another traditionalist group by the deposed priests, the Society of St. Pius V, and to lengthy litigation over the control of several chapel locations. Following the archbishop's excommunication in 1988, nearly thirty priests and seminarians also left the SSPX and become members of the Society of St. Peter, a Vatican-approved organization set up to reincorporate Lefebvre clergy into the church. Controversies have also arisen among traditionalist Catholics over "bogus" priests or clerics with proported connections to the Old Catholic movement that broke away from Rome in 1870 following the First Vatican Council.

Impact on Contemporary Culture

The traditionalist movement in the United States has had marginal public repercussions and limited public visibility over the last several decades—in contrast to the situation in France, where Catholic traditionalism is more militant and publicly linked with right-wing political causes, most notably Jean-Marie Le Pen's National Front. The American situation is, in part, attributable to the size and diffusion of the movement and to its character as an introversionist sect focused on internal church-related issues rather than a world-transforming one. Nor does the traditionalist movement in the United States have overt organizational ties with the Protestant Religious Right. This situation derives from the fact that traditionalism is vehemently anti-ecumenical and composed of ideological purists unlikely to make common cause with "heretics." Whether the current round of culture wars and especially the escalating abortion issue will make the possibility of such an alliance between the Protestant and Catholic far right a more

fluid matter remains to be seen. However, while traditionalism is not primarily a movement of religiously motivated political activism, its ideology, as previously noted, both reiterates and reinforces much of the social and cultural agenda of the Protestant Religious Right.

Catholic traditionalism's lack of media visibility also stems from the fact that, unlike other new religious movements such as ISKCON and the Reverend Sun Myung Moon's Unification Church, traditionalism has not been the focus of public controversy over alleged brainwashing practices or deceptive recruiting strategies that have provoked anticult initiatives elsewhere. Although there have been isolated instances in which brainwashing charges have been brought against specific traditionalist groups,[8] the movement as a whole has not been the subject of widespread public controversy in this regard. As previously noted, however, there has been some public litigation concerning ownership of church property along with media airing of disputes within local traditionalist groups.

Conclusion

As much of the contemporary scholarship attests, the global situation of religion today includes the repoliticalization of religion, the militant resurgence of religious traditionalism, and the proliferation of enclaves of religious totalism.[9] Movements on the Catholic right need to be situated in this wider macrosocial context. These movements are one cultural manifestation of the problematic character of Catholic identity in the culture of modernity.

While Catholic traditionalism is unlikely to grow in any substantial way in the decades ahead, neither is the movement likely to disappear. In the United States, traditionalism has emerged as a subcultural element in the contemporary Catholic experience, albeit one that has lost much of its connection to mainstream Catholicism. Nevertheless, Catholic traditionalism has assumed a distinctive place in America's dynamic sect and cult milieu.

Notes

1. For studies of the turmoil among Catholics in the postconciliar era, see Joseph Fichter, "Restructuring Catholicism," *Sociological Analysis* 38 (Summer 1977): 154–66; Andrew Greeley, *Crisis in the Church* (Chicago: Thomas More, 1979); John Seidler and Katherine Meyer, *Conflict and Change in the Catholic Church* (New Bruns-wick: Rutgers University Press, 1989); William McSweeney, *Roman Catholicism: The Search for Relevancy* (New York: St. Martin's, 1980).

2. See Robert Wuthnow, *The Restructuring of American Religion* (Princeton: Prince-ton University Press, 1988).

3. For a more extensive treatment of Catholic traditionalism, see William D. Dinges, "Roman Catholic Traditionalism," in *Fundamentalisms Observed*, ed., Martin E. Marty and R. Scott Appleby (Chicago: University of Chicago Press, 1991), 66–101.

4. See James Hitchcock, "Catholic Activist Conservatism in the United States," ibid., 101–27.

5. See Gabriel Daly, "Catholicism and Modernity," *Journal of the American Academy of Religion* 53, no. 3 (1985): 773–96.

6. In addition to these traditionalist chapels, there are nearly 160 additional locations in the United States in which priests are offering mass under the 1984 Indult, or as members of the Society of St. Peter.

7. Several American traditionalist sedevacantist priests have been consecrated as "bishops" through the initiative of Archbishop Pierre Martin Ngo-Dihn-Thuc. For a discussion of the sedevacantist wing of traditionalism see Michael Davies, "The Sedevacantists," *The Angelus* (February 1983): 10–12.

8. See, for example, *The Washington Post* (23 July 1988) for a story of a woman abducted from St. Joseph Novitiate Convent in Round Top, New York (run by the Society of St. Pius V), who was purportedly brainwashed. Lawsuits have also been initiated charging "cult-like" practices against a traditionalist organization called the Latin Rite Catholic Church (formerly Fatima Crusade) in Coeur D'Alene, Idaho, founded in 1968 by "Archbishop" Francis K. Schuckardt.

9. See Thomas Robbins and Roland Robertson, "Studying Religion Today: Controversiality and 'Objectivity' in the Sociology of Religion," *Religion* 21 (1991): 319–37.

Suggestions for Further Reading

Coleman, John. "Who Are the Catholic Fundamentalists?" *Commonweal,* 27 January 1989.

Cuneo, Michael. "Conservative Catholicism in North America: Pro Life Activism and the Pursuit of the Sacred." *Pro Mundi Vita: Dossiers* (January 1987): 2–27.

Davies, Michael. *Apologia Pro Marcel Lefebvre: Part I, 1905–1976.* Dickinson, Tex.: The Angelus Press, 1979.

Dinges, William D. "Ritual Conflict as Social Conflict: Liturgical Reform in the Roman Catholic Church." *Sociological Analysis* 48, no. 2 (Summer 1987): 138–58.

———. " 'We Are What You Were': Catholic Traditionalists in America." In *Being Right: Conservative American Catholics,* edited by Mary Jo Weaver and R. Scott Appleby. Bloomington: Indiana University Press, forthcoming.

Lefebvre, Marcel. *A Bishop Speaks: Writings and Addresses, 1973–1975.* Edinburgh: Scottish *Una Voce,* 1976.

10

HASIDISM AND ITS EFFECTS ON ALTERNATIVE JEWISH MOVEMENTS IN AMERICA

S. Daniel Breslauer

The Jewish mystical movement Hasidism has exerted a strange fascination on modern Jews in the last four decades.[1] The name "Hasidism" can be translated as "pietism." It derives from a biblical term, used most often in the Book of Psalms, describing those "zealous" for God. An individual pietist is a "Hasid," several are called "Hasidim," and the movement is "Hasidism." Although Jewish history records several different groups claiming that title, in modern times it refers to a movement that arose in Eastern Europe in the eighteenth century, associated with stories about a charismatic leader called Israel ben Eleazar, Baal Shem Tov. The last phrase is a title, translated sometimes as "Master of the Good Name," and sometimes as "Good Master of the Name." The title seems to refer to the magical abilities and personal qualities of its holder. In its original context Hasidism became a major alternative for Jews faced with rapidly changing social and intellectual options brought by political emancipation, Enlightenment philosophy, and the lure of secular nationalism. Whether following in the footsteps of its putative founder or striking out on new paths, the leaders of Hasidism challenged the status quo maintained by traditional Jewish authorities.[2] At first, the traditional Jewish leaders, recognizing in Hasidism a threat to their authority, reacted with hostility. Rabbis associated with official authorities, for example Elijah

Gaon of Vilna (now Vilnius, in Lithuania), the leading Jewish legalist of the time, pronounced a ban on the new movement. Hasidic leaders, in turn, often castigated many of the innovations current among Jews of their times—religious reforms, Zionism and other nationalistic movements, secularism, and Jewish socialism.[3] Eventually European Jewish traditionalists agreed to present a united front opposing the innovations of Reform Judaism, Jewish Enlightenment, and secular movements such as Zionism and socialism. As part of this coalition of traditional forces, Hasidism gained some respectability. By World War II it had become the bulwark of traditional Judaism in Europe.

The antagonism of various Jewish orthodoxies toward innovative movements in general, and toward Zionism in particular, should be stressed. As a modern, secular, and humanistic movement Zionism contradicts several theological tenets of traditional Judaism. It removes God as the active agent bringing the Messiah and makes human action central. It denies the transcendent importance of obedience to Jewish law and substitutes political and practical action for traditional legal injunctions. It advocates Jewish political activism rather than faith in divine help. While some Hasidic groups have made peace with the Zionist movement, particularly after the creation of the State of Israel, other groups have not (an ambivalence paralleled in Orthodox Judaism generally). The divisions within Orthodoxy and Hasidism toward Zionism symbolizes the condition of both movements today. Despite efforts to portray themselves as a single block, the Orthodox, generally, and Hasidism in particular display tendencies toward factionalism and divisiveness, tendencies found in Hasidism since its beginnings.

The movement developed as a set of often-competing groups each organized around a charismatic figure, a rebbe. Different Hasidic groups were characterized by distinctive practices, theologies, and opinions about other Jews. One of the earliest groups to come to the United States was also one of the most unusual. In 1903 a prominent European rebbe, the Lelover, sent one of his disciples to America, a disciple who settled in Boston, thus creating the "Bostoner" Hasidim. The followers of this group imbibed much of American thought and theory and today represent a liberal wing in Hasidic life.[4] Other Hasidim followed and, while not as liberal as the Bostoner Hasidim, also succeeded in gaining a foothold in the new country and adapting to its particular style and approach to religion.

During the 1930s and 1940s, Hasidic communities emigrated to the United States either to escape Hitler's forces or to avoid the aftermath of World War II. The groups generally identified themselves by the places from which their leader came; thus, for example, one refers to Lubavitcher, Bobover, Satmar, or Bratzlaver Hasidism. By the end of this period, much of American Jewish life had been transformed due to these new immigrants. Jenne Weismann Joselit reported that, because of this influx of a new type of Orthodox Jew, the character of American Jewish Orthodoxy had been radically altered. This alteration had both a positive and negative effect as a study of Jewish life in the Williamsburg neighborhood of Brooklyn, New York, demonstrates. Joselit notes that while the original Jewish inhabitants of Williamsburg retained their Orthodoxy by giving it an Americanized flavor, the Hasidim refused to exhibit any signs of accommodation. This refusal, she infered, made

life uncomfortable for some Jews who had assimilated American ways but also maintained a high standard of Jewish self-consciousness. This self-consciousness stemmed the tide of suburban flight that often undermined the Jewish nature of urban communities. As Joselit commented, "the postwar Hasidification of Williamsburg not only left its distinctive stamp on that community but also saved it from physical deterioration."[5] As in Europe, the American Hasidim began by arousing hostility and were seen by many other Jews as alien, but eventually became accepted as models of traditional Judaism.

Hasidism accomplished this acceptance by building its own structures and institutions, thereby ensuring its survival. Solomon Poll studied the institutional network of Hasidic Jews in Williamsburg, New York.[6] Using a functionalist analysis, he suggests that Hasidic institutions succeed because they serve the basic needs of their constituency. Poll points out that Hasidic Jews recognize that they do not fit easily into the American environment. He shows how they justify their willingness to remain alien and unassimilated by reference to supernatural belief. They appeal to divinely sanctioned laws as an explanation for the apparent oddity of their ways. In addition to this supernatural reinforcement of their way of life, their practice has, Poll contends, the sociological effect of strengthening their resolve to remain different. Through their collective ritual they reinforce social ties. By making every action a concrete referent to a specific religious value they invest life with meaning. By an elaborate system of reward and punishment, of official and unofficial approval or disapproval, Poll suggests, they use social pressure to enforce their cultural system.[7] Whether Poll's analysis is accurate or not, the Hasidim did in fact succeed in maintaining their own identity and increasing their prestige in America. This continued success startled many social analysts who expected all immigrant communities to adapt to their new environment and gradually assimilate to it. One scholar of Jewish mysticism, Joseph Dan, notes that "The new flourishing of Hasidism took historians by surprise so that they need to re-evaluate previous ideas."[8]

One key to this success lies in Hasidic theology—in its explicit appeal to the Jewish mystical tradition. Three primary elements, all of them rooted in earlier mystical thought, characterize Hasidic theology.[9] The first emphasizes the cosmic importance of Jewish activities. Hasidim claim that whatever Jews do here on earth causes repercussions in the heavenly sphere. From this perspective when things go wrong in daily life the cause springs from what Jews have done. This theology proclaims that there is no unimportant Jewish action. This basic tenet of Hasidism underlines the essential importance of traditional living. Given its claims, when the world seems corrupt and unsatisfying the most helpful response is that of performing Jewish commandments, of fulfilling the traditional precepts, the *mitzvot*. While these actions are tied to tradition, the second aspect of Hasidic theology emphasizes individual piety. The Hasidim hold that the crucial act is that of cleaving to the divine, of *devekut*. They aver that an individual's act of devotion draws down heavenly powers and, if properly directed, can bring redemption to humanity and transform human experience. Here Hasidism focuses on the individual's sense of personhood, on the self-image of each individual Jew striving to perform those actions needed to bring salvation to the world. Finally the Hasidim emphasize that not everyone can attain the heights of *devekut* nor can all discern the true means of attunement to the heavenly forces. According to their view every Jew needs the assistance of an exalted leader, of a rebbe. In this way Hasidism legitimates community and communal loyalty through insisting upon the inherent necessity for leaders with spiritual powers. By joining a Hasidic community and through loyalty to its leadership, they maintain, a Jew actualizes that grace which the divine has already provided.

The claim to cosmic relevance helps explain the persistence and attractiveness of Hasidism in the modern American context. Modern Orthodox Jewish leadership, best exemplified by leaders arising from the Young Israel movement, vacillated between what Jeffrey Gurock has called "resisters"

and "accommodators."[10] The development of the Young Israel movement shows that vacillation well. Begun in 1912 as a response to Americanization the movement originally sought accommodation with modernity. American Jews, accused of criminal behavior and uncivil nature, had formed an internal communal structure, the New York Kehillah movement.[11] As one outgrowth of this movement, Young Israel sought a double goal. It used adaptation to American values to stem the defection of Orthodox Jewish youth to Reform Judaism. Until World War II this accommodationist stance continued with Young Israel acting as a bridge between the traditional Orthodox community and modernized Jews who had rejected the tradition. Since then, however, its Council of Young Israel Rabbis has emphasized greater traditionalism, resistance to modernity, and intensive programs of classical Jewish learning. Throughout this transformation, however, Young Israel articulated a traditional Orthodox theology. This theology maintained that the Torah as interpreted by traditional Jewish leaders represents a literal revelation given to Moses at Mount Sinai. From its perspective God desires Jews to follow the laws and commandments given in the Torah. The leaders of Young Israel insist that Jewish survival depends upon fidelity to these *mitzvot*.

Hasidism does not disagree with these basic principles. Nevertheless its enunciation of a more transcendent purpose in Jewish observances helps explain its attractiveness in contrast to the alternative exemplified by Young Israel. In the 1950s a number of sociologists discerned disturbing aspects of American Jewry. Oscar Handlin and Will Herberg agreed that there was a "pragmatic" and social orientation to American Jewishness which belied the so-called "revival" of religion.[12] Herberg, however, remarked on the theological sensitivity that moved many younger Americans, uncomfortable with secularization. Herberg noted that while many Jews find pragmatism and assimilation fully satisfying, "among some American Jews there was perplexity and restlessness" since all the material success and social comfort

Jews and achieved could not answer the spiritual questions about human existence and the meaning of life that trouble the intellectually sensitive.[13] According to Herberg, Hasidic theology addressed this restlessness better and seemed more sensitive to the dilemma it expressed than did the theologies associated with modern Jewish Orthodoxy. As Herberg had expected, the appeal of Hasidic groups grew beyond their own boundaries and attracted many originally non-Hasidic Jews. One observer remarked that the Hasidim "have been doubling their numbers every decade since the nineteen-fifties."[14] Demographically, then, the Hasidim have increased in numbers and prominence in the United States. Not only did Hasidism become more visible; it also gained respectability. The theological claim that Jewish survival has consequences for the universe as a whole lent legitimacy to the choice of such a particularistic way of life as that advocated by Orthodox Judaism.

In the 1960s and 1970s Hasidism, perhaps as a result of this demographic and ideological success, became more activist and attracted a large number of young Jews. A recent commentator has suggested that "new generations of American-born Jews of Reform, Conservative, and unaffiliated parents carry on Hasidic tradition in America."[15] Hasidism is not monolithic, so a generalization hardly applies to every subgroup within the movement. Nevertheless, a variety of Hasidic groups among American Jewry seems to be flourishing. These groups have a new activism—both politically and religiously—and reach out to all American Jews.[16] This activism apparently contrasts with the personalized and individualistic focus of Hasidic piety. Modern Hasidim, however, manage to maintain a commitment to the experience of *devekut,* of a personal devotionalism which confirms Jews in their individuality, in their selfhood, in their sense of distinctiveness. Such self-confirmation not only draws Jews into Hasidic groups but also cements the Hasidic community itself.

William Shaffir studied the Lubavitcher community in Montreal.[17] Shaffir contrasted this community with another Hasidic group, the Satmar, who also live in the city. He showed how the Hasidim came from being alien outsiders to models of the Jewish way of life. He connected this with their energy in propagating Judaica practice. He placed the Lubavitch outreach to nonobservant Jews in the context of "their role as super-Jews."[18] His analysis claimed that the high visibility the Hasidim achieve in their efforts to spread observance of Jewish practices reinforces their image as bulwarks for the tradition. Shaffir also noted that this outreach campaign is an effective means to maintain control over Hasidic youth who might be tempted to leave the movement.[19]

What are the implications of these developments in Hasidism? Sociologist Stephen Sharot concluded that Hasidism in modern society has become an introversionist sect.[20] Such a sect looks inward rather than outward to others for its legitimacy and authenticity. It rejects the external world because that world is irrelevant to the truth and meaning the sect experiences in its life. Sharot marshalled evidence to support his claim. He argues that Hasidim separate themselves from other Jews and proclaim that their form of Judaism manifests a greater fidelity to Jewish religion than do those of other Jewish movements. Sharot emphasized the Hasidic conviction of the "sacredness of the community" which underlies their separatist mentality.[21] This sense of separatist community provided him with a basis on which to define the type of sectarianism Hasidism represents in the modern world.

Not every analysis agrees with Sharot's conclusions. Hasidim themselves often presented their movement as an all-inclusive one intending to unite Jewry under one banner. When the movement described its own history it emphasized that type of inclusiveness.[22] It portrayed itself as reaching out to other Jews so that they too can share in the holiness of the Jewish community. It claimed that it extends an invitation to those estranged from Judaism, offering a path back home. The Hasidim affirmed that they seek out Jews to encourage them to fulfill the precepts of Judaism—men should pray using the traditional instruments of prayer *(tefillin)*, women should light candles on the Sabbath and holidays, rituals associated with holidays such as Tabernacles and Hannukah should be performed. Lubavitcher Hasidim described how they organize crusades to visit universities and enable Jews estranged from the tradition to return to Jewish practice. In this way Lubavitcher Hasidism presented itself as part of a broader movement—that of the Baal Teshuva, or repentant Jew who returns to a faithful Jewish life. Hasidism appealed to American Jewish youth because it offered a clear set of values, an unambiguous picture of the ideal Jew, and an evident model of behavior. The Hasidim actively sought out other Jews to convince them to accept this Hasidic paradigm of Judaism as the basis for their lives.

Hasidism has succeeded but only as one alternative among many different Jewish movements concerned with structuring a new personal identity to integrate political, cultural, and sociopsychological aspects of the self. The Baal Teshuva movement addressed these same issues. Men and women attracted to Orthodox Judaism articulated a vision of renewed selfhood. M. Herbert Danzger, studying this phenomenon, commented on the affinity between the ideals of the counterculture and the values of Orthodox Judaism. He identified this affinity as a basis for the attraction American Jewish youth feel toward Orthodoxy generally, not only toward Hasidism. He noted that the norms taught to these newly observant Jews often differ from those of modernity, but nevertheless attract youth seeking to establish their own identity and sense of selfhood.[23] Danzger focused primarily on men who returned to Judaism. Debra Renee Kaufman studied women who entered Orthodox Judaism from a nontraditional background. She discovered that many such women often explain their change by appealing to values of family and feminism. She demonstrated that such women need not enter a Hasidic community to find in traditional Jewish practice a refuge from what they see as modern culture's "confusion and ambivalence toward women, women's sexuality, family and gender roles."[24] Tradition of-

fers a way out of the dilemma created by modernity's open society.

Yet Hasidism itself faces a dilemma precisely because of its traditional views of sexuality and gender. Women with unconventional views of their role, male and female homosexuals, discover that the Hasidic welcome does not extend to them. Gay and lesbian Jews express their frustration with Orthodox Judaism.[25] Lis Harris describes the pain felt by homosexual Jews within a Hasidic community. They are both drawn toward the communal support offered and repelled, knowing that they cannot honestly express themselves. They often live frustrated lives by controlling their sexual desires or act out deviant behavior in secret, hounded by guilt.[26] Many heterosexual women sympathize and identify with this experience. The Ezrat Nashim movement reflects this frustration among mainstream Jewish women and the efforts to cope with it. Although originally, in 1971, the movement subsisted within the Conservative movement in Judaism, it soon grew to national proportions.[27] Judith Plaskow, associated with the Jewish woman's movement and Ezrat Nashim almost from its inception, expressed its theological concerns. She denied the compartmentalization of her life—she is not a woman and a Jew but a Jewish woman. A Judaism that will fit her selfhood must be constructed anew, rebuilding the basic concepts of Jewish thought.[28] She described her task as a religious Jewish woman using the technical phrase "repairing the world," a theological expression most associated with Jewish mysticism and often used by the Hasidim. At this point Plaskow noted the appeal of Hasidism to newly observant Jewish women. She pointed to what she found as the irony of feminist *"baalot teshuvah."* When they seek to enter traditional Jewish communities they find their theological concerns rebuffed. If they become too articulate in their questioning, she observed, "they are referred to the Hasidim."[29] Plaskow interpreted this effort by traditionalists to brand theology as mysticism a symptom of insensitivity. She claimed that the Orthodox Jewish community relegates religious searching to a sectarian tributary, a nonmainstream aspect of Jewish life.

The automatic response which associates sensitivity to Jewish theology with Jewish mysticism generally and with Hasidism in particular, however, also shows an advantage held by the Hasidim over other groups of Orthodox Jews reaching out to nontraditional Jewish populations. The mystical background of the Hasidic movement endows its social and political agenda with a theological rationale not found in other movements. Hasidism attracts Jews not just because of its traditionalism or its emphasis on personal piety. It also creates a sense of community through the personality and charisma of a leader said to possess special divine sanction, charismatic empowerment by God: the rebbe. The importance of the rebbe as the center of Hasidic community cannot be overestimated. Rabbi Herbert Weiner interviewed young Jews who entered Bratzlaver Hasidism. He asked why they chose the Hasidic way rather than any other normative and traditional form of Judaism and received the reply that they were attracted to " 'eytsos,' concrete personal guidance through the example of and the teachings of a rebbe."[30] These young Jews selected Hasidism because they found that the rebbe, through practical advice, offers a clear blueprint for community, a program that creates social bonding.

Such bonding arises in various ways. Study groups, for example, often establish an atmosphere of social interaction. Samuel Heilman investigated traditional ways of "learning Torah," of studying traditional Jewish texts. He described, as one example, the effect of the Bratzlaver Hasidic approach to Torah study in this way. The Bratzlavers are unique among Hasidic groups since they revere a dead rebbe, Rabbi Nahman of Bratzlav, a descendent of the Baal Shem Tov. Because they have no living leader, they use the books bequeathed from Rabbi Nahman as the central hub around which they organize their community.[31] At a particular study session Heilman observed, various members of the group studied different texts; they moved from the classical rabbinic books such as chapters of the Mishnah or tractates of the Talmud to esoteric mystical works and concluded with the writings of Rabbi Nahman himself. After reading from these works they broke out into dance, a dance which Heilman interprets as a "tie sign" indicating how the act of study itself, irrespective of the intellectual effect of such study, unifies the group into a cohesive community. Such a ritual, Heilman remarked, reaffirms communal unity. He concludes that for the Hasidim the commandment to study Torah becomes a means of confirming communal solidarity.[32]

Hasidism, of course, is not the only modern Jewish movement to focus on the creation of community. The Havurah movement which began in the 1970s is another alternative. It developed as a group of small fellowships, loosely connected in a nationwide network. A National Havurah Coordinating Committee now sponsors conferences and regular interchange among the fellowships. It not only articulates a distinctive theory and practice but has also provided a source book of "Jewish experience."[33] Despite the movement's appeal, many of its participants—especially those who find its sexual egalitarianism disquieting—eventually leave it for Orthodoxy.[34] Hasidism's willingness to reach out to such Jews gives evidence of its activist position.

The pro-active stance became even more evident in the late 1970s and throughout the 1980s. Hasidic groups agitated for greater political power in both the United States and Israel. Activism found within Hasidic neighborhoods in both countries illustrates how charismatic leaders mobilize a community, using the social and political opportunities of modern life to further their own aims. Jerome Mintz analyzed this phenomenon and claimed that American democracy presented Hasidim with a novel opportunity. They were able to participate in civil life without forgoing their distinctive characteristics. For the first time, he suggested, "the Hasidim in the New world were able to engage in dialogue with a government sympathetic to minority needs."[35] Hasidism took advantage of government-sponsored programs meant to strengthen education, to combat poverty, and to reduce ethnic violence as a means of reinforcing their own particular institutions of learning and welfare, their dominance in certain neighborhoods, and their programs for outreach to non-Hasidic Jews.

The ambivalent environment of the State of Israel also gave Hasidim an unprecedented political opportunity. While some Hasidic leaders assaulted Zionism as a heretical option, others made a "tactical alliance with Israel" so that while they remained theoretically opposed to the state they could also use leverage to gain advantages from it.[36] The Hasidim have an ambivalence toward Israel because, while they recognize its ability to support them in their quest to create a holy community, they also know that its secularity challenges their definition of such a holy community. The search for community is reinforced by rituals no less than by politics. A description of a Hasidic celebration

of the Jewish holiday of Purim explores how it confirms social boundaries and re-affirms communal identity.[37] Both politics and ritual unite to help the Hasidim respond to an outside world that seems inherently individualistic and atomistic, that lacks a sense of community. By using the various elements of the Jewish tradition in a unique way the Hasidim "preserve a value system in their own way . . . to define . . . clear boundaries between themselves and others."[38]

The three theological concepts of cosmic value, cleaving to God, and charismatic leadership provide interlocking factors that attract new members to Hasidism and retain established membership. At different stages in the development of Hasidism one or another of these factors appears most prominent. Each concept, however, has an analog in other American Jewish movements. The unique combination of all three suggests the special appeal of Hasidism as an alternative Jewish movement for American Jews.

Notes

1. See the survey of recent studies given by Joseph Dan, "Hasidism: The Third Century," (Hebrew) *World Union of Jewish Studies Newsletter* 29 (1989): 29–42, which discusses the evaluation of Hasidism and how it has changed from the beginnings of the movement to the present day.

2. See the discussion throughout Abraham Joshua Heschel, *A Passion For Truth* (New York: Farrar, Straus and Giroux, 1973). Heschel focuses on two early leaders—the Baal Shem Tov and Rabbi Menachem Mendel of Kotzk. He claims that both, in different ways, were iconoclastic figures.

3. See the various essays included in Gershon David Hundert, ed., *Essential Papers on Hasidism: Origins to Present*, Essential Papers on Jewish Studies, Robert M. Seltzer, general editor (New York: New York University Press, 1991) and Raphael Mahler, *Hasidism and the Jewish Enlightenment* (Philadelphia: Jewish Publication Society of America, 1985).

4. See Amnon Levi, "Anglo-Saxon *Haredim:* Can They Serve as a Bridge between *Haredim* and Non-Religious?" in *Religious and Secular: Conflict and Accommodation between Jews in Israel,* ed. Charles S. Liebman (Jerusalem: Avi Chai, 1990), 12–13.

5. Jenna Weissman Joselit, *New York's Jewish Jews: The Orthodox Community in the Interwar Years* (Bloomington: Indiana University Press, 1990), 147.

6. Solomon Poll, *The Hasidic Community of Williamsburg* (New York: The Free Press of Glencoe, 1962).

7. Ibid., 249–51.

8. Dan, "Hasidism: The Third Century," 31.

9. For background on this theology see essays in the following works: Louis Jacobs, *Hasidic Prayer,* Littman Library of Jewish Civilization (New York: Schocken, 1973); Bezalel Safran, ed., *Hasidism: Continuity or Innovation* (Cambridge: Harvard University Press [for] Harvard University Center for Jewish Studies,

1988); Gershom G. Scholem, *The Messianic Idea in Judaism* (New York: Schocken, 1971); Joseph Weiss, *Eastern European Jewish Mysticism,* Littman Library of Jewish Civilization, David Goldstein, ed. (Oxford: Oxford University Press, 1985).

10. See Jeffrey S. Gurock, "The Orthodox Synagogue," in *The American Synagogue: A Sanctuary Transformed,* ed. Jack Wertheimer (New York: Cambridge University Press, 1987), 37–84.

11. See the study of this movement by Arthur A. Goren, *New York Jews and the Quest for Community: The Kehillah Experiment 1908–1922* (New York: Columbia University Press, 1970).

12. See Oscar Handlin, "Judaism," in *The Shaping of American Religion,* ed. James Ward Smith and A. Leland Johnson, Religion in American Life, vol. 1, Princeton Studies in American Civilization, no. 5 (Princeton, N.J.: Princeton University Press, 1961), 122–61, and Will Herberg, *Protestant-Catholic-Jew: An Essay in American Religious Sociology* (Garden City, N.Y.: Doubleday and Company, 1955).

13. Herberg, *Protestant-Catholic-Jew,* 198.

14. Lis Harris, *Holy Days: The World of a Hasidic Family* (New York: Summit, 1985), 167.

15. Solomon Poll, "The Impact of Hasidism on American Judaism," in *The Dimensions of Orthodox Judaism,* ed. and with an introduction by Reuven P. Bulka (New York: Ktav, 1983), 209.

16. See Abraham D. Lavender, ed. and comp., *A Coat of Many Colors: Jewish Subcommunities in the United States,* Contributions in Family Studies, no. 1 (Westport, Conn.: Greenwood Press, 1977), sect. 4, "Hasidism," 175–207.

17. William Shaffir, *Life in a Religious Community: The Lubavitcher Chassidim in Montreal,* Cultures and Communities: A Series of Monographs, Community Studies, Gordon B. Inglis, general editor (Toronto: Holt, Rinehart and Winston of Canada, 1974).

18. Ibid., 190.

19. Ibid., 192.

20. See Stephen Sharot, *Messianism, Mysticism, and Magic: A Sociological Analysis of Jewish Religious Movements,* Studies in Religion, Charles H. Long, ed. (Chapel Hill: University of North Carolina Press, 1982), 189–205.

21. Ibid., 191.

22. See Lubavitch Foundation of Great Britain, *Challenge: An Encounter with Lubavitch-Chabad* (London: Vallentine Mitchell, 1970).

23. See M. Herbert Danzger, *Returning to the Tradition: The Contemporary Revival of Orthodox Judaism* (New Haven: Yale University Press, 1989).

24. Debra Renee Kaufman, *Newly Orthodox Jewish Women* (New Brunswick: Rutgers University Press, 1991), 22.

25. See Christie Balka and Andy Rose, eds., *Twice Blessed: On Being Lesbian, Gay, and Jewish* (Boston: Beacon, 1989).

26. See Harris, *Holy Days,* 233–37.

27. See the discussion in Reena Sigman Friedman, "The Jewish Feminist Movement," in *Jewish American Voluntary Organizations,* ed. Michael N. Dobkowski (Westport, Conn.: Greenwood Press, 1986), 575–601.

28. See Judith Plaskow, *Standing Again at Sinai: Juadism from a Feminist Perspective* (San Francisco: Harper and Row, 1990).

29. Ibid., 249.

30. Herbert Weiner, *Nine and a Half Mystics: The Kabbala Today* (New York: Collier Books, 1971), 213.

31. On Rabbi Nahman see Arthur Green, *Tormented Master* (University, Ala.: University of Alabama Press, 1979).

32. Samuel C. Heilman, *The People of the Book: Drama, Fellowship, and Religion* (Chicago: University of Chicago Press, 1983), 222–24.

33. See Bernard Reisman, *The Chavurah: A Contemporary Jewish Experience* (New York: UAHC, 1977) and his *The Jewish Experiential Book: The Quest for Jewish Identity* (New York: Ktav Publishing House, 1979).

34. Kaufman, *Newly Orthodox Jewish Women,* 5.

35. Jerome R. Mintz, "Ethnic Activism: The Hasidic Example," *Judaism* 28 (1979): 453. The entire essay is reprinted in Bulka, *Dimensions of Orthodox Judaism,* 225–41.

36. See Allan L. Nadler, "Piety and Politics: The Case of the Satmar Rebbe," *Judaism* 31 (1982): 135–52. Nadler is not an unbiased observer. He feels that both the anti-Zionist Satmar and the "fair-weather friends of Zionism" like the Lubavitcher are neither valuable to nor friends of the Jewish state.

37. See Shifra Epstein, "Drama on a Table: The Bobover Hasidim *Piremshpiyl,*" in *Judaism From Within and From Without: Anthropological Studies,* ed. Harvey E. Goldberg (Albany: State University of New York Press, 1987), 195–217.

38. Ibid., 215.

Suggestions for Further Reading

Dan, Joseph, With the assistance of Robert J. Milch. *The Teachings of Hasidism*. New York: Behrman House, 1983.

Green, Arthur, and Barry W. Holtz, eds. *Your Word Is Fire: The Hasidic Masters on Contemplative Prayer*. New York: Schocken, 1987.

Hundert, Gershon David, ed. *Essential Papers on Hasidism: Origins to Present*. Essential Papers on Jewish Studies. New York: New York University Press, 1991.

Mintz, Jerome R. *Hasidic People: A Place in the New World*. Cambridge, Mass.: Harvard University Press, 1992.

Zalman, Shneur, of Lyady. *Likute Amarim*, 2 volumes. Translated by Nissan Mindel. 3rd revised ed. Brooklyn, N.Y.: "Kehot," 1969.

11

GOD AND RACE: BRITISH-ISRAELISM AND CHRISTIAN IDENTITY

William L. Ingram

British-Israelism is a theology which teaches that the Anglo-Saxon peoples and their present-day descendants are the literal offspring of the "lost tribes" of ancient Israel. While British-Israelism had its beginnings in early-nineteenth-century England, it has found its most fertile soil in twentieth-century America, where it is sometimes called Anglo-Israelism. The high value placed on a direct bloodline with "God's chosen people" underscores a racial elitism that, in its more sedate form, projects a relatively benign paternalism at non–Anglo-Saxons. In its more activist form, called Christian Identity, this racial elitism fosters suspicion, hatred, and violence toward nonwhites, and especially Jews.

The modern origins of British-Israelism can be traced to John Wilson's *Lectures on Our Israelitish Origin,* published in England in 1840. There may have been a political as well as a religious motivation to Wilson's claim that the British people, and particularly the monarch, had an "Israelitish Origin." F. Wallace Connon, a British-Israel author, writing nearly one hundred years after Wilson, places special emphasis on the hereditary authority of the English monarchy. Connon attempts to show that the coronation of ancient Hebrew kings was performed with the new king sitting on a sacred stone, and that English kings and queens (including Queen Elizabeth II) were crowned sitting over a special stone, called

the "Stone of Scone."[1] He attempts to trace the journey of this sacred coronation stone of King David, along with its biblical authority, from Jerusalem to England.

According to Connon and other British-Israel writers, the Jewish prophet Jeremiah removed this sacred stone to Ireland soon after 588 B.C.E., when Zedekiah, the last king of Judah, was taken prisoner to Babylon. From Ireland the stone was moved to Scotland by Fergus II a few years before his death in 502 C.E., and from Scotland the stone was removed by Edward I to England, in 1296 C.E. The English monarchy is, then, directly linked to the ancient Hebrew monarchy and the sacred coronation stone of King David is the very same one utilized by contemporary English rulers.[2] Certainly, British-Israelism argues, an English monarch who sits on an ancient Hebrew throne must rule over British people who are themselves descended from ancient Israelites.

This historical revisionism was never adopted by the Church of England, but neither was it fiercely attacked, perhaps because a belief in an "Israelitish Origin" contributed to, rather than detracted from, nineteenth-century British imperialism.[3]

Within thirty years of Wilson's 1840 work, British-Israel thought had established itself in America.[4] But the groundwork for a belief that America was connected to ancient Israel, through its British roots, had been laid long before the nineteenth century. A religious typology which depicted America as a land where "God had founded a new Israel" was being preached almost from the moment the *Mayflower* landed at Plymouth in 1620.[5] Later Puritan colonies in Connecticut, Massachusetts Bay, and New Haven came to see "themselves as the Israelites in God's master plan."[6] These early Puritan (and later republican) connections between America and Israel, while fervently believed, were spiritual and symbolic in nature. In America, there was no attempt to cast the ancient Israelites as the direct flesh-and-blood ancestors of Americans until the late nineteenth century.

British-Israel teachings were adopted by Charles A. L. Totten, a U.S. Army lieutenant, in 1883. The four-year proselytizing mission to America of Edward Hine, an English preacher of British-Israelism, begun in 1884, brought Hine and Totten together and began a surge of British-Israelism in America. Both Hine and Totten were prolific authors of tracts which were to serve as a basis for later American Anglo-Israel teachings.[7]

By 1900, Charles Fox Parham, a Kansas evangelical who later founded Pentecostalism, and J. H. Allen, who would assist in founding the Church of God (Holiness), were believers and teachers of British-Israel doctrine.[8] Allen's *Judah's Sceptre and Joseph's Birthright* (1902) "became the single most important instrument in spreading Anglo-Israel thought into Adventist and independent Bible student circles."[9] It is out of the Adventist movement, specifically the Church of God (Seventh-Day), headquartered in Stanberry, Missouri, that emerged that most prolific and successful proponent of Anglo-Israel thought, Herbert W. Armstrong (1892–1986).

Armstrong writes in his autobiography that by 1927 he had researched and "PROVED that the so-called 'Lost Ten Tribes' of Israel had migrated to western Europe, the British Isles, and later the United States . . . "[10] He also claims to have been the first to have discovered this "new truth" and, upon delivering a three-hundred-page manuscript on the topic to a church leader at Stanberry, claims he

was told that "God surely had a special reason for revealing this new truth to me."[11] In 1931, Herbert W. Armstrong was ordained as a minister into a separately incorporated splinter sect of the Stanberry Church of God (Seventh-Day), which called itself the Oregon Conference of the Church of God, in Salem, Oregon. In 1933, he split from the Oregon Conference of the Church of God and founded the Radio Church of God, which changed its name in 1968 to the Worldwide Church of God.

While Herbert W. Armstrong denied ever attending an Adventist church, many of his teachings are in agreement with Adventist doctrine—e.g., the Bible as the inspired and infallible Word of God (especially the biblical account of creation), denial of the Trinity, salvation through faith, baptism by full immersion, and the imminent return of Jesus to the earth to set up a utopian millennium. His teachings, which are not usually associated with Adventism, include observance of the annual cycle of holy days from Leviticus, to which Armstrong adds his interpretation of New Testament meanings. The Worldwide Church of God, like the Church of God (Seventh-Day), is also sabbatarian, holding that the Sabbath begins at sundown on Friday and ends at sundown on Saturday. New Year's Day, Valentine's Day, Easter, Halloween, Christmas, and personal birthdays are denounced as pagan in origin and are not observed.[12] Dietary prohibitions concerning the consumption of pork and shellfish were strongly enforced before Herbert W. Armstrong's death.

Herbert W. Armstrong believed that the history of the true church of God could be traced back to Jesus and that God's "chosen people" could be genetically traced back to Adam. He agreed with dispensational teachings that the seven churches described in the book of Revelation were indicative of seven eras of the true church.[13] Armstrong taught that the Church of God (Seventh-Day) was the dispensation to the "Sardis" church, and his own Worldwide Church of God was the historical dispensation to the "Philadelphia" era of the true church. It is his strong emphasis on his version of historical events which is the driving element of his British-Israel teachings.

British-Israel theology is based on biblical fundamentalism, with particular emphasis on the story of Abraham as patriarch of God's chosen people.[14] In Genesis 12:2, God is reported to have promised Abraham that he would be the founding father of "a great nation" and in Genesis 17:4 Abraham was again proclaimed by God to be the founding "father of many nations." Historically, Abraham has been accepted as the founding father of the Jewish people by people of the Jewish faith, through his son, Isaac, and Isaac's son, Jacob. Abraham has also been accepted as the founding father of the Arab people by people of the Islamic faith, through his son, Ishmael. British-Israelism argues that Abraham is also the ancestor of all the people of northern and western Europe[15] through his male descendants Isaac, Jacob, and Jacob's twelve sons.

One of Jacob's sons, Joseph, had two sons of his own, Ephraim and Manasseh. Nearing the end of his life, Jacob, whose name had been changed by God to Israel, adopted Joseph's sons and passed his own name of Israel, along with the "birthright" of Abraham, onto Ephraim and Manasseh.[16] This event of Jacob/Israel's adopting of his grandsons is important because Judah, the patriarch of the Jewish people and another son of Jacob/Israel, did not inherit the name of Israel. That name was given only to Ephraim and Manasseh. Therefore, according to British-Israel theology, the true inheritors of the birthright and name of Israel can be found today as the "white, English-speaking peoples," the descendants of Ephraim and Manasseh: Great Britain and the United States.[17]

Various proofs of the "true" ancestry of white, English-speaking peoples include some tortured etymology. British-Israelism teaches that the "house of Israel is the covenant people."[18] The word for "covenant" in Hebrew is *"beriyth"* "berith," and the word for "man" in Hebrew is *"iysh"* or *"ish."*[19] Because "in the original Hebrew language vowels were never given in the spelling," the *e* is dropped from *berith,* and when the *h* is dropped because "Hebrews ... never pro-

nounced their 'h's,' " the combined phrase, "covenant man," becomes "British."[20] Further creative etymology involves the word "Saxon." Herbert W. Armstrong taught that the Anglo-Saxon peoples, who settled in England, are a genetically different breed than the Old Saxons of Germany. "Drop the 'I' from 'Isaac,' " writes Armstrong, because, "(vowels are not used in Hebrew spelling), and we have the modern name 'SAAC'S SONS,' or, as we spell it in shorter manner, 'SAXONS!' "[21]

Another "proof" offered as a trace of at least one of the "lost tribes" of Israel is that they left their name everywhere they went. As the tribe of Dan moved around Europe, before it eventually settled in Ireland, it named places after itself, e.g., Danube, Denmark, or any other place that has *D*-(vowel)-*N* in its name. Herbert Armstrong shows himself to be a convinced diffusionist when he writes, "and in Ireland we find ... Dans-Laugh, Dan-Sower, Dun-dalk, Dun-drum, Don-egal Bay, Donegal City, Dun-gloe, Din-gle, Dunsmor (meaning 'more Dans'). Moreover, the name Dunn in the Irish language means the same as Dan in the Hebrew: judge."[22]

The racial chauvinism intrinsic to British-Israelism is not always covert. During the civil unrest in the United States following the assassination of Dr. Martin Luther King, an evangelist of the Worldwide Church of God explained that "the man or men behind the rioting are the Jews and/or the Negroes exploiting their own people."[23] While Jews and other ethnic minorities were not openly despised within the Worldwide Church of God during Herbert W. Armstrong's lifetime, they were perceived as being outside the normal bounds of human interaction. Armstrong taught that racial strife would increase in "the last days" and that, after World War III had begun, a race war would commence with the white, English-speaking peoples fighting against "the yellow and brown hordes of Asia, with a sprinkling of black people."[24] After the second coming of Jesus puts "a stop to that attempt of Satan to crush Israel ... the White, English-speaking world, with other tribes of Israel will really begin to shoulder the 'White Man's Burden' and bless the world with peace . . ."[25]

The Worldwide Church of God was, during Herbert W. Armstrong's lifetime, the only group of British-Israelists to successfully grow into a sect with a significant following. During its height, in the 1960s and early 1970s, the membership was upward of 120,000 people around the world. The upheaval of the middle and late 1970s greatly reduced that number, with many small splinter groups breaking away and forming their own churches. Garner Ted Armstrong's Church of God, International, formed in 1979, is the largest of these and growing. Although the Worldwide Church of God has altered many of Herbert W. Armstrong's teachings following his death, many of the splinter groups are continuing his British-Israel teachings.[26] But out of the turbulent 1970s grew another version of British-Israelism, Christian Identity, and its brand of racial chauvinism is by no means covert.

Christian Identity is currently the dominant religious affiliation of the extreme right-wing political movement in America, and it has been growing since the early 1970s. Conservation of the status quo, in the face of social changes perceived to be confusing and frightening, has been the province of the right wing since the French Revolution. Christian Identity perceives the threat to the status quo as being racial in nature and orchestrated by a conspiracy of international Jews.

The rise of the Ku Klux Klan from 1915 to 1930, with its peak of five million members in 1925, focused primarily on anti-Catholic rhetoric. The Christian God was strictly a Protestant one. Klan perceptions of threats to the status quo also targeted blacks and Jews, but anti-Catholic rhetoric was foremost until after World War II.[27] Prior to World War II, William J. Cameron published "The International Jew" and the ersatz *Protocols of the Elders of Zion* in Henry Ford's Dearborn *Independent*.[28] These early attempts at blaming political problems on conspiracies among international Jews were later to be transformed into beliefs that all Jews are the literal descendants of Satan, and Jews should be harassed at every op-

portunity until the return of Jesus Christ, when they must all be destroyed.

Gerald L. K. Smith (a Huey Long crony, publisher of *The Cross and the Flag,* and founder of the Christian Nationalist Crusade), Wesley Swift (a Klan organizer and defrocked Methodist minister), William Potter Gale, and Bertrand Comparet came together in southern California in the 1950s to give a new face to Jewish conspiracy theories.[29] The great war for Anglo-Saxon hegemony would not be between whites and blacks, but between Protestant Christians and Jews, with Jews controlling the Papacy. The problems Anglo-Saxons faced in the decade of the 1950s because of racial desegregation were caused by an international conspiracy of communist Jews.[30]

Richard Butler, a former parishioner of William Potter Gale, inherited Wesley Swift's church in 1970 and moved it to Hayden Lake, Idaho.[31] There Butler's Church of Jesus Christ Christian has "served as the headquarters for a white supremacist plot to overthrow the United States through bombings, robberies, assassination, and sabotage."[32] William Potter Gale went on to form the Posse Comitatus, and was convicted in 1987 of "conspiring to mail death threats to Internal Revenue Service officials and a federal judge."[33]

Organizations such as the Aryan Nations, the Ku Klux Klan, the White Aryan Resistance, the Order, the Confederate Hammerskins, and the American Nazi Party have all incorporated Christian Identity into their belief structures. Attempts to form an overarching organization have been and are currently being formulated so that energy, money, and time can be more profitably utilized.[34]

Christian Identity has taken a dramatic tack away from other manifestations of British-Israelism. Herbert W. Armstrong operated a highly centralized organization, with himself in absolute control. He taught that the laws of the land must be respected, up to the point of their interfering with his interpretation of the laws of God. He taught that any participation in political activities would be futile at best and disruptive to God's purposes at worst. Physical violence of any kind, except corporal punishment of children and capital punishment of criminals, was strongly discouraged. The proper place for "God's elect" during the "Great Tribulation," which immediately precedes the Second Coming of Jesus, was in "a place of safety" far from the mayhem.[35]

Christian Identity rejects "the legitimacy of all central government."[36] They have no respect for the laws of the land, because they consider those laws to have been made by Jews for the advancement of Jews. And they seem to have no problem with physical violence. Adherents to Christian Identity have become highly involved in American politics in recent years, because they consider themselves to be in a war for racial survival. They also differ from British-Israelism in that they believe that their place during "the end time" is in the battlefield, killing Jews and fighting for their God. Identity's disgust with racial integration and loathing of Jews poses problems not only for non–Anglo-Saxons, but for Anglo-Saxons who would "betray" their race. As

one Identity author writes, "Voluntary fraternization with mud-races *is* race-mixing. Race-mixing *is* race treason. Race treason is a *capital* offense to your nation. So if you ain't stopped doing it, you'd better."[37]

Racial chauvinism is central to both British-Israel and Identity teachings, but the method of expression, certainly toward Jews, is vastly different. For British-Israelist premillennial dispensationalism, Jews are important principal protagonists in the drama of the apocalypse. For Identity eschatology, Jews are the true antagonists.

The predilection toward violent teachings among Christian Identity believers, and the nature of self-fulfilling prophecies in general, demands careful study of Christian Identity beliefs and activities. As mainstream American power structures move toward repudiating any form of racial and ethnic chauvinism, British-Israel and Identity teachings will certainly evolve as well.[38] The directions this evolution will take can keep researchers of British-Israel and Christian Identity busy for years to come.

Notes

1. Michael Barkun, "From British-Israelism to Christian Identity: The Evolution of White Supremacist Religious Doctrine," *Syzygy: Journal of Alternative Religion and Culture* 1, no. 1 (1992): 56. Some elements of British-Israel thought existed long before 1840. Richard Brothers (1757–1824) claimed to be a descendant of King David and, according to his genealogical calculations, the rightful heir to the throne of England. Brothers was committed to an asylum for the insane and his ideas were not given serious consideration in his lifetime. See J. Gordon Melton, *Encyclopedic Handbook of Cults in America* (New York: Garland, 1986), 53.

The myth of the Stone of Scone's being Jacob's "pillow" for his dream in Genesis 28 was introduced into England soon after 1600. A plaque inscribed "Jacob's Pillar" is currently resting over the Stone of Scone in Westminster Abbey. F. Wallace Connon, *The Stone of Destiny: Or the Stone that Binds a Commonwealth* (London: The Covenant Publishing Co. Ltd., 1951), 13.

2. Connon, *Stone of Destiny,* 39–46. British-Israel authors often quote 2 Samuel 7:13, 2 Chronicles 13:4–5, and Psalms 89:3–4, as biblical "proofs" of the continuing physical presence of the throne of David on earth. See Herbert W. Armstrong, *The United States and Britain in Prophecy* (Pasadena: The Worldwide Church of God, 1980), 52–53. Garner Ted Armstrong, Herbert W. Armstrong's estranged son, states that the coronation ceremony includes a statement which the Archbishop of Canterbury prays over the new monarch request that "thy people Israel may prosper." Garner Ted Armstrong, "Russia in Prophecy" (taped sermon, 7 September 1991).

3. Barkun alludes to this possibility in "British-Israelism to Christian Identity," 59.

4. Ibid., 56.

5. Nathan O. Hatch, *The Sacred Cause of Liberty: Republican Thought and the Millennium in Revolutionary New England* (New Haven: Yale University Press, 1977), 16. Hatch offers an intriguing view into how the idea of America as the "New Israel" changed in the latter half

of the eighteenth century from America as God's Israelitish "kingdom" on earth, to one which viewed Israel as "the ancient world's model republic." Hatch, 90–96.

6. Martin E. Marty, *Pilgrims in Their Own Land: 500 Years of Religion in America* (New York: Penguin, 1988), 58–59.

7. Barkun, "British-Israelism to Christian Identity," 58.

8. Ibid. Barkun notes the significance of geography in the development of British-Israelism's popularity in the United States. It was in the Pacific northwest that the beginnings of the theological cracks between British-Israelism and Christian Identity appeared, although developments in Massachusetts and Michigan were not far behind. Reuben H. Sawyer, a clergyman from Portland, Oregon, was influential in the growth of both Anglo-Israelism and the Oregon Ku Klux Klan in the 1920s. Sawyer was also influential in the formation and growth of Howard Rand's Anglo-Saxon Federation of America, which held a "national convention in Detroit in 1930." Ibid., 57.

9. Melton, *Encyclopedic Handbook*, 53.

10. Herbert W. Armstrong, *Autobiography of Herbert W. Armstrong, vol. 1* (Pasadena: Worldwide Church of God, 1986), 362. Emphasis in original. Armstrong's autobiography comes in two large volumes, totalling over 1300 pages. In it he claims, among other extraordinary things, to have pioneered the field of public opinion polls; become a millionaire twice and lost both fortunes; become an expert in the ancient Greek and Hebrew languages, as well as in the fields of biology, paleontology, and geology; and to have become learned in the works of Darwin, Haeckel, Spencer, Huxley, and Vogt, and subsequently to have disproved evolutionary theory.

11. Ibid., 363. Herbert W. Armstrong does not credit Allen or any of his British-Israel predecessors, although Garner Ted Armstrong does credit Allen's *Judah's Sceptre and Joseph's Birthright* as a source for his father's work. Garner Ted Armstrong also teaches that "eighty percent of the Anglican bishops were teaching that England was the direct descendant of Ephraim at the end of the seventeenth century." Garner Ted Armstrong, "Russia in Prophecy." Merritt Dickinson is credited by Melton as introducing Anglo-Israel thought into the Church of God (Seventh-Day). Melton, *Encyclopedic Handbook*, 53.

12. This was also the teaching of William S. Crowdy, a black visionary from Lawrence, Kansas, who founded the Church of God and Saints of Christ in 1896. Sometimes called Black Jews, this organization teaches sabbatarianism, and holds beliefs about Jesus which are consistent with Armstrong's views. See Frank S. Mead, *Handbook of Denominations in the United States*, rev. by Samuel S. Hill, 9th ed. (Nashville: Abingdon Press, 1990), 85.

13. Revelation 1:20–3:22. Dispensationalism is a form of premillennialism which began in the early 1800s with the Plymouth Brethren in England. Michael Barkun's concise definition of dispensationalism is that it "makes the history of the Jewish people central to the fulfillment of Christian eschatological hopes." "Racist Apocalypse: Millennialism on the Far Right," *American Studies* 31, no. 2 (Fall 1990): 125.

14. In British-Israel doctrine, the different human races originated with Noah's sons. According to Herbert W. Armstrong, all black people derive from Noah's youngest son, Ham, who was cursed by Noah because he "saw his [drunken] father's nakedness" (Genesis 9:21–25). Ham was seen as a direct descendant of Cain and Cain's curse was continued on him. Herbert Armstrong taught that all people descended from Noah's middle son, Japheth, became the Asiatic race. Noah's eldest son, Shem, was the purported ancestor of all "white" people. Garner Ted Armstrong differs only a little from his father on this point and teaches that the races were formed prior to Noah and that Noah's sons married racially diverse women. Note that it is from the name Shem that we get the word Semite.

The manner of "birthright" succession is male primogeniture, where the eldest living son inherits his father's possessions. Note that it is from the ancient Biblical patriarchs that we have fashioned the word patriarchy.

15. For Herbert and Garner Ted Armstrong, this excludes Germany. They believe that modern Germans are the descendants of the Assyrians who first took the Israelite nation into captivity, and are thus the "natural" enemies of true Israelites. H. Armstrong, *The United States and Britain in Prophecy*, 144.

16. Ibid., 42–43. Herbert Armstrong argues that Jacob/Israel had to adopt Joseph's sons because they had an Egyptian mother and,

because his eldest son, Reuben, "had defiled his father's bed," Jacob/Israel didn't want the birthright of Abraham to pass through Reuben. Armstrong traces the current descendants of Reuben to the French people, because they "have the very characteristics of their ancestor, Reuben." Ibid., 144.

17. Ibid., 95. The current descendants of the other sons of Jacob/Israel are described by Worldwide Church of God teachers as: Reuben-France; Simeon and Levi-scattered and unknown; Judah-scattered and in Israel; Zebulun-Netherlands; Issachar-Finland; Dan-Denmark and Ireland; Gad-Switzerland; Asher-Belgium and Luxembourg; Naphtali-Sweden; and Benjamin-Norway. Roderick C. Merideth, sermon, September 1968.

18. H. Armstrong, *The United States and Britain in Prophecy*, 95.

19. Ibid., 95.

20. Ibid., 95. That the ancient Ephraimites had difficulty pronouncing their *h*'s is recorded in Judges 12:6. We get the word *shibboleth* from this biblical passage.

21. Ibid., 96. Emphasis in original. Note how vowels are dropped when it is convenient to do so, and kept when it is not. *The Oxford Dictionary of English Etymology* disputes British-Israelist origins of the terms "British" and "Saxon." Armstrong makes no attempt to explain the "Anglo-" prefix of Anglo-Saxon, but perhaps he believed that his explanation of "Saxon" was sufficient. "To Abraham, God said, 'In ISAAC shall thy seed be called,' " and this name is repeated in Romans 9:7 and Hebrews 11:18. In Amos 7:16 the Israelites are called 'the house of Isaac,' " 96.

22. Ibid., 97. It is just because the "Danites" are prone to be so judgmental that they are left off the list of the protected 144,000 "elect" who are spared the tribulation at the end of the current age. Roderick Merideth, sermon, September 1968. See Revelation 7: 1–8.

23. Dean C. Blackwell, sermon, 17 April 1968.

24. Herman L. Hoeh, *The TRUTH about the RACE QUESTION (sic)* (Pasadena, Calif.: Radio Church of God, 1957), 11. Hoeh is the current executive editor of *The Plain Truth*, the chief organ of the Worldwide Church of God, and author of the intricate and convoluted historical revision, *Compendium of World History* (Pasadena, Calif.: Ambassador College, 1962).

25. Ibid., 11.

26. The cover story of *The Plain Truth* 58, no. 2 (February 1993), was titled, "Christian Must Challenge Racism." Within the article is a reprint of excerpts from Dr. King's "Letter From Birmingham Jail." This would have been a most unlikely publishing event during Herbert Armstrong's lifetime.

27. See Kenneth T. Jackson, *The Ku Klux Klan in the City: 1915–1930* (New York: Oxford University Press, 1967).

28. Barkun, "From British-Israelism to Christian Identity," 57.

29. Ibid., 59. Smith writes excoriating missives against "the counterfeit state of Israel" in his *The Cross and the Flag*. An example can be found in volume 1, no. 11 (February 1973): 16.

30. Kenneth Goff, *Reds Promote Racial War* (Englewood, Colo.: Soldiers of the Cross, 1958). Every communist identified by Goff is Jewish. The ascent to the papacy of Pope John Paul II, whose mother was Jewish and who came from communist Poland, has added fuel to the fire of Identity eschatology.

31. Swift taught that all nonwhites were brought to earth by "evil forces from the far reaches of the galaxy," and that all Jews are the progeny of Satan's cohabitation with Eve. Barkun, "Racist Apocalypse," 129. British-Israel teachers, especially Garner Ted Armstrong, strongly disagree with Identity cosmology of racial origin. See Vance A. Stinson "The 'Seed of Satan': Does the Devil Have Offspring on this Earth?" (Tyler, Tex.: The Church of God, International, 1990).

32. The Southern Poverty Law Center, "The Ku Klux Klan: A History of Racism and Violence," 4th ed. (Montgomery, Ala.: Klanwatch, 1991), 46.

33. Ibid., 46.

34. David Duke's National Association for the Advancement of White People is one example. Another is the White Separatist Banner, under which Identity believers have gathered in Oklahoma, Arkansas, and Texas.

35. For Herbert W. Armstrong's Worldwide Church of God, the "place of safety" was Petra, an ancient rock city in what is now Jordan. Although Petra is the site of the legendary "Well of Moses," there isn't much water there.

36. Barkun, "Racist Apocalypse," 125.

37. "Editorial Thunder," *The Oklahoma Separatist* (May/June 1988). Emphasis in original. The author is anonymous.

38. Most Identity groups reacted to the decreasing acceptance of racial chauvinism in American society over the past twenty years by secreting themselves in "survivalist" hideaways. Identity believers have become more vocal in recent years, and have dug in their ideological heels against social change. Please note that violence is advocated by Identity teachers as a response to their expectations of future events, and rarely as a way of behaving in current society.

Throughout most of its history, the Worldwide Church of God only allowed new converts to attend services after a lengthy screening process. No one was allowed to walk into services off the street and guards were placed at the door to prevent such an occurrence. This policy was changed in 1992, probably because of changes in expectations of the social climate of mainstream America.

Suggestions for Further Reading

Armstrong, Herbert W. *The United States and Britain in Prophecy*. Pasadena: The Worldwide Church of God, 1980. A concise description of British-Israelism which is easily obtained.

Barkun, Michael. "Racist Apocalypse: Millennialism on the Far Right," *American Studies* 31, no. 2 (fall 1990).

————. *Religion and the Racist Right: The Origins of the Christian Identity Movement*. Chapel Hill: University of North Carolina Press, 1994.

12

THE CHILDREN OF GOD

David E. Van Zandt

The Children of God (now known as the Family or the Family of Love) is probably the most radical of all the major groups to emerge from the Jesus People movement of the late 1960s. David Berg (called Moses David or Father David by members) is the charismatic leader, who claims to be God's prophet of the end time and has controlled the group's ideology and organization for most of its history. Despite numerous organizational changes and geographic movements, the Children of God (COG) has consistently adhered to a basic ideological core that requires members to spread God's word (or at least the COG's version of it) throughout the world in what the COG believes are the last days. In accomplishing this goal, the COG has experimented with a number of proselytization techniques and living arrangements, many of which are highly controversial and have attracted substantial negative publicity. Its early members were some of the first targets of deprogramming efforts.

History of the COG

The COG began as the Teens for Christ in Huntington Beach, California, in 1967. Berg and his children brought twenty to thirty wayward "hippies" into their home and preached a message of personal salvation and millennial beliefs. Berg, who in his childhood had travelled the South

with his evangelical mother and who had a short-lived tenure as a minister in the Christian and Missionary Alliance, tailored his message to the radical milieu of that day. This small commune quickly grew as the Berg family and its followers embarked on a series of public demonstrations and "church visitations" that criticized established Christianity and attracted wide attention, some of it negative.

In 1969, Berg led his group on nomadic wanderings through the United States and Canada, gathering new members along the way. The group continued the public demonstrations, this time at "sackcloth vigils," in which members donned sackcloths, carried staffs, and declared that American society was doomed for turning its back on God. It was during this period that Berg introduced to a small group of select members his unorthodox ideas on sex and marriage. He announced to them that his relationship with his wife Eve was standing in the way of God's work, and that he had started a new sexual relationship with a young member named Maria. It was not until the mid-1970s, however, that most members of the group became aware of these activities.

By early 1970, the group had grown to 200 members, and Berg arranged for them to live on an abandoned ranch near Thurber, Texas, owned by his former mentor. A small number of members also moved into an old mission building on Skid Row in Los Angeles. At both places, the COG established large communal living centers that they used as bases for recruiting new members. In August of that year, Berg and Maria left the Texas commune to travel to Israel. That trip began a pattern that persists to this day. Berg and Maria lived and travelled alone or with a small group of household helpers and communicated with the rest of the group via eight-to-ten-page letters known as "Mo letters."

In September 1971, Berg, through Mo letters, directed members to break up the large communes in Texas and Los Angeles and establish smaller communes or "colonies" in cities and towns throughout the United States. In addition, he urged members to form small teams to "pioneer" into Western Europe and South America. By January 1973, Berg claimed that there were over 2,400 "disciples" (full-time members) in 140 colonies in 40 countries. In this different environment, the COG adopted a new proselytization method called "litnessing": members distributed Mo letters in train stations, shopping malls, and other public areas in exchange for donations. Berg, who initiated the innovation, wrote a flood of letters for distribution on topics such as God's love, political affairs, movies, and the end time. Not only did litnessing get the COG message to a much wider audience, but it also proved to be a consistent means of financial support for the individual colonies.

Another side effect of litnessing was a reduction in the flow of new members. Berg sought to counter this by reemphasizing one-on-one witnessing, and in May 1976, he announced another proselytization innovation: Flirty Fishing. For a number of years, Berg and Maria had been experimenting secretly with the practice of sending COG women into bars and nightclubs to meet potential converts. In some cases, the members would take the targets (called "fish") to bed if necessary to obtain a conversion. In the late 1970s, a series of Mo letters described Berg's and Maria's Flirty Fishing adventures and urged members to adopt the technique. By the late 1970s, the press got wind of the practice and made the most of it. In addition, the practice caused a significant number of COG members to leave the group.

To quell rebellion in the ranks and to assert more direct control over the group, Berg ordered a radical reorganization of the COG (now called the Family by members) in late 1977. He removed most of the old leaders of the group from their positions and set individual colonies (now called "Homes") free to do as they pleased subject to the commands of Berg delivered through Mo letters. Berg also directed that the sexual liberality that Berg, Maria, and the highest leaders had enjoyed for some time should be extended to all members. Members were now free to engage in casual sexual relations with other members if the participants consented (called "sexual sharing"). Because the COG does not believe in birth control, the number of children born from informal liaisons or Flirty Fishing interactions (called Jesus Babies) increased. By April 1981, the COG claimed 2,188 Homes in 76 countries with a total of 8,715 members.

The effect of all these changes was a destruction of the communal organization of COG. A Home often consisted of two or three adults and their many children travelling nomadically in a camper. The Home would stop for a short period outside a town, engage in litnessing and some Flirty Fishing, and then move on. Some members returned to their native homes and took jobs until they could save enough money to head off to a new location. Berg, in May 1980, warned that the world was close to a nuclear war and urged members to move to the relative safety of South America and the Far East. All this movement eliminated the social support that the more centralized organization had provided previously. Moreover, most Homes were surviving hand-to-mouth; even Berg claimed financial straits. Another effect was due to the democratization of sexual practice. While sexual sharing formally required consent, there was social pressure in the Homes to engage in it. Moreover, some members interpreted statements by Berg to condone sexual sharing between adults and children that even included incidents of incest. While disgruntled ex-members of the group most likely exaggerate the frequency of these practices, it is clear that they caused substantial disruption for and discontent among the growing ranks of younger members in the group.

To reassert their control, Berg and Maria in 1985 reestablished a more centralized organization led by a central office called World Services. The new phase emphasized litnessing and the sale of other COG products such as posters and musical cassettes and videos, which improved the financial position of the Homes, and was accompanied by a more defined and authoritarian leadership structure. Berg and Maria appointed a number of Visiting Servants to monitor Homes. Homes became more communal, with the typical Home housing eight to ten adults and as many as twenty-five children. Berg and Maria also clamped down on excessive sexual practices. Maria, in particular, concerned about the treatment of younger members, set up Teen Training Camps (TTCs) to remove pre- and young teens from the sexual and other pressures of the Homes. Berg, according to the COG, expressly banned incest and child sex in late 1987. At the same time, he also prohibited Flirty Fishing, citing the dangers of AIDS.

Underlying these changes in organization was a more important if subtle change in the focus of the COG. Instead of growing by recruiting adults, the COG has now turned inward to grow by bearing and nurturing its children. By July 1988, the COG claimed to have 12,390 full-time members of which 6,833 were children, most of whom were born into the COG. For Berg and Maria, the COG teenagers are the future and the new leaders of the group. The second function of the TTCs is to prepare these teens for this new role and to secure their allegiance to the group. This can mean separating them from the influence of their parents. In fact, after completing a six-month session at a TTC, the teen is considered a full adult member of the group and is moved to a new Home to begin his or her adult proselytizing career.

These changes have brought renewed and negative press attention to the COG. In both Spain and Australia, local authorities have temporarily taken COG children into custody after allegations of child abuse. Moreover, a number of ex-COG members have attempted to obtain custody of children they left behind with the other parent in the group. They have done this either by invoking legal process or hiring persons to seize their children physically. Despite its longstanding strategy of keeping a low profile and avoiding direct confrontation, the COG has recently not been shy in invoking the legal process itself, to defend its children, citing principles of religious freedom. To date the COG has prevailed in all custody battles.

The COG Ideology

The COG ideology is rooted in the southern Protestant evangelical tradition in which Berg was raised. It is created and controlled by Berg and a small number of high leaders and is laid out in the Mo letters that now number over 2,500. Berg claims and members believe that the Mo letters are valid sources for determining God's will and at times even overrule the Bible and its rules. Berg identifies himself as God's Prophet of the End Time, a human vessel through whom God can speak. Berg admits, however, that while divinely inspired, the Mo letters are fallible and that some of his disconfirmed prophecies were based on his misunderstanding of what God had told him.

The written ideology consists of several strands, the most important of which is the traditional southern Protestant emphasis on personal salvation. In order to be saved from eternal damnation at the coming Judgment, a person has only to accept God's love offered through Jesus. This is a personal decision that, once made, guarantees a place in the Kingdom of God. Subsequent good works will determine the position that the saved person will have in that kingdom. The Mo letters also occasionally refer to the Pentecostal doctrine of the baptism in the Holy Spirit, but that aspect is muted.

A second strand is strident criticism of society and contemporary social relations—

referred to derogatorily by the COG as the System. Berg espouses a type of Christian socialism as an antidote to capitalism. In the COG view, America is the epitome of the degenerate capitalist system, with Western Europe not too far behind. Another target of his criticism is Israel and the Jews. In contrast, Berg sees more merit in third-world, particularly Arab, societies, and has visited and promoted Colonel Moammar Khadafi of Libya. Because of the System's corruptive power, the COG ideology urges members not to become too entangled with it.

This leads to the third strand, the demand for total commitment from group members. The only true and complete way to follow God is through total commitment to his work. In practice, this means that COG members are to forsake all: quit their jobs or schools in the System, surrender almost all possessions to the COG, cut almost all ties with nonmembers, live full-time in a COG commune, and engage in full-time proselytization. While the status of associate member or friend of the COG has been recognized at times, it has always been clear that total commitment is the norm.

The millennial beliefs of the COG are striking if rarely completely understood by members. Initially, Berg laid a fairly precise timetable for the end; when the dates he stated passed, however, he backed off specific predictions, but largely maintained the substance of his predictions. The Great Tribulation will begin with the world's being racked by wars and economic collapse. A great socialist leader will rise out of Egypt, and he will end the wars, take over the world, and establish a benevolent socialist dictatorship. After three and one-half years of this reign, he will show his true face as the Antichrist: he will demand to be worshipped, will exterminate those who refuse (particularly COG members), and will destroy all Bibles and Mo letters. Christ will return after another three and one-half years, lift up all living saved believers, defeat the Antichrist, and subdue Satan. There will be a general resurrection of deceased believers, and Christ will establish a physical millennium on earth and rule over it with the help of COG members.

After the thousand years, Satan will be released for one last rebellion. God will imprison Satan in a lake of fire, and conduct the Judgment in which all who did not accept Jesus during their lives will be sent to live with Satan. God will send New Jerusalem, a city one thousand miles high, long, and wide, to earth, and all those who did accept him will live in this perfection on earth. Children of God members and the saints will have proselytization missions on other worlds.

Finally, the COG ideology refers to an active spirit world, coextensive with the material world and populated by the spirits of deceased figures. These spirits have little impact on the material world. Instead, they usually provide inspiration and information to Berg. In some cases, however, Berg has attributed the disobedience of members to evil spirits and conducted exorcisms to attempt to change their behavior.

The written COG ideology is quite detailed and lengthy, and while all members claim to believe it, most members only vaguely understand the ideology and certainly do not grasp all of its details. This is most pronounced in the area of the end time. Most members simply believe that Jesus is coming soon, despite the numerous pages of Mo letters devoted to explaining the details of the group's eschatology. The one overriding aspect of the ideology that members do consistently understand is the call to full-time proselytization. Not to proselytize is seen by every member as an abdication of responsibility. The rest of the ideology is used pragmatically by members as the circumstances require.

Composition of Membership

Through the early 1970s, the COG recruits were generally middle to upper-middle class whites in their late teens or early twenties. Males greatly outnumbered females, and nonwhites were few and far between. Most recruits had attended a university, but not completed their degrees. A fair number had been involved in drugs and many considered themselves part of the counterculture. These people tended to have a liberal, nonactive religious background, whether Protestant, Catholic, or Jewish. A large minority were young people from fundamentalist Christian backgrounds who saw Berg and his group as authentic followers of Jesus.

Recruitment patterns shifted once the COG moved to Europe in the middle 1970s. The most likely European recruit was a lower-middle-class teen who was not headed to a university, but instead faced a clerical or similar career. As in America, some had more fundamentalist backgrounds, but most were liberal and nonactive religiously. Drug use among the European converts was lower. With the advent of Flirty Fishing in the late 1970s and into the 1980s, the COG actively recruited older, educated professionals. The number of new members from this group, however, was never great. By the late 1980s, aggressive recruitment of outsiders ceased, and the COG focused on growing internally.

Relationship to Society

Throughout its history, the COG's relationship to the rest of society has been highly oppositional. Given its beliefs about the System, the COG has always viewed the wider society at best with indifference and more often as a source of persecution. Some of this perception is well founded. From its earliest days, the COG has been the target of criticism from more traditional religions, unhappy parents, and sensation-seeking journalists. The original targets of modern religious deprogramming were COG members. On the other hand, the oppositional stance is one that the COG adopted from the very beginning with its use of public demonstrations such as the sackcloth vigil, its insistence on nonconventional living arrangements, and its later sexual practices. In the past, COG members also tended to ignore laws (such as compulsory education laws and bans on solicitation) that they find make their work more difficult. More recently, because of their growing population

of children, more sedentary life, and consequent vulnerability to authorities, members have been much more scrupulous about adhering to local laws and regulations.

Because of these factors, COG members' interactions with the wider society have been largely instrumental and circumscribed. Children of God members do spend large blocks of time interacting with nonmembers, but those interactions are for specific ideological or practical purposes. Most interactions are attempted proselytizations, whether through litnessing or one-on-one proselytization. Other interactions are motivated by the need to buy supplies or obtain other necessities of life. Even when COG members simply engage outsiders in conversation, it is usually to keep up with current trends and topics to make their proselytization efforts more efficacious.

At times, the COG are forced to confront the wider society more directly, particularly when the press or law enforcement officials intrude. Members have been arrested or challenged at various times on allegations of child abuse, truancy violations, immoral behavior, illegal demonstrations, and illegal solicitation. The basic COG strategy over the years has been to respond to such intrusions by denial and flight. The first example of this occurred in Huntington Beach. After some of the members were arrested for demonstrating on public school grounds, Berg packed up the whole group and moved out of state without facing trial. At one point, the COG did sue a group of disgruntled parents, but dropped the suit once the legal process of discovery began. Since then, whenever challenged by adverse publicity or law enforcement officials, the COG have quickly closed up and moved on. Only recently, in child custody battles with authorities, have the COG mounted any sustained legal efforts.

The result of all this is that the COG remain highly marginal in modern society. They do not expose themselves to the forces that might lead to a denominationalization process. In fact, Berg has expressly recognized this danger in Mo letters and warned against it. The cultivation of the group's children is also based on this recognition. If anything, the COG is becoming more insular.

Now that it does not have to look outside to replenish its membership, the need for contact with the wider society is even less.

The Future of COG

The engine of the COG has been David Berg, who is now well into his seventies. Upon his death, the group may lose its central focus. On the other hand, several factors point to its continued vitality. First, his consort, Maria, is a charismatic figure in her own right, and has day-to-day control of the group. It is conceivable that Maria will be able to continue Berg's charismatic leadership indefinitely.

The second factor is the COG's internal organization. Most of the adult members of the COG joined during the 1970s when they were in their late teens or early twenties, before finishing their educations or acquiring job skills. A great number are Americans who now live in foreign lands. For all their adult lives they have lived as COG members. The COG has provided them with sufficient material and emotional support. In doing so, it has also insulated them from acquiring the skills and social support they would need if they were to return to conventional society. Finally, most adult COG members have as many as five or more children. The thought of leaving the COG and supporting such large families in the System is both frightening and impractical.

Nor will the COG children be the weak link that causes the organization to begin to unravel. Part of the classic denominationalization process is the effect of the second generation. In the case of the COG, the second generation is often even more committed than their parents. The COG has carefully cultivated a high degree of commitment among the children. Because of their separation from wider society, COG children do not have more than a glimpse of the conventional life experienced by the parents in their pre-COG lives. The children's primary allegiance is to the group. Moreover, they quickly acquire adult status, often around the age of twelve. Many will have their first children by their mid to late teens. It is unlikely that many of these young members will leave the COG on their own.

While it is difficult to predict the future course of the COG, neither an immediate disintegration or a gradual shift to the status of an established sect is in the cards. Instead, the most likely outcome is that the COG will grow more and more insular and secretive. If Berg is not replaced and the group loses its central organizing force, individual communes will continue but will perhaps drift off in a variety of religious directions. If Berg is replaced, the COG could continue for an extended period as an isolated, cohesive, nonconventional alternative religion. In the latter case, the only limit to its growth will be its ability to retain and train its children as committed members.

Suggestions for Further Reading

Van Zandt, David E. *Living in the Children of God.* Princeton, N.J.: Princeton University Press, 1991.

Wallis, Roy. "Sex, Marriage and the Children of God." In *Salvation and Protest: Studies of Social and Religious Movements,* 74–90. London: Frances Pinter Ltd., 1979.

Wangerin, Ruth. "Women in the Children of God: 'Revolutionary Women' or 'Mountin' Maids?' " In *Women in Search of Utopia: Mavericks and Mythmakers,* edited by Ruby Rohrlich and Elaine Baruch, 130–39. New York: Schocken Books, 1984.

13

THE BOSTON CHURCH OF CHRIST

Russell Paden

In the past decade few religious groups have gained as much attention from the media and the anticult forces as the Boston Church of Christ. Controversial recruiting practices, high commitment expectations of members, use of discipleship partners, and teachings on church authority have brought a barrage of criticism from outsiders and ex-members alike.

Boston Church of Christ is the name given to a religious movement that began with a single congregation in Boston, Massachusetts. This movement has been known by a variety of names (the Crossroads movement,[1] Multiplying Ministries, the Discipling movement, and the International Churches of Christ, among others), but for the purposes of this study, the term "Boston movement" will be used for two reasons. One, for the sake of clarity, it is useful to distinguish between the founding church in Boston and the churches worldwide that affiliate themselves with the Boston Church of Christ. Two, the name is not chosen arbitrarily, for those in the Boston movement both think of and refer to themselves as a movement and, indeed, the term "Boston movement" appears in much of their literature.

Early History

Although the Boston Church of Christ officially came into existence in 1979, its roots

run much deeper. The Boston movement is born of the traditions of the nineteenth-century Restoration movement in America. Leaders of the Restoration movement such as Thomas Campbell, his son Alexander, and Barton Stone sought a return to first-century Christianity. Their two main objectives were to do away with denominational divisions and to return to the Bible as the sole authority for the faith and practice of the church.

The Restoration movement pledged itself to the axiom "Where the scriptures speak, we speak; and where the scriptures are silent, we are silent,"[2] but applying this interpretive rule was problematic. When some Restorationists began using musical instruments in the worship service and instituting missionary societies, a small conservative faction felt that neither had biblical precedence or authority. This faction, which became the traditional or mainline Churches of Christ, separated itself from the remainder of the Restoration movement. Major doctrinal differences developed among Restorationist leaders as early as the 1860s,[3] and the Churches of Christ officially went their own way in 1906, growing from 160,000 members[4] to 1.2 million in the United States by the 1990s.[5]

In 1967, the 14th Street Church of Christ in Gainesville, Florida (later renamed the Crossroads Church of Christ), borrowing and adapting some techniques learned from Campus Crusade,[6] began a "pilot project [at the University of Florida] for a campus ministry program with a strong evangelistic thrust."[7] Under the direction of the minister, Chuck Lucas, the campus ministry, called Campus Advance, grew rapidly. Campus Advance was not without critics. Two practices in particular, "soul talks" and "prayer partners," led to accusations of cultism. Soul talks, evangelistic Bible studies with prayer and sharing, were held in student residences.[8] Each soul talk had a leader who was given delegated authority over the members of his group.[9] "Prayer partners" was the term used for the practice of pairing up a new Christian with a more mature Christian so that the new Christian could be given one-on-one direction.[10] Both practices emphasized "in-depth involvement of each member in one another's lives,"[11] and critics thought the practices led to manipulation and abuse of members.

In 1972 a freshman at the University of Florida, the future leader of the Boston movement, Kip McKean, was converted through Campus Advance. The impact of the campus ministry of the Crossroads Church of Christ on him was significant:

> The innovations of "one another Christianity," evangelistic small group Bible studies, and the vision of dynamic campus ministries were put on my heart through the powerful preaching of Chuck Lucas and his associate, Sam Laing. The seeds of discipling were placed in my life as I saw personally how one man could affect another's daily lifestyle and eternal destiny for God.[12]

McKean trained at Crossroads while finishing his education at the University of Florida. He left Crossroads and served as campus minister at other mainline Churches of Christ until, in 1979, he was invited to take over as the pulpit and campus minister of a struggling, thirty-member church in a Boston suburb, the Lexington Church of Christ.

Growth

The Lexington Church of Christ was renamed the Boston Church of Christ and saw tremendous growth under McKean's tutelage. By 1981, the 30-member church had grown to a membership of 300. In 1981–82 Kip McKean felt the Lord had placed on his heart a "vision for the world." His vision was to establish "pillar churches" in key metropolitan centers of the world that could in turn evangelize the cities around them.[13]

In 1982 the Boston Church of Christ planted churches in Chicago and London and in 1983 in New York City. This heavy emphasis on evangelism and the trend of church plantings continued, until by 1993 the movement had grown to 42,855 members in 130 congregations worldwide, with 27,055 members and 48 congregations in the United States. The largest congregations, New York and Boston, both currently have a Sunday morning attendance over 5,000, while the Los Angeles congregation has attendance over 4,000.[14]

Much of the movement's vision has been fueled by the perceived lethargy of denominational churches, particularly the mainline Churches of Christ from which it originated. Church growth has become the litmus test of a true church. While members would probably concede that there are false religions that experience growth, they would contend that a true church of God *must* be experiencing growth.

Lack of growth among the mainline Churches of Christ provided much of the impetus for the Boston movement. Between 1945 and 1965 the mainline Churches of Christ was one of the fastest growing religious movements in America. By the 1970s, however, the Churches of Christ saw a decrease in conversions and a decline in growth until the net annual growth rate was less than 1 percent.[15] Kip McKean stated that he visited numerous mainline Churches of Christ between 1976 and 1979 and found their spiritual condition "ranged from lukewarm to disgusting."[16] It was this attitude, plus the decline in growth of the Churches of Christ, that spurred him on in his belief that Christ's church had to be revitalized and restored.

Beliefs and Practices

Many of the beliefs and practices of the Boston movement would fit easily within the evangelical tradition in America. A typical Sunday morning service consists of singing, praying, preaching, and the taking of the Lord's Supper. Members of the movement accept the inspiration of the Bible, the virgin birth, the substitutionary atonement, the bodily resurrection of Jesus, the Trinity, and the Second Coming.

However, the movement is very exclusivistic, believing that it alone has "rediscovered" numerous first-century Bible doctrines and that it is virtually impossible to be among the elect outside the ranks of the Boston movement. Movement leaders have a vision for converting the whole world by training individual members to be highly evangelistic and very submissive to the leadership of the church.

Part of their commitment to evangelism is seen in their financial practices. Very rarely will a congregation affiliated with the movement own a church building. A congregation will typically rent a facility to meet in on Sunday morning (the Boston Church of Christ meets in the Boston Garden); the money that would have gone toward a church mortgage is funneled into paid staff, the majority of whom are involved directly or indirectly in evangelistic efforts.

Discipleship

Key to understanding the Boston movement is the concept of discipleship. The movement sees a sharp distinction between "the world's" view of a Christian and a true disciple of Christ. Marty Wooten, missionary and leader in the Boston movement, has written,

> In the Boston movement, "disciple" was soon to gain momentum and come to represent those who are faithfully following Christ in contrast to someone in another congregation who had been immersed [baptized] for the forgiveness of sins but never repented and took on

the lifestyle and purpose of the early disciples, that is, making disciples of all nations.[17]

Boston movement missionary Andrew Giambarba echoed those sentiments:

> Every single member of every congregation must be committed to making disciples. If any are not, then they are not disciples themselves. And if they are not disciples themselves, then they will not be going to heaven.[18]

As these quotations show, the most important characteristic of a disciple, according to the Boston movement, is making other disciples. Part of the process of making disciples includes the use of discipleship partners. McKean felt that the practice of prayer partners that was employed at the Crossroads Church of Christ was not "directive enough," since Crossroads members chose their own partners. At Boston, McKean decided it was better for the leaders of the congregation to arrange for "older, stronger Christians to give direction to each of the younger, weaker ones."[19] Discipleship partners were always of the same sex and were to have daily contact and meet weekly.[20]

Discipleship partners are not considered optional:

> Similarly we expect every member to be discipled by a more spiritually mature Christian who is given the authority to teach him to obey everything that Jesus commanded.[21]

Kip McKean writes:

> We need to make it abundantly clear . . . that every brother in the congregation needs to have a discipleship partner. To not have a discipleship partner is to be rebellious to God and to the leadership of this congregation.[22]

The soul talks concept from Crossroads was also continued in Boston, renamed "Bible talks." Bible talks are held once a week at regular times and places, and attended consistently by an average of six to ten members.[23] Some Bible talks are for men or women only, while others are mixed.

Each Bible talk has a Bible talk leader and assistants who are given authority over the members of the group by the elders and evangelists of the congregation to see that the leadership's "expectations" are implemented by the members of the group.[24] The Bible talk is the main outreach instrument of the local congregations, and members are expected to bring visitors with them. In many ways, the Bible talk is the foundation of the movement, for if the Bible talks do not grow, the local churches do not grow.[25]

It should be noted that this concept of discipling is not new. Other religious movements have made use of this system of training and close personal supervision. Two parachurch organizations, Campus Crusade for Christ and the Navigators, use variants of this system. Similar "shepherding" movements arose within charismatic circles during the 1970s under the names Christian Growth Ministries and Maranatha Christian Churches.

Baptism

There is probably no biblical passage that is more important or more pivotal to the teachings of the Boston movement than Matthew 28:19–20:

> Therefore go and make disciples of all nations, baptizing them in the name of the Father and of the Son and of the Holy Spirit, and teaching them to obey everything I have commanded you. And surely I am with you always, to the very end of the age.[26]

This passage (often called the Great Commission) reiterates the movement's commitment to evangelism; it also is used as a source outlining the proper form of baptism. There are two important things to know about the movement's teachings on baptism: (1) The only acceptable form of baptism is immersion, and (2) although adherents deny that they teach baptismal regeneration, they do in fact believe that one is saved at the time of baptism.[27] Using Matthew 28:19–20 as their proof text,

they further contend that one must be a disciple *first,* before baptism, for the baptism to be valid. Their reasoning is that since "make disciples" comes before "baptizing" in the text, the one must precede the other.[28]

Since salvation is dependent upon a correct and valid baptism, a person who was baptized in any other religious group (including the mainline Churches of Christ) is almost always rebaptized upon joining the Boston movement. Often, a member who was initially baptized within the Boston movement will decide he or she did not have a proper understanding of baptism or was not a true disciple at the time of the first baptism, and will be baptized a second time.[29] This was particularly true in the fall of 1986 and spring of 1987. It was during this time that the current understanding of Matthew 28:19–20 began to be taught: that a person had to be a disciple first, before baptism, for the baptism to be valid.[30] Kip McKean stated that he and other leaders in the church "rediscovered" this first-century Bible doctrine.[31] With its discovery came a rash of rebaptisms throughout the movement, including rebaptisms of many of the top leaders of the church.

Organization

Based on its interpretation of the second and third chapters of the book of Revelation, the movement adheres to a "one church, one city" concept. They believe it is unscriptural to have more than one congregation per city. Typically, but not always, a church affiliated with the Boston movement will simply take the name of the city as its name, such as the Los Angeles Church of Christ or the Chicago Church of Christ.

There is a very clear hierarchy in the Boston movement. In 1988 Kip McKean established nine world sector leaders who would each be responsible for the churches in a portion of the world. World Sector Administrators were also appointed to oversee the administration and finances of each world sector. Elders and evangelists make up the leadership core of individual congregations. Although the terminology differs from congregation to congregation, each church is usually divided geographically into sectors or quadrants with a sector or quadrant leader. The sectors are further subdivided (again, geographically) into zones, and the sector leader oversees the zone leaders. The zone leader then oversees the individual Bible talks and the Bible talk leaders. Typically, anyone in the position of zone leader or higher is a paid employee of the church.[32]

Kip McKean founded the Boston Church of Christ and continues as its undisputed leader today. In 1988 McKean removed himself from the position of lead evangelist of the Boston Church of Christ so that he could focus his attention on the newly appointed world sector leaders. In 1990 he moved to Los Angeles to oversee the Los Angeles Church of Christ and continue to serve as missions evangelist for the movement worldwide.

Those within the movement enthusiastically follow McKean as leader and have nothing but the highest praise for him. Andrew Giambarba says,

> In spanning twenty centuries of history it is my belief that there has never been a disciple since the apostle Paul who has given spiritual sight to so many.[33]

Steve Johnson, world sector leader and evangelist for the New York City Church of Christ, writes:

> With eyes wide open I'm following Kip McKean; Consciously, Intentionally; Thankfully. I guess I'm just not as strong as some folks and I need help in following Jesus. And so far, I've found no better help, no better leader, no more righteous a man—no better friend than Kip.[34]

Controversy

While the Boston movement is untainted by sexual scandal or financial impropriety, it has been the focus of intense controversy. The mainline Churches of Christ disavowed the Boston movement in the mid-1980s and are now ardent opponents of it; numerous universities around the country either restrict or bar Boston movement activities on their campuses; anticult forces charge the movement with mind control and abusive practices; and many ex-members have taken up personal crusades against the movement.

The majority of the controversy surrounding the Boston movement centers on the commitment level that is expected of church members and the authority the church exercises in members' lives. It is clear from *Making Disciples* (a manual to train potential converts) that members are expected to put the church above all else, including job, friends, and family.[35] Each week the average member attends at least four or five meetings for worship and/or Bible study. Those in any position of leadership (assistant Bible talk leader and up) might also attend a leadership meeting on a weekly basis. Every member is involved with a discipleship partner, and many, if not most, are involved with multiple discipleship partners.[36] Partners usually meet once a week and keep in daily contact. In many congregations Saturday night has been set aside as a time when singles are expected to date other singles in the church.[37] Members are expected, on a daily basis, to contact people with the intention of recruiting; some leaders set guidelines as to how many contacts a member is to have each day. As Nick Young said in a sermon in Tulsa, Oklahoma,

> You are going to go out with the gospel of Jesus, and you're not going to have a problem with inviting thirty a day. . . . I have heard that some of you have actually had an attitude about having to share with thirty people a day. That makes me sick! And you know, it makes God sicker! Where is your heart? You've lost your faith. You've lost your heart. You can't even take a simple challenge like sharing with thirty people a day and not get all bent out of shape about it.[38]

Many congregations make use of accountability sheets that each member is to fill out and turn in on a weekly basis. For each day of the week members are to indicate whether they spent time praying (alone and with spouse), studying the Bible, and sharing their faith. Accountability sheets from some congregations have also included checklists for such things as whether they had sex with their spouses, whether they went to bed and arose on time, and how much sleep and exercise they were getting.[39]

It is these intrusions into private areas of people's lives that are cited by critics and ex-members alike. Ex-members charge that church leaders dictated to them regarding the use of their money, how they spent their free time, whom they dated and for how long, and with whom they associated. Critics believe that the church attempts to isolate members from anyone who might cause them to question the teachings of the Boston movement. As support for this contention, critics claim that members are encouraged to live together and to limit their contact with non-member family and friends. They also note that college students are often urged not to go home for the summer if there are no Boston movement churches near their homes.[40]

It is clear that the movement does maintain rigid teachings on authority: part of being a disciple is submitting to the leadership of the church. It is asumed that someone in a leadership position knows what is best for an individual even more than the individual does. As Kip McKean has said,

> Let me tell you this, the people that are easiest to disciple are those individuals who are the ones who most want to imitate you. Because the moment you start saying, "Well, there are some parts about this brother I am a little bit unsure of," what that person begins to do, is they begin to filter through the direction and advice that's given to them. And when they start filtering through, they begin to filter out. And when they start filtering out, they're going to filter out what seems best to them, and the whole point of being a disciple is that they don't know what is best for them. But their discipler knows what is best for them. And so I

believe a challenge for us is to say, "Listen, I really love and appreciate my Zone leader. But more than that, I want to be like him."[41]

He further states:

> The only time [the evangelist] is not to be obeyed is when he calls you to disobey Scripture or disobey your conscience and even if he calls you do something that disobeys your conscience, you still have an obligation to study it out and prayerfully change your opinion so you can be totally unified.[42]

Critics of the Boston movement believe the church's teachings on authority, its influence in members' daily lives, and the discipling relationships have all led to emotional abuse of members. It should be noted that the leadership of the Boston movement recognizes that abuses of authority have occurred, and it has retracted some of its earlier teachings on authority and submission.[43] However, while the movement claims it has attempted to "readjust what was previously taught,"[44] those who have recently left the movement claim that the old teachings and practices regarding authority in the church persist.[45]

Along with the tremendous growth there has been a tremendous drop-out rate as well. Although more people come into the Boston movement than leave it, large numbers leave the movement every year. Although 22,135 people joined the movement in 1991, the total growth for the year was only 8,880, indicating that 13,255 people left the movement.[46] Kip McKean states that the drop-out rate for the movement is 50 percent[47] while ex-Boston Elder Jerry Jones has put the figure at 59 percent.[48]

Many ex-members have proven quite nettlesome to the movement. Those who leave are often "marked" as people that members are to have no contact with. Ex-members routinely recount their stories (which usually portray the movement in a negative light) to the media, and others such as Jerry Jones and Rick Bauer have produced books denouncing the movement.[49] Kip McKean has pronounced any publications critical of the Boston movement as "spiritual pornography,"[50] and in a recent article stated, "Listening to men like Jerry Jones is ultimately in violation of Scripture."[51]

Conclusion

The challenge facing the Boston movement in its second decade is sustaining its tremendous growth. While the movement continues to increase its numbers each year, its percentage of growth declines.[52] Many of the larger congregations are experiencing a leveling off of their membership growth. For a movement that is theologically centered on expansive evangelism and that often justifies its existence and its practices based on its numerical growth, a substantial decline in growth could raise serious questions among members as to the righteousness of the movement.

It is unlikely that critics will become fewer in number as the Boston movement expands. The movement has already experienced a few cases of forcible deprogramming and will continue to have to deal with the ranks of ex-members, critics, and anticult forces. But the strong opposition encountered by the movement has done little to diminish its zeal and in fact often strengthens the conviction that this is truly a movement of God.

Notes

1. This term has been used due to the key role of the Crossroads Church of Christ in the history of the Boston movement. The term is a misnomer since the Crossroads and Boston Church of Christ have severed all ties and the Boston movement has become its own distinct movement.

2. First spoken by Thomas Campbell in 1809. Robert Richardson, *Memoirs of Alexander Campbell*, vol. 1 (Philadelphia: J. B. Lippincott), 1868; reprint, (Indianapolis: Religious Book Service, n.d.), 236.

3. David Edwin Harrell, Jr., *Emergence of the "Church of Christ" Denomination* (Athens, Ala.: Christian Enterprises International, 1972), 9.

4. United States Department of Commerce and Labor, Bureau of the Census, *Religious Bodies, 1906* (United States Printing Office, 1910), 236.

5. Mac Lynn, comp., *Churches of Christ in the United States* (Nashville: Gospel Advocate Co., 1991), xiii.

6. Flavil R. Yeakley, ed., *The Discipling Dilemma: A Study of the Discipling Movement Among Churches of Christ* (Nashville: Gospel Advocate Co., 1988), 137. Campus Crusade for Christ International is an evangelistic organization committed to spreading the gospel throughout the world, particularly among college students. Daniel G. Reid, ed., *Dictionary of Christianity in America* (Downers Grove, Ill.: InterVarsity Press, 1990), s.v. "Campus Crusade for Christ International," by K. L. Staggers, 215.

7. Rick Rowland, "The History of Campus Ministry," *Campus Journal* 32 (Summer 1990): 8.

8. Ibid., 9.

9. Unless all the participants of the soul talk were female, then the meeting was always led by a male.

10. Rowland, "History of Campus Ministry," 9.

11. Martin Edward Wooten, "The Boston Movement as a 'Revitalization Movement'" (D.Min. thesis, Harding Graduate School of Religion, 1990), 86–87.

12. Kip McKean, "Revolution Through Restoration," *UpsideDown* 1 (April 1992): 6.

13. Ibid., 8–9.

14. Attendance figures are as of February 1993. Roger Lamb, managing editor *UpsideDown* magazine, private correspondence to Russell R. Paden, 24 March 1993.

15. Flavil R. Yeakley, Jr., *Why Churches Grow* (Broken Arrow, Okla.: Christian Communications, Inc., 1979), 1.

16. K. McKean, "Revolution Through Restoration," 6.

17. Wooten, "The Boston Movement as a 'Revitalization Movement,'" 70.

18. Andrew Giambarba, *Bent on Conquest* (Boston: Boston Church of Christ Printing, 1988), 7.

19. K. McKean, "Revolution Through Restoration," 8.

20. Ibid., 8–9.

21. Al Baird, *Boston Bulletin*, "Authority and Submission," part 5, 4 October 1987.

22. Kip McKean, 1988 Leadership Conference (Boston), "Discipleship Partners," audio cassette.

23. Lamb, private correspondence.

24. Wooten, "The Boston Movement as a 'Revitalization Movement,' " 86.

25. Sarah Bauer, *A Time to Speak: A Personal Journal of My Years in the Boston Movement* (Upper Marlboro, Md.: Freedom House, Inc., 1992), 24.

26. I have used the New International Version due to its popularity within the Boston movement.

27. Randy McKean, ed., *Making Disciples* (Woburn, Mass.: Kingdom Media Resources, 1991), 22.

28. Biblical scholars have noted that the Boston movement's rendering of this passage is problematic in an English translation, but is particularly dubious in the original Greek. See J. Paul Pollard, "An Analysis of Matthew 28:19–20" in *The Boston Movement: Analysis, Commentary, and Media Reports* (Upper Marlboro, Md.: Freedom House, Inc., 1992), no page number.

29. "Letter to Boston Leaders from Scott and Robyn Deal" in Jerry Jones, *What Does the Boston Movement Teach?* vol. 3 (Bridgeton, Mo.: By the author, 1993), 73.

30. Jones, *What Does the Boston Movement Teach?* 3: 7.

31. K. McKean, "Revolution Through Restoration," 8.

32. Susan McGunnigle Condon, *A Diary: Why I Left the Boston Movement* (Atlanta: By the author, 1991), 9.

33. Giambarba, *Bent on Conquest*, from the dedication, no page number.

34. Steve Johnson, "A Tribute to the Boston Church of Christ," *Discipleship Magazine* 1 (Spring 1989): 26.

35. R. McKean, *Making Disciples*, 45.

36. Giambarba, *Bent on Conquest*, 9.

37. Both the Boston and Chicago congregations have printed "Dating Guidelines" for singles to use. Jones, *What Does the Boston Movement Teach?* vol. 1 (reprint, 1991), 9, 88.

38. "Tulsa Reconstruction," (Tulsa, Okla.) August 1992, audio cassette.

39. Photocopies of accountability sheets appear in Jones, *What Does the Boston Movement Teach?* 1: 16–17, 128, 163; 2: 117.

40. Carlene B. Hill, "Church Grows Amidst Controversy," *New England Church Life* (December 1987): 10.

41. Kip McKean, 1988 Leadership Retreat (Boston), audio cassette in Jones, *What Does the Boston Movement Teach?* 1: 13.

42. Kip McKean, 1987 World Mission Seminar (Boston), "Why Do You Resist the Spirit?" audio cassette.

43. K. McKean, "Revolution Through Restoration," 15; Wooten, "The Boston Movement as a 'Revitalization Movement,' " 157; Al Baird, "A New Look at Authority," *UpsideDown* 1 (April 1992): 18–19, 49.

44. Baird, "A New Look at Authority," 18.

45. "Open Letter from Daniel Eng" in Jones, *What Does the Boston Movement Teach?* 3: 75.

46. Using statistics from the *Boston Bulletin*, Jerry Jones has provided growth figures in tabular form. Ibid., 34.

47. K. McKean, "Revolution Through Restoration," 8.

48. Jones, *What Does the Boston Movement Teach?* 3: 34.

49. They have also set up ministries to aid those leaving the Boston movement.

50. Roger Lamb, Tom Jones, and Declan Joyce, "Who's Brainwashing Who?" *UpsideDown* 2 (January 1993): 24.

51. Ibid., 30.

52. Wooten, "The Boston Movement as a 'Revitalization Movement,' " 194. See also growth statistics in Jones, *What Does the Boston Movement Teach?* 3: 34.

Suggestions for Further Reading

Jones, Jerry. *What Does the Boston Movement Teach?* vols. 1–3. Bridgeton, Mo.: By the author, 1990–93.

McKean, Kip. "Revolution Through Restoration," *UpsideDown* 1 (April 1991): 6.

Martin, Edward. "The Boston Movement as a 'Revitalization Movement,' " D.Min. thesis, Harding Graduate School of Religion, 1990.

Yeakley, Flavil R., ed. *The Discipling Dilemma: A Study of the Discipling Movement Among Churches of Christ.* Nashville: Gospel Advocate Co., 1988.

14

FROM HOLY ORDER OF MANS TO CHRIST THE SAVIOR BROTHERHOOD: THE RADICAL TRANSFORMATION OF AN ESOTERIC CHRISTIAN ORDER

Phillip Lucas

Historical Introduction

The twenty-year (1968 to 1988) transformation of the Holy Order of MANS, a Rosicrucian-style monastic community, into a traditionalist Eastern Orthodox sect provides a paradigmatic example of the processes of maturation, conventionalization, identity stabilization, and adjustment to the death of a charismatic founder that the alternative religious movements of 1960s America have undergone during their founding generation.[1]

The order emerged in the culturally innovative milieu of mid-1960s San Francisco. Its founder, Earl Blighton, was a retired electrical engineer and social worker who had been affiliated with the Freemasons, Spiritualist churches, the Ancient and Mystical Order of the Rosae Crucis (AMORC), the Subramuniya Yoga Order, and the Theosophical Society. At the height of the counterculture explosion that swept the Haight-Ashbury in 1966 and 1967, Blighton began to teach a hybrid brand of "esoteric Christianity" to a small following of young persons who were disillusioned with the excesses of the hippie lifestyle and committed to a search for spiritual community and drug-free mystical experience. Out of this core of followers evolved a monastic-style service and teaching order that was formally incorporated in the state of California in July of 1968.[2]

The order's teachings and spiritual practices were a synthesis of traditional Christian monasticism, New Thought philosophy, the Western esoteric tradition, Tantrism, and a theosophically inspired millenarianism. Blighton's central proclamation was that the earth was moving into a golden age of spiritual illumination and that the Holy Order of MANS had been divinely ordained to prepare people for this new era through its open transmission of ancient Christian "mystery teachings" and initiations. Blighton's signature initiation, called the "illumination," was understood to be an infusing of the physical and subtle bodies of the initiate with the light of the universal Christ spirit. It was the order's mission to bring as many people as possible into this "higher state" of spiritual functioning so as to ameliorate the disorienting conditions that Blighton claimed would accompany the emerging planetary "lift in vibration."[3]

In a series of green-covered books that the brotherhood published beginning in 1968, Blighton and his wife, Ruth Blighton, articulated their doctrines of psycho-spiritual unfoldment, contemplative practice, and theosophical Christianity. The most important of these works, *The Golden Force*, taught Blighton's "universal law" of mental dynamics. This law had purportedly been taught by the "Master Jesus" to his early followers but had been suppressed by institutional Christianity as part of its plan to make people "totally dependent on the church hierarchy." Blighton tied the Christian doctrine of the Trinity to the three steps of this law—which was essentially a New Thought-inspired method of creative visualization.[4]

In the first step, the student established meditative contact with the Creative Life Force (the Father) that was believed to animate all things. The second step was to mentally image a picture of what was desired and to ask for this "in the name of Our Lord Jesus Christ" (the Son). The last step (related to the action of the Holy Spirit) was to thank the Creator for this gift and to continue one's normal life activities in the complete assurance that what had been prayed for would be manifested "on the material plane" according to inexorable universal law.[5]

The brotherhood was organized hierarchically along the lines of Catholic teaching orders like the Jesuits. At the top of this hierarchy were the offices of director and co-director general (Earl and Ruth Blighton). These two functionaries oversaw the order's temporal and spiritual affairs, which were administered by a board of directors and an "esoteric council," respectively. The esoteric council was composed of the nearly two hundred priests Blighton ordained between 1968 and 1974. The director general elaborated a complex myth of origins for this priesthood that tied it to the biblical Order of Melchizedek and the theosophical Great White Brotherhood.[6]

The movement spread quickly throughout the United States between 1969 and 1974, establishing seminaries, mission stations, and training centers in over sixty major cities. Members took both temporary and lifetime vows of poverty, service, obedience, purity, and humility. They also observed regular periods of prayer and fasting, wore clerical clothing (in public) and monastic robes (inside the "brotherhouses"), and held all assets in common. Unlike monastic communities of the past, the order established itself in largely urban settings, accepted a coeducational membership, ordained women to its priesthood, and adopted an eclectic assortment of spiritual practices.[7]

During the early 1970s, the movement expanded its outreach to include lay persons who wished to study under the renunciate brotherhood's auspices while remaining financially independent. Members of the Discipleship movement could enroll in the *Tree of Life* correspondence course and receive training in the use of spiritual "tools" at yearly seminars and retreats. Lay families who wished to establish local chapels for daily communion and classes could pool their resources and become chartered by the order as Christian Communities. The renunciate brotherhood then sent priests to act as teachers, celebrants, and counsellors for these communities—which during the late 1970s numbered about thirty.[8]

Blighton also created the Immaculate Heart Sisters of Mary and the Brown Brothers of the Holy Light in the early 1970s. Students in these celibate suborders spent a year dedicated to service work, missionary outreach, and Marian devotional practices. The blue-and-brown-robed brothers and sisters could be seen in nursing homes, hospitals, youth centers, emergency wards, and on "street patrols" throughout America's larger cities between 1973 and 1982. Members of the suborders also staffed the order's Raphael Houses, which were pioneering efforts to provide shelter for victims of domestic violence. The large Raphael House in San Francisco was so successful that Mayor Diane Feinstein declared the last week of November, 1980, as Raphael House Week.[9]

In April of 1974, Blighton died suddenly while on a private retreat at the Pacific Coast. After several years of interim leadership, he was succeeded as the group's director general by Andrew Rossi, an early disciple. The movement's combined membership peaked at about three thousand in 1977 and began to decline quickly in the wake of the cult hysteria generated by the Jonestown suicides of November 1978. Like many of the period's new religious movements, the order began to appear on the "cult lists" published by the anticult movement and to receive increasingly hostile coverage from both local and national media. This was an upsetting turn of events for a group that had previously enjoyed a largely positive public image and had been the focus of favorable media attention because of its charitable activities.

To address this negative publicity and a corresponding dropoff in the rate of new recruits, Rossi and his closest aides decided to distance the order from its early identity as a school of esoteric Christian initiation and to move toward a more mainstream Christian self-representation. The movement also consolidated itself into ten large centers in the United States and Europe and shifted its focus from missionary expansion to the creation of an exemplary Christian-based subculture. The keynotes of this subculture were spiritual community, family life, appropriate technology, and the preservation of traditional values. In concrete terms, this included the founding of private schools for the group's children, the collective celebration of seasonal festivals, the promotion of an ethic of ecology, the practice of traditional arts and crafts, and the creation of small businesses.[10]

In the early 1980s, Rossi undertook an exhaustive study of Christian history as part of his attempt to find a niche for the order in the mainstream Christian tradition. At a critical juncture in this search, he underwent a personal religious conversion to Eastern Orthodoxy. Rather than resigning his post as director general and joining a local Orthodox church, he and his Orthodox mentor, Father Herman Podmoshensky (the abbot of the Saint Herman of Alaska Russian Orthodox Brotherhood) decided to orchestrate a gradual process in the order through which a number of its key identity markers were replaced with Orthodox Christian beliefs and practices. Although no member was forced overtly to participate in the newly instituted Orthodox liturgies, those who resisted the changeover became marginalized within the order's power structure or were pressured to leave altogether. Several groups of order members broke away during the 1980s and have attempted to perpetuate Blighton's legacy through private initiatory training, publication of his writings and sermons, and public classes.[11]

The renunciate brotherhood's "journey to Orthodoxy" was completed in May of 1988, when its remaining one thousand members were baptized and received into a small, independent Orthodox archdiocese headquartered in Queens, New York. As part of the arrangement Rossi negotiated with the metropolitan of this archdiocese, Pangratios Vrionis, the director general was left in charge of the order's assets and given continued autonomy in matters of internal polity. The group changed its name to Christ the Savior Brotherhood (CSB) and recently (1991) joined its lay and renunciate branches together into conventional Orthodox parishes governed by local priests.[12]

In 1990, Rossi was challenged by disgruntled priests within the group's hierarchy for his alleged failings as a pastor and administrator. After a long and bitter battle of wills, he agreed to relinquish his authority and accept CSB's financial support for his doctoral studies at Oxford University. With Metropolitan Pangratios and Father Podmoshensky now firmly in control, CSB has reconceived its purpose to be the missionizing of America (and especially New Agers) for Eastern Orthodoxy in preparation for the imminent Last Judgment.[13]

Internal and External Drivers of Change

The rapid transformation of the order during its founding generation raises the question of what specific internal and external forces may have been responsible for its radical alterations in doctrine and identity.

The most important internal force of change was probably the shift in membership profile during the late 1970s from a primarily young, single, and mobile corps of self-styled "spiritual shock troops" to a collection of middle-aged married couples whose primary considerations were childrearing and the creation of stable religious communities. Between 1975 and 1984, all but a few of the order's brothers and sisters married and began families. Coupled with this development was the consolidation of the group's small mission stations into large-scale intentional communities. These shifts in membership demography and communal living arrangements meant that the practical support of families, the efficient indoctrination of children, and the strengthening of affective group ties replaced the early order's focus on heroic missionary outreach, individual initiatory attainment, and imminent millennial transformation.

As the value of communal affective ties became paramount in the order, the doctrinal eclecticism of the Blighton era was increasingly viewed as a threat to group unity. The order's leadership therefore made it their top priority to articulate a more defined and cohesive system of doctrines. In the process of creating this system, the movement came to the realization that the general tenor of its original teachings placed it squarely within the Western esoteric tradition and in opposition to the dogmas of Orthodox Christianity. The brotherhood's aging members were faced with a difficult choice at this point— whether to remain loyal to the vision of their founder (and thus continue in his eclectic and esoteric trajectory), with all the risks of disunity and outside persecution that such a course entailed—or to return to the more culturally legitimate Christian doctrines of their early upbringings.[14]

Since Blighton had never explicitly condemned traditional Christianity as such and had in fact utilized a wide array of Christian symbols, writings, and practices in his ongoing construction of the order, such a leap was not so radical as it might at first seem. In addition, few of the group's members were conversant enough with the history of Christian theology to be aware of the magnitude of the shift that was being contemplated. Since the rank and file were focused primarily on building stronger affective ties within their new communities, they were more than willing to delegate the task of doctrinal self-representation to the order's more theologically sophisticated leadership.

With the shift from missionary outreach to community building, a change in the movement's overall conception of its mission also occurred. The early order's emphasis on individual initiatory attainment as a prelude to planetary apotheosis faded into the background and was replaced by the communitarian ideal of creating an exemplary "city on a hill," a perfect social form that would slowly transform the surrounding culture by quiet example. Since building an exemplary Christian community would now be the brotherhood's chief activity, Blighton's nontraditional religious system came to be viewed as a potentially damaging distraction from the core of what the group really had to offer. As such, it became expendable.

External factors also played an important role in the order's transformation. One such factor, the anticult hysteria that followed in the wake of the Jonestown tragedy, has already been mentioned. Another significant factor was the decline of the counterculture during the mid-1970s and the resulting disappearance of the brotherhood's main pool of recruits. The rapid early growth in the order's membership had been fueled by the sizeable number of rootless counterculture youths living in large cities near universities between 1968 and 1976. The movement had strategically located its new centers in the vicinity of universities to take advantage of this fact.[15]

As these counterculturists began to drop back into society, a new generation appeared who were far more pragmatic and conventional than the early baby boomers. This new cohort pursued college degrees and sought employment in the nation's mainstream businesses and institutions. As a whole, its members were disinclined to join nontraditional religious communities, particularly in the aftermath of Jonestown. The order was aware that this new youth cohort had more conventional values and attitudes and sought to refurbish its public image— first in the direction of evangelicalism, and finally in the direction of Christian Orthodoxy—at least partially to appeal to it.[16]

A third societal condition that had a significant impact on the brotherhood's transformation relates to what Jean Baudrillard has argued is our era's "domination of simulation." What Baudrillard means by this is, first, the growing tendency of postmodern culture to produce and disseminate simulations or images, which in turn come to mediate all human experience. Along with the ever-increasing production of images has occurred the lifting of the requirement that these simulations have any verifiable relation to the everyday world of concrete experience. What has resulted, according to Baudrillard, is a confusion of random simulations floating through the collective consciousness of the postmodern world, turning the human struggle for an authentic identity into a slippery walk through a jungle of dissociated images and reflections. This cultural trend, aided by such electronic technologies as video cameras, digital sound, and computer graphics, has funneled power in our society to those who are masters of image production and dissemination.[17]

The order was forced to enter this postmodern arena of image production in order to combat the negative portrayals of itself that were being formulated by both the anticult movement and the national electronic and print media. Through the development of propaganda organs like *Epiphany* journal, *Tree of Life* magazine, and *Sonflowers* magazine, the order created an increasingly sophisticated apparatus for recreating and refining its public self-representation. The temptation, once this apparatus was in place, was for the group to produce a series of subtly nuanced simulations of itself in word and picture, many of which did not conform to the brotherhood's actual practices and teachings.

This image-making apparatus proved so successful in crafting a respectable public image for the order that Rossi and his advisors were later able to utilize it to indoctrinate the brotherhood itself into Eastern Orthodoxy. Most members were not entirely sure what the group's teachings were in the period between 1978 and 1986, since what they saw represented on the printed page and heard in public pronouncements barely resembled the conception of the movement they had developed between 1968 and 1977. This state of affairs, coupled with Rossi's skillful telling and retelling of the brotherhood's early history, left many members asking whether their own conception of the order had ever actually corresponded to its objective reality. Such confusion left most members more than willing to follow Rossi into Orthodoxy,

since this path seemed to promise them a coherent institutional identity rooted firmly in a culturally legitimate tradition.

This conservative trajectory also conformed nicely to the widespread revalorization of tradition that swept the United States during the Reagan era. By becoming more conservative and orthodox than its most vocal critics, the group outflanked the anticult movement and effectively neutralized its attacks.

Continuities

This focus on the radical changes in the order brings up an important question. To what extent can a new religious movement (NRM) move beyond its original doctrines and practices and still survive in the contemporary religious marketplace? According to sociologists like Rodney Stark, NRMs that compromise their original cultural content and accommodate themselves too quickly to societal norms (in the hopes of gaining respectability) run the danger of losing their market viability. In short, why would anyone convert to a new movement that offers the same doctrines and practices as older, more established traditions?[18]

The Holy Order of MANS presents an interesting test case for Stark's hypothesis. On the surface, few elements of Christ the Savior Brotherhood have continuity with the early order. The present community repudiates Blighton's ecumenism and his corollary belief that all religions present legitimate pathways to the Divine. It has completely jettisoned the Western esoteric foundations of his early cosmology and Christology and adheres strictly to the dogmas of Eastern Orthodoxy. The brotherhood also considers the "revelatory messages" received by Blighton as, at best, the effluent of his own subconscious and at worst the teachings of the demonic hosts. The group has substituted Orthodox liturgies for the early order's "new age" initiatory rites and has democratized its internal governance. Christ the Savior Brotherhood members have moved beyond the order's early communalism, choosing instead to live as nuclear families in conventional neighborhoods. Blighton's pioneering effort to ordain women as priests has given way to a strict proscription of women in sacerdotal roles. Finally, the early order's optimistic expectation of an imminent new age of spiritual illumination has been replaced by a darkly apocalyptic vision of a coming Antichrist who will lead most of humankind to perdition.[19]

Christ the Savior Brotherhood's radical accommodations to Orthodox norms of belief and practice are not the whole story, however. Throughout its revisionist "journey to the heart of the Christian tradition" the order has managed to maintain several key values from its earliest days. The first of these is the group's commitment to charitable service. From the earliest hotel and food vouchers it distributed to indigents in 1966 through its establishment of temporary shelters for victims of domestic violence, the brotherhood never lost its ethic of service to the needy. Christ the Savior Brotherhood continues to administer these shelters and sees this work as a salutary prod to other Eastern Orthodox jurisdictions to expand their charitable activities beyond their own ethnic enclaves.[20]

A second continuity relates to the group's enduring respect for the monastic vocation. The early order's monasticism included such elements as the five vows administered to recruits, a daily rule of prayer and meditation, the members' common robes, and a generally abstemious lifestyle. The monastic ideal could also be recognized in the suborders' vows of celibacy and in the brotherhood's self-conception as a religious elite whose spiritual attainments would inspire lay followers. Several members have remarked that the movement was attracted to Eastern Orthodoxy because of this tradition's reverence for monastic spirituality. Father Podmoshensky, who is hugely popular in CSB, upholds the rigorous traditions of Orthodox monasticism in both his teaching and lifestyle. Although most of CSB's members now live in conventional nuclear families, they attempt to infuse their householders' lives with the spirit of traditional Russian monasticism.[21]

A third important continuity is the brotherhood's ongoing interest in initiatory spirituality and light mysticism. The early order's mystical rites of baptism, illumination, and self-realization were easily adapted to Eastern Orthodoxy's initiatory path of baptism, chrismation, and *theosis* (divinization). In addition, the light mysticism underlying the "illumination" was understood by Rossi to be congruent with the Neoplatonic light mysticism taught by the elders of Orthodox monasticism.[22]

A final important continuity concerns a primitivist strain that has always been present in the group. Blighton claimed that the path he taught was the ancient apostolic form of the Christian mysteries. He also claimed that many of the order's members were reincarnations of such early Christian leaders as the apostles James, Philip, Paul, and Andrew. This primitivist theme has been carried through to the present in CSB's claim to be the preserver and transmitter of the earliest traditions of Christian mystical spirituality. Father Podmoshensky has told the brotherhood that the monastic spirituality he teaches can be traced through an oral line of transmission back to the "catacomb church" of the first century. Of course, Eastern Orthodoxy itself claims to embody and transmit the earliest forms of Christian doctrine and practice.[23]

Thus, even as the order underwent a radical metamorphosis, it retained substantial continuities with its earliest ethical ideals, spiritual striving, and primitivist self-conception. It is likely as a result of these continuities that the brotherhood has been able to preserve an undeniable coherence and solidarity as a community between 1968 and 1992. With regard to Stark's thesis, it is probably too soon to predict whether CSB can survive in the long term as a discrete religious movement after having abandoned so much of its original religious and cultural content.[24]

Future

The future trajectory for CSB appears to be in the direction of increasing conventionalization and accommodation to societal norms. In 1992 unofficial meetings were held with officials of the Orthodox Church in America regarding CSB's eventual unification with that mainstream jurisdiction. The brotherhood has found, much to its dismay, that both Metropolitan Pangratios and Father Podmoshensky have been defrocked by mainstream Orthodox jurisdictions and that, as a consequence, their baptisms and ordinations are considered invalid by the Standing Conference of Orthodox Bishops in America. It is likely that CSB will seek to rectify this legitimacy problem in the near future by coming under the auspices of a more recognized Orthodox jurisdiction.[25]

The danger this poses for CSB is clear. What will prevent current members from simply leaving their small, quasi-legitimate parishes and joining more established local Orthodox churches (as many have already done)? On the other hand, if CSB remains under the influence of marginal Orthodox leaders such as Metropolitan Pangratios and Father Podmoshensky, its chances of long-term growth and survival are slight. Under their tutelage, the movement has developed into a highly conservative sect whose men sport long beards and Russian peasant shirts and whose women wear plain frocks and hair tightly bound under linen bonnets. In addition, CSB observes the ancient Julian calendar, eschews makeup and jewelry, encourages the home-schooling of its children, and is engaged in an ongoing round of mutual criticism with other Orthodox jurisdictions. It is unlikely that this sectarian subculture will have much appeal to the general American public. Whichever way it decides to go, it is clear that CSB will ultimately lose any resemblance to the new age school of Christian initiation founded by Earl Blighton in 1968.

Notes

1. MANS was a secret acronym denoting the group's overall mission and identity. It was revealed only to movement insiders.

2. Earl Blighton, "A History of the Holy Order of MANS," general letter, June 1970.

3. John McCaffery, interview with author, Syracuse, N.Y., 13 October 1991.

4. Holy Order of MANS, *The Golden Force* (San Francisco: Holy Order of MANS, 1967), 71–72, 106.

5. Holy Order of MANS, Tree of Life Lessons, "Symbolism," Level 2, 1, 3; "Prayer," Level 1, 1.

6. Holy Order of MANS, "The Cosmic Orders and Their Purposes," unpublished, undated manuscript, 5-9; "Book of Alchemy," 1974, unpublished, 82; "The Discovery," unpublished, undated manuscript, 14, 35.

7. Holy Order of MANS, *Uniting All Faiths* (San Francisco: Holy Order of MANS, 1973).

8. Holy Order of MANS, *Christian Community* (San Francisco: Holy Order of MANS, 1976); "Steps Along the Way" (San Francisco: Holy Order of MANS, undated). This latter publication was a brochure introducing the Discipleship movement.

9. Holy Order of MANS, *Uniting All Faiths;* "Why a Raphael House?," brochure detailing Raphael House's services, 1981.

10. McCaffery, interview.

11. Mark and Mary Anderson, interview with author, Sandy, Oregon, 9 October 1987; Herman Podmoshensky, interview with author, Forestville, California, 8 June 1991.

12. Ibid.; Andrew Rossi, transcript of meeting with Christian Community of Portland, 22 February 1988.

13. Matthew Tate, interview with author, Milwaukie, Oregon, 12 Sept. 1991; Apostolic Council report, April 25–27, 1991, 15–20.

14. McCaffery, interview.

15. Ruth Woodhead, interview with author, Goleta, California, 25 June 1991.

16. It should be noted that the Holy Order of MANS was not the only new religious movement to have to contend with this drying up of potential converts. Movements like the International Society for Krishna Consciousness, the Unification Church, and Transcendental Meditation also saw their recruitment rates begin to decline in the late 1970s—and were forced to make changes in self-representation

and internal structure as a result. See Anson Shupe and David G. Bromley, "Apostates and Atrocity Stories: Some Parameters in the Dynamics of Deprogramming," in *The Social Impact of New Religious Movements,* ed. Bryan Wilson (New York: Rose of Sharon Press, 1981), 209–211; William S. Bainbridge and Daniel Jackson, "The Rise and Decline of Transcendental Meditation," in *The Social Impact of New Religious Movements,* 151–52.

17. Jean Baudrillard, "The Precession of Simulacra," in *Simulations,* trans. Paul Foss and Paul Patton (New York: Semiotext[e], 1983), 1–79.

18. Rodney Stark, "How New Religions Succeed," in *The Future of New Religious Movements,* ed. David Bromley and Phillip E. Hammond (Macon: Mercer University Press, 1987), 23–24.

19. McCaffery, interview; Tate, interview.

20. Ibid.

21. Podmoshensky, interview.

22. Michael Hoffman, interview with author, Forestville, California, 8 June 1991.

23. John Anderson, interview with author, Midwoud, Holland, 1 August 1991; Rossi, transcript of meeting with Christian Community; Ya'qub Ibn Yusuf, "The Living Tradition of Catacomb Christianity: An Interview with Father Herman," *Gnosis Magazine* (Summer 1990): 23.

24. For a comprehensive analysis and interpretation of the order's history, see my book, *The Odyssey of a New Religion: The Holy Order of MANS from New Age to Orthodoxy* (Bloomington: Indiana University Press, 1995).

25. Official Decision of the Ecclesiastical Court of the Western-American Diocese Regarding Abbot Herman [Podmoshensky], 16 June 1988; Don Lattin, interview with author, San Francisco, California, 9 March 1992.

Suggestions for Further Reading

Fracchia, Charles. *Living Together Alone: The New American Monasticism.* San Francisco: Harper and Row, Inc., 1979.

Lucas, Phillip. "Social Factors in the Failure of NRMs: A Case Study Using Stark's Success Model." *Syzygy* 1 (Winter 1992): 39–53.

———. *The Odyssey of a New Religion: The Holy Order of MANS from New Age to Orthodoxy.* Bloomington: Indiana University Press, 1995.

15

THE BRANCH DAVIDIANS: A SOCIAL PROFILE AND ORGANIZATIONAL HISTORY

David G. Bromley and Edward D. Silver

The Branch Davidians can trace their roots to the nineteenth-century Millerites.[1] When the failure of a series of William Miller's prophecies of the end of the world caused his movement to collapse in 1844, a number of splinter groups arose from the disorder. One of these groups, inspired by Hiram Edson, a New York farmer, believed that Christ had not left his heavenly sanctuary to return to earth at the predicted time, but rather had entered a new sanctuary to judge the lives of the faithful. The Second Coming would immediately follow the completion of that task. It was this group that eventually formed the Seventh-Day Adventist Church (SDA), which continues to expect Christ's imminent return. The Seventh-Day Adventists, like many other Protestant denominations, experienced a number of schisms. This chapter sketches Branch Davidian history beginning with the initial schismatic break from the SDA. The history is divided into three segments—the Houteff, Roden, and Koresh periods—that correspond to the leadership groups during those periods. (We shall refer to the succession of groups that culminated in the Branch Davidians as the Davidians and to Vernon Howell as David Koresh throughout, although he did not legally adopt this name until 1990.)

The Houteff Period

The group that gave birth to the Branch Davidians was founded in 1929 by Victor Houteff, a Bulgarian immigrant. Houteff arrived in the United States in 1907 when he was twenty-one years old and converted to the Seventh-Day Adventist Church twelve years later.[2] By 1929 he had become disillusioned with the church, and in that year Houteff challenged SDA theology in his theological manifesto, "The Shepherd's Rod." Houteff asserted that the SDA was indeed the authentic church of the remnant, but that the church and its leadership had forsaken scriptural teachings and become overly materialistic and worldly. Houteff believed that he had been selected as a divine messenger to reveal new spiritual truths and to lead the purification process that would permit Christ's return. He had two divinely appointed missions. The first was to unlock the secrets to the end time, recorded in the Seven Seals (contained in the book of Revelation). The second was to gather the 144,000 faithful, who would be delivered at the Second Coming of Christ when sinners would be destroyed and the Kingdom of David would be erected in Palestine. Houteff clearly expected that he would complete his missions within a short time.

When Houteff found an audience receptive to his message within SDA ranks, church leaders responded with sanctions and theological rejoinders. These measures failed to deter Houteff, however, and he was disfellowshipped in 1934. A year later, Houteff and a small group of followers established the Shepherd's Rod, informally named after his manifesto. He purchased a tract of land on the Brazos River near Waco, Texas, and named the farm community he established there the Mt. Carmel Center. Houteff believed that Mt. Carmel was but a temporary waystation. He predicted that within a year the saved remnant would found a theocratic Kingdom of David in Palestine, proclaim the true gospel to the world, and be transported into heaven upon the return of Christ.

When the expected migration to Palestine did not take place, the group began turning its attention toward creating a more permanent organization. Over the next twenty years Shepherd's Rod adherents cleared the land, erected buildings, and constructed a community infrastructure. The rest home, dispensary, publication center, and ministerial school reflected the group's SDA roots, as did the community's practices of vegetarianism, evangelism, and intense devotionalism. The residents at Mt. Carmel distanced themselves from the outside world by growing their own food, creating a community-run school, limiting external sources of news, and even printing their own internal currency. Houteff instituted a system of double tithing to support the community's religious mission and the various social services it sought to offer adherents.

Because Houteff's followers accepted the basic tenets of SDA theology, they evangelized among Seventh-Day Adventists almost exclusively. However, because Shepherd's Rod teachings were of interest only to those who accepted SDA theology, the group grew only to perhaps one hundred members by the late 1930s, even with intensive evangelizing. In 1942 Houteff finally severed his relationship with the SDA, renamed his group the Davidian Seventh-Day Adventists (DSDA) and created a separate formal organization. During the 1950s, Houteff began seeking converts around the globe wherever the SDA had taken root, with the result that the Shepherd's Rod developed a small but committed international membership.

The DSDA was organized theocratically. Houteff possessed personal veto power over all decisions, and his wife and mother-in-law held the positions of secretary and treasurer on the executive council.[3] In an effort to maintain a spiritually committed community, he decreed that members must abandon marriages with spouses who refused to adopt the faith. Despite such measures, Houteff's control of DSDA members was limited, since most adherents did not reside at Mt. Carmel. As a result, the tightly organized core community was buttressed by a more loosely integrated network of supporters having varying degrees of commitment to the DSDA. Independent families also constituted a countervailing powerbase. For example, a family named Hermanson financially underwrote the formation of the Mt. Carmel community by purchasing the original tract of land and selling it to the group for a nominal price; in 1937 the Hermansons' seventeen-year-old daughter, Florence, married the fifty-two-year-old Houteff.

Houteff died in 1955 after a decade of declining health. This event surprised his followers, who had expected him to reign over the imminent establishment of the Kingdom of God that he had predicted. After a brief power struggle among competing factions, Florence Houteff assumed the mantle of DSDA leadership.[4] She sold the original Mt. Carmel property and used the proceeds to purchase a new, larger, and much less expensive tract of land several miles outside of the city. The move both shored up the DSDA's financial base and allowed the residents of the (New) Mt. Carmel community to maintain their distance from an expanding urban center. The DSDA's proceeded to rebuild their community, but again they constructed temporary structures since they expected to occupy the property only briefly.

In 1955 Florence Houteff announced that, based on a revelation gained from her reading of the Bible, she had unlocked the biblical code contained in the book of Revelation through which the timing of the Second Coming could be known. She then proclaimed 1959 "The Year of the Kingdom" and predicted April 22 as the exact date on which God's earthly kingdom would be established. As a prelude to the founding of God's kingdom in Jerusalem, the DSDAs expected a war in the Middle East and the purification of the SDA. Only God's chosen faithful would avoid being destroyed at the time the new kingdom was established, and many DSDAs believed that Victor Houteff would be resurrected at this time to assume leadership of the city of God. In the wake of this prophecy, group membership swelled to as many as 1,000 to 1,500, and between 500 and 1,000 believers sold their homes and possessions and moved to Waco in 1959 in anticipation of the end time. When April 22 passed uneventfully, the faithful began to scatter or form splinter groups; a year later only about 50 members remained at Mt. Carmel. The new prophet stunned the faithful in 1962 with the announcement that her teachings contained errors. Shortly after this announcement she closed the new center, moved away, and sold most of the Mt. Carmel property.

The Roden Period

There was a struggle for control of the DSDA following Florence Houteff's failed prophecy. One of the contenders for DSDA leadership during the 1955 succession struggle had been Benjamin Roden. He claimed to have received a spiritual revelation that he had been divinely ordained to assume the mantle of DSDA leadership and warned DSDA members to "Get off the dead Rod, and move into a living Branch," thereby anticipating the Branch Davidian movement. (The term "Branch" was used only sporadically, however; during the Koresh period the group members most frequently called themselves the "Students of the Seven Seals," and expressed puzzlement when the media accounts of the siege consistently referred to them as

Branch Davidians.) Roden even predicted divine destruction of the community if his claim went unheeded. Florence Houteff's failed prophecy presented Roden with another opportunity to contest for power. Within a short time, the fifty-seven-year-old Benjamin Roden won the loyalty of most of the remaining Davidians, gained legal control over the remaining seventy-seven acres of Mt. Carmel property, and renamed the group the General Association of Davidian Seventh-Day Adventists (GADSA). Roden enunciated his mission as creating a Christlike moral character in the ranks of the faithful. He taught that the Second Coming would occur soon after his followers had achieved sufficient moral rectitude under biblical law. In 1970 Roden announced a spiritual vision which his followers came to view as the beginning of the rule of God on earth, and he also pronounced himself the successor to the biblical King David. Moreover, he sought to begin a realization of the goal of establishing God's kingdom in Israel. In 1958 Roden and his wife, Lois, actually visited Israel, established a commune, occupied the site briefly, and urged followers to consider relocating there.

It appeared that Benjamin Roden would be successful in heading off another succession crisis. He arranged to vest the power to name the successor to GADSA leadership in the chairman of the executive council, a position Roden himself held, and he installed his son, George, as second in command and heir apparent.[5] However, the basis was laid for another succession struggle in 1977 when Lois Roden began having spiritual visions. She first announced that the Holy Spirit was in fact female and then elaborated on this vision, asserting that God is both male and female and that at the second coming the Messiah would assume female form. Later she founded a magazine, **She**kinah, to propound her theological views. Soon after her vision she began intensive scriptural study and subsequently was awarded GADSA ministerial credentials. When Benjamin Roden died on October 22, 1978, Lois Roden quickly laid claim to the mantle of GADSA leadership. However, a substantial proportion of GADSA members defected as a result of political infighting and her controversial theological doctrines. Further, George Roden was determined to regain what he believed to be his rightful position as leader of GADSA.[6] When his appeals to Mt. Carmel residents and the courts were unsuccesful, the feud between mother and son became so bitter that Lois Roden ultimately obtained a court order barring George from the Mt. Carmel property. It was into this contentious political situation that David Koresh came.

The Koresh Period

David Koresh was born Vernon Howell to a single mother in Houston, Texas, in 1959. He lived with his grandmother during the first five years of his life until his mother remarried. A learning disability created continuing academic problems through his early school years, and he ultimately dropped out of school before completing the tenth grade. His passions as a teenager were playing the guitar and studying the Bible. He memorized long sections of the New Testament, preaching to anyone who would listen. In the years that followed he held a succession of short-term, menial jobs, devoting most of his attention to playing the guitar and restoring cars. In 1979 Koresh began participating in study sessions at a Seventh-Day Adventist church in Tyler that his mother attended. However, after a succession of incidents in which he announced that God intended for him to marry the pastor's daughter, continually preached his own version of SDA theology to other church members, and even took over the pulpit to propound his own theological views, he was disfellowshipped in April, 1983.

While attending the SDA Church, Koresh learned of the Branch Davidians from an SDA friend. His initial association with the Mt. Carmel community was as a handyman at Mt. Carmel in 1981. He soon became a favorite of Lois Roden, then sixty-seven years old, and rumors soon began circulating that the two were lovers. The relationship served the interests of both parties as Koresh's status was significantly elevated and Lois Roden gained an ally in her struggle with her son. Koresh and George Roden competed for power, both claiming divine inspiration and revelations. Lois Roden attempted to resolve the power struggle in 1983 by naming Koresh her successor and inviting Branch Davidian adherents to come to Mt. Carmel to listen to his teachings and prophecies. The following year Koresh strengthened his powerbase by marrying fourteen-year-old Rachael Jones. Her father, Perry Jones, was one of the most senior and respected members of the Davidian community, having been one of the earliest and most loyal followers of Benjamin and Lois Roden. Over the next five years the couple gave birth to a son, Cyrus, and a daughter, Star.

The struggle for power with George Roden was not over, however. Koresh suffered a setback when in 1985 George Roden was able to organize and win an election for the presidency of the Branch Davidians. Roden ousted Koresh and his followers at gunpoint from Mt. Carmel and renamed the community Rodenville. Koresh and his few dozen followers, about half of whom were children, succeeded in obtaining property in nearby Palestine, eking out a precarious existence in crude shelters that they constructed. Koresh suffered a further setback when his ally Lois Roden died in 1986. Nevertheless, despite his victories, George Roden's position became increasingly desperate on several fronts. Only two or three dozen residents remained at Mt. Carmel, and Koresh now enjoyed the loyalty of most of the community. The Branch Davidians' financial position also had deteriorated to the point that they were unable to pay school and county property taxes. Finally, the 1979 injunction Lois Roden had obtained against George prior to her death remained in effect, and so the Koresh faction was in a position to have George Roden found in contempt of court and to displace him once again from Mt. Carmel.

In the end, George Roden largely caused his own downfall. He countered judicial actions against Koresh by filing a series of legal motions and suits filled with such vituperation and profanity that the justices ultimately issued contempt citations against him. Further, in a desperate effort to assert spiritual supremacy over Koresh, Roden proposed a spiritual contest to raise from the dead Anna Hughes, who had died twenty years earlier at Mt. Carmel. Koresh declined the challenge and instead, on November 3, 1987, he and a group of followers infiltrated the Mt. Carmel center seeking a photograph of Hughes's remains that would serve as evidence to prosecute Roden. A gun battle ensued between Roden and the Koresh group in which Roden was slightly wounded. In the subsequent legal proceedings, attempted murder charges against Koresh and his followers were dismissed. Roden, however, was imprisoned for violating earlier restraining orders and for continuing to file profanity-filled legal suits and motions. The day after Roden's incarceration, Koresh and his followers reoccupied Mt. Carmel, and shortly thereafter he convinced a well-to-do Branch Davidian family to pay the back taxes on the property.

BRANCH DAVIDIAN THEOLOGY

Branch Davidian doctrines closely reflected the groups's SDA heritage. The Branch Davidians retained a biblical base for teachings, but the Bible was supplemented, and in certain respects supplanted, by revelations of the living prophet. They regarded themselves as the remnant church, which would operate as a bridge between the old and new orders. They expected the imminent return of Christ and the inauguration of the millennium. They observed a Saturday sabbath. They proscribed meat, alcohol, caffeine, and tobacco. They avoided worldliness, defined as consisting of such things as ostentatious dress and grooming, birthday celebrations, and television viewing.[7] And they followed Koresh as his authority was consolidated and new doctrines were enunciated.

Koresh—heretofore Howell—symbolized his spiritual status by legally changing his name to David Koresh in 1990. "Koresh" is the Hebrew for "Cyrus," the Persian king who defeated the Babylonians five hundred years before the birth of Jesus. In biblical language, Koresh is *a* (as opposed to *the*) messiah, one

appointed to carry out a special mission for God. By taking the first name David, Koresh asserted that he was spiritually descended from the biblical King David, the ancestor of the new messiah. David Koresh, then, was a messianic figure carrying out a divinely commissioned errand.

Koresh taught that his messianic role was crucial to human salvation because Christ had died only for those who lived prior to his crucifixion; Koresh's mission was necessary to permit the salvation of all subsequent generations. Further, in contrast to Christ, who was sinless and therefore embodied an impossible standard for inherently sinful humans to achieve, Koresh was a "sinful messiah." By personally experiencing sin like all other humans, Koresh asserted, he could judge sinners more fairly. Koresh taught that human sinfulness does not prevent humans from attaining salvation; there was another route to salvation that involved following him as he carried out the opening of the Seven Seals.[8] Koresh believed that it was his special mission to open the Seven Seals, cryptically described in the New Testament book of Revelation, an action believed to be the prelude to the end of the world (which Branch Davidians referred to as the downfall of Babylon). His disciples regarded themselves as the "wavesheaf," God's faithful, courageous followers who are the elite that will ascend to heaven prior to the 144,000 exemplary souls selected to reign with the Messiah during the millennium.[9]

According to Koresh, the world had already entered the period of tribulation that was to precede the final cleansing of the earth. Following this process, the earth would be transformed into an eternal, divinely ruled abode for humankind. In his early prophecy, Koresh instructed his disciples that the Branch Davidians would migrate to Israel where they would begin converting the Jews; this would trigger international tumult and a war that would lead to an invasion by the American army. These events would signal the beginning of Armageddon, and Koresh would be the cleansing angel who would prepare the earth to receive the New Jerusalem. Koresh later informed his followers that

Armageddon would begin in the United States with an attack on the Branch Davidians.[10] In fact, Koresh renamed the Mt. Carmel community "Ranch Apocalypse" in 1992.

It is in regard to his role as a messianic figure who would create a new beginning for humanity that the controversial "New Light" doctrine that Koresh first enunciated in 1989 must be understood. Drawing on the book of Revelation, Koresh asserted that in his role as a messiah he became the perfect mate of all the female adherents. Central to his messianic mission, Koresh taught, was the creation of a new lineage of God's children from his own seed. The children created through these unions would erect the House of David and ultimately rule the world. The implication of the New Light doctrine was that all of the female Branch Davidians potentially became spiritual wives to Koresh. Male adherents would also be united with their perfect mates, but in heaven. In fact, the future mates of male members were already part of them physically, just as Eve was physically a part of Adam before her creation. It was therefore the duty of male adherents to await the bestowal of their perfect mates in heaven.[11] This doctrine had the effect of annulling all marriages, at least with respect to spousal sexual exclusivity.

RECRUITMENT AND MEMBERSHIP

The ranks of the Branch Davidians had been seriously depleted by the ongoing conflicts within the group since 1960, and so Koresh launched several recruitment campaigns to rebuild the membership base. Beginning in 1985, the group recruited both nationally and internationally, travelling to Hawaii, Canada, England, Israel, and Australia. These campaigns almost exclusively targeted current or former Seventh-Day Adventists, and those who converted were often disfellowshipped by the SDA. The Branch Davidians were willing to challenge SDA theology, even disrupting church services to gain a hearing for their message. While there were some efforts at more general street recruiting, not surprisingly, these endeavors were unsuccessful. These campaigns yielded several dozen converts,

and created an international, interracial community at Mt. Carmel.[12]

One significant contrast between the Koreshian and previous eras was that Koresh apparently was able to attract young adults to the group due to his own youthful, countercultural demeanor and his musical and automotive interests. These young adults most often were members of families the Branch Davidians recruited from SDA ranks. However, their conversions appear to have been individual rather than familial. During one of his Australian trips, for instance, Koresh converted Bruce and Lisa Gent and also their son and daughter, Peter and Nicole. Lisa Gent recalls that "Peter pretty well got impressed right away. . . . The change in Peter seemed almost miraculous. He quit smoking, drinking and doing drugs . . . "[13] Converts point to Koresh's biblical knowledge more than any other single factor in explaining their own attraction to the Branch Davidians. For example, Paul Fatta, who ran the Davidians' weapons business, traced his commitment to Koresh to the latter's biblical prowess: "I believe David is the Messiah. . . . He has shown me over and over that he knows the book, and he presented Scriptures showing how the last day's events would happen."[14]

These various recruitment campaigns expanded the number of Branch Davidians living at or around Mt. Carmel to around one hundred adherents. By 1993 the sex ratio of adults was relatively evenly balanced between males and females. More than one-third of the population was composed of children, which is not surprising given the concentration of the adult population in the twenty- to forty-five-year-old age range. It was a multiracial and multinational community, reflecting the diversity in the SDA church, the primary target of Branch Davidian evangelizing. Blacks, Mexicans, and Asians constituted about half of the Branch Davidian community. Although Americans were the largest nationality, there was a sizeable contingent from the United Kingdom and smaller groups from Australia/New Zealand, Canada, Jamaica, and the Philippines.

ORGANIZATION AND LEADERSHIP

During the Roden era, the property at Mt. Carmel had fallen into considerable disrepair. Koresh organized a major clean-up campaign and a construction project that considerably improved the quality of life and expanded living quarters. Some of the men held paying jobs in the local manufacturing plants, and several of the women worked as nurses in local hospitals. On a regular basis, members who worked outside the community contributed their wages, and older members turned over their food stamps and Social Security checks. Relatively well-to-do members gave substantial sums of money, and sometimes property, to the group. Members attempted to be as self-sufficient as possible, growing a considerable portion of their own food and even making some of their own clothing. The community also operated an automobile repair/renovation enterprise, Mag Bag, through which Koresh purchased more than a dozen high performance cars that were restored for sale in California.[15] Through the weapons business, which was primarily operated by Paul Fatta, Davidians purchased gun and hunting-related products by mail and sold them at gun shows.[16] As Koresh began to prepare for an apocalypse that he increasingly concluded would occur in America rather than Israel, the group began adopting a survivalist outlook, stockpiling large amounts of food, weapons, ammunition, and fuel.

Daily life at Mt. Carmel became much more communal in nature during the Koresh era than it had been earlier, and members lived relatively disciplined lives. On an average day members rose around 6:00 A.M. and then congregated in the communal dining room for breakfast. During the day men and women devoted their energy to community-building, occupational, and childrearing activities necessary to sustain the community. At some times children were educated in local schools; at others they were home-schooled within the community. Following dinner there were regular evening Bible study periods that sometimes lasted long into the night, and morning and afternoon study sessions might be held as well. Indeed, portraits of daily life by Branch Davidians who lived at Mt. Carmel during the Koresh era suggest that devotional activity was at the center of community life. Apostate Branch Davidian Marc Breault recalls that "We lived, ate, and breathed the Bible. . . . It was the whole center of our being. We would have these long studies."[17] The religious zeal of Mt. Carmel was probably critical to its vitality, for the communal, quasi–self-sufficient lifestyle was rigorous indeed. Despite major improvements in the community's infrastructure and economic base, life at Mt. Carmel remained arduous in a number of respects. Even the new buildings lacked central heating, air conditioning, and most indoor plumbing; as a result, members were forced to pump water from a well on the grounds and remove waste from the buildings on a daily basis.

The single most significant restructuring of the Davidian community during the Koresh era occurred in conjunction with his New Light doctrine. About three years after marrying Rachel Jones in 1984, Koresh began taking "spiritual wives" from among the young, unmarried women in the group. It appears that in most cases Koresh received the blessing of the parents either before or after the relationship commenced. For example, Koresh received permission from Australian Branch Davidians Bruce and Lisa Gent to begin a sexual relationship with their nineteen-year-old daughter, Nicole. Bruce Gent acknowledges that "At that point in time, yes I was very influenced. . . . Nicole had spent four days with him being convinced of the message. It wasn't for me to say yes or no . . . she was going to have children for the Lord."[18] Koresh later expanded these relationships to include the wives of male Branch Davidian adherents. Koresh requested permission to initiate sexual relations with Lisa Gent, and Bruce and Lisa Gent both assented after considerable deliberation. Although he was troubled, Bruce Gent asserts that he gave his wife to Koresh because of "what they were going to accomplish in the kingdom."[19] Even where Koresh did generally gain the approval of family members, agreement likely followed a period of considerable ambivalence and soul-searching. Koresh also obviously did

pressure some individuals to comply with
his doctrine, and sometimes was met with
overt resistance. Marc Breault started con-
templating defection in 1989 when he began to fear that Koresh was going to claim
as a spiritual wife his young Australian
bride, Elizabeth Baranyai, who had decided
that she could not comply. Both apparently finally concluded that their resistance
would make it impossible for them to remain in the group on acceptable terms.

Koresh's spiritual status within the
Davidian community rose rapidly. His
charismatic authority rested primarily on
his ability to produce converts and compelling spiritual revelations. As a result of
the conversion campaigns, a substantial
proportion of the Mt. Carmel residents were
recent converts who looked to Koresh as
their personal spiritual leader. The leader-
follower relationship was further strengthened as new converts took up residence at
Mt. Carmel and the community moved
toward communal organization. Perhaps
most importantly for his ongoing charismatic authority, Koresh led daily Bible studies during which he unlocked spiritual
mysteries for his followers, creating a compelling sense that the group was in the
midst of revelatory activities which would
culminate in end-time events. This rapid
status escalation yielded an increasingly
asymmetrical power relationship, with
Koresh claiming ever-greater spiritual authority and his disciples owing him ever-
greater allegiance.

Continuities in the Davidian Tradition

Surprisingly little is known about the
Branch Davidians, considering how much
national attention they attracted during
their confrontation with federal law enforcement agencies. Contrary to popular
press accounts, which presented beliefs
and practices out of context, however,
there is considerable continuity in the
group's history. Much of the theology and
organization can be traced directly to the
group's Adventist roots. Throughout
Davidian history the adherents maintained separation from the larger society
and lived an intensely devotional lifestyle.
During each period there also was a pattern of strong, centralized leadership. At
the same time, considerable instability is
also evident in Davidian history. The
Davidians experienced repeated succession
conflicts and never achieved a large full-
time membership base. Further, they never
developed a viable economic base. The
Branch Davidians seemed to be moving
in a new direction under David Koresh.
He was moving the group toward communal organization, assuming greater
charismatic authority, and scripting the
creation of the Kingdom of God (by opening the Seven Seals and beginning a new
spiritual lineage).[20] It will never be known
where this path might have led the Branch
Davidians, for the confrontation with federal authorities sealed their fate in an
apocalypse of human rather than divine
origin.

The 1993 conflagration at Ranch
Apocalypse received saturation media
coverage, and does not need a detailed
recounting here. To oversimplify a deeply
complex series of events, accusations of
misbehavior on the part of Koresh and
some other residents of the Branch
Davidian headquarters began to circulate among anticult activists and others.
The accusations were not unlike those frequently levied against many unconventional religions by their opponents, in this
case most frequently alleging child abuse
and possession of firearms. Local authorities investigated the child abuse allegations and found them groundless, but the
federal Bureau of Alcohol, Tobacco, and
Firearms (AFT) of the Department of the
Treasury eventually obtained search and
arrest warrants on weapons charges. Approaching the complex with a force of
seventy-six agents on February 28, 1993,
the ATF raid quickly turned into a
shootout between its agents and the
Branch Davidians, who had learned of
the raid in advance and who apparently
regarded the attack as part of a larger,
divinely mandated millennial scenario.
The resulting standoff turned into a fifty-
one-day siege that ended on April 19,

when federal agents launched a new attack on the Davidian complex using military equipment to batter holes in the buildings through which noxious gas was injected in an attempt to force the Davidians outside. A fire was somehow ignited, and over eighty Branch Davidians perished in the ensuing conflagration. Some of the surviving members of the group were tried for the murder of the four federal agents who were shot in the original raid; they were found innocent of the most serious charges.

The surviving Branch Davidians for the most part continue to adhere to their millennial faith, although they have not at this writing regrouped into a single organization. Other wings of the greater Davidian movement, resulting from some of the schisms discussed above, continue their work as well. The largest of them, the Davidian Seventh-Day Adventist Association, was established in the wake of Florence Houteff's failed prophecy of 1959 and was never related to the leadership of David Koresh. Headquartered near Exeter, Missouri, these Davidians, who number several thousand in some twenty-five countries, continue to espouse a fairly standard Seventh-Day Adventist point of view.

Notes

1. For a discussion of this early history, see Jonathan Butler, "From Millerism to Seventh-Day Adventism: Boundlessness to Consolidation," *Church History* 55 (1986): 50–64; Ruth Doan, *The Miller Heresy, Millennialism, and American Culture* (Philadelphia: Temple University Press, 1987); Michael Pearson, *Millennial Dreams and Moral Dilemmas* (Cambridge: Cambridge University Press, 1990).

2. The best sources on the early history of Davidian groups are Brad Bailey and Bob Darden, *Mad Man in Waco: The Complete Story of the Davidian Cult, David Koresh, and the Waco Massacre* (Waco: WRS Publishing, 1993); Bill Pitts, "Davidians and Branch Davidians," in *Armageddon in Waco: Critical Perspectives on the Branch Davidian Conflict*, ed. Stuart Wright (Chicago: University of Chicago Press, 1994).

3. Pitts, "Davidians and Branch Davidians."

4. For a discussion of the political maneuvering for control of the group, see Bailey and Darden, *Mad Man in Waco*, 37.

5. Ibid., 60–61.

6. Ibid., 68–69.

7. Jordan Bonfante and Sally B. Donnelly, et al., "Cult of Death," *Time* (15 March 1993): 38.

8. James Tabor, "Apocalypse at Waco: Could the Tragedy Have Been Averted?" *Bible Review* (October 1993): 25–32.

9. Clifford Linedecker, *Massacre at Waco, Texas: The Shocking Story of Cult Leader David Koresh and the Branch Davidians* (New York: St. Martin's, 1993), 88.

10. Ibid., 151.

11. Mark England, Mark McCormick, and Darlene McCormick, "The Sinful Messiah: Parts 3–7," *Waco Tribune-Herald*, 1 March 1993, A8.

12. Marc Breault and Martin King, *Inside the Cult* (New York: Signet, 1993), 122.

13. Bret Tate, "Officials Dig Up Cultist's Body," *Waco Tribune-Herald*, 5 May 1993, 1A, 4A.

14. Michael de Courcy Hinds, "Cult Member Gives Details of Life Inside Waco Compound," *Fort Worth Star-Telegram*, 12 March 1993, A6.

15. James Pinkerton, "Sect's Money Was Welcome, Source Unclear," *Fort Worth Star-Telegram*, 7 March 1993, A23.

16. Bob Mahlburg, "Cult Member Sold Items at Gun Shows, Dealers Say," *Fort Worth Star-Telegram*, 14 March 1993, A17.

17. England, McCormick, and McCormick, "The Sinful Messiah," 9A.

18. Ibid., 5A; Breault and King, *Inside the Cult*, 118–19.

19. England, McCormick, and McCormick, "The Sinful Messiah," 9A.

20. For a discussion of the various forms of organization in Davidian groups through their histories, see David Bromley and Edward Silver, "The Davidian Tradition: From Patronal Religious Clan to Transformative Religious Movement," *Armageddon in Waco*.

Suggestions for Further Reading

Lewis, James, ed. *From the Ashes: Making Sense of Waco.* Lanham, Maryland: Rowman and Littlefield, 1994.

Wright, Stuart, ed. *Armageddon in Waco: Critical Perspectives on the Branch Davidian Conflict.* Chicago: University of Chicago Press, 1994.

Part III
Religions from Asia

Asian religions began to be noticed in the United States in the nineteenth century, becoming organized societies devoted to versions of Indian religion soon after the visit to the United States of Swami Vivekananda in 1893. Chinese and other Asian immigrants had practiced Buddhism and other Eastern religions even earlier, although their impact hardly reached beyond their ethnic groups. Both Hinduism and Buddhism grew slowly throughout the twentieth century, boosted in the latter case by American-Japanese contacts just after World War II.

The much larger impact of Eastern religious traditions came during and after the 1960s, with the arrival of many new Eastern teachers at a time of cultural upheaval, when many Americans were seeking alternatives to their inherited cultural traditions. Soon the American seeker had dozens of Asian options from which to choose.

Most of the religions presented in these chapters are movements within Hinduism or Buddhism, the foundational traditions behind the majority of the Asian-based religions now active in the United States. Their stories begin with the above-mentioned visit by Swami Vivekananda in 1893 and his subsequent founding of the Vedanta movement. He was followed to the United States in 1920 by Paramahansa Yogananda who, like Vivekananda, had been influenced by the important nineteenth-century Indian spiritual leader Ramakrishna Paramahansa. Yogananda founded the Self-Realization Fellowship, which has since become one of the largest Asian-derived religious movements in the United States. More Indian teachers arrived in the 1960s and thereafter, founding, among others, the groups discussed in the chapter by Gene Thursby. By far the largest movement, at least in numbers of persons who have participated at one time or another, is Transcendental Meditation, which claims to be not a religion at all but a scientific relaxation technique that improves one's health and overall life. Smaller but still influential groups with strong ongoing presences in the United States are the Himalayan Institute (founded by Swami Rama), Kripalu Yoga (Yogi Amrit Desai), Integral Yoga (Swami Satchidananda), and Siddha Yoga (founded by Swami Muktananda Paramahamsa and now led by Swami Chidvilasananda, known to her disciples as Gurumayi). A separate chapter here is devoted to the International Society for Krishna Consciousness, in membership probably no larger than most of the groups listed above but flamboyantly prominent—and controversial—in the United States since the late 1960s.

Buddhism made few inroads among nonimmigrant Americans until about a half-century ago, but since the 1940s it has grown considerably. The chapter on Buddhism that opens this section deals primarily with the three most prominent strains of Buddhism operating in the United States today: Zen, mainly from Japan and Korea and known for its austere simplicity;

Tibetan, which took root here only after the 1959 Chinese invasion of Tibet that scattered the spiritual teachers long resident there; and Nichiren Shoshu, a Japanese "new religion" that has spread its brand of Buddhism with enormous missionary zeal.

The final chapter in the section presents the only movement here not Buddhist or Hindu in origin, the Unification Church, which has roots in Korean Christianity but has been influenced also by indigenous Korean religious traditions and even touches of Taoism and Confucianism. The Unificationists, who had dis-patched missionaries to the United Kingdom by 1954 and the United States by 1959, share with the Hare Krishnas the dubious honor of being widely and loudly denounced by anticultists, although in recent years, they have had some success in building bridges to other organizations and movements, especially conservative political groups.

Hundreds of distinct movements of Asian origin are now active in the United States. These chapters provide only a small sampling of some of the more prominent ones.

16

BUDDHISM IN AMERICA: THE DHARMA IN THE LAND OF THE RED MAN

Jane Hurst

Guru Padmasambhava, the missionary who converted Tibet to Buddhism in the seventh century, predicted that the spread of this way of life would some day move beyond Asia. He said:

> When the iron bird flies, and horses run on wheels,
> The Tibetan people will be scattered like ants across the World,
> And the Dharma will come to the land of the Red Man.[1]

From the Buddhist point of view, this prophecy has come to pass. The Dharma (teaching of the Buddha) can be found throughout the United States, from California and New York to New Mexico, Ohio, Georgia, Arkansas, Texas, Maryland, Virginia, Oregon, Colorado and more. In America now there are representatives of all the major streams of Buddhist thought and practice, including American-born practitioners of Buddhism. Within an hour's drive of Washington, D.C., there are Buddhist temples and monks to staff them from Thailand, Vietnam, Japan, Korea, Sri Lanka, and Tibet. To complete the circle, in Bristol, Vermont, is the Sunray Meditation Society, founded by a Native American elder Dhyani Ywahoo, which combines the wisdom teachings of the "Red Man" with those of Tibetan Buddhism.

How has Buddhism come to be so widespread in America? In actual numbers, its membership is small and statistics are unreliable. Very few groups include more than a few hundred members and many have far fewer than that. One study estimates that there are "a million people in America who call themselves Buddhists . . . ,"[2] with the vast majority most likely of Asian Buddhist heritage.[3] The best estimate of this researcher, based on contact with various Buddhist groups, is fifty- to one-hundred thousand non-Asian, American-born converts now practicing Buddhism, with an uncertain number of Asian Americans and recent Asian immigrants still practicing the Buddhism of their ancestors.

Buddhism is taught differently depending on the cultural context in which it is found. As a global religion, like Christianity and Islam, this has meant a great deal of regional variation resulting in movements within Buddhism since its founding during the life of Siddartha Gautama, the Buddha (563–483 B.C.E.). *Theravada,* the Path of the Elders, has preserved the teachings of the Buddha in the original Pali texts. It is all but gone from India, where it began, but is now to be found in Sri Lanka and Southeast Asia. *Mahayana* Buddhism, the Greater Vehicle, spread to East Asia, especially China, Korea, and Japan. Its scriptures, such as the Lotus Sutra, the Perfection of Wisdom Sutra, and the Pure Land sutras, were recorded in Sanskrit. It includes the Zen and Nichiren schools. The third major movement is *Vajrayana,* the Diamond Vehicle, also known as Tantric Buddhism. Tibetan and Mongolian Buddhism are Vajrayana Buddhism.

In spite of many historical and cultural differences among these Buddhist movements, there is a central core of teaching on which all are agreed. When he sought enlightenment, Gautama the Buddha was searching for the meaning of suffering and a cure for it. In his experience of Enlightenment, he discovered the Four Noble Truths, which are the basis of all forms of Buddhism. First, Buddha discovered that life involves suffering *(Dukkha).* There is no human being born who does not experience some suffering in life. Second, suffering is caused by desire. Attachment to experience and even to life itself means that we are never fully free of wanting what we do not have. Nothing is ever enough. Life is impermanent, and in our wanting it to be otherwise, we suffer. Third, then, the cure for suffering is to give up desire and embrace impermanence. When one is free from wanting, one is free to live without attachment and without suffering. Fourth, the Eightfold Path can lead us from suffering to Enlightenment. It involves right view, right thought, right speech, right action, right livelihood, right effort, right mindfulness, and right concentration (meditation).

The various movements and schools of Buddhism, while agreeing on the central teaching of the Four Noble Truths, have emphasized different aspects of the teachings. Some schools focus on certain sutras (writings) to the exclusion of others. Meditative practices are by no means uniform. In addition, the methods used to experience Enlightenment, the ending of suffering, vary widely from group to group. All emphasize some form of chanting the sutras and/or meditation, but these practices look, sound, and even smell quite different from temple to temple. What is of interest to us here is that these differences within Buddhism have all been brought with Buddhist teachers here to North America. Just as the differences within Christianity mean that a Georgia Baptist and a New England Episcopalian would feel equally alien in each other's milieu,

so do differences within Buddhism separate one community from another.

Buddhism has come to America in three different ways: through immigration of Buddhists, as an influence on intellectual life, and as a missionary movement. First, Buddhism arrived with immigrants from China and Japan in the nineteenth century, and then from other Buddhist countries in the twentieth century. Beginning with the California Gold Rush in 1849, thousands of Chinese and Japanese people settled in the western part of the United States bringing a variety of Asian religions, including Buddhism, with them. In this form Buddhism did not proselytize, but it stayed within immigrant communities which built temples and supported monks to staff them. World War II and America's contact with Japan during the Marshall Plan and later during the Korean War brought Japanese Buddhism via American soldiers, many of whom had learned Japanese and had developed an interest in Asian culture, and their Japanese brides. The Vietnam War and its aftermath brought another era of contact with some parallels to World War II. In addition, many thousands of refugees from Southeast Asia came to the United States after 1975, especially to the West Coast and the Washington, D.C., area, bringing several unique forms of Buddhism with them.

Second, Buddhism has travelled via its intellectual influence on American thinkers.[4] The New England Transcendentalists Ralph Waldo Emerson and Henry David Thoreau read what few Buddhist texts were available to them in the 1840s in their search for Truth. The Theosophists H. P. Blavatsky and New Yorker Colonel Henry Steel Olcott not only read Buddhist texts, they travelled to the East where they formed a chapter of the Theosophical Society in India and fostered a revival of Buddhism in Sri Lanka. Their dedication to the "wisdom of the East" was total, and despite the unusual method of learning from the Ascended (i.e. deceased) Masters as their teachers, Blavatsky's Buddhist-influenced book *The Secret Doctrine* remains influential as a spiritual text and in print after more than a century.

The World Parliament of Religions held in 1893 in conjunction with the Chicago World's Fair invited representatives of the major religious traditions to meet together in that forum. At that time, Soyen Shaku, a Japanese Rinzai Zen monk, Anagarika Dharmapala, a Sri Lankan monk who had studied with Colonel Olcott, and monks from several Japanese sects including Nichiren spoke for Buddhism. Although the motives of the organizers were perhaps less to see the Light common to all religions than to prove that in comparison with others, Christianity held the one Truth, Buddhism was for the first time recognized as a legitimate tradition worthy of discussion and study in America.

Buddhism has had an impact on two other intellectual movements in America. Psychotherapy has been influenced by Buddhism initially through the works of Carl Jung, who understood Zen and psychotherapy as sharing the goal of ending human suffering, and through the Jungian movement in this country. Buddhism has continued to influence other schools of therapeutic thought such as Transpersonal Psychology. In the 1950s, the beat poets adopted Zen along with jazz and existentialism, which in turn had a strong influence on the counterculture of the sixties.

Third, Buddhism has arrived here as a missionary movement led by Buddhist monks who desired to bring the eternal Truth to a culture badly in need of it. They have missionized Americans of European, African, and Asian ancestry. They have built centers and temples throughout the United States. The first Buddhist missionaries were two Japanese Pure Land priests who established the Buddhist Mission of North America in San Francisco in 1899, renamed the Buddhist Churches of America in 1942. Their purpose was to convert Japanese immigrants who had stopped practicing their religion back to Buddhism.[5]

Buddhism was one of the first Asian "products" imported to America after World War II. In a sense it is a forerunner of the opening up of global economic and cultural interconnectedness in the late twentieth century. To understand the Buddhists' motivation in coming here, it is useful to see from the Buddhist perspective that America is a land of intense suffering due to our materialistic and social attachments (the Second Noble Truth). The social ills that beset our prosperous nation—ill health, poverty, inadequate parenting, homelessness, violence, crime, addiction—are from the Buddhist point of view the logical result of a culture focused on wanting and having. If we could but follow the Eightfold Path we would be able to put an end to this suffering.

We will now consider the three most influential Buddhist movements in America today: Japanese Zen, the Japanese Nichiren Shoshu and Soka Gakkai movement, and Tibetan Buddhism. These are important for their intellectual influence and in the number and quality of converts each has attracted. Springing from a common source, each has interpreted the teachings of the Buddha in a unique way.

Zen

Zen Buddhism is one of the first successful Japanese exports to America in the twentieth century. From the first two Rinzai centers founded by Nyogen Senzaki in California in 1928 and 1929, today Zen centers can be found across the country. In addition, the impact of Zen ideas on poetry, art, and intellectual life in general has been profound.

At about the same time that Zen teachers appeared on the West Coast, the Buddhist Society of America was founded by Shigetsu Sasaki, known as Sokei-an, in New York City. Sokei-an was part of the Rinzai school as well, and the center was renamed the First Zen Institute of America in 1945. It was run by his widow Ruth Fuller Sasaki after his death and then later by Mary Farkas. The existence of a Zen center in New York City was crucial because it was here that poets Allen Ginsberg and Gary Snyder and other members of their literary circle could come to explore their interest in Buddhism.

Zen teaches that through meditation, sitting *zazen,* one can cut through the illusion of reality and the illusion of the ego to the truth that underlies all things. Through the process of clearing the mind, all illusion falls away and one is left with direct experience of reality. In this way, one is freed to take actionless action, to live without attachment, to experience life purely in the now. This is the right meditation mentioned in the Fourth Noble Truth. It can result in the experience of *satori,* sudden Enlightenment, which in turn leads to that state of *nirvana* in which human suffering is no longer experienced.

The characteristics of Zen that appealed to the beat poets and writers are simple, and yet complex. Zen offered a way to liberation, a freedom from everyday suffering, and a sense of the paradoxical and absurd that made sense to people questioning the very foundations of the Western mind. However, Zen also offered a difficult spiritual practice requiring dedication and discipline of its practitioners and so it offered an anchor to keep sheer anarchy at bay. Zen offered freedom for the mind and structure for the body. For the beats, it ripped established concepts of reality wide open.

This exciting intellectual atmosphere surrounding Zen was encouraged by the prolific writings of two persons in particular. Alan Watts, an Englishman who was a convert to Buddhism and later an Episcopal priest (a career which lasted from 1944 to 1950), wrote several books on Zen, relating it to art, psychotherapy, and the life of the mind. Watts published *The Way of Zen,* the first Buddhist bestseller, in 1957; it made Zen accessible to many young people, especially college students. He also had success as a lecturer. Daisetz T. Suzuki, a Rinzai Zen monk who knew English and had interpreted for Soyen Shaku at the World Parliament of Religions, wrote about Zen for Western audiences. He was fascinated by the intellectual juxtapositions of Zen and psychoanalysis, Zen and mysticism, and Zen and Christianity. No student of Zen in the 1960s would have been without Watts' *The Way of Zen* or Suzuki's *An Introduction to Zen Buddhism* and *Essays in Zen Buddhism* on his or her bookshelf.

Students of Zen in the 1960s could not only read about Zen, they could practice it. In the 1950s, Soyu Matsuoka Roshi founded the Chicago Buddhist Temple of Soto Zen. The San Francisco Zen Center was founded by Shunryu Suzuki Roshi, a Soto Zen master, in 1961. This center was and continues to be very successful with a program of lectures, classes, and retreats. Its facilities include the breathtaking Tassajara Zen Mountain Center in northern California. In 1968 Eido Tai Shimano opened the New York Zendo Shoboji Rinzai Zen center. In 1969 Shasta Abbey was founded at Mt. Shasta, California, by Jiyu Kennett Roshi, a Soto Zen teacher.[6]

Today there are several other major Zen centers including the Zen Center of Los Angeles under the direction of Zen Master Taizan Maezumi Roshi, who is trained in the Soto and Rinzai lineages; the Maria Kannon Zen Center of Dallas, Texas, under the direction of Ruben Habito; the Kwan Um School of Chogye Zen in Cumberland, Rhode Island, under the direction of Zen Master Seung Sahn who is Korean; the Diamond Sangha in Honolulu; and Zen Mountain Monastery in Mt. Tremper, New York, under the direction of John Daido Loori, which combines the teachings of Chinese and Japanese Zen.

None of these schools or centers are very large; none has more than a few hundred or at most a few thousand members. Yet these are vital Zen Buddhist communities that continue to attract those interested in sitting *zazen* and seeking release from suffering. There have been controversies surrounding the ethics of several of these Zen centers. Scandals involving sexual improprieties have emerged from the Zen Studies Center of New York, the San Francisco Zen Center, the Zen Center of Los Angeles, and the Kwan Um Zen School. These improprieties revolve around supposedly celibate priests' being accused of seducing women students. Each of these communities has dealt with these accusations and survived with renewed determination not to repeat the behavior which caused them. In the case of the San Francisco Zen Center, Richard Baker Roshi was

Nichiren Shoshu and Soka Gakkai

In 1960 Daisaku Ikeda, the president of the Nichiren Shoshu Buddhist organization Soka Gakkai, came to San Francisco. His purpose was clear: He wanted to bring his Japanese Buddhist practice to America and expected to convert one-third of the population. This missionary movement had the support of more than a million Soka Gakkai member families in Japan. Although Ikeda's original goal was not reached, either in America or in Japan, Soka Gakkai, as of 1993, probably had between 5 and 8.5 million member families in 115 countries throughout the world.[8]

Nichiren Shoshu Buddhism dates back to the thirteenth-century prophet Nichiren Daishonin. After his death, several sects of Nichiren Buddhism were established; Nichiren Shoshu is one of them. In broad Buddhist terms, it intends to eliminate suffering by aligning the believer with the sacred law of cause and effect. Its focus is on the Lotus Sutra alone. Soka Gakkai, a layman's organization dedicated to the practice and spread of Nichiren Shoshu Buddhism, was founded in 1937 by educator Tsunesaburo Makiguchi. It nearly died out during World War II but was revived by Josei Toda after the defeat that left Japan in need of a new structure of meaning and opened the way for the flowering of many new postwar religions. Soka Gakkai has been the largest of these and has had political influence through Komeito (Clean Government Party), which it founded but from which it is technically now separate.

Soka Gakkai, as a religious group, was able to attain a certain legitimacy through its relationship with the Nichiren Shoshu priesthood. The priests initiated all members in a *gojukai* ceremony during which they were each given a copy of a sacred scroll, the Gohonzon, upon which Nichiren Daishonin had inscribed a mandala with the words *Nam-myoho-renge-kyo*. The Gohonzon is the center of Nichiren Shoshu practice. Each day members chant sections of the Lotus Sutra, called *gongyo*, in a Japanese transliteration of the Chinese translation of the original Sanskrit work. They also chant *daimoku*, repetition of the phrase *Nam-myoho-renge-kyo*, which is literally means "devotion to the Lotus Sutra." Soka Gakkai members translate this phrase with an expanded interpretation: " . . . devotion to *(Nam)* the Mystic Law of the Universe *(Myoho)* creates the vital life-force which includes the simultaneous cause and effect *(Renge)* of putting human life into rhythm with the universe *(Kyo)*."[9] This is the central Buddhist teaching in the group, and the Lotus Sutra and the writings of Nichiren Daishonin make up the whole of the study materials used by members.

Nichiren Shoshu Sokagakkai of America, or NSA, as the group has called itself for most of its American incarnation, has enjoyed remarkable success. It is the largest of the Buddhist groups in America. The original group began as 300 or so members in the early 1960s, most of whom were the Japanese wives of American servicemen returning from the Japanese occupation or having been stationed in Japan during the Korean War. At the height of the movement in America in 1976, it claimed 500,000 members, which is incorrect. This number probably represents the number of people who were at one time initiated in a *gojukai* ceremony and who at one time chanted to the Gohonzon. As of 1992, the group claimed 150,000 members. From a study of community photographs, subscriptions to the group's newspaper *The World Tribune*, and attendance at national conventions, an educated guess would put current membership near 50,000 members.

The Soka Gakkai in America have thus had great success in attracting members initially but, like nearly all alternative religions, have had great difficulty keeping them in the group. Their method of recruiting members is called *shakubuku*. In Japanese this literally means "break and subdue," and this has been one of the more controversial features of the movement. In the late 1960s and early 1970s, *shakubuku* was a high-pressure sales pitch to prospective members involving a great deal of personal persuasion for people to join. Because Soka Gakkai does not expect members to break all previous social and familial ties, nor does it expect a lifestyle change of any kind, the charge of brainwashing has only been made by a few disillusioned former members. However, its group energy was always very intense, and could be perceived as quite obnoxious to members' family and friends who were not interested in religious conversion. Today, *shakubuku* is understood as a quite different concept. Members expect that the example of their changed lives will attract new members. There are no more *shakubuku* meetings or *shakubuku* campaigns with numerical goals for recruiting new members.

Another change in Soka Gakkai thinking has been a different emphasis on the goal of Buddhist practice. In the early intense *shakubuku* days, prospective members were told that they could chant *Nammyoho-renge-kyo* and get whatever they wanted by aligning themselves with the cause-effect energy of the universe. Members would join and chant for cars, girlfriends, jobs, and a variety of material goals. This was extremely off-putting to many people, although the group always stressed that it was a superficial practice and that a deeper level would follow. Now, the emphasis on materialism is gone. This may be the function of an aging membership, for whom the acquisition of the goods of American life is not the same object of preoccupation as it is for people in their early twenties. It is also a response to criticism from within and without. Today, the deeper practice of changing your life-condition through chanting is what is talked about in discussion meetings. Long term members all report that this is the greatest benefit they have received from chanting to the Gohonzon.

The concept of *kosen-rufu* has likewise undergone a transition. It was originally taught as the world peace that would result when at least one-third of the world's population had converted to Nichiren Shoshu Buddhism. By knowing true religion, "Each country can achieve prosperity without any harm to, or discord with any other country."[10] For those who still remembered the imperialistic designs of Japan during World War II, this was perceived as a very threatening statement. Although Soka Gakkai founder Makiguchi had opposed the war and died in prison because of it, Americans were suspicious of the motives of this group. As time has passed, the group's expectations of worldwide mass conversions have diminished, and the concept of *kosen-rufu* has been modified to mean "Promotion of peace, culture, and education through Buddhism." International efforts for world peace, led by Soka Gakkai International President Daisaku Ikeda, have included antinuclear activism, United Nations–affiliated cultural programs promoting peace, and even a call for peace just as the 1991 Gulf War was breaking out.

The movement has gone through some rather dramatic changes as well. Phase I, from its founding in America to the late 1970s, was high energy, high pressure, and very involving for the members. As NSA, the group sponsored nightly meetings and yearly conventions, great extravaganzas involving parades and culture presentations with a cast of thousands. Much of the labor for these activities was donated by members. After the Jonestown mass suicide/murder in 1978, NSA was quite distressed by the possible dark side of mass movements. This coincided with organizational struggles in Japan. At this point, Phase II was initiated. Activities were scaled back. Conventions became regional meetings. Street *shakubuku,* soliciting new members off the street, was discontinued. The movement began to lose members in increasing numbers.

By the mid-1980s, an attempt was made to revive the energy and enthusiasm of Phase I. This enabled the membership to stabilize, but with a different mix than before. The group has become increasingly less Asian and white and increasingly older. Presently it is the only Buddhist group in America to attract African-American and

Hispanic members in any sizeable numbers. In some communities such as Washington, D.C., they are the majority of members. This is a big change from the days when the faces at NSA conventions, though always multicultural, were mostly those of white, middle-class, young people.

Soka Gakkai's American organization has always been under the leadership of the Japanese organization, and has probably been funded by it as well. The talent for organization which we have seen in Japanese business enterprises is certainly in part responsible for Soka Gakkai's success. In 1991 a major rift occurred in the group between the seven-hundred-year-old Nichiren Shoshu priesthood and the lay members of Soka Gakkai. The major causes of this split are disagreements over interpretations of Nichiren Daishonin's teachings, the authority and the power of the leadership of each branch of the movement, and certain financial issues. In November 1991 the Nichiren Shoshu priesthood excommunicated all of the millions of Soka Gakkai members. Soka Gakkai reorganized as Soka Gakkai International (SGI). In America the group is now called SGI-USA. The major impact of this split is that SGI cannot give Gohonzons to new members; this is a ritual performed by the priesthood only. Therefore they allow new members to join and to practice without the Gohonzon until such time as this split is resolved. Some priests have left the Nichiren Shoshu priesthood but have not yet begun to perform *gojukai* ceremonies for SGI members.

The six Nichiren Shoshu temples in America are controlled by the priesthood and have reorganized with their own layman's group, Hokkeko, associated with them. They probably have one thousand to three thousand members, but this is an educated guess and not an official statistic. This separation has been less traumatic to SGI-USA than to those associated with the temples. Those who have joined Hokkeko at the temples have often been disaffected former members of SGI and they carry a suspicion of outsiders that is palpable. One can expect that with time this will dissipate, and the temples will attract members in their own right. They have already begun to do so, although some

Hokkeko members have returned to SGI. The entire SGI organization has taken the official stance that they wish to open a dialogue with the priesthood and they expect a resolution of the current split to eventually occur.

For its own part, SGI-USA has once again reevaluated itself. It has shifted into the most democratic form of leadership in its thirty-year history, with a national advisory board and greater membership participation in decision making. Its fifty-six community centers still function as centers of SGI-USA activity. Soka Gakkai International–USA has moved from the enthusiastic energy of its initial founding to the more secure, middle-aged energy of an established group.

Tibetan Buddhism

Tibet, although for millennia a great trading nation in Asia with contacts throughout that continent, had extremely limited contact with Europe until the Chinese Communist invasion of Tibet in 1950. Karma (the law of cause and effect) works in strange ways. Were it not for that invasion, thousands of Tibetan refugees, including His Holiness the Dalai Lama in 1959, would not have fled their homeland to exile in India. Tibetan lamas (teachers) would not have learned English, studied in foreign universities, and felt the pull of America as missionary territory. But this is how it happened, and how Guru Padmasambhava's prophecy was fulfilled with the spread of the Dharma to the land of the Red Man.

Tibetan Buddhism is part of the Vajrayana school of Buddhism, though influenced by Theravada and Mahayana teachings as well. With its combined practices of meditation, visualization, chanting of mantras, and elaborate rituals, it is considered by some to be an occult form of Buddhism. Yet these methods allow practitioners to achieve deep spiritual states and a profound sense of release from suffering. Tibetan Buddhism satisfies the seeker who truly desires to experience something as a result of meditation. In addition, it teaches that the highest spiritual state is not just personal relief from suffering but to become a *boddhisattva* who serves others to relieve their suffering as well. Tibetan Buddhism teaches a kind of compassionate action that fulfills the ethically hungry heart.[11]

Tibetan Buddhism has attracted only a few thousand practitioners in America, and yet its influence has been profound for several reasons. First, it has attracted a well-educated and literate group of American believers, and so several excellent books from a Western point of view have been written about it. Second, Tibetans are a healthy-minded and positive lot. They are in general friendly and not at all defensive. They are approachable and open to dialogue with other religions. His Holiness the Dalai Lama has participated in many American seminars in dialogue with other religious traditions including Hinduism, Judaism, Christianity, Islam, and other forms of Buddhism. Third, the meditation centers and schools established in North America by Tibetan Buddhists have become centers of both scholarly and religious practice. A large publishing industry of scholarly texts on Tibetan Buddhism has grown up around these centers, including Shambhala Press, Station Hill Press, Wisdom Publications, Dhama Publishing, and divisions of many major publishers. Many centers have started presses to publish texts central to their own lineages.

One feature of Tibetan Buddhism imported to the United States, the tradition of the *tulku,* has been the source of rivalry between different schools. A *tulku* is a lama who dies and when he or she is reincarnated is recognized for who he or she was and then taught by his or her own (former) students. As a Tibetan Buddhist your religious Sangha (community) is therefore truly your family of several centuries' duration. The *tulku* tradition creates lineages of teachers and students stretching for centuries and to which its believers are fiercely loyal. The major sects are Nyingma, Kagyu (including Karma Kagyu and Drikung), Sakya, and Gelug. The competition that had existed in Tibet between these groups

was brought to the United States. At times the rivalry is put aside for common purpose: representatives of all the schools joined together to protest the conditions in Tibet in a march to the Chinese Embassy at the time of the Tienamen Square uprising. On the other hand, the rivalry can seem to be downright silly, as when on the Dalai Lama's visit to Washington, D.C., chairs were reserved for each of the five Tibetan Buddhist groups attending a special audience with His Holiness. Members were careful to sit in their own sections and were corrected when they did not.

America has been frequently visited by the two highest teachers in Tibetan Buddhism. His Holiness the Sixteenth Karmapa Rangjung Dorje (1923–1981) of the Karma Kagyu School first visited the United States in 1976. The Karmapa tradition is one of the most intellectually and spiritually important in Tibet, and the Sixteenth Karmapa's frequent visits to America and his support of the Vajradhatu movement and the Karma Triyana Dharma Center in Woodstock, New York, have had a great impact here. He died in America in 1981 in Zion, Illinois, leaving many followers. Ugyen Thinley, a Tibetan boy, has been recognized as the reincarnated Karmapa and was installed as the Seventeenth Karmapa in 1992.

His Holiness Tenzin Gyatso, the Fourteenth Dalai Lama, has also often visited America. The Dalai Lama is considered to be a "manifestation of Avalokiteshvara, or Chenrezig, Bodhisattva of Compassion, holder of the White Lotus . . . " He has said himself that he feels "spiritually connected both to the thirteen previous Dalai Lamas, to Chenrezig, and to the Buddha himself."[12] He first visited America in 1979 and has made many visits to lecture on Buddhism and lobby on behalf of the plight of the Tibetan people since that time. The Dalai Lama was in California at an interreligious conference called "Harmonia Mundi" when he was awarded the Nobel Peace Prize in 1989.

There are two large, established schools of Tibetan Buddhism in America today. The first is the Nyingma Institute of Berkeley, California, established by Tarthang Tulku in 1969 under the name Tibetan Nyingma Meditation Center. Tarthang Tulku is a Tibetan-born refugee who received education in India as well as in his home monastery. This center has served two constituencies: those who desired to become Buddhists as a full-time commitment and those who wished to learn enough about Tibetan Buddhism to apply its teachings to their own fields of study or professions. In the early days the former group was served by a traditional program of meditative practices and study of Tibetan texts and teachings. The latter group was served by a Human Development Training Program aimed at teaching the principles of awareness and compassion to professionals, especially in the field of psychology and therapy.[13] Today the Nyingma Institute still exists under the direction of Tarthang Tulku, who is no longer active as a teacher, with Barry Schrieber as its dean. It sponsors many programs in Tibetan Buddhism for a variety of audiences. It is one of the few schools to teach *Kumnye*, a meditative physical exercise system designed to bring meditation into the body.

The second and larger school is Naropa Institute in Boulder, Colorado. Naropa was founded in 1974 by Chogyam Trungpa, a Tibetan refugee to India who was trained as a lama and at Oxford University. Naropa is in the Karma Kagyu lineage and also has ties with the Nyingma lineage. It is a center for Buddhist studies a well as an accredited university offering graduate and undergraduate degrees. Naropa stands as the major intellectual center of Buddhism in the United States. It has invited teachers of several religious traditions to be part of its programs and has attracted writers, poets, psychologists, and artists as teachers and students.

Chogyam Trungpa was a charismatic and entertaining teacher who departed from what many expected in a spiritual teacher. He ate meat, drank alcohol, and somewhat openly carried on liaisons with female students. He also was able to attract a large and serious membership in his Vajradhatu movement. It currently has several regional meditation centers. Trungpa was a writer as well, and his

books *Meditation in Action* (1969) and *Cutting Through Spiritual Materialism* (1973) presented Tibetan Buddhism in an accessible form. During his lifetime, Trungpa Rinpoche, as he was known to his students, attracted the most followers of any lama in the West, before or since. At one time he had thousands of students. When he died in 1987 he left his movement in the hands of Regent Osel Tendzin (the former Thomas F. Rich from New Jersey).

It was under the leadership of Osel Tendzin that Vajradhatu faced its greatest challenge. In late 1988 it was revealed that the regent was infected with the AIDS virus and had been for nearly three years. Although he was sexually active within the community, he had "neither protected his sexual partners nor told them the truth."[14] One young man was infected by the regent and he in turn infected his girlfriend. The revelation of this tragedy caused a serious rift in the movement. Some members left; others stayed to reevaluate and revision the group. The organization survived this experience. Osel Tendzin died in 1991 while on retreat. The leadership of Vajradhatu passed to Osel Mukpo, the eldest son of Trungpa Rinpoche, who is a teacher and scholar in his own right.

There are many other Tibetan Buddhist teachers and centers in America today. These centers are usually small but have attracted energetic and dedicated memberships. There are probably between fifty and one hundred lamas in residence at these various centers and many others who periodically travel here from their exile in India. Most of these centers are headed by Tibetan-born lamas and are found throughout the country. One exception is the Kunzang Palyul Choling (KPC) founded in 1982 by Michael and Catharine Burroughs in Poolesville, Maryland. Catharine Burroughs was recognized in 1987 as a *tulku*, was enthroned as a reincarnated lama in the Nyingma lineage, and was renamed Jetsunma Akhon Lhamo. Michael Burroughs has left the center and Jetsunma has remarried, but KPC continues as a monastery and teaching facility. As at some of the centers discussed here, there have recently been problems at KPC around leadership, finances, and the faithfulness of the teaching to the Tibetan tradition from which it springs. It shares the potential to erupt into the controversy that other groups have already experienced.

Conclusion

We have seen that the major controversies surrounding Buddhism in America have touched on the age-old human weaknesses, sex and money. Sexual scandals have been the most obvious among the Zen and Tibetan Buddhist communities. Unethical behavior by Buddhist teachers has been a serious problem in America. Its causes are several. The teachers themselves are outside their own cultural contexts, with their own psychological limitations, and the restraints of the traditions they left behind are not present here. In Asia, men and women are usually separated in their meditative practice. In America, students meditate in mixed groups and are often themselves far from home and in an experimental stage of life.

In addition the students bring into the Buddhist community their own unresolved psychological issues, some spawned by dysfunctional families, and often project onto the teacher the "perfect parent" and thus deny that any less than perfect behavior is problematic. They excuse unethical personal behavior because they respect the spiritual authority of the teacher. And, finally, the American attitude toward sexuality and spirituality is confused and complex. Some students misunderstand spiritual power and believe that by sharing a sexual experience with the teacher they will also share spiritual experience and the transmission of spiritual power and understanding. All of these factors together have led to ethical abuses by many, though certainly not all, Buddhist teachers in America. The positive development in Buddhist America is that publicity surrounding these scandals has meant an end to denial for most groups and an insistence on ethical behavior by all members of the community, teachers and students alike.

A second area of controversy involves money. Most Buddhist centers in America are small, shoestring operations. Larger institutions are always prey to the temptation to empire building, and Buddhist centers have at times given in to this temptation. Money has been spent unwisely and leaders have not always been held accountable. There has been no focused research on this issue, only concerns expressed to the author from current and former members of several different Buddhist groups. This is an area that warrants observation and further research.

In this survey of Buddhism in America, we have touched on the major movements: Zen, Nichiren Shoshu/Soka Gakkai, and Tibetan Buddhism. Due to limitations of space, we can only mention several other important groups. The Buddhist Churches of America, with headquarters in San Francisco, is the oldest American Buddhist group (1899) and possibly the largest. Its members are primarily Oriental Americans. The Buddhist Vihara Society in Washington, D.C., was founded in 1966. It was the first Theravada center in America and is staffed by Sri Lankan monks. It serves Theravada Buddhists in the international community and a number of American-born converts. The Insight Meditation Center in Barre, Massachusetts, was founded in 1976 by Joel Goldstein and Jack Kornfeld. It teaches Vipassana meditation in the Theravada tradition. It is a highly respected center and continues to attract serious mediation students. The Tibetan Buddhist Learning Center (formerly the Lamaist Buddhist Monastery of America) trains monks in New Jersey. Two successful traditional lamas are Gyaltrul Rinpoche in Ashland, Oregon, and Chagdud Tulku in Junction City, California. There are many other groups across the country, from Cambridge to Boulder and Cleveland to Arizona.

One final person should be mentioned. The Venerable Thich Nhat Hanh is a Vietnamese Buddhist monk, a teacher of sound Mahayana practice. Although his retreat center is in Europe, he teaches frequently in America. Of special note is his work in healing the wounds of the Vietnam War for both sides of the conflict. For example, in 1990 he led a walking meditation retreat at the Vietnam War Memorial in Washington, D.C. He has inspired many as a teacher of peace. His books include *Peace Is Every Step: The Path of Mindfulness in Everyday Life* (1991) and *The Diamond That Cuts Through Illusion: Commentaries on the Prajnaparamita Diamond Sutra* (1992).

Guru Padmasambhava's prophecy has come true. The Buddha's teachings are now spread, in many different forms, throughout the land of the Red Man. One can certainly predict that most of the centers of practice and learning discussed here will continue to teach the Dharma. These also may become important cultural libraries in which ancient traditions are preserved

when political problems have threatened them in their native lands. In economic terms, Buddhism in America has produced many thriving businesses such as publishing, audio tape production, meditation supplies and t-shirt retailers, and travel. In addition, many meditation centers support relief programs for Buddhists throughout the world through such programs as the International Buddhist Children's Relief Program. In this era of global economic interconnectedness, it seems that global cultural interconnectedness is occurring as well. Buddhism, a twenty-five-hundred-year-old religious tradition, has become one of Asia's greatest intellectual exports. Certainly we can predict that Buddhism will be part of the global flow of ideas that will shape the next century and beyond.

Notes

1. *Annals of the Nyingma Lineage in America,* vol. 1, 4. Quoted in Charles S. Prebish, *American Buddhism* (North Scituate: Mass.: Duxbury Press, 1979), xx.

2. *The National Survey of Religious Identification,* conducted by the City College of New York Graduate Center between 1989 and 1990. Cited in Rick Fields, *How the Swans Came to the Lake,* 3rd ed. (Boston: Shambhala, 1992), 424.

3. J. Gordon Melton estimates that there are one to three million Buddhists in the United States as of 1990 from 109 "Buddhist centers and organizations" and six interfaith Buddhist organizations. J. Gordon Melton, *Religious Bodies in the United States: A Directory* (New York: Garland, 1992), 133. This would mean that there are ten to thirty thousand members in each of these groups. This has not been born out by direct observation. The *1992 World Almanac and Book of Facts,* citing the *1991 Yearbook of American and Canadian Churches,* says that in 1989 there were one hundred thousand Buddhists in the United States, and in 1990 there were nineteen thousand. No explanation is given for the variation in this number. *The World Almanac and Book of Facts* (New York: Pharos Books/World Almanac, 1992), 725.

4. Historical information for this section comes from Fields, *Swans,* chapters 4, 6, and 7.

5. Prebish, *Buddhism,* 58.

6. More information on some of these groups can be found in Prebish, *Buddhism,* and Helen Tworkov, *Zen in America: Profiles of Five Teachers* (San Francisco: North Point Press, 1989).

7. For more information see Katy Butler, "Encountering the Shadow in Buddhist America," *Common Boundary* (May/June 1990): 14–22.

8. For detailed information and further references for this section see Jane Hurst, *Nichiren Shoshu and Soka Gakkai in America: The Ethos of a New Religious Movement* (New York: Garland, 1992).

9. *NSA Handbook,* no. 4, 1972, 25.

10. *The Sokagakkai,* 2d ed. (Tokyo: Seikyo Press, 1962) 16.

11. Tibetan Buddhism shares this emphasis on the *boddhisattva* motivation with most branches of the Mahayana school and recently with the Theravada school as well.

12. Tenzin Gyatso, the Fourteenth Dalai Lama, *Freedom in Exile: The Autobiography of the Dalai Lama* (New York: HarperCollins, 1990), 11.

13. For a detailed description of this group see Fields, *Swans,* 313–15.

14. Butler, "Encountering the Shadow," 16.

Suggestions for Further Reading

Fields, Rick. *How the Swans Came to the Lake: A Narrative History of Buddhism in America.* 3d ed. Boston and London: Shambhala, 1992.

Hurst, Jane. *The Nichiren Shoshu and Soka Gakkai in America: The Ethos of a New Religious Movement.* New York: Garland, 1992.

Layman, Emma McCloy. *Buddhism in America.* Chicago: Nelson-Hall, 1976.

Prebish, Charles S. *American Buddhism.* North Scituate, Mass.: Duxbury, 1979.

Tricycle: The Buddhist Review. (Fall 1991–) New York: The Buddhist Ray, Inc., 163 West 22nd St., New York, N.Y. 10011.

17

HINDUISM ARRIVES IN AMERICA: THE VEDANTA MOVEMENT AND THE SELF-REALIZATION FELLOWSHIP

Catherine Wessinger

In the late eighteenth and nineteenth centuries, one product of imperialism was the assault of Christian missionaries on what they viewed as the heathen Hindu religion. At that time in Western history, everything progressive, modern, and moral was associated with the superiority of Christian civilization. This antagonistic attitude toward Hinduism can be contrasted with that of contemporary Indian Christians who are engaged in a project of inculturation, the conscious incorporation of Hindu ideas and practices into their Christianity. Their intent is to produce a form of Christianity that fits comfortably into the Indian context and that affirms Hindu modes of spirituality.[1] Similarly in America, two Hindu groups, the Vedanta societies and the Self-Realization Fellowship, are engaged in a project of inculturation. The Vedanta movement since 1893, and the Self-Realization Fellowship (SRF) since 1920, are adapting Hindu ideas and practices to the American, predominantly Christian, context. These two Hindu groups in America have numerous similarities, along with significant differences.

Both the Vedanta movement and the Self-Realization Fellowship are rooted in the reevaluation of the Hindu tradition in the nineteenth century that has been termed the Hindu renaissance. Both have responded to Christian exclusivism by asserting religious universalism and preaching tolerance. Each self-consciously presents an alternative religious viewpoint in America, particularly in the claim that the individual can have direct experience of ultimate reality. As of 1995, both are mature and well-established representatives of alternative religion in America. The Vedanta movement and the Self-Realization Fellowship differ in the ways that they combine ideas and practices drawn from the Hindu tradition, as well as in their organizational structures.

Forerunners

There were a number of important forerunners to the arrival of Hinduism in America.[2] Ever since the 1830s and 1840s when Transcendentalists such as Ralph Waldo Emerson and Henry David Thoreau began to read translations of the Hindu scriptures, certain Americans have been drawn to Eastern thought. Edwin Arnold's poetic interpretation of the life of Gautama Buddha, *The Light of Asia,* was published in 1879, and Arnold's *The Song Celestial* (1885), a translation of the Hindu text, Bhagavad Gita, was widely available to Americans. The Transcendentalist poetry and literature and Arnold's presentation of the wisdom of the East prepared many Americans for the messages of Swami

Vivekananda and Swami Yogananda, the founders of the Vedanta movement and the Self-Realization Fellowship respectively. In 1875, the Theosophical Society was founded in New York City; with its strong Neoplatonic cast, it was rooted in the Western occult tradition. It was not long before Theosophy developed clear-cut connections with Hinduism. In the same year, Mary Baker Eddy published her work *Science and Health with Key to the Scriptures* and later established the headquarters of her Church of Christ, Scientist, in Boston, the center of Transcendentalism. Christian Science bears a strong resemblance to the Hindu philosophy called Advaita Vedanta. Vivekananda, Yogananda, and other Indian speakers in America found a ready hearing among persons influenced by Theosophy, Christian Science, and the New Thought movement. The New Thought movement harkens back to the mental healing work of Phineas P. Quimby in the 1860s, was further developed by Christian Science teachers who split with Mary Baker Eddy, and has been strongly influenced by Theosophy. Yogananda, in particular, adjusted his presentation to emphasize more strongly the principles of healing and positive thinking taught by these American movements.[3]

The Vedanta movement and the Self-Realization Fellowship were not the only, or the first, representatives of Hinduism in America. Since the 1880s, Indian lecturers had been visiting America. Due to limitations of space, it is not possible to discuss thoroughly the precursors of Hinduism in America, or other Hindu lecturers in America from the 1890s on. Instead this chapter will focus on the Vedanta movement and the Self-Realization Fellowship, since these have had the strongest influence in America in terms of institutional presence and literature produced.

Bengali Neo-Vedantic Renaissance

Both Swami Vivekananda (1863–1902) and Paramahansa[4] Yogananda (1893–1952) came from Bengal in northeast India. At that time, the British seat of power in In-

dia was located in Calcutta, the major city of Bengal, so that region was the focus of stresses produced by the incursion of Western culture into India. Bengalis played a leading role in the wider Hindu renaissance, producing what can be termed the Bengali "Neo-Vedantic renaissance,"[5] the attempt on the part of men educated in British-run schools to reconcile rationalism, science, and Christianity with their own diverse Hindu heritage.

"Vedanta," meaning "the end of the Vedas," refers to the scriptures in the corpus known as the Vedas ("knowledge") that are called the Upanishads (composed approximately 600–300 B.C.E.). The term Vedanta in its broadest sense refers to the philosophical systems that have been derived from the Upanishads by later interpreters. Both the Vedanta movement in America and the SRF rely most heavily on the Advaita (nondual) Vedanta formulated by Shankara (ninth century C.E.), but also have strong affinities with Vishishtadvaita (nondualism with qualities) Vedanta articulated by Ramanuja (1017–1137 C.E.).[6] They both also strongly rely on religious texts outside the Vedic corpus, such as the Bhagavad Gita and the Yoga Sutras of Patanjali.

The Bengali proponents of Neo-Vedanta and their American heirs see the monistic outlook of Vedanta as offering a worldview that is compatible with contemporary science and experience, and as providing plausible answers to basic, perennial human questions: Who are we? What is our purpose? Why do we suffer? How can permanent happiness be achieved?

Swami Vivekananda and the Vedanta Movement in America

Vivekananda was the primary evangelist, organizer, and theologian of the religious movement sparked by the life of his master, Ramakrishna Paramahansa (1836–1886). Ramakrishna was a village Brahmin who was a priest to the Goddess Kali at the temple at Dakshineswar, just outside of Calcutta. In Bengal, God is most often worshipped as the Goddess Kali, Outwardly, her form is horrific. She may be depicted as a naked black woman, wearing a garland of severed heads and a skirt of severed arms, her long tongue and fangs dripping with blood, brandishing a bloody sword and a severed head. She represents the force that creates life and destroys it, i.e. time. However, in Bengal, she is called "Ma" (Mother) and her devotees regard her as their loving Divine Mother. Ramakrishna was a lover of God in the Indian tradition of God-intoxicated, mad saints. His desire to see the Goddess overwhelmed his ability to function normally. After he achieved the direct experience of Kali he would often experience a state identified as *samadhi*. *Samadhi* is described as a consciousness of unity with the divine which transcends sense perceptions. To the observer, the person experiencing *samadhi* is unconscious to the outer world. Ramakrishna's frequent experiences of *samadhi* and transitions relating to it made him appear intoxicated. He acted strangely and reported that he perceived the image of Kali in the temple as a living being with whom he interacted. Although many people were concerned for his sanity, a conference of Hindu scholars decided that he was an *avatar* ("one who has descended"), an incarnation of God. Upon hearing the verdict of the final scholar, Ramakrishna reportedly remarked, "So he really thinks that! Well—anyway, I'm glad it's not a disease!"[7] Although Ramakrishna was married, the marriage reportedly was never consummated and he took monastic vows of renunciation *(sannyasa)*. His wife, Sarada Devi (1853–1920), similarly came to be regarded as a divine incarnation, the Holy Mother.[8]

According to the account of Ramakrishna's life prepared for Westerners, previous to the stabilization of his God-consciousness, Ramakrishna engaged in a variety of spiritual disciplines relating to several of the world religions as well as the Hindu tradition. He sought and obtained visions of various Hindu deities, and he was instructed by a series of spiritual teachers. His devotion to Kali, as a personal expression of God, is described as initially hindering him from attaining the Advaitic

experience of *nirguna Brahman* (the ultimate without qualities). When his teacher stuck a bit of glass between his eyebrows and told him to meditate on that point, Ramakrishna was able to go beyond the form of his beloved Mother Kali to experience *nirvikalpa samadhi* (the highest unitary experience in which there is no object consciousness). Ramakrishna also had religious experiences relating to non-Hindu religions. For three days, he dressed and ate as a Muslim, constantly repeated the name of Allah, and had a vision of a man merging into God. While gazing at a picture of the Madonna and Child, he saw the picture emit rays of light which entered his heart. He later saw Jesus Christ, "the great yogi," who embraced him and then merged into his body. On the basis of his experiences, Ramakrishna concluded that the various religions and sects are simply different paths that lead to the same goal.

Ramakrishna as a local saint attracted the attention of educated and westernized men from Calcutta, who began to go to him for religious instruction. It was in these circles that an eighteen-year-old college student, Narendra Nath Datta, who would become Swami Vivekananda, met Ramakrishna. Naren, a student at Scottish Church College, was a skeptic, and had concluded that God's existence could only be proved by direct experience. He repeatedly asked holy men if they had seen God. Ramakrishna was the only one who answered in the affirmative.

It is recounted that Ramakrishna instructed Naren to read books on Advaita Vedanta, and initially Naren concluded that Advaita Vedanta was no different from atheism. Naren laughed at the idea of nondualism, and said "Can it be that the waterpot is God, that the drinking vessel is God, that everything we see and all of us are God?" At that moment, Ramakrishna touched him, and, suddenly, his awareness changed:

> I was aghast to realize that there really was nothing whatever in the entire universe but God.... [F]rom then on, I kept having the same experience, no

matter what I was doing—eating, drinking, sitting, lying down, going to college, strolling down the street. It was a kind of intoxication; I can't describe it. If I was crossing a street and saw a carriage coming towards me I didn't have the urge, as I would ordinarily, to get out of its way for fear of being run over. For I said to myself, "I am that carriage. There's no difference between it and me."

When that first intoxication lost part of its power, I began to see the world as though it were a dream. When I went for a walk around Cornwallis Square, I used to knock my head against the iron railings to find out if they were only dream-railings or real ones. The loss of feeling in my hands and feet made me afraid that I was going to be paralyzed. When I did at last return to normal consciousness, I felt convinced that the state I had been in was a revelation of non-dualistic experience. So then I knew what is written in the Scriptures about this experience is all true.[9]

In a subsequent episode, Naren is described as also attaining the experience of God with form (*saguna,* with qualities). When Ramakrishna instructed him to go into the temple to make a request of Kali, Naren saw that her statue was a living Being. Prostrating himself, he prayed "Mother—grant me discrimination, grant me detachment, grant me divine knowledge and devotion, grant me that I may see you without obstruction always!"[10]

Naren and fifteen other young men became Ramakrishna's immediate circle of disciples.[11] Ramakrishna encouraged them to renounce "woman and gold," explaining that the goal, the unmediated knowledge of unity of self and the ultimate, can only be achieved by renouncing all desires associated with the world. Shortly after Ramakrishna's death, the young men took vows of *sannyasa* and undertook a monastic lifestyle. Naren embarked on a three-year period of wandering throughout India, during which time he became acutely aware of the suffering of the masses of India. He heard that there was to be held in 1893 a World Parliament of Religions in Chicago in conjunction with the Columbian Exposition, and he resolved to attend this parliament as a representative of Hinduism. His plan was to raise funds in the West to alleviate the poverty of India, and, in return, to offer India's spiritual wisdom. Naren arrived in America with a new monastic name—he was Swami Vivekananda (one who has the bliss of discrimination).

After a series of adventures and mishaps, Swami Vivekananda on September 11, 1893, made his first address to the parliament. Vivekananda at age thirty made a striking appearance, a strong brown figure dressed in vividly colored robes (orange and red) and turbans and with an aggressive style of speaking. His addresses, delivered during the seventeen days of the parliament, attracted considerable favorable response from the audiences. Later, a disciple reported that people began to ask, "Why send missionaries to a country which produces men like this?"[12] Vivekananda thus became the first Hindu teacher to attract the widespread attention of the American public.

After the parliament, Vivekananda continued to receive extensive newspaper coverage for his lectures in the midwestern and eastern United States and in England. Due to missionary portrayals of the evils of Hinduism, Vivekananda decided against his earlier plan to highlight the material neediness of India. Instead, he emerged as the vigorous defender of the value of Hindu thought for the world, who was ready to cross verbal swords with Christian missionaries. His message, which he termed Vedanta, was that each individual was able to achieve the direct experience of God-realization, and that the diversity of various religions and sects merely meant that they were different paths to the same goal. Vivekananda particularly conducted classes and lectured in New York City and Boston. In order to train workers to perpetuate Vedanta in America, Vivekananda spent two quiet months in the summer of 1895 at Thousand Island Park on the St. Lawrence River intensively instructing twelve students. The first Vedanta Society was organized in New York City in 1896.

When Vivekananda returned to India in 1896, he was welcomed as a hero who had reversed the tide of Christian proselytization by winning American converts to Hinduism. Vivekananda and his *gurubhais* (spiritual brothers) buckled down to the task of organizing the Ramakrishna Math (monastic order) and the Ramakrishna Mission to provide social services to India's poor. Vivekananda returned to the United States and in 1899 to 1900 he spent six months lecturing to Unitarian and New Thought groups in the Los Angeles and San Francisco areas. After his return to India, Vivekananda, suffering from diabetes and asthma, increasingly withdrew from activity to devote himself to spiritual practice, and passed away on July 4, 1902, at age thirty-nine.

The Vedanta movement that Vivekananda started in America grew slowly but steadily. Swamis from the Ramakrishna Order were sent to teach in independent urban centers and to give lectures to outside groups. These included four direct disciples of Ramakrishna, Swamis Saradananda, Turiyananda, Trigunatita, and Abhedananda. Abhedananda remained in the West for the longest period, 1897 to 1921. Working primarily out of New York City, Abhedananda was prolific in his lecturing and writing. Under the leadership of Trigunatita, the San Francisco center completed the first Hindu temple in America in 1906, and made the first experiment in establishing monastic communities for men and women. The three outstanding second-generation swamis were Paramananda (1884–1940), Prabhavananda (1893–1976), and Nikhilananda (1895–1973).

Coming to the West in 1906, Paramananda established centers in Boston and Los Angeles, and lectured in Europe and all over the United States, particularly Cincinnati, Dayton, St. Louis, and Louisville. In 1923 he established an *ashrama* (retreat center) north of Los Angeles at La Crescenta, which he named Ananda Ashrama. At Ananda Ashrama, the Temple of the Universal Spirit was constructed; it honors the variety of world religions. A group of American women disciples and his young niece, Gayatri Devi,

were Paramananda's partners in ministry. In 1927, Paramananda began to give lectures on radio, and in 1939 he resorted to airplane travel to maintain his outreach.

Swami Prabhavananda, after founding a successful center in Portland, established the Vedanta Society in Hollywood in 1930. This would become the Vedanta Society of Southern California that would grow to include a monastery in Orange County, a convent and monastery in Santa Barbara, a monastery in San Diego, and the Vedanta Press, bookstore, and monastic quarters adjacent to the Hollywood temple. In the late 1930s, Prabhavananda attracted to Vedanta the British writers Gerald Heard, Aldous Huxley, and Christopher Isherwood, who were living in Los Angeles. Prabhavananda's published works include a widely distributed interpretation of *The Sermon on the Mount According to Vedanta*,[13] translations in collaboration with Christopher Isherwood of the Bhagavad Gita, *The Crest-Jewel of Discrimination* by Shankara, and a translation of the Yoga Sutras of Patanjali with commentary. In collaboration with Frederick Manchester he produced a translation of Upanishads.

Swami Nikhilananda established the Ramakrishna-Vivekananda Center in Manhattan in 1933, and lectured widely in New York City. The author of many books, Nikhilananda made important contributions to the literature of the Ramakrishna movement, including an English version of Mahendra Nath Gupta's *The Gospel of Sri Ramakrishna*.[14] He attracted distinguished disciples, including Margaret Woodrow Wilson, daughter of the president, the comparative mythologist Professor Joseph Campbell, and Chester Carlson, inventor of the xerographic process.

Paramahansa Yogananda

The infant who would become Paramahansa Yogananda was born as Mukunda Lal Ghosh on January 5, 1893, the same year that Vivekananda addressed the Parliament of Religions. Although a fellow Bengali, Yogananda was a very different personality. Vivekananda, "the cyclonic Hindu" who liked to meditate on the heart of a lion, was concerned to present Hinduism as a "manly" religion, and he constantly stressed the need for self-reliance in the struggle toward enlightenment. In contrast, Yogananda, with his round face and shoulder-length wavy hair, evoked a softer presence in his physical appearance as well as in his teachings. In his emphasis on the devotional aspects of the Hindu tradition, he was more similar to Ramakrishna than Vivekananda. He was regarded by his disciples as a *premavatar,* an incarnation of divine love. However, Yogananda shared with Vivekananda the ability to communicate effectively in English and strong organizational talents. Yogananda's treatise, *The Science of Religion,* demonstrated his ability to engage in philosophical analysis.[15] Yogananda has presented his life's story in his *Autobiography of a Yogi,* which was first published in 1946, and has since been translated into eighteen languages.[16]

Since his father was a railway executive, Mukunda grew up in materially comfortable circumstances. His parents were described as devout disciples of Lahiri Mahasaya (1828–1895), who was an accountant for the British government in India. Lahiri Mahasaya was a guru who had retained the householder lifestyle, with its attendant duties of work, marriage, and raising children. He taught a spiritual technique known as *kriya yoga* that was revealed to him by his guru, the everyouthful Himalayan *avatar* (divine incarnation) known as Babaji. From childhood, Mukunda expressed a resolve to be a yogi in order to know God.

Mukunda grew up in the Bengali environment in which worship of the Divine Mother was natural, and which had been strongly shaped by the spirituality of Ramakrishna. Yogananda recounted that "M." or Mahendra Nath Gupta, the author of *Srisriramakrsnakathamrta* (which Nikhilananda shaped into *The Gospel of Sri Ramakrishna*), had his residence and school in the Calcutta house that had formerly been the Ghosh family home. It was in this house that Mukunda's mother died

when he was eleven. M. was Mukunda's early spiritual teacher, and they often would travel together to worship at the Dakshineswar temple. One day, M. took Mukunda to see a "bioscope," an early motion picture being shown at the Calcutta University. Afterwards on the sidewalk, M. perceived that Mukunda had found the bioscope to be dull. M. tapped Mukunda's chest over the heart. Suddenly, on that busy street, all noise was silenced. Mukunda could see the pedestrians, all the vehicles on the street; he could even see what was taking place behind him—but all was silent. It was like a movie in which there was no sound. Underneath it all, he could perceive a luminescent glow. His own body, as well as those of the others, seemed to be a mere silent shadow. The experience with its accompanying bliss was terminated when M. again tapped his chest, noting that Mukunda seemed to like that bioscope better. This experience, similar to that of the young Naren, presaged Yogananda's teaching to his Western audiences that the physical world has the reality of a motion picture or a dream. Reinforcing his connection to the Ramakrishna movement, later in his college years, Mukunda had a vision of the Goddess Kali while meditating at the Dakshineswar temple.

Mukunda met his guru, Swami Sri Yukteswar (1855–1936), in 1910 when he was seventeen. Yukteswar, a direct disciple of Lahiri Mahasaya, had his *ashrama* at Serampore, a long-time base for Christian missionaries twelve miles north of Calcutta. He had taken *sannyasa* after fulfilling his householder duties. Yukteswar insisted that Mukunda complete his college education, so Mukunda attended the Scottish Church College for two years. He completed his A.B. degree at Serampore College, which was affiliated with Calcutta University. After his graduation, Mukunda took *sannyasa,* becoming Swami Yogananda (one who has bliss through divine union). In 1917, Yogananda founded a boys' school administered by an organization he called Yogoda Satsanga Society of India. (Satsanga means "fellowship with truth" or "good company," and Yogoda was a term coined by Yogananda meaning "that which imparts union.")

Autobiography of a Yogi describes Yogananda's spiritual lineage as being particularly concerned with integrating Hindu spirituality with the emerging modern lifestyle influenced by the West. Lahiri Mahasaya was a householder-guru to demonstrate that the highest spiritual attainment can be achieved while living fully in the world. *Autobiography* describes Yukteswar in 1894 meeting Babaji, the guru of his guru, at the *kumbha mela* (religious fair) at Allahabad. When Yukteswar expressed his wish that the scientists of the West benefit from the spiritual knowledge of India, Babaji predicted that he would have a disciple who would take yoga to the West. In the meantime, Babaji instructed that Yukteswar should write a book on the harmony of Hindu and Christian scriptures. Many years later, Yogananda, while seated in meditation at his boys' school, had a vision of the faces of his American disciples. The next day he received an invitation to address the International Congress of Religious Liberals convening in Boston under of the auspices of the American Unitarian Association. Funded by his father, Yogananda travelled to the United States. He delivered his address, "The Science of Religion," on October 6, 1920.

Yogananda found Boston to be receptive to his message and he settled there for three years.[17] In his early years in America, he continued to use the Indian name for his organization, Yogoda Satsanga Society. By 1922, he had established an *ashrama* near Boston at Waltham, Massachusetts. In 1924, he began a transcontinental speaking tour, attracting large crowds in major cities. In January 1925, the three-thousand-seat Philharmonic Auditorium in Los Angeles was filled to capacity for Yogananda's lectures, with thousands turned away. In the same year, an estate was acquired on Mount Washington in Los Angeles to be Yogananda's headquarters. During this time, the California horticulturalist Luther Burbank became Yogananda's disciple. In January 1927, Yogananda attracted record crowds to his lectures in Washington, D.C., and was received by President Coolidge at the White House.[18] Yogananda's organization was incorporated in 1935 as the Self-

Realization Fellowship. In 1935, Yogananda visited India, during which time his guru passed away, and Yogananda gave *kriya* initiation to Mohandas Gandhi. Upon his return to America in late 1936, Yogananda devoted himself to writing and the training of his most committed American disciples. A hermitage was established at Encinitas, and a temple in San Diego and the Church of All Religions in Hollywood were constructed. The beautiful Lake Shrine was dedicated in 1950 at Pacific Palisades, at which a portion of Gandhi's ashes were enshrined.

Autobiography of a Yogi describes Yogananda's many encounters with saints, Eastern and Western. It is filled with accounts of visions, healings, materializations, and resurrections. This is to demonstrate that the miraculous is not confined to the life of Jesus Christ alone, but that supernormal powers are available to yogis in all traditions who understand the underlying universal laws. His devotees believe Yogananda's departure from earthly life *(mahasamadhi)* to be a demonstration of his supreme yogic control of bodily function.[19] On March 7, 1952, Yogananda addressed 240 people at a banquet at the Biltmore Hotel held by the India Association of America in honor of India's ambassador to America. Yogananda welcomed the ambassador to Los Angeles, and made a short speech expressing his hope for a "United World" that would combine the best qualities of "efficient America" and "spiritual India." He concluded with a few lines from his poem, "My India"; then his body slipped to the floor. The mortuary director of the Forest Lawn Memorial Park later certified that Yogananda's body did not evidence the normal signs of decay during the twenty days before it was entombed. (The body was embalmed, but emulsion was not applied to the skin.)

Leadership of the SRF was taken up by James J. Lynn, who after taking *sannyasa* was known as Rajarsi Janakananda. He served as president of the SRF from 1952 until his death in 1955. Sri Daya Mata, who met Yogananda when she was a teenager in Salt Lake City, has served as SRF president since 1955.

The Attraction of Neo-Vedanta for Americans

Although the worldview and religious methods of the Vedanta movement and the Self-Realization Fellowship are not identical, their common roots in the Bengali Neo-Vedantic renaissance make them similar enough to warrant discussion together of the positive features they offer to Americans. When persons turn to a religious group that is foreign to their culture, the foreign religion must be offering something that people find to be meaningful.

First and foremost, the Vedanta movement and the SRF offer to the West a positive understanding of human nature. The view that each human partakes in divinity was forcefully expressed by Vivekananda at the Parliament of Religions as an alternative to the Christian doctrine of original sin:

> Allow me to call you, brethren, by that sweet name—heirs of immortal bliss—yea, the Hindu refuses to call you sinners. We are the Children of God, the sharers of immortal bliss, holy and perfect beings. Ye divinities on earth—sinners! It is a sin to call a man so; it is standing libel on human nature. Come up, O lions, and shake off the delusion that you are sheep; you are souls immortal, spirits free, blest and eternal; ye are not bodies; matter is your servant, not you the servant of matter.[20]

Vivekananda is here expressing the Advaitic concept that the true human self, the *atman,* is eternally free, perfect and divine. It is identical with the unmanifest Absolute, *nirguna Brahman.* The material world, including the body, is a secondary, impermanent, and deluding existence *(maya).* Yogananda was fond of explaining that Jesus Christ was not the only Son of God. Jesus' command, "Be perfect, therefore, as your heavenly Father is perfect" (Matthew 5:48), should be taken seriously by every person, since each has the capacity to realize the Christ Consciousness within and to know oneself to be the perfect child of God.[21]

The doctrines of reincarnation and karma are integral components of this positive anthropology. Karma, meaning "action," refers to the universal law of cause and effect. Every action, including thought and speech, produces a result, either in the present lifetime or in a future lifetime. Therefore, an individual creates the specific circumstances of his or her life. Vivekananda urged individuals to shoulder responsibility for their destiny. If you suffer, then the responsibility is yours alone, and only you can undo the suffering. The doctrines of karma and reincarnation are seen as resolving the dilemma of the existence of evil, so that there is no need to placate "a hideous, cruel, and ever-angry God." According to Vivekananda, "There is no other way to vindicate the glory and the liberty of the human soul and reconcile the inequalities and the horrors of this world, than by placing the whole burden upon the legitimate cause—our own independent actions, or Karma."[22] Therefore, both the Vedanta swamis and Yogananda teach human free will and the necessity of self-effort.

The Neo-Vedantic positive view of human nature is correlated with a monistic cosmology in which there is one reality, which is God. This is to be contrasted with the Christian God seen as separate from his creation, who either wrathfully judges it or is inexplicably unresponsive to its suffering. Christopher Isherwood vividly describes his alienation from the Christian tradition:

> I hated Christianity—the kind of Christianity I had been taught—because it was dualistic. God, high in heaven, ruled with grim justice over us, his sinful and brutish subjects, here below. He was good. We were bad. We were so bad that we crucified Jesus his son, whom he had sent down to live amongst us. . . .
>
> Who—I furiously exclaimed—wouldn't rebel against the concept of such a God? Who wouldn't abhor his tyranny? Who wouldn't denounce the cruel unfairness of this test he had set us: one short human life in which to earn salvation or damnation? Who wouldn't detest his Son, who had come to us—like a vice squad officer bent on entrapment—

wearing a hypocritical mask of meekness in order to tempt us to murder him?[23]

Neo-Vedanta in America offers a monistic view of reality that is ambiguous about whether the ultimate reality is personal or impersonal, whether the material world is real or unreal. The Vedanta movement in America, following Vivekananda, tends to view the ultimate reality as the unmanifest *nirguna Brahman*, but following the example of Ramakrishna, devotion *(bhakti)* to a personal expression of deity is considered to be the most efficacious path to realization of the ultimate. When Vivekananda was visiting St. Peter's Basilica in Rome, his companion, who was astonished to see him being "so reverential to the symbols of the Roman Church," asked, "Swami, you don't believe in a Personal God; why do you honour this so much?" He replied, "But Alberta, if you do believe in a Personal God, surely you give it your best."[24] As in India, Neo-Vedanta in America has scope for the Absolute to be conceived in personal or impersonal terms—the personal being either male or female. God is Mother, Father, Friend, Lover, Creator, Artist, the Cosmic Director of the universal play. The traditional Vedantic formula indicating the nature of *nirguna Brahman* is *sat-chit-ananda*—pure existence, pure consciousness, pure bliss. While upholding this view, Yogananda preferred to opt for a personal but abstract conception of God. He taught that the unmanifest absolute can and does assume a personal aspect as the object of human yearning. He argued that since humans are created in God's image (Genesis 9:6), God must possess "the spirit of reciprocity"[25] found in human beings.

The Indian Vedantic tradition includes a variety of views on whether or not the material world is real. Neo-Vedanta tends to blur the distinction between the Advaita position that the one reality is *nirguna Brahman,* and that the manifest universe is the result of superimposition, a false perception, and the Vishishtadvaita position that ultimate reality is *saguna Brahman,* and that the material universe is real and can

be spoken of as being part of God's body. Both positions are agreed that the realm of material existence is characterized by impermanence and suffering, and that permanent bliss can only be discovered in the *atman* (self) which is one with *Brahman* (either *nirguna* or *saguna*).

Yogananda seemed at times to take the Vishishtadvaita view, speaking of the Divine Spirit as creating the manifested universe as his physical body, so that creation consists of the vibrations of God's energy.[26] But Yogananda taught that once the highest realization *(nirvikalpa samadhi)* is achieved, the material world will be perceived as an illusion, the dream of God, or to use his favorite simile, a movie show projected by light onto the screen of consciousness for the entertainment of the viewers.[27] The same sort of ambiguity can be found in Vivekananda. For him, the ultimate reality was *advaita* (nondual), and the material world was *maya* (illusion). Vivekananda also explained *maya* by the metaphors of a dream, a picture, and a play. However, the Vishishtadvaita position formed the basis for what Vivekananda called "practical Vedanta," providing the rationale for the social service in India of the Ramakrishna Mission. This position states that the natural expression of the perception of unity is the desire to help. However, Vivekananda was adamant that the social worker should never believe that she or he was actually improving the world, which is, after all, illusory. Service should be performed without attachment to the final results. In this manner, social service becomes karma yoga, the discipline of action, that ultimately brings spiritual benefits to the server, not to those being served.[28] Ultimately, there can only be individual transformation rather than social reform.

An important attraction of Neo-Vedanta for Americans is its compatibility with science. Vivekananda addressed Americans at a time when scientific discoveries and theories had dealt severe blows to traditional Judeo-Christian theism and biblical authority. Vivekananda's addresses, and those of the swamis after him, were peppered with references to scientific data. This concern with science continues into the twentieth century. Yogananda, who lived through the two world wars, often stated that he was presenting a cosmology for the "Atomic Age." The writings of Christopher Isherwood and Gerald Heard discuss how the Neo-Vedantic cosmology is compatible with information presented by physics and astronomy. Further, they express keen awareness that humans need to develop the moral maturity to put the power of the atom and advanced technology to peaceful uses.[29]

Neo-Vedanta is seen as a "Science of the Soul"[30] that is empirical and experimental. It is emphasized that there is no need to accept Neo-Vedantic teachings on blind faith. The Vedanta movement in America and the SRF offer techniques for spiritual realization, and ask only that they be tried. While the experiment is being conducted, one need only to accept as a "minimum working hypothesis" that the divinity of the real Self can be known. One can discover the truth for oneself through immediate experience. Similarly, doctrines such as karma, reincarnation, and *avatars* should be regarded as hypotheses to encourage intelligent inquiry. Although in the Hindu tradition there is the tendency to rely on the authority of the guru, regarded as a God-realized individual, Ramakrishna encouraged his disciples to test him, and Vivekananda warned against trusting a teacher who says, "I have seen, but *you cannot.*" Brother Anandamoy, a direct disciple of Yogananda, explained that a true guru points beyond herself or himself to God.[31] The Vedanta societies and the SRF are agreed that the ultimate goal is the realization of God, or the realization of the Self. It is the experience that the Self is one with God.

An important attraction of Neo-Vedanta for Americans is that it offers practical techniques to achieve direct spiritual experience. In the Hindu tradition, the term "yoga" designates the various methods of spirituality. "Yoga" has many connotations, but it can mean "union" and also "discipline." Since the advent of *hatha yoga* instructors in the 1950s, Americans usually associate the term with the hatha yoga discipline of the body. Both the Vedanta movement and the SRF view hatha yoga as a preparation for meditation, and focus primarily on other types of yoga. Similarly, they both regard adherence to basic moral precepts as an essential preliminary.[32]

The Vedanta movement teaches that different yogas are suitable for different temperaments. The purpose of all the yogas is to detach the practitioner from false identification with the desires of personality and body to come to the realization of the true Self. If a person chooses to be instructed by a swami at a Vedanta center, the swami will offer the spiritual guidance he deems suitable for that individual. However, the Vedanta movement encourages the simultaneous practice of four yogas, the first three of which are derived from the Bhagavad Gita. Karma yoga is work done without attachment to the fruits of action. Nonattachment is achieved by offering the results of one's labor to God. Jnana yoga is the discipline of knowledge, in which one constantly discriminates the permanent reality from the impermanent phenomena. This process is supplemented by scriptural study and philosophic inquiry. Bhakti yoga is intense love and devotion for a personal expression of deity. The fourth, *raja yoga,* the kingly yoga, encompasses the eight steps taught in the Yoga Sutras of Patanjali. The object is to eliminate distracting movements of the body and mind so that *nirvikalpa samadhi* can be achieved. The senses are withdrawn from outer objects so that the inner reality can be discovered. The Vedanta movement further encourages practices relating to bhakti yoga such as *japam,* the repeating of a *mantra* or name(s) of a personal deity to which one should show special devotion. At initiation (*diksha*) by a swami, a disciple receives the *mantra* for the aspect of God upon which she or he is instructed to meditate. It is believed that through repetition, the *mantra* brings the vision of the personal deity. At some Vedanta centers, there is daily ritual worship (*puja*) of Ramakrishna and Sarada Devi. On special occasions, Ramakrishna's foremost disciples, Vivekananda and Brahmananda, and teachers such as Jesus Christ and Buddha may also be worshipped. Householder devotees may keep an altar at home at which they can perform *puja* and meditate. Jnana yoga is regarded as the most difficult method, but intellectual inquiry is present in the study of Hindu scriptures in classes and the Sunday lectures offered at the centers.[33]

The Self-Realization Fellowship provides a similar combination of methods, but with different emphases. Yogananda greatly stressed the deep emotional longing for God associated with *bhakti yoga*. He liked to cite Jesus' saying that the greatest commandment is "you shall love the Lord your God with all your heart, and with all your soul, and with all your mind, and with all your strength" (Mark 12: 30), which leads naturally to loving your neighbor as yourself (Mark 12: 31). But one should additionally follow the steps outlined by Patanjali: the keeping of positive and negative moral precepts; quieting and discipline of the body; control of breath; withdrawal of senses from outward objects thus reversing the outward flow of life force; concentration and meditation.[34]

The SRF offers initiation in a technique termed kriya yoga that is said to immensely speed up the process of spiritual evolution. The disciple must prepare to receive the kriya technique by undertaking the study and practices offered in the Self-Realization Fellowship Lessons, a home-study course compiled from Yogananda's classes. In continuity with the Upanishadic practice of teachings being conveyed only to properly prepared students, the SRF disciple must sign a pledge promising not to reveal the contents of the lessons. In the SRF, bestowal of the kriya technique constitutes *diksha* (initiation) by the guru, Paramahansa Yogananda. In most cases, this is done through the *kriya* initiation rite conducted by an SRF authorized representative. When it is not possible for the disciple to attend such a rite, the technique may be received in the printed kriya yoga lessons that are mailed to the disciple.[35]

Important attractions of the Neo-Vedantic methods are that they offer direct religious experience, a sense of personal control over one's destiny, and a means to achieve calm and inner peace which seems particularly needed in today's hectic and stressful world. For the strongly motivated, the SRF and the Vedanta societies offer monastic training. The SRF monastic order for men and women is headquartered at the Mount Washington estate in Los Angeles. All of the Vedanta centers in America offer monastic training for men. The Vedanta Society of Northern California and the Vedanta Society of Southern California also offer monastic training for women. Though at present there is no plan for the Ramakrishna Order to accommodate more convents in America, several other Vedanta centers have purchased houses for women who wish to lead dedicated lives according to Vedantic ideals. These women, though under the close supervision and spiritual guidance of the swami in charge of their center, are not nuns. Though single, many are older women who have had families. Financially independent, these women usually hold outside jobs, but devote the remainder of their free time to spiritual practices and center-related activities.

Another attraction of Neo-Vedanta for Americans is its universalism. In an age in which exclusive claims to truth are becoming less tenable, and in which various religions and nationalities increasingly impinge on each other, Neo-Vedanta offers a way to make sense of diversity. The various religions are seen as different paths to the same goal—diversity in practice and even dogma are external concerns only. It is asserted that the mystical experiences of the saints of all the world's religions point to the same ultimate reality, so the Vedanta movement bookshops carry books on saints in diverse traditions. Yogananda in his *Autobiography* recounts his intense interest in meeting Western and Eastern saints. Neo-Vedanta finds truth in the Bible, and Jesus is seen as a great yogi, and as one of the many *avatars*. At the Parliament of Religions, Vivekananda told the story of a frog in a well, who thought his well was the whole world. One day, a frog from the sea fell into the well. He tried to tell the first frog about the sea, but the first frog responded "nothing can be bigger than my well; there can be nothing bigger than this; this fellow is a liar, so turn him out."

Vivekananda said that the devotee of an exclusive religion is like the frog who thinks that his well is the whole world. "I have to thank you of America for the great attempt you are making to break down the barriers of this little world of ours, and hope that, in the future, the Lord will help you to accomplish your purpose."[36]

Neo-Vedanta thus offers to Americans a new understanding of their traditional religions without requiring that they be left behind. An additional sense of familiarity can be found in the Protestant style of the public Sunday services held by the Vedanta centers and the SRF. These services include a sermon delivered by a monastic and singing either by the congregation or by a small choir.

A final important attraction of Neo-Vedanta for Americans is the role of the guru. *Diksha* marks that the initiate has become a disciple of his guru (spiritual teacher) and that the guru agrees to assume responsibility for that disciple's spiritual welfare. In the Vedanta movement, any swami who conveys *diksha* is a guru. Christopher Isherwood has testified that the guru-disciple bond, which gave deep meaning to the beliefs and practices of Vedanta, was a primary attraction for him.[37] In the SRF, Yogananda is believed to stand within a lineage of gurus that includes Babaji, Lahiri Mahasaya, and Sri Yukteswar. Krishna and Christ are revered as the two great gurus from whose teachings the SRF beliefs are derived. Yogananda instructed that with his passing, his writings, especially the SRF Lessons, would serve as the guru-given means of spiritual instruction. The SRF exists to preserve and disseminate Yogananda's teachings. Yogananda promised that the SRF president would always be a God-realized person, but Yogananda remains the guru. Devotees regard Yogananda as a living guru who has taken responsibility for their spiritual welfare and who communicates with them through their meditations and intuitions, as well as through his writings.[38] The guru and the saints of all traditions are important in the Vedanta movement and the SRF as exemplars of God-identification. They demonstrate that the ultimate goal can be achieved.

Who Is Attracted

In the late nineteenth century, Vivekananda's work was supported by wealthy upper-class persons, particularly women. People of this sort were the first to have the time and leisure to inquire into alternative religions. Neo-Vedanta offers to women alternative views, which include belief in goddesses, to the Judeo-Christian God the Father. Additionally, Neo-Vedanta stresses that the *atman* has no gender and that distinctions of sex are only temporary. But women have often been the benefactors of new religious movements, and Neo-Vedanta appealed to working-class men as well as wealthy women.[39] Two of Yogananda's early devotees were a dentist and his wife, Doctor and Mildred Lewis, and a core of professional men were his supporters. Probably Yogananda's greatest financial benefactor was James J. Lynn, a self-educated farmboy from Louisiana who by virtue of his diligence and native intelligence became a very wealthy businessman. He often testified that he suffered from "nervousness" before he discovered *kriya yoga*.

When I attended public meetings of the SRF in the Los Angeles area, and those of the Vedanta Society of Southern California, in June 1992, I observed greater racial diversity at the Vedanta Society. There were Indians, East Asians, African Americans, Hispanics, and whites, from the age of about thirty-five up. The SRF Sunday service at the Lake Shrine attracted a large crowd of Hispanics and whites and some Asians. This crowd, however, was much more diverse in age, with more young people, and parents with their children.

Wendell Thomas in 1930 characterized the American followers of Neo-Vedanta as intellectual and venturesome, whose work ranged from manual labor to white collar. At that time, the American Neo-Vedantists were primarily white, women predominating, and the SRF disciples were somewhat younger than people affiliated with the Vedanta societies. It would still seem to hold true that both the Vedanta societies and the SRF "clearly operate in the great middle class,"[40] but currently these groups reflect the increasing ethnic diversity of the American middle class. The constant factor in the diversity of Americans attracted to Neo-Vedanta would seem to be a certain level of literacy and intelligence. The SRF disciple must be able to study the words of Yogananda, and Vivekananda noted difficulty lecturing to unintelligent audiences.

Controversies

Swami Vivekananda and the swamis who followed him to America often encountered racist attitudes. They were dark skinned and odd looking in their native costumes, and Americans often responded negatively. Moreover, Swami Vivekananda, as a result of his lecturing successes, elicited a deep hostility from Christian missionaries. Ministers countered the invasion of Hindu heathenism by sermons and pamphlets directed against Vivekananda and the movement he instigated. A common charge was that the swamis mainly attracted gullible wealthy women, and a 1912 article asserted that "Eve is eating the apple again." When Mrs. Sara Bull of Boston left her fortune in 1911 to the Ramakrishna Order, her will was overturned on the basis that her practice of Hindu methods of spirituality surely indicated insanity.[41] The Reverend Reeves Calkins told of his initial encounter with Vivekananda on a ship travelling to India in 1900. Vivekananda asked:

"You are an American?"

"Yes."

"A missionary?"

"Yes."

"Why do you teach religion in my country?" he demanded.

"Why do you teach religion in my country?" I countered.

The least quiver of an eyelash was enough to throw down our guards. We both burst out laughing, and were friends.[42]

That this confrontation was resolved amicably foreshadows the cordial relations that would eventually develop between the urban Vedanta centers and representatives of American mainstream denominations. For example, the Vedanta Society of Southern California currently participates in the Interreligious Council of Southern California. Swami Sarvagatananda in Boston conducts a Friday afternoon service at the MIT chapel, and he is a member of the United Ministry of Harvard University.

When Swami Paramananda died in 1940, his disciples, including a group of consecrated women, decided that they preferred that his niece, Gayatri Devi, continue his work instead of a swami sent out from the Ramakrishna Order. Rather than sanction the religious leadership of a woman, in 1941 the Ramakrishna Order ruled that Paramananda's centers were no longer its affiliates.[43] The leadership and even the presence of women religious remains an issue for the Vedanta societies, since in India it is not considered appropriate for men and women religious to be part of the same order. Though Western women religious are not listed on the official register of the Ramakrishna Order, they are monastic members of the American Vedanta societies which are affiliated with the Ramakrishna Order, and they receive their vows from a Ramakrishna Order swami. In 1947, the Vedanta Society of Southern California established the Sarada Convent in Santa Barbara on the first occasion of *brahmacharya* vows (preliminary to *sannyasa*) officially administered to women in America. The Vedanta Society of Northern California established a convent in San Francisco shortly thereafter. In contrast to the dual monastic arrangement in America, the Sri Sarada Math for women established in 1954 in India is completely separate from the Ramakrishna Order. It had been Vivekananda's intent that the women of India establish an organization separate from the men's Math. In 1959 in southern California, five American women were the first to take the vows of *sannyasa* with the full sanction of the Ramakrishna Order. Women who have taken *sannyasa* in the Vedanta movement in America and in India receive the title "pravrajika" (renunciant).[44] In recent years in the United

States, American pravrajikas and swamis have begun to participate in the public teaching functions that have been carried out by the Indian swamis. Unresolved is the full legitimacy of women's religious leadership, as well as that of American men, since swamis sent from India continue to head the various Vedanta centers in America. It must be noted that these Indian swamis come at the invitation of the Americans in the centers.

The Self-Realization Fellowship has experienced difficulties in preserving the confidentiality of the lessons offered in its home-study course. Other individuals and groups offer similar lessons. The SRF has responded by including in all of its publications a very strict copyright statement and a statement that Yogananda established the SRF as the instrument for the dissemination of his teachings.

In 1962, a direct disciple of Yogananda, J. Donald Walters or Kriyananda, separated from the SRF. Walters was formerly a minister of the SRF Church of All Religions in Hollywood, and was vice-president of the SRF and member of its board from 1960 to 1962. In his autobiography, he explains that the problem involved his "eccentricity," which he values as thinking for oneself, and the dilemma of how to get his own written works published.[45] In 1968 Walters established a cooperative community now called Ananda World Brotherhood Village in Nevada City, California, and he currently offers an extensive selection of books, pamphlets, audio and video tapes, and his own home-study course through Crystal Clarity Publishers. Walters/Kriyananda frequently lectures with popular New Age teachers such as Shakti Gawain, Louise Hay, and Dr. Bernie Siegal.

The perennial problem of accommodating talented and independent-minded individuals within a single religious institution often results in the founding of separate institutions, and that was the final outcome of Swami Paramananda's organization. In the Vedanta movement, Abhedananda from 1910 lectured in America independently of the direction of the Ramakrishna Order. When he returned to India, he founded a separate organization.

Impact of Neo-Vedanta in America

The influence of the Vedanta movement and the Self-Realization Fellowship on Americans is diffuse and impossible to gauge with precision. The impact goes far beyond mere membership statistics. Both groups do not pressure individuals for conversion. They present their message via public lectures and publications. If someone wants to become a committed disciple, he or she must initiate contact with the organization. The impact on the many who attend a few worship services, attend some lectures or classes, or read some books cannot be measured, but is surely significant.

The Vedanta movement in America consists of twelve independent centers, plus their officially associated subcenters, convents, and monasteries. The main Vedanta centers are located in Berkeley, San Francisco, Sacramento, Hollywood, Chicago, Boston, St. Louis, Portland, Providence, and Seattle, and there are two centers in New York City. The convent near Santa Barbara has a lovely temple which hosts public services and a fine bookstore. The Chicago center has a monastery and retreat center at Ganges, Michigan. There are many unofficial centers scattered around the United States, which hold regular meetings and at least once or twice a year host a Vedanta swami to lecture and hold classes. There are also Vedanta centers in Argentina, Canada, England, France, the Netherlands, Switzerland, Japan, and the former Soviet Union. Total membership in America is about 2,200, but the collective mailing lists of the centers include about four times that number. The Vedanta centers attract a church attendance that is largely non-member. The bookstores operated by the Vedanta societies carry books on all aspects of Asian religions as well as Western religious traditions. Thus, in America, the Vedanta societies are instrumental in promoting an appreciation of the mystical aspects of all religions, particularly the Eastern. An important instrument for outreach is the Vedanta Catalog that is put out by members of the Hollywood center and offers books on all religions, especially Eastern.

About ten thousand catalogs are distributed each year. The Vedanta Press Trade List, also from Hollywood, is annually distributed to approximately six thousand people, schools, libraries, and yoga groups. The Chicago and San Francisco centers also distribute book catalogs. Books produced by the Vedanta movement are widely distributed in America. For instance, Prabhavananda and Isherwood's translation of the Bhagavad Gita, all editions, has sold over a million copies.

The work of Yogananda and SRF have similarly had a much wider impact on religion in America than can be discerned from membership statistics. Jane Dillon's dissertation reports that as of 1992 the SRF membership included several hundred thousand *kriyabans* (kriya initiates), but she also demonstrates that among the *kriyabans* there are varying levels and types of commitment. The SRF has exerted a widespread influence through publication of *Autobiography of a Yogi,* its magazine, and the SRF Lessons. The SRF publication work appears to be going very well since the organization has recently moved into a 57,000 sq. ft. building on a four-acre site. The publication facility employs fifty full-time workers and prints about two thousand items. The modest pricing of the SRF publications seeks only to cover costs.

Whereas the metaphysical movement in America[46] (which includes Theosophical, Christian Science, and New Thought groups) was the most receptive to the Indian swamis, Yogananda was particularly open to adopting emphases from these groups. In turn, his teachings are widely disseminated within the metaphysical movement in the form of both SRF literature and outside publications. In several pamphlets popular in New Thought circles, Yogananda explained that when the individual consciousness was united with the consciousness of God, directed thought could control atoms and cause material change. Matter was described as resulting from the vibration of God's energy or thought. Congruent with the Hindu concept of karma, Yogananda asserted that humans create their own destinies by what they think. Yogananda did not disparage

resorting to medical treatment, but he taught that healing required mental change. According to Yogananda, material prosperity was a legitimate aim when it entailed the concern to help others, and it could be achieved by cultivating right thoughts.[47] An SRF worship service is similar to the services of the New Thought denomination, Unity, in that both contain meditation and positive verbal affirmations.

Conclusion

The work of the Ramakrishna swamis and Yogananda helped to establish Hinduism in America as a viable religious alternative for Americans. Their introductory work set the stage for the growth of American interest in Hindu philosophy, meditation, and yoga that blossomed in the 1960s and 70s. The Vedanta societies and the Self-Realization Fellowship continue to provide a space for serious religious practitioners. The SRF literature and techniques, in particular, have a strong influence on Americans whose spirituality has been shaped by the metaphysical movement.

The difficulty of defining Hinduism has often been noted,[48] and some scholars have proposed abandoning the term altogether. The Hindu tradition can be seen as a kaleidoscope containing many elements, including but not limited to basic key terms, such as yoga, karma, guru, and *samadhi.* Individuals and specific groups put their own emphases and interpretations on these terms, and use them as building blocks to construct their own worldview that have as their backdrop the constantly changing components of the wider Hindu tradition. As the kaleidoscopic components of the Hindu tradition are incorporated into American culture, and into the emerging international culture, it is not clear when a religion ceases to be Hindu and becomes something else. Ethnic Hindus with American citizenship can easily be termed Hindu Americans. But there are also Americans who are not ethnic Hindus who have adopted Hindu outlooks and practices, who can be termed American Hindus. As with the Indian Christians who found *ashrams*, have gurus, and practive yoga, the question remains as to how far the process of inculturation can go before you have something radically different from the originating religious tradition. An American monastic in the Ramakrishna Order who travelled to India in the 1950s felt that he participated in the Hindu tradition as a believer and that he had very little in common with the Europeans and American Christian missionaries that he met in India. Such a person can be considered an American Hindu. Subsequent to their initial amazement, Indian Hindus acknowl-

edged that he was an authentic practitioner within their religious tradition.[49] The Self-Realization Fellowship also has strong ties with India, and a number of prominent Indians have acknowledged that they find in the American SRF president, Sri Daya Mata, an authentic exemplar of Hindu spirituality.[50] A former ambassador of India to the United States has noted that subsequent to the phenomenon of Indian gurus with Western followers, we are beginning to see the phenomenon of American Hindu gurus who are attracting Indian followers.[51] This is the inevitable result of the globalization process that began when Columbus set out to find a new way to India.

Notes

1. Catherine Cornille, *The Guru in Indian Catholicism: Ambiguity or Opportunity of Inculturation?* (Louvain: Peeters Press, 1991).

2. Information on forerunners is drawn from Robert Ellwood, ed., *Eastern Spirituality in America: Selected Writings,* Sources of American Spirituality Series (New York: Paulist Press 1987), 5–43; Wendell Thomas, *Hinduism Invades America* (New York: The Beacon Press, Inc., 1930), 177–245; Carl Thomas Jackson, "The Swami in America: A History of the Ramakrishna Movement in the United States, 1893–1960," Ph.D. diss., University of California, Los Angeles, 1964, 26–79; Carl T. Jackson, *The Oriental Religions and American Thought: Nineteenth-Century Explorations* (Westport, Conn.: Greenwood Press, 1981). A more detailed description of forerunners to Hinduism in America can be found in these works.

3. Thomas, *Hinduism Invades America,* 145, 147, 156. Yogananda himself approved Thomas's chapter on his work in America.

4. Paramahansa means "supreme swan" and is a title indicating the highest spiritual attainment. When Yogananda first arrived in America, as a Hindu monk he was known as Swami Yogananda. In 1935, he was given the title "Paramahansa" by his guru. The title Paramahansa was also applied to Swami Vivekananda's guru, Ramakrishna. The title "swami" (lord) is commonly given to Hindu monks who have taken vows of renunciation

(*sannyasa*). Monks take a new name, usually a compound ending in *ananda* (bliss).

5. Ellwood, *Eastern Spirituality in America,* 45–48.

6. Advaita or nondual Vedanta is a monistic philosophy that stresses that the one reality, *Brahman,* is permanent, unmanifest, and unchanging. *Brahman* is *nirguna,* without qualities. Therefore, Advaita Vedanta sees the impermanent and constantly changing material world as illusory and personal deities as being on the level of illusion. Ramanuja, as a monotheist, argued that *brahman* is *saguna,* with qualities. In his Vishishtadvaita, "qualified nondualism," he retains a monistic perspective, but God is personal; the material world is real and is part of God's body.

In this chapter, Sanskrit words that are names or that are well-known in the English-speaking world are not italicized. Diacritical marks are omitted.

7. Christopher Isherwood, *Ramakrishna and His Disciples* (1959; reprint, New York: Simon and Schuster, 1965), 96. The following account of Ramakrishna's religious experiences relies on this work. For an in-depth evaluation of Ramakrishna in relation to the Bengal Tantric tradition, see the 1993 Ph.D. dissertation by Jeffrey Kripal, University of Chicago.

8. This usage is ambiguous, but clearly Sarada Devi in being called the Holy Mother

is identified with the divine feminine that is believed to be manifested also in Kali. In Hinduism, the female divine principle is *shakti*, most often translated as "power," the creative force that produces material existence.

9. Isherwood, *Ramakrishna and His Disciples*, 206–7.

10. Ibid., 214.

11. Subsequent information on the Ramakrishna movement in the West, except when referenced otherwise, is drawn from Harold W. French, *The Swan's Wide Waters: Ramakrishna and Western Culture* (Port Washington, N.Y.: Kennikat Press, 1974), and Jackson, "The Swami in America."

12. Sister Christine, "Swami Vivekananda as I Saw Him," in *Reminiscences of Swami Vivekananda*, by His Eastern and Western Admirers (Calcutta: Advaita Ashrama, 1983), 185.

13. Swami Prabhavananda, *The Sermon on the Mount According to Vedanta* (New York: New American Library, 1963).

14. Swami Nikhilananda, trans., *The Gospel of Sri Ramakrishna* (New York: Ramakrishna-Vivekananda Center, 1984).

15. Paramahansa Yogananda, *The Science of Religion* (Los Angeles: Self-Realization Fellowship, 1982).

16. Paramahansa Yogananda, *Autobiography of a Yogi*, 12th ed. (Los Angeles: Self-Realization Fellowship, 1990).

17. Most of the following information is taken from the *Pictorial History of Self-Realization Fellowship (Yogoda Satsanga Society of America)* (Los Angeles: Self-Realization Fellowship, 1975).

18. Swami Abhedananda of the Vedanta movement, who was introduced to President McKinley, was probably the first Indian swami to be introduced to an American president. See Jackson, "Swami in America," 213.

19. *Paramahansa Yogananda: In Memoriam* (Los Angeles: Self-Realization Fellowship, 1958).

20. Swami Vivekananda, *Chicago Addresses* (Calcutta: Advaita Ashrama, 1989), 18.

21. Yogananda, *Autobiography*, 198–99.

22. Swami Vivekananda, *Life After Death*, 11th ed. (Calcutta: Advaita Ashrama, 1989), 34.

23. Robert Adjemian, ed., *The Wishing Tree: Christopher Isherwood on Mystical Religion* (San Francisco: Harper and Row, 1986), 9.

24. Josephine MacLeod in *Reminiscences of Swami Vivekananda*, 231.

25. Paramahansa Yogananda, *How You Can Talk With God* (Los Angeles: Self-Realization Fellowship, 1985), 14.

26. Ibid., 22–23.

27. Yogananda, *Autobiography*, 310–22, 330, 360–61, 494–95.

28. George M. Williams, *The Quest for Meaning of Swami Vivekenanda: A Study of Religious Change* (Chico, Calif.: New Horizons Press, 1974), 82–95; Swami Vivekananda, *Inspired Talks, My Master and Other Writings* (New York: Ramakrishna-Vivekananda Center, 1958), 30, 32–33, 37, 82, 99, 101.

29. Adjemian, *The Wishing Tree*, 67; Gerald Heard, "My Discoveries in Vedanta," in *Vedanta for the Western World*, ed. Christopher Isherwood (Hollywood: Vedanta Press, 1945), 59–63.

30. The term comes from Swami Abhedananda as quoted in Jackson, "Swami in America," 240.

31. Adjemian, *The Wishing Tree*, 19, 48, 51, 57, 69; Isherwood, introduction to *Vedanta for the Western World*, 11; Aldous Huxley, "The Minimum Working Hypothesis," in *Vedanta for the Western World*, 33–35; Isherwood, *Ramakrishna and His Disciples*, 223; Vivekananda, *Inspired Talks*, 26; conversation with Brother Anandamoy on 3 June 1992.

32. Richard Leviton, "How the Swamis Came to America," *Yoga Journal* (March/April 1990): 42–128.

33. Swami Prabhavananda, *Religion in Practice* (Hollywood: Vedanta Press, 1968).

34. Paramahansa Yogananda, "How You Can Approach God" in *The Divine Romance* (Los Angeles: Self-Realization Fellowship, 1986), 360–68. For SRF practices, see also the chapter "Learning to Behave," in the forthcoming Ph.D. dissertation in sociology by Jane Dillon on the SRF, University of California, San Diego.

35. The Self-Realization Fellowship, 3880 San Rafael Avenue, Los Angeles, California, 90065.

36. Vivekananda, *Chicago Addresses*, 6–7.

37. Christopher Isherwood, *My Guru and His Disciple* (New York: Penguin Books, 1981).

38. Dillon.

39. Jackson, "Swami in America," 299.

40. Thomas, *Hinduism Invades America*, 116–17, 173–74.

41. Sara Ann Levinsky, *A Bridge of Dreams: The Story of Paramananda, A Modern Mystic, and His Ideal of All-Conquering Love* (West

Stockbridge, Mass.: The Lindisfarne Press, 1984). Quotation on 126.

42. *Reminiscences of Swami Vivekananda,* 387.

43. Srimata Gayatri Devi, *One Life's Pilgrimage* (Cohasset, Mass.: Vedanta Centre, 1977), 115–20.

44. *Vedanta in Southern California: An Illustrated Guide to the Vedanta Society,* rev. ed. (Hollywood: Vedanta Press, 1960), 59–60.

45. J. Donald Walters, *The Path: A Spiritual Autobiography* (Nevada City, Calif.: Ananda Publications, 1977), 310, 578–82.

46. J. Stillson Judah, *The History and Philosophy of the Metaphysical Movements in America* (Philadelphia: The Westminster Press, 1967).

47. See the following booklets by Paramahansa Yogananda published by the SRF: "How You Can Talk With God" (1985); "The Law of Success" (1972); "Scientific Healing Affirmations: Theory and Practice of Concentration" (1981); "Metaphysical Meditations" (1964).

48. C. J. Fuller discusses the history of the term in *The Camphor Flame: Popular Hinduism and Society in India* (Princeton: Princeton University Press, 1992), 10–11.

49. John Yale, *A Yankee and the Swamis* (London: George Allen and Unwin Ltd., 1961).

50. Binay Ranjan Sen, foreword to *Finding the Joy Within You,* by Sri Daya Mata (Los Angeles: Self-Realization Fellowship, 1990), xiii–xv; Chakravarthi V. Narasimhan, preface to *Only Love,* by Sri Daya Mata (Los Angeles: Self-Realization Fellowship, 1976), v–vi; Swami Shyamananda Giri, "Kriya Yoga and the Spiritual Meaning of the Bhagavad Gita," *Self-Realization* (Fall 1989): 38; Sri Nani A. Palkhivala, " 'Only Love'—Book Review," *Self-Realization* (Summer 1980): 34–36.

51. Karan Singh, "American Gurus: The Bridge Builders," *Bhavan's Journal* (1 November 1985): 53–55.

Suggestions for Further Reading

Burke, Marie Louise. *Swami Vivekananda in America: New Discoveries.* 2 vols. Calcutta: Advaita Ashrama, 1958.

———. *Swami Vivekananda: His Second Visit to the West: New Discoveries.* Calcutta: Advaita Ashrama, 1978.

Kripal, Jeffrey J. "Ramakrishna's Foot: Mystical Homoeroticism in the *Kathamrta.*" In *Religion, Homosexuality and Literature,* edited by Michael L. Stemmeler and Jose Ignacio Cabezon. Las Colinas: Monument Press, 1992.

———. "Kali's Child: The Mystical and the Erotic in the Life and Teachings of Ramakrishna Paramahansa." Ph.D. diss., University of Chicago, 1993.

Neevel, Walter G. "The Transformation of Sri Ramakrishna." In *Hinduism: New Essays in the History of Religions,* edited by Bardwell L. Smith. Leiden: E. J. Brill, 1976.

Roberts, John Edward. "The Philosophy and Psychology of Paramahansa Yogananda as the Basis for a Unified Psychology: A First Look." Ph.D. diss., University of Southern California, 1986.

Swami Vivekananda. *The Complete Works of Swami Vivekananda.* 8 vols. Mayavati Memorial Edition. Calcutta: Advaita Ashrama, 1989.

Williams, George M. "The Ramakrishna Movement: A Study in Religious Change," and "Svami Vivekananda: Archetypal Hero or Doubting Saint?" In *Religion in Modern India,* edited by Robert D. Baird. New Delhi: Manohar, 1981.

18

HINDU MOVEMENTS SINCE MID-CENTURY: YOGIS IN THE STATES
Gene R. Thursby

> Having traveled further in the direction of spiritual alienation than any other people in history (and having drawn the rest of the world after us in our course), it now becomes our task to reclaim the human potentialities we have denigrated and sacrificed along the way.
>
> —Theodore Roszak

> We always find some form of Yoga whenever the goal is *experience of the sacred* or the attainment of a perfect *self-mastery*, which is itself the first step toward magical mastery of the world. It is a fact of considerable significance that the noblest mystical experiences, as well as the most daring magical desires, are realized through yogic technique, or, more precisely, that Yoga can equally well adapt itself to either path.
>
> —Mircea Eliade[1]

Introduction

The yogi best known to most Americans at mid-century was a fellow Yankee. His haphazard and colorful commentaries on the national pastime were widely quoted. Cartoonists played on his fame to create a landmark character for the newly emerging medium of children's television. They contrived a mythic landscape for him that soon gave shape to a network of tourist parks and campgrounds along the nation's highways. Americans, who had been deeply confused about the identities of Indians and India for centuries, were further confounded by these comic images that mixed a baseball player and an imaginary bear with a traditional Indian title of honor. Over the next quarter century, actual yogis who arrived from India helped to revive the title's traditional meanings

and ancient prestige—but could do little to resolve longstanding contradictions within the American experience.[2]

Many of the older attitudes toward a distant India that persisted through mid-century were informed by the heroic narrative tradition that told of the feats of European adventurers who had dared travel to the East. Travelers' tales shaped popular misperceptions that were further distorted in films that freely mixed fanciful elements from sources such as the *Arabian Nights,* Marco Polo, Jules Verne, and Rudyard Kipling. This India of heroic tales and Hollywood images was pictured as a dangerous and fabulous land. Paul Brunton built on this popular tradition with his book *A Search in Secret India.*[3] But rather than merely using India to turn himself into a hero figure, Brunton reported on living sages and yogis. His accounts of

Ramana Maharshi (1879–1950) and others drew American attention to the aims of real Indian spiritual masters. Later, the type of search that Brunton exemplified was taken up again and more rigorously by modern scientists. Medical practitioners and biofeedback investigators invited yogis to the United States to serve as case studies for their research. In return, a few American scientists travelled to India themselves and, without a sense of the irony of it, some of them made their contributions to the heroic quest literature, too.[4]

A period of rapid social and technological change around mid-century brought India closer to America. The United States government became concerned about India's position as a leader among nations not aligned with either Western or Communist countries. Appreciation for the importance of these nonaligned nations resulted in extensive agricultural assistance provided during the Eisenhower era, the appointment of John Kenneth Galbraith as ambassador to India by President Kennedy, and the creation of the Peace Corps. American popular culture became similarly preoccupied during the 1960s. When the Beatles went to India to practice Transcendental Meditation, both the place and the practice gained new interest in the West. Low excursion fares on jumbo jet aircraft allowed more people to make the journey to and from India. Increased traffic between the United States and India influenced fashion in general (Nehru jackets, tie-dyed skirts) and supplied raw materials for the language and style of the hippie and New Age subcultures.[5]

America's popular culture and its image of India shortly after mid-century also were affected by research with human subjects that was supported by several United States government agencies, including study of the effects of psychotropic or psychedelic substances. Research conducted by Timothy Leary and Richard Alpert, who were licensed to use LSD as an adjunct in experimental types of therapy, was highly publicized and became so controversial that it drove the two from academic life and made further scientific investigation all but impossible. However, both of them went on to make unusual contributions to ongoing American involvement with India. Leary and some associates became advocates for a kind of psychedelic religion that drew its expressive imagery partly from Indo-Tibetan traditional sources. Alpert went to India, became the devotee of a Hindu spiritual master, and adopted a new identity as Baba Ram Dass. When he returned he began a life of social service and inspirational lecturing that included innovative activities in support of South Asians and Americans afflicted with serious illness. He became a practicing yogi.[6]

At the same time, a broader affinity between American life and Hindu spiritual values was becoming evident due to concern for basic human rights. Popular movements arose in the United States during the 1960s to support the demands of African Americans for equal access to public resources and to oppose an undeclared Southeast Asian war in the nations emerging from colonial Indochina. Most leaders of those movements advocated civil disobedience, and some of them found encouragement and direction in the tactics of nonviolent action that had been devised by Rabindranath Tagore (1861–1941) and Mohandas Karamchand Gandhi (1869–1948) earlier in the century to oppose British colonial power in India. Their importance was acknowledged, for example, by the civil rights leader Martin Luther King, Jr., and antiwar activist Joan Baez.[7]

Since the middle of the twentieth century, Americans have responded in a rich variety of ways to the spiritual attraction of Hindu India. Much of the variety can be understood in relation to differences in personalities, organizational styles, and motivations. Among the typical motives of Americans who have been drawn toward Hindu spirituality have been a wish to help a suffering humanity, a need to engage in social action, an urge to experience a more real "inner world" beneath surface consciousness, and even a desire to attain some kind of conventional success in the ordinary world. A representative number of Hindu teachers who have arrived here since mid-century, have found resources in their tradition to address these motives, and whose organizations seem likely to maintain a place in American culture well into the next century are described in this chapter.[8]

Transcendental Meditation

What Dr. Eric Berne's Transactional Analysis (TA) was to psychotherapy in the 1960s and 1970s, Maharishi Mahesh Yogi's Transcendental Meditation (TM) was to spirituality. Berne derived his basic principles from a complex tradition of scientific inquiry into human nature. He drew insights from theories of Sigmund Freud, Alfred Adler, and Harry Stack Sullivan; pared them down to a few essentials; and expressed them in ways that were appealing and immediately understandable. The result was a revolution in popular culture. Effective techniques for psychological analysis seemed simple enough so that nearly anyone could begin to put them into practice and benefit from them. Berne's TA even became a fad for a few years, but persisted through that period and remains a creative movement today. In fact, most of the celebrated self-help teachers who have come along after him—concerned that you nurture your inner child, learn to pull your own strings, and recover from addictions by realizing the independent adulthood that is your very birthright—have borrowed heavily from Berne. Maharishi's TM is similar to Berne's TA in that it takes a few principles from traditional Hindu teachings, uses simple techniques, was a fad for a time, and continues to be taught today by a movement that seeks to confirm the effectiveness of its techniques by scientific measures.[9]

The Maharishi (a title of honor that means Great Sage) was born in the Indian town of Jabalpur on 12 January 1917. In his youth he studied physics at Allahabad University and soon after graduation met the highly respected Hindu monk, Swami Brahmananda Saraswati (1868–1953). When they met in 1940, the swami recently had returned to public activity after two decades of solitary contemplative life and

was about to assume the traditional teaching office of the Shankaracharya of Jyotir Math in northern India. Swami Brahmananda became the Maharishi's guru or spiritual preceptor, and the Maharishi in turn developed great devotion toward him, and served him all through the Shankaracharya years to the end of the swami's life. Then he withdrew to the mountains for an extended period of contemplation. After two years in the Himalayas, the Maharishi felt called to visit the temples of south India and set out on a pilgrimage that eventually took him all the way to Kanyakumari on the subcontinent's far southern tip. Along the return journey, he was persuaded to give a talk in Trivandrum, Kerala. It was so well received that his hosts turned it into a lecture series and then an extended speaking tour around the state.[10]

His presence attracted followers who founded the Spiritual Regeneration movement and organized a conference at Cochin. They brought out a commemorative book for the conference and named it *Beacon Light of the Himalayas* in honor of their visitor from the mountains. The book announced "a happy new era in the field of spiritual practices" and a talk on "Mind Control, Peace, and Atmananda through simple and easy methods of Spiritual Sadhana," by Maharishi Bala Brahmachari Mahesh Yogi Maharaj. Among these honorific and descriptive titles by which the book identified Maharishi, the term "Brahmachari" means a person who is unmarried and intentionally remains celibate. It indicates that the Maharishi had not become a monk but nevertheless was living a mode of life consistent with *sadhana* or the spiritual practices and disciplines that lead to *atmananda* or realization of unqualified bliss that is the nature of the indestructable inner Self. All this is consistent with the teachings of the ancient Upanishads that Self-realization requires energies that ordinarily go into sexuality, marriage, and family life should be redirected to *sadhana*. In short, the combination of the titles given to the Maharishi and to his talk would have assured the Indian audience that a competent teacher would be speaking on topics of traditional concern.

The principles that he taught while on the Kerala tour continue to be the main assumptions of his movement. First, spiritual development and eventual Self-realization are the natural birthright of every human being. Second, modern science is essentially compatible with ancient wisdom, and together they reveal a series of lawful states of consciousness and levels of reality. Third, a few simple techniques, regularly and correctly applied, will result in the opening of higher consciousness and ultimately will yield full Self-realization. Fourth, the general spread of this knowledge will inaugurate a new age of peace and happiness for all of humanity.

After the Kerala tour, he continued to carry the same message across India for the next two years, and then he set out through Southeast Asia to the West. The culmination of the India-wide phase of the movement came in a three-day religious seminar in Madras at the end of 1957 that attracted an audience of ten thousand people. The Maharishi called an extra meeting on the fourth day to announce on 1 January 1958 that he was about to take the Spiritual Regeneration movement worldwide. He completed preparations for travel and left India in April. By the time he returned in 1961 from this first of many world tours, he had set up an organizational framework sufficient to introduce the movement to small numbers of people in what was then Burma, Malaya, and Singapore, as well as in Thailand, Hong Kong, Hawaii, the continental United States, and western Europe. Nevertheless, it took several years more to make TM, Maharishi Mahesh Yogi, and his movement widely known here.

The small circle of seekers who became involved with the Maharishi during his first visit to the United States was similar to the kind of spiritual group that is common in Hindu India, composed of a guru surrounded by disciples. But he was not able to spend much time in the United States as the years went by, and the movement in American eventually was restructured on the pattern of a diversified corporation.

From the middle of the 1960s onward, various tasks were allocated by adding several new organizations. Some of them were responsible for introducing TM to a particular segment of society in the United States: the American Foundation for the Science of Creative Intelligence was directed toward leaders in education, business, and industry; the International Meditation Society was intended for the general public; and the Students International Meditation Society was for students from high school through university. These functional divisions of the movement were directed with considerable energy and enthusiasm by Americans such as Jerry W. Jarvis, who established and led the latter two organizations through the period of their greatest numerical growth in the 1970s. The restructuring also required supporting staff, especially people to teach TM in their local communities. Before 1966 there had been only one American who was authorized by the Maharishi to initiate people into TM practice, and intensive teacher training courses had to be designed and conducted.

To attract widespread positive interest in TM the right message was required, too. With restructuring, the ideal of spiritual regeneration moved toward the background, and greater emphasis was placed on immediate practical advantages to be gained from becoming skilled in meditation. Transcendental Meditation was presented as a technique, like speed reading, that could help the practitioner perform more effectively in the world. At the same time, the costly fallout from the 1960s consciousness revolution made Americans more motivated to find a safe way to "expand the mind" that would be a lawful alternative to dangerous drugs. Scientific studies conducted by R. Keith Wallace, Herbert Benson, and others, suggested that TM does produce an altered state of consciousness—one marked by deep rest which restores energy and may be of general benefit to physical and mental health. By the early 1970s the means, the motivation, and the moment had converged to make TM seem to be a panacea that could deliver America from all sorts of individual and social problems.[11]

The number of new initiates to TM per year in the United States reached its peak in 1975, after Merv Griffin heavily endorsed it on his television program, bringing the cumulative total of Americans who had begun the practice to about a million. By then TM had an American center for higher education, Maharishi International University, founded in California in 1971 and moved to Iowa in 1974. But the world headquarters and two institutions for advanced study, Maharishi European Research University and Maharishi Vedic University, were established in western Europe. The Maharishi settled there, seldom visiting the United States, and from 1972 onward formulated visionary plans that look toward a world government based on higher consciousness. He also began making what seemed to be magical claims about the potential consequences of meditation practice. The most difficult for the public to accept, and a real crisis for the movement's image in America, was the TM-Sidhis program that was introduced in 1976 to prepare meditators to be able to levitate. It put TM through an unprecedented period of media controversy.[12]

Nevertheless, the movement has continued to be confident that the power of higher consciousness to affect conditions at every level can be clearly demonstrated. The Maharishi Effect, which was proposed at the European Research University in 1974 and extended in 1978, builds on that assumption and asserts that when at least the square root of 1 percent of the population engages in meditation practice and the TM-Sidhis program then a condition of positive orderliness will be induced in the population at large. To generate the effect, large numbers of meditators gather at specified times and places in the hope of creating a more orderly world for the good of all.

The progressive optimism of the movement has been evident recently in politics and medicine, too. Organized as the Natural Law Party, it has participated in electoral politics in North America and in Europe. In the United States, the party succeeded in being listed on the ballot in several states during the presidential election of 1992. With award-winning physicist Dr. John Hagelin as its presidential nominee, and describing itself as the first American political party to be based on scientific principles and research, the 1992 platform of the party cited evidence of the positive effects of TM practice on social life and individual health. In medicine, the TM version of the traditional healing system of India, called Maharishi Ayur-Ved, has been made available to the public through consultation and treatment at holistic health clinics in major cities and in products sold in health food stores and by mail order. The best-known medical advocate of the system and its benefits is Deepak Chopra, M.D. His workshops and popular books offer the possibility of "quantum healing" and "perfect health."[13]

The movement's involvement in these seemingly diverse activities might be unexpected if one were to persist in identifying TM too narrowly with a simple meditation technique intended to attain limited objectives. But from the perspective of its history they are evidence of the basic continuity of the contemporary movement with what the Maharishi started among people in southern India some forty years ago. Today the movement supports those same basic principles, seeks to practice them in order to bring about the regeneration of humanity at every level, and values them as manifestations of the wisdom of the Maharishi and of the grace of his guru, Swami Brahmananda.

Himalayan Yoga

What immediately distinguishes Swami Rama from other yogis is that his powers of bodily control have been carefully tested by scientists. When he accepted an invitation to visit the Voluntary-Controls Project at the Menninger Foundation in March 1970, he was taken into the laboratory and was connected to devices that recorded his brain waves, heart action and blood flow, respiration, muscle tension, skin resistance and potential, and temperature. The monitoring devices indicated that when asked he was able to produce specific brain wave patterns. They showed that within a few minutes and without moving or using muscle tension he could cause a temperature differential of 10°F between the thumb and little-finger side of his right palm, presumably by exercising differential control over the blood flow through the radial and ulnar arteries in his wrist. They recorded an atrial flutter in his heart that he intentionally induced and that raised its rate from 70 to 300 beats per minute, effectively obliterating his pulse and briefly interrupting the flow of blood. The laboratory results from the visit were sufficiently interesting that he was asked to return for a longer stay and an extended series of experiments.

He did return from September to December 1970 to serve as a consultant to the Voluntary-Controls Project and as one of its main research subjects. In the laboratory he demonstrated that he could designate a brain-wave frequency (theta, delta, beta, or alpha) and specify a length of time he would produce it, as if he were a skilled musician who could play all the right notes at their proper tempo. In fact, before long he became bored with routine laboratory testing, but generated some unusual effects when challenged. In one instance he seemed to have psychokinetic power—the power to move an object by will. In the experiment, he was carefully masked to prevent air flow and seated five feet from a set of crossed knitting needles that were glued together and attached to a moveable bead over a 360° protractor. Behind his mask, he repeated a mantra (a set of Sanskrit sounds) and the needles moved 10°. He was asked to make the needles move again, and they did. But what was perhaps the most unexpected feature of this experiment, and of all the Swami Rama experiments, was the response of many of the research scientists. If they were open to the possibility of extended human potential before the experiments, they concluded that an exceptional skill was being demonstrated and that it deserved further study. If not, they concluded that the experimental results could have no significance for science.[14]

Outside the laboratory, the swami showed other special qualities including what appeared to be precognition. He was highly energetic, needed little sleep, and kept a busy schedule well beyond his role as a research subject. He was living at the home of researchers Elmer and Alyce Green and their son Doug Boyd, where he led meditation classes. He also gave public talks in Topeka and lectures at meetings in other cities. By the time he left for India in December, there were enough people who appreciated his abilities so that he could return to the United States as the director of his own teaching and research institute.[15]

Relatively little is known about Swami Rama's life before he first arrived in the United States. He relates that he was born in a high valley of the Himalayas in 1925. His father was over sixty and his mother over forty-five years old at the time, and they experienced the birth of a son as a blessing from the guru his father had found a few years earlier while on a trip into the mountains. His parents died while he was still a child, and he was raised by that guru—who usually is referred to simply as the master or the Bengali Baba. The master arranged a spiritual apprenticeship, a traditional education in India, and a modern one at Oxford for him. At age twenty-four, Swami Rama was selected for a high religious office at Kavirpitham in southern India, but served just three years and then left the position in order to pursue his own path of inner development. With the aim of sharing the wisdom of the Himalayan sages, eventually he found his way to Europe, then Japan, and finally the United States.[16]

Swami Rama returned from India in 1971 to organize the Himalayan Institute of Yoga Science and Philosophy in Glenview, Illinois. By 1978 the work had prospered enough that it was possible to move the institute's national headquarters to a four-hundred-acre complex in the Poconos to the north of Honesdale, Pennsylvania. Today the national headquarters coordinates a dozen branch or affiliated centers in this country and several abroad, and conducts its own teaching programs.

There are workshops and classes in meditation, psychology and relationships, diet and nutrition, hatha yoga, and health. Teacher training and certification in hatha yoga is available along with membership in the Himalayan Institute Teachers' Association. Comprehensive programs include a ten-day work-study retreat; a month-long retreat that combines classes, work, and quiet time for self-transformation; and longer-term residential programs.

In addition to teaching, the institute conducts research in its Dana Research Laboratory and provides holistic healthcare that seeks to integrate knowledge from allopathic and homeopathic medical traditions. One of the goals of the healthcare program is to empower people to manage their lives more effectively on their own. For that reason, treatment programs may include addictions recovery, weight loss, and stress assessment components. Swami Rama is skilled in homeopathic medicine, and there are several staff and cooperating physicians with allopathic certification, headed by Rudolph Ballentine, M.D. When it will benefit patients, Dr. Ballentine and others refer them from practices in New York and Chicago metropolitan centers to the institute for consultation and for short- or intermediate-term programs. Since the institute is oriented toward holistic care, staff members and cooperating professionals include psychologists, an anatomy and body therapy specialist, a graduate homeopathic physician, a nurse, and a pharmacist to manage what is one of the most comprehensive homeopathic pharmacies in North America.

Himalayan Yoga, like most of the other movements described in this chapter, has an integrated multimedia publishing program. The press at the national headquarters regularly produces the magazine *Yoga International,* many books, the quarterly guide to the institute's programs, and audio and video tapes. Distribution is primarily by direct mail order and through East West Books. Altogether the teaching, research, and publication make a big enterprise to manage.

Swami Rama, however, is not a "business as usual" kind of person. Though he is now entering his seventies, in his recent years he has been more embattled and busier than ever before. Having offered his special capacities to the West and contributed toward the growth of scientific knowledge in this country, in recent years he has been completing the circle by enlisting international support for needs in northern India and his native Himalayan region. Because the Himalayas are the earth's highest and youngest mountains, the plates that formed them are unstable and susceptible to severe tremors and quakes. The swami endangered his own health after a recent earthquake by engaging in the Gandhian practice of fasting to appeal to government leaders in India to release relief funds intended for the victims but not reaching them. In addition to disaster relief, he is working for long-term improvement of health for the people of the region through the Himalayan Hospital Trust which plans to complete a 350-million-dollar medical center and rural improvement program in the foothills. The project envisions a hospital, medical research units, and colleges of medicine, nursing, and medical technology. It also includes 250 earthquake-resistant homes for villagers. But apart from threats from disease and overpowering acts of nature, human malice is what creates the greatest danger for most people. Among his many acts to alleviate intolerance, Swami Rama has worked to improve relations between Hindus and Sikhs in India and abroad by translating and publishing important devotional works from the Sikh tradition.

In the West, what the swami has been attempting to establish is far more subtle and potentially more important than the scientific credibility of yoga—even though he has made a major contribution toward that goal. A few years ago he stated in the following words his more central intent as a teacher, guide, and guru in the tradition of Himalayan Yoga:

> As far as I am concerned, I have no doubt about the authenticity and efficacy of these practices. However, I have not been able to accomplish my prime purpose for coming to the West because there is no laboratory with equipment

sophisticated enough to help me scientifically examine and verify meditation and kundalini exercises. I have been facing a serious difficulty: either I meet material scientists or I meet religionists and philosophers, but not aspirants who are prepared to evaluate and verify the effects of these practices. I hope that one day this science will be popular and available for the true seekers in modern society.[17]

His unfinished task here in the United States is something like the sensitive and delicate procedure of completing a graft or a transplant. However urgent, the process can be slow and the results may take time to reveal themselves. Swami Rama is attempting to bring resources from an ancient initiatory tradition that was developed, preserved, and transmitted in the mountain retreats of the Himalayas, and to impart them to reliable aspirants who will be able to maintain them in the far different conditions of life that characterize the contemporary West.

Integral Yoga

Swami Satchidananda, even at eighty, looks like the veritable image of the quintessential spiritual teacher from the East. Along with his irrepressible sense of humor, his appearance has been both an immediate asset and a liability to his work in the West. In modern consumer society where nothing is safe from being turned into a commodity, his stylized image on posters drawn by Peter Max and his photogenic presence at the opening of the 1969 Woodstock Festival may have made him seem familiar and domesticated, like some brand-name product. But attention to the causes to which he has given himself through the years, the life at his ashram along the banks of the James River in Virginia, or his immediate presence will quickly sweep away that merely surface impression.

He was born on 22 December 1914 as the second son in an accomplished family that lived on their extensive agricultural lands near Coimbatore in southern India. From an early age he had a keen interest in learning how things work. He directed his curiosity equally toward language, society, and mechanical devices. At seven he prepared a speech on nonviolence that he gave at a regional spiritual conference to which his father, an excellent poet, took him. In his youth he saw the futility of the traditionally strict distinction between high caste and low in south Indian social life. By early adulthood, he studied scientific agricultural techniques, became the first south Indian expert welder, worked for companies that produced automobiles and distributed films, and for a time managed a temple. At twenty-three, he was newly married, was regularly motorcycling between his home and factory, and was well prepared for the full responsibilities of a long and productive family life. But after only five years that way of life was ended by the death of his wife, which left him a widower with two young sons.

His family saw him through a radical transition during the next six years. The sons were well cared for at the household of his parents while he withdrew from active life and moved to a secluded garden cottage well suited to an extended period of deep contemplation, austerity, and study. Regular practice of hatha yoga and a single midday meal provided the structure for a disciplined routine. After a time he began to visit nearby holy places and spiritual teachers, including a few siddhas—rare beings who may go unrecognized because they are apt to live a simple, strange, or inexplicable lifestyle but can manifest extraordinary powers for the good of others. He became ready for another change, and in 1946 he entered the Ramakrishna Mission at Tiruparaitturai and was initiated into the Brahmacharya life of intentional celibacy, study, and service. Not long after his initiation, he moved on to other ashrams and centers of learning—like a university student who studies with experts at several institutions in order to pursue an advanced research project.

His transition was completed and a new way of life begun when he reached the ashram of Swami Sivananda (1887–1963) at Rishikesh. Located on the banks of the Ganges River where it comes out of the Himalayas, Rishikesh is a gathering place for great sages, strange siddhas, and every sort of real or seeming saint and aspirant. Among all of them, Swami Sivananda had a unique place. He was born in south India and became a monk after a successful career as a medical doctor. He was a big man in every good way—tall, broad, and the embodiment of generosity. Large and strong enough to support many kinds of projects and activities, he had an inclusive or integrative attitude that made him one of India's best models of how to be a monk under conditions of modern life. In 1936, he organized his work by founding the nonsectarian Divine Life Society. Several of the students who came to him, including Swami Satchidananda whom he initiated into the monastic life in 1949, later became senior teachers in India and in other parts of the world.[18]

Master of Yoga (Yogiraj) was the title Sivananda bestowed on Satchidananda, who taught in the Yoga Vedanta Forest Academy at the Rishikesh ashram until 1951, when he set out on a year-long tour of India. The teaching work and the tour alike were twin fruits of his many years of regular spiritual practice and of learning to remain free from attachment to people or place. But perhaps because he still showed some preference for withdrawal from worldly life, his master instructed him to go to Sri Lanka to open a branch of the Divine Life Society in 1953 to serve the island's people. Finding it a place divided by differences in caste, language, and religion, he was successful in adapting the integral approach of his master to local circumstances. He developed the traditional July festival in honor of the guru into an All Prophets Day that honored masters from all religions. His innovative work for interreligious understanding and for peace between Tamils and Sinhalese earned him the title of Revolutionary Monk. Where no more could be done, he and his followers built temples and conducted services for those in prison. Soon he was one of the best-known people in Sri Lanka and was asked to travel around the island in a regular circuit in order to be available to all who needed him. Having become a major public figure, Satchidananda intensified his experience of the inner aspects of spiritual life in 1958 by making an arduous pilgrimage to Mount Kailash high up in the Himalayas.

In the years following, he was called upon to make more distant journeys. In 1959, he gave public lectures and yoga demonstrations in Hong Kong for the Divine Life Society. In 1961, he made a more extensive teaching tour to the Philippines, Malaya, Hong Kong, and Japan. His experience of foreign lands and people, along with his practice of detachment, were called upon again in 1965 when a wealthy young filmmaker from the United States named Conrad Rooks came to Sri Lanka. Rooks began recording Swami Satchidananda on film, but was recalled to Paris. He sent an air ticket and asked the swami to come to Europe to continue the filming. Satchidananda agreed to a working tour that would also take him to several great spiritual centers: Jerusalem, Cairo, Mount Athos, and Rome. When he got to Paris the way opened for him to travel even farther West.

On the invitation of artist Peter Max, he arrived in New York City at the end of July 1966. By October his following had grown from a few friends who gathered at the Max apartment, to people who began enrolling for formal classes, to the founding membership of the Integral Yoga Institute. Despite the extraordinary interest in his teaching in America, he decided that he had to return to his responsibilities in Sri Lanka at the end of the year. When he got there, a stack of letters from New York was waiting for him. He helped to reorganize the religious center in Sri Lanka under new leadership and was back in the United States before the end of May.

It is now approaching thirty years since Swami Satchidananda answered the demand from Americans to stay and teach. He arrived, returned, and then remained here in response to the needs of others. After he was able to arrange for the work in Sri Lanka to be continued without him and was free to teach in the United States, his commitment to be here made history. At the insistence of his Integral Yoga students he applied for and received the first permanent resident visa ever issued for the entry of a "Minister of Divine Words." Although thousands of Americans are sent out for ministerial service elsewhere in the world, not one entering person had been granted formal permission to reside in the United States for that purpose until 25 July 1968. The visa application file was filled with letters that described ways the swami had helped bring positive changes into the lives of people in this country. Later, during the 1976 bicentennial year and almost a decade after being invited to New York, Satchidananda became a citizen of the United States.

The swami's life as an American has followed almost the same pattern as in Sri Lanka. The continuity demonstrates his conviction that spiritual essentials are universal and go deeper than any differences created by religion or culture. Harmony among religions is the hallmark of his approach. Brother David Steindl-Rast and Rabbi Joseph Gelberman have been among the long-term interfaith friends with whom he has conducted many workshops, carried on dialogues, and officiated at ritual celebrations. He was twice received by the late Pope Paul VI. When he was blessed by Pope John Paul II, he described himself by saying, "Mainly I'm working in the ecumenical field." Tending that field has been strenuous and has required him to travel across the country and the world for most of the years he has been here. Although he came to stay, that has not meant remaining in one place.

The practice of Integral Yoga has brought people together at urban teaching centers and more recently at a rural retreat center that reflects the values of Swami Sivananda's ashram on the Ganges at Rishikesh. For several years short-term retreats were held on some college campus, at a leased facility, or in an ashram of another teacher. The Ananda Ashram of the accomplished medical doctor, yoga psychologist, and Sanskrit language teacher Rammurti S. Mishra (who later took the name Swami Brahmananda when he

entered monastic life in 1983) was particularly welcoming. But by 1979, after several years of hard work and various interim arrangements, it became possible to purchase 750 acres along the James River in Virginia as a permanent home for the Satchidananda Ashram and an extended residential community called Yogaville. Most of its residents can be grouped under one or another of five categories. A few people have taken preliminary or final vows to enter a service-oriented monastic life, following the example of Swami Satchidananda. Others are preparing or have completed preparation for ordination as ministers. They have a discipline as do the monks, but unlike the monks they can marry and share the responsibilities of family life. A third category includes married and unmarried people who are not seeking to be ministers or monks but who find the practice of yoga meaningful, who are devoted to Swami Satchidananda, and who want to participate in a community that has a basis in spiritual values. Next are short-term visitors—people who come to the ashram to attend a course, take a workshop, or see what it is like to follow that way of life. Finally, casual or day visitors come to the ashram in order to visit a family member or friend who is in residence or to see the LOTUS.

LOTUS is an acronym for Light of Truth Universal Shrine. Dedicated in 1986, its distinctive design expresses Swami Satchidananda's ecumenical vision. The outward shape of the building is based on the lotus flower. That flower is an ancient symbol of higher truth because its surprising beauty so surpasses its apparent source in a plant that grows up from mud and through brackish water to emerge in the light. The opening petals of the flower are also a sign of the process of transformation by which every individual's spiritual nature becomes evident. Within the LOTUS building the central point of interest in the shrine is a column of moving light, an image inspired in part by Swami Satchidananda's admiration for the nineteenth-century south Indian saint Ramalinga Swamigal. The saint himself invoked the supreme reality as Infinite

Grace-bestowing Light (Arutperum Jyoti), a term of great inspirational power but free from sectarian trappings, and consecrated a Light Temple in 1869. In the LOTUS, the light in the central column moves upward to the ceiling and then radiates outward to the several altars that represent particular religious traditions and are located around the perimeter of the circular shrine.

Yogaville, although in some ways exotic, is a good example of the intentional or ideal-guided communities that are intrinsic to the American tradition. To live there one must get acquainted with its values and rules, feel that they are helpful for guiding one's life, offer services to the community, and above all want to be there. The food is strictly vegetarian. (Dean Ornish credits Swami Satchidananda with inspiring his research on diet and health.) The governance combines authority with democracy, the traditional with the modern. Although Swami Satchidananda has been taking a less-active role in day-to-day questions, he is the final authority. Officers of the ashram include a president, vice-president for finance, and vice-president for administration, each of whom is a monk or minister. Community meetings are held regularly so that questions of mutual concern can be discussed and resolved. Along with the individuals who live in the ashram, about thirty-five families have homes in the immediate community and a few commute from nearby towns and cities. There is a community school for children up to age twelve (the Yogaville Vidyalayam), a fine arts society, and a credit union. Members voluntarily contribute their time and material resources to help meet human needs in the surrounding county, too. Yogaville itself has another memorable symbol in addition to the LOTUS. A monumental bronze image of the Lord of the Dance (Shiva Nataraja) stands at the top of a hill named for Mount Kailash. Presented by Karan Singh, former Indian ambassador to the United States, the image is a reminder of the connection between India and America that made it possible for there to be a place like Yogaville, Virginia. The figure of the danc-

ing Lord also beautifully expresses Integral Yoga ideals for living—attention, balance, courage, skillful movement, surpassing of self-limitations, and compassion for all.[19]

Kripalu Yoga

Yogi Amrit Desai is the founder and master of the Kripalu Yoga movement. He was born on 16 October 1932 in the Gujarat region of northwestern India, where his father was working as a village shopkeeper. His family were followers of the Vaishnava branch of Hindu tradition, and his father began each day by offering ritual worship to God in the form of Krishna before opening his shop. When Amrit was ten, the family moved from the village into the town of Halol. At the time, Amrit found the change rather difficult because he was recovering from the effects of typhoid fever. But as he regained strength, he began to find benefits in urban life. There were better schools, more resources to support the family, and his maternal relatives lived there, too.

During his youth in Halol, Amrit was attracted to all sorts of self-improvement activities. In his teens he read the Gujarati version of Dale Carnegie's *How to Win Friends and Influence People* and tried to put its teachings into practice. He also hiked, became an enthusiastic competitor in games and sports, and practiced body building. But this interest took a new direction when he met a Hindu monk who was on one of his periodic visits to the town. Amrit was in the process of teaching himself hatha yoga from posture charts on the wall of a local exercise center while the visiting Swami Kripalvananda (1912–1981) was making temporary use of a private room in the same building for his daily meditation. When he saw the youth's affinity for yoga, the swami immediately appreciated it, and further encouraged it by giving Amrit a personal demonstration of his own practice of the traditional postures.

Eventually Swami Kripalvananda began to serve as a spiritual guide to Amrit's family, giving them counsel about all aspects of living. He proposed a developmental path for Amrit that was to include a five-year period of Brahmacharya (continence combined with spiritual practice) followed by a traditionally arranged marriage. The Desai family took the swami's guidance, but that did not oblige Amrit to be otherwise secluded from experience of the world. He completed school, tried out the training required for a career as an engineer, then left it for the air force, and after military service he returned to take up teaching at a high school in Halol. Once settled there, he was married in 1955.

A year later the young couple moved to Ahmedabad, one of the largest cities in the region, so that Amrit could attend art school. In the next four years, he completed the requirements for an art diploma, secured a teaching position at Saint Xavier's High School in Ahmedabad, and saved money to travel to the United States for further education. Even so, all the money that could be saved and borrowed amounted to just enough to bring him here on his own and to pay his tuition at the Philadelphia College of Art, with very little left to meet basic living expenses for himself in the States and for his family in India. But at least he was able to count on one full meal a day by washing lunch dishes at the college, and when the United States immigration service issued him a work permit he found a night job at a paper bag factory. On weekends he taught a fashion design class and yoga classes at a local adult education center. After a year and a half of nearly nonstop activity, he was well enough situated to bring his wife, first-born son, and younger brother to join him in this country.

When he graduated from the Philadelphia College of Art in 1964, Amrit Desai already had a loyal following from his first years of yoga teaching. Although he worked for textile and design firms after graduating, and continued to paint and to exhibit his art, he was pressed to meet the demand from aspiring students of yoga. Matters reached a turning point in 1966, marked by his first return to India since coming to the United States. Swami

Kripalvananda received him at Bhiwandi near Bombay, giving him initiation, instruction, and advice on how he should teach in America. With full support from his wife and brother, that year he determined to devote himself full time to yoga. The non-profit Yoga Society of Pennsylvania that he established became so successful that within a few years it was sponsoring more than 150 classes a week taught by Amrit Desai and others he had trained.

He attributes that early success as well as the subsequent maturing of his teaching to his master, Swami Kripalvananda, whom he returned to India repeatedly over the next decade to visit. The swami gave Amrit Desai a special blessing and the title of "yogi" at the end of a period of advanced instruction in 1969, and in 1971 gave him a type of initiation called Shaktipat Diksha by which a rare master can awaken the spiritual energy (the *prana, kundalini,* or *shakti*) in a properly prepared disciple. What the swami gave Amrit Desai through a combination of instruction and initiation enabled him to pursue his practice of yoga in a way that produced a gain in bodily control and also a gain in awareness of a more subtle energy. What the Swami taught him was not just a set of techniques to master the body, which some consider to be the proper aim of hatha yoga, but a process leading to awakening.

The value of the master's guidance became evident to Yogi Desai during a regular round of practice one morning in 1970:

That morning my body moved of its own volition, without my direction, automatically performing an elaborate series of flowing motions. Many of these "postures" I had never seen even in any yoga book before. It was the movements of my body—which ordinarily are thought to be an obstruction to concentration—that drew my outgoing attention inward and brought about the inner stillness of deepest meditation. This induced an expanded state of consciousness that revealed new dimensions of life and filled me with ecstasy. Later my joy was even greater when I found I was able to enter the same experience again and again during my daily practice.[20]

On the basis of that extraordinary experience, he developed an approach to yoga that seeks to incorporate both control and surrender in order to generate awakening and to contribute toward ongoing inner development. In honor of his master, Yogi Desai called it Kripalu Yoga. For the next fifteen years he continued to refine his understanding, and then presented it in detail in the two volumes of *Kripalu Yoga: Meditation-in-Motion* in 1985. There he describes the path of Kripalu Yoga as a bridge between two highly respected formalized approaches to yoga practice, the way of willful discipline in Ashtanga Yoga (e.g., as summarized in Patanjali's *Yoga Sutra*) and the way of initiation and surrender in Kundalini Yoga (e.g., the basis for the great texts of Kashmir Shaivism). The first represents the preliminary and the second the advanced stage envisioned in Kripalu Yoga. A student must begin with practice of the yoga of will and then can advance toward the yoga of surrender. In the early 1990s, Yogi Desai noted that some students tend to avoid vigorous practice of the correct postures that constitute the beginning stage, and so he gave it a renewed emphasis. He also invited Bikram Choudhury to the new Kripalu Center in Lenox, Massachusetts, to serve as a consulting teacher who would help foster a more intense style of basic yoga practice.

During the years that he was moving toward his mature understanding of the Kripalu path, Yogi Desai also was maintaining a balance between his life as a householder and as a spiritual guide. Family life as a husband and father of three children had to be integrated with his individual yoga practice, his teaching, and his effort to design activities that would assist others in advancing their spiritual evolution. In 1970 he found the site for a residential setting that would bring these several strands of life together in one place, and purchased the sixty-eight-acre parcel of land located just thirty-five miles northwest of Philadelphia at Sumneytown, Pennsylvania. For more than a decade it was

the major center for Kripalu Yoga activities. In 1972, after two summers there, he and his family moved to the property. By that time he had begun to give formal initiation to small numbers of disciples, and he permitted a few of them to share the Sumneytown property as year-round residents of the Kripalu Yoga Ashram. Improving the site, creating facilities suitable for a spiritual retreat center, and living together in close promixity with others required a good deal of physical labor and a set of behavioral guidelines. In 1973, Yogi Desai formulated the basic requirements for ashram living, including Brahmacharya. In the winter of that year he decided that his own inner work would benefit from a period of solitude, and he withdrew into a private room inside the ashram for three months, which gave his disciples the opportunity to learn to manage their lives within the patterns he had established for them but without his personal direction. They regarded him as their "Gurudev" or divinely inspired spiritual master. He had given them a formal initiation which included a Sankrit spiritual name and the mantra passed down from his teacher, *"Om Namo Bhagavate Vasudevaya"* ("I surrender to the Lord"), and on their behalf he continued to apply traditional teaching methods and adapt contemporary ones to guide them.

The movement's membership and resources continued to grow rapidly during the decade from 1974 through 1983. The ashram at Sumneytown was enlarged in 1974, and its ownership was transferred from Yogi Desai to a non-profit corporation. In 1975 the Kripalu Yoga Retreat, a 250-acre site suitable for summer programs, was purchased at Summit Station, Pennsylvania. In 1983, a former Jesuit seminary on a several-hundred-acre wooded hillside across from the Tanglewood Music Center in Lenox, Massachusetts, was acquired. Now, as the Kripalu Center for Yoga and Health at Shadowbrook, it is the main home of the movement and has been described as the world's largest holistic health and yoga complex. The Kripalu Community at Sumneytown also currently functions as an intentional community for residents and as a place where visitors can attend workshops and obtain holistic health services that are designed to assist in recovery and to provide resources for life enrichment.

Yogi Desai understands the meaning of "yoga" in a very broad and inclusive sense, and as a result his American movement has been dynamic and experimental through its history. At the same time, he has maintained respect for the roots of this branch of yoga in India. He has returned to India many times, either alone or with disciples, and has been honored there. In 1974 the Shankaracharya of Dwaraka in western India awarded him the honorary standing of Doctor of Yoga Science, and in 1982 the centenarian Swami Gangeshwarananda gave him the title of Maharishi. But doubtless more important for him, his own master Swami Kripalvananda in 1980 designated him a yogacharya or master teacher of yoga. Even more remarkably, the swami consented to leave India, where he had kept a regimen of silent meditation for nearly twenty years, and came to the United States to spend his last years with Yogi Desai and his disciples in their American ashram.[21]

Siddha Yoga

The Siddha Yoga movement is led by a small, vital, energetic monk named Swami Chidvilasananda. She was born in southwestern India on 24 June 1955, and from early childhood was guided in her spiritual development by Swami Muktananda Paramahamsa (1908–1982), the guru who brought Siddha Yoga to America. Muktananda came to the United States for a brief visit in 1970, then returned here for longer stays as part of his 1974 to 1976 and 1978 to 1981 world tours. Chidvilasananda served as his translator during the world tours. Her role required her to stand for hours beside her master and to express without delay everything that he wished to communicate—from his most subtle teachings to his down-to-earth humor. She had to do it in a way that was

accurate and yet understandable to a person who had no prior knowledge of yoga, spiritual disciplines, or Hindu tradition. That experience proved to be as arduous, intense, and effective a preparation for leadership as could be devised.

The movement that she leads was shaped mainly by the influence of Bhagawan Nityananda (d. 1961), the great guru of her master Swami Muktananda. It is likely that he was born somewhere in southwestern India in the late nineteenth century, but the details of his early life are lost in legend. He seems to have entered a monastic order while a youth and then as a young man took up the life of an avadhut—one who wanders about freely and with no concern for comfort, social custom, personal loss or gain. He was a large, dark, and striking figure who rarely wore anything more than a small loincloth. Because of his strange appearance, he was little understood and not very well treated. Most people tended either to avoid him or else mercilessly pursue him to get benefits from what they believed were his auspicious powers. Even now there are people who report that some member of their immediate family was cured of an affliction or came into great wealth as a result of a blessing from Nityananda.

In his middle years he moved northward and settled in Ganeshpuri, then a remote village along the Tansa River some fifty miles inland from Bombay. He lived simply, bathed in the local hot springs, and generally was respected by the local people. Word about him eventually reached the city, and by mid-century many urban residents of Bombay were making pilgrimages out to Ganeshpuri in order to have the *darshan* of Bhagawan Nityananda—literally, to be able to see him and be improved by being in his presence. He spoke little, was neither a philosopher nor a preacher, and did not write books, but undeniably was a special presence.

At about the same time Swami Muktananda, who was himself from the southwest but had come north to visit the shrines of saints that dot the countryside of that region and had settled further inland at Yeola, was advised to visit Bhagawan

Nityananda. The visit was the start of a spiritual apprenticeship that went on for many years and that Muktananda has described in detail in his autobiography *Play of Consciousness*. At the conclusion of the long process, Nityananda arranged for Muktananda to be accommodated in a small ashram of his own alongside the main road leading into Ganeshpuri. During his last years, Nityananda sent some of the visitors who came to see him to Muktananda who was adept at making clear the meaning of Nityananda's few words, was well trained in traditional philosophy and medicine, was an insightful listener, and was able to give practical advice in response to the most vexing personal problems. By the time Bhagawan Nityananda left his body in 1961, Swami Muktananda could be regarded as his successor.

Ganeshpuri began to attract a few foreign visitors during the 1960s, and by the end of the decade Swami Muktananda had determined to come to the West to make his guru known here. Muktananda, like Nityananda, was a charismatic figure. He continued the practice of making *darshan* the central feature of the master-disciple relationship but expanded and explained it by setting it in the context of the cosmology of Kashmir Shaivism. He characterized Siddha Yoga as the yoga of the guru's grace (*guru-kripa* yoga). Grace becomes available through the presence of an already realized being, the Siddha guru, who awakens the dormant *kundalini-shakti* and enables the disciple to make spiritual progress toward full realization of the inner Self (Shiva). Having awakened to the reality of the inner Self, one is able to recognize the Self in all. That was what Muktananda believed had taken place in the apprenticeship that he served under Bhagawan Nityananda, and afterward found it confirmed by the traditional texts of the nondual philosophy of Kashmir Shaivism.

Muktananda became known in the West as "the guru's guru" in part because he was able to evoke an immediate experience of the Self, even in people who were unprepared for it and perhaps thought they were not interested. He had enormous

confidence in the grace of Bhagawan Nityananda, whom he saw as the personal form of that divine power which enabled him to give thousands of people the otherwise rare form of initiation known as Shaktipat Diksha. The surprisingly informal and unexpected way that Muktananda could give people the *shaktipat* experience that made them aware of their spiritual potential remains today the source of numerous anecdotes. He also designed a suitable formal setting, the Intensive, in which there would be an appropriate degree of respect and appreciation for what was taking place when the *kundalini* was awakened. Among the published reports by Americans of their *shaktipat* experiences, a brief account by Christina Grof makes clear that for her the charismatic touch of Swami Muktananda during a meditation retreat generated an enormous burst of transformational energy:

> Suddenly I felt as though I had been plugged into a high-voltage socket as I started to shake uncontrollably. My breathing fell into an automatic, rapid rhythm that seemed beyond my control, and a multitude of visions flooded my consciousness. I wept as I felt myself being born; I experienced death; I plunged into pain and ecstasy, strength and gentleness, love and fear, depths and heights. I was on an experiential roller coaster, and I knew I could no longer contain it. The genie was out of the bottle.
>
> During the next few months, my whole life changed. My neat, restricted worldview was shattered, and I began to discover new possibilities within myself as my meditation experiences continued.[22]

While Grof had an experience of considerable intensity, reports by others indicate that the *shaktipat* brought about by a master of Siddha Yoga may have a more subtle or slow-acting quality. Nevertheless, it is difficult to determine in advance what short-term manifestations could accompany *kundalini* awakening, and it is important to recognize that present scientific knowledge is insufficient to predict with confidence what might take place. Because a powerful catharsis and realignment may be felt at a physical, emotional, and mental level, it is only reasonable to proceed with caution and to give oneself and these mysterious energies proper respect.[23]

Shaktipat, whether it comes as a dramatic sudden shock or a subtle unfolding process, is just one part of Siddha Yoga's larger framework of meaning that Swami Muktananda called *maha-yoga*—a spiritual path that is composed of many aspects that work with one another in harmony. At the center is the Siddha guru. *Darshan* and spiritual transformation under the guidance of the guru are basic components. Devotion is celebrated and cultivated in song and service, too. Siddha Yoga has a well-developed liturgy. The *Guru Gita,* its most honored Sanskrit-language text, is chanted at dawn each day. Other long and short chants give devotional order to the rest of the daily routine. Siddha Yoga is a chanting yoga. It is also a yoga of service in which work freely offered for the guru and for the welfare of humanity is regarded as a religious activity. Hatha yoga is encouraged as an auxiliary discipline that can help one to gain strength, become supple, and sustain the other practices.

When Swami Muktananda came to the West, he said that he was bringing about a meditation revolution. Contemplation and meditation are central activities in Siddha Yoga, but by the time Muktananda arrived in America there had been several teachers of meditation from India here already, most notably Maharishi Mahesh Yogi. How was it possible at that point to make a meditation revolution? One answer is suggested by the characterization of Siddha Yoga as *guru-kripa* yoga. Like the early modern cosmological revolution that put the sun at center, the Siddha Yoga meditation revolution puts the Self—embodied in the form of the Siddha guru—at center. The *shakti* or spiritual energy of the guru is believed to attract disciples to meditation and to initiate the meditative state. As a result, meditation should take place easily, naturally, at times spontaneously. The master's felt presence rather than any particular technique is the key to the Siddha meditation that Swami Mukta-

nanda brought to the West. Siddha Yoga affirms a "charismatic" rather than a "technical" approach to meditation.[24]

During the years since Swami Chidvilasananda succeeded Swami Muktananda as the presiding Siddha guru, she has paid tribute to her predecessors and has enlarged the range of their influence in several ways. She has had a beautiful temple in honor of Bhagawan Nityananda constructed at the main Siddha Yoga ashram in South Fallsburg, New York. She has expanded the movement's home ashram in Ganeshpuri, and has contributed toward the improvement of the nearby village. She has fostered a charitable organization, which builds on the work that was begun by Bhagawan Nityananda and was carried forward by Swami Muktananda, to provide supplemental nutrition, clothing, and healthcare for rural poor in India. She has arranged for the posthumous publication of a large collection of writings of Swami Muktananda. And she has continued the meditation revolution, taking it to new parts of the world by making far-reaching tours and by the innovative use of satellite-transmitted television.

Swami Chidvilasananda, called Gurumayi by her devotees, has gone to great lengths to maintain the continuity of her movement. She also has made small adjustments, like a careful navigator embarked on a very long voyage, that seek to preserve the balanced and comprehensive character of Siddha Yoga teachings. For instance, she has given renewed attention to the Advaita Vedanta philosophy that provides an astringent complement to the more world-accepting orientation of Kashmir Shaivism. And for several years she has been interpreting and commending the teachings of the Bhagavad Gita, particularly for their relevance to questions of proper behavior and the value of perseverance. Her work has been conservative—all the more remarkable because she is the youngest of the leaders described in this chapter. She is also the only one of them who has been tested by a major crisis of succession and has seen it through to resolution. There is every indication that she could continue to lead Siddha Yoga right through to the next mid-century.[25]

Conclusion

I conclude that all five movements described in this chapter are instances of alternative religion that merit further study. They derive from diverse segments of a major cumulative tradition which for convenience may be termed Hinduism. Each of them represents a particular style of partial adaptation to conditions in what Anthony Giddens calls late modernity. None of them has sought to adapt completely to the modern science and the pattern of contractual relations that characterize (post-) industrial society. All of them—not- withstanding TM's emphasis on the harmony of science with religion—hold that the highest and final authority is the spiritual master or guru, whether honored as a maharishi, swami, gurudev, or gurumayi.[26]

Clifford Geertz's now-classical interpretation of a religious system could provide a starting point for more detailed study of any one of these movements. Geertz's analysis turns on twin assumptions about the role of authority in religion. First:

It seems to me that it is best to begin any approach to this issue with frank recognition that religious belief involves not a Baconian induction from everyday experience—for then we should all be agnostics—but rather a prior acceptance of authority which transforms that experience.

The second concerns ritual:

For it is in ritual—that is, consecrated behavior—that this conviction that religious conceptions are veridical and that religious directives are sound is somehow generated. It is in some sort of ceremonial form—even if that form be hardly more than the recitation of a myth, the consultation of an oracle, or the decoration of a grave—that the moods and motivations which sacred symbols induce . . . and the general conceptions of the order of existence which they formulate . . . meet and reinforce one another.[27]

A more recent characterization offered by Geertz, which he applied to fields of study in the social sciences and humanities, could be applied to these movements, too. They represent a region of "blurred genres." The resistance of some of them to being classified by scholars as religions or religious represents one area in which genres are blurred. The seemingly discrepant ways in which the various movements actively seek to identify themselves—to the public, to their participants, to courts of law, to local and state tax authorities, and to the IRS—suggest that the genres or categories are blurred along several lines.[28]

The categories could be clarified to some extent by utilizing the distinction between "covenant" and "contract" based relationships. Identities constructed by these movements for themselves and for their followers tend to be determined by a paradigm in which the covenantal and central relationship is the one between the master and an apprentice. This echoes the patterns typical in transmission of roles and skills in a traditional society, family, or craft. With outsiders, relations are more likely to be regulated by a variety of formal patterns determined by the contract model.[29]

Meditation and yoga at any rate function in all five movements as a way in which a sense of self and world, perhaps unfamiliar but believed to be a more real one, is meant to be awakened: they are spiritual disciplines. Current popular interest in America in what are known as "health spas" and the allied notion that yoga is simply another physical activity that can contribute to good health are impediments to understanding what these movements profess to be their fundamental aims, ideals, and assumptions. Kripalu Yoga and Siddha Yoga, for instance, routinely inform new patrons and remind old followers that their ashrams and centers profoundly differ in their intended role from a health spa or recreational resort. All five movements may best be understood as alternative religions.[30]

The movements described in this chapter, and many similar ones, have been relatively neglected in the field of religious studies. Each of them is sufficiently important to merit a book-length phenomenological treatment. One may also hope that they might someday be included in a large-scale cooperative study undertaken along the lines of the Fundamentalism Project coordinated by Martin Marty or the Religious Pluralism Project organized by Diana Eck—an Alternative Religions Project.

Notes

1. Theodore Roszak, *Unfinished Animal: The Aquarian Frontier and the Evolution of Consciousness* (New York: Harper and Row, 1975), 11; Mircea Eliade, *Yoga: Immortality and Freedom,* tr. Willard R. Trask, 2d ed. (Princeton: Princeton University Press, 1970), 360. Roszak and Eliade share a sense of the urgent need for the sacred, but Eliade's interpretive framework is devolutionary while Roszak's is evolutionary. Roszak, 5–6:

> For all the seeming irrelevance and perversity of their style, those who step to the Aquarian tempo of life may sense with a unique vividness that our much endangered interval in history demands more of us than mere survival (as much as that might be to ask), more than social revolution (as necessary as that might be). It demands a regeneration of life at some finer, more vibrant level of being, a qualitative leap forward of the species whose outcome we can only fantastically prefigure by outlandish assertions of the strange and awesome.

See Sheldon R. Isenberg and Gene R. Thursby, "Esoteric Anthropology: 'Devolutionary' and 'Evolutionary' Orientations in Perennial Philosophy," *Religious Traditions* 7–9 (1984–86): 177–226. Encouragement from Dr. Isenberg and Dr. Linda E. Olds, as well as a critical reading by J. C. Orr, M.A., assisted in the preparation of the chapter.

2. The term "yogi" refers to one who practices or is a master of some form of yoga. The baseball player–commentator was Lawrence Peter "Yogi" Berra (b. 1925). The cartoon figure was Yogi Bear, from the animation studios of William D. Hanna and Joseph R. Barbera, who was nationally syndicated in 1958. On image and myth, see Harold R. Isaacs, *Scratches on Our Minds: American Images of China and India* (New York: John Day Co., 1958); and Mircea Eliade, *Myth and Reality,* tr. Willard R. Trask (New York: Colophon-Harper, 1975). The "contradictions" are discussed by John P. Hewitt, *Dilemmas of the*

American Self (Philadelphia: Temple University Press, 1989); and Charles Taylor, *Sources of the Self: The Making of the Modern Identity* (Cambridge, Mass.: Harvard University Press, 1989).

3. Paul Brunton, *A Search in Secret India* (London: Rider, 1934; New York: E. P. Dutton, 1935). Brunton's collected works are kept in print by Larson Publications in Burdett, New York. He became an influential and highly regarded figure who also attracted a few unrelenting critics. For a brief appreciation and an extended critique, see Georg Feuerstein, *Yoga: The Technology of Ecstasy* (Los Angeles: Jeremy P. Tarcher, Inc., 1989), xi; and Jeffrey Moussaieff Masson, *My Father's Guru: A Journey through Spirituality and Disillusion* (Reading, Mass.: Addison-Wesley Publishing Company, 1993).

4. For example, Barbara Brown, *Travels through the Mind of India* (Dallas: Saybrook Publishing Company, 1986). An informal work by a noted biofeedback researcher, the book both extends and subverts the old heroic narrative tradition. The author shares with Rollo May, the estimable editor of the series in which her book was published, the ability to convey insights despite misinformation about India. In *The Cry for Myth* (New York: W. W. Norton and Company, 1991, 22n), May rails against Eastern-derived "new cults" and their leaders—including one he dubs Radachristian.

5. Americans who have lost their equilibrium over India, either here or there, have been subjected to harsh satire ever since the spurious travelogues of Mark Twain. Recent examples include a memoir by Gita Mehta, *Karma Cola: Marketing the Mystic East* (New York: Simon and Schuster, 1979) and a novel by John Updike, *S* (New York: Alfred A. Knopf, 1988).

6. For survey and analysis, see Bernard Aaronson and Humphrey Osmond, eds., *Psychedelics: The Uses and Implications of Hallucinogenic Drugs* (Garden City, N.Y.: Anchor-Doubleday, 1970) and David C. McClelland,

Power: The Inner Experience (New York: Irvington Publishers, Inc., 1975), 203–51. The last scientist licensed to conduct LSD research with human subjects apparently was Stanislav Grof, M.D. American-born Franklin Jones (b. 1939), who subsequently adopted a Hindu mode of religious teaching as Bubba then Da Free John and more recently as Da Avabhasa, has commented on a time in his youth when he participated in government-sponsored drug research. See Da Avabhasa, *The Knee of Listening*, new standard ed. (Clearlake, Calif.: The Dawn Horse Press, 1992), 50–55. On the spiritual master who made Ram Dass a yogi, see Dada Mukerjee, *By His Grace: A Devotee's Story* (Santa Fe, N. Mex.: Hanuman Foundation, 1990).

7. See, e.g., Amiya Chakravarty, "Satyagraha and the Race Problem in America," in *Gandhi India and the World* ed. Sibnarayan Ray (Philadelphia: Temple University Press, 1970), 300–18.

8. References to the broader religious and social context are available in Martin E. Marty, "Religion in America since Mid-century," *Daedalus* 111, no. 1 (1982): 149–63; and Frances FitzGerald, *Cities on a Hill: A Journey through Contemporary American Cultures* (New York: Simon and Schuster, 1986), 383–414.

Historical information and terms introduced in the chapter by Catherine Wessinger will help the reader understand the movements treated here. For instance, all five utilize the Advaita Vedanta philosophy of Shankara, the Bhagavad Gita, and other traditional texts. In three, the leader is a monk in one of the monastic orders said to have been founded by Shankara; another is led by an unmarried disciple of a great acharya or teacher in the Shankara tradition; and another by a married householder who is a gifted disciple of a remarkable monk. Two movements have sponsored initiation of non-Indian men and women into monastic life, and all of them represent regions of origin in India other than Bengal.

"Hindu" and "Hinduism" (as well as "religion" itself) are contended terms that serve as problematic heuristic devices. For a brief discussion with references to relevant literature, see my "Islamic, Hindu, and Buddhist Conceptions of Aging," in *Handbook of the Humanities and Aging,* ed. Thomas R. Cole, David D. Van Tassel, and Robert Kastenbaum

(New York: Springer Publishing Company, 1992), 175–96. Any close analysis of the first two terms also should take into account Robert Eric Frykenberg, "Constructions of Hinduism at the Nexus of History and Religion," *Journal of Interdisciplinary History* 23 (1993): 523–50.

The position taken by the Transcendental Meditation movement is that none of the three terms should be applied to them, while the opposite conclusion is drawn by J. Gordon Melton, *The Encyclopedic Handbook of Cults in America* (New York: Garland Publishing Company, 1986), 187ff. One complicating factor is the claim sometimes put forward that TM should be defined as a method of meditation that can be considered apart from the larger agenda of the movement. See Robert M. Oates, Jr., *Celebrating the Dawn: Maharishi Mahesh Yogi and the TM Technique* (New York: G. P. Putnam's Sons, 1976). Another is that while the central practices and assumptions of TM (method and movement alike) derive from a "Hindu" background, Indic traditions reckon "religious identity" rather differently than do the exclusive monotheisms from Asia Minor and Arabia. See Paul Dundas, *The Jains* (London and New York: Routledge, 1992), 3–6.

9. Berne originated TA and made it a popular phenomenon by writing *Games People Play* (New York: Grove Press, 1964). His close followers used his categories but had some fundamental disagreements. Claude M. Steiner's *Scripts People Live: Transactional Analysis of Life Scripts* (New York: Grove Press, 1974) as well as Muriel James and Dorothy Jongeward's *Born to Win* (Reading, Mass.: Addison-Wesley, 1971) follow Berne in affirming humanity's innate integrity. Thomas A. Harris's *I'm OK—You're OK* (New York: Harper and Row, 1969) takes the view that humans start life inwardly divided but can be made whole. Many Protestant churches in that period were open to new trends in secular psychology and adopted one or the other version of TA for their adult programs.

In contrast, TM stimulated Catholic leaders to adapt their own traditions of spiritual formation, previously restricted mainly to religious orders, and make them available to the laity. The success of the Centering Prayer movement, for example, probably owes much to the ways in which TM made the public receptive. See M. Basis Pennington, *Daily We*

Touch Him: Practical Religious Experiences (Garden City, N.Y.: Image-Doubleday, 1979) and *Centering Prayer: Renewing an Ancient Christian Prayer Form* (Garden City, N.Y.: Doubleday, 1980). Other instances of Roman Catholic openness to Hinduism after mid-century include J. M. Dechanet, *Christian Yoga* (New York: Perennial-Harper, 1972); Edward Stevens, *An Introduction to Oriental Mysticism* (New York: Paulist Press, 1973); and Anthony de Mello, *Sadhana, A Way to God: Christian Exercises in Eastern Form* (Garden City, N.Y.: Image-Doubleday, 1984). Similar spiritual traffic between India and Eastern Orthodoxy is exemplified in *Yoga and the Jesus Prayer Tradition* (Ramsey, N.J.: Paulist Press, 1984) by Thomas Matus, who artfully compares Symeon the New Theologian and Abhinavagupta the great Kashmir Shaiva philosopher.

10. On the Maharishi and the spread of TM, see Else Dragemark, *The Way to Maharishi's Himalayas* (Stockholm: Author, 1972); and *His Holiness Maharishi Mahesh Yogi: Thirty Years Around the World, Dawn of the Age of Enlightenment*, vol. 1, 1957–1964 (Netherlands: MVU Press, 1986). On the Maharishi and the Shankaracharya, see William Cenkner, *A Tradition of Teachers: Sankara and the Jagadgurus Today* (Delhi: Motilal Banarsidass, 1983), 126–27.

11. An account of TM training that reflects the early 1970s is Patricia Drake Hemingway, *The Transcendental Meditation Primer* (New York: David McKay Company, Inc., 1975). Enthusiasm about TM's implications for education is evidenced by the December 1972 issue of *Phi Delta Kappan*, but a law suit in New Jersey put a stop to incorporation of TM into public school classes. Early scientific studies are heavily cited by Jack Forem, *Transcendental Meditation: Maharishi Mahesh Yogi and the Science of Creative Intelligence* (New York: E. P. Dutton, Inc., 1974), and more recent references are available from the Department of Psychology, Maharishi International University, Fairfield, Iowa. See also Patrick Tierney, "The Mechanics of Mysticism," *Omni* (November 1990): 84–88. Benson went on to popularize his own form of meditation, which is featured in "Can Your Mind Heal Your Body?" *Consumer Reports* (February 1993): 107–15. Patricia Carrington's *Freedom in Meditation* (Garden City, N.Y.: Anchor-Doubleday, 1977) is a helpful treatment of the whole subject, which she brings up to date in her contribution to *Principles and Practice of Stress Management*, 2d ed., ed. Paul Lehrer and Robert Woolfolk (New York: Guilford Publications, 1993). She distinguishes "practical" from "spiritual" meditation and develops a nonreligious kind called Clinically Standardized Meditation that anyone can practice or use in research.

12. Similar assessments of the movement's reorganization, growth, and peak are offered by Hank Johnston, "The Marketed Social Movement: A Case Study of the Rapid Growth of TM," *Pacific Sociological Review* 23 (1980): 333–54; William Sims Bainbridge and Daniel H. Jackson, "The Rise and Decline of Transcendental Meditation," in *The Social Impact of New Religious Movements*, ed. Bryan Wilson (New York: Rose of Sharon Press, Inc., 1981), 135–57; and Eric Woodrum, "Religious Organizational Change: An Analysis Based on the TM Movement," *Review of Religious Research* 24 (1982): 89–103.

13. On controversies surrounding these activities, see Christopher Anderson, "Physicist Running for President Is Accused of Distorting Science to Fit Guru's Ideas," *Nature* 359 (10 September 1992): 97; Doug M. Podolsky, "Pulse Reading, Herbs and Oil Massage," *American Health* 7 (July 1988): 78–81; Andrew A. Skolnick, "Maharishi Ayur-Veda: Guru's Marketing Scheme Promises the World Eternal 'Perfect Health,'" *JAMA: The Journal of the American Medical Association* 266 (2 October 1991): 1741–50, along with responses published in subsequent numbers. On Deepak Chopra, see Catherine Winters, "Guru on the Go," *American Health* 11 (January 1992): 43–46.

14. Elmer and Alyce Green, *Beyond Biofeedback* (New York: Delta-Dell, 1977), 197–218.

15. For more about Swami Rama's personality, see Doug Boyd, *Swami* (New York: Paragon House, 1990).

16. Some recollections from his early life along with a number of teaching stories are collected in Swami Ajaya, ed., *Living with the Himalayan Masters: Spiritual Experiences of Swami Rama* (Honesdale, Pa.: Himalayan International Institute of Yoga Science and Philosophy, 1978).

17. Swami Rama, *Path of Fire and Light: Advanced Practices of Yoga* (Honesdale, Pa.: The Himalayan International Institute of Yoga Sci-

ence and Philosophy of the U.S.A., 1986), 7. The term *kundalini* refers to a repository of energy that may be manifested in a human being during spiritual development or transformation. It is believed to be activated by divine grace, by the power of some gurus, or by certain kinds of yogic practices. It is a major theme in some Hindu movements, especially Siddha Yoga. Discussion of it has been stimulated by the writings of Gopi Krishna (1903–1984), too. See Gopi Krishna, *Kundalini: The Evolutionary Energy in Man*, intro. by Frederick Spiegelberg and psychological commentary by James Hillman (Berkeley: Shambhala, 1971); Gene Kiefer, ed., *Kundalini for the New Age: Selected Writings of Gopi Krishna* (New York: Bantam Books, 1988); John White, ed., *Kundalini, Evolution and Enlightenment* (New York: Paragon House, 1990).

18. There are many works by and about Swami Sivananda. For representative examples, see: Swami Venkatesananda, *Sivananda Yoga*, ed. Lakshmi (Shivanandanagar: The Divine Life Society, 1983); *Autobiography of Swami Sivananda* (Shivanandanagar: The Divine Life Society, 1989); Swami Sivananda, *The Science of Pranayama* (Shivanandanagar: The Divine Life Society, 1992). On his students in North America, begin with Richard Leviton, "How the Swamis Came to the States," *Yoga Journal* (March-April 1990): 53–55.

19. The best source on Swami Satchidananda is by Sita Bordow and others, *Sri Swami Satchidananda: Apostle of Peace* (Yogaville, Va.: Integral Yoga Publications, 1986) which is a revised and enlarged version of Sita Wiener, *Swami Satchidananda: His Biography* (San Francisco and New York: Straight Arrow Books, 1970). I rely on it. More recent and supplemental information is available in the journal *Integral Yoga*. See, e.g., Peter Max, "My First Meeting with Swamiji," *Integral Yoga* 23, no. 4 (Winter 1991): 29–32. There also is a Satchidananda Ashram-Yogaville newsletter. Integral Yoga Distribution carries the books and pamphlets of Swami Satchidananda. An audacious and delightful guide to living by an early disciple is Vijay Hassin, *The Modern Yoga Handbook: A Complete Guide to Making the Spiritual and Physical Disciplines of Yoga Work in Your Life* (Garden City, N.Y.: Delphin-Doubleday, 1978).

20. Yogi Amrit Desai, *Kripalu Yoga: Meditation-in-Motion*, vol. 1 (Lenox, Mass.: Kripalu Publications, 1985), 7. See also Meredith Gould, "Kripalu's Flowing Yoga," *Yoga Journal* (November-December 1991): 62–66, 104–05.

21. Every movement described in this chapter understands "yoga" in an inclusive way, and there is traditional precedent for it, e.g., in the Bhagavad Gita. One accomplished translator made a case for rendering "yoga" in that context simply as "discipline." See Barbara Stoler Miller, tr., *The Bhagavad-Gita: Krishna's Counsel in Time of War* (New York: Bantam Books, 1986). Each movement is distinctive in its style and emphasis, too.

On the life and work of Yogi Desai, see Sukanya Warren with Frances and Peter Mellen, *Gurudev: The Life of Yogi Amrit Desai* (Summit Station, Pa.: Kripalu Publications, 1982). An account of life at Kripalu, Yogaville, and Mt. Madonna in California, is provided by Corinne McLaughlin, "In the Spirit of Service," *Yoga Journal* (March-April 1987): 34–40, 62–66. See also the following articles by sociologist Stephen R. Wilson, based on his research at Sumneytown: "In Pursuit of Energy: Spiritual Growth in a Yoga Ashram," *Journal of Humanistic Psychology* 22 (1982): 43–56; "Becoming a Yogi: Resocialization and Deconditioning as Conversion Processes," *Sociological Analysis* 45 (1984): 301–14; "Therapeutic Processes in a Yoga Ashram," *American Journal of Psychotherapy* 39 (1985): 253–62.

22. Christina and Stanislav Grof, *The Stormy Search for the Self: A Guide to Personal Growth through Transformational Crisis* (New York: Perigee-Tarcher-Putnam, 1992), 11–12. Also see Lucy DuPertuis, "How People Recognize Charisma: The Case of *Darshan* in *Radhasoami* and Divine Light Mission," *Sociological Analysis* 47 (1986): 111–24.

23. In reading a recent case study of a woman from Mexico who received *shaktipat* from Swami Chidvilasananda, it became clear to me that most modern cultures are impoverished insofar as they fail to recognize and to make provision for support to the person who is undergoing this type of transition. The *cultural* context, as much as any psychological correlate, may require the category of "Premature Kundalini Awakening." In the case study, the woman's awakening was considered "premature because it triggered a host of symptoms she was unable to handle or assimilate smoothly at the time. . . . " See Jon Ossoff, "Reflections of *Shaktipat*: Psychosis or the Rise of Kundalini? A Case Study," *The*

Journal of Transpersonal Psychology 25 (1993): 29–42.

What may be considered "cultural impoverishment" complicates the process of acknowledging, appreciating, and taking benefit from the opportunities that may be presented by *shaktipat* or similar transformational situations. Christina Grof, cited above, founded the Spiritual Emergence Network in order to provide support to people who are passing through one or another form of "spiritual emergency."

24. Dick Anthony proposed a typology that supports this interpretation of the meditation revolution by identifying Transcendental Meditation and Siddha Yoga as contrasting types. He presents it in Dick Anthony, Bruce Ecker, and Ken Wilber, *Spiritual Choices: The Problem of Recognizing Authentic Paths to Inner Transformation* (New York: Paragon House, 1987), 35–105. It is summarized and critiqued in Thomas Robbins, *Cults, Converts and Charisma: The Sociology of New Religious Movements* (London: Sage Publications, 1988).

25. For another description of Siddha Yoga that complements this one, discusses the succession crisis, and contains extensive references to relevant literature, see Gene R. Thursby, "Siddha Yoga: Swami Muktananda and the Seat of Power," in *When Prophets Die: The Postcharismatic Fate of New Religious Movements*, ed. Timothy Miller (Albany: State University of New York Press, 1991), 165–81.

26. See Anthony Giddens, *Modernity and Self-Identity: Self and Society in the Late Modern Age* (Cambridge: Polity Press, 1991).

27. Clifford Geertz, "Religion as a Cultural System," in his *The Interpretation of Cultures* (New York: Basic Books, Inc., 1973), 109, 112.

28. Clifford Geertz, "Blurred Genres: The Refiguration of Social Thought," in his *Local Knowledge: Further Essays in Interpretive Anthropology* (New York: Basic Books, Inc., 1983) 19–35. Another (and crucial) area of blurring concerns the nature of the spiritual master in each of these movements. Some are claimed by their followers to be beyond error, to be perfectly realized, or to be incarnations of the divine. One may be reminded of Isherwood's observation, derived from Swami Saradananda, that "even an avatar, when he assumes a body and enters the sphere of Maya, must suffer some blurring of his spiritual insight." Christopher Isherwood,

Ramakrishna and His Disciples (New York: Simon and Schuster, 1965), 201.

29. David G. Bromley and Bruce C. Busching, "Understanding the Structure of Contractual and Covenantal Social Relations: Implications for the Sociology of Religion," *Sociological Analysis* 49 (1988): S15–32. Note, too, that Robert Bellah and associates have made extensive use of the distinction between covenant- and contract-based relations in their study of modern American society, and that Thomas Robbins and associates have sought to draw out some of the implications of the distinction for analysis of new religious movements or alternative religions.

30. See, e.g., Mary Talbot with John Schwartz, "Trends—Om Is Where the Heart Is: Fed Up with Aerobics, the Boomers Turn to Yoga," *Newsweek* (3 February 1992): 71; Dana Wechsler Linden, "Boot Camp by the Sea," *Forbes* (17 February 1992): 140–41; Stephanie von Hirschberg, "The New Mind Spas," *New Woman* (April 1990): 80–82. The second reports on "The Ashram" which actually is a spa in Malibu, while the last includes a Maharishi Ayur-Ved health center.

Reports in the press and popular periodicals tend to ignore or be cynical about the religious dimensions of these movements, and reduce the focus to questions of economic interests, health outcomes, or sexual practices. TM, for example, is treated as a new arena for economics: Jeff Bloch, "Cities/Fairfield, Iowa—We Got Mantras Right Here in River City," *Forbes* (24 March 1986): 74–78; Patricia King and Penelope Wang, "The Karma of Capitalism: A Guru's Followers Transform an Iowa Farm Town," *Newsweek* (3 August 1987): 44; Elizabeth Corcoran, "Entrepreneurial Spirit," *Scientific American* 259, no. 2 (August 1988): 99; Duncan Campbell, "Heaven on Earth," *New Statesman and Society* 3, no. 120 (28 September 1990): 10–11.

Even positive reports adopt a street-wise or hard-edged tone perhaps in order to assure the reader of the "objectivity" of the author. See, e.g., Daniel Asa Rose, "The Enlightened Traveler—Have You a Mind to Travel?" *Esquire* (June 1988): 40; Pamela Weintraub, "Masters of the Universe," *Omni* (March 1990): 43–46, 86–90; and Jean Callahan, "Spiritual Adventures in the Borscht Belt," *New Age Journal* (May-June 1993): 76–79, 131–36. The first is a coarse but appreciative account of a visit to the

Kripalu Center, the second reviews the work of Baba Ram Dass and Swami Satchidananda among others, and the third reflects on experiences of the author while visiting the main Siddha Yoga ashram. Along similar lines is a sensationalized but apt warning about risks

of involvement with alternative religions: Stephen Rae, "The Guru Scene," *Cosmopolitan* (July-September 1991): 176–79, 238. On a more serious level, see Gregory C. Bogart, "Separating from a Spiritual Teacher," *The Journal of Transpersonal Psychology* 24 (1992): 1–21.

Suggestions for Further Reading

Ajaya, Swami, ed. *Living with the Himalayan Masters: Spiritual Experiences of Swami Rama.* Honesdale, Pa.: Himalayan International Institute of Yoga Science and Philosophy, 1978.

Bordow, Sita, and others. *Sri Swami Satchidananda: Apostle of Peace.* Foreword by Father Thomas Keating. Yogaville: Va.: Integral Yoga Publications, 1986.

Campbell, Anthony. *Seven States of Consciousness: A Vision of Possibilities Suggested by the Teaching of Maharishi Mahesh Yogi.* New York: Perennial-Harper, 1974.

Desai, Yogi Amrit. *Kripalu Yoga: Meditation-in-Motion.* 2 vols. Lenox, Mass.: Kripalu Publications, 1985.

Giddens, Anthony. *Modernity and Self-Identity: Self and Society in the Late Modern Age.* Cambridge: Polity Press, 1991.

Hayes, Peter. *The Supreme Adventure: The Experience of Siddha Yoga.* Preface by Gurumayi Chidvilasananda. New York: Delta-Dell, 1988.

Mahesh Yogi, Maharishi. *The Science of Being and Art of Living.* Delhi: Allied Publishers Private Ltd., 1963.

———. *Maharishi Mahesh Yogi on the Bhagavad-Gita: A New Translation and Commentary with Sanskrit Text, Chapters 1 to 6.* London: Arkana-Penguin, 1990.

Mandelkorn, Philip, ed. *To Know Your Self: The Essential Teachings of Swami Satchidananda.* Yogaville: Integral Yoga Publications, 1988.

Muktananda, Swami. *Play of Consciousness (Chitshakti Vilas).* 2d ed. Intro. by Gurumayi Chidvilasananda. South Fallsburg, N.Y.: SYDA Foundation, 1978.

Warren, Sukanya, with Frances and Peter Mellen. *Gurudev: The Life of Yogi Amrit Desai.* Summit Station, Pa.: Kripalu Publications, 1982.

White, John, ed. *Kundalini, Evolution and Enlightenment.* New York: Paragon House, 1990.

Wuthnow, Robert. *The Restructuring of American Religion: Society and Faith since World War II.* Princeton: Princeton University Press, 1988.

19

HARE KRISHNA IN AMERICA:
GROWTH, DECLINE, AND ACCOMMODATION

E. Burke Rochford, Jr.

It is a truism that religious movements and their organizational forms undergo change over the course of their histories. Many new religions burst onto the scene without fully articulated ideologies, established objectives, or stable organizational structures. But neither do these groups over time reach what might be thought of as developmental endpoints, unless, of course, they fail altogether. Rather the careers of new faiths are guided by a dialectical interplay between internal movement forces and external societal influences.[1] While scholars recognize that change in "new" and "established" religions takes place, we know much less about the specific processes that promote social change in religious organizations. This case study of the International Society for Krishna Consciousness (hereafter ISKCON), more popularly known as the Hare Krishna movement, attempts to extend empirical and theoretical understanding of how new religious movements develop in the American context.[2]

Origins, American Beginnings, and Religious Beliefs

The presence of Hare Krishna in America comes from the inspiration of one man, A. C. Bhaktivedanta Swami Prabhupada. Bhaktivedanta, or Srila Prabhupada, as he is called by his followers, travelled to the United States from India in 1965, at the age of sixty-nine, to spread Krishna Consciousness to the Western world. One year after his arrival, Prabhupada founded ISKCON in New York City. Within a decade, Prabhupada and his followers had established a worldwide movement. Before his death in 1977, Prabhupada initiated nearly five thousand disciples into Krishna consciousness and attracted tens of thousands of other less-committed followers.

Prabhupada was born in 1896 with the name of Abhay Charan De. His family adhered to a strict Krishna-conscious lifestyle. After graduating from the University of Calcutta with majors in English, philosophy, and economics, Prabhupada was employed as a manager in a chemical firm, where he worked until his retirement in 1954. In 1922, Prabhupada met his spiritual master, Bhaktisiddhanta, from whom he ultimately took initiation in 1933. Prior to Bhaktisiddhanta's death in 1936, he instructed Prabhupada to carry the teachings of Krishna Consciousness to the West. In the years prior to his departure for America, Prabhupada raised a family and continued to promote the teachings of Bhaktisiddhanta. During this period he started publishing *Back to Godhead* magazine, which he would later use to promote his movement in America. Prabhupada took the order of *sannyasa* at age fifty-nine, thereafter retiring from family life. Until his death, Prabhupada focused his energies on translating and writing commentaries on ancient Vedic scriptures such as the Bhagavad Gita and the Srimad Bhagavatam. His many books were published by ISKCON's Bhaktivedanta Book Trust in Los Angeles.

The historical roots of the Hare Krishna movement in America can be traced to Bengal, India, in the sixteenth century. While aligned with the more prevalent forms of Hinduism, the Krishna Consciousness preached by ISKCON's founder traces its beginnings to the Krishna *bhakti* movement founded by Sri Caitanya Mahaprabhu. Caitanya revived the devotional form of Hinduism (*bhakti* yoga) emphasizing that love and devotional service to God were the means by which one could gain spiritual realization. Instead of seeing him as one of several gods, Caitanya and his followers made Krishna the supreme manifestation of God. In a major split from other forms of Hinduism, Caitanya preached that all people, regardless of their caste or station in life, could be self-realized through their activities performed in the service of Krishna.

Caitanya also developed another practice unique to Hinduism, which has proved a trademark of the Krishna movement in America. Growing out of his intense religious passion, Caitanya initiated *sankirtana,* a practice requiring his followers to venture out into the streets to dance and sing their praises of Lord Krishna. When Prabhupada began his movement in America, *sankirtana* (preaching, book distribution, and chanting in public) became the principal means of spreading Krishna Consciousness.[3]

The spiritual goal of Hare Krishna devotees is to escape birth in the material world and go back to Godhead. Because of material contamination, the soul is forced to assume a continuous succession of rebirths. To escape the laws of *karma* and break the cycle of reincarnation, devotees seek to perfect their spiritual lives by controlling their senses. This is done under the direction of a spiritual teacher, or guru. The *bhakti* yoga process involves a number of religious prac-

tices directed toward purifying the soul. Central to this process of self-realization is chanting the Hare Krishna mantra: Hare Krishna, Hare Krishna, Krishna Krishna, Hare Hare, Hare Rama, Hare Rama, Rama Rama, Hare Hare. At the time of initiation from a guru, devotees commit themselves to chant sixteen rounds of the Hare Krishna mantra daily, on a string of *japa,* or prayer beads. They must also abstain from eating meat, illicit sex (sex other than for the propagation of God-conscious children), taking intoxicants (i.e., cigarettes, alcohol, tea, coffee, drugs), and gambling. Although no longer a mandatory requirement, many ISKCON devotees take part in a morning worship program beginning in the temple at 4:30 A.M. There they worship the deities on the altar, a spiritual plant *Tulasi,* and their founding guru Srila Prabhupada. One male devotee leads the others in singing various Sanskrit verses to the beat of music provided by devotees playing *mrdanga* drums and *karatals* (small hand cymbals). Men and women are strictly segregated in the temple, with men generally standing nearest the altar and women behind them. Between each of the four morning ceremonies devotees busily chant their daily rounds. Punctuating the end of the morning program is a class on Prabhupada's commentaries on the Vedic scriptures.

ISKCON's Growth and Development in America

The fortunes of the Krishna movement have changed rather dramatically since its introduction to America in 1965. From very humble beginnings in New York City, Prabhupada and his followers recruited thousands of members. Along with success, however, came public scrutiny and controversy. By the mid-1970s, ISKCON and other new religions of the period felt the effects of a countermovement of anticultists bent on halting what they saw as the "evil" influence of "cults." Under attack, and facing a downturn in its recruitment and economic fortunes, ISKCON began to decline as a religious organization. Prabhupada's death, in 1977, further aggravated the movement's growing sense of crisis. ISKCON's efforts to deal with its decline brought with it negotiation, compromise, and change.

GROWTH AND EXPANSION

The early history of the Hare Krishna movement in America mirrors in many respects the career of the 1960s and 1970s counterculture. The war in Vietnam, and the peace movement that grew in opposition to it, sparked the growth of numerous social movements. American values and ways of life faced critical questioning by many young people who began experimenting with a range of alternative value systems and lifestyles. Studies of ISKCON have demonstrated how the movement's early growth in the United States was sustained by recruiting alienated youth from the counterculture. From the counterculture ISKCON attracted mostly Anglo-Americans in their late teens and early twenties from middle- and upper-middle-class families. But with the end of the war, the counterculture began to fade from the American landscape and ISKCON's growth leveled off; membership began to decline in 1974.[4]

The Hare Krishna movement began modestly in New York City in 1965. Prabhupada, or the Swami as he was known by his early followers, turned his proselytizing efforts to the young people living on the Bowery on the Lower East Side. After Prabhupada was observed chanting in Tompkins Square Park word spread amongst the musicians and bohemian crowd of the area. Within a short time, several of Prabhupada's followers helped him establish a small temple on Second Avenue. During this first year in New York, Prabhupada initiated nineteen disciples.[5]

ISKCON underwent radical change after Prabhupada relocated to the emerging hippie community in the Haight-Ashbury district of San Francisco. Having located a temple in the heart of the district, ISKCON recruited an estimated 150 to 200 converts during its first two years.[6] Because many of these new recruits had

only recently migrated to the area, and were without permanent or stable residences, ISKCON's communal structure emerged as a means to hold the young countercultural youth being attracted to Krishna Consciousness. ISKCON's San Francisco organization served as a model for the many devotees who were deployed to other cities across America to establish Krishna temples and recruit members. Being a missionary movement, ISKCON was opportunistic in its recruitment strategies, successfully recruiting in public places and through social networks.[7] By the end of 1975, ISKCON had established nearly forty communities and preaching centers in North America and many more worldwide.

Economically, ISKCON was largely supported by *sankirtana,* the public distribution of religious literature. During the late 1960s and early 1970s devotees distributed incense or *Back to Godhead* magazines to the public in exchange for donations. The economics of *sankirtana* changed greatly in 1971 and 1972, as devotees began to distribute Prabhupada's books in public locations, first in shopping malls and parking lots, and then at major American airports. Book distribution expanded yearly through 1978 and provided large sums of money to bankroll ISKCON's worldwide expansion. One conservative estimate is that ISKCON's communities in North America grossed over thirteen million dollars between 1974 and 1978 on hardback books alone.[8]

Along with ISKCON's successful expansion came charges of brainwashing by anticultists. Although social science evidence provides little or no support for brainwashing explanations of conversion to new religions, such charges did have an impact on ISKCON's American development.[9] Anticult propaganda, widely disseminated by the media, helped reshape the public's definition of Hare Krishna; from a peculiar, but essentially harmless movement. ISKCON came to be identified as threatening and dangerous.[10] Defined as a dangerous cult, ISKCON found it all the more difficult to attract new members and to secure the economic resources necessary to sustain its communities.

DECLINE AND POLITICIZATION

The late 1970s and the 1980s was a period of decline, conflict, and change within ISKCON. Recruitment declined significantly and ISKCON witnessed a sharp downturn in its economic fortunes. Prabhupada's death, in 1977, only intensified ISKCON's decline as the movement faced years of conflict and instability in America.

By 1982, the level of ISKCON's North American book distribution was less than half its 1978 peak. The corresponding decline in *sankirtana* revenues had a devastating effect on ISKCON's communities. In an effort to bring much-needed revenue into its communities ISKCON developed a number of alternative economic strategies in the late 1970s. In addition to distributing books in public places, devotees began selling record albums, artwork, candles, food, and various buttons supporting sports teams and rock bands. During the Christmas season, ISKCON members dressed as Santa Claus and solicited donations from an unsuspecting public. Book distribution declined sharply when these new and highly profitably forms of enterprise gained favor among most ISKCON leaders. While profitable, these practices also proved controversial both within and outside of the movement. The movement's critics interpreted these changes as evidence of a basic transformation in ISKCON's purpose in America: finances and maintenance concerns had come to replace the goal of expanding Prabhupada's Krishna Consciousness movement.[11]

The death of a charismatic leader is often a turning point in the history of any religious movement, and ISKCON is no exception. Prabhupada's death brought about widespread factionalism, substantial defection, and schism. In the months preceding his death Prabhupada appointed eleven of his closest disciples to serve as initiating gurus for ISKCON. Following his death, ISKCON's new gurus took spiritual and political control over specific areas of the world. Each was responsible for initiating disciples in his zone. Beginning in 1978, ISKCON faced a series of guru controversies that threatened to splinter the organization entirely. ISKCON's political stability was also jeopardized by a growing number of ex-ISKCON members who challenged the very idea that Prabhupada had actually appointed successor gurus.[12]

In 1982, Jayatirtha, the ISKCON guru in England, defected with as many as one hundred of his disciples, after a failed attempt to have one of Prabhupada's Godbrothers from India brought into ISKCON as an initiating guru. Other leading devotees also left ISKCON to join Sridara Maharaja in the early 1980s; some of these established communities in America.[13] In 1983, after years of controversy that included allegations of drug use and weapons violations in the Berkeley Temple, the guru Hansaduta was expelled from ISKCON. During 1986 and 1987, three other gurus were forced to resign their guruships after charges of sexual misconduct were brought against them. In a well-publicized legal case, ISKCON's West Virginia farm community, New Vrindaban, witnessed murder and a resulting state and federal investigation. In 1987, ISKCON excommunicated New Vrindaban's leader Kirtanananda, and no longer recognized his community as part of ISKCON. The community now blends Krishna conscious theology with Christian millenarianism.

After years of controversy, a reform movement emerged in America during the fall of 1984 in an effort to change the existing guru system. The reformers were senior Prabhupada disciples, many of whom were temple presidents in North America. Finally, in 1987, changes were made to the then-existing guru system: ISKCON's international governing body ruled that all qualified ISKCON members could become initiating gurus and that henceforth gurus could no longer control exclusive geographical zones over which they exercised total political and spiritual authority. The latter arrangement had effectively undermined ISKCON as the appointed gurus were essentially leading their own movements more or less independently of ISKCON. By the end of 1993, ISKCON had more than seventy initiating gurus worldwide. Although reform of the guru system quieted protest throughout much of the movement, controversy remains. An outspoken minority of Prabhupada disciples hold the position that since none of the new gurus are actually *maha-bhagavata* (qualified gurus) they should initiate disciples only on Prabhupada's behalf. Newly initiated devotees should be considered Prabhupada disciples, rather than disciples of any one of the present gurus.[14]

NEGOTIATION AND ACCOMMODATION

ISKCON's declining position in America resulted in a number of strategic decisions by the leaders to bring much-needed resources into the movement and its communities. ISKCON faced the need to find a new constituency from which it could enlist new members and mobilize financial support. Without adequate finances, ISKCON also found it difficult to sustain its totalistic communal world: Exclusivity gave way to more flexible and inclusive boundaries as the movement sought negotiation and compromise with the conventional culture.

With declining financial resources available to its communities ISKCON faced a significant turning point in its North American history. No longer could ISKCON afford to maintain its communal lifestyle: Lacking a viable means of internal support most ISKCON members had little choice but to seek outside employment. A 1992 survey of 271 ISKCON members in the United States revealed that over half were employed by non-devotee businesses, or were self-employed. Fewer than a third worked for an ISKCON business, or for a local ISKCON community. Fewer than 5 percent distributed books, or sought donations in public locations. Having outside jobs, many, if not most, devotees have become increasingly independent of ISKCON. Two-thirds of the surveyed devotees resided in housing outside of an ISKCON community, although many did live nearby. Findings from the survey also revealed that ISKCON members employed in outside jobs, as compared to those working in devotee environments, were less likely to regularly chant their rounds, attend religious functions at the temple, or to contribute time working in their local ISKCON community. More than two-thirds reported that work and/or family obligations made it difficult for them to commit more time toward these activities. As these findings suggest, ISKCON's previous sectarian lifestyle and purpose has given way to domesticity: Jobs, family responsibilities, educating children, and the like now largely define the daily concerns of the average ISKCON devotee. This everyday reality has forced ISKCON members to recraft their identities to reflect their involvement in two social worlds previously experienced as hostile to one another. As this has occurred at the individual level, ISKCON's social organization has changed accordingly from a monastic lifestyle to the creation of broad-based, pluralistic communities.

ISKCON has also changed in recent years because of the growth of its East Indian congregation. During ISKCON's early days in America, Prabhupada made little effort to involve East Indian immigrants in his movement. He sought to avoid ISKCON's becoming identified as an ethnic Hindu movement. Prabhupada's goal was to reach out to a wider audience, though, in the end, his movement in America appealed largely to white middle-class youth. The first significant involvement of East Indians occurred in the face of efforts by anticultists to suppress ISKCON in the mid-1970s. For strategic purposes, ISKCON had sympathetic Indian people come forward to counter anticultists' claims that ISKCON was a dangerou cult. Members of the Indian community effectively argued that anticult efforts to suppress ISKCON represented little more than overt acts of persecution against all Hindus in America. Thereafter, ISKCON made a more concerted effort to encourage the involvement of East Indians. ISKCON's temples became places of worship for many thousands of East Indians in America, though few in fact have become initiated disciples of any of ISKCON's gurus. Most limit their involvement to attending the Sunday program at a local ISKCON community where they worship and socialize with other Indian people. Most importantly for ISKCON, its East Indian congregation contributes significant funding to help support local temples. In a few locations (e.g., Houston, Detroit, Vancouver), Indian people have taken on leadership positions as temple presidents. It is likely that the present "Indianization" of ISKCON will continue in the future, with the possibility that some ISKCON temples in America will become ethnic churches.

Conclusion

Throughout much of ISKCON's North American history the movement has found itself in a relatively high state of tension with the surrounding conventional society. During the 1970s and early 1980s the general public was suspicious and even outwardly hostile toward ISKCON and some other new religious movements of the period. As a result, ISKCON faced difficulty in mobilizing the resources (i.e., people, power, and money) required to underwrite its expansionary aims. Facing decline, ISKCON undertook a number of strategies requiring it to alter its relationship with the surrounding culture. Without its own economic institutions in place, ISKCON relaxed its formerly rigid boundaries to allow its members to seek outside employment. It also went about the business of building a congregation of East Indian members. By changing in these ways, ISKCON became inclusive and pluralistic, its members as much involved in the conventional society as within ISKCON.

It seems likely that ISKCON's future development will involve still further changes and growing secularization. ISKCON's congregation (i.e., lay as opposed to full-time membership) seems destined to expand as the movement's second generation shows little interest in taking up a monastic lifestyle. This and related trends seem destined to further erode ISKCON's sectarian purposes and lifestyle. As a result, ISKCON's uniqueness and overall mission may be threatened. As Rodney Stark reminds us, "To succeed, a new religious movement must not make its peace with this world too rapidly or too fully. A faith too accommodated to worldliness lacks power for continued conversion."[15]

Notes

1. David G. Bromley and Phillip E. Hammond, *The Future of New Religious Movements* (Macon, Ga.: Mercer University Press, 1987).

2. The question of change in religious organizations is of longstanding interest to scholars of religion. Much of this inquiry has focused on how sects become institutionalized as churches, or more precisely denominations. See, for example, Max Weber, *The Sociology of Religion* (Boston: Beacon Press, 1963); H. Richard Niebuhr, *The Social Sources of Denominationalism* (New York: Meridian, 1929). For an application to ISKCON, see E. Burke Rochford, Jr., *Hare Krishna in America* (New Brunswick, N.J.: Rutgers University Press, 1985), 214–20.

3. For discussion of ISKCON's roots in India, see Charles R. Brooks, *The Hare Krishnas in India* (Princeton, N.J.: Princeton University Press, 1989), 27–55; Steven Gelberg, ed., *Hare Krishna, Hare Krishna* (New York: Grove Press, 1983);

Stillson J. Judah, *Hare Krishna and the Counterculture* (New York: Wiley, 1974), 18–68.

4. For a discussion of ISKCON's ties to the counterculture, see Gregory Johnson, "The Hare Krishna in San Francisco," in *The New Religious Consciousness*, C. Glock and R. Bellah (Berkeley: University of California Press, 1976), 31–51; Judah, *Hare Krishna and the Counterculture*; Rochford, *Hare Krishna in America*, 60–68, 153–60.

5. Satsvarupa dasa Goswami, *Planting the Seed: New York City, 1965–1966* (Los Angeles: The Bhaktivedanta Book Trust, 1980).

6. For a discussion of ISKCON's growth in San Francisco, see Johnson, "The Hare Krishna in San Francisco"; Judah, *Hare Krishna and the Counterculture*; Satsvarupa dasa Goswami, *Only He Could Lead Them: San Francisco/India, 1967* (Los Angeles: Bhaktivedanta Book Trust, 1981).

7. See E. Burke Rochford, Jr., "Recruitment Strategies, Ideology, and Organization in the

Hare Krishna Movement," *Social Problems* 29, no. 4 (1982): 399–410.

8. See Rochford, *Hare Krishna in America,* 174–75.

9. For critical assessments of brainwashing explanations of conversion, see Eileen Barker, *The Making of a Moonie: Choice or Brainwashing?* (Oxford: Blackwell, 1984); David G. Bromley and James T. Richardson, eds., *The Brainwashing-Deprogramming Controversy: Sociological, Psychological, Legal and Historical Perspectives* (New York: Edwin Mellen, 1983); E. Burke Rochford, Jr., Sheryl Purvis, and NeMar Eastman, "New Religions, Mental Health and Social Control," in *Research in the Social Scientific Study of Religion,* ed. M. Lynn and D. Moberg (Greenwich, Conn.: JAI Press, 1989), 57–82; Larry D. Shinn, *The Dark Lord: Cult Images and the Hare Krishnas in America* (Philadelphia: Westminster, 1987), 122–43.

10. See E. Burke Rochford, Jr. "Shifting Public Definitions of Hare Krishna," in *Collective Behavior,* Ralph Turner and Lewis Killian (Englewood Cliffs, N.J.: Prentice-Hall, 1987), 258–60.

11. Rochford, *Hare Krishna in America,* 171–220.

12. Ibid., 221–55; E. Burke Rochford, Jr., "Factionalism, Group Defection, and Schism in the Hare Krishna Movement," *Journal for the Scientific Study of Religion* 28, no. 2 (1989): 162–79.

13. Rochford, *Hare Krishna in America,* 245–253; Shinn, *The Dark Lord,* 130.

14. See Karnamrta dasa, ed., *Living Still in Sound* (Washington, Miss.: New Jaipur Press, 1990).

15. Rodney Stark, "How New Religions Succeed: A Theoretical Model," in *The Future of New Religious Movements,* Bromley and Hammond, 11–29.

Suggestions for Further Reading

Daner, Francine. *The American Children of Krsna: A Study of the Hare Krsna Movement.* New York: Holt, Rinehart and Winston, 1976.

Judah, Stillson. *Hare Krishna and the Counterculture.* New York: Wiley, 1974.

Rochford, E. Burke, Jr. *Hare Krishna in America.* New Brunswick, N.J.: Rutgers University Press, 1985.

Shinn, Larry D. *The Dark Lord: Cult Images and the Hare Krishnas in America.* Philadelphia: Westminster, 1987.

20

THE UNIFICATION CHURCH
Eileen Barker

The Unification Church or, to give it its full title, the Holy Spirit Association for the Unification of World Christianity, was founded in Korea in 1954. Although the members prefer to be called Unificationists, they are referred to in the media and popularly known as "Moonies"—a label derived from the name of the movement's founder, Sun Myung Moon.

Moon was born in what is now North Korea in 1920 to a family which converted to Christianity when he was ten years old. It is claimed that on Easter Sunday, 1936, Jesus appeared to Moon and told him that God had chosen him for the special mission of restoring His Kingdom of Heaven on earth. For the next nine years, through prayer and spiritual communications with other religious leaders (such as Jesus, Moses, and Buddha), Moon sought to solve the fundamental questions of life and the universe, and, through spiritual communication with God Himself, he received the revelations that were later to form the basis of Unification theology.[1] Having studied electrical engineering in Japan, and then worked as an electrician in Korea, Moon started his own church after the end of World War II; but, always a controversial figure, he found himself arrested on several occasions, and spent over two and a half years in a communist labour camp, from which he was liberated by the Allies at the end of the Korean War.

Missionaries were sent by Moon to the West in the late 1950s. They met with limited success at first,[2] but, from the early 1970s, when Moon and his family came to live in the United States, the Unification Church became one of the new religions with the highest profile throughout the West. "Moonies" became familiar figures, selling literature, flowers, candy and other goods in the streets, shopping malls and airports, and "witnessing" on campuses to potential converts, inviting them to visit a local centre to learn more about the movement. Moon himself became a household name, largely as a result of his speaking at a number of rallies, his supporting Nixon's continuing presidency at the time of Watergate, and the movement's being the subject of an investigation by a congressional committee in the late 1970s.

The Unification movement has given rise to innumerable organizations and projects, among which one might, almost at random, name the Korean Folk Ballet, the Unification Theological Seminary, the Washington Institute, the *Washington Times,* the International Religious Foundation, the Collegiate Association for the Research of Principles (CARP), CAUSA, and a projected international highway that includes a tunnel between Japan and Korea. It has also acquired a number of valuable properties, including the New Yorker hotel and the old Tiffany building in Manhattan.

One of the features of the movement has always been its internationalism. Couples from different cultures, sometimes unable to speak in a common language and with little in common apart from their membership of the movement, have been married to each other; young converts have not infrequently been expected to travel to another country at a moment's notice. Unificationists are now to be found in over 150 countries throughout the world, although sometimes there may be no more than a small handful of members, occasionally living "underground" if, as in some Muslim societies, active proselytizing is illegal. Since 1989, members of the Unification Church, like members of many other new religious movements (and, indeed, mainstream American Evangelicals), have been active in eastern Europe and some of the erstwhile Republics of the Soviet Union—particularly in Russia.

Since the early 1970s, but more vociferously following the Jonestown tragedy in 1978, the media and the anticult movement have publicised a number of accusations about the church—that it was amassing large fortunes for its leaders, that it was engaged in nefarious political activities, that it brainwashed and exploited its members, that it was breaking up families and carrying out all manner of other deceptive and sinister practices. In some circles, such accusations have been taken as a justification for the expensive and illegal practice of "deprogramming" to which a considerable number of Unificationists have been, and continue to be, subjected.

Moon himself has been the object of more suspicion and enmity than almost any other contemporary religious leader. He has been attacked for his theology, which has been described as bizarre, heretical and/or blasphemous, for his political beliefs, which are strongly anticommunist, and for his accumulation of real estate and vast business empires which include the manufacture of parts for armaments in Korea. Despite a number of *amicus curiae* briefs submitted in his defence by the mainstream churches, Moon was convicted of conspiracy to evade taxes in 1982, and was sentenced to prison for eighteen months. Since his release, he has spent most of his time in the East, although he still visits the United States and has made a number of appearances both on semi-public occasions, such as at conferences that the movement has organised, and, more privately, when addressing his American followers.

Unlike many new religious movements, the Unification Church has an elaborate and comprehensive theology, based on Moon's particular interpretation of the Old and New Testaments. The more publicly accessible part of the belief system is to be found in the *Divine Principle,* a book in which his followers wrote down his teachings. This reveals that God created Adam and Eve in the hope that they could establish a God-centred family. However, before they were sufficiently mature to be married, the Archangel Lucifer, who was jealous of God's love for Adam, seduced Eve into having a spiritual sexual relationship with him. Eve then had an illicit physical relationship with Adam. The Fall was, thus, the result of the misuse of the most powerful of all forces: love; and the children born of this Lucifer-centred union have been contaminated by Fallen Nature—which is, roughly, the Unificationist equivalent of original sin.

The *Divine Principle* interprets history as a series of attempts by key figures to restore the world according to God's original plan. Jesus was meant to perform this mission, but he was murdered before he was able to marry and set the foundation for the ideal God-centred family; he was, as a consequence, able to offer only spiritual salvation to the world. According to Unification theology, a careful reading of history since the time of Jesus demonstrates that the Lord of the Second Advent was born in Korea between 1917 and 1930. Unificationists believe that Moon is this Messiah and that, through his marriage to his present wife in 1960, he has laid the foundation for establishing the Kingdom of Heaven on earth. The final battle between God and Satan has been revealed to be that taking place between "godism," as exemplified by the Unification Church, and atheistic communism. A further elaboration of the theology, centring mainly on Moon and his family, and making abundant use of significant numbers and dates, is disseminated to the members in the form of transcripts of Moon's speeches. It has frequently been stated that Moon has received many more revelations that have yet to be released.[3]

The most important Unification rite is the mass wedding ceremony, or "Blessing," during which several thousands of couples whom Moon has "matched" are married. Shortly preceding the wedding ceremony, there is the Holy Wine Ceremony, during which, it is believed, the matched couples' blood lineage is purified, enabling them to bear children untainted by Fallen Nature. The marriages are not consummated for some time (ranging from a few days to several years) after the Blessing, but when they are, there is a special "three-day ceremony" performed by each couple. Further ceremonies, equivalent in some ways to infant baptism, are performed after the birth of "blessed" children.

Members observe a Pledge service at 5 A.M. on the first day of each week, month, and year. Also on Sundays, there is a mid-morning and/or evening service which non-members might attend at some of the larger centres. Five major Holy Days (God's Day, Parents' Day, Children's Day, the Day of All Things, and True Parents' [Reverend and Mrs. Moon's] Birthday) are celebrated each year. A number of other rituals, many of them commemorating happenings and accomplishments of theological significance, have emerged during the years and become part of what is known as the Unification Tradition.[4]

While the basic tenets of Unification theology have not changed significantly since they were first taught in America in the 1960s, there have been several elaborations and a number of significant additions. It could be argued that there have been modifications in the movement's eschatology— for example, many of the early members in America were expecting an apocalyptic event in 1967. When nothing much seemed to have happened, several members left the movement, but to those who remained it was explained that it had been a misguided understanding on the part of some of the leaders that had led to an expectation of a visible change—rather than the

significant spiritual change that had, it was claimed, been accomplished. With the passage of time, imminent dates of great import have continued to hold out promises (on February 23rd, 1977, Moon declared the beginning of the new age),[5] but the members' understanding of the changes anticipated for each successive date seems, at least to an outsider, to have become progressively less apocalyptic. Very generally speaking, it has been possible to observe a shift from a movement with millennial expectations that God was going to bring about a miraculous change, to one in which a utopian ideal might be established by following the leadership of the Messiah, to a movement whose members are more reformist in their visions of the future, accepting that if changes are to take place, then they themselves are responsible for bringing these about. Moon's claims of important victories being actually accomplished continue, however. One comparatively recent such declaration was made following Moon's meeting in December 1991 with the late Kim Il Sung, the president of North Korea, who had allegedly tried to kill Moon at least three times:

> The natural subjugation of Kim Il Sung, who symbolizes all the evil, satanic qualities, including false parenthood, means false parents have finally surrendered in front of the True Parents. Father [Moon] has completely fulfilled God's dispensational history.[6]

One of the more significant additions to the theology, which was to lead to what might be termed a revivalist movement within the church, was revealed after the Reverend and Mrs. Moon's seventeen-year-old son, Heung Jin Nim, was involved in what proved to be a fatal car accident in America. Moon has told his followers that he had the power to save his son, but that he had let him die: Heung Jin Nim's death was the culmination of a final showdown between Moon and Satan, who, having been unable to "invade" Moon himself, had turned to Moon's family. Through this sacrifice, Heung Jin Nim had become the bridge between the spirit world and the physical world, and within the spirit world, we are told, "Jesus is now known as the old Christ and Heung Jin is the young Christ."[7]

Shortly after Heung Jin's death on January 2nd, 1984, a number of members began to receive messages from him from the spirit world. One of the most well known of these spiritual mediums is a British woman, Faith Jones, who reports that soon after his death, Heung Jin Nim told her, "You must become my body, Faith, I need your body to walk, talk and speak, your body must become my body."[8] Another "channel" was an American man through whom Heung Jin Nim gave a series of well-attended lectures in New York towards the end of 1987. Some of the other members were less successful—a small group in Germany left the movement after it was decided that the messages coming through from Heung Jin Nim did not match the statements made by the local leader.

Later, Heung Jin Nim took over the body of a young Unificationist from Zimbabwe who had been practically unknown to anyone outside Africa at the time. Soon, however, the news had spread that Moon and his family fully accepted that this was indeed Heung Jin Nim, and the movement took on a revivalist character as "Second Self Heung Jin Nim" spoke at meetings to the membership, making a tremendous impression on nearly all those who saw him in action. He told the Bible stories from a new, robust perspective which included some interesting African embellishments. Special meetings were convened at which particular categories of members, such as the "blessed couples," were expected to confess to their sins and were given "conditions," such as fasting or abstention from sex for varying periods of time, according to the severity of the sins. Even the most senior members of the movement did not escape his wrath at their misdemeanours, and at one time physical punishment was meted out to miscreants: Col. Pak, Moon's chief interpreter and one of his top aides, was, it is said, hit so severely that he was in hospital for several days. Second Self Heung Jin Nim also arranged for couples to con-

ceive and bear children for other Unification couples who had found themselves unable to have children.[9]

But as time passed, Second Self Heung Jin Nim began to have revelations that differed, not just in interesting embellishments but in more fundamental ways, from Moon's revelations. Claims were made about the circumstances of the Fall, for example, that had serious implications for the movement's theodicy. About this time, Second Self Heung Jin Nim left the United States and went on a world tour of Europe and the East. His speeches were no longer distributed (as "Second Self Heung Jin Nim"). Soon after, it appears, Heung Jin Nim left the Zimbabwe brother's body, the Zimbabwe brother returned to Zimbabwe, and the excitement of the revival died down.

An early observer of the Unification Church, John Lofland, noted that those who joined the movement on the West Coast of America in the early 1960s were "primarily white, Protestant, young (typically below age thirty-five), some had college training, most were Americans from lower-middle-class and small town backgrounds, and the rest were immigrants."[10] With the advent of the 1970s, and as the movement increasingly concentrated on converting college students, the social class and educational attainments of the membership rose. By the time of my own study in the mid- to late-1970s, those joining the movement were disproportionately male (2:1) and disproportionately from the upper-middle and middle-middle classes, and the average age of joining was 23.[11] Although the average age of membership does not increase by one year every twelve-month (due to the high turnover and the fact that new converts tend to be young), the average age of those who converted to the movement is now around the late-thirties—but the average age of all those in the movement has become much younger with the advent of a second generation. A few of the older "blessed" children are now young men and women, a handful of whom have themselves been blessed in marriage by Moon, but the majority of those born to Americans will not have reached their teens by the mid-1990s.

It has never been easy to assess the number of Unificationists at any one time. This is partly because, for different reasons, both the movement and its opponents have tended to exaggerate the figures and to discount the large turnover rate—the members because they wanted to seem more successful than they are, and the anticultists because they wanted to stress the threat of the movement and to deny the possibility that the "brainwashed" members are able to leave of their own free will. In fact, it is unlikely that there have ever been ten thousand core members at any one time in the West. Although many more may have flirted with Unificationism for a short time, the majority of those who have joined have left within a comparatively short time. A few of those who leave do so because they have been expelled or forcibly "deprogrammed," but the vast majority leave because they themselves no longer wanted to stay—sometimes because they had become disillusioned with the leadership or because they no longer believed that what they were doing was actually going to produce the promised results. Some, still believing, have found the life too hard, or have wanted to escape from a particular situation or group of people—or, perhaps, from the partner chosen for them by Moon.[12] Yet others have just wanted to move on—to return to college, perhaps, or to enjoy more control over their own lives.[13]

The high drop-out rate among the membership, and the fact that around 90 percent of those who have been interested enough in the Unification Church to attend one of its residential seminars were perfectly capable of saying that they did not want to join the movement,[14] does, of course, seriously challenge the popular hypothesis that the Unification Church uses irresistible and irreversible techniques of brainwashing or mind control to obtain and keep its members. It would, on the contrary, seem that if sinister techniques are being used (and there is no evidence that any of the processes involved in proselytising differ qualitatively from processes that are to be found in "outside" society), they are pretty ineffective.[15] Furthermore, comparative analysis has indicated that those who (according to a number of criteria independent of the fact that they had expressed an interest in the movement) might be considered particularly inadequate or suggestible were in fact unlikely to join, or they would join for a short period—of a week or so—and then leave.[16]

During the 1970s, it was easy to know who was and who was not a "real Unificationist," and anyone who left the movement was likely to be shunned by the remaining members. With the passage of time, however, unambiguous labels have become more difficult to apply to a number of individuals on the periphery of the movement, some of whom are not themselves very sure whether or not they still accept enough of the movement's beliefs to continue to call themselves Unificationists, but who, nonetheless, keep in touch with the more committed membership and may attend the occasional Unificationist function. This blurring of the boundaries between "them" and "us" is in part a reflection of changes that have taken place both within the movement and in its relationship with the rest of American society.

Various levels of Unification membership have, however, existed for some time, the "core" members being those who have attracted the most attention and whose parents have been most anxious about their intensity of commitment. In America, where it has been predominantly single people rather than families who have joined the movement, the members tended to live together in communities, which have ranged in size from small apartments to the vast New Yorker hotel. Given the movement's theological position, it is not surprising that there are strict rules about the relationship between the sexes, with members segregated in dormitories and expected to regard each other as brothers and sisters whose marriage partners are chosen for them by Moon.

Around 1972 the majority of members in the West started to work full-time for the movement (sometimes for up to eighteen hours a day), often travelling in Mobile Fund-raising Teams (MFTs). Unificationists are also expected to try to bring "spiritual children" into the movement by "witnessing" to potential converts, but there are various other activities in which members may be involved, including such "missions" as public relations, working for one of the movement's publications or one of its businesses (such as the fishing industry or selling ginseng products), or organising the large number of conferences that have been arranged for theologians, clergy, academics, politicians, army personnel, and journalists. While many stories in the media have been gross distortions of the truth, there can be little doubt that life in the Unification Church has been, and continues to be, one in which the rank-and-file members have enjoyed far fewer of the material comforts of this world than they would have been likely to have done were they not members.

Towards the end of the 1970s, the category of "House Church" member was introduced to accommodate those (often older Unificationists with young families) who preferred to live in their own homes and to continue to work outside the movement. At a much less committed level are people who may be referred to as "Associates," some of whom may attend occasional services or keep spasmodically in touch with some members, but many of whom have done little more than sign a piece of paper at some time stating that they were in sympathy with one or other of the movement's tenets. More recently, "core members" have been living with their young children as self-contained units, or in semi-self-contained apartments in a centre with other Unificationists—or, in some instances, with or close by their non-Unificationist parents, having been encouraged to move to their home towns and to find outside work or to set up small businesses with other members, tithing a percentage of their income to the movement.

It would be foolhardy to anticipate what the future holds for the Unification Church, but the demographic factors of a membership which has shifted from one of young, idealistic persons, eager to sacrifice themselves for the cause of restoring the Kingdom of Heaven on earth, to a middle-aged membership with more immediate responsibilities towards their young families has meant that many changes have already occurred, only the more obvious of which have been mentioned in this short chapter. Although Moon seems to be in excellent health, he himself is aware that he cannot live forever, and he has started to make plans for a future without his presence in the physical world. His wife, twenty years his junior, has recently started to play a far more significant role in the movement. Exactly what will happen when Moon dies does, of course, remain to be seen; there are a number of possible scenarios, including the probability that there will be some schisms. But it is unlikely that the Unification Church will disappear completely from the American scene, at least within the foreseeable future.

Notes

1. Chung Hwan Kwak, *Outline of the Principle: Level 4* (New York: HSA-UWC, 1980), 1–2.

2. J. Lofland, *Doomsday Cult: A Study of Conversion, Proselytization, and Maintenance of Faith* (New York 1966; London: Irvington, 1977) and Michael Mickler, "A History of the Unification Church in the Bay Area: 1960–74," MA thesis, Graduate Theological Union, Berkeley, California.

3. See, for example, Kwak, *Outline of the Principle*, 2.

4. Chung Hwan, *The Tradition* (New York: HSA-UWC, 1985).

5. *Reverend Sun Myung Moon Speaks on The Age of New Dispensation* 14 (May 1978): 17.

6. *Today's World* (February 1992): 36.

7. "Day of Victory of Love," talk by Sun Myung Moon on 2 January 1987, *Today's World* (March 1987): 14. See also page 8 of

the original transcript of the talk and Young Whi Kim *Guidance for Heavenly Tradition,* vol. 2 (Morfelden-Walldorf: Kando, 1985), ch. 22.

8. "Faith Jones—Experiences with Heung Jin Nim," Friday, 24 February 1984. Duplicated typescript, p. 1.

9. *The Home Front: Newsletter of the 8000 Couples Blessed Family Association* (Spring 1988): 4.

10. Lofland, *Doomsday Cult,* 32.

11. E. Barker, *The Making of a Moonie: Brainwashing or Choice?* (Oxford: Basil Blackwell, 1984; reprint, Aldershot: Gregg Revivals, 1993).

12. It is perfectly possible for members to reject the partner chosen for them and to stay in the movement.

13. David G. Bromley, ed., *Falling from the Faith: Causes and Consequences of Religious Apostasy* (Beverly Hills: Sage, 1988), chs. 9 and 10.

14. Barker, *Making of a Moonie,* 146; M. Galanter, "Psychological Induction into the Large Group: Findings from a Modern Religious Sect," *American Journal of Psychiatry* 137, no. 12 (1980): 1575.

15. Barker, *Making of a Moonie;* Lofland *Doomsday Cult;* and D. Bromley and A. Shupe, *"Moonies" in America: Cult, Church and Crusade* (Beverly Hills: Sage, 1979).

16. Barker, *Making of a Moonie,* ch. 8.

Suggestions for Further Reading

Barker, Eileen. *The Making of a Moonie: Brainwashing or Choice?* Oxford: Basil Blackwell, 1984; reprint, Aldershot: Gregg Revivals, 1993.

Bromley, David, and Anson Shupe. *"Moonies" in America: Cult, Church and Crusade.* Beverly Hills: Sage, 1979.

Lofland, John. *Doomsday Cult: A Study of Conversion, Proselytization, and Maintenance of Faith.* 1966. Reprint. New York and London: Irvington.

Mickler, Michael. *The Unification Church in America: A Bibliography and Research Guide.* New York: Garland, 1987.

Part IV
Religions from the Middle East

Christianity and Judaism, the religions at the heart of the American mainstream, are Middle Eastern in origin (and still have a presence in their homeland) but have been heavily influenced by over a thousand years of development in Europe and the Americas. In relatively recent times newer Middle Eastern religions have arrived, among them Islam and several independent groups with at least some historical ties to Islam. Islam may be the fastest-growing religion in the United States, at least in percentage terms, because immigration from Islamic parts of the world continues to be strong and because nonimmigrant Americans, especially African Americans, are converting to the faith in much larger numbers than was once the case.

This section begins with a general survey of Islam's presence in the United States in its varied forms. It then turns to examinations of several groups derived from or influenced by Islam (with varying degrees of resemblance to the more prevalent forms of Islam), religious movements whose homelands range from the Caucasus to Indonesia. The Bahá'í Faith arose in Persia in the mid-nineteenth century; Muslims have tended to regard it as a pernicious Muslim heresy, but the Bahá'ís themselves see their faith as a new world religion based on revelations to its prophetic founder and stress, over all, the unity of the people of the world. The Sufis represent a mystical strain of Islam. Arising some twelve centuries ago, Sufism has been influenced by religions other than Islam and today appeals to a diverse constituency that in many cases sees itself only slightly, if at all, Islamic.

This section concludes with two chapters on groups whose ties to Islam and other Middle Eastern religions are thinner yet. Growing up in Asia Minor, George I. Gurdjieff was exposed to Eastern Orthodoxy and Sufism as well as to numerous other religious groups and movements. His own work, which he early characterized as "esoteric Christianity," first attracted followers in Russia in the years before the Bolshevik Revolution and later gained the attention of artists and intelligentsia in England and America. Subud was brought to the West in the 1960s by an Indonesian Muslim who taught what he called not a religious system but a technique for spiritual self-awakening that was compatible with any religion, Islamic or otherwise. These chapters fit here better than they would in any other section of the book, but remind us that the development of clear-cut categories in which to group religions is always difficult.

21

EXPRESSIONS OF ISLAM IN AMERICA

Gisela Webb

The 1990s may be the last decade in which Islam is viewed as a "non-mainstream" religious tradition in America. At its current rate of growth, by the year 2015 Islam will be the second largest religion in the United States, following Christianity. There are approximately four million Muslims in the United States and 650 mosques.[1] Foreign-born Muslims and their descendants constitute about two thirds of those numbers; indigenous Americans (born in America), mostly African Americans, constitute the other third.[2] Islam is already the world's second largest religion, with 900 million members—about one sixth of the world's population—living in geographic regions that include, but extend far beyond, the Middle East. Islam is either the major religion or has large populations in such diverse cultural environments as Africa, Malaysia, and Indonesia, the former Soviet Union, Turkey, India and Pakistan, northwestern China and Europe.

Yet there is surprisingly little awareness or understanding of Islam in the American consciousness. What Americans do think about Islam tends to be formed by media images, specifically by the presence of one-sided negative imagery on the one hand ("Arab terrorists," "Islamic fundamentalists"), and by the absence of positive, or even neutral images on the other. American Muslims often express frustration over a situation that seems to be the last bastion of tolerated stereotyping. Clearly, the poor relationship between Islam and the "Chris-

tian West" has its roots in the confrontational and competitive history which Christianity and Islam have shared since Islam arose as a religious and political challenge to Christianity in the seventh century. The roots of confrontation also lie in the remembered history of the Crusades, in the relationship established during the colonial and the post-colonial periods (including the loss of Palestinian lands to Israel) and, now, in the heightened rhetoric and mistrust created by Muslims and "Westerners" alike, who would present Islam and "secular democracy" as polar opposites. Ideologues on both sides would like to present an image of a monolithic "Islam" with a unified agenda and clear leaders.

The reality is that the situation of Islam worldwide and in the United States, in particular, is extremely complex and shifting. Islam developed its forms of orthodoxy in the early history of the community.[3] There were, of course, different interpretations of basic principles derived from sacred scripture which led to a number of contending discourses in Islam (theological, juridical, philosophical, mystical, popular, political) as well as differing "styles" of Islam depending on the cultural milieu into which Islam was introduced. This complex reality is also the "process" of Islam in America. There have already been a number of stages in the development of an "American" Islam as well as a number of different groups and styles that constitute the Muslims of America.

There are three major constituents of Islam in America: immigrants, who bring Islam from their homelands; African-American converts to Islam; and the Sufi groups, the "spiritual confraternities" of Islam. This chapter will introduce the reader first to the central tenets of Islamic faith and practice and then to the historical development of certain segments of the Islamic community in America, namely, immigrant groups and African-American groups that see themselves as members of traditional or "orthodox" Islam. Sufism will also be treated in a separate chapter in this volume. It will be evident that there are a number of important issues facing American Muslim communities and individuals at this time, but they all point to the overarching question of how to define and manifest what "Islam" means in the midst of a secular, pluralistic, contemporary American culture.

Beliefs and Practices

The Islamic religion had its historic origin in the figure of Muhammad Ibn Abdullah. Muhammad was born in the Arabian city of Mecca in 570 C.E. and was a member of the Quraysh tribe. According to traditional accounts, Muhammad was in the trading business, Mecca being a crossroads for many of the overland trade routes of the day, and was married to Khadija, his former employer who was fifteen years his senior. He was a reflective man and often meditated in a cave near Mt. Hira. From 610 through 632, when he died, Muhammad experienced a number of visions and "hearings," which he came to understand as true revelation (wahy) from the one God, Allah, which was communicated through the angel Gabriel.[4] These "revelations" began as warnings directed at the Meccans for their forgetfulness of God, for their polytheism and idolatry, and for the social and economic injustices of Meccan society. The revelations also warned of an inevitable judgment that all human beings would experience at the "Final Hour," an idea which was alien to the prevailing view of life and death in Arabian tribal culture. Muhammad understood his role to be that of the final prophet and messenger of God, and his message of submission (islam) to God's will as the same message that had been revealed to Abraham, Moses and all the other prophets of Jewish and Christian Scriptures as well as to the "prophets" of other peoples from the beginning of time. Jesus was seen as a prophet, born of the virgin Mary, and a special model of sanctity; but Christian claims of Jesus' divinity and "sonship" were rejected. The collection of Muhammad's revelations is the sacred book of Islam, the Quran. Muslims traditionally accept it as the authoritative word of God which "preexisted" eternally with God.

Muhammad began to preach in Mecca and, as a result of persecution, emigrated with a number of his followers to the city of Medina, where he established the paradigmatic "Islamic" community. The emigration (hijra) to Medina in 622 C.E. marks the beginning of the Islamic calendar. Muhammad eventually returned victorious to Mecca, clearing the Ka'ba—the pilgrimage site used by the many Arabian tribes—of all idols in a symbolic act of reviving the original intention of the Ka'ba, which, according to tradition, had been built by Abraham and his son Ishmael to worship the One God, Allah.

The Quran and the example (sunna) of Muhammad became the main sources for the development of belief and practice in Islam. The Quran established the main articles of belief and practice, which are known as the Five Pillars of Islam. The first pillar is the shahada, the affirmation that "There is no God but God (La ilaha illa Allah), and Muhammad is His Prophet." The shahada is normally understood as stressing the utter transcendence and distinction of God "above" all created orders, although the Sufis would traditionally interpret the shahada as affirming that ultimately only God can be called "the Real." The shahada is also seen as affirming the authenticity of God's prophets and holy books, the angels, the jinn (invisible creatures created out of "fire"), and the final judgment of one's deeds and consignment to heaven or hell. The five pillars also include the basic duties of Muslims. Thus, the second pillar consists of the *salat,* the liturgical prayers said in Arabic five times daily, facing Mecca. On Fridays, Muslims gather in mosques for congregational recitation of prayers. The *salat* prayers create the basic orientation of time and space for Muslims. Arabic became the sacred language of Islam and an important unifying element for Muslims throughout the world. With the third pillar, the *zakat,* or charity tax, Muslims are required to pay a yearly tax of 2.5 percent of one's holdings for the care of the society's poor. The fourth pillar is *sawm,* or fasting—refraining from all food and liquid—from sunrise to sunset each day during the lunar month of Ramadan. It is a time of inner reflection and training of the *nafs,* the "lower self," as well as of experiencing something of the hunger of the poor. Finally, Muslims are required to make the *hajj,* the pilgrimage to Mecca once in their lives so long as it is not a financial burden. The primary ritual of the *hajj* is the circumambulation of the Ka'ba, which is seen as a reenactment of Muhammad's "clearing the idols" as well as symbolic of the ideal of the "unity of humankind" that has attracted so many marginalized peoples to Islam. Muslim men and women arrive in Mecca from virtually every race, class, and ethnic group, shedding their outer garments for a plain white shroud—a symbol of equality as well as the Muslim death shroud—and begin their common "journey to the center."

In principle, there is no division between religious and secular law in Islam. All of life is to be oriented toward the Divine Will. The *shariah,* or Islamic law, was developed to provide specific guidelines for all areas of life, from religious ritual (e.g., requirements in prayer) to sexuality (e.g., no premarital sex) to political principles (e.g., rules of war) to dietary restrictions (e.g., no pork, no alcohol). Of course, the *shariah* is based on interpretation of the Quran, the remembered history of Muhammad's actions, and the cultural customs of the geographic regions in which the *shariah* developed during the eighth and ninth centuries. It is not surprising that a major area

of contemporary discussion among Muslims is the issue of reinterpreting the *shariah* in light of considerations of modernity. The variety of Islamic "revival" and "reform" movements that have emerged in the contemporary Islamic world (often inaccurately lumped together under such terms as "radical" or "fundamentalist")[5] have tended to see the political, social, and economic ills of the Islamic world as indications that Muslims have fallen away—because of infatuation with the West or corruption of their own leaders—from the moral and civic principles of the *shariah,* and that a return to an "Islamic" way of life, the *shariah,* would revitalize both Islamic society and, ultimately, the world community. However, it is this same activist spirit that has led to disagreement over "what," or "whose," version of Islam is correct, as well as how the *shariah* should be implemented.[6] The issue of interpretation is particularly crucial in the area of the rights and treatment of women. Muslim women writers, both in America and abroad, often point to the curtailed role of women in the post-Muhammadan community in comparison with the egalitarian thrust of the Quran itself and the more active participation of women in the early Muslim community.[7] Thus, the issue of "women and the veil" is symbolic of discussions that have become particularly important for Muslims in America. In addition to the *shariah,* many customs have spread throughout the Islamic world which Muslims see as rooted in the example of Muhammad, and which they feel incumbent to cultivate—for example, modesty, hospitality, and respect for teachers and elders.

Two major branches of Islam developed early in the community's history in response to the question of succession of authority after Muhammad's death. Sunni Islam and Shi'ite Islam reflect two approaches to politics and rule. Shi'ites believe that Muhammad's charisma—and, hence, political and spiritual guidance—was continued in the bloodline of Ali (Muhammad's cousin and son-in-law) and his descendants, the Shi'ite imams (leaders). Shi'ites believe in the continued guidance from the final imam (although different sects of Shi'ites disagree on whether that was the fifth, the seventh, or the twelfth in the line of succession), and tradition maintains that he will return as the *mahdi* to usher in the Day of Judgment. About 20 percent of all Muslims, mostly from Iran and southern Lebanon, are Shi'ites.[8] The other 80 percent, the majority of Muslims, are Sunnis, for whom selection of leaders is supposed to take place through representatives (originally the tribal elders) of the people.[9] Both Sunnis and Shi'ites are considered "orthodox."

Within both Sunni and Shi'ite communities of Islam there emerged spiritual confraternities, the Sufi groups, or *tariqas,* which were centered on the teachings of certain pious individuals. These charismatic figures taught a "subtle wisdom" tradition of interpreting the Quran and the traditions of the Prophet. The Sufi groups developed a variety of approaches to Islamic spirituality—ecstatic, contemplative, devotional, poetic, musical, chivalrous—the goal of which was both purity of devotion and attainment of a unitive experience of God. The Sufis contributed much to the development of the esoteric sciences of the medieval period (alchemy, subtle psychology), popular forms of piety, and the arts—literary, visual, musical, and poetic. While the Sufis at times strained the boundaries of "orthodoxy" with some of their teachings, their presence has been a historical constant in Islamic societies. They are recognized for their importance as transmitters of Islam to lands far from the original "heartland" of Islam. See "Sufism in America" in this volume.

The beliefs and practices of Sunnis and Shi'ites, of Sufis and non-Sufis, came to the shores of America with the arrival of immigrant populations, traditions brought by slaves, and popular Sufi teachers from "the East."

Muslims in America—Immigrant Communities

About two thirds of all Muslims in the United States are immigrants and their descendants.[10] Muslim immigrants, both Sunnis and Shi'ites, arrived in waves beginning in the late 1800s, the first groups coming from what are now Syria, Lebanon, Jordan, and Palestine. Communities began to form in the industrial centers of the Midwest—Toledo, Cedar Rapids, Detroit, Michigan City, and Chicago. Most of these immigrants were uneducated and unskilled workers who sought economic opportunities in the United States. The extended families of these immigrants became the founders of the first mosques in North America. These first mosque communities functioned primarily to maintain social bonds, offer solidarity in this new land, and provide community space for rites of passage.[11]

Another wave of immigrants arrived between 1947 and 1960 and included Muslims from the Middle East as well as from India, Pakistan, Eastern Europe, and the Soviet Union. Some were children of ruling elites; some were refugees; many came solely for higher education.[12]

The individuals comprising the last wave, from 1967 to the present, have come for both political and economic reasons. Many, especially Pakistanis and Arabs, are educated professionals. Substantial numbers of Iranians came prior to and after their country's revolution. A number of other countries are represented in this wave: Yemen, Lebanon, Egypt, Jordan, Turkistan-Turkey, Kuwait, Saudi Arabia, Iraq, and Afghanistan.[13] The most recent arrivals are from the Sudan, Uganda, Guyana, Bermuda, and the former Yugoslavia.

Development of Islamic community life in America corresponded to the political and social concerns of particular immigrant groups. Earlier Muslim immigrants saw mosque life mostly in terms of social needs, and *imams* (leaders) of local congregations were not always trained as religious teachers. Thus, little emphasis was placed upon strict observance of traditional mosque functions. Adaptations were made to conform to American church patterns, such as scheduling congregational prayers on Sundays and allowing "mixed" (men and women) social functions, such as dances.

Later groups of immigrants brought the heightened religious and political self-consciousness that has been part of the legacy of the loss and occupation of Palestinian lands.[14] These Muslims came with commitments to a variety of religio-political ideologies and with more religious training, usually more conservative, than their predecessors in America. Tension points developed in some of the earlier mosque communities as more recent and conservative Muslim arrivals attempted to correct their more Americanized brothers and sisters in areas of Islamic practice and custom.

In general, Muslims in America who have been raised in traditional Muslim cultures speak of the tension they experience in trying to remain close to linguistic, cultural, ethnic, and religious roots while trying to develop a sense of belonging in their adopted home. American societal patterns are often at odds with needs of Muslim life and practice: Work schedules do not easily allow for the five-times-daily *salat* prayers or Friday congregational prayers. Institutional eating facilities (schools, prisons, military) are not set up for Muslim dietary practices. The pervasiveness of alcohol in America and the cultural acceptance of sexual permissiveness and immodesty (in clothing and comportment) are seen as negative influences on the faith community, particularly on its young people.[15] The *shariah,* however, continues to be held as the ideal pattern of life to be striven for, somehow, in the midst of contemporary American culture.

Mosque governance in America appears to be taking the pattern of some Protestant denominations, such as the Baptists, in which each community has autonomy in deciding its local leadership and ideological orientation, but in which each member and each community shares a commitment to sacred scripture as the ultimate source of guidance in areas of belief and practice.[16] American mosques, unlike mosques in Islamic countries, are self-supporting, and therefore they must rely on membership contributions or fund-raising activities. The *imam* of the American mosque often finds himself in a role that goes beyond the traditional function of reciter of prayers. He may assume additional roles, common to American pastors, such as administrative and counseling responsibilities.

There are a variety of styles and emphases in mosque communities of the United States. Some mosques function in the way of America's small, urban ethnic churches, in which ethnic ties are emphasized, cultivated, and preserved. These communities function as centers for learning and sharing information about surviving in America as much as they function as centers for prayer. Other mosques, while being centers for prayer and social activities, also emphasize "outreach," utilizing the Islamic cultural tradition of hospitality in order to establish communication and goodwill with the surrounding community.[17] Mosques in the Midwest, such as the Islamic Center of Toledo, Ohio, are known for this approach. More recently established mosque communities, such as the Islamic Society of Central Jersey, have taken this approach as well, particularly in light of escalating fears of Islam and Muslims.[18] The focus of their work is in correcting misunderstandings about Islam by inviting non-Muslim groups to their facilities and by offering lectures and programs. Finally, a new trend has emerged in America: the large "mega-mosques" that serve the needs of large, rapidly growing, racially and ethnically diverse communities, such as in the Los Angeles area.[19] These mosques most clearly reflect the historical pluralism within the Islamic community as well as the continually widening ethnic pluralism of the United States.

There are a number of active Islamic organizations that exist alongside the mosque communities. In the middle of this century, the Muslim population was still small and dispersed over the continent. The need for a unifying organization led second-generation Muslim immigrants to form a federation of mosques that would provide a pooling of resources and contact with other communities.[20] It was originally called the Federation of Islamic Organizations; today it is the Federation of Islamic Associations in the United States and Canada, and its headquarters are in Detroit.

While the federation of mosques was taking shape within the earlier ethnic communities, Muslim student organizations were forming on college campuses. In 1963 the Muslim Student Association (MSA) was created to coordinate activities of the student groups. The MSA symbolized the international diversity of Islam as well as the ideological concerns of a more activist Islam worldwide. For these students, Islam was a way of life, a mission, and the organization's goal was to help create an ideal community and to serve Islam.[21] The MSA is still one of the largest and most well-organized Islamic organizations, and it has led to the creation of a number of other service and professional organizations designed to meet the needs of Muslims beyond the student community. Among them are the Muslim Community Association, American Muslim Social Scientists, Muslim Youth of North America, American Muslim Scientists and Engineers, Islamic Teaching Center, Islamic Medical Association, and the American Muslim Mission. These and other groups are now under the umbrella organization of the Islamic Society of North America (ISNA). The groups have their own committees and boards, but their administrative, legal, and financial affairs are linked at the center by ISNA's legislative body, the Majlis al-Shura.[22] ISNA groups sponsor national, zonal, and profession-specific congresses, where members engage in social, business, and intellectual exchange while maintaining connections with the larger international Islamic community.

One of the most important developments that characterizes the current Islamic community in America is the movement in the direction of political activity in the United States. While ISNA's leadership always tended to be individuals with affiliation to or backing by politically minded "Islamist" groups, such as the Ikhwan al-Muslimin and the Jammati-Islami,[23] there was never agreement on the appropriateness or the form of political action in the United States. Some of the more "ultra-orthodox" movements (such as the Sala-fiyya, comprised mainly of Gulf Arabs and some African Americans) and some of the African-American "utopian separatists" felt reluctant to participate in the *kufr* ("unbelieving") American governmental system.[24]

Nevertheless, in trying to offer some balance to the influence of the many pro-Israel political action committees, a number of Muslim PACs have emerged since 1985, including ISNA's own ISNA-PAC. In addition, a number of Muslim groups, such as the United Muslims of America and the Islamic Society of Greater Houston have encouraged participation in such mainstream American activities as registering and voting in elections, actively supporting candidates, and even running for office. One of the results of this public visibility in the political system is that Muslim candidates sometimes find criticism coming from conservative elements within the Muslim community for such things as not using an Islamic name, dressing in an "overly Western" manner, or making other concessions to American secular culture.[25]

There are a number of Muslim organizations and activities which are not specifically political. Among them are *da'wa* (missionary, education, ministry) oriented groups, such as the Muslim World League and the Shi'ite-based Islamic Societies of Georgia and Virginia; the Muslim "think-tanks," such as the International Institute of Islamic Thought, formed in 1982 to promote "Islamic" scholarship and methodologies; and the National Committee on Islamic Affairs, which has begun to utilize the media as a forum for Muslim discussion on affairs in the Middle East.

There are also many Muslim "activist-scholars" in America who are engaged in critical examination of a wide variety of issues and assumptions related to "tradition" and "modernity" in Islam. These scholars often find themselves caught between cultures: they find it difficult to take scholarship back home to countries where ideological concerns rule the academic discourse; but they also find it difficult to challenge ideological assumptions that exist in American academia.

African-American Islam

Most of the "non-immigrant" Muslims in America are African-American converts to Islam. For many African Americans, Islam has become a means of self-definition and of "choosing" to identify with a religio-cultural system that was other than the one (the Christian West) that had failed in establishing a truly racially inclusive society.[26] Certainly the phenomenal growth of Islam among African Americans, even the injection of Islamic themes into black popular culture (such as rap music),[27] is related to the meaning that "Islam" holds for many African Americans, namely, identifying with a religious faith that has affirmed their African heritage.

The roots of a "black Muslim" perspective can be traced back to Timothy Drew (Noble Drew Ali) and the founding of the Moorish American Science Temple in Newark in 1913, as well as to the emergence of the Elijah Muhammad and the Nation of Islam. Certainly the most well-known convert to the Nation of Islam was Malcolm X, whose expositions of Elijah Muhammad's teachings were most influential in bringing membership to the Nation. (See Timothy Miller, "Black Jews and Black Muslims," this volume.) There were/are some themes taught in the Nation of Islam that reflect traditional Islamic teachings: submission to Allah, the repudiation of such vices as alcohol, sex outside of marriage, the eating of pork, and gambling. However, such teachings as the "white man as devil" and the quasi-scientific theory of the origins of human history run counter to traditional Islamic accounts of human history and purpose. It was Malcolm X's pilgrimage to Mecca and his experience of a "universal brotherhood" in submission to Allah without color lines that helped make permanent his break with Elijah Muhammad and the Nation of Islam in favor of what he regarded as "true Islam." Malcolm X's teachings after his trip to Mecca became a major catalyst for moving many African Americans in the direction of "orthodox" Islam. Elijah Muhammad's own son, Warith Deen Muhammad, was one of these.

After the death of his father, Warith Deen Muhammad took over the Nation and formally brought the organization into mainstream Islamic belief and practice. He rejected the preaching of racial hatred, including the "white man as devil" idea. He instituted the use of traditional Islamic rituals, and he repudiated teachings that identified Elijah Muhammad as a prophet. The organization went through a number of name changes. It had been the Lost-Found Nation of Islam in the Wilderness of North America, then the Nation of Islam. It then became the American Bilalian Community, then the World Community of Islam in the West, and, finally, the American Muslim Mission. In 1985, Warith Deen Muhammad decentralized the organization, delegating the central responsibilities to local imams. He encouraged the merging of African-American Muslims into the worldwide Islamic community. These directives were not accepted by all members of the Nation. Louis Farrakhan is the best-known current spokesman for Elijah Muhammad's teachings, maintaining both the name, the Nation of Islam, and the centralized form of the organization. Farrakhan tends to draw more media attention than the American Muslim Mission, confirming the conviction of many Muslims, African American and immigrants alike, that normative Islam is rarely depicted in the U.S. media.

In reality, there are hints of an increased public awareness of African-American Muslim activity beyond Farrakhan's "Nation." There is increased reportage on mosques being built in American cities. Furthermore, the American Muslim Mission's nationwide system of schools, the Clara Muhammad Schools, has received media attention for the positive contribution to the quality of life and education they are providing in the larger urban areas where they are situated as alternatives to the public schools. There are over sixty of these academically certified schools. Also of significance in the development of American Islamic communities is the fact that these schools are drawing children of recent immigrants into already established African-American communities, thereby fostering a sense of community across ethnic lines. The teachers tend to be immigrants themselves, often with advanced degrees in their native countries. Islamic studies are interwoven with subjects such as English, history, and science, and Arabic is taught from kindergarten. They espouse a philosophy that is racially inclusive and religiously tolerant.[28]

The Clara Muhammad Schools are an example of the growing ties emerging between indigenous and immigrant Muslims. As mentioned, tension does occur when new immigrants attempt to make changes in already established mosque communities, whether they are predominantly African American or immigrant, and this friction has become somewhat heightened in the present climate of growing emphasis on cultural self-affirmation of minority groups in America (mirroring the worldwide self-affirmation of ethnic identity). However, the larger pattern that seems to be emerging is one of increased cooperation, interaction, and even intermarriage between indigenous and immigrant Muslims.

Another important segment of the African-American Muslim population that must be mentioned in any consideration of current developments in America is the unprecedented numbers of African Americans who are converting to Islam while in prison. For these (mostly) men, Islam is an important means of identity formation. Many mosques, including Sufi communities, are involved in ministry to prisons, forging community support systems for these prisoners. Furthermore, Muslims in prison are raising important legal questions with regard to freedom of expression of religion for "non-conventional faiths" within prison walls. Issues of whether Muslim prisoners should be entitled to consideration in terms of space and time for worship, dietary restrictions, and wearing beards are being argued in the courts presently. Certain accommodations in the area of religious expression are already permitted in the case of Christian and Jewish prisoners.[29]

The Islamic community in America includes the many mosque communities which are attempting to find ways to accommodate both traditional religious norms and changing constituencies within the cultural context of American society. It includes Muslim "conservatives" and "traditionalists," whose ideologies put them at odds with American secular values, and Muslim "modernists" who wish to be transmitters of Islamic values while working within the framework of the American democratic tradition. The Islamic community includes individual Muslim women and men in every American mosque community who are struggling with the tension between traditional practices and modern secular Western views about the rights and role of women. American Muslims include African-American groups who have chosen to be integrated in the larger Islamic community, but who seek affirmation and respect for their African-American cultural identity. There are those African-American and immigrant Muslim communities that are combining their resources to improve the conditions of recent immigrants and the marginalized poor of the inner cities. Finally, it is evident that the distinction between immigrant and indigenous Islam is rapidly becoming meaningless as "foreign-born" Muslims and their American-born children share mosque community life with growing numbers of American-born Muslims and their children. The Islamic community in America is becoming the major melting pot of the wide variety of racial and ethnic groups that constitute the "traditional" Islamic world. Islam has long been regarded by Westerners as the religion of "the other." Clearly, this perception of Islam will undergo revision in America as Muslim communities grow, and as America comes to re-define itself in terms of its increasingly multicultural and multireligious nature.

Notes

1. "Mosque," the Muslim "house of prayer" is derived from the Arabic *masjid,* "place of prostration."

2. Terms such as "indigenous" and "immigrant" are categories of differentiation that are currently under scrutiny as they become

less helpful in describing sociological changes that have taken place in Muslim communities. "Immigrant" communities are becoming "establishment," children are growing and intermarrying, foreign-born Muslims are becoming American citizens, demarcation between the "older" immigrants and the new African and Asian immigrants taking on racist overtones. However, until there is a consensus in the scholarly community on this issue, these terms will be used.

3. The term "orthodoxy" is understood to mean the beliefs and practices that became normative in the community. However, in Islam there is no official body or council that defines "orthodoxy."

4. "Allah" is simply the Arabic word referring to "God." Christians whose native language is Arabic also speak of God as "Allah."

5. As John Esposito points out in *Islam: The Straight Path* (New York: Oxford Press, 1991), there are a number of variations of "fundamentalist"—or "back to the fundamentals"—movements in the Islamic world, from "moderate" voices who seek reconciliation of traditional Islam and certain aspects of the modern West, to "radical" voices who see the West as a major enemy of Islam with no reconciliation possible, and who condone the use of violence to bring about an Islamic society. See chapter 5.

6. See Esposito, *Islam: The Straight Path*, chapters 5 and 6.

7. See Fatima Mernissi, *The Veil and the Male Elite* (Reading, Mass.: Addison-Wesley Publishing Company, Inc., 1991) and Leila Ahmed, *Women and Gender in Islam* (New Haven: Yale University Press, 1992).

8. "Twelver Shi'ism" is the largest of the Shi'ite groups; other sects include the Ismailis (the "Seveners") and the Druze. See Annemarie Schimmel, "The Shia and Related Sects," in *Islam: An Introduction* (Albany: State University of New York Press, 1992).

9. Fredrick Denny, *An Introduction to Islam* (New York: Macmillan Publishing, Co., 1985), 135–36.

10. Yvonne Haddad and Adair T. Lummis, *Islamic Values in the United States* (New York: Oxford Press, 1987), 3ff.

11. Ibid.

12. Ibid. Among the immigrants were a number of Palestinians who went to Puerto Rico. It is estimated that there are ten thousand Muslims in San Juan alone.

13. Ibid.

14. Ibid., 14.

15. John Voll, "Islamic Issues for Muslims in the United States," in *The Muslims of America,* ed. Yvonne Haddad (New York: Oxford University Press, 1991), 205 ff.

16. Frederick Denny, "Emerging Forms of the Muslim Community" (paper delivered at the American Council for the Study of Islamic Societies Annual Meeting, 1992).

17. Frederick Denny, *Islam* (San Francisco Harper and Row, Publishers, 1987), 111 ff.

18. At the time of this writing, the February 1993 bombing of the World Trade center had just occurred.

19. Frederick Denny, "Emerging Forms of Muslim Community" (paper delivered at the American Council for the Study of Islamic Societies Annual Meeting, 1992).

20. Gutbi Mahdi Ahmed, "Muslim Organizations in the United States," in *The Muslims of America,* 12.

21. Ibid., 14.

22. Ibid., 15–16.

23. Steven A. Johnson, "Political Activity in Muslims in America," in *The Muslims of America,* 112. These are very ideologically oriented Islamic revivalist groups with roots in Egypt and Pakistan, but they have to a great extent become "mainstream" in these countries, renouncing violence as they seek their goal of creating a modern "Islamic" society. There are a small but clearly significant number of Islamic "extremist" groups who affirm the use of violence as a means of fighting "the satanic West." In light of the bombing of the World Trade Center, investigations are underway to locate possible formal connections between American Muslim individuals or groups with these most extremist of "Islamic" groups.

24. Ibid., 113.

25. Ibid., 114–19.

26. See Abubaker al-Shingiety, "The Muslim as the 'Other': Representation and Self-Image of the Muslims in America" in *The Muslims of America.*

27. See Prince-a-Cuba, "Black Gods of the inner City," *Gnosis Magazine,* no. 25, (Fall 1992): 56–63.

28. Ari Goldman, "Reading, Writing, Arithmetic, and Arabic," *New York Times,* 3 October 1992.

29. Kathleen Moore, "Muslims in Prisons: Claims to Constitutional Protection of Religious Liberty" in *The Muslims of America,* 150–51.

Suggestions for Further Reading

Denny, Frederick. *An Introduction to Islam.* New York Macmillan Publishing Co., 1985.

————. *Islam.* San Francisco: Harper and Row, 1987.

Haddad, Yvonne, ed. *The Muslims of America.* New York: Oxford University Press, 1991.

Haddad, Yvonne, and Adair T. Lummis. *Islamic Values in the United States.* New York: Oxford Press, 1987.

Haddad, Yvonne, and Jane Smith, eds. *Muslim Communities in North America.* Albany: State University of New York Press, 1994.

Prince-A-Cuba. "Black Gods of the Inner City." *Gnosis Magazine,* no. 25 (Fall 1992): 56–63.

22

THE AMERICAN BAHÁ'Í COMMUNITY IN THE NINETIES
Robert H. Stockman

The Bahá'í Faith arrived in the United States in 1894 and is now a century old. Its American membership, which in 1899 consisted of about 2,000 persons, mostly of white Protestant background, has grown to almost 120,000.[1] Initially located in a few score towns and cities, today Bahá'ís can be found in about 7000 localities in the United States. Worldwide, 1992 membership stands at about 5 million, with Bahá'ís located in every country on the planet.

Diversification is an ever-present theme in American Bahá'í history. From two black members in 1899, the African-American membership rose to 5 percent of the community by 1936.[2] Efforts to teach the religion to rural populations in the early 1970s, especially in South Carolina, increased the African-American population to perhaps 30 percent of the American Bahá'í community. Native Americans have been attracted to the Bahá'í religion in increasing numbers since the 1940s; currently there are several thousand Indian and Eskimo Bahá'ís, especially in rural Alaska and on the Navajo and Sioux reservations. Hispanics have also joined and constitute a thousand or two members.[3]

Immigration has profoundly shaped the American Bahá'í community's ethnic composition. During the war in Vietnam the Bahá'í Faith in Southeast Asia particularly attracted ethnic Chinese and Hmong hill people; they have been especially numerous among the groups fleeing Vietnam.

Bahá'í teaching efforts in refugee camps attracted thousands of Cambodians and Laotians to the Bahá'í Faith as well, and many of them came to the United States. As a result the American Bahá'í community has several thousand Bahá'ís of Southeast Asian background; no one knows exactly how many there are. In some cities—such as Portland, Oregon, and Lowell, Massachusetts—Southeast Asian Bahá'ís are a majority or substantial minority of the Bahá'í community. The Islamic revolution in Iran also forced tens of thousands of Bahá'ís to flee that country and about ten thousand have settled in the United States, especially in greater Los Angeles.

What attracted this remarkably diverse community to a single religion? The Bahá'í teachings consist of the ideas enunciated by Bahá'u'lláh (1817–1892), whom Bahá'ís regard as the bearer of a new revelation from God and the fulfillment of the prophecies of the previous religions. His teachings have been interpreted, clarified, and expanded by a line of successors: 'Abdu'l-Bahá (1844–1921), Shoghi Effendi (1897–1957), and the Universal House of Justice (a nine-member body elected every five years, starting in 1963). The writings of all three are considered authoritative and binding on all Bahá'ís worldwide.

Central to the Bahá'í religion's appeal have been two teachings: the oneness of religion and the oneness of humanity. The tenet of oneness of religion asserts that each of the major religions of the world was

243

founded by a manifestation of God whose teaching constituted a divine revelation. Thus Bahá'u'lláh is viewed as only the latest manifestation in a list that includes Abraham, Moses, Jesus Christ, Muhammad, Zoroaster, Krishna, and Buddha. The oneness of religion also involves a corollary principle that all the religions of the world have promised a messiah figure who would come and usher in a golden age; those promises, Bahá'u'lláh asserted, were fulfilled by him and his religion. Bahá'u'lláh specifically claimed to be the return of Christ and to fulfill biblical prophecy. This claim was the principal reason two thousand Americans became Bahá'ís between the years 1894 and 1900; it remains a popular aspect of Bahá'í teaching in the rural South today. The Bahá'í claim to fulfill Islamic, Zoroastrian, and Jewish prophecies attracted thousands to the faith in nineteenth-century Iran; the more general Bahá'í claim that all religions ultimately can be traced to a divine revelation and that they all promise the coming of Bahá'u'lláh were factors in attracting Southeast Asians and Native Americans to the fold.

The Bahá'í principle of the oneness of humanity has been another consistent source of appeal. The American Bahá'ís early recognized that the oneness of humanity meant that they had to teach their religion to all types of people, and that they could not form racially or ethnically segregated Bahá'í communities. The Washington, D.C., Bahá'ís took the lead in teaching African Americans the Bahá'í Faith in 1903; by 1909 about a dozen blacks had become Bahá'ís (in a community with about seventy Bahá'ís altogether) and in spite of resistance by some white Bahá'ís, who maintained the time for integration had not come, the African Americans were integrated into the white community. In 1911 the Washington Bahá'ís elected Louis G. Gregory, the leading black Bahá'í, to the local Bahá'í governing body; in 1912 Gregory was elected to the national Bahá'í coordinating body as well by delegates representing all the Bahá'í communities in North America. In 1912 Gregory married a white Bahá'í. The union was the first racially integrated marriage in the American Bahá'í community; 'Abdu'l-Bahá, who was visiting the United States at the time and who had actively encouraged their courtship, praised interracial marriage as a demonstration of the love that is possible between the races.[4] 'Abdu'l-Bahá also spoke extensively about the dangers facing the United States if it did not overcome its racial divide; he set the tone for future Bahá'í concern about the issue.

While integration of races and ethnic groups in the American Bahá'í community has never been perfect or without controversy, it has consistently been a priority of the American Bahá'ís, and explains why persons of varied ethnic backgrounds have been able to coexist in local Bahá'í communities. Intermarriage among these groups is a sign of their acceptance of each other. The American experience has helped set the tone for Bahá'í communities worldwide.

While the American Bahá'í community has influenced many Bahá'í communities around the globe through its travelling Bahá'í teachers, its "pioneers" (unpaid voluntary missionaries), and its publications, other communities have strongly influenced the Americans as well. This is especially true of Iran; Persian Bahá'ís have settled in the United States since 1901 and have been active as leaders in the American Bahá'í community. But undoubtedly the strongest source of influence from outside the United States has been the head of the faith ('Abdu'l-Bahá from 1892 to 1921, Shoghi Effendi from 1921 to 1957, and the Universal House of Justice since 1963), located in Haifa, Israel. Because the head of the faith has binding authority to interpret the Bahá'í scriptures, set major policies, and overrule decisions of local and national Bahá'í governing bodies, the development of the Bahá'í Faith worldwide is coordinated. If the understanding of the Bahá'í Faith in one country develops in a direction that the head of the faith does not desire, the head will take steps to correct the situation. Consequently any study of the American Bahá'í community cannot treat it in a vacuum, but must consider the role of the Bahá'í World Center.

Contemporary Issues in the American Bahá'í Community

Any discussion of the American Bahá'í community in the 1990s must include a discussion of which issues are "hot" in the Bahá'í community and which are not. But such a discussion must begin with the recognition that the Bahá'ís, within their own community, do not think in terms of "issues." Their primary concern is with community priorities, which are largely set by their institutions, not by the Bahá'ís individually. Furthermore, the American Bahá'í community has been heavily, but by no means completely, insulated from the intellectual trends in American society by the consistent focus of the Bahá'ís on their scriptures and their obedience to their elected Bahá'í institutions.[5] Finally, the Bahá'í religion has elaborate rules of discourse that strongly direct and sharply limit the nature of discourse among Bahá'ís.

For over sixty years, the highest priority of the National Spiritual Assembly—the nine-member elected governing body of the Bahá'í Faith in the United States—has been teaching the Bahá'í Faith to others. Each American Bahá'í is encouraged to set a goal of bringing one new person into the Bahá'í Faith each year; to host an informal meeting in his or her home for teaching others (called a fireside) at least once every Bahá'í month; and by word and deed to proclaim the Bahá'í Faith in an appropriate fashion to everyone he or she can. American Bahá'ís fall far short of the teaching ideals set for them: growth currently averages about 3 percent a year, not 100 percent, and the majority of the nation's population still knows little or nothing about the Bahá'í religion. While the high expectations generate some discouragement, American Bahá'í are generally optimistic that in the future the Bahá'í Faith will grow rapidly in the United States and eventually—in centuries—it will become the predominant religion of the country. Monthly Bahá'í community meetings are usually dominated by reports of teaching successes or by consultation on new efforts to take the message of Bahá'u'lláh to the public. A new technique that has stimu-

lated successes has been "teaching institutes": any group of Bahá'ís can come together to form these informal teams to study the Bahá'í scriptures together and teach the faith to others, and each institute sets its own goals and makes its own plans. Such team efforts have strengthened individual initiative by providing it with a peer support network.

The second priority of the National Spiritual Assembly—especially over the last decade—has been fostering racial unity and equality in the American Bahá'í community itself. Shoghi Effendi identified racism as "the most challenging issue" facing the American Bahá'ís, and his phrase has become a watchword. Many local Bahá'í communities hold one or more meetings every year where the Bahá'í standard of racial equality is discussed.

In the last decade Bahá'í efforts to combat racism in American society have also greatly increased. Bahá'ís have long been involved in the NAACP, the Urban League, and the civil rights movement; in the first two they have provided local leadership. In the last decade increasing numbers of Bahá'ís have been asked to serve on city human relations commissions; more and more local Bahá'í communities are collaborating with religious and human rights groups to sponsor projects to educate the public about racism. In 1991 the National Spiritual Assembly of the Bahá'ís of the United States issued *The Vision of Race Unity,* a public statement of the Bahá'í understanding of the racial challenges facing America; a campaign was initiated to give copies of it to government officials and leaders of thought. A second, more ambitious statement is in the planning stage. One result of the Bahá'í Faith's growing visibility in the area of race relations was the appointment, in 1992, of a representative of the National Spiritual Assembly to the rank of commissioner on the Martin Luther King Federal Holiday Commission.

There are other "official" issues in the American Bahá'í community of lesser importance, such as the role of women in the Bahá'í Faith and educating Bahá'í children in the religion, but space does not allow a discussion of them. Unofficial issues also exist but describing them systematically is impossible because no polls of Bahá'í attitudes have ever been taken, and no relevant statistics have been collected.[6] Furthermore, the Bahá'í rules of discourse emphasize that discourse must occur in such a way as to maximize unity and minimize disunity. The Bahá'í scriptures make it clear that unity is incompatible with the creation of special interest groups within the Bahá'í community or the division of the Bahá'ís into competing factions. Unity is currently understood by the Bahá'í community to mean that Bahá'í institutions can be publicly criticized only in ways that are respectful of their authority; that individuals are almost never publicly criticized; that all discussion of issues must avoid polarization; and that all arguments made in a Bahá'í context must be built on principles articulated in the Bahá'í scriptures. Under such circumstances many issues current in American society—such as which politicians to vote for in elections, or eliminating sexist language in publications, or the Bahá'í position on abortion, or the role of homosexuals in civil society—are discussed little or not at all in a "public" Bahá'í context.

Bahá'í Impact on American Culture

It is always difficult to assess the impact of a particular movement on American society or American culture as a whole. Ideas may be borrowed from the movement by society, but sometimes the borrowing goes from society to the movement instead, and sometimes an idea arises almost simultaneously in both.

Though it has steadily grown over the last century, the American Bahá'í community remains small, perhaps one twentieth of 1 percent of the total American population. There are many examples of small movements' having noticeable impacts on American culture or American religion; Unitarianism, Theosophy, and Vedantism are good examples. But for a small movement to produce a large impact on the American scene, three conditions usually

must be fulfilled. First, the movement must advocate ideas—usually a few simple ones—that resonate strongly with existing trends in the culture. Second, the movement must be able to advocate those ideas in a language that is appropriate and effective in the society outside it. Third, the movement must have articulate spokespersons who are also leading intellectual or literary figures in the culture. Usually the presence of the first two virtually assures the third.

Historically, the Bahá'í community has rarely been able to fulfill these three requirements for influence. The basic Bahá'í teachings are usually expressed in a Bahá'í terminology that is difficult to translate into mainstream language. Further, the ideas usually are part of a much larger complex of Bahá'í teachings and cannot be separated from them. For example, the application of the principle of interracial and interethnic unity to society is difficult because Bahá'í scripture prohibits Bahá'ís from partisan political activity and breaking the law.[7] Consequently few prominent blacks and few civil rights leaders have been attracted to the Bahá'í Faith.

The Bahá'í vision of a united, peaceful world, similarly, has been of limited appeal outside the Bahá'í community because it cannot be established through partisan political efforts. Furthermore, the Bahá'í conception of world unity and of interreligious relations are dominated by the belief that the new world order envisioned by the Bahá'í scriptures can occur only if the world accepts Bahá'u'lláh as its Lord.

In spite of these caveats, the Bahá'í Faith has had some impact on American culture in the areas of racial integration and the peace movement. The fact that the American Bahá'í community has been racially integrated since its establishment has been an encouraging example to others. Bahá'ís generally bring an optimistic idealism to efforts to foster interracial unity or world peace which is usually appreciated and welcomed. In both areas the Bahá'í Faith has attracted a few converts from among prominent thinkers and has influenced the thinking of non-Bahá'ís somewhat.

Current Priorities and Concerns

Currently the American Bahá'í community is enjoying better public recognition than ever before. Newspaper articles mentioning the Bahá'í Faith have increased in number considerably in the last few years, and now the majority of articles do not focus on the persecution of Iranian Bahá'ís, but on the American Bahá'í community itself.[8] Anti-Bahá'í materials (usually produced by Fundamentalists) are still relatively rare. The United States Congress has passed five resolutions condemning the persecution of Iran's Bahá'í community and has even held three congressional hearings on the treatment of Iran's Bahá'ís, which concretely demonstrates that the American Bahá'í community has been able to muster some political influence on Capitol Hill. The Bahá'ís have also collaborated with other human rights organizations such as Amnesty International in their efforts to secure congressional ratification of the United Nations Convention on Genocide, and are currently working on the ratification of four other treaties.

April 1992 to April 1993 is a Holy Year for Bahá'ís because it marks the centenary of the passing of Bahá'u'lláh. Only one other Bahá'í Holy Year has ever been proclaimed before: 1953, the centenary of the beginning of Bahá'u'lláh's mission. During 1992–93 Bahá'ís are to reflect on Bahá'u'lláh's mission; the National Spiritual Assembly has also called on the American Bahá'ís to rededicate themselves to the establishment of racial unity. The Holy Year began with the election of twelve new National Spiritual Assemblies, primarily in countries of the former Soviet bloc where the Bahá'í Faith was severely proscribed until a few years ago. On 29 May 1992 several thousand Bahá'ís gathered in Haifa, Israel, to commemorate Bahá'u'lláh's passing at his mausoleum.

In late November 1992 the second Bahá'í World Congress was convened in New York; 27,000 Bahá'ís from around the world attended the four-day event.[9] The themes of the congress were a celebration of Bahá'u'lláh's mission, of his establishment of a covenant to maintain the unity of the Bahá'í Faith, and of the growing strength and diversity of the Bahá'í world community.

In February 1993 the first official translation of the Kitáb-i-Aqdas, Bahá'u'lláh's book of laws, was released to the world; the book is expected to have a deep impact on the Bahá'ís, and will probably shift their emphasis from an enunciation of Bahá'í social principles toward a proclamation of the significance of Bahá'u'lláh and his teachings to humanity. The Holy Year also saw the application for the first time of an important law of the Kitáb-i-Aqdas to Bahá'ís outside of the Middle East: the law of *huqúqu'lláh,* which calls for the payment of a 19 percent tithe on one's surplus income to the Bahá'í World Center.[10] So far the American Bahá'í community has greeted the law quite positively, and contributions to the other Bahá'í funds have not declined significantly.

The Future

History has shown that great increases in the numbers of American Bahá'ís occur when social turmoil is high; the Bahá'ís experienced large increases in the late 1960s, the 1930s, and the 1890s. If American society enters another period of turmoil, a substantial increase in Bahá'í numbers may occur. If, on the other hand, society remains more or less as it is now, Bahá'í growth is likely to remain in the range of 3 to 5 percent per year for the foreseeable future. Even at that rate the American Bahá'í community is likely to reach a quarter million members in about fifteen years, and a half million members in about thirty years.

Growing size and influence will also spark a much more thorough investigation of the American Bahá'í community by outsiders. One result of that investigation will be the asking of tough questions about the many ways the Bahá'í religion's teachings deviate from cultural norms. The Bahá'í rules of discourse, discussed in cursory fashion above, are only one example of an aspect of the Bahá'í Faith that differs markedly from accepted practice in the United States. If the Bahá'í religion is ever to have substantial influence in the United States, the Bahá'í distinctives—both

positive ones from a cultural point of view, such as racial integration, and negative ones, such as restrictions on discourse—will also have to be explored and sharply debated.

Notes

1. The Bahá'í population of the contiguous forty-eight states was about 110,000 in 1992, but Alaska, Hawaii, and Puerto Rico together have about 6000 more. Reconstructing the membership figures for the American Bahá'ís decade by decade is complicated by changing definitions of membership and poor data collection, but the following numbers have been determined: From 1899 to 1921 the number of Bahá'ís ranged between 1500 and 2500, depending on how many of the Bahá'í sympathizers one includes. In 1936 the membership had risen to 2584; in 1944, to 4800; in 1956, to 7000; in 1963, to 10,000; in 1969, 13,000; in 1971, 31,000; in 1974, 60,000; in 1979, 75,000; in 1987, 100,000.

2. Gayle Morrison, *To Move the World: Louis G. Gregory and the Advancement of Racial Unity in America* (Wilmette, Ill.: Bahá'í Publishing Trust, 1982), 204.

3. No comprehensive ethnic survey of the American Bahá'í community has ever been undertaken. The numbers of minorities given in this chapter are estimates made by various offices at the Bahá'í national headquarters in Wilmette, Illinois.

4. The life of Louis Gregory is thoroughly documented in Morrison, *To Move the World.*

5. This is a generality; one exception are those Bahá'ís who engaged professionally in the external affairs work of local and national Bahá'í governing bodies.

6. I refer to such issues in American society as abortion, euthanasia, party politics, and homosexuality; without surveys of Bahá'í attitudes it is impossible to discuss in a scholarly way the role of these issues in the Bahá'í community. There is also the question of "schismatic" Bahá'í groups; four small ones (with a total membership of about a thousand) exist in the

United States. But Bahá'ís have almost no contact with these groups and the issues that brought them into existence thirty or more years ago are of no contemporary interest to Bahá'ís.

7. The reason partisan political activity and violation of the law are prohibited is because of the Bahá'í emphasis on the concept of unity. Partisanship divides political elites into competing factions, whose chief loyalty is to maintenance of their own power, not to what is right or what is best for society. The rule of law is essential for the maintenance of social order, and therefore for maintaining unity. Consequently the exalted standard of unity which Bahá'ís proclaim precludes Bahá'ís from joining political parties, taking positions in partisan issues, and breaking the law in order to change social practices.

8. The Office of Public Information at the Bahá'í National Center supplied the following statistics: from May 1989 through April 1990, 4340 newspaper and magazine articles appeared in the United States; from May 1990 through April 1991, 3628; from May 1991 through April 1992, 3855; from May 1992 through November 1992, 5202. The increase in 1992 reflects publicity generated by the Bahá'í Holy Year.

9. An excellent summary of the World Congress's purpose and its events may be found in *One Country* 4 (July-September 1992): 3. A thorough description of the events, with numerous photographs, may be found in *The American Bahá'í* 23 (31 December 1992): 19.

10. The huqúqu'lláh is paid on nonessential property and assets; it is not paid on one's food, lodging, clothing, transportation, and other essentials. Many Bahá'ís never are able to pay any *huqúqu'lláh* at all. It functions more like a religious "luxury tax" than a tithe.

Suggestions for Further Reading

Hatcher, William S., and J. Douglas Martin. *The Bahá'í Faith: The Emerging Global Religion.* San Francisco: Harper and Row, 1984.

Smith, Peter. *The Bábí and Bahá'í Religions: From Messianic Shí'ism to a World Religion.*

Cambridge: Cambridge University Press, 1987.

Stockman, Robert H. *The Bahá'í Faith in America, Volume One: Origins, 1892–1900.* Wilmette, Ill.: Bahá'í Publishing Trust, 1986.

23

SUFISM IN AMERICA

Gisela Webb

Introduction

Sufism, or *tasawwuf,* is the "mystical" dimension of Islam. The term refers to a variety of modes of spirituality that developed in the Islamic world, including ascetic-social-critical movements, esoteric and poetic interpretations of the Quran, and spiritual confraternities. The goal of Sufism has always been deepened devotion, spiritual transformation, and, ultimately, the interiorization of the basic tenet of Islamic belief, that "there is no God but God" or, in the classic Sufi interpretation, "Only God is the Real; Only God exists." Sufis have been major transmitters of Islam to regions far beyond the religion's "Middle Eastern" origin, especially in Africa, the Indian subcontinent, and the Malay-Indonesian world. In a sense, it is quite in the spirit of "the tradition" that Sufis have continued that role in the United States.

The fact that there has been little scholarly attention to Sufism in America can be attributed to three factors. First, there has been a tendency among academics, anticult groups, and traditional Muslims alike to lump the American-bred Sufi groups into categories such as "cults," "New Age," "popular," or "unorthodox," thereby dismissing Sufism as a serious topic in the study of religion. Second, the historical situation of Sufism itself, both inside and outside the Islamic world, complicates the issue of understanding the relationship of present-day Sufi movements to traditional Islamic practice. That is, Sufism has always been an "alternative" discourse in the Islamic world, existing in tension with stricter, legalistic elements in the tradition, and there continue to be voices in Islam that would deny the legitimacy and the pervasiveness of Sufism in Islamic culture.[1] Third, to further complicate the situation, there are many Americans involved in Sufi movements who emphasize classical Sufism's goal of the transcendental unity beyond all distinctions (including religious differences) to the point of denying any essential connection of Sufism with the religion of Islam.

The goal of this chapter is to shed light on the development of Sufi groups in America, first by discussing fundamental aspects of Sufism as it has been practiced in the Islamic world, and second by looking at particular American Sufi groups that represent differing models of relationship between Sufism and Islam. The group that bears the name the Sufi Order, founded by Hazrat Inayat Khan, incorporates a wide variety of holistic and spiritual systems under the umbrella of Sufism with little intention of linking their activities and goals to "exoteric" Islam. The Bawa Muhaiyaddeen Fellowship is a community whose founding teacher moved his mostly American membership in the direction of clearer identification with traditional Islamic (and Sufi) ritual and customs, a shift that has resulted in growing numbers of Muslims from traditional Islamic countries' joining in community activities. There are a number of other groups functioning as transmitters of Sufism and Muslim cultural values in the contemporary American context, but they will be discussed only briefly.

"Traditional Sufism"

Sufism had its historic origins in second-century Islam (eighth century C.E.), as numbers of devout Muslims began to criticize the accumulation of wealth and power—and the concomitant "forgetfulness of God"—that the Ummayad conquests had brought to Islamic society. These pious individuals began to devote themselves to ascetic practices such as nightly vigils, fasting beyond religious requirements, giving up worldly possessions, and wearing simple cloaks of wool (Arabic, *suf*), the latter from which the term "Sufi" derives.[2] It is well known that the example of Christian and Buddhist monks, and even Indian Vedantic theory, may have been factors in the development of Sufism. Whatever the historical influences were, by the tenth century the Sufis were well on their way to developing a lexicon of Islamic mystical concepts derived from and legitimated in Quranic language and exegesis.

The earliest preachers of this popular movement, such as Hasan al-Basri (d. 728 C.E.) of Iraq, emphasized fear of God's punishment, the need for repentance, and the *jihad,* or internal struggle against the *nafs,* the lower soul, in the attainment of purity of devotion *(ikhlas)*. With the figure of Rabi'a of Basra (d. 801), Islam found an important representative of devotional, or love, mysticism, as well as an important model of women's spirituality. By the ninth century, the Sufi movement included Muhasibi, a teacher in Baghdad (d. 857), who formulated an analysis of the human soul with its "states and stages" of spiritual development, and Dhu'n-Nun (d. 859), a Nubian in Egypt, who taught the sacredness of nature and defined the goal of spiritual knowledge in terms of *ma'rifa,* or gnosis, that is, non-discursive, intuitive knowledge. With al-Tustari (d. 896) we

have the beginnings of Sufi discussion on the human heart *(qalb)* as the locus of union and knowledge of God and on the "light of Muhammad" as the primal cosmic origin of the human race. The famous al-Hallaj (d. 922) represents the Islamic mystics whose ecstatic utterances brought criticism and sometimes persecution from the theological or juridical authorities of Islam. Al-Hallaj was executed for declaring "Ana al-Haqq," "I am the Truth," as an expression of his own unitive experience with God, which he described as meaning that his own separateness from God, his I-ness, had been annihilated *(fana)* in God.[3] Most Sufis were more "sober" than al-Hallaj in their expressions of spiritual realization.

By the twelfth century, formal religious orders *(tariqas)* began to crystalize around revered teachers, and a number of characteristic institutions developed. Each order was headed by a spiritual master *(shaykh,* or *pir)* whose lineage was claimed to go back to the original founder of the order and, ultimately, to Prophet Muhammad, through a chain of transmission *(silsilah)*. There was a very close bond between *shaykh* and disciple *(murid,* or dervish), with the disciple owing absolute obedience to the *shaykh,* and the *shaykh* acting as teacher and guide *(murshid)* for the disciple on his/her inward journey of the soul to God. Disciples met in lodges *(khanaqah)* for their rituals and often lived in the proximity of the compound *(zawiyyah,* or *dergah)* of the *shaykh.* One could be married or take the vow of celibacy—a much rarer situation—in becoming a member of a *tariqa.*

The role of the *shaykh* was to inculcate in the disciple the spiritual virtues that were necessary for, and reflections of, spiritual progress. The virtues included such attitudes as trust, repentance, patience, contentment, gratitude, poverty, love, sincerity, faith *(iman)*, and absolute surrender *(islam)*. Codes of noble and polite conduct, based primarily on the example of Muhammad as recorded in traditional accounts, informed the "rules" adopted by the Sufi orders as well as the medieval orders of "chivalry," or *futuwwah* in the Islamic world. Especially important were the acquisition of the qualities of modesty, hospitality, generosity, and loyalty.

The Sufi orders developed their own particular communal rituals and practices (based on the teachings of the *shaykh*) to complement and deepen the understanding of the basic requirements of Islamic worship. There were initiation rituals (usually involving the clasping of the *shaykh's* hand), night vigils, litanies of prayers, and times of seclusion and retreat. Perhaps the most central Sufi practice to develop was the *dhikr* (or *zikr*), the ritual of "remembrance of God," which always included the invocation of the Name of God. Some groups developed a "silent *dhikr*," such as the silent, rhythmic repetition of the *"La ilaha illa Allah"* ("there is no God but God"/ "only You, O God, exist") as an aid toward surrendrance and annihilation of the *nafs,* the lower self, the ego. Other groups utilized spoken *dhikrs,* in which blessings on the prophets and the saints and the "ninety-nine most beautiful names of Allah" (the Compassionate, the Just, etc.) were repeated hundreds of times, often with the aid of a *tasbih* (rosary-like counting beads). Many groups came to utilize both types of *dhikr.*

Some groups developed the use of rhythmical instruments to accompany singing and movement. The spiritual concert *(sama)* became an important part of Sufi practice in many parts of the Islamic world, with theologians and poets writing on both the benefits and dangers of its use. It is described as "listening with the ear of the heart to music" while being in a special state of love of God[4] (lest it become simply sensual music and a detriment to the listener). The "dance" became a part of some orders' practices, such as the Mevlevis (the Whirling Dervishes), while other orders permitted it only if movement arose spontaneously. Sufi gatherings sometimes included inspired poetry recitation and musical compositions, which were intended to express and cultivate a certain *hal,* or spiritual feeling.

Popular Sufi piety came to include the practice of making pilgrimages to the shrines *(mazar)* of Sufi teachers, saints, and *qutbs* (the spiritual poles of their ages). Because of its association with folk-religion, superstition, and the idea of mediation between God and humans, saint veneration has been controversial in the Islamic world, and it is discouraged or repudiated by religious leaders in certain Islamic countries today, such as Saudi Arabia. Nevertheless, the holy personage has been a central focus of popular religious and devotional life in virtually every region of the Islamic world, as can be seen by the number of shrines and pilgrimage sites which dot the Islamic landscape.

Traditional Sufi orders were named after their founders. Among the earliest was the Qadiriyyah order, based on Abd al-Qadir al-Jilani of eleventh century Baghdad. It is still the largest order, with members from West Africa to Indonesia. Other orders include the Naqshbandiyyah order, important in Central Asia and India. The Chistiyyah order of India created a bridge for discussions between Hindus and Muslims on the Unity of Being. The Shadhiliyyah order emerged in North Africa, and the Mawlawiyyah (or Mevlevis, the Whirling Dervishes), Khalwatiyyah, and Bektashiyyah orders represent living spiritual orders in Turkey. The Nimatullahis have had a long history in Iran; the Tijaniyyahs are prominent in West Africa. All of these traditional orders are represented in North America today.

The American Orders

The development of Sufi groups in America has gone through three major phases, roughly corresponding to three distinct periods of interaction between Euro-American and Asian worlds in this century. The first period, beginning in the early 1900s, is characterized by the interest of Americans (and Europeans) in "Oriental" wisdom, which grew out of the contact that Europeans had with Asian cultures during the colonial period. Alongside the negative aspects of "the Orient-as-Other" that characterized the period, the interaction of cultures did produce a number of teachers trained in both traditional learning and

European institutions, who saw a spiritual lack and longing in the West and who felt compelled to bring their teachings to the West. Clearly there were few authentic masters among them; nevertheless, this wave of spiritual teachers from "the East" had a receptive audience in the United States. Among Sufi teachers, Hazrat Inayat Khan, the founder of the Sufi Order in the West, is representative of this first wave.

The second phase of Sufi activity in the United States coincided with the 1960s' countercultural movement in which large numbers of (mostly) young middle-class Americans located the cause of racism, the Vietnam War, and the evils of technocracy in a spiritual sickness that establishment religions in America had not only failed to solve, but had fostered.[5] They sought teachers of traditional wisdom from "the East," often with little knowledge or concern as to the historical foundations of systems associated with Zen, Sufism, or Yoga. Their goal was to find a therapeutic system that would lead to individual and, one hoped, global spiritual transformation. A number of Sufi groups flowered in America during this period of the late 1960s and 1970s, including the Bawa Muhaiyaddeen Fellowship, the Khalwatiyyah-Jerrahiyyahs, the Nimatullahis, and the Sufi Order in the West under the new leadership of Hazrat Inayat Khan's son, Pir Vilayat. Members of these groups (whether still active or not) describe this era as consisting of lively networks of guru or spiritual "seekers," always ready to attend the next lecture by a visiting guru (or Sufi shaykh, zen master, poetic visionary, hassidic master) at the local university campus or Unitarian church. The Sufi groups that developed in this period varied considerably in the degree to which they aligned themselves with traditional Sufi doctrine and practice.

The present period of Sufi activity in America is characterized by the less-visible but continued existence of a number of the Sufi groups established during the 1960s and 1970s, intersecting with the reality of increasing numbers of immigrants coming to the United States from traditional Muslim countries.[6] A small percent-

age of the new immigrant arrivals seek out Sufi communities or teachers. In some cases, the Sufi community simply represents the availability of a mosque for congregational prayers. Some of the newer immigrants, however, come with affiliations with Sufi orders in their home countries. In addition, Sufi mosque communities in America tend to be ethnically heterogeneous and non-political, and they tend to affirm cultural forms of polite and modest behavior *(adab)* important to traditional Muslims, whether they are Sufi-oriented or not. Some Muslim immigrants say that they are attracted to Sufi communities because they affirm their Islamic religious heritage while allowing them to cultivate a form of religiosity *different*—possibly deeper—than that they would have had in their native countries, where forces of routinization, ethnic rivalry, or ideological thinking prevail. They sometimes admit a sense of surprise and pride in finding that some Americans have come to appreciate teachings that most of them learned at their mother's knee. Traditionally educated Muslims admit concern, on the one hand, over a certain "laxity" regarding *shariah* (Islamic legal) requirements they find in some groups. On the other hand, many of them join Sufi communities because they see Sufism, with its heritage of an inner and flexible interpretation of the Quran, as the best alternative to resolving the competing demands of tradition and modernity.

THE SUFI ORDER IN THE WEST
The earliest phase of an American interest in Sufism began with the figure of Hazrat Pir-O-Murshid Inayat Khan (literally, Master, Shaykh and Guide Inayat Khan). Inayat Khan came to America and founded the Sufi Order in 1910, believing that he was meant to bring the Sufi Message for the modern era. He saw his philosophy as one that would unite East and West through its teachings of universal brotherhood and attunement to the unitive structures of reality both at the macro and microcosmic levels.[7] Inayat Khan's autobiographical accounts reveal his early attraction to the life of the Sufi dervishes of India, with their vigils, songs of devotion

at dawn, and meditation with music in the evenings, and the circumstances of his initiation by the Chisti master, Khwaja Abu Hashim Madani.[8] Hazrat's teachings embodied elements characteristic of Chistiyyah Sufism, in particular the melding of (Hindu) Advaita Vedanta and Islamic *wahdat al-wujud*/"unity of being" philosophical perspectives as well as the belief that the sacred character of traditional music could aid in the elevation and "attunement" of the human soul. Thus, he maintained that "Moslem or Hindu are only outward distinctions," that "their Truth is one."[9] He was an accomplished musician trained in classical Indian music, as well as Western music, and his fame at the turn of the century was based as much on his musical talents as on his spiritual teachings. His first visit to America consisted of talks and musical concerts (in which his brothers participated). The importance attached to sacred music and dance continues to be a major attraction of the Sufi Order in America.

Hazrat Inayat Khan's observations of American, European, and Indian peoples—their attitudes (how in the West "there are no disciples, only teachers"), prejudices (how Americans disparaged his skin color, Islam, and anyone coming from the East), and social structures (his audiences drew heavily from wealthy and artistic elites)—form an insightful commentary on early twentieth-century "spiritual searchers" as well as East-West interactions of the period.[10] Hazrat believed destiny had called him to spread the "Universal Message of the time," which maintained that Sufism was *not* essentially tied to historical Islam, but rather consisted of timeless, universal teachings related to peace, harmony, and the essential unity of all being (and beings). One sees in Hazrat Khan's writings the imprint of traditional teachings and imagery of the classic Sufis, such as Ibn Arabi and Rumi[11] as well as the untraditional conviction that he should create new universal forms of worship in which people could experience spiritual growth within the context of affirmation of the integrity and common inner truths of the world's religious faiths. After initiat-

ing a number of American *murids* (disciples), he returned to India, visiting the United States again in 1923 and 1925. Fairfax California, was the site of the first Sufi Order *khangah* (lodge) in America, the Kaaba Allah. After his death in 1927, small groups of *murids* in America continued to work to pass on "the Message" of Hazrat Inayat Khan, but disagreement among a number of *murids* with regard to leadership, administration of property, and philosophies (particularly after the Kaaba Allah burned) had its impact on the group. Rabia Martin, an early disciple of Hazrat's and owner of part of the organization's properties, turned over Sufi properties to Meher Baba, whom she believed to be the Avatar of the Age. Meher Baba adapted and universalized Sufi Order teachings; the school still exists as Sufism Reoriented under Murshida Ivy O. Duce.[12]

A new wave of interest in the East brought a rejuvenation of Hazrat Inayat Khan's teachings during the 1960s and 1970s. The Sufi Order grew rapidly with the arrival of Hazrat Khan's European-educated son, Pir Vilayat Inayat Khan, born of the union of Hazrat Inayat Khan and the American-born Ora Begum. Pir Vilayat began giving lectures and leading meditations in New York during the mid-1960s. This was a period when some members felt "invaded by flower children," while others appreciated "the influx of energy and . . . expansion."[13] One of those flower children told me of the mutual perplexity experienced by the very formal Pir Vilayat and his motley, laid-back hippie audience upon their first encounter. This member summarized the early days of Pir Vilayat in America: "We all had to learn to relax a little. He changed and we changed."

While Pir Vilayat headed (and still heads) the Sufi Order in the West, providing the focal point of transmission of his father's teachings through retreats, lectures, and writings, the order has expanded and diversified the organization and its teaching modes. In the late 1960s and early 1970s one of the *murids*, Shahabuddin Less, began to lead Sufi dancing (now known as Dances of Universal Peace) at the cathedral of St. John the Divine in New York.

These dances, created by Sam Lewis, the West Coast disciple of Hazrat who is remembered as a sufi/zen/yoga/hassidic master of the late 1960s, introduced thousands of people to "the Message." Another marked increase in membership occurred in 1975, as the Sufi Order, along with the Temple of Understanding (another of the universal brotherhood groups) sponsored a Cosmic Mass at New York's St. John the Divine Cathedral as part of the Spiritual Summit Conference celebrating the thirtieth anniversary of the United Nations. Rehearsals were seen as vehicles of "attuning" the participants (gaining harmony and sensitivity within oneself, between self and others, and between self and world).[14] During this period a *khanaqah* was opened in New York, which was used for weekly Universal Worship, Amnesty International meetings, morning prayers, and *zikr (dhikr)*. The *khanaqah* closed in 1982 as the trend toward decentralization, further changes in leadership, and a certain decline of energy ensued.

During the 1970s land had been purchased in the Berkshire hills of upstate New York for the site of "the Abode of the Message." The land had been part of the Shaker village that served as headquarters of the Shaker movement in its heyday (Mt. Lebanon). The 430 acres of mountain and farm land are still used to accommodate "Universal Worship" services, host consciousness-raising and holistic healing activities, and provide weekend retreat space both for visitors and the community of about fifty adults and fifteen children who live and maintain a school on the land. The diversity of activities at the abode indicates the trend of the Sufi Order to incorporate numerous spiritual systems and teachings—clearly not limited to traditional Sufism—which are seen as compatible with the goals of Hazrat Khan's teachings. Examples include Intensive Retreat (with Pir Vilayat), Chi Kung Healing Workshop, Bridging Psychotherapy and Spirituality, Easter Retreat, Mountain Work Camp, and Sacred Music Camps (in preparation for Pir Vilayat's conducting Bach's entire B-Minor Mass in the year 2000!). Membership includes differing levels of participa-

tion, from very active, to occasional participants at workshops, to subscribers to *Hearts and Wings*, the organization's quarterly publication. The total membership presently affiliated with the Sufi Order, which can mean simply subscribing to literature, is given as fifty thousand. Clearly, the model of Sufism that has evolved with the Sufi Order is a spiritual resource center with a number of teachers and teachings, with Hazrat Inayat Khan functioning as its inspiration. Not surprisingly, most Islamic communities do not regard it as orthodox. Membership and energy of the Sufi Order's sixties and seventies era has dissipated somewhat, but those still involved describe it as "a change," a "transformation" to more individual modes of application of Hazrat's message of love, creativity, peace, and manifestation of the Divine Will. Some of those who say they were inspired by Hazrat Khan's writings gravitated toward other Sufi groups that had a more "traditional" *shaykh*/disciple and communal relationship.

THE BAWA MUHAIYADDEEN FELLOWSHIP

Bawa Muhaiyaddeen was a well-known teacher of wisdom to both Hindus and Muslims in Sri Lanka beginning in the 1940s. His talks were always in Tamil, and he was at ease in using both Hindu Puranas and Islamic Hadiths (stories and sayings of Muhammad) to teach the virtuous qualities of justice, charity, and wisdom. He also gave instruction on the tendencies of the human being that cause illusion and separation, from other humans and from God, and he taught practices that would aid in realizing the essential unity that human beings have with God, that only God exists. In Sri Lanka he was known as a former wandering ascetic, a holy man and inspired teacher, who established an ashram to care for the poor and to cure their spiritual (and sometimes physical) illnesses. In 1955 he laid the foundation for a mosque near Mankumban. This event established a clearer connection between Bawa's teachings and Islam, although he insisted that at his talks there was to be no distinction between people due to race, color, class, or religion and, furthermore, that men and women of all religions could pray in the mosque as long as non-Muslims respected the *salat* times of Muslim prayer.

Bawa was invited to America by a young woman who, in her own search for a spiritual teacher, had heard of Bawa from an Asian graduate student who was studying in Philadelphia. A small group of interested, mostly hippie-type, seekers were waiting for him when he arrived in Philadelphia in 1971, but the membership of "the Fellowship" grew rapidly to about one thousand. Virtually all of the original members describe their attraction to Bawa's "embodiment of pure love," his ability to teach "what we needed, when we needed it, and how we would be able to hear it," and his unceasing "giving" of his time. Many say that he "cleaned us up and got us off drugs." His discourses and counsel were available day and night, and members note his complete openness to public interest and scrutiny throughout his fifteen years in the United States. This openness accounts for the existence on audio and video tape of virtually all of his discourses, which were often spoken or sung to the community's members gathered at his bedside.[15] It appears that Bawa did not identify himself with institutional Islam in the early days in the United States, although many members also say that, in looking back, it is clear that many of his teaching stories were traditional Sufi wisdom and hadiths, and he consistently spoke of acquiring the "state of islam," the "state of Muhammad," meaning the state of absolute surrender and the state of the perfected human, the *insan al-kamil* "who perfectly mirrors the totality of the Divine Names and Qualities." It is evident that Bawa taught a classic, complex Sufi metaphysics of the unity of being and a silent *dhikr* as a means to attain it but, as with his Sri Lankan audiences, his teaching was done in accordance with the language and the "capacity" of the listeners. In a sense, he taught the esoteric, subtle dimension of Islam and end goal of traditional Sufism first (the inner meaning of the *shahada*), and he established a more articulated connection to "exoteric" Islam later, namely in

the building of the community's mosque in 1982–83, where congregational prayers were to be practiced in strict accordance to the *shariah*. He encouraged the practice of *mawlids*, celebrations in honor of Muhammad and Abd al-Qadir al-Jilani, the "patron saint" of this Qadiriyyah order. Moreover, the community sees an identification of Bawa and Jilani in their role as *qutb*. Bawa's model was that of the ascetic, loving, father-teacher, and *jnana-sheikh*, who taught the nature of human existence through such metaphors as cooking (the alchemy of the soul) and farming (the cultivation of the divine qualities), while literally teaching members of "his funny family" to cook and farm. (The fellowship has a farm in Coatesville, Pennsylvania.) Despite his death in 1986, he is experienced as present and as "guide" in the lives of his original disciples as well as in the lives of many newer members who never knew Bawa while alive. Transmission of his teachings is continued through meetings in which members discuss Bawa's teachings and their own experiences, through children's meetings and camps, through listening to tapes and watching videos of his talks, by the publication of his discourses, and through ministry to prisoners. His reputation as an authentic *shaykh* and *qutb* seems to be gaining wider acceptance in the larger Muslim community as evidenced by increasing numbers of pilgrims from both the fellowship and other Sufi groups in Muslim countries to the *mazar*, the shrine where Bawa is interred in Coatesville. Many of the members of the fellowship were young and in transition when they met Bawa, and he insisted on their learning skills to support themselves. The community today is represented by the widest array of professions—carpenters, doctors, psychologists, educators, and entrepreneurs, as well as full-time caretakers of the mosque and fellowship facilities.

If one can locate tensions or transition points in the community, they lie in the interpretation of Bawa's teachings, particularly in light of the building of the mosque. Did Bawa intend a general movement toward Islamic religious practices (e.g. *salat* prayers) as an outer manifestation of inner maturity and discipline, or did he intend it as a "concession" to the human need for unifying cultural forms, despite the "illusory" quality of religious distinction, or both? Bawa did not leave a successor-*shaykh* but did appoint two *imams* to lead traditional Friday prayers. Mosque attendance has grown considerably, with increasing numbers of foreign-born Muslims as well as Muslims from the larger African-American community (who are not necessarily Sufi-oriented) attending congregational prayers and religious festivals. Some of the newer members of the mosque community become interested in teachings and activities related to Bawa. Others do not. A few will question the devotion to Bawa and utilize traditional *shariah*-oriented arguments to criticize certain of Bawa's teachings. Thus far, these differences have remained friendly tensions, and Bawa's own teachings on the peace of Islam are utilized to clarify issues related to the meaning of *islam, iman* (religious faith), and *ittihad* (unity).[16] The overall pattern in recent years, then, has been to establish increasing interaction with the Islamic establishment, both city-wide and worldwide, but to maintain the close communal structure and transmission of wisdom teachings as instituted by Bawa.

THE JERRAHIYYAH ORDER
OF DERVISHES

There are other *tariqas* in the United States that are actually branches of larger traditional orders whose living masters do not live in the United States. These masters provide spiritual guidance and authority through the appointment of local *shaykhs* and *shaykhahs* (female). To exemplify this type of Sufi order, we will briefly look at a branch of the Khalwatiyyah-Jerrahiyyah Order, an active *tariqa* in Turkey that exists as well in Spring Valley, New York.[17]

The Jerrahiyyah Order in Spring Valley has about fifty dervishes in its membership, but their mosque draws many additional participants from non-Sufi (especially immigrant) Muslim populations for Friday congregational prayers and other activities. In terms of Sufi belief and prac-

tice, these dervishes are heirs to the perspectives of the well-known Sufis Junayd and Ibn Arabi, and they emphasize fasting, vigils, ritual cleanliness, silence, invocation of the name of God, and *khalwah* (retreat). Their teachings include traditional discussions of the states and stages of the spiritual path, and their practices include communal invocation and sacred dance *(al-hadrah)*. The Jerrahi *dhikr* is said out loud, using rhythm and musical compositions derived from various *tariqas*. The mosque architecture is clearly designed to convey the "fragrance" of Turkish spirituality. Arabic calligraphy and traditional carpets adorn the mosque, whose shape recalls the Central Asian *yurt*. Men perform their prayers, including the circular sacred dance, under the dome of the mosque, while the women perform their prayers and accompany the sacred dance through chanting and rhythmic movements in rows behind a partition that divides the social space but allows a view of and proximity to the men's area. Communal activities, such as discourses and counsel given by the group's *shaykh*—and shared meals—are regular events of the community of dervishes. As is the case with many of the Sufi communities in America, while the initial flurry of interest and growth characteristic of the sixties and seventies has subsided, the growing immigrant and African-American Muslim populations have contributed to increased numbers, at least in Friday mosque attendance.

The traditional closeness of the *shaykh*-disciple relationship is very evident in the community of dervishes. Tosun Bayrak, the *shaykh* of the Spring Valley *dergah* and son of a Turkish military officer, was educated in the West (he was a well-known artist in New York during the sixties) before returning to his roots in Turkey to look for traditional teaching and teachers. He entered the Jerrahiyyah order, eventually returning to the United States and gathering members in the Spring Valley area during the late seventies. He is seen as a father-figure, teacher, counselor, and authority in all local matters, spiritual and administrative.

The revered leader of the main Jerrahiyyah *dergah* in Istanbul, the late Hajj

Shaykh Muzaffereddin al-Jerrahi al-Khalwati, came to the United States himself to institute this first Jerrahiyyah order in the West. Sefer Efendi of Istanbul is the present international head of the order. His visits to the American *dergah* are occasions of special celebrations, prayer, and traditional counsel, which may include the traditional practice of dream interpretation.

Shaykh Tosun "Baba" as well as other learned members of this *dergah* have contributed much in the way of valuable translations of traditional Sufi literature,[18] which has in fact become a major vehicle of Sufi outreach to both popular and academic audiences.

While the media attention on "radical" and "militant" elements of Islam continues to propagate a monolithic and one-sided image of Islam, the Sufi groups in America, continuing their historic role as transmitters of Islamic piety and devotion, have provided a crucial bridge between American culture and the traditional Islamic world.

Notes

1. The puritanical Wahabi movement that emerged in what is now Saudi Arabia in the eighteenth century, whose ideology became for some Muslims a sort of measuring stick of Islamic ultra-orthodoxy, denounced and outlawed virtually all forms of Sufi teachings and practices in Saudi Arabia. Most particularly criticized was the practice of veneration of saints, the "friends" *(awliya)* of God, through pilgrimages to shrines. The influence of Wahabi revivalist thought continues to endure in some segments of Islamic society. See John Esposito, *Islam: The Straight Path* (New York: Oxford Press, 1991), chapter 4.

2. The term *sufi* may also be related to the word *safa* (Arabic, purity).

3. *Fana* and other terms associated with Sufi mystical experience and doctrine are often drawn from Quranic eschatological imagery. *Fana* is the annihilation of the world at the "end time." For the Sufis, the experience refers to the end, the surrendrance *(islam)*, of self-will and ego, which renders the unity of the human/divine being and will.

4. Dr. Javad Nurbaksh, *In the Tavern of Ruin* (New York: Khaniqahi-Nimatullahi Publications, 1978), 32ff.

5. See Theodore Roszak, *The Making of a Counter Culture* (New York: Anchor, 1969).

6. See chapter on Islam in America in this volume.

7. One ought to be aware of the fact that for many contemporary Muslims of formerly colonized countries, Sufism became associated with passivity and other-worldliness and, hence, with the forces that *contributed* to internal decay and outer domination by the modern, "rational" West. The fact that American and European audiences "patronized" these teachers (such as Hazrat Inayat Khan) further contributed to anti-Sufi feelings among some modernist and reform-minded Muslims. On the other hand, in some Muslim countries, particularly in Africa, Sufism was associated with anti-colonial political political movements. Thus, in Islamic countries, attitudes toward Sufism vary.

8. *Biography of Pir-O-Murshid Inayat Khan* (London: East-West Publications, 1979), 107.

9. *Wahdat al-wujud* (unity of being) is the philosophical interpretation of *"tawhid"* (the Islamic doctrine of God's "oneness") rendered by important Sufi expositors and poets, such as Ibn Arabi (d. 1240) and Rumi (d. 1273). It maintained that while the created order is "plunged in God," God is beyond all form and that all forms and distinctions in the world are ultimately relative. It is important to note that while these original expositors of the "transcendent unity of being" did maintain the illusory quality of religious differences, they clearly assumed—and wrote about—the participation in the "external" forms of their Islamic religion.

10. Ibid.

11. See Hazrat Khan's discussion of Rumi's teaching of the *nafs*, the lower or "false" ego, quoted in Jelaluddin Rumi, *This Longing* (Poetry, Teaching Stories, and Selected Letters), trans. Coleman Barks and John Moyne (Putney, Vt.: Threshold Books, 1988), xiv–xv.

12. Meher Baba, born Merwan Sheriar Irani in Poona, India in 1894, was a spiritual master who declared himself the avatar (de-

scent of God into human form) of this age. From 1925 to the end of his life, Meher observed silence, communicating through pointing to letters on an alphabet board and through gestures. He believed this action would bring about a universal transformation of consciousness through a release of divine love into the world. His followers have grown considerably since his death in 1969, particularly in India, America, Australia, and Europe. The disciples feel themselves guided in their spiritual journey to eliminate the ego and to realize God as the "true self." His followers gather informally to share experiences of his love and guidance. See "Meher Baba," by Charles C. Haynes in *Encyclopedia of Religion* (New York: Macmillan, 1987). Also C. B. Purdom, *The God-Man* (Crescent Beach, S.C.: Sheriar Press, 1971) and William Donkin, *The Wayfarers* (San Francisco: Sufism Reoriented, 1969). Jacob Needleman, *The New Religions* (New York: Doubleday, 1970) contains a chapter on Meher's life and work.

13. *Hearts and Wings,* quarterly publication of the Sufi Order (Spring 1992): 4.

14. Ibid.

15. The fact that Bawa often spoke, in lotus position, from his bed is an indication of his austerity (he had few pieces of furniture—a bed and two chairs) and his constant availability (and the members' presence) for counsel and prayer, day or night, even during his many bouts of respiratory illness.

16. Bawa Muhaiyaddeen, *Islam and World Peace* (Philadelphia: Fellowship Press, 1989). See Gisela Webb, "Tradition and Innovation in Contemporary American Islamic Spirituality: The Bawa Muhaiyaddeen Fellowship," in *Muslim Communities in North America,* ed. Yvonne Y. Haddad and Jane I. Smith (Albany: State University of New York Press, 1994).

17. Other branches of the Jerrahiyyah Order exist in a number of cities in North America, including New York City, Toronto, and San Francisco.

18. For example, see *Journey to the Lord of Power,* a translation by Rabia Harris of Ibn Arabi's book on Retreat *(Khalwah),* and *The Way of Sufi Chivalry,* a translation by Tosun Bayrak of Ibn al-Husayn al-Sulami's collection of sayings on *adab* and *futuwwah* (chivalry). Both are available through Inner Traditions International. Expositors of Sufi teachings in the academic community, such as the pioneer Seyyed Hossein Nasr; the contemporary translations of Sufi writings, such as Coleman Barks' superb interpretations of Rumi's works; the expositors of Sufism who seek to present Sufi teachings in more Western-oriented concepts, such as Kabir Helminski; as well as the number of publications related to Sufism, such as *Sufi Review* and *Sufi,* Omega Press Mail-Order Bookstore, have all contributed to the accessibility of Sufism to the American audience.

Suggestions for Further Reading

Bawa Muhaiyaddeen. *Questions of Life, Answers of Wisdom.* Philadelphia: Fellowship Press, 1991. A number of other publications are available through this press.

Biography of Pir-O-Murshid Inayat Khan. London: East-West Publications, 1979.

Muzaffer Ozak al-Jerrahi, Sheikh. *The Unveiling of Love.* New York: Inner Traditions International, 1981.

Nasr, Seyyed Hossein, ed. *Islamic Spirituality: Manifestations.* New York: Crossroad, 1991.

Nurbakhsh, Javad. *In the Tavern of Ruin: Seven Essays on Sufism.* New York: Khaniqahi-Nimatullahi Publications, 1978.

Schimmel, Annemarie. *Mystical Dimensions of Islam.* Chapel Hill: University of North Carolina Press, 1975).

Webb, Gisela. "Tradition and Innovation in Contemporary American Islamic Spirituality: The Bawa Muhaiyaddeen Fellowship" in *Muslim Communities in North America,* edited by Yvonne Haddad and Jane Smith. Albany: State University of New York Press, 1994.

24

GURDJIEFF IN AMERICA: AN OVERVIEW

George Baker and Walter Driscoll

George I. Gurdjieff was born in Trans-caucasia in about 1866. He grew up in an Orthodox Christian home but was exposed to a diverse Middle Eastern and European religious milieu. Almost nothing is known about his first forty years apart from what he related in his philosophically instructive autobiography, *Meetings with Remarkable Men*[1] (1963). Verifiable information dates only from his arrival in Moscow around 1911; major accounts of the period between 1915 and 1929 were written by disciples P. D. Ouspensky, Thomas and Olga de Hartmann, and Fritz Peters.

Gurdjieff was in Russia and Georgia until 1920; he emigrated to western Europe via Istanbul. In 1922 Gurdjieff and his followers moved to Fontainebleau, south of Paris. His center, called the Institute for the Harmonious Development of Man, operated into the early 1930s. At his institute the study of consciousness took many forms, some strenuous and many unexpected. One characteristic activity was the study of Gurdjieff's choreographed dances, known as "sacred gymnastics" and, later, "movements."

Gurdjieff with some forty of his pupils first travelled to the United States in early 1924. He presented public demonstrations of his movements in New York and laid the groundwork for the opening of the first branch of his institute. In mid-year, however, shortly after his return from the United States, Gurdjieff suffered a nearly fatal automobile accident. Owing to the long period of his recovery Gurdjieff was forced to scale back the activities of his institute, and his plans for the opening of the New York branch were delayed.

In the winter of 1930, Gurdjieff returned to the United States, having left, since 1924, the former London editor O. R. Orage in New York as his representative. There he reorganized the groups that Orage had led.[2] For the decade 1924 to 1934 Gurdjieff dedicated himself to writing books to communicate his ideas. From the early 1930s until his death in 1949 Gurdjieff lived in Paris, with occasional trips to America.

Ouspensky, the most prominent of Gurdjieff's disciples, died in 1947 in England; many of those who had been introduced to Gurdjieff's ideas through him then journeyed to Paris, where they joined Gurdjieff himself for the last two intense years of his life.

Gurdjieff died in 1949; the following year saw the publication of *An Objectively Impartial Criticism of the Life of Man, or Beelzebub's Tales to His Grandson,* the first volume of the proposed three-volume work *All and Everything.*[3] Written in the format of an epic science fiction novel, the book is meant to upset the worldview of the reader, and in the end to evoke feelings of compassion and hope. Some Gurdjieff groups today regard *Beelzebub's Tales* as a canonical text to be interpreted, although many disdain that approach, holding that the book must be received directly by individuals.

Consider chapter 27: here, in the literary vehicle of a grandfather's instructive reflections to his grandson, Gurdjieff describes a prehistoric saint's transformation of the religious, social, and political outlooks of his people. The transformation was effected by the saint's reformation of the spiritual outlook of his countrymen, as a result of which the feeling of conscience, normally scarcely noticed in the course of everyday life, came to participate more richly and organically in the social, political, and even economic transactions of society. Moral scourges of society (slavery, social castes) briefly disappeared.

In digesting this account the reader is left with multiple impressions: everyday human relationships are largely governed by considerations of power, class, race, and personal ambition, but here Gurdjieff invites the reader to visualize a different social order. The chapter calls into question our assumptions about religious structures in ancient civilizations; the reader may experience, in personal terms, a question about the appearance of conscience in his or her own life.

To students of Gurdjieff, who taught by example that life was to be lived in the present moment, the master's life is much less important than his ideas, music, and sacred gymnastics. Whereas in Christianity every detail of the life of Jesus is made the object of commentary and interpretation, in the Gurdjieff communities the historical Gurdjieff is infrequently discussed. Some students, however, say that learning how Gurdjieff interacted with society and with individuals of different temperaments is subtly, indirectly instructive. To them, the harmonic of his fearless and uncompromising attitude still resounds in firsthand accounts of episodes in his life.

Gurdjieff Pupils

Gurdjieff recruited six or seven key persons who were in large measure responsible for the transmission of his ideas, music, movements, and texts. The best known of them was Ouspensky, who expounded "the System" from the early 1920s until his death in 1947. His book *In Search of the Miraculous,* published posthumously with Gurdjieff's authorization, recounts the years from 1915 to 1924.[4] Ouspensky succeeded in capturing on paper Gurdjieff's system of interconnected ideas and in expressing, as no other pupil did, the power of Gurdjieff's way of working with people through ideas. Ouspensky spread Gurdjieff's ideas in the United States while taking refuge there during the Second World War. His wife, Sophia Ouspensky, who lived in the United States from the Second World War until her death in the early 1960s, continued to shape American interest in the Gurdjieff teachings.

Another key pupil was the composer Thomas de Hartmann, with whom Gurdjieff worked in the 1920s to compose the Gurdjieff/de Hartmann music. Meanwhile, Jeanne de Salzmann, Jessmin Howarth, and Rose Mary Nott preserved Gurdjieff's sacred gymnastics when, in the late 1920s and early 1930s, the master had turned to other pursuits. Decades later de Salzmann conceived of a feature film, *Meetings with Remarkable Men,* which was completed under director Peter Brook and released in 1979. The film effectively conveys the energy of Gurdjieff's early spiritual quest.

Gurdjieff's writings would not have materialized without the collaboration of Olga de Hartmann, the aristocratic wife of the composer, and the editor Alfred R. Orage, previously mentioned. Gurdjieff dictated many of his writings to de Hartmann, who worked with Orage and others to render the Russian text of *Beelzebub* and *Meetings with Remarkable Men* into publishable English.

American pupils also became prominent in the 1920s and 1930s, among them many writers and editors including Jane Heap, Jean Toomer, and Gorham Munson. Other American writers were in contact with Gurdjieff in France. Especially significant was Heap, who first visited Gurdjieff's institute near Paris in 1925 and was at the center of a group of women that included Gertrude Stein. Later, at Gurdjieff's request, Heap in 1935 moved to London and directed Gurdjieff groups there for many years.

Post-Gurdjieff Developments

The Gurdjieff Foundation of New York, established in the mid-1950s, and the other centers soon thereafter established in other cities, faced as an early task the bringing together of followers of Orage, Ouspensky, and Gurdjieff himself. A key leader in the development of the Gurdjieff foundations was Henry John Sinclair (Lord Pentland), a pupil of long standing of Mr. and Mme. Ouspensky. Pentland, who was in contact with Gurdjieff during the last two years of Gurdjieff's life, oversaw the posthumous publication of a number of Gurdjieff's and Ouspensky's works, and, for over thirty years, until his death in 1984, was a major force in the Gurdjieff movement in America.

As of late 1994, several of Gurdjieff's own pupils remained actively involved in the work that he began, although responsibility for day-to-day activities largely has devolved into the hands of second-generation followers. In addition to the Gurdjieff foundations in New York, Los Angeles, San Francisco and other metropolitan areas, a number of smaller Gurdjieff study centers have been located in rural areas. Some of these latter centers were founded by persons who studied with Mr. Gurdjieff (as he is often referred to in first-person accounts), among them Annie Lou Staveley in Oregon, John G. Bennett in West Virginia, and Louise March and Willem Nyland both in New York State. Other organizations invoke Gurdjieff's name but have no connection with either the Gurdjieff foundations or any pupil who worked directly with Gurdjieff.

Methodology

Scholars seeking to formulate clear categories for the ideas, practices, and participants of the Gurdjieff movement seem unable to complete their task. Indeed, the only consistent finding seems to be that Gurdjieff followers believe that the ideas in the Gurdjieff oral tradition cannot be communicated accurately outside the activities of the Gurdjieff foundations. This feature was apparent to Ouspensky in his capacity as an early outside observer of Gurdjieff groups. Looking back on an early meeting in 1915, Ouspensky recalled that it was difficult to reconstruct the beginning of his conversation with Gurdjieff's pupils. "I tried to discover in what their work consisted, but they gave me no direct answers, insisting in some cases on a strange and, to me, unintelligible terminology. . . . They spoke of 'work on oneself' but in what this work consisted they failed to explain." Leaving that initial meeting at dawn of the next day "produced in me an unexpected desire to laugh, to shout, to sing, as though I had escaped from school or from some strange detention."

Contemporary Gurdjieff followers similarly tend to believe that little is to be gained from discussing the ideas and activities of the Gurdjieff work with outsiders using the terminology of the oral tradition. Indeed, such discussions could put at risk the specificity of meaning of the Gurdjieff language. They point, for example, to the symbol of the enneagram that Gurdjieff first discussed with Western pupils in 1916, which in the 1970s and 1980s was relatively indiscriminately incorporated into New Age psychology and spirituality, divorced from its specific Gurdjieffian meaning. (Witness the plethora of groups and books generated almost entirely through the psychologizing of the enneagram by groups such as Arica, Esalen, and the Jesuits.) Other borrowings from the language of the Gurdjieff oral tradition could lead to similar confusion about the ideas themselves. The problem of communicating between those inside and outside the Gurdjieff work that was described so clearly and honestly by Ouspensky is in part a result of the nature of the work itself. Indeed, Lord Pentland once described it as a non-verbal teaching, a rather startling definition considering the amount of writing and talking that accompanies a Gurdjieffian's pursuit of his or her aims. It becomes less startling if one considers Gurdjieff's description of the nature of man.

Gurdjieff taught that there are several distinct sources of intelligence in the human body, each responsible for its own area of activity. In addition to the mind-of-thought located in the brain, there is mind-of-feeling located in the solar plexus and the mind-of-movement located in the spinal column. Gurdjieff followers believe that it is possible to have a conscious awareness of the relative participation of each of these three minds, or brains, in any given moment of experience. They try to practice this participatory awareness of the functioning of all three brains during any sort of exchange with each other, for example, in group meetings.

An individual is assigned to a group of about ten to fifteen persons that will meet weekly for an hour during most of the year. An individual may stay in the same group for many years. The purpose of the weekly meeting is to give the individual an opportunity to reexperience him or herself, above everything else, as a seeker. The organization of the meetings is outwardly similar to those of Quaker meetings. At some point, typically after an initial period of silence, someone speaks about a recent specific experience in which a dimension of the Gurdjieff teaching was attainable, or, as is often the case, visible, but not attainable. The person speaking as well as those listening try to engage all three minds and, when this occurs more or less successfully, the communication is as much or more non-verbal than verbal.

Another way to consider this question lies in Gurdjieff's frequent exhortation to his students that in order to really understand anything, one must not only think about it with one's intellectual apparatus but also sense it with one's body and feel it with one's heart. Only in this way can knowledge be transformed into understanding. Thus, when someone in a group meeting speaks, he or she is trying also to speak from those other silent parts so that what is transmitted can be received in the same way.

To an outsider, such as Ouspensky on that evening in Moscow in 1915, the effect of this kind of inner discipline can be strange, discomforting, if not jarring.

Three conclusions follow. One, some Heisenberg-like Uncertainty Principle may be at work in research on the Gurdjieff phenomena: the reliability of the field data may vary inversely with the specificity of the content of the data. Two, it may not work to approach the data in the manner of a descriptive linguist bent on capturing the idiom and syntax of a language. Three, it may be better to concentrate on issues than on beliefs and practices of followers.

Gurdjieff Issues

The principal Gurdjieff "issue" is the study of the underlying conditions of one's life from the point of view of the possibility of inner unity. Gurdjieff observes that conscience, while latently present, is rarely active in an individual's daily life. How, then, may conscience be brought to participate in the ordinary exchanges and engagements of life?

One's own life, Gurdjieff says, offers the best material for the study of the core issues of the human condition. Gurdjieff himself gave a few close pupils numerous exercises intended to increase their sense of self-presence. One, for example, entailed the pupil's inward saying of the words "I AM." When saying "I" the pupil was to be aware of his state of feeling; when saying "am" he was to be aware of his total state of sensation. This exercise was to be carried out once an hour; yet, as with most of the exercises, it is either incomprehensible or impossible to experience outside the teacher-pupil relationship.

All of Gurdjieff's teachings are to be verified in the individual's own experience. For example, Gurdjieff insisted that an individual usually has no volition of his or her own, but functions through cultural conditioning, instincts, and the idiosyncratic workings of the personality. Only rarely does an individual authentically express his or her body, feelings, and mind in a single, unified act or gesture. The Gurdjieff teaching, then, must be verified in light of the pupil's experience.

The study of Gurdjieff issues must be undertaken in association with others; Gurdjieff held group work important to both the seeker and the person guiding the group. At Gurdjieff centers in North America, including Mexico, teams often practice various crafts (such as weaving and pottery) and traditional disciplines (such as translations of sacred texts).

Finally, the age-old mind-body paradox is addressed through a study of the attentiveness, or presence, of the human body through experimentation and discussion. The body, the link between the cosmos and the individual, must be sensed and felt in a new way; the goal is balance among mind, feeling, and presence-of-the-body. One's physical existence is a key to receiving higher or divine influences.

Liturgy

From a Gurdjieffian point of view, religion may be considered the art of invoking liturgical order in human affairs; it must invoke sacred time, space, and order. The year and the day are important time dimensions. In the United States the Gurdjieffian year follows the school year, from September to June; a study center typically offers members various weekly activities, such as movements classes, seminars, and craft work. Most institutional activities are suspended for the summer. However, followers are encouraged to practice individual meditation each morning of the year. The Gurdjieff program makes demands on the follower's time and attention similar to those made by most churches on their members. Perhaps its signature is that it offers a life not of prayer or devotion but of service to oneself, others, and the universe through study and verification. Through engagement with outer forms the individual may reconnect to an inner order of balance and conscience.

Special Topics

At several points the Gurdjieff approach to spiritual direction can be compared to that of mainline religions and human potential movements. The Gurdjieff movement resembles Judaism and Islam, for example, in using spatial metaphors—e.g., path, way, direction—for spiritual ideas. Gurdjieff also spoke of "remembering oneself," referring to moments in which thought, feeling, and sensation of one's physical presence were in an unmistakable relationship. A core problem in modern life, Gurdjieff said, is that people do not "remember" or experience themselves in this reintegrated state; his teachings were intended to provide people with the needed special conditions in which such reintegrated moments of "I am" become possible. An individual in talking about everything he or she does mainly refers to habits and fears ingrained from childhood, plus newly acquired resentments and petty conquests, and has all but forgotten the sense of "I" that impartially accepts life as it is. This quiet sense-of-I is occasionally experienced in impressions of impartiality and compassion in relation to one's own life and its circumstances.

No ordered words or ceremonies can help a person remember him or herself at this deeper level. There is, therefore, no Gurdjieff Book of Common Prayer. That is not to say there is no basis for ethical or moral philosophy, but only that such a basis cannot be codified in ways religions and philosophies have tried in modern times. The experience Gurdjieffians seek lies at the intersection of the personal and impersonal; the Gurdjieff teaching mainly provides tools for studying the impersonal.

Conclusion

Religions say that a human being lives from two sources of energy, natural and divine, or chemical and alchemical. The great debate in religion seems to center on the nature and fluid mechanics of alchemical energy. Christians rightly warn that alchemical energy is wholly other than chemical energy and urge believers to discriminate between ordinary life, the life of sin, and the higher, or Christian, life.

Many new religious movements have intuited that established forms of religion have in some central way mixed gold with alloy, that they have let an earlier discernment of two sources of energy degenerate into mere instruments of personal or institutional power. New religions are typically also willing to respond to that situation by claiming that they can overcome that degeneration, that by some technique, practice, or set of ideals they can lead us out of this Egyptian captivity, this maze of sensory and mental impulses that make up our lives. What is interesting about the Gurdjieff teaching is its unusual quietness, approaching silence, about what awaits the spiritual seeker who would ask, what do I have to do?, for what am I responsible?

With the problem cast in this way, the aims of the Gurdjieff teaching may be expressed in two or three essential points: first, the individual is in profound need of purification in his or her understanding of the difference between the flows of chemical and alchemical energy in life. Second, the individual is responsible for maintaining working relationships with others who, also, seek verification of the inner and outer conditions in which contact with alchemical energy becomes more likely. Finally, the probability that an individual will succeed in gaining even a partial discrimination between the two rivers of life, as Gurdjieff called them, will directly vary with the intensity and sincerity of his or her association with others similarly embarked on the path of verification.

Gurdjieff followers seem to be saying that their approach to a spiritualized life offers a new basis for interest-in-life, a new reason for living. For them, the Gurdjieff community provides opportunities to associate with others on a new basis of sincerity and inner relaxation not elsewhere found in North American society. Gurdjieff followers claim (although not in so many words) to have rediscovered in a practical way the possibility of contact with the sacred mystery of one's own life and, by extension, that of the lives of others.

Gurdjieff seems to have foreseen much of the present state of confusion in religious inquiry in the West. His teaching invites the religious seeker to develop in him or herself a moral sensitivity that is nourished not as much by techniques or metaphysical inquiry as by a lucid, if almost ineffable, opening to oneself and others.

Notes

1. G. I. Gurdjieff, *Meetings with Remarkable Men* (New York: E. P. Dutton, 1963).

2. The year 1930 might well be called the Year of the Great Earthquake in Gurdjieffian circles, as a reading of the five lectures given by Gurdjieff at that time will readily show. This collection of lectures, published as a kind of prologue to the unpublished—and presumably destroyed—manuscript of the third volume of Gurdjieff's trilogy, gives a lucid account of Gurdjieff's approach to the study of consciousness. The lectures also indicate the basis of Gurdjieff's special interest in the development of his ideas in the United States. See G. I. Gurdjieff, *Life Is Real Only Then, When "I Am."* (New York: Dutton/Triangle Editions, 1975).

3. G. I. Gurdjieff, *All and Everything: Beelzebub's Tales to His Grandson* (New York: E. P. Dutton, 1950).

4. Peter D. Ouspensky, *In Search of the Miraculous: Fragments of an Unknown Teaching* (New York: Harcourt, Brace and World, 1949).

Suggestions for Further Reading

Bennett, John G., and Elizabeth Bennett. *Idiots in Paris: Diaries of J. G. Bennett and Elizabeth Bennett, 1949*. York Beach, Maine: Samuel Weiser, 1991.

Butkosky-Hewitt, Anna. *With Gurdjieff in St. Petersburg and Paris*. New York: Samuel Weiser, 1978.

Driscoll, Walter, and the Gurdjieff Foundation of California. *Gurdjieff: A Bibliography*. New York: Garland, 1985.

Gurdjieff, G. I. *All and Everything: Beelzebub's Tales to His Grandson*. New York: E. P. Dutton, 1950.

———. *Meetings with Remarkable Men*. New York: E. P. Dutton, 1963.

Hands, Rina. *Diary of Mme. Egout Pour Sweet: With Mr. Gurdjieff in Paris, 1948–49*. Aurora, Ore.: Two Rivers Press, 1991.

Kherdian, David. *On a Spaceship with Beelzebub: By a Grandson of Gurdjieff*. New York: Globe Press Books, 1990.

Moore, James. *Gurdjieff: The Anatomy of a Myth*. Shaftesbury, England, and Rockport, Maine: Element, 1991.

Ouspensky, Pyotr D. *In Search of the Miraculous: Fragments of an Unknown Teaching*. New York: Harcourt, Brace and World, 1949.

Patterson, William Patrick. *Eating the "I": An Account of the Fourth Way—The Way of Transformation in Ordinary Life*. San Anselmo, Calif.: Arete Publications, 1992.

Peters, Fritz. *Boyhood with Gurdjieff*. New York: E. P. Dutton; Penguin Books, 1972.

Speeth, Kathleen. *The Gurdjieff Work*. 2nd ed. Los Angeles: Jeremy P. Tarcher, 1989. The second edition provides a speculative genealogy of Gurdjieff groups in the United States.

Vaysse, Jean. *Toward Awakening: An Approach to the Teaching Left by Gurdjieff*. San Francisco: Far West, 1978; Harper and Row, 1979.

Webb, James. *The Harmonious Circle: The Lives and Works of G. I. Gurdjieff, P. D. Ouspensky and Their Followers*. London: Thames and Hudson; New York: G. P. Putnam's, 1980.

25

SUBUD

Gisela Webb

Introduction

Subud is a spiritual movement that had its origins in Indonesia during the 1920s when a Javanese Muslim, Muhammad Subuh,[1] or "Bapak" (in Indonesian, respected elder or father), as Subud members call him, had a series of inner revelatory experiences that he perceived as no less than a contact with the power of God. During the course of these experiences, he came to believe that this contact was meant to be shared with all mankind without deference to religion, race, nationality, or gender. Bapak maintained that he was not a prophet or teacher, that religions had already brought what humans needed to know about morality and culture, and that what was needed in this era was a way to experience for oneself the inner content of oneself and one's religion, a way to relinquish negative qualities, and a way to become a "true human being." Bapak described the true human being as one who lived the life of *"Susila Budhi Dharma."* These three Sanskrit words became the name of the organization (Subud is an acronym), denoting character and conduct that are "truly human" *(susila),* awareness of the inner force present in all creatures that draws them in the proper path *(budhi),* and the attitude of "sincerity, patience, and surrender" to the will of God awakened in the individual by the power of God *(dharma).*[2]

It is difficult to place Subud among America's alternative religious movements. The organization does not consider itself a religion, since practicing members of many religions as well as people without religious ties are part of this association. Subud is not actually Middle Eastern, except that it originated in a Muslim country and its founder was Muslim. Islam was brought to Indonesia mainly by the "mystics" of Islam, the Sufis, who lent a certain character to traditional understandings about the cosmos and the human being. Subud is mystical in character; it focuses on the immediate intuitive experience, inspiration, and knowledge from "deep within the innermost depths of [the] heart," free from the influence of the thinking mind and the desires.[3] Bapak utilized many traditional Sufi concepts in his discourses (e.g., the experience of the *haqiqat,* or inner content of religions; the training and subduing of the *nafs;* the attainment of the station of the true human being, or *insan al-kamil;* and the inner or subtle *[batin, latif]* understanding of Islamic and other sacred scriptures). Many of his initial revelatory experiences of the 1920s and 1930s occurred while saying the *salat* prayers or private *dhikr,* or included spiritual events and inner journeys reminiscent of Muhammad's paradigmatic ascension experience *(mi'raj).* Indeed, Bapak was born at dawn on Muhammad's birthday. Subud may be Islam-inspired, but it is not a Sufi order.[4]

This chapter will briefly outline the historical development of Subud from its early days as one of Java's many mystical associations to its present situation as a sparsely populated, but widely spread, international organization with groups in about seventy countries. A major theme that permeates Subud's history and development has been how to build and maintain community in a multicultural organization whose philosophy eschews authority figures, dogma, and common cultural forms (e.g., dress, eating, rites of passage). For, despite Muhammad Subuh's rejection of the title of teacher, his living presence made it possible to utilize his personal example and to appeal to him directly for guidance or settling disagreements. Subud members speak of the current challenge as learning to "stand on our own two feet," to be guided from "within," which is what Bapak had always described as being the purpose of the Subud practice.

History

As has been mentioned, Bapak described his early ecstatic experiences as a contact with the power of God. He also understood the contact to be the experience of a vibration, divine grace, inspiration, revelation, and spirit.[5] These ecstatic experiences took the form of spontaneous bodily movements, dance, chants, and singing, as well as visionary and aural phenomena. Bapak felt that he was undergoing a kind of inner training, or *latihan kejiwaan,* a cleansing of his entire being and a receiving of divine guidance.[6]

At first Bapak shared his experience with close friends and relatives. A number of Indonesians, some of them members of Sufi groups, came to hear of Bapak and asked him for this "training," this *latihan.* He began to initiate, or "open" them to the practice. There was no formal organization; people would simply gather in fellowship, at first in the Indonesian towns of Semarang and Yogya, often in Bapak's sitting room, to do the latihan. In 1947, there were some

three hundred persons in Indonesia practicing the latihan. Bapak made no requirements in terms of religion or previous spiritual knowledge. He maintained that only the act of surrendering, and simply being in the presence of one who was already doing the latihan, would evoke the individual's own latihan, and that one might expect a spontaneous arising of movement, sound, or inner calm. The outer form that the latihan took in each person was simply a mirroring of inner work being effected by God's power. Furthermore, the effects of the cleansing and guidance received in the latihan would be manifested in the participant's everyday life.

An English-educated Levantine Muslim would be the bridge for Subud to the West. Hussein Rofe, a linguist and journalist, arrived in Jakarta in 1951 to conduct research on Sufi groups in Indonesia. He was told about Bapak, located him, asked to be opened, and inadvertently became the first ambassador for Bapak as he began to both practice the latihan and write articles about Subud in many of the seventeen languages in which he was fluent. In a 1951 article in *The Islamic Literature,* Rofe describes Muhammad Subuh as a famous mystic of Java, a "perfect Muslim," who "freely welcomes non-Muslims to his circle of disciples without asking them to abandon their faith."[7] His presentation was in part directed at Muslim audiences in Indonesia and at their concerns as to where to situate Bapak and Subud.[8]

Rofe's articles caught the attention of a number of Westerners and Asians.[9] Bapak began to receive letters from persons who were interested in being opened. In response, Bapak asked Rofe to take the latihan abroad. In 1954 Rofe travelled to Japan where he opened the first Subud members in a foreign country.[10] He went to Cyprus and opened a number of Europeans.

Through Hussein Rofe, John Bennett, a major teacher of Gurdjieff's and Ouspensky's works,[11] was opened in England. In 1957, Bennett invited Bapak to Coombe Springs, England, and within a few months, hundreds of people entered Subud.[12]

Gurdjieff members (as well as other self-described searchers) in America and other countries—including many in Europe—heard about Subud and began inviting Bapak and his wife to their centers. Now Bennett himself became an emissary for Subud in America, speaking and writing about the latihan, opening members, and preparing the way for Bapak's arrival in 1959. By the end of 1959, there were groups in many parts of the United States: San Francisco, Los Angeles, Carmel, Sacramento, Kansas City, Detroit, Denver, Washington, D.C., New York, and Florida. With many of the early Subud members being former Gurdjieff followers, it was perhaps inevitable that a rift would develop between Gurdjieff and Subud groups. Each group saw the other's system as antithetical to its own. A major theme of Gurdjieff had been the need to develop the faculty, or power, of the "observing self," the "inner witness" who could see and evaluate one's own actions without attachment or influence (a Sufi-inspired idea). Gurdjieff saw this as involving the development of the will. Bapak had spoken of the inner witness as well; but he maintained the necessity of surrendering the will to its divine source.

There was no census taken during the early years, but indications are that about two thousand people were opened in the United States in the first two years. Some who were opened did not remain in Subud for even a short time. Others, like Bennett himself, left after a few years. Still others of the first American groups have remained actively engaged in Subud. Subud census information suggests that after its initial period of growth, Subud has tended to remain at about the same number, with about eight thousand participants worldwide and about twenty-five hundred in the United States. Bapak attributed the attrition rate to "the influence of the world."[13] Subud's pattern of development may be tied to other factors as well. For example, Bapak instructed that there should be no proselytising or advertising in Subud. While some members say they were attracted by Subud's low profile, others criticize its near invisibility and inaccessibility. It should be mentioned that there has been a very recent surge in membership as children born to Subud parents during the 1960s and 1970s are being opened.[14]

Another factor is the necessarily subjective way members judge the "progress" made through the exercise. Bennett's description of his own process of leaving marks one kind of pattern of involvement and departure.[15] His initial experience of the *latihan* was marked by sudden and dramatic experiences of change, such as deep feelings of unity, peace, even healings and the like. Then he entered a stage in which he felt that the "opening of the heart" needed to be balanced by finding a way to develop the will and the mind, and so he left to search for other systems that he felt would do this. Indeed, a number of people leave Subud for other methods or groups that offer more direction by teacher, therapist, or communal structure. However, some leave Subud because they feel that there has developed too much structure; that guidelines had become rules, that helpers had become authorities, and that the spontaneous character of the earlier days had changed. Members who have remained active over the years consistently attribute their staying to the capacity of the latihan to effect, in both subtle and profound ways, needed changes and realizations in their lives. The issue of outer authority/routinization vs. inner authority/spontaneity is a major area of current discussion in Subud.

A summary of developments over the past three decades of Subud in America would have to include discussion of the practice of the latihan group life and structure, crisis points, and present activities.

The Latihan: The Practice

The latihan has always been the core and only essential activity of Subud life. The general pattern of Subud practice is that twice a week Subud members go their local centers to participate in the group latihan. Men and women "latihan" in separate rooms. Codes of modesty in dress are normative. After a few minutes one of the "helpers" (an experienced Subud member designated to open people and care for members' needs) asks people to stand and says, "Begin." The helpers have already explained that one should not mix other activities with the latihan, such as meditation or use of drugs, but simply intend to surrender to the will of God. One is advised not to expect any particular thing or to do anything except "what arises from within." One is not to pay attention to others in the room, each of whom is doing his or her own latihan. Non-Subud members may not participate in the latihan, but if one sits outside a latihan room, one hears the rising of discordant voices, lyrical singing, sounds of movement, laughter, sobbing, chanting. After about thirty minutes the helper says, "Finish." Subud members come out of the latihan rooms, sometimes socialize, and then leave for home or work.

Subud members' descriptions of the latihan are as diverse as the sounds one hears. Members say they have at times experienced some particular insight during latihan, perhaps even a visionary experience. Occasionally someone describes having a "wild latihan," or a "difficult latihan," or a "very deep latihan." More often, members describe their latihan as leaving them feeling "cleansed," "centered," "at peace," or "energized." Sometimes a member has a very explosive and sustained negative latihan, which might indicate the person is going through a serious spiritual or psychological crisis and needs special attention from helpers, family, or professional counselors. Bapak spoke of the group latihan as being a "training" or exercising of the "spiritual muscles" which, like physical exercise, has its effects in our conduct and feelings in ordinary life. The latihan, he said, would affect an understanding and transformation of the self such that all of life was experienced as worship.

There are other kinds of latihan beyond the group latihan. Members may do the latihan alone at home. Moreover, if a member feels the need for guidance in a particular situation in life—personal, family, work related—he or she may ask to do a short latihan with other members, prefacing the latihan with a prayer and a request for guidance on that issue. This form of latihan is called "testing" and is described as the possibility of receiving the truth about a situation if, and only if, one can ask with absolute surrender and no interference by what one wishes or imagines the answer or guidance should be.

Members furthermore speak of experiencing "spontaneous latihans"; how in the midst of some ordinary activity, they will suddenly feel the latihan as a state of love, tranquility, or "feeling moved to do something." One member described it as "feeling aware of every nerve, blood vessel, and bone in my body."

Developments in Group Life and Culture

It appears that from Subud's earliest days there were always some members who felt a close personal loyalty to Bapak and his family and adhered to Bapak's words as authoritative, while other members emphasized those talks in which Bapak characterized his words as advice based on his own experience and culture, asking people to not accept anything until they received it for themselves. During the sixties and seventies in particular, Subud reflected a kind of culture of Indonesian Muslim flavor (batik shirts, clove cigarettes). Some members converted to Islam. Many people in Subud asked (and this is still quite common) Bapak (now his daughter, Ibu Rahayu) for new names, often Muslim. Subud members, even if not Muslim, would fast during the Islamic month of Ramadan, fast on Mondays and Thursdays, celebrate *selametans* (the Indonesian tradition of a communal meal in honor of the deceased), and appropriate Muslim views of modesty (long dresses, no bare shoulders) and gender roles. These Javanese and Islamically oriented patterns have lessened somewhat in the post-Bapak period except for Muslim and/or Indonesian Subud members.

Since Bapak's death, and with apparently less inclination among new members to read or listen to talks of Bapak, the issue of the status of Bapak's advice has come into the foreground. There is discussion of updating the language in Subud literature and reducing unfamiliar Javanese, Sanskrit, or Muslim terms unless they are essential. Of course, establishing which of Bapak's teachings are essential for the progress in the latihan and which are culturally or situationally contextual will be the issues of this decade.[16]

The Organizational Structure

The beginnings of a delineation of the structure of Subud national organizations began as early as 1959 in talks Bapak gave to the First International Congress of Subud, held near London. There would be a distinction between the administrative and the spiritual sides, that is, between "committee" and "helpers."[17] Each group would have a committee which would handle the practical needs of the membership: providing a place for latihan, overseeing communications, looking after the financial side. (Bapak maintained that groups should collect only voluntary donations.) Each group would also have its *kejiwaan* side, a helpers' group, to assist in the spiritual needs of the membership: openings, guidance, support, and answering questions that arise for members in the course of their experiences in the latihan. It was at this time that Bapak also began delineating his long-range goals of "human welfare projects": "establishing schools, hospitals, and homes for those in distress" which were to be funded by profits made in Subud business ventures.[18]

During a 1971 visit to the United States, Bapak established a still more formal structure for helper and committee work that included local, regional, national, "zonal," and international bodies. Except for some reorganizational adjustments in 1989 at the first Subud World Congress after Bapak's death, the basic pattern has remained the same. Every four or five years, the World Subud Association holds a world congress to review activities and formulate future projects. Representatives from all countries with Subud membership attend. Headquarters of the Subud International Committee, which administers Subud communications and activities between congresses, moves to a new country at the end of every congress to ensure that the "Subud democracy" functions, that the "voices of members everywhere" can be heard.[19]

Subud members speak of the 1970s as a period of crisis and purification. Many members, in an attempt to follow Bapak's advice to give evidence of Subud in the world, joined in business enterprises (including a bank, a hotel, craft stores, and production of bean-sprouting kits). Many of the enterprises failed, and most members interpret these failures as the result of too much listening to inner feelings, not enough common sense, and not a small amount of ego. In an effort to find ways of manifesting the latihan, Subud has shifted its attention to supporting small-scale, but thus far successful, social welfare projects around the world that are created and staffed by Subud professionals. They include medical clinics, a medical supply group, schools, and shelters. The social welfare wing of Subud (Susila Dharma) has gained legitimacy through its recent acceptance in the United Nations as a nongovernmental organization. Financing at all levels of the organization seems to be an ongoing difficulty and threatens to collapse the entire structure. Yet the organization has thus far maintained Bapak's advice not to ask for membership fees.

Subud members speak of the current era as a time of transition. Clearly, one of the major challenges is how to maintain the delicate balance between the spontaneous and individual character of the latihan and the practical needs (e.g., how to finance, how to discuss and transmit knowledge about Subud) of the culturally diverse Subud community.

Notes

1. The name "Subuh" is only coincidentally related by sound to "Subud." Subuh's complete name was Muhammad Subuh Sumohadiwidjojo. *Subuh* means "dawn"; he was born at dawn on 22 June 1901 in the village of Kedungjati in central Java. He was a civil servant of the municipality of Semarang when his spiritual experiences began. He died on June 23, 1987, outside Jakarta. See Matthew Sullivan, *Living Religion in Subud* (East Sussex: Humanus Ltd., 1991), 7. Sullivan's book discusses Bapak's life, the coming of the *latihan,* and the Subud experience from the perspective of individuals who belong to various religions. Also Robert Lyle, *Subud* (Kent, England: Humanus, 1983).

2. Lyle, *Subud,* 14.

3. "Bapak's Talk in Sydney, 5 June 1958," trans. by Sofyan Brugger, *Subud Journal* 11 (March 1992): 2.

4. See "Sufism in America" in this volume. One sees that a major difference between Subud and Sufism lies in Sufism's traditional (teacher)/disciple relationship. For information of Bapak's cosmological framework, including the various macrocosmic and microcosmic levels of spirit (*ruh* in Arabic, *roh* is the usual transliteration in Subud literature) or life forces, see Muhammad-Subuh, "The Hierarchy of Life Forces" in *The Way Ahead* (U.K.: Subud Publications International, 1976), 33–42. Also "Excerpts from Bapak's Talks" (at the Subud Bogor House, 4 December 1982 and in Bandung, 15 February 1968) printed in *Asia Pacific: The Newsletter of Subud World Zones One and Two* (April 1992): 1–11. See also John Bennett, *Concerning Subud* (London: Hodder and Stoughton, 1958). Most accessible is Muhammad Subuh Sumohadiwidjojo, *Susila Budhi Dharma* (A poem received and written down in High Javanese and Kawi, and later rendered into Indonesian, with the Javanese and Indonesian and English translations) (England: Subud Publications International, 1975).

5. Talk given at Subud Bogor House, 4 December 1982, printed in *Asia Pacific.* It is important to note that for Bapak, these terms (power, grace, inspiration, revelation, spirit) have particular connotations in his Javanese and Islamic milieu. All of these terms, which he uses in the Arabic (respectively, *qudrah, rahmat, ilham, wahyi, ruh*) are connected to the idea of the *anzala* or the "descent" of the Quran to the Prophet Muhammad. It seems that, much in line with traditional Muslim (and Jewish and Christian, for that matter) concerns to affirm the origin of prophetic or mystical experience in an outpouring of God's radiance and mercy—as opposed to mere human volition or emotion—Bapak compares that latihan to the "content" of the prophetic experiences (*wahyi,* revelation) of the past. Although not in the scope of this chapter, there are numerous elements in Bapak's talks that reveal the complex historical development of Javanese mystical or spiritual *(kejiwaan)* movements since the colonial period. See Paul Stange, "The Sumarah Movement in Javanese Mysticism" (Ph.D. diss., University of Wisconsin, Madison, 1980), 33–83, for an excellent historical discussion of Javanese mystical sects, including such groups as Subud and Sumarah. Most Subud members are not aware of the connections between Bapak's movement and other Javanese movements except for his statements distinguishing Subud from the *kebatinan* groups. Stange accurately points out the religio-political context which has influenced the language of self-definition among these groups. For example, there were a number of universalistically oriented movements that originated in Indonesia in the colonial and post-colonial periods; Subud has been the only Javanese movement to go international on a large scale (74). But what most of these groups shared was a language that distanced them from a *kebatinan* label because of the modernist association of *kebatinan* with superstition, animism, syncretism, and magic. (The word is derived from the Arabic *batin,* with its Sufi association of the "inner" as distinct from the "outer" or apparent aspect of things.) The language would also walk a fine theological line between monistic (Indic) and dualist (Islamist) ontological tendencies in deference to the santri/orthodox Muslim sensibilities. Another commonality of the *kebatinan*-type movements is that in using the term *kebatinan,* the emphasis on a dimension of being is conveyed (namely, the inner dimension) rather than a person, such as the Indic term, guru, and the Javanese term, *paguron,* would suggest (52). This tendency is clearly evident in Bapak's many statements, quoted in Subud's literature, in which he distances himself from the titles of teacher, guru, *shaykh,* prophet.

6. Sullivan, *Living Religion in Subud,* 7–10.

7. P. H. Rofe, "Muhammad Subuh: Mystic of Java," *The Islamic Literature* (June 1951): 5–9.

8. See Frederick Denny, *An Introduction to Islam* (New York: Macmillan, 1985), 371. The Indonesian audiences included at least three major groups (and classes): the *santris,* who are the most "orthodox" of Javanese Muslims; the *abangan,* the majority, who are Muslim but syncretized with traditional beliefs and customs; and the *priyayi* class, Muslims, deeply influenced by their aristocratic past as Javanese, with older Indian-influenced attitudes and behavior patterns. In fact, Bapak's writings seem to reflect awareness and connection to all three classes: he never encourages leaving traditional religious practices, yet he feels at home in utilizing episodes and characters from *wayang* stories, based on the Sanskrit epic poems, the Ramayana and the Mahabharata, to illustrate points in his talks. See Laura Lathrop, *Wayang Heroes in the Pewarta* (series of published talks), available through Subud USA National Office, 13701 Bel-Rd. Suite B, Bellevue, WA 98005. Bapak's own major poetic work was a poem that he received in high Javanese, which is translated into Indonesian and English in his *Susila Buddhi Dharma.* And Bapak's own translation of the Hindic words *susila, buddhi, dharma,* used in the organization's name, reflect a "monothe-ized" or Islamized usage of these Sanskrit terms.

9. The sixties interest in the "East" may be seen as a culmination, rather than the beginning, of tendencies—beginning ironically with colonialism—toward integration of Eastern and Western philosophies. This can be seen in such diverse early twentieth-century figures as Hazrat Inayat Khan and G. I. Gurdjieff, and the emergence of such groups as the Theosophical Society. See "Sufism" in this volume.

10. Sullivan, *Living Religion in Subud,* 11–12.

11. See the chapter on Gurdjieff in this volume. John Bennett created a school of thought dedicated to the "Harmonious Developments of Man" and founded the Institute for the Comparative Study of History, Philosophy, and the Sciences, Limited, at Coombe Springs, England.

12. John Bennett, *Witness: The Autobiography of John Bennett* (London: Turnstone Books, 1974), 320. Bennett's chapter on "The Subud Experience" is a vivid description of the early days of Subud in the West, which corresponds to accounts of Subud members regarding the earlier tendencies toward explosive *latihans,* healings, and ecstatic experiences. John Bennett would eventually resign from Subud, going back to Gurdjieff work and becoming a devotee of Idries Shah, who in 1965 pressed Bennett to give him Coombe Springs as an offering (Bennett and other members saw it as an opportunity to break his "attachment.") No sooner had Shah taken possession of it than he banned the Gurdjieff members from visiting (361).

13. Muhammad Subuh, "What Use Is the Latihan Kejiwaan?" *Pewarta Kejiwaan Subud* (International Subud Committee) 13, no. 5 (April 1977): 169.

14. Subud children are not opened until after they are seventeen, and they must request it on their own.

15. See John Bennett, *Witness* (1975 edition), chapters 25 and 26 on the remarkable effects of the latihan in his life ("illuminations" about love, humanity, prayer, pp. 344–48) and chapter 27 written fifteen years after he first wrote *Witness,* particularly p. 350 " . . . the realization came to me that I had ceased to work on myself and had relied upon the latihan to do what I should be doing by my own effort."

16. Issues under current reflection in the community include Bapak's discussions on sexuality and sexual orientation.

17. Muhammad Subuh, *Subud and the Active Life.* Talks given at the Subud International Congress 1959 (Great Britain: Subud Brotherhood, 1961) 17.

18. Ibid.

19. Pamphlet, "Subud International." Published by the International Subud Committee, Kawasake-shi, Japan, n.d.

Suggestions for Further Reading

Lyle, Robert. *Subud.* Kent, England: Humanus, 1983.

Needleman, Jacob. *The New Religions.* New York: Doubleday, 1970.

Sullivan, Matthew. *Living Religion in Subud.* East Sussex: Humanus Ltd., 1991.

Part V
African-American Freedom Movements

The overwhelming oppression of slavery has left a strong imprint on the religions of persons of African descent throughout the Western Hemisphere. Today a large majority of religious African Americans are Protestant Christians, members of Baptist, Methodist, Pentecostal, and many other churches. Many others, however, have rejected the Christianity they associate with slaveowners in favor of religions with more distinctively black identities.

Several patterns of African-American religiosity are represented in the following chapters. Santería, vodou, and the Rastafari all have roots in the Caribbean. The former two, centered in Cuba and Haiti, respectively, represent the correspondence of African religions with Christianity during slavery and its aftermath, having incorporated African and Christian elements into new religious forms. The Rastafari, who developed in twentieth-century Jamaica, represent post-slavery longings for the recovery of ethnic roots and stress repatriation to Africa under the aegis of the late Ethiopian emperor Haile Selassie, who is held to be still living and divine.

The black Jews and black Muslims arose in the United States, products of the wave of black nationalism that swept through African America in the early twentieth century. The earlier form was Judaism, adopted by several small groups generally headed by charismatic leaders. By the 1910s the focus for African Americans seeking religions other than slavery-tainted Christianity began to shift toward Islam with the rise of the Moorish Science Temple under Noble Drew Ali. The shift was accelerated with the emergence of the Nation of Islam, or Black Muslims, in the 1930s; Islam has, in diverse organizations and forms, gone on to win the allegiance of increasing numbers of African Americans in subsequent years.

The quest for freedom from oppression had other religious expressions as well. Father Divine was perhaps the most prominent of many independent religious leaders who created new religious systems to meet the real needs of African Americans who were still far from participating fully in the American dream, more so than ever during the bleakest years of the Depression. Themes that were in some respects similar were played out several years later in the Peoples Temple, which, until its tragic end, was a beacon of hope for its many African-American members.

26

BLACK JEWS AND BLACK MUSLIMS

Timothy Miller

The period from the 1890s to the 1930s saw the flourishing of a great assortment of African-American religious movements, ranging from the large Baptist and Methodist denominations to Pentecostalism to Father Divine's Peace Mission movement to vodou (voodoo). Many elements of the African past (including cosmologies, healing practices, and a strong sense of being in touch with the unseen spiritual world) continued to undergird the black spiritual ethos, but at the same time new leaders and new institutions reconfigured the religious landscape.

One part of this new landscape was occupied by emergent Jewish and Islamic movements that, although never large in membership, became potent symbols of rejection of the religion of the slave-owners. By and large they were part of a surge, in the early twentieth century, of American black nationalism—a recurring movement seeking black self-determination, economic independence, and, often, repatriation to Africa, born of the grim poverty and ongoing racial oppression in which many African Americans lived. Islam, in particular, eventually came to have an influence in the African-American community second only to that of the Protestant denominations. This chapter outlines the rise of new forms of Judaism and Islam among African Americans.

Black Jews

The Church of God and Saints of Christ

Most of the black Jewish and Muslim groups have been based in urban America, but the first of them emerged in the small Midwestern town of Lawrence, Kansas.[1] William Saunders Crowdy (1847–1908), a cook who worked for the Santa Fe railroad, began to have visionary experiences in 1893, and began preaching on the streets of Lawrence in the fall of 1896. Long an itinerant, he travelled the surrounding area and founded churches in twenty-nine other Kansas towns by 1899. The church, despite its Christian-sounding name, had Jewish content from the first, at least in a sense of identification with ancient Israel. Crowdy preached that Africans were the descendants of the lost tribes of Israel and thus the true surviving Jews.

Crowdy spread the faith tirelessly. Shortly after the turn of the century he purchased land in Belleville, near Portsmouth, Virginia, that some years later became the headquarters of the movement. There for many years the core members of the church lived communally.[2] Within a few years of its founding the movement opened foreign missions, especially in South Africa and Jamaica. The largest numbers of members, however, live in cities in the eastern United States.

Especially under Crowdy's successors the church's theology became a mixture of Jewish, Christian, and black nationalist precepts.[3] Jewishness is present in such matters as observance of the Sabbath and the use of Jewish terminology to describe leaders, buildings, and observances. Here as in many other African-American religions a key theme is the Exodus, the liberation of people in bondage. The ceremonial year culminates in Passover, a week-long national homecoming in Belleville with a richly ceremonial Seder. On the Christian side, Jesus is invoked as an advocate of racial equality (although not as the Lord; the Christ of the church's name refers to the still-awaited Messiah). The church sees no contradiction in its admixture of the two religions, but considers itself Christian only in the sense that Christianity is a seamless extension of Judaism.

The membership of the church in the United States is estimated at 30,000 to 40,000 members in slightly over 200 churches, and it may be growing.[4] The original black Jews are alive and well and practicing their distinctive religion.

Later Black Jewish Groups

Most subsequent black Jewish groups, as well as the black Islamic groups that arose soon afterwards, were urban, typically flourishing in Chicago and the Northeast. They were the products not only of the visionary experiences of their founders, but of many other currents in the urban ghettoes, notably that of black nationalism. Many had direct connections to the influential black nationalist leader Marcus Garvey and his Universal Negro Improvement Association (UNIA). Once the existence of the Ethiopian "Falasha" Jews became known shortly after the turn of the century their mystique was incorporated as well: most black Jewish groups claimed descent from these Ethiopians who, although cut off from the rest of Judaism thousands of years ago, still used the Torah and claimed as their ancestors King Solomon and the Queen of Sheba.[5]

The Temple of the Gospel of the Kingdom

A second black Jewish group emerged shortly after Crowdy's founding of the Church of God and Saints of Christ. Around 1900 Warien Roberson founded, in Virginia, a communal black Jewish religious movement known as the Temple of the Gospel of the Kingdom (derisively called the "Live Ever, Die Never" society by reporters, after Roberson's teaching that his followers would live forever). Emulating Orthodox Judaism, Roberson's followers learned Yiddish and adopted Jewish cultural patterns.[6] By about 1917 the group had relocated its headquarters to Harlem; there and in several other places it established communal "kingdoms"—households—for members, who reportedly numbered about 150 in all.[7] One kingdom near Atlantic City became a center of scandal when it was reported that it was actually a "baby farm" where women bore Roberson's children (a rule of celibacy bound followers, but apparently not the leader). Roberson was charged with violation of the Mann Act, which forbade the transportation of women across state lines for "immoral purposes," in 1926. He pleaded guilty and was sentenced to eighteen months in the Atlanta Penitentiary.[8] The movement collapsed. However, despite its leader's ethical failings, during its quarter-century of life it provided real uplift for its poverty-stricken adherents, and its development of communal "kingdoms" would become the model for the much larger movement of Father Divine a few years later.

Church of God

Not long after Roberson's appearance on the scene a third group of black Jews appeared, this time led by Prophet F. S. Cherry, who had been influenced by both the Church of God and Saints of Christ and the Temple of the Gospel of the Kingdom. The Church's history, beliefs, and practices are only sketchily documented. Its history is especially obscure; of its founding it is only known that it took place in Philadelphia, which remained the headquarters of the movement, in 1915.[9] Never large, it continues its work under the leadership of Cherry's son Prince Cherry.

Cherry's most distinctive contribution to the black Jewish/black Muslim tradition may have been his teaching of racial origins that appears to be the model on which that of the Nation of Islam was later based. Cherry taught that God, who is black, created black original humans; the first white person was Gehazi, whose complexion resulted from a curse. Prophet Cherry's followers believe, as do members of the Church of God and Saints of Christ, that they are the true Jews, and that those more commonly acknowledged as Jews are impostors.

Cherry's theology mixed Christianity and Judaism. He read both Hebrew and Yiddish and based his teachings on the Jewish Bible and the Talmud. Jewish elements of church practice are strong, with a Saturday Sabbath, a liturgical year that focuses on Passover, and a prohibition of eating pork.

Rabbi Matthew and the Commandment Keepers

One of the most prominent black Jewish groups has been the Commandment Keepers Congregation of the Living God, which emerged in 1930 under Rabbi Wentworth A. Matthew (1892–1973). Matthew was ordained to his position by Arnold J. Ford (discussed in more detail below), who had started his own black Jewish movement a few years earlier. Like most other black Jews, the Commandment Keepers believe that they are the lineal descendants of the ancient Hebrews by way of the Ethiopian Jews. Matthew taught themes familiar in black Judaism and Islam—that the temporary ascendancy of whites was nearly over; the end of white domination and the restoration of the true Israelites would come with a devastating atomic war in the year 2000. (Whether or not the Commandment Keepers are around to triumph, however, is a matter of conjecture; their numbers are believed to have declined substantially since the death of Matthew, and some scholars regard the movement as moribund.[10])

The Commandment Keepers take their Judaism seriously, maintaining some contact with the mainstream Jewish community in New York City and observing a version of the kosher diet. The study of the Hebrew language is an integral part of the group's program. Services are held on the Jewish Sabbath; the men wear yarmulkes and prayer shawls. Jewish holidays are observed, the greatest festive occasion of the year being Passover. As with other black Jewish groups, however, the observances and rituals of the Commandment Keepers diverge to a fair degree from those of mainstream Jews.[11]

Other Black Jews

Dozens of small, usually localized groups have at various times identified themselves as black Jews in the United States. Space prohibits discussion of all of them, but among those that have been the subject of some scholarly investigation are the Hebrew Israelites, the House of Judah, the Moorish Zionist Temple, the Nation of Yahweh, the Original Hebrew Israelite Nation, the Pan African Orthodox Christian Church, the United Hebrew Congregation, the B'nai Zakin Sar Shalom, the Beth B'nai Abraham congregation, and the Gospel of the Kingdom Temple.[12] A comprehensive list of the groups would include dozens more. Yet another type of black Judaism is found among the Rastafari, whose story comprises a separate chapter in this book.

Black Muslims

The Moorish Science Temple of America

Black Islamic groups began to appear shortly after the urban black Jewish groups did, and were similarly the products of racial oppression, poverty, and black nationalism. As early as 1913, or perhaps sometime in the decade thereafter, Noble Drew Ali (born Timothy Drew in 1886) created a new racial variety of Islam with the founding of the first Moorish Science Temple. Drew Ali asserted that the Americans commonly called Negroes were racially not Africans but Asiatics, descended from the Moors who settled the northern and western shores of Africa, and that he had been commissioned by the King of Morocco to teach Islam to black Americans.[13] Early in his career he published a short book called *The Holy Koran,* an idiosyncratic mixture of Islamic, Christian, and black nationalist teachings.[14] Although Drew Ali's work may have predated the arrival in the United States of Marcus Garvey in 1917, once exposed to Garvey's ideas Drew Ali placed them at the center of his movement's ideology. Garvey reportedly came to be eulogized as the movement's John the Baptist,[15] and after Garvey's deportation in 1927 the Moors aggressively and with good success wooed his followers.[16]

Although he seems to have found some following in his early years in Newark, Pittsburgh, and Detroit, Drew Ali only came to real prominence in Chicago in the 1920s. His movement adopted beliefs and practices that to a large degree presaged those of the later Nation of Islam. Members wore bright red fezzes and converted their "slave" surnames into new ones by adding to them the suffix "Bey" or "El." The membership of the movement may have reached twenty or thirty thousand.[17]

Drew Ali died under mysterious circumstances in 1929. One of his lieutenants had been killed after trying to oust Drew Ali from the leadership, and Drew Ali had been arrested for the crime.[18] He vanished while out on bond awaiting trial. His following was splintered; several of his leading assistants, some of them claiming to be Drew Ali reincarnated, established successor movements. One of those assistants may have been W. D. Fard, with whom the story of the Nation of Islam begins (see below). The Moorish Science Temple itself continues to exist as a somewhat decentralized national organization.

The Ahmadiyya Movement

An anomaly among the black Islamic groups in the early twentieth century was the Ahmadiyya movement, which was not an original black-American creation but a movement that had been founded in northern India in the late nineteenth century. The movement's most distinctive claim was that Jesus had not died on the cross, but had gone to Kashmir in later life and died in old age there; his reputed tomb at Srinagar is today a popular pilgrimage site.[19]

The first stirrings of the Ahmadiyya movement in the United States came in the 1880s, as the movement reckons its history, with the conversion to Islam of Alexander Russell Webb as a result of his correspondence with the Indian founder of the movement, Hazrat Mirza Ghulam Ahmad. The movement's visibility increased somewhat in 1901 with the establishment of its English-language magazine, *Review of Religions*.[20] Finally in 1920 the first Ahmadiyya missionary to America, Dr. Mufti Muhammad Sadiq, arrived and began propagating his faith through lectures. In the fall of that year he purchased property for a mosque in Chicago, and the next year he began publishing the periodical *Moslem Sunrise*. He found fertile ground among the Garveyites and converted dozens of them to his movement. Today the movement has both African-American and Asian immigrant (principally Pakistani) members. Never large, the movement provided another Islamic model for later religious black nationalist groups to follow. Two branches continue to operate today.[21]

The Nation of Islam

The most influential of the black Islamic movements arose in Detroit in 1930. In that year a mysterious peddler, perhaps from the West Indies or Africa or Arabia, appeared with silks and other goods from what he said were black homelands overseas, as well as stories of life in those faraway lands. As interest in his wares and tales grew, he became increasingly strident in denouncing the white race. The stranger used a variety of names; most commonly he is referred to as W. D. Fard or Master Wali Farrad Muhammad.

Fard disappeared in 1934. Various speculations involved his demise at the hands of the Detroit police or of his dissident followers, or perhaps his departure overseas, but the truth remains a mystery. In any event Elijah Muhammad, Fard's top lieutenant, became leader of the burgeoning movement. He moved the headquarters to Chicago and oversaw an expansion that included the opening of not only temples and mosques but schools, housing projects, stores, restaurants, and farms.[22]

In Elijah Muhammad's theology, Fard was elevated from prophet to deity, Allah himself.[23] An imaginative creation myth, one that echoed similar myths in other black Jewish and Islamic groups, helped explain the present-day oppression of blacks: blacks were the original humans, but Yakub, a rebellious scientist, had produced and released genetically weakened pale stock. The resulting whites were given six thousand years to rule—a period that ended in 1914, leaving only a few years of grace before "original" humans would again reign.[24] In the meantime, most Muslims were to use "X" as a surname, indicating that their original African names had been lost in slavery. Blacks, naturally morally stronger than whites, were to prepare for their return to their rightful social and political estate by disciplined living, avoiding such worldly pleasures as pork, alcohol, tobacco, nonmarital sex, dancing, and gambling. War might be necessary to overthrow the decadent white devils, but until the officially announced propitious movement had arrived, no one was to engage in any threatening behavior that might allow the white slavemasters a pretext for suppressing the Muslims.

Other Islamic groups emerged from schisms in the Nation of Islam. One prominent example came when Malcolm X, the charismatic leader of the New York Temple, was expelled for speaking approvingly of the assassination of John F. Kennedy—or perhaps for publicizing, within the movement, the sexual improprieties of Elijah Muhammad.[25] Malcolm, after a pilgrimage to Mecca during which he experienced true interracial harmony, abandoned the theme of black racism and formed a more traditionally Islamic group, the Muslim Mosque, Inc.[26] But before many months had passed Malcolm was killed by Nation of Islam gunmen.

Following Elijah Muhammad's death in 1975 his son Wallace Muhammad (now known as W. Deen Mohammed) ascended to the leadership. The younger Muhammad steered the movement toward orthodox Islam and abandoned his father's antiwhite rhetoric. In 1985 the national organization, then known as the American Muslim Mission (AMM), was dissolved, and the approximately two hundred local centers now function as independent mosques. In the late 1970s a conservative old guard under the leadership of Louis Farrakhan broke away from the AMM, reconstituting a Nation of Islam that closely resembles the movement built by Elijah Muhammad. Several other splinter groups and newly founded Islamic groups continue to exist as well, including the Ansaru Allah Community of Brooklyn and the Hanafi Madh-Hab Center, Islam Faith, in Washington, D.C.[27]

A SINGLE MOVEMENT?

While all of these groups tended to have charismatic founders who claimed original revelations or other ahistorical origins and did not credit those mortals who actually inspired them, specific connections among some of them do exist. Howard Brotz, writing in 1964, tried to forge a specific link between the two basic types, Jews and Muslims, through the person of Arnold J. Ford, who, he speculated, just might have been one and the same as W. D. Fard. Ford had studied Hebrew and had much to do with introducing talmudic traditions to the black Jews who previously had used the Jewish Bible as the sole authority for faith and practice. In the 1920s he was an active Garveyite and helped promote the black nationalism that continued, following the collapse of Garvey's movement, in the black Jewish and Muslim groups. Ford also had sympathies for Islam; his *Universal Ethiopian Hymnal* contained a hymn based on African lyrics entitled "Allah-Hu-Ak Bar."[28] But where from there? Expelled by Garvey in 1923, he soon founded the Beth B'nai Abraham congregation, which suffered financial problems and collapsed in 1930, whereupon he left New York. Brotz speculated that Ford simply vanished from New York as a black Jew and soon thereafter appeared in Detroit as a black Muslim.[29] Actually, however, Ford's later story was more prosaic: he emigrated to Ethiopia and worked as a musician in Addis Ababa.[30] Fard, for his part, was probably not an African American but an Arab.

Other ties, however, do connect black Judaism and Islam. Elijah Poole, for example, was reportedly an early associate of Wentworth Matthew who broke with him when Matthew refused to switch from black Judaism to black Islam. Poole joined the Nation of Islam, soon becoming its head, Elijah Muhammad.[31]

Whatever web of relationships may connect all of these groups, it is clear that they influenced each other and had the same constituency. The beliefs and rhetoric of black Jews and Muslims were strikingly similar. The movements offered powerful ideas to African Americans: an identity untainted by slavery; a sense of pride in an ancient tradition; a hope for liberation; a myth of origins depicting blacks as the ur-humans and explaining the current degradation of African Americans. Crowdy, Garvey, Ford, Fard, Matthew, Cherry, and the rest, in short, wrote an important, ongoing chapter in the history of African America.

Notes

My sincere thanks go to Professors James E. Landing and Catherine Wessinger for making valuable comments on an earlier draft of this paper.

1. The definitive work on the movement is Elly Wynia-Trey, "The Church of God and Saints of Christ: A Black Judeo-Christian Movement Founded in Lawrence, Kansas in 1896," senior honors thesis, University of Kansas, 1988. A revised version of the thesis is scheduled to be issued soon by Garland Publishing. All information pertaining to the movement is taken from Wynia-Trey's thesis except as otherwise attributed.

2. A few elderly members still live on church property in Belleville. See Rosemary Armao and Greg Schneider, " 'Black Jews' Step Out of the Shadows," Virginian-Pilot (Norfolk), 1 April 1988, A1, A6–A7.

3. The church experienced schism after Crowdy's death in 1908. William H. Plummer became leader of the larger faction; he and members of his family promoted increased Judaizing in the movement. See Wynia-Trey, "Church of God and Saints of Christ," 56–61; James E. Landing, personal communication, 1993.

4. A 1952 report says that there were then 204 congregations and 34,710 members. See Benson Y. Landis, ed., Yearbook of American Churches (New York: National Council of Churches, 1952), 29–30. The church itself has only infrequently released statistics. As of 1988 plans were being laid for extensive development of the Belleville acreage. See Armao and Schneider, " 'Black Jews' Step Out of the Shadows."

5. "Falasha" is used in quotation marks here because in Ethiopia it is a pejorative. "Ethiopian Jews" is a more neutral usage.

6. Roberson's detractors say that a prime motivation for his Judaizing of the movement was to attract donations from sympathetic white Jews. See Albert Ehrman, "Explorations and Responses: Black Judaism in New York," in A Coat of Many Colors: Jewish Subcommunities in the United States, ed. Abraham D. Lavender (Westport, Conn.: Greenwood, 1977), 214.

7. Ira De A. Reid, "Let Us Prey!" Opportunity: A Journal of Negro Life 4 (September 1926): 274–78.

8. "Negro Elder Held in $50,000 Bail," New York Times, 16 April 1926, 12; " 'Black Messiah' Gets 18 Months," New York Times, 20 May 1926, 27.

9. This sketch is based primarily on information in Arthur Huff Fauset, Black Gods of the Metropolis: Negro Religious Cults in the Urban North (Philadelphia: University of Pennsylvania Press, 1944), 31–40. The founding date of 1915 is provided by Israel J. Gerber, The Heritage Seekers: American Blacks in Search of Jewish Identity (Middle Village, N.Y.: Jonathan David Publishers, 1977), 70.

10. Landing, personal communication, 1993.

11. The standard study of the Commandment Keepers, written while Rabbi Matthew was still alive, is Howard Brotz, The Black Jews of Harlem (New York: Free Press/Macmillan, 1964).

12. Of these smaller groups, Wardell J. Payne lists House of Judah, Nation of Yahweh, Original Hebrew Israelite Nation, and United Hebrew Congregation. (See Wardell J. Payne, ed., Directory of African American Religious Bodies: A Compendium by the Howard University School of Divinity [Washington: Howard University Press, 1991], 132–36.) Payne's infor-

mation appears to be largely distilled from that provided by J. Gordon Melton, who in his work lists House of Judah, Nation of Yahweh (Hebrew Israelites), Original Hebrew Israelite Nation, Overcoming Saints of God, Pan African Orthodox Christian Church, and United Hebrew Congregation. (See J. Gordon Melton, *The Encyclopedia of American Religions* 4th ed. [Detroit: Gale, 1993], 868–71). Wynia-Trey (pp. 22–23) provides a reference to an unpublished paper on the Moorish Zionist Temple: Arthur Dobrin, "A History of Negro Jews in America," Schamburg Collection, New York Public Library. Arnold Ford's Beth B'nai Abraham congregation is discussed below in this chapter; see Gerber, *Heritage Seekers*, 14–16. For a brief note on the Gospel of the Kingdom Temple, see Ehrman, "Explorations and Responses," 214. For B'nai Zakin Sar Shalom, see Gerber, *Heritage Seekers*, passim.

13. E. U. Essien-Udom, *Black Nationalism: A Search for Identity in America* (Chicago: University of Chicago Press, 1962), 34.

14. Noble Drew Ali, *The Holy Koran of the Moorish Science Temple of America* (n.p., n.d.). For a brief synopsis see Fauset, *Black Gods of the Metropolis*, 45–47.

15. Arna Bontemps and Jack Conroy, *They Seek a City* (Garden City, N.Y.: Doubleday, Doran, 1945), 175.

16. Moors did so well at converting Garveyites that in 1935 one group of the latter actually petitioned the government to readmit Garvey to counter the work of this group converting UNIA members "on the pretense that they are doing Garvey's work, as he no longer can return." See Tony Martin, *Race First: The Ideological and Organizational Struggles of Marcus Garvey and the Universal Negro Improvement Association* (Westport, Conn.: Greenwood, 1976), 77.

17. Bontemps and Conroy, *They Seek a City*, 176; C. Eric Lincoln, *The Black Muslims in America* (Boston: Beacon, 1961), 51.

18. Fauset, *Black Gods of the Metropolis*, 43.

19. Melton, *Encyclopedia*, 890.

20. Yvonne Yazbeck Haddad and Jane Idleman Smith, *Mission to America: Five Islamic Sectarian Communities in North America* (Gainesville: University Press of Florida, 1993), 59–60.

21. Martin, *Race First*, 75–76. For further information on the ongoing groups see Melton, *Encyclopedia*, 889–90.

22. Lincoln, *Black Muslims*, 16.

23. Actually, Muhammad began proclaiming Fard's divinity during Fard's lifetime. See Martha F. Lee, *The Nation of Islam, an American Millenarian Movement* (Lewiston, N.Y.: Edwin Mellen, 1988), 33.

24. Lincoln, *Black Muslims*, 76–77.

25. See Lawrence H. Mamiya, "From Black Muslim to Bilalian: The Evolution of a Movement," *Journal for the Scientific Study of Religion* 21 (1982): 138–52.

26. Malcolm X with Alex Haley, *The Autobiography of Malcolm X* (New York: Grove, 1965), 315–17.

27. For information on these groups as well as on the various Nation of Islam splinters, see Melton, *Encyclopedia*, 889–95; Payne, *Directory*, 136–43.

28. Martin, *Race First*, 75.

29. Howard Brotz, *The Black Jews of Harlem* (New York: Free Press/Macmillan, 1964), 12.

30. For a discussion of the evidence that seems to prove Ford's emigration to Ethiopia, see Robert G. Weisbord, *Ebony Kinship: Africa, Africans, and the Afro-American* (Westport, Conn.: Greenwood, 1973), 93–94; Gerber, *Heritage Seekers*, 16.

31. Gerber, *Heritage Seekers*, 16–17.

Suggestions for Further Reading

Essien-Udom, E. U. *Black Nationalism: A Search for Identity in America*. Chicago: University of Chicago Press, 1962.

Fauset, Arthur Huff. *Black Gods of the Metropolis: Negro Religious Cults in the Urban North*. Philadelphia: University of Pennsylvania Press, 1944.

Lincoln, C. Eric. *The Black Muslims in America*. Boston: Beacon, 1961.

Yvonne Yazbeck Haddad and Jane Idleman Smith, *Mission to America: Five Islamic Sectarian Communities in North America*. Gainesville: University Press of Florida, 1993.

27

FATHER DIVINE'S PEACE MISSION MOVEMENT
Robert Weisbrot

The Peace Mission is an interracial religious organization that affirms the divinity of its founder, a black minister known as Father Divine (1879–1965). The membership, though it has dwindled since its peak of perhaps ten thousand in the 1930s, still upholds Divine's strict moral code, including celibacy. Disciples hope in this way to identify more closely with the divine spirit that they believe inheres in all creation.

The banquet table serves as the central place both of worship and fellowship for Peace Mission disciples. Heaping dishes of food, of great variety and in seemingly endless succession, recall the free Sunday feasts that helped propel this movement to national fame during the Great Depression. The meals may last for hours, and feature lively, jazz-inflected hymns to Father Divine, thanking him for all good things and pledging devotion to his ideals of equality and brotherhood. Many at the tables feel moved to testify, at times confessing to lives of sin, and recounting how Father Divine (personally or "in the spirit") enabled them to be reborn.

The Peace Mission's theology is rooted in Christianity but also draws eclectically on other traditions. Pantheistic notions color the Peace Mission's Christian faith, as in the teaching that "Christ is in every joint, every sinew, every limb, every bone, every vein and fiber, every cell and atom of your bodily form."[1] The movement also accords an honored place to the works of

Robert Collier and other exponents of New Thought.[2] These volumes from the early twentieth century encourage readers to realize a universal human potential for earthly success by visualizing positive images and tapping a world of divine power. And, like the Christian Scientists, Peace Mission members trust that perfect faith will ensure good health, though in recent decades the movement has eased its strictures against consulting physicians.

Members pay supreme reverence to the messages of Father Divine, which number in the thousands and are reprinted in the Peace Mission's various publications. Disciples order their lives around Divine's exhortations to strive for unity with God by denying their egos in order to let the divine spirit become manifest. Followers must master their physical desires, as evidenced by a renunciation of tobacco, alcohol, drugs, and sexual relations. Disciples believe that Father Divine left a perfect "sample and example" of righteous conduct, embodying to perfection the divine spirit. They declare that he did not die, despite his apparent physical demise, but rather rules the universe through his spirit.

A strict ethical code complements the Peace Mission's stringent morality. Honesty is a watchword of the movement, and members abjure even credit purchases, preferring to pay at once for any good or service. Their scrupulous behavior draws on Father Divine's teaching that there is no such thing as a small or harmless theft, for all crimes stem from the same evil impulses: "He who would steal an apple, would steal an elephant, if he could get him in his pocket, and get away with it, and he who would steal an egg would steal an ox, if he could get away with it."[3]

The Peace Mission's central tenet that everyone can live a godly life complements an equally strong social creed: that all people, as repositories of the divine spirit, should be treated with dignity regardless of background or complexion. Disciples reject the concept of race as a falsehood that has had terrible social consequences. The Peace Mission's communal residences, banquet tables, and other facilities all promote racial integration. No disciple will say "black" or "white" to describe an individual; such "negative" thinking would detract from appreciating the inner person. On occasion members may resort to such euphemisms as "light-complected" and "dark-complected," while still avowing that there is no race except the human race. In this, the movement today maintains the central concern of its founder: to link religious faith with the struggle for racial justice.

Father Divine, who for many years was the Peace Mission's indispensable driving force, was born George Baker, in Rockville, Maryland, in 1879, to a poor black family.[4] Raised a Baptist, he imbibed many religious traditions. In 1906 he visited the Azusa Street Revival in Los Angeles, where he joined other worshipers in glossolalia, or speaking in tongues. Later that year, he studied with a black preacher in Baltimore named Samuel Morris, who interpreted literally a New Testament phrase, "Know ye not that ye are the temple of God, and that the spirit of God dwelleth in you?" In 1912 Baker headed south and, as "the Messenger," preached on this theme of inner divinity to blacks who hailed him as a messiah. He urged them to make a heaven on Earth, not wait for an afterlife, and assured them of their infinite worth regardless of color or origin.

Baker's preaching in Georgia seemed subversive to white authorities, who in 1914 jailed him and later briefly placed him in an asylum. Returning north, Baker moved to New York before settling, as "the Reverend M. J. Divine," in a previously all-white suburb in Long Island called Sayville. He and his small coterie of followers lived communally, a practice that pared expenses while emulating the early Christian apostles. Then in 1929 the Great Depression, creating widespread desperation, provided an outlet for Divine to construct his vision of an egalitarian heaven on Earth.

As his modest communal movement continued to prosper during the Depression, Divine welcomed all visitors, presenting free Sunday banquets and often finding jobs for needy guests. Crowds came from Harlem and Newark, venerating this mysterious provider as a heaven-sent deliverer. By the early thirties bands of disciples, some whites among them, were forming communal centers throughout the ghettos and beyond. Late in 1931 Sayville authorities arrested Divine and some eighty disciples for disturbing the peace by praying too loudly, and on June 8, 1932, a blatantly racist judge sentenced him to prison. But three days later the judge suddenly died, and Divine soon after emerged from jail with his stature enhanced, as a martyr who had spectacularly resurrected his leadership. Relocating to Harlem, he presided over what had become a burgeoning national movement.

The Peace Mission's bolt to prominence coincided with a crisis in black religious leadership. Legions of destitute blacks looked to their churches—the central community institutions—to provide relief. Yet during the first years of the Depression many pastors in the established black churches shifted only haltingly from their otherworldly outlook. The ghetto's numerous cult figures often ministered more effectively to poor blacks than established ministers did, but most confined their anodynes largely to emotional catharsis. Father Divine, by contrast, emphasized a socially conscious, present-centered religion, saying, "I would not give five cents for a god that could not help me here on the earth."[5]

The Peace Mission became known for its aggressive efforts to desegregate American society. It featured integrated services at a time when more than 99 percent of American congregations were segregated. Divine also used whites as secret emissaries to circumvent restrictive housing covenants and acquire homes, hotels, and beachfronts for his interracial following in northern white neighborhoods, including over two thousand acres of choice property far from the city slums. The Peace Mission gained fame as well for many thriving cooperative businesses. Drawing on pooled funds, disciples opened inexpensive hotels, restaurants, clothing stores, and numerous other businesses, volunteering their labor and sharing all income. By the mid-1930s Peace Mission members were handling millions of dollars in business annually.

Father Divine increasingly encouraged political activism, at a time when ghetto residents generally were becoming more assertive in reform causes. In January 1936 Divine guided a Peace Mission convention in New York City that issued a "Righteous Government Platform" for a more just society. It proposed the abolition of racial segregation, lynching, and capital punishment, and urged an expanded government commitment to end unemployment, poverty, and hunger.[6] In 1940 Peace Mission members gathered 250,000 signatures on a petition to pass federal antilynching legislation. Divine praised American democratic principles, but in militant tones. "If the White House or the Capitol does not do right, it can be picketed!" he told his Harlem followers. "Every American citizen has a right and if he does not get it one way, he can protest. . . . "[7]

The Peace Mission's successes came at the cost of persistent controversy. Critics scoffed that Divine was simply a racketeer, though the newfound material security enjoyed by many disciples tended to blunt such charges. Divine also faced several lawsuits by spouses of converts who had left their homes—at times taking their children with them—and entered Peace Mission residences. Divine weathered these court battles, showing that the children received ample care, and testifying that he urged married couples to remain together, though chastely. The movement also contended with violence and harassment by whites

outraged at the integration of their neighborhoods. Yet throughout the Depression decade the Peace Mission expanded, till it numbered over 150 "[heavenly] kingdom extensions," including several branches overseas.

The Peace Mission evolved after 1940 from a mass movement wholly dependent on its founding father to a formal sect featuring an elaborate bureaucracy. While such trends often overtake charismatic movements after the passing of the original leader, the Peace Mission changed while Father Divine still lived and firmly controlled its affairs. Under the pressures of advancing age and growing legal problems, Divine increasingly focused on building institutional guarantees for the movement he had once sustained through sheer vitality and seemingly endless ingenuity. The result of these changes was that the Peace Mission proved able to survive even the great trauma of Father Divine's death in 1965, but at the cost—exacted well in advance—of virtually all the movement's original social energy and impact.

The catalyst spurring the Peace Mission's conservative shift was a bitter court fight, spanning more than five years and exposing the fragility of the movement's financial and legal state. A former follower, Verinda Brown, sued in 1937 for money allegedly given to Father Divine in trust while a disciple. Partly to discourage further such actions, Divine incorporated several Peace Mission centers during the early 1940s. This marked a decisive break with his earlier stress on an "invisible" church, but it allowed each center to deed property in its own name, so that no disciples could henceforth claim any of the Peace Mission's assets on leaving the movement. And, rather than pay Brown "an unjust judgment" of $7,000, as a New York court ordered, Divine instead left Harlem permanently, in July 1942, and made Philadelphia his new headquarters.

Divine's sudden self-exile from the heart of his black constituency, just when renewed national prosperity and high employment were eroding the Peace Mission's economic appeal, led to a sharp decline in his following. Yet the minister was by then becoming absorbed with consolidating his corporate creation, to the neglect of mass-based activity. Divine's sermons, though still championing civil rights, increasingly reflected the Peace Mission's accommodation with the wider society. Tirades against communists and unions, often in combination, revealed the minister's utopian vision shading into the most profoundly conservative prayers of the cold war era.

As the Peace Mission lost its former scope and influence, it cultivated its status as a disciplined religious institution. There arose new orders of the devoted, each with its own elaborate code of conduct and special liturgical functions. "Rosebuds" included young women disciples, "Lily-buds" somewhat older women, and "Crusaders" men of all ages. If one already lived a celibate life, as Father Divine advocated, it was not difficult to attain membership in one of these orders: about half the active disciples belonged. Nor were these "privileged" orders except in leading hymns of praise to Father Divine. Initiates did, however, wear special uniforms, brightly colored to distinguish them unmistakably from their brethren in the organization. A small move, it underscored the advent of the Peace Mission as an established church rather than simply a bustling and spontaneous evangelical assembly.

Institutional continuity became a priority to Father Divine in his twilight years. In August 1946 he announced his marriage to a twenty-one-year-old white disciple called Sweet Angel, thereafter called Mother Divine. He assured his followers that this was not a conventional marriage but a spiritual union to symbolize interracial harmony and uphold a standard of chaste conduct. By exalting his "spotless virgin bride" who represented his "church" on earth, Divine invested her with the mystique and authority needed to rule eventually in his stead. Mother Divine became a nearly coequal partner in guiding the Peace Mission, and followers who once reflexively thanked "Father" for all blessings now exclaimed, "Thank you, Father and Mother!"

Father Divine died in September 1965. Disciples were stunned and saddened, but not to the point of mass desertion. The minister had been seriously ill and largely out of public view for several years, during which time Mother Divine had prepared followers for the day when "Father will not be with us personally." But Mother Divine did not view Divine as subject to death. Rather, she announced (dressed in white) a day to celebrate that "Father" had shed his mortal body to rule purely in the spirit. Peace Mission members continue to refer to Father Divine as still living, and they reserve a place for him at all their banquets.

In recent decades the absence of aggressive proselytizing, coupled with the stricture of celibacy, has severely depleted the Peace Mission membership. There remain several hundred followers, concentrated in six incorporated churches in Philadelphia and Newark, but also scattered across the United States and in foreign countries (chiefly Switzerland).[8] Although blacks are still well represented in the major centers, the throngs of poor ghetto residents who once flocked to the Peace Mission for physical as well as emotional sustenance have long since faded into history. Today's members are overwhelmingly middle class, in aspiration if not always in affluence. And the leadership has imposed a more decorous tone to the worship, in place of the uninhibited emotional displays that once attracted the most desperate among Harlem's underclass.

The current headquarters of the Peace Mission movement is a seventy-two-acre estate called Woodmont, outside Philadelphia, which Father Divine proclaimed "the mount of the house of the Lord" on moving there in 1953. Mother Divine supervises church business from this estate, gives tours and interviews, and leads study groups. Visiting Angels pay special homage at Woodmont's Shrine to Life, a structure designed by Mother Divine: it surrounds a red marble crypt that holds the body of Father Divine.[9]

Outside of Woodmont the most active Peace Mission community resides in Philadelphia, where members operate cafeterias, dry-cleaners, and printshops, as well as two clean, comfortable, and extremely inexpensive hotels, the Divine Tracy and the Divine Lorraine. The hotels enforce Father Divine's

International Modest Code, which forbids smoking, drinking, and profanity, and requires women to wear dresses and hose and men to wear dress pants and shirts. Floors are segregated by gender, and men and women may mingle only in the entrance lobby.[10] Most other properties that once formed a thriving network of Peace Mission cooperatives have been sold off, not from financial distress but for lack of personnel. The movement's newspaper, the *New Day*, originally appearing twice weekly during the 1930s, suspended publication in 1992.

The decline of the Peace Mission has seemed, paradoxically, to facilitate its acceptance by the wider society. The end of mass conversions to the movement also effectively ended the lawsuits by irate outsiders seeking to wrest former spouses and children from Peace Mission residences. Similarly, the cessation of social activism and expansion reduced displays of hostility by outsiders toward unwelcome neighbors. And the growing conservatism of the movement encouraged officials in Pennsylvania and other states to praise the Peace Mission as a pillar of moral and social responsibility.

The Peace Mission's theology has evolved, though modestly, to account for changes in the movement. Most notably there has been a rethinking of the significance of death, which had once seemed to Peace Mission members the ultimate disgrace, resulting from a sinful state of mind. "[I]f you die, you are not of me. If you are an invalid you are not of me," Divine had often stated.[11] Yet as the demise of veteran followers became too frequent to ignore, the movement reinterpreted death as a natural occurrence, even for the faithful, involving the migration of a person's spirit into a more perfect body. A letter from a female disciple in Panama, telling of her brother's passing, reveals the impact of this new teaching: "We that were around him did not feel much distressed, but were in the realization that his passing was but the means to a happy end."[12]

In asking, in effect, "Death, where is thy stigma?" the Peace Mission made theological provision for its institutional future. It ensured that the passing of the whole first generation of disciples, who joined in the 1930s, would not discredit the movement's central tenet that God resides in every individual. The concept of immortality simply became more heavily spiritualized, a development that accorded well with the movement's general trend toward a more socially passive and aloof character.

The Peace Mission has also reinterpreted its mission to the world, reflecting its dramatic decline in membership, wealth, and social activism. During the 1930s the young, dynamic, and expanding movement boasted that it was fast converting the world; but today's members instead perceive themselves as a saving remnant, vigilant for the return in bodily form of their founding leader. They stress their indifference to numbers, or, like the Shakers with whom they sometimes compare themselves, they express pride in forming part of an elite, winnowed by the demands of righteous living to a select few.

The daily administration of the Peace Mission has fallen to Mother Divine, working closely with an able secretarial staff. Although not an innovator or social crusader as Father Divine had been in his prime, Mother Divine has proved an effective unifying symbol for a movement seeking to maintain organizational stability amid waning numbers. She has chosen simply to revere, rather than revive, Father Divine's earlier social radicalism; but within the Peace Mission's own centers Father Divine's vision of a chaste, integrated communal society goes on as before. As one follower, Blessed Mary Love, explained, "Father has freed us from within."[13]

Notes

1. Jill Watts, *God, Harlem U.S.A.: The Father Divine Story* (Berkeley: University of California Press, 1992), 175.

2. Divine's sermons reveal much of the philosophy and phrasing of Robert Collier's writings. See, for example, Collier's *The Book*

of Life, 7 vols. (New York: Robert Collier, 1925); *The Secret of Gold*, 2 vols. (New York: Robert Collier, 1927); and *The Life Magnet*, 6 vols. (New York: Robert Collier, 1928).

3. Sermon of 29 July 1936, in *Spoken Word*, 18 August 1936, p. 27.

4. Watts, *God, Harlem U.S.A.*, 1–4, traces Divine's likely roots.

5. Sermon of 20 February 1938, in *New Day*, 3 March 1938, p. 20.

6. The Righteous Government Platform was first printed in a Peace Mission journal, the *Spoken Word*, 14 January 1936, pp. 7–16.

7. Sermon of 18 March 1940, in *New Day*, 21 March 1940, p. 15.

8. See "Combined Reports of the Annual Meetings of the Peace Mission Churches for the Fiscal Year 1991–1992," *New Day*, 31 October 1992, pp. 12–17, on the status of Peace Mission branches throughout the world.

9. Watts, *God, Harlem U.S.A.*, 176–77.

10. Ibid., 176.

11. See, for example, sermon of 12 September 1938, in *New Day*, 15 September 1938, p. 76.

12. Disciple identified as "E.E.M." to Father Divine, 5 February 1959, in *New Day*, 28 February 1959, p. 21.

13. R. W. Apple, "Father Divine Shuns Rights Drive," *New York Times*, 10 May 1964, 65.

Suggestions for Further Reading

Harris, Sara, with the assistance of Harriet Crittendon. *Father Divine*. Enl. ed. New York: Collier Books, 1971.

Hoshor, John. *God in a Rolls-Royce: The Rise of Father Divine, Madman, Menace, or Messiah* . . . New York: Hillman-Curl, 1936.

Parker, Robert Allerton. *The Incredible Messiah: The Deification of Father Divine*. Boston: Little, Brown, 1937.

Watts, Jill. *God, Harlem U.S.A.: The Father Divine Story*. Berkeley: University of California Press, 1992.

Weisbrot, Robert. *Father Divine and the Struggle for Racial Equality*. Urbana: University of Illinois Press, 1983. The volume contains an annotated bibliography, pp. 224–32.

28

SANTERÍA AND VODOU IN THE UNITED STATES
Joseph M. Murphy

In 1797 a Martiniquean traveller, Médéric Louis Moreau de St. Méry, described a religious ceremony that he had observed among the slaves of the French colony of St. Domingue, soon to be independent Haiti. In some five pages of careful description he notes the specific African origins of the ceremony, the connections between dance, music and sacrifice, and the authority of priests and priestesses over the participants. He concludes his account with a warning about the revolutionary potential of such religious activity among the slaves:

> In a word, nothing is more dangerous, according to all reports, than this cult of Vaudoux, based on this extravagant idea which can become a terrible weapon, that the ministers of this so-called god can know everything and do anything.[1]

Moreau's observations of *vaudoux*, usually rendered "voodoo" in English texts and "vodou" in official Haitian Créole, have set the pattern for the history of discourse about African-derived religious traditions in the Americas. Religions like vodou in Haiti and *santería* in Cuba have been observed through the dark glasses of colonial failure and slave revolt, and so have been portrayed as threatening, dangerous, and evil. With the arrival of large numbers of Haitians, Cubans, and other Caribbean peoples to the United States in the last decades of the twentieth century, the images created by Moreau are still relied upon to

evoke feelings of threat and provoke responses toward containment.

In this short chapter I will provide some alternative views of vodou and santería and show how they offer creative strategies for living in the multicultural world of twenty-first-century America.

African religious traditions came to the Americas with the very first Africans. Ivan van Sertima makes a fascinating case that Africans made regular voyages to Central America centuries before Columbus.[2] Afro-Spaniards accompanied Spanish explorers in the first voyages of discovery and conquest in the sixteenth century. Slaves and indentured servants were brought from Africa to Latin America early in the sixteenth century and to North America before the *Mayflower* in the seventeenth. By the end of legal slavery in Brazil in 1888, at least ten million African men, women, and children had survived the terrible passage from Africa to work and die in the plantation economies of the Americas.[3]

In the United States the African religious heritage of the slaves came to inform a distinctive vision of Christianity. Divided by design from their fellow countrymen and proselytized first by white and then black preachers, African Americans created an alternative Christianity from that of the white slaveholders. It was grounded in the biblical struggles of the Hebrews from slavery to freedom and realized in the extraordinary consciousness of the spirit-filled ceremonies of the black church.

In the Caribbean and South American colonies the African religious heritage often took different forms. In Haiti and Cuba, some Africans from the same ethnic groups were able to reconstitute fragments of their individual "nations" *(nanchon, nación, nação)* in religious communities dedicated to the spirits brought from Africa. Where these "houses" of the African spirits survived the periodic persecutions and harassments by the official powers, they preserved the traditions now known as Haitian vodou and Cuban santería. Since the Cuban revolution of 1959, over one million Cubans have come to the United States, many of them priests and priestesses of *santería.* Probably a million Haitians have also come north since that time, especially since the fall of the Duvalier regime in 1986. Particularly in New York and Miami, but also in other large North American cities, Cuban and Haitian immigrants have reestablished houses for the veneration of the African spirits. While the focus of many of these houses was and continues to be the mutual aid and orientation of fellow immigrants, the power of the religions has brought African Americans and white Americans to them.

Vodou and santería are similar, but not identical. Their similarities come from their origins in contiguous parts of West Africa, while the differences stem from their historical developments in the Americas. Vodou is a word meaning "spirit" in the language of the Fon people of present-day Benin. The enslaved Fon priests and priestesses who were brought to Haiti in the eighteenth century transplanted large elements of their systems of veneration of the spirits. In Haiti the Fon ideas and practices came in contact with elements of other African religious traditions, and with the Catholicism of the French, to produce a variety of Fon-centered traditions that we call vodou.

Santería has its origins among the Yoruba people, who are neighbors to the Fon and share many traditions with them. In the early nineteenth century the Yoruba were enslaved in even greater numbers than the Fon and they were able to form Yoruba-speaking communities in Cuba and Brazil. Yoruba priests and priestesses created new lineages of initiates dedicated to the Yoruba spirits called *orishas,* which was translated as *santos* in Spanish. In this way people called the Yoruba traditions in Cuba "santería," the way of the saints.

Both vodou and santería recognize a remote and almighty Supreme Being, who might best be understood as a personification of fate or destiny. In vodou this God is called Bondye, a Créole rendering of the French "Bon Dieu." In santería God is invoked by the Yoruba title Olodumare, the Owner of all Destinies. The entire cosmos receives its *telos* and individuals are given their own destinies by Bondye or Olodumare. Yet in order to fulfill these destinies with grace and power an individual will require guidance from a variety of spirits called *lwa* in vodou and *orishas* in santería. The religions of vodou and santería are systems of actions toward the development of ever-closer relationships with *lwa* and *orishas.* The relationships are shown by increasingly complex exchanges of sacrifice and praise on the part of human beings and power and wisdom on the part of the spirits.

Human beings and spirits interact through divination and sacrifice. Trained priests and priestesses consult oracles to determine the sacrificial foods and actions necessary to secure the power and presence of a *lwa* or an *orisha.* In both traditions one particular *lwa* or *orisha* will begin to assert itself as an individual devotee's patron or "master of the head." When the spirit wills it, and when the devotee can afford it, he or she will undergo a costly and irrevocable initiation into the mysteries of his or her patron spirit. This initiation will constitute the member's entry into the priesthood of vodou or santería and give him or her the authority to found his or her own house and consecrate other priests and priestesses. The spirit will be symbolically identified with the devotee's "head" or inner self, and this new relationship of intimacy will offer the devotee health, success, and wisdom.

The spirits are venerated through a variety of symbolic media: each has its own special colors, numbers, songs, rhythms and foods. Feasts for the spirits involve complex arrangements of these media to incarnate and modulate the presence of the spirit in the community. The most dramatic media for the *lwa* and *orishas* are the bodies of their human devotees, who, in the midst of the proper combination of rhythms and songs, lose individual consciousness and manifest the divine personalities of the spirits who are the "masters of their heads."

When vodou and santería first came to the United States with Haitian and Cuban immigrants the appeal of the religions was primarily to fellow immigrants who were familiar with the traditions in their homelands. The traditions had been maintained primarily by poor and black Haitians and Cubans who sustained the religions despite brutal campaigns of suppression. The houses became the dispensaries of services denied to their members in the racially stratified worlds of their homelands.

In the United States the houses of the spirits offered similar services for cultural survival, mutual aid, and spiritual fulfillment. Vodou and santería houses provided natural community centers where familiar idioms could be enjoyed. Priests and priestesses, trained as diagnosticians and herbalists, offered avenues for healthcare in the new and largely unresponsive environment. And the houses offered strategies of power, formulae for aligning the individual with the force of the *lwa* or *orishas* to secure a job, win a lover, or revenge an injustice. While the houses of the spirits continue to provide these services for the American-born children of the original immigrants, they have also offered spiritual opportunities to a variety of outsiders who have come in contact with the traditions for the first time in the United States.

An influential nonimmigrant initiate of African traditions is an African-American priest who has taken the name Oseijeman Adefunmi. In his own account of his initiation Oseijeman Adefunmi speaks of his involvement in the African nationalist movements in the New York of the 1950s.[4] Finding Christianity inalterably compromised by its participation in the enslavement and colonization of Africans, he was excited by the liberating philosophies of African statesmen such as Kwame Nkrumah and Léopold Senghor. He was looking for a spirituality that would speak to black men and women and found himself amazed to discover it among his Cuban neighbors in Harlem. He went to Cuba in 1959 and was initiated a priest of the *orisha*. He founded his own Yoruba Temple in New York and later a Yoruba village in the heartland of North America's African cultural roots, coastal South Carolina.

Oseijeman Adefunmi is one of many African Americans who have sought to re-Africanize the Caribbean traditions by attempting to remove the European elements that the traditions have gathered over their histories in Cuba or Haiti. Many African Americans have travelled to Africa to receive initiations there and thus establish lineages independent of the Caribbean teachers who first inspired men and women like Oseijeman Adefunmi. While the decision of any individual to commit himself or herself to a new religion is based on innumerable factors, for Oseijeman Adefunmi and many African Americans, spiritualities from Africa offer a return to roots, an authentic religion for black men and black women that will free them from the tyrannies of white cultural values.

White Americans as well as black Americans have been finding their way to vodou and santería houses. Though there are relatively few white initiates, it is likely that there will be many more as the religion becomes better known and spreads further beyond its immigrant roots. In a remarkable film, *Legacy of the Spirits* by Karen Kramer, several vodou initiates in New York speak before the camera of their involvement in the religion. A white woman speaks of her devotion to drumming and finding in vodou a place to express her love of music, of nature, and of the ritualism dear to her from her Catholic childhood. She concludes:

> We're not all blood relatives. In the house that I belong to ... I think that I'm probably the first white initiate ... but we have members from Barba-

dos and all over the West Indies and all over this country as well. So we're not all Haitians. But in the eyes of the *lwa* that doesn't matter because we're all one.[5]

While the most venerable priests and priestesses of vodou and santería are likely to be older, black, working people, who have emigrated from Haiti and Cuba, the next generation of initiates reflects the Americanization of the traditions. These newer members are much more likely to be middle-class, educated individuals—often intellectuals—who are finding in the movement not only urban survival skills but cultural empowerment and aesthetic pleasure. For the members of the traditions, beyond all these functions stands the reality of the *lwa* and *orishas,* life forces for the fulfillment of destiny.

The movement of the religions beyond the communities which brought them to the United States has brought a number of challenges to the traditions. Teaching within vodou and santería has been done orally, in the face-to-face context of initiation. The teachings are secret and available only to those who have been chosen by elders to receive them. With the arrival of the traditions in the mobile and frequently unstable social environment of North American cities, more and more charlatans are pretending to initiations which they have not undergone. These unsupervised impostors will often demand large sums of money for bogus services and the performance of initiations about which they know little. One solution to this crisis of authority may be resolved in the production of ritual texts. More and more houses are producing texts for the instruction of their initiates and the education of outsiders. It is likely that institutions will arise to attest to the reliability of the texts, preserve their transmission, and sanction their use.

As the existence of vodou and santería in the cities of the United States has come to the attention of outsiders, municipal authorities and mass media have reacted in much the same way that Moreau de St. Méry did nearly two hundred years ago. The perception of independent African spirituality is so deeply embedded in images of irrational violence that it is nearly impossible for outsiders to see the religions as they are. The most controversial element of vodou and santería in the eyes of outsiders is the slaughter of animals as part of feasts for the *lwa* and *orishas.* As with every communal interchange between spirits and human beings in vodou and santería, the symbolic elements are arranged according to rules that take many years to master. Most of the more important ceremonies require a feast to be prepared for the spirits and to be enjoyed by the assembled community. In order to fix the meal to the spirit's specifications, the foods must not only be prepared and cooked according to strict recipes, but they must be properly consecrated with certain prayers and rhythms. Animals for the feast—fowl, goats, and sheep—must be slaughtered by a priest or priestess initiated specially to this task, in the presence of the community, and to the accompaniment of the correct chants.

In the urban centers of the United States, particularly in the crowded neighborhoods of New York and Miami, this insistence on animal slaughter has caused a number of problems. Even when the ceremonies are conducted with traditional rigor and expertise, problems with the storage of the animals before the ceremony and the disposal of the remains afterward have spurred concerns on the part of municipal authorities. Yet these concerns have been molded by the history of fearful images of African spirituality. In 1987 the city of Hialeah, Florida, enacted a ban against "animal sacrifice," directly aimed at the growing santería community of the city. One santería house decided to challenge the ban and, despite losses in lower courts, brought the case before the Supreme Court in 1992. The city maintained that all the concerns of the wider community, issues of sanitation and animal cruelty, centered on the practice of "sacrifice," and thus a ban on "sacrifice" would meet these legitimate needs. The appellants argued that they were willing to satisfy all the health and humane interests of the community, through state inspections of slaughter and lawful disposal of remains, but that a ban on "sacrifice" was an infringement on the free exercise of religion. In June of 1993 the Supreme Court unanimously reversed the judgment of the lower courts and declared the Hialeah ordinances unconstitutional. The mayor of Hialeah said the city will initiate no further actions against the santería house, and its leaders look forward, in their words, to "institutionalizing the Santería religion."

Vodou and santería have yet to make a direct impact on the wider culture of the United States beyond the stereotypes of black magic and insurrection. A case could be made that the idioms of popular American music have their origins in the alternative spirituality of Southern black culture and so are informed by "voodoo." But it is only the stereotypes of irrationality and violence that have been accepted by the mainstream. George Bush's critique of Ronald Reagan's economic theories as "voodoo economics" continues to have currency as a term of contempt. I have been arguing that the tenacious fidelity to this image of African-derived traditions is more than ignorance, it is a willful ignorance that deliberately places independent black power "beyond the pale." Yet, as we have seen, many African Americans, and white Americans as well, are finding in vodou and santería a "righteous place." As America comes to terms with the multiple cultures which are shaping it, the traditions of vodou and santería are creating models for pluralistic views and modes of action. The *lwa* and *orishas* are providing a kind of archetypal imagery to compare, contrast, and integrate a variety of cultural experiences. Every year in New York and Miami conferences are held, public ceremonies are offered, and texts are produced by growing vodou and santería communities.

It will be interesting to see how houses of vodou and santería respond to this role. Already there are signs of strain in the movements between those who would "rectify" the religions through a return to strictly African models of practice and those who have accepted the multiple cultural layers that the religions have constructed.

In the first case the religions have the opportunity to become empowering foci for an alternative identity in an America dominated by white and "Anglo" power. In the second case the religions may offer what art historian Robert Farris Thompson calls the antidote for cultural balkanization, a way of corresponding the values of Fon and the Yoruba, African and European, white and black, Latino and Anglo.[6]

A possible future for the development of vodou and santería in the United States might be found in the rise of the Umbanda tradition in Brazil. Umbanda is a deliberately syncretic religion which uses the images of the *orishas* to construct a theological unity from the European, African, and Indian heritages of Brazil. Since its formulation in Rio de Janeiro in the 1920s Umbanda has grown to be considered the "national religion of Brazil," boasting thousands of independent houses throughout the country.[7] Umbanda's theology is flexible, and it can be quite complex, but its rituals are much-simplified versions of the African models of those for the *orishas*. Umbanda also eschews the more controversial elements of other African-derived traditions such as secret teachings and animal sacrifice.

While it is unlikely that the United States will witness in vodou and santería the amazing growth that Brazil has experienced in Umbanda, there are elements of Umbanda's modifications of African traditions that are likely. It is foreseeable that many houses will simplify the demanding ritual rules that have been in force. The spirit of entrepreneurship in Umbanda and the reliance on instruction by spirits rather than by human teachers will produce new houses with many modifications and innovations of the original doctrines. Finally Umbanda's rejection of animal sacrifice is already being taken up by reformist houses in the United States. Given the cultural and legal pressure against the practice, it is likely that many more people will consider themselves children of the spirits without offering the spirits the traditional sacrifices. Workshops in vodou and santería spirituality are already being offered in New Age retreats. It is likely that more and more white and middle-class Americans will become familiar with elements of the traditions in these denatured contexts.

Of course no tradition is "pure" and unaffected by the historical experience of those who pass it on. The vodou of the eighteenth century served very different people than that of the late twentieth. What began as a movement of cultural resistance and empowerment may become the focus for cultural integration. It may remain an inassimilable force for an alternative worldview, or it may be coopted to become another commodity in the spiritual supermarket. Whatever the changes, vodou and santería, by whatever names they come to be called, are in the United States for good. They are not a fad for their initiates who appreciate the history of their transmission and preservation against the racist powers that have tried to crush them. There will continue to be traditional houses where this history is understood and the veneration of the *lwa* and *orishas* is carried out with the dedication of the ancestors.

Notes

1. M. L. E. Moreau de St. Méry, *Description Topographique, Physique, Civile, Politique, et Historique de la Partie Francaise de l'Isle de St Domingue* (1797; reprint, Paris: Libraire Larose, 1958), 68–69.

2. Ivan van Sertima, *They Came Before Columbus* (New York: Random House, 1976).

3. Philip Curtin, *The Atlantic Slave Trade: A Census* (Madison: University of Wisconsin Press, 1969).

4. Oseijeman Adelabu Adefunmi, "The Orisha Tradition among Afro-Americans" (paper read at the First World Conference on the Orisha Tradition, Ife, Nigeria, 1981). See also Carl M. Hunt, *Oyotunji Village: The Yoruba Movement in America* (Washington, D.C.: University Press of America, 1979).

5. *Legacy of the Spirits,* produced and directed by Karen Kramer. Distributed by The Film Library, Wyckoff, N.J., 1986.

6. Robert Farris Thompson, "Divine Countenance: Afro-Atlantic Altars" (panel discussion on "Things that Do Things: Objects, Altars, and Sacred Spaces as Artistic Creations," National Museum of African Art, May, 1993).

7. See Diana DeG. Brown, *Umbanda: Religion and Politics in Brazil* (Ann Arbor, Mich.: UMI Research Press, 1986).

Suggestions for Further Reading

Barrett, Leonard E. *Soul Force: African Heritage in Afro-American Religion.* New York: Doubleday/Anchor, 1974.

Brown, Karen McCarthy. *Mama Lola: A Vodou Priestess in Brooklyn.* Berkeley: University of California Press, 1991.

Herskovits, Melville J. *The Myth of the Negro Past.* 1941. Reprint, Boston: Beacon Press, 1958.

Murphy, Joseph M. *Santería: An African Religion in America.* Boston: Beacon Press, 1988.

Simpson, George E. *Black Religions in the New World.* New York: Columbia, 1979.

Thompson, Robert Farris. *Flash of the Spirit: African and Afro-American Art and Philosophy.* New York: Random House, 1983.

29

THE RASTAFARI ABROAD

Barry Chevannes

In 1953 Rastafari was a small sect almost entirely confined to the west end of Kingston, the capital of Jamaica. Forty years later, in 1993, there were people in many parts of the world identifying themselves as Rasta. Following a brief introduction, this chapter presents a survey of the Rastafari outside of Jamaica, including the United States, and explains the factors accounting for this internationalization.

On the coronation in 1930 of Ras Tafari Makonnen as the Emperor of Ethiopia, Haile Selassie I, certain Jamaicans influenced by the popular teachings of Marcus Garvey, but equally also influenced by traditional African-Jamaican beliefs, concluded that Tafari was none other than the Returned Messiah. They based their arguments primarily on an alleged prophecy of Garvey that black people were to look to Africa for the crowning of a king as the sign that their redemption was at hand; but they were also moved by the biblical roots of the new emperor's titles and claims: King of Kings, Lord of Lords, Elect of God, Light of the World, Conquering Lion of the Tribe of Judah—biblical titles referring to the Messiah. The Ethiopian royal family in actual fact claimed descent from the Jewish King Solomon and the Kushite Queen Sheba.

From this simple origin, the Rastafarians,[1] as they eventually became known, grew into an important social and religious movement among rural migrants in the city of Kingston. The conviction that the black man, Selassie, was God was the main cornerstone on which they erected a new consciousness, for it empowered them to reject the popular conception of God as white, and of black skin color as a debility. Along with this belief came their well-known agitation for repatriation, that is the return to Africa, from where blacks were unlawfully and involuntarily forced into slavery by the Europeans. It is with this latter tenet in mind that most scholars have described the movement as millenarian, overlooking its profound impact as a cultural force in Jamaica and the African world generally. By the 1960s Rastafari became the most important social force among the urban youth and retained this position throughout the 1970s.[2]

Beginning late in the 1940s, a group of young militants, impatient with their elders, started a new trend that earned the designation "Dreadlocks," since their most distinguishing mark was their long matted hair, a symbol of their alienation from and aggressive attitude toward the society which they designated "Babylon," in reference to the biblical kingdom that had enslaved the nation of Israel.[3] By the 1970s Dreadlocks became synonymous with Rastafari.[4]

The aggressive attitude towards Jamaican society found expression in three attempts late in the 1950s to force repatriation to Africa. The last, the Claudius

Henry affair,[5] was blown up into a national crisis, the aftermath of which was to have a profound impact on the cultural development of the country. Rex Nettleford made himself available both as one of the three scholars to study the Rastafari in Kingston[6] and as one of the emissaries on a technical mission to Africa to conclude arrangements for the emigration of Jamaicans there. Nettleford followed closely the developments through the 1960s and argues that Rastafari agitation was in reality a dialogue with the society over the question of the cultural identity of Jamaica.[7] Given the Eurocentric biases and orientation of the upper and middle classes, Rastafari builds on and extends the Afrocentrism of the lower-class African majority in a struggle for supremacy. As such the African majority is up against the continuing racism that values everything white and devalues everything black. Or, as he put it, Jamaican culture is the "melody of Europe and the rhythm of Africa, or 'every john crow t'ink him pickney white,' " in reference to a Jamaican proverb which alludes disapprovingly to the tendency among some blacks to think that they are white (the "john crow" being a buzzard).

The results of this struggle are still unfolding, but progress has been recorded in getting Jamaicans to shed much, though by no means all, of their colonial legacy of mental enslavement and to identify positively with being black and a part of the African diaspora.[8] Now Rastafari has become an upwardly mobile movement that has attracted members of the middle classes,[9] not only because of its struggle on the question of racial identity, but also because of its philosophy of "ital livity." "Ital livity" rejects the artificiality of modern Western consumerism and opts for relationships and activities that harmonize more closely with nature: food grown without chemical fertilizers and cooked without salt, herbal remedies instead of manufactured pills and medicines, sexual intercourse without prophylactics, and so on; and on the moral level, a life guided by principles of integrity and straightforwardness. Indeed, these are some of the achievements of the Rastafari that make the group appealing on the international level.

Internationalization

As Ken Bilby has already observed, the spread of Rastafari outside of Jamaica has been due to the external migration of Jamaicans and to the internationalization of reggae music.[10] Bilby is correct of course, but to these must be added the role of the Caribbean integration movement, since Caribbeans were the first non-Jamaicans to adopt Rastafari. The circumstances facilitating this were twofold. First, there was the University of the West Indies, whose main campus located in Jamaica hosted hundreds of students from other islands. With Rastafari ideas becoming more and more commonplace in Jamaican cultural and political life throughout the 1960s and 1970s, inevitably many students were influenced and returned home the bearers of a new light. Second, there was the fleet of federal boats that used to ply the Caribbean, facilitating inter-island contact. Rastafari ideas were first taken back to St. Kitts in this way. By the time the reggae artistes were staging shows in the islands, the way had already been prepared. Dominica and Grenada were two islands in which Rastafari were making—some would say a negative—political impact by the end of the 1970s.[11]

But the first part of the world outside of the Caribbean where the Rastafari drew the attention of the establishment was Great Britain. There the children of Caribbean immigrants, confronted with racism and ethnocentricity, found in Rastafari an ideal source of cultural pride and identity, and a weapon with which to fight back. British society, unable to withstand the aggressive critique of a morally powerful social movement, at first retaliated by trying to criminalize it.[12] Both have since found common ground, and the Rastafari have been declared an ethnic group, with the right to wear their dreadlocks without fear of discrimination.[13]

Another European country to receive Caribbean migrants was the Netherlands. A few of the Surinamese who have settled in Amsterdam, Rotterdam, Utrecht, and other cities were Rastafari prior to leaving Suriname. Similarly, it is believed that many of the Rastafari in Paris were already Dreadlocks before leaving Martinique or Guadeloupe.

While migration may account for some Rastafari in the metropolitan countries, without doubt the main factor responsible for the growth of the movement there was the internationalization of reggae from a national music that evolved in Jamaica during the 1960s. During that evolution reggae became an ideal vehicle for the expression of Rastafari alienation from Jamaican society, what with the music's inherited tradition for social commentary. With Kingston already overcrowded by rural immigrants, unemployment doubling during the decade, and health, sanitation and other social conditions in the ghettoes at subhuman levels, the youth turned to the Rastafari, bringing into the movement the newly emerging music but taking from it the trenchant critique of the society. By the start of the 1970s, very few nationally recognized artistes were not also Dreadlocks. Among them was Bob Marley, the charismatic genius whose exposition of reggae was to become to many a listener the sacred presentation of all that mattered about life. To them Marley's music was not about Marley, but about Jah, about Rastafari, about truth, about justice.

Reggae music first made its international debut in England among the Caribbean immigrants, and from there it developed a following in Europe, where groups such as Boney M became exponents of reggae. In between local groups and touring bands and artistes from Jamaica, reggae aficionados could satisfy their tastes with the hundreds of recordings produced by an industry whose center gradually shifted from Jamaica to Britain by the 1980s. Reggae music is no longer exclusively Jamaican, though its leading artistes and composers are, and the association with Jamaica remains.

As a result of the internationalization of reggae, Rastafari has spread as far east as Japan and Australasia. Its presence in Africa is due primarily to the "reggae ambassadors,"[14] the Rastafari artistes, whose strong sense of identity with Africa resonates through the music. Zimbabweans had camped outside the stadium in Harare days before Bob Marley's concert there. And when Nelson and Winnie Mandela visited Jamaica in 1991 they paid tribute to the many Jamaican singers and composers whose songs they said gave succor to their struggle against apartheid. If Rastafari, many of them white, may be found outside Durban,[15] chances are that others may be found in the black townships of South Africa. In Zambia, at a park outside Lusaka, every September Zambian Rastafari stage their own version of the Jamaican summer festival called "Reggae Sunsplash." And in West Africa there are Rastafari in most countries of the region, including even some that are also Islamic.[16]

Although they are by no means a major factor, mention should be made of the presence of "missionary" groups of Jamaican Rastafari on the continent. The settlement at Shehamane in Ethiopia has been well known. In gratitude to the African diaspora for their support during the Italian invasion of Ethiopia, Emperor Haile Selassie made a grant of several hundred acres of land available to all those who wished to settle there. Rastafari from Jamaica have been there since the 1950s. In Ghana, the group of Rastafari known in Jamaica as the Bobo has established a presence.[17] It is not known what success they may be having in winning over Ghanaians and other Africans.

The growth of the Rastafari in the United States, like its growth elsewhere, is due to the factors cited above. However, owing to the fact that a larger number of Americans are themselves of African origin, its rootedness promises to be far deeper in the United States than in any other industrialized country. It also is more recent. None of the publications on new religious movements in the United States in the 1980s, by Petersen, Choquette, Melton, or Ellwood, make any mention of Rastafari.[18]

Although reggae artists from Jamaica were already touring the United States from the early 1970s, it was through an alleged criminal link that the American establishment began taking public notice of the Rastafari.[19] It began in 1979 with national exposure of a Miami-based group known as the Coptics, suspected as much for their prolific use of marihuana as for their trafficking in it. This was followed quickly by the leaking to the press of a "secret report" on the Rastas prepared as early as 1977 by the New York Police, and attributing to them the criminal violence of the Jamaican posses. What the author of the report if not the American press should have understood was that in Jamaica no one made the mistake of confusing the Rastafari and the urban youth, even though the street language and dreadlocks hair styles of the latter made them appear the same as the former. Thus, notwithstanding the rise of violent crimes in Jamaica, Rastafari has remained completely untarnished, thanks to the quiet and resourceful affirmation of "ital livity," which has become the badge of identification distinguishing "Rasta" from "Rascal," as the people themselves put it. In the United States, however, for most of the 1980s the American establishment, including the media to a large extent, tried to link the violence of the Jamaican posses to the Rastafari. Rastafari use of marihuana as a sacrament, likened to the communion wine of the Christian churches,[20] made it easier to do so.

Although much damage was done as a result of adverse publicity, Rastafari is set to win out in the end, as Americans come to understand the various aspects of the concept of livity. For this Rastafari owe much to the reggae ambassadors, in particular Bob Marley. As a new and attractive sound, reggae developed its own American following and soon many Americans were making the connection that others had been making in other parts of the world between reggae and Rasta.

Especially significant, particularly for African Americans, have been the dreadlocks. This public statement with one's hair could not be made without one's having first made an internal decision about one's identity, since dreadlocks take some time to grow.[21] Some members of the African-American intelligentsia and artistic community have taken this step, aided by increasing contact with migrant Rastafari leaders from Jamaica, or with Jamaica itself, through which the deeper dimensions of the Rasta lifestyle and position are realized.

Nevertheless, Rastafari at the international level is not the same as Rastafari in Jamaica. The most profound difference lies in the position of Haile Selassie. In Jamaica, belief in the divinity of the emperor has remained the most central aspect of Rastafari beliefs, even after his death. It could be argued that such profound impact as the Rasta movement has had in Jamaica could not have been possible without so fundamental a change in one's conception of God, that this is the origin and font of one's "emancipation from mental slavery." Outside Jamaica, on the other hand, very few hold to this belief in Haile Selassie, among them some Ethiopian Rastafari. Indeed, few non-Jamaican Rastafari would maintain the belief that he has not died. At best, most seem to think him a ruler who did much for Africa and for world peace.

Although research on the Rastafari diaspora has only just begun, it would seem that a second difference lies in the ritual process. In Jamaica, the Rastafari constitute a loose community of believers who are nurtured by a network of association formalized around a *nyabinghi,* or *binghi.* This is a ritual which brings together Dreadlocks several times a year on events in the Rastafari liturgical calendar, such as the anniversary of Haile Selassie's coronation or of his visit to Jamaica, for celebrations lasting at least three days. Ritual reasoning throughout the day and chanting to the beat of the drums at night are its main hallmarks. There is no evidence yet of formal religious worship among Rastafari outside of Jamaica, except in cities such as London and Atlanta where Jamaican Rastas have established themselves.

A third difference lies in the place of marihuana. Rastafari sacralization of this substance was culturally rooted in Jamaica. Brought to the country by Indian indentured laborers in the nineteenth century, marihuana, or *ganja,* the Indian name it goes by in Jamaica, was incorporated into the folk pharmacopoeia as a panacea. The Rastafari modified the Indian way of smoking it, turning it into an entirely different ritual.[22] Although the complete suppression of *ganja* is impossible because of its rootedness in folk practices and beliefs, official recognition of the Rastafari has been blocked because of their use of this illegal substance. In the United States, however, not much emphasis is given to the sacramental character of *ganja,* especially not when it is assumed that its users are also quite likely addicted to dangerous substances like cocaine, crack, and heroin.

Conclusion

Rastafari is a Third World religion that has won adherents in other parts of the world, especially the industrialized countries. Other Third World religions making similar headway are those from India and the Middle East, the various forms and offshoots of Hinduism and Islam. Rastafari represents a first for black Africa.

As the movement spreads outside Jamaica, it will undergo change. Already certain beliefs are being modified, for example those concerning Haile Selassie's divinity and immortality. These developments will have an impact on the movement even in Jamaica itself, as efforts will be made to establish networks and linkages between all its various manifestations.

Notes

1. They at first called themselves the "King of Kings" people. Today they prefer the designation "Rastafari" or "Rastas."

2. See Barry Chevannes, "The Rastafari and the Urban Youth," in *Perspectives on Jamaica in the Seventies,* ed. Carl Stone and Aggrey Brown (Kingston: Jamaica Publishing House, 1982).

3. See Barry Chevannes, *Rastafari: Roots and Ideology* (Syracuse: Syracuse University Press, 1994). Prior to this period most Rastafari, identifying black people as the biblical children of God, the Israelites, adopted the Nazarite vow—they combed but did not cut their hair.

4. On the significance of the hair, see "The Phallus and the Outcast," in *Rastafari and Other African-Caribbean World Views,* ed. Barry Chevannes (London: Macmillan, 1995).

5. See my "Repairer of the Breach: Reverend Claudius Henry and Jamaican society," in *Ethnicity in the Americas,* ed. Frances Henry (The Hague: Mouton, 1976).

6. See M. G. Smith, Roy Augier, and Rex Nettleford, *Report on the Rastafari Movement in Kingston, Jamaica* (Kingston: Extra-Mural Department, University of the West Indies, 1960).

7. Rex Nettleford, *Mirror, Mirror: Identity, Race and Protest* (Glasgow: Collins-Sangsters, 1970).

8. See Barry Chevannes, "The Case of Jah versus Jamaican Middle-Class Society," Institute of Social Studies Working Paper Series, no. 68 (The Hague, 1990).

9. See Frank Jan van Dijk, "The Twelve Tribes of Israel: Rasta and the Middle Class," *New West Indian Guide* 62, nos. 1 and 2 (1988).

10. Kenneth M. Bilby, "Black Thoughts from the Caribbean," *New West Indian Guide* 57, nos. 3 and 4 (1983).

11. For a survey of Rastafari in the Caribbean, see Horace Campbell, *Rastafari and Resistance: From Marcus Garvey to Walter Rodney* (London: Hansib Publishing Ltd.).

12. See E. E. Cashmore, *Rastaman* (London: George Allen and Unwin, 1979), and his "The De-Labelling Process: From 'Lost Tribe' to 'Ethnic Group,'" in *Rastafari and other African-Caribbean World Views,* ed. Barry Chevannes. Cashmore argues that Rastafari and British police (society) have both undergone internal and externally propelled changes that make them now able to live together.

13. Cashmore, "The De-Labelling Process."

14. The title of a song by Third World.

15. Personal communication from a South African student at the Institute of Social Studies in The Hague, July 1989.

16. Personal communication from Neil Savishinsky.

17. The Bobo are the only Rastafari to live a communal life. They distinguish themselves from mainstream Dreadlocks principally by wearing a turban at all times and a flowing robe sometimes, and by peddling brooms made of straw.

18. William J. Petersen, *Those Curious New Cults in the 80s* (New Canaan, Conn.: Keats, 1982); Diane Choquette, *New Religious Movements in the U.S. and Canada* (Westport, Conn.: Greenwood, 1985); J. Gordon Melton, *The Encyclopedic Handbook of Cults in America* (New York: Garland, 1986); Robert S. Ellwood and Harry B. Partin, *Religious and Spiritual Groups in Modern America,* 2d ed. (Englewood Cliffs, N.J.: Prentice-Hall, 1988).

19. See Chevannes, *Rastafari Origins,* for a more detailed survey of the Rastafari in the United States.

20. The *chillum* pipe is called a "chalice." To "lick a chalice" is to partake in a communal sharing of ideas, as the chalice passes from hand to hand. This sacred ritual is called a "reasoning."

21. Even the instant dreadlocks that may now be woven by hair stylists are not without their own statement. If nothing else, blacks, as never before, are finding pleasure in their own hair.

22. Indian men smoked *ganja* using the *chillum* only; Indian women smoked tobacco using the *huka* or water pipe. The Rastafari merged the two.

Suggestions for Further Reading

Barrett, Leonard E., Sr. *The Rastafarians.* Boston: Beacon Press, 1988.

Caribbean Quarterly Monograph: Rastafari. Kingston: University of the West Indies, 1985.

Chevannes, Barry. *Rastafari: Roots and Ideology.* Syracuse: Syracuse University Press, 1994.

———, ed. *Rastafari and Other African-Caribbean World Views.* London: Macmillan, 1993.

30

PEOPLES TEMPLE

John R. Hall

The two central questions about Peoples Temple have always been these: why did the murders and mass suicide take place? And what is their cultural significance? Peoples Temple began like many American religious groups—in the mind of a self-styled visionary prophet. But it ended in an apocalypse without precedent in U.S. religious history. On November 18, 1978, over nine hundred people from the United States died in the small, poor South American country of Guyana. On that day gunmen from Peoples Temple's communal settlement of Jonestown murdered five people who had just left their jungle community—a visiting U.S. congressman, three newsmen, and a young defector. Back at Jonestown, Jim Jones, Peoples Temple's white charismatic leader, was orchestrating a "revolutionary suicide" at which the members of the agricultural community—mostly black, some white—drank a deadly potion of Fla-Vor Aid laced with poison. How many people willingly gave up their lives at Jonestown? The question will always be open to debate. Certainly young children could not have fully understood the consequences of drinking the potion, and during the suicide council, one woman pleaded against Jones's proposal. But many people supported the plan—mothers marching up to have their children killed, elderly people telling Jones they were ready to go, the sharpshooters who had killed the congressman. Wittingly, unknowingly,

or reluctantly, virtually everyone present took the poison. At the very end, Jim Jones and a close aide died by gunshots to the head, consistent with suicide.[1]

If these tragic events had not occurred, Peoples Temple might never have become the subject of widespread attention. But with the murders and mass suicide, the group became infamous. A film, a television docudrama and more than twenty books enshrined Jim Jones in popular culture as the image incarnate of the AntiChrist, Peoples Temple as the paragon of the religious "cult." Like other religious communal movements—both historical and contemporary—Peoples Temple practiced a way of life alien to mainstream America. Like other collectivist organizations such as religious orders and the military, the Temple demanded individual submission to collective authority and it used social control to forestall internal dissension. Temple staff carefully monitored the commitment of members, and they held public meetings for "catharsis," allowing the assembled populace to determine punishments for wrongdoers and backsliders. Like other religious social movements Peoples Temple practiced a communal socialism that flew in the face of the dominant American ideology that embraces capitalism, individualism, and the nuclear family.

In the early years, the Jones family expanded through adoption. Eventually,

Peoples Temple as a group took on the functions of an extended family. More significantly, Jim Jones was bisexual, and he led the way in exploring unconventional relationships. Sex became something like a currency Jones used, supposedly, "for the cause." With it, he gave some people intimacy, and controlled or humiliated others. The offspring of Jones's sexual unions included Stephan, the one child born (in 1959) to Jones's wife Marcie. In addition, Jones was the father of Carolyn Layton's son Kimo Prokes, and he was widely believed to be the father of John Victor Stoen, born in 1972 to Grace Stoen, wife of Temple attorney Tim Stoen.

Quite apart from his controversial sexual practices, Jones called his followers to what Max Weber has termed an "ethic of ultimate ends": he recruited only the most highly committed individuals, and he insisted that followers pursue the cause of Peoples Temple selflessly, tirelessly, without compromise. Members of Peoples Temple in effect took a path that black activist Huey Newton had once described as "revolutionary suicide": they gave up their previous lives, friends, and commitments, and became born again to a collective struggle against economic, social, and racial injustice that had no limits other than victory or death. This radical stance deepened the gulf between Peoples Temple and the wider society and set the stage for a protracted conflict with organized opponents who were equally committed to their own cause. It was specifically this conflict that led to the murders and mass suicide. How, then, did it develop? This question can only be addressed by tracing the biography of Jim Jones and the historical emergence of his movement.

James Warren Jones was born in east central Indiana in the time of the Great Depression, May 13, 1931. The only child of working-poor parents, he grew up with a strong sense of resentment toward people of wealth, status, and privilege. He was exposed to a variety of Protestant churches, from the mainstream Methodists to the pacifist Quakers, the Holiness-movement Nazarenes, and the then-marginal Pentecostalists with their revivalist-style

worship and speaking in tongues. In his high school years, Jones was seen preaching on the street in a factory neighborhood of Richmond, Indiana, to an audience of both whites and blacks. By the summer of 1949, Jim Jones had married Marceline Baldwin, a young nurse from a Richmond family of Methodists and Republicans. Marcie was shocked, Jones later recounted, when he revealed his sympathies with political communism and his disdain for the "sky god."

Jim and Marcie Jones moved to Indianapolis in 1951, and soon Jones was on his way to becoming a preacher. Along this path, Jones forged a volatile mix of theology and practice. Exposed variously to the Methodists' liberal social creed, communist ideology, and the apocalyptic vision of the Pentecostalists, he preached racial integration and a veiled communist philosophy within a Pentecostal framework that emphasized gifts of the spirit—discerning of spirits and faith healing. Jones displayed a knack for preaching, and he learned some tricks of the Pentecostal revival circuit—how to convince audiences of his abilities in matters of discernment and faith healing by sleights of hand and fakery. More important, he gradually discovered a formula for building a social movement out of a church. Over the years, out of an unlikely amalgamation of disparate ideas and practices, Jones forged the mantle of a prophet who foresaw capitalist apocalypse and worked to establish a promised land for those who heeded his message.

Organizationally, Jones started in Indianapolis with a small church called Community Unity. After visitors took in his services following a revival appearance, Jones was invited to preach at the Pentecostalist Laurel Street Tabernacle. A crisis ensued when Jones brought blacks to the service of the racially segregated church, and after witnessing his preaching and healing performance, a substantial segment of the Tabernacle voted with their feet, leaving their congregation to walk with Jones. Together, on April 4, 1955, they established Wings of Deliverance, the corporate vehicle of what was to be called

Peoples Temple. Combining the Pentecostalist ethic of a caring community with the social gospel of liberal denominations, Peoples Temple became a racially integrated community of believers in practical service under the umbrella of a church. Jones modelled Peoples Temple partly after the Peace Mission of American black preacher Father M. J. Divine, who, in the 1920s and 1930s, had established a racially integrated religious and economic community with himself at the center. Like Father Divine, Jones took to being called "Father," or, sometimes, "Dad." Like the Peace Mission, Peoples Temple was to become an extended family that offered its communal fellowship as a shelter from the uncertain world beyond. In turn, Jones used the organization of Peoples Temple as a springboard to social action, establishing care homes for the elderly, running a free restaurant to feed the hungry, maintaining a social service center to help people with needs to get their lives back together, and precipitating public confrontations to promote racial integration. The unconventional congregation attracted the attention of the Christian Church (Disciples of Christ), which long had been committed to a social ministry. In 1960, Peoples Temple became affiliated with the Disciples of Christ, and in 1964 Jones was officially ordained a minister.

Peoples Temple not only prospered in Indianapolis, it provoked controversy. The city was not a progressive one, and there was staunch resistance to racial integration in some quarters. By publicly challenging segregationist policies, Jones antagonized this opposition and enhanced his own status as a civil rights leader. To demonstrate what a threat he was to white racists, he also staged incidents in which his family and he were objects of harassment. But some of the harassment was real, and Jones does not seem to have held up well under the pressure. In the face of the public tensions, he was hospitalized for an ulcer in the fall of 1961. After his release, he began to seek a way out of Indianapolis. Leaving his congregation in the care of associate pastors, Jones and his family visited British Guiana (pre-independence

Guyana), and spent two years in Brazil. Even as he returned to Indianapolis in 1964, Jones already was laying the groundwork for a collective migration to California by his most committed followers. Tired of racial intolerance and citing fears of nuclear holocaust, they moved to the quiet town of Ukiah, in the Russian River valley of northern California. About seventy families, half white, half black, made the journey in the summer of 1965.

Jones's congregation became reestablished slowly, counting only 168 adult members by 1968. But in 1969 the congregation completed its own church building in the hamlet of Redwood Valley, about eight miles north of Ukiah. The church began to attract the interest of a wide range of people—hippies, socially concerned progressive professionals, fundamentalist Christians, political activists and militants, street people, delinquents, and the elderly. Propelled by these diverse streams of membership the Temple grew rapidly in the 1970s, establishing churches in San Francisco and Los Angeles, running a fleet of buses to carry followers to church functions, running a "human services" ministry of "care" homes for juveniles and the elderly, and using the care homes as a nucleus for promoting a communal orientation among followers.

By its California heyday in the mid-1970s, Peoples Temple had become a collectivist organization that pooled the economic resources of highly committed members. In return, the Temple offered them an extended, collectivist "family," economic security, and a meaningful life. By the power of their organized efforts, it energized an activist religious social movement committed to racial integration, social and economic justice, peace, and other progressive and radical political causes. In comparison to both conventional churches and retreatist countercultural communal groups of its day, Peoples Temple was an anomaly—a relatively disciplined religiously radical collective that successfully pursued an activist politics within the society at large. By 1975 Peoples Temple was a formidable force in the left-liberal political surge that propelled George Moscone into office as mayor of San Francisco. In 1976 the Temple reaped political rewards: Temple attorney Tim Stoen was called from his position as assistant district attorney in Mendocino County to prosecute voter fraud for the San Francisco district attorney; and Jim Jones was appointed to the San Francisco Housing Authority Commission by Mayor Moscone.

Peoples Temple was a dynamic, growing group by the mid-1970s, but its success depended on using public relations techniques to create a facade that hid its more radical aspects. And for all its worldly success, its status in the larger society was precarious. Because of the Temple's complex communal economic practices, its leadership began to be concerned in 1975 that the group would be charged with tax evasion by the U.S. Internal Revenue Service. Moreover, like many other alternative religious social movements, both historical and contemporary, Peoples Temple garnered considerable opposition—both from defectors and from scandalized outsiders.

Beginning in Indianapolis, Jones projected the belief that his racially integrated group of followers could not survive in their surroundings. Like Moses and the ancient Jews searching for a land of "milk and honey," like the Puritans who fled to North America from England to found a "city on a hill," Jones sought redemption for his followers in collective religious migration to a promised land. Indeed, Jones explicitly borrowed the term "promised land" from Father Divine, who had established a series of agricultural communities called the Promised Land in upstate New York during the 1930s. Divine himself was one of a series of "black messiahs" (another was Marcus Garvey) who promised blacks salvation from the racism of a country to which their people had been brought forcibly as slaves.[2] But Jones's promised land was not only to be a refuge for blacks; it came to represent a sanctuary from the United States, portrayed by Jones as Babylon.

Peoples Temple operated *in* the world, yet Jones never expected acceptance *from* the world. From the Indianapolis years on-

ward, he promised his followers that Peoples Temple would protect them from a hostile outside world. To accomplish that protection, and to separate the truly committed from backsliders, Jones twice drew on the enduring recipe of those (like the Puritans) who claim to be victims of religious persecution—collective migration. First, the Temple moved to California. There, Jones used internal defections and small incidents of external "persecution" during 1972 and 1973 as the warrant to establish Peoples Temple's "Promised Land"—an "agricultural mission" eventually called Jonestown—in a remote corner of Guyana, an ethnically diverse, socialist-governed South American country oriented toward the Caribbean.

At its inception, Jonestown was just a pioneer camp. But even before the site was established in early 1974, a memo by Temple attorney Tim Stoen suggested that the Temple should methodically prepare for collective migration by consolidating its property holdings and other affairs in the United States; the group was to remain in California "until first signs of outright persecution from press or government," then "start moving all members to mission post." In practice, the Temple followed the basic thrust of this plan. The initial settlers devoted most of their efforts toward construction of housing and other facilities to accommodate a large influx of settlers, while Temple operatives in Guyana's capital of Georgetown used their public relations and political skills (and sexual allure) to establish secure political alliances with members of the patrimonial socialist regime of the black prime minister, Forbes Burnham.

In the summer of 1977 Jones ordered the collective migration for which the Temple had begun preparing years earlier. At the time, it was widely believed that they left California because of press exposés appearing in California's *New West* magazine and other media outlets. The exposés were fueled in part through information provided by Temple defectors and outside relatives, and in part by conservative efforts to unseat liberal San Francisco mayor George Moscone, with whom Jones and the Temple were allied. It was the defectors who offered the inside view: they accused Peoples Temple of shady financial dealings, faked healings, and atrocities of psychological catharsis and physical punishment.

In addition to their other concerns, in the press exposés the opponents raised the issue of custody rights over children in Peoples Temple. Most notable of these was the child born to Grace Stoen, John Stoen, who had been raised communally within the Temple as a son of Jim Jones. In July of 1976 Grace Stoen had defected from the Temple, leaving her husband and her son behind. In the fall of 1976, the legal father, Grace's husband Tim Stoen, signed a power-of-attorney form for John Stoen, appointing Jim Jones and others "to exercise all powers and rights, that I might do in connection with said minor." The four-and-a-half-year-old boy was then taken to live at Jonestown. These events set the stage for a custody struggle over John Stoen, and this struggle became the most celebrated among a series of custody battles that eventually raised the question of whether adults at Jonestown were there of their own free will.

Although the collective migration took place during the press exposés, it would be a mistake to assume that the exposés caused the migration. There was a different sequence of events, driven by other aspects of the conflict between Peoples Temple and the small but increasingly coherent group of grassroots opponents. The leadership of Peoples Temple actually undertook the migration because of their concerns about a U.S. government investigation of the Temple's tax status. In the years of preparing for migration, the Temple had gone to considerable lengths to keep "black people's money" out of the hands of the Internal Revenue Service. By the standards of poor people, they had created substantial collective wealth (between ten and fifteen million dollars) by collectivizing the financial and housing donations of committed members who "went communal." The Temple was using the resources to finance Jonestown and the migration, and it was shifting millions of dollars into overseas bank accounts beyond the reach of authorities in the United States.

In early 1976, the Temple sought to clarify its tax situation with the IRS. Over a year later, in early March, 1977, the IRS finally notified the Temple that it had been denied tax-exempt status. Soon thereafter, the opponents unintentionally substantiated the Temple's longstanding concerns about its tax status: in late March of 1977, they revealed to a Temple ally, American Indian Movement (AIM) leader Dennis Banks, that the Temple was the subject of a U.S. Treasury Department investigation (itself initiated by a reporter, George Klineman, who had close ties to the Temple's opponents). Mistakenly, the Temple leadership took their opponents' "treasury agent" to be connected with the Temple's tax situation (the opponents actually had talked with a Customs Service agent). Faced with what they regarded as a serious governmental threat to their organization, Temple leaders launched final preparations for the migration. In the glare of the media spotlight, the collective migration began in earnest in July of 1977 and was effectively completed by September (a steady trickle of immigrants continued to arrive in Jonestown through October of 1978).

There is no way of knowing how Jonestown would have developed as a communal settlement in the absence of its conflict with opponents. The migration to Guyana did not cut the Temple off from its detractors; it simply shifted the dynamics of a struggle that eventually culminated in the murders and mass suicide. In the aftermath of the 1977 migration, the increasingly organized opponents continued to feed information about the Temple to reporters and government investigators; they filed requests that the U.S. embassy in Guyana check on the welfare of their relatives in Jonestown; and they initiated court proceedings both in the United States and Guyana to try to obtain legal custody of Jonestown children. One father even tried to kidnap his adult daughter from the communal settlement.

The most famous case was that of the "child-god," John Victor Stoen. In the summer of 1978, Temple attorney Tim Stoen, the legal father by California law, went over to the camp of Temple opponents. On August 26 a California court granted custody to Grace Stoen. Her lawyer then travelled to Guyana. When people at Jonestown refused to hand over John Stoen, the lawyer obtained a court summons for Jim Jones and the child. In Jonestown, Jones responded with a dramaturgical state of siege. Reaffirming his paternity of John Stoen, he threatened death: "I related to Grace, and out of that came a son. That's part of the deal. The way to get to Jim Jones is through his son. They think that will suck me back or cause me to die before I'll give him up. And that's what we'll do, we'll die." Through political and legal maneuvering, Temple staff managed to vacate the court order (it had been made despite the fact that Grace Stoen had never revoked a standing grant of custody to a Temple member). The crisis abated.

In the aftermath, the legal process in Guyana seemed to stall, and in the months that followed, the frustrated Temple opponents, with the increasingly active participation of Tim Stoen, turned to methods that Peoples Temple had used so effectively in the United States—political pressure and public relations campaigns. Calling themselves the "Concerned Relatives," they wrote to members of Congress, they met with State Department officials, they organized human rights demonstrations. In the face of these efforts, the Temple's siege mentality hardened. In March, 1978, a Temple letter to members of Congress stated, "I can say without hesitation that we are devoted to a decision that it is better even to die than to be constantly harassed from one continent to the next. I hope that you can protect the right of over 1,000 people from the U.S. to live in peace." A woman who defected from Jonestown in May of 1978, Debbie Blakey, told an embassy official and the Concerned Relatives that Jonestown was developing plans for a mass suicide and the murder of resisters. In turn, the Concerned Relatives publicized the diehard threats to raise the alarm against Jonestown. For the most part, their efforts accomplished nothing. United States

embassy officials in Guyana checked up on the status of relatives in Jonestown, but they did not find evidence for the opponents' charges of mass starvation and people living in bondage. One embassy consul observed, "The Concerned Relatives had a credibility problem, since so many of their claims were untrue."

Frustrated in both their legal efforts and their attempts to get the U.S. State Department and its embassy to take their side in the complex dispute, yet propelled by the belief that Jones had to be stopped, the Concerned Relatives increasingly pinned their hopes on political intervention. In Washington they attracted the active support of Leo Ryan, a San Mateo congressman already sympathetic to the U.S. anticult movement. In December, 1977, Congressman Ryan had written U.S. Secretary of State Cyrus Vance, asking him "to investigate what action might be taken in connection with Mr. Jones." The State Department had responded by describing the situation as a legal controversy that did not warrant any "political action without justification." Ryan rejected this view. In May of 1978 he wrote to Peoples Temple, "Please be advised that Tim Stoen does have my support in the effort to return his son from Guyana." Then Ryan began to work with members of the Concerned Relatives to organize a visit to Jonestown.

The expedition formally was billed a congressional delegation (although it did not meet congressional criteria). Diverse motives shaped it. At least two opponents, Tim Stoen and Steve Katsaris, wanted to retrieve their relatives "by force if necessary," as Stoen put it. A less-clandestine strategy hinged on the opponents' accounts about desperate conditions at Jonestown; in this scenario, the presence of visiting relatives together with outside authorities would break Jones's discipline and result in a mass exodus. The press had agendas too. Don Harris, a soldier-of-fortune journalist, organized an NBC crew to cover a story about people trapped in a jungle commune. With a congressman and the newsmen making the trip, the expedition promised to confront Jones with the choice of either submitting to external scrutiny or precipitating a flood of bad press and governmental inquiry.

When Peoples Temple staff first learned of the planned expedition, they sought to negotiate conditions about press coverage and the composition of the congressional delegation. But Ryan considered the negotiations a delaying tactic, and he decided to proceed to Guyana with the group of Concerned Relatives and the news reporters. They would try to gain access to Jonestown once they reached the capital, Georgetown. But there, Ryan met further resistance. With time running out before he would have to return to the United States, he flew with the reporters and a subgroup of the Concerned Relatives to Port Kaituma, a small settlement near Jonestown. Faced with a fait accompli, Jones acquiesced to the visit.

At Jonestown, Jim Jones already had coached his community for days about how to respond to the visitors. On the evening of November 17, Jonestown offered Ryan and the others an orchestrated welcome, serving up a good dinner and musical entertainment from The Jonestown Express. But during the festivities, a message was passed to NBC reporter Don Harris: "Help us get out of Jonestown." The note was signed "Vern Gosney." On the reverse side was the name "Monica Bagby." The next day, Jonestown staff tried to occupy the visitors with public relations activities. But Ryan and embassy staff began to make arrangements for Gosney and Bagby to leave. Don Harris then tipped off Leo Ryan's assistant, Jackie Speier, about members of the Parks family, who also might want to leave. Jones pleaded with the Parkses not to depart with his enemies; he offered them $5,000 to cover transportation if they would wait several days. But they decided to leave with Ryan. "I have failed," Jones muttered to his lawyer, Charles Garry. "I live for my people because they need me. But whenever they leave, they tell lies about the place."

As a dump truck was loaded for departure, Ryan told Jones that he would give a basically positive report: "If two hundred people wanted to leave, I would still say you have a beautiful place here." Ryan spoke about the need for more interchange with the outside world. Suddenly blood spurted across his white shirt as bystanders disarmed a man attacking Ryan. Jones stood impassively by. Ryan was disheveled but unhurt; the attacker was Don Sly, former husband of a Concerned Relative named Neva Sly; he had accidentally cut himself, not Ryan. "Does this change everything?" Jones asked Ryan. "It doesn't change everything, but it changes things," Ryan replied. "You get that man arrested." Then embassy official Richard Dwyer led Ryan to the departing truck, and they piled in with the reporters, the four representatives of the Concerned Relatives, and sixteen people who had decided to leave Jonestown.

When the truck reached the Port Kaituma airstrip and the travelers started loading into two planes, a Jonestown man posing as a defector pulled out a pistol in the smaller plane and started shooting. Simultaneously, a tractor came up pulling a flatbed; from it the Jonestown sharpshooters shot toward the other plane. Left dead were Congressman Leo Ryan, NBC reporter Don Harris, two other newsmen, and defector Patricia Parks. At Jonestown, Jim Jones told the assembled community that they would no longer be able to survive as a community. With a tape recorder running, Jones argued, "If we can't live in peace, then let's die in peace." Medical staff set up cauldrons of Fla-Vor Aid laced with cyanide and tranquilizers while Jones called taking the poison "a revolutionary act." One woman named Christine Miller spoke up against the plan, but she was outnumbered by others who argued in favor. Amidst low wails, sobbing, and the shrieks of children, people walked up to take the "potion," then moved out of the pavilion to huddle with their families and die. In the confusion, two black men slipped past the guards. The community's two American lawyers, Charles Garry and Mark Lane, sequestered at a perimeter house, plunged into the jungle. Everyone else died.

The proximate cause of murder and mass suicide was the refusal of Jim Jones, his staff, and the loyalists among his followers to brook compromise with opponents whom they believed were out to bring Jonestown as a community to an end. Rather than submit to external powers that they regarded as illegitimate, they chose to stage the airstrip murders as revenge and shut out their opponents by ending their own lives. Their socialist community unraveling in the face of pitched opposition, they sought revolutionary immortality. In the popular mind, they achieved infamy instead. The stigma of the mass deaths carved this infamy in the narrative structure of myth. If Jim Jones were anything other than a megalomaniacal madman or AntiChrist, if Peoples Temple were anything but a cult of brainwashed robots, then the stigma of avoidable carnage would not necessarily fall on Jones and his accomplices alone. Either the story of Jonestown would have to be told as an atrocity tale or an unthinkable question would have to be posed: Did the people of Jonestown have the right to live in isolation from the intervention of opponents who sought to dismantle their community?

Roland Barthes once observed that myth has an important quality: "The reader lives the myth as a story at once true and unreal."[3] Put differently, history is much messier than any story that reduces it to myth. Thus, the popular accounts of Peoples Temple have been displaced by the accumulation of careful scholarly research on Peoples Temple by theologians, historians, sociologists, and other students of religion. Compared to our knowledge of many other alternative American religions, we have a quite detailed historical record. To be sure, there is still much potentially important research to be done. Particularly important issues are the factual question of the biological paternity of John Stoen and the broader question of the role of government agencies in the opposition. Much anecdotal evidence suggests that Jim Jones was indeed the biological father of John Stoen: this view was held even by certain people outside the Temple who knew Grace and Tim Stoen at the time of the child's birth. It was affirmed in an affidavit by Tim Stoen in 1972 shortly after the birth, taken as fact within the

Temple, and only publicly denied by Tim Stoen much later, when he took the side of Grace Stoen in the custody battle. To date, the evidence is not completely conclusive, but the weight of it leans, in my view, to Jones as the father. If this is so, then one of the Concerned Relatives' central atrocity contentions—that Jones amounted to a kidnapper—would lose its moral force, and one significant element of their campaign against Peoples Temple would turn out to be based on a public construction of reality that differed from privately held knowledge.

The second controversy—about government agencies—is even murkier. The Concerned Relatives mobilized some governmental interest in Peoples Temple. But some government initiatives preceded the advent of the Concerned Relatives, and the inquiries of various government agencies fed on one another. In particular, early on the U.S. embassy in Guyana had diplomatic and strategic concerns that led to monitoring the Jonestown settlement. Both because the government might have been able to prevent the tragedy and because it may have acted in ways that propelled it, there has been considerable speculation about the government's role. One book weaves together some well-established facts with highly questionable inferences to raise the question of whether Jonestown was a "CIA medical experiment."[4] Whatever the truth of the matter, such accounts cannot be easily assessed because the U.S. government has suppressed information about its dealing with Peoples Temple, partly on the basis of the sensitivity of its diplomatic and geopolitical interests in relation to the socialist government of Guyana. Opening the government files on Peoples Temple might well yield significant reassessments of its history (the same holds for the NBC video "outakes" from the Jonestown coverage).

Whatever comes of further research, the popular myth about Peoples Temple already has been substantially revised. Immediately after the mass suicides, popular accounts portrayed the Concerned Relatives, Leo Ryan, and the press that visited Jonestown as tragic heroes. Yet it is now evident that their own actions were consequential in affecting the course of events. Thus, the murders and mass suicide cannot be adequately explained except as the outcome of an unfolding and interactive conflict between two diametrically opposed groups—Peoples Temple and the Concerned Relatives. In this conflict, the Concerned Relatives were able to marshall to their side significant allies within the established social order—the press, governmental investigators, a congressman. It is now possible to see more clearly what was obscured by the popular myth. The apocalypse at Jonestown is an extreme case of a more general pattern of religious conflict between a new religious movement and established social interests. In this pattern (found in the history of the Puritans and the Mormons, for example), collective religious migration is a strategy employed by the religious movement when conflict erupts between the movement and opponents who regard it as threatening to an established social and moral order.

Peoples Temple ended with the mass suicides. It made its historical mark not like the Puritans and the Mormons, by success, but by dramatic failure. Yet this organization was infused with many of the contradictions of American culture, and in these terms its cultural legacy is defined by the public understanding of Peoples Temples. It is a legacy that keeps changing. After the murders and mass suicide, Jonestown became the quintessence of the "cult." Jonestown undoubtedly shifted the circumstances of other alternative religions in subtle yet profound ways, for it confirmed the most dire warnings of the anticult movement. But Jonestown has also inspired radically different understandings. The cultural significance of the movement is deeply intertwined with certain central issues of American social history, most notably, (1) the status of blacks within a racially divided society, (2) the character and mission of religion in an increasingly secular society, (3) the agendas and strategies of left-liberal political movements, and (4) social and ethical issues about the character of welfare, bureaucratic organization, social control, politics, and public relations in a society where Jones borrowed many of his most questionable practices from the wider culture, but directed them to countercultural purposes. Because of the complex connections between Jones's world and ours, Peoples Temple is a benchmark by which to chart American cultural practices and religious development.

Notes

1. Information for the present chapter is drawn largely from my book-length study, John R. Hall, *Gone From the Promised Land: Jonestown in American Cultural History* (New Brunswick, N.J.: Transaction Books, 1987).

2. William Jeremiah Moses, *Black Messiahs and Uncle Toms: Social and Literary Manipulations of a Religious Myth* (University Park: Pennsylvania State University Press, 1982).

3. Roland Barthes, *Mythologies* (New York: Hill and Wang, 1972), 128.

4. Michael Meiers, *Was Jonestown a CIA Medical Experiment?* (Lewiston, N.Y.: Edwin Mellen Press, 1988).

Suggestions for Further Reading

Chidester, David. *Salvation and Suicide: An Interpretation of Jim Jones, the Peoples Temple, and Jonestown.* Bloomington: Indiana University Press, 1988.

Hall, John R. *Gone from the Promised Land: Jonestown in American Cultural History.* New Brunswick, N.J.: Transaction, 1987.

———. Afterword to "The Apocalypse at Jonestown." In *Gods We Trust*, edited by Thomas Robbins and Dick Anthony, 290–293. New Brunswick, N.J.: Transaction, 1988.

Moore, Rebecca, and Fielding McGeehee III, eds. *New Religious Movements, Mass Suicide, and Peoples Temple.* Lewiston, N.Y.: Edwin Mellen Press, 1988.

Part VI
Ancient Wisdom and New Age Movements

Since the mid-nineteenth century many alternative religions have arisen claiming to have acquired new spiritual insight and wisdom from heretofore hidden sources, some allegedly of ancient vintage, or to have reconstructed longstanding religious teachings in ways believed to be especially suited to the contemporary world.

The earliest of the movements treated in the following chapters was Spiritualism, which is usually traced to "rappings" heard by two sisters in 1848. In the following years it became a cultural phenomenon, gathering a formidable following and igniting a good deal of controversy; then it subsided somewhat, only to be revived in the 1970s and 1980s under the name of "channeling." Out of the nineteenth-century phase of Spiritualism emerged Theosophy, formally organized in 1875 as the Theosophical Society, which combined Western Neoplatonism and occultism with other esoterica and insights from Eastern religions, notably Hinduism, and which continues to flower in diverse places and ways. A related development that appeared about the same time as Theosophy was New Thought, which emphasized the power of mind over all physical reality and which like Theosophy has had a strong following ever since, although the following has been split among many diverse organizations and locations. In the twentieth century the psychic Edgar Cayce stood out among the many investigators of the paranormal; his work has been carried on by the Association for Research and Enlightenment.

The great cultural explosion of the 1960s saw several new additions to this religious panorama. Many elements of existing ancient wisdom and metaphysical groups were leavened by hippie culture and combined with innovative insights and approaches to produce the nearly indefinable cluster of schools of thought known as the New Age movement. Paul Twitchell announced the arrival of ECKANKAR, which had roots in the Indian Radhasoami tradition and offered its adherents nearly limitless spiritual power, including that of soul travel to other worlds. At the same time the mystical, eclectic spirituality propounded by the hippies in America and elsewhere helped spawn the largest wave of communal living in American history, one whose thousands of outposts were predominantly spiritual—in some sense—in nature; hundreds of them, including the largest, the Farm in Tennessee, are still alive and well today.

Yet another array of new religions arrived on the scene in the 1960s and 1970s under the heading of neo-paganism. Many of its adherents called themselves witches, determined to rehabilitate that long-standing pejorative, and they found a substantial following attracted to their program of a mystical experience of nature, preservation of the environment, and strong feminism. In all, the groups and movements presented in this section are marvelously diverse and ever-changing representatives of the ongoing spiritual quest of humankind.

31

THEOSOPHY
Robert S. Ellwood

The modern Theosophical impulse has been among the most influential of new religious and spiritual movements in the nineteenth and twentieth centuries. Since its founding in New York in 1875, the Theosophical Society in its several branches and devolutions has not only itself been spiritual home to thousands of persons of alternative religious interests, it has also provided models and doctrines for many subsequent groups. Probably more than any other single activity, it has been Theosophy that has made several generations of Americans reasonably familiar with such concepts as astrology, karma, and reincarnation, together with the general idea of spiritual masters and inner spiritual initiations. Through travelling lecturers and gifts of books to public libraries, Theosophy brought the attention of seekers to its offerings not only in such redoubts of the esoteric as Boston, New York, or Los Angeles, but also in smaller towns and cities across the country. In 1900, for example, there were branches of the Theosophical Society in such places as Pierre, South Dakota, and Sheridan, Wyoming, busy with discussions on matters like karma and the astral plane.

Spiritual movements can be traced back through almost infinite regressions, and Theosophy is no exception. Its particular version of the Ancient Wisdom (as it likes to call its doctrine), containing material from Neoplatonism, the Kabbala, and East-ern sources, became mother to much that came later. But Theosophy in turn was the daughter of much that went before. Setting aside for the moment its ultimate primordial sources, the teaching associated with the 1875 society was a synthesis of current occultism—as was freely acknowledged—together with, added a few years later, new teaching coming in from the East.

Most directly, Theosophy was the offspring of the mid-century vogue for Spiritualism. Helena Blavatsky, catalyst and co-founder of the Theosophical Society, and Henry Steel Olcott, another co-founder, had both previously taken an avid interest in Spiritualism, and in fact met at the home of the dour Eddy brothers in Vermont, where Spiritualistic phenomena were allegedly taking place, in 1874. Much early Theosophical writing, especially by Blavatsky, is designed to show the difference between Spiritualist doctrine and practice and that of Theosophy, while pointing to the former's importance as precursor.

The Spiritualism which began in 1848 with mysterious rappings at the modest home of the Fox sisters, and the writings of Andrew Jackson Davis, can itself be considered an amalgamation of the visionary instruction of Emanuel Swedenborg, the Swedish seer, concerning the life of the soul and other worlds, with the trance-inducing practice of Anton Mesmer, the father of modern hypnotism. Both were in vogue in America in the 1830s and 1840s. It was a natural combination; mesmeric trance easily became trance-mediumship, by which those departed to the other worlds could speak again through the lips of a living communicator.

Spiritualists, Theosophists contended, were on to something very important evidenced by this apparent communication. It at least showed that human beings have a spiritual (technically, ultra-refined material) component, and a consequent origin and destiny far greater than their present mortal life. But, according to Theosophists, the mediumistic faith possessed only shallow information concerning the nature of the other worlds and planes; Spiritualists frequently confused mere fragmentary discarnate entities with the deceased person, and stood in need of the depth of insight they could gain from wise masters of all ages, including some now living. Yet Spiritualism was a start that had released many from their dogmatic slumbers.

As for Mesmer, he himself thought that he had discovered not only the art of Mesmerism that bears his name, but something else beyond it, a universal occult energy he called "animal magnetism" that could be accessed through mesmeric trance. This energy, also called Vril and Odic force by such nineteenth-century writers as Bulwer-Lytton and Reichenbach, was also of great importance to Helena Blavatsky, who devoted much of her first major work, *Isis Unveiled,* to exposition of it as the natural but little-known source of what is called magic. Mesmerism, she said, was the most important key to magic and, indeed, the true base of all that appears magical or miraculous.[1]

In addition, Theosophy was heir to the century's revival of interest in the European occult tradition, associated with the Kabbala (in both Christian and Jewish wings), eighteenth-century figures like Cagliostro and Saint-Germain as well as Swedenborg, Freemasonry and its mystique, and the almost-contemporary writings of the French esotericist Eliphas Levi; this was the tradition which would, around 1890, coalesce in the famous Hermetic Order of

the Golden Dawn. Theosophy also drew from a growing interest in Asiatic religion, especially Hindu and Tibetan at first, reflected both in the American Transcendentalists and the burgeoning scholarly orientalism of Europe. Among the eclectic and fascinating list of books Blavatsky used in composing *Isis Unveiled* were such titles as C. W. King's *The Gnostics and Their Remains,* Hargrave Jenning's *The Rosicrucians,* Moor's pioneer *Hindoo Pantheon,* various works of Eliphas Levi, of the Indologist L. Jacolliot, as well as of scholars, scientists or philosophers of the rank of Max Muller, T. H. Huxley, Herbert Spencer, and John Tyndall—persons with whom she sometimes took issue, but whose writings she and Olcott consulted.

Also in the background was romanticism, a vast and complex movement of which two facets are particularly relevant here: the exaltation of feeling and imagination (above all of feelings of openness toward the infinite and the ultimate to which the mystical language characteristic of Theosophists and others was very conducive); and the fascination with the exotic, with the distant and past (above all as reservoirs of forgotten mysteries and wisdom). It was an age of great advances in archaeology, which delighted in stories of lost and buried cities; it could be even more impressed by resuscitations of the wisdom that had died with them.

There could be a present use for resurrected wisdom. One great issue that troubled nearly all thinking Victorians was the "conflict" of science and religion, so much abetted by Darwin and the arguments over evolution versus scriptural authority, or as some would have it, of God versus geology. Henry Steel Olcott's 1875 inaugural address as president of the Theosophical Society was not the first to touch on the problem in the way he did, but he put the issues succinctly and showed a Theosophical way out:

> If I rightly apprehend our work it is to aid in freeing the public mind of theological superstition and a tame subservience to the arrogance of science. However much or little we may do, I

think it would have been hardly possible to hope for anything if the work had been begun in any country which did not afford perfect political and religious liberty . . .

Our Society is, I may say, without precedent. From the days when the Neoplatonists and the last theurgists of Alexandria were scattered by the murderous hand of Christianity, until now, the study of Theosophy has not been attempted.

To the Protestant and Catholic sectaries we have to show the origin of many of their most sacred idols and most cherished dogmas; to the liberal minds in science, the profound scientific attainments of the ancient magi. Society has reached a point where *something* must be done; it is for us to indicate where that something may be found.[2]

Here we find a perception of a need in relation to time and place that explains much. On the one hand, thinking people find that conventional Christianity is out of touch; on the other, the science that has done so much to discredit the traditional faiths fails to meet all human needs and displays its own "arrogance." What is called for is "something" new that is also old, coming from a day when universal wisdom and the human heart were less at odds, which shows the common ground of all religion while undercutting the pretensions of both sanctuary and laboratory. Finally, we note that only in America could this new stage of spirituality fully mature, for only here is found adequate freedom of thought and faith.

We must then turn to the background of those principal founders. The two contrast mightily. Helena Petrovna Blavatsky, nee de Hahn, was of Russian aristocratic family.[3] Her father, of German descent, was an officer in the army of the czar; the tomboyish Helena was close to him and loved riding with him and his troops across the steppes. Her mother, connected to the princely Dolgorouky house, was a popular novelist whose works inevitably involved the suffering of women at the hands of callous men; she died while Helena was still a child, and the future Theosophist spent much of her youth on the vast estates of her maternal grandfather, a provincial governor.

Helena was always a headstrong, difficult child, if imaginative and bright. Though she often disparaged marriage, in 1849 (some sources say 1848) she impulsively married Nikofer Blavatsky, a widower twice her age who was vice-governor of Erivan (Armenia). She left him before the end of the honeymoon, however, and made her way to Constantinople. This adventurous move began many years of wandering, concerning which accounts vary markedly. By her own version, she eventually made her way to central Asia where she received very high occult initiations.

In any event, it was clear that by the time Blavatsky surfaced and came to New York in 1874—drawn, she said, as a Muslim to Mecca by a desire to observe Spiritualism in its modern homeland—she had acquired an impressive familiarity with the spirit-faith and with occultism generally. It was by now the burning passion of her life, and she was determined to gain still more experience with it.

Her companion in that quest, and in the subsequent venture to disseminate wisdom to the world through the Theosophical Society, was Henry Steel Olcott (1832–1907).[4] Of sturdy American middle-class background, his world was outwardly very different from hers. After service for the Union in the Civil War, where he acquired the title colonel in connection with his role in prosecuting fraudulent military suppliers, he pursued a career in law and journalism in New York. But though reasonably successful, despite a failed marriage, some unanswered yearning obviously festered within him. When he met Helena Blavatsky at the Eddy farm, almost immediately his life and hers intertwined around their mutual fascination with hidden wisdom and latent powers. Their series of flats—one famous as "The Lamasery"—became magnets for the city's coteries of seekers, bohemians, and mystics. Many were fascinated by the portly, mysterious Russian woman, with her exotic accent, razor-sharp tongue, large deep eyes, and tales of mystic wonders.

By September of 1875, the crowd around Blavatsky and Olcott was prepared to establish a society for the study of ancient wisdom, comparative religion and science, and the "powers latent in man"; it was called the Theosophical Society (TS). Olcott was first president, and Blavatsky corresponding secretary—though obviously the real drive behind the movement, she hated formal public positions and never held higher outer office than this, nor did she ever give public lectures. Olcott, on the other hand, an outgoing, energetic man of affairs, was a natural for such roles.

Their first venture, after the founding of the Society, was the composition of *Isis Unveiled.* This rambling, erudite, and often fascinating work besets the reader with intriguing instances of seemingly magical occurrences past and present, and from around the world; interprets them as signs of a subtle force which, as we have seen, is identical with Mesmer's "animal magnetism" or Reichenbach's "Odic force"; and finally presents an image of the human being as tripartite, made up of matter, spirit, and that quasi-material, quasi-spiritual energy. In the process Blavatsky delivers numerous missiles, some quite well aimed, at conventional religion and science. She also allows other ideas to slip in which were to become standard Theosophical doctrine: that the universal truths are contained, though veiled, in myths, legends, and doctrines of all peoples; that the universe is in a continual process of evolution; that there is validity in such arcane arts as astrology, magic, and mediumship, though their meaning goes far beyond crude popular representations of them.

However, though *Isis,* on its publication in 1877, sold well and received much critical attention, favorable and unfavorable, the Theosophical Society did not correspondingly prosper. Indeed, within a year of its founding it had declined to little more than a paper organization. On the other hand, a branch was formed in London, and Olcott and Blavatsky were in correspondence with Swami Dayananda in India, the founder of the Hindu reformist Arya Samaj movement. All this led the founders to turn their thoughts to India,

which they believed to be the chief outer storehouse of the Ancient Wisdom. Late in 1878 they set sail for that fabled subcontinent, stopping en route in London and arriving in Bombay the next year. For them, as for many spiritual pilgrims, it was not only Walt Whitman's "Passage to India" but also the poet's "Passage to more than India!"—to the wonder, the wisdom, and the masters of the wisdom, of which geographical India was only the facade.

The "Theosophical Twins," as Olcott liked to call himself and his companion, dwelt briefly in Bombay, had a disillusioning encounter with Dayananda, met and talked with goodly numbers of both native Indians and British elite, and in turn were the subjects of much conversation in both communities. They started magazines and established a permanent headquarters at an estate called Adyar, on the outskirts of Madras. Blavatsky, though by now a U.S. citizen, was suspected by the British raj of being a Russian spy and was shadowed; many Indians, and some liberal Englishmen like Octavian Hume, later a founder of the Congress Party, were drawn to the Theosophists both because of their universalism and their respect for India's spiritual traditions. A number of TS chapters were founded in India.

In India, Theosophical teaching developed. Although they had been spoken of before, now Theosophists increasingly talked of the Masters, Adepts, or Mahatmas, persons said to be much ahead of others in spiritual evolution, and who guided the development of individuals and the world by inner means. Many were in the flesh; the Himalayas, and beyond that towering range mystic Tibet, were home to many of the most important. Blavatsky was in touch with them, both psychically and by more ordinary means, as were some other Theosophists who received letters as well as subjective promptings from these elder brothers of the race.

Other Indic doctrines appeared also. Karma and reincarnation, though barely mentioned in *Isis Unveiled,* came more and more to the Theosophical center. An elaborate picture of the world's spiritual evolution, based in part on Hindu and Buddhist mythologies and first presented in detail in *Esoteric Buddhism* (1883) by A. P. Sinnett (an Anglo-Indian journalist and convert), was subsequently developed in Blavatsky's *The Secret Doctrine* (1888).

Problems arose, however. In 1884 Adyar was rocked by charges, brought by former employees and published in a Christian missionary paper, that Blavatsky had fraudulently produced many of her psychic phenomena, especially the so-called "Mahatma Letters," supposedly from masters and conveyed to certain Theosophists (especially Sinnett) by means of a box in the Shrine Room at headquarters. An investigation by Richard Hodgson, sent by the Society for Psychical Research, was unfavorable to the Theosophists. Amid the furor, Blavatsky, now in failing health, reluctantly returned to Europe, leaving the Adyar work in the hands of Olcott.

Before her death in London in 1891, Helena Blavatsky managed to complete her masterwork, *The Secret Doctrine,* a compendium of occultism which is certainly one of the landmarks of the genre. Fundamentally an esoteric history of the universe, the world, and the "root races" of humankind, it also surveys a remarkable range of the world's religions and arcane lore for clues to those inner realities.

On the institutional side, the 1888 publication of this work, together with attractive magazines and news from the successful (except for 1884, and even that generated much publicity) labors in India, bore fruit around the world. Theosophy met some inner need of the 1890s, and grew rapidly in the United States, England, Ireland, Australia, New Zealand, and elsewhere. With growth, however, came more difficulties.

The revived society in the United States was now under the presidency of a third of the original founders, the Irish immigrant William Q. Judge. Tension arose between him and the international president at Adyar, Henry Olcott, including accusations that Judge was falsely claiming personal letters from the Masters. A deeper issue was the direction Theosophy was to take after the death of Blavatsky. Judge charged that the Adyar headquarters in India was moving Theosophy away from its original universalist nature and in a Hindu direction; Olcott countered that Judge wanted to make it a "Blavatsky sect."

Also involved was the role of two women of strong character who would become dominant figures in Theosophy's second generation, Annie Besant (1847–1933) and Katherine Tingley (1847–1929). Besant, an Englishwoman, ardent reformer, and Hindu sympathizer, was believed by many Americans to be the force behind Olcott's accusations; she succeeded him as international president in 1907.[5] Tingley, another fervent reforming activist, had her own dreams for the movement's future. The American society separated from Adyar in 1895. Thereafter events moved swiftly. Judge died in 1896; Tingley was then the real power in her society, becoming officially its leader in 1898.

In 1897 Tingley with her supporters purchased land at Point Loma, in San Diego, and commenced building a utopian community. She summoned members of the American TS to join her there; augmented by favorable publicity for relief efforts Tingley organized in connection with the Spanish-American War the next year, the Point Loma experiment at first flourished. Most U.S. Theosophists who did not support the communal project, on the other hand, reverted to the Adyar leadership, leaving Point Loma in splendid isolation. "Lomaland" was, however, a magnificent vision, famous for its advanced pioneer experiments in childraising, education, and agriculture, and for the zeal with which its happy citizens, lured from around the world, pursued a cultural as well as Theosophical life of high quality. It was, seemingly, an advanced soul's dreamland, full of books, concerts, drama, and stirring lectures amid Grecian theaters and futuristic glass-domed lodges by the sparkling blue Pacific.

But the community encountered financial difficulties in the 1920s, and declined after Tingley's death in 1929. Utopia was finally closed in wartime 1942. After a brief move to Covina, California, the remnants of Point Loma eventually became the non-communal Theosophical

Society headquartered in Altadena. Although it does not sponsor branches or hold extensive meetings, this organization manages an excellent Theosophical library in Altadena, and publishes Theosophical literature.[6]

A third American Theosophical group, after Adyar (the United States branch of which is the Theosophical Society in America, headquartered in Wheaton, Illinois) and the Point Loma/Altadena Theosophical Society, is the United Lodge of Theosophists. This group, with its central lodge in Los Angeles, was founded in 1909 by Robert Crosbie to unite Theosophists who wished to remain independent of both the other contending factions. It emphasizes a conservative, Blavatskian approach to Theosophy.

In the meantime, new developments were shaking the Adyar organization, by far the largest worldwide. Much of it centered on the controversial Charles W. Leadbeater (1854[7]–1934), a former Anglican priest who joined the society in 1883. By the turn of the century he was a prominent member, living at Adyar off and on but lecturing widely. He was, however, forced to resign in 1906 when charges of homosexuality involving boys entrusted to his charge were laid against him. He was reinstated in 1909 after Annie Besant, a close associate, became president.

Although charges on the same matter were levied recurrently, particularly in the early 1920s, Besant supported her colleague. Together they developed what has been called Neo-Theosophy. Expressed in the extensive writings of both Besant and Leadbeater, it propounded an elaborate and schematic vision of reincarnation, the subtle constituents of human nature, the evolution of worlds, and the "hierarchy" of the Masters who comprise the "inner government of the world." Much of it was based on Leadbeater's claimed clairvoyance.

The most interesting and significant development of all was the promotion of a young Hindu boy, Jiddu Krishnamurti (1895–1986), to the messianic role of "vehicle" for a coming world teacher. Discovered by Leadbeater's clairvoyance, this initially unprepossessing youth was carefully nourished by Theosophists on three continents, and amid mounting excitement in the 'teens and 'twenties was expected soon to declare himself. A worldwide organization, the Order of the Star in the East, was set up to prepare the way for his coming. But in 1929, at a great conclave of enthusiasts in Holland, Krishnamurti astounded his followers by dissolving the order and renouncing all formal titles or organizations. Until his death, Krishnamurti then pursued independent spiritual work as lecturer and educator, emphasizing, as he put it in his 1929 address, that "truth is a pathless land," and advocating a mode of consciousness he termed "choiceless awareness."[8]

Leadbeater was involved in yet another controversial venture, the establishment of the Liberal Catholic Church. In 1916, having become persuaded that Theosophy needed a liturgical expression, Leadbeater (then esconced in his own Theosophical center in Sydney, Australia), was consecrated bishop in an Old Catholic church of Theosophical leanings by James Ingall Wedgwood. Within the next two years, he and Wedgwood devised a liturgy and ceremonial of Catholic type but with concessions to Theosophical concepts, for this churchly body, and named it the Liberal Catholic Church. That body was quickly planted around the world, and can still be found in many major cities. In 1923, after Wedgwood was compelled to resign his office as Presiding Bishop of the Liberal Catholic Church following homosexual scandals of his own, he was succeeded by Leadbeater. Some Theosophists, raised on the anti-clericalism of early Theosophy, were appalled by the ecclesiastical development; others found it satisfied a heretofore unmet thirst for Theosophical worship as well as ideas.

This brings us to the area of "spin-off" movements from Theosophy. These may be divided into three types: Allies of Theosophy, Liberal Theosophy, and New Revelation Theosophy. Two important examples of each will be cited. The first, the Allies, are groups which have a goodly number of Theosophists among their members. Membership in them is widely considered compatible with allegiance to the (Adyar) Theosophical Society, and frequently represents a desire to supplement lodge Theosophy with religious or ritual expression of the same worldview. The prime example is the already-mentioned Liberal Catholic Church. Another is Co-Masonry, a Masonic Lodge open to women as well as men. Although founded in France, when it entered the English-speaking world early in the twentieth century, it quickly acquired a largely Theosophical membership, the same James Wedgwood who was first Presiding Bishop of the Liberal Catholic Church being also a prominent Co-Mason.

Liberal Theosophy is represented chiefly by the Krishnamurti Foundation, headquartered in Ojai, California, and its equivalents around the world, designed chiefly to promote Krishnamurti's teachings through books and tapes, and to support the several schools he founded. Today a number of Theosophists see themselves able to appreciate Krishnamurti's experience, though others are less sympathetic. Another liberal movement is the Anthroposophical Society, founded by the Austro-German Rudolf Steiner (1861–1925), one-time head of the German section of the TS. Becoming disillusioned with the Eastern drift of Adyar Theosophy under Besant and Leadbeater, and in any case a powerful occult thinker and visionary in his own right, Steiner established the new organization in 1912. He emphasized Western and Christian mysticism, particularly the idea of consciousness as the inner source of the world's outward expression, and so evolution as fundamentally an evolution of mind.[9] Though small in the United States, Anthroposophy has been noted for its highly regarded Waldorf schools and other works.

New Revelation Theosophy depends on alleged new teachings from the Theosophical masters. One example is the Alice Bailey or Arcane School groups. Alice LaTrobe Bateman Bailey (1880–1949) was an Englishwoman who, after a difficult life despite a privileged background, came to Theosophy in California in 1915.[10] She joined the society and, in 1917, moved to Hollywood, California, where she worked in the vegetarian cafeteria at Krotona, the Theosophical study center. She there met Foster Bailey, national secretary of the Theosophical Society, whom she subsequently married.

Alice Bailey's relationship to Theosophy soon suffered strains. This was first the result of her claimed reception of new communications from Masters in the Theosophical tradition. In November, 1919, as she was walking in the Hollywood Hills near Krotona, she believed she was contacted by one of the Masters, Djwhal Khul, known popularly as "The Tibetan," who wanted her to serve as his amanuensis. The first book produced in this manner, *Initiation: Human and Solar,* was commenced in 1920 and appeared in 1922; it was followed by numerous others, presenting Theosophical teaching together with a particular emphasis on the coming "reappearance of the Christ" in the form of a new world teacher or era, and the need to prepare for that event by guided meditation. It was, one might say, eschatological Theosophy. Followers of the Alice Bailey tradition meet at every full moon for the work of group meditation.

The "I Am" movement was founded by Guy W. Ballard (1878–1939) and his wife Edna W. Ballard (1886–1971). Guy Ballard reported that, in 1930, he encountered one of the Theosophical Masters, Saint Germain, on the slopes of Mt. Shasta in California; the experience and teaching are presented in *Unveiled Mysteries* (1934). The I Am activity offers a combination of New Thought type teaching on the power of mind with Theosophy and colorful accounts of Ascended Masters. There is emphasis on reincarnation and also on the power of one who is truly purified to ascend directly to the supernal realms. I Am was a vigorous and much-publicized movement in the late 1930s, but it suffered from Guy Ballard's sudden death at the end of 1939, and then from a series of court cases stemming from charges of mail fraud; these were eventually dismissed by the U.S. Supreme Court in 1944 in an important religious liberty decision.[11]

A subsequent group clearly modelled on I Am in important respects is the Church Universal and Triumphant, incorporated in 1974. It had its beginnings in the Summit Lighthouse, founded in 1958 by Mark L. Prophet to publish messages allegedly received from Ascended Masters of the Great White Brotherhood, generally the same as those of Theosophy and I Am, including Saint-Germain, Jesus, and the Buddha. In 1961 Prophet was joined by Elizabeth Clare Wulf, whom he later married. The Summit Lighthouse was moved to Colorado Springs in 1966. After Mark Prophet's death in 1973, Elizabeth Clare Prophet became its leader, transforming it into the Church Universal and Triumphant (CUT) the next year. Under her dynamic personality, and with the help of her vibrant channeled messages from the Masters, the new denomination flourished. It gained a tightly knit band of dedicated adherents who have followed its headquarters to various sites: from Colorado to Pasadena and then Malibu, California, and finally to Corwin Springs, Montana, near Yellowstone, in 1986. The group's colorfully printed posters, flyers, and books have been disseminated widely. The fundamental teachings center on belief that through inner initiations and the use of prayers, mantras, and "decrees" one can realize one's divinity and eventually "ascend" to the ranks of the Masters. Reincarnation is affirmed. Like I Am, the CUT has engendered much controversy, and has identified itself with stalwart American patriotism and with causes generally regarded as politically "right wing."[12]

The heyday of "classical" Theosophy was certainly the period between, approximately, 1890 and 1930. At this time it was relatively new, dynamic, and generally identified with the liberal, reformist, even utopian spirit of an important segment of society, those who wished to combine universalism in religion with social reform. Among the signs of its influence was the influence of Theosophy on certain "symbolist" artists, such as Mondrian and Roerich, or poets such as Yeats and George Russell (known as "Æ"), not to mention political figures from Gandhi (indirectly)

to George Lansbury, Theosophist and leader of the British Labour Party in the early 1930s.

Basically, it seems fair to say that Theosophy represented a spiritual home for persons like Blavatsky, Besant, Tingley, Olcott, or Bailey who came from respectable, in some cases high-status, backgrounds but who nonetheless found themselves intellectually and spiritually ill at ease. Typically they seem to have been people of deep mental interests in religious and philosophical topics, but without conventional education in them—perhaps without access to it. They were the kind of people who read a lot of serious books, but in the library or the home rather than the university classroom. They were "status inconsistent"—persons whose outward life, however comfortable, was at odds with what they inwardly sensed themselves to be: a woman with a gift for religious leadership, a lawyer like Olcott with a missionary call but no interest in the conventional church. Yet they were of a class and character that gave them some confidence they could make it in a different and better venue.

Theosophy, against a backdrop of personal and often cultural religious crisis, gave such people a platform and something to say, something that could be as startling and far-reaching as the changes moderns felt within and saw all around. For that very reason Theosophy was the subject of controversy far out of proportion to its small numbers, for if it became home to those few, it also gave shape to the anxieties of a religious era. Much of the controversy was, at least on the surface, related to Theosophy's numerous scandals and colorful individuals—the "Mahatma letters" case, the Leadbeater charges, the Krishnamurti episode. But there is reason to think the movement's capacity to provoke high-decibel charges and countercharges went even deeper; and in any case, Theosophists tended to answer the *ad hominem* (or, more often, *ad feminam*) arguments of opponents with an acknowledgment its leaders were not perfect, but the important thing was what they said. "Read the books, not the persons," they might implore critics. But what Blavatsky, Besant, and the others had to say was, for some, provocative enough.

Theosophy, though minuscule, nonetheless represented an egregious and visible example of many things traditional Christianity now had to contend with in an age of doubt, Darwin, social change, and incipient globalism. Often these presences were amorphous yet threatening clouds, but in Theosophy they seemed personified in their most extreme shape. It is little wonder the society drew lightning. From 1890 to 1930 was a time of increasing uncertainty in religion, and of deepending polarization in churches between liberal and conservative wings. But on the issues at hand—evolution, the Bible, the claims of rival world religions—Theosophy took a more advanced position than even the most progressive churchmen, speaking of cosmic evolution in the most sweeping terms as embracing everything from atoms to consciousness, of the Bible as at best only a partial and distorted version of the Ancient Wisdom, of all religions—and especially some of those most despised by the orthodox, such as Gnosticism and Hinduism—as bearers of the occult light.

On top of this, Theosophy challenged the Christian ecclesiastical establishment structurally, in its provision for lay and particularly female leadership. In the main-line churches and academies of the day, women could not hope for positions of intellectual or institutional leadership equivalent to those that obviously brilliant and capable persons of their gender like Blavatsky, Besant, or Tingley held in the new movement. Nor, in many cases, could males who were not of appropriate background. (Even a man like Leadbeater would not likely have become an Anglican bishop in Victorian England. Though ordained in the Church of England, he came from a lower-class family and had not graduated from Oxford or Cambridge. But he wore the full panoply of episcopal cope and mitre in the Liberal Catholic Church.)

The Theosophical movement, then, was a remarkable combination of things new and old that helped provide bridges between several worlds: ancient wisdom and a new age, traditional society and a reformist era, West and East, gender- and class-based religious institutions and a new vision of spirituality yearning to breathe free of such distinctions. Finally, in a time when liberal social and intellectual concerns were too often cloaked in gray modernity, or tied to iron ideologies, Theosophy offered progressives who could resonate with its immense cosmic vision a sense of wonder and a deep past to go with the new earth they envisioned here below.

Notes

1. H. P. Blavatsky, *Isis Unveiled*, 2 vols. (Wheaton, Ill.: Theosophical Publishing House, 1972; facsimile of first edition, New York: J. W. Bouton, 1877), 1:129.

2. "Inaugural Address of the President of the Theosophical Society," facsimile centenary edition (Theosophical Society of America, Wheaton, Ill.: 1975).

3. Unless otherwise indicated, titles following are published in Adyar and Wheaton, Ill., by the Theosophical Publishing House. Virtually all of Blavatsky's published work and a number of her letters can be found in Helena P. Blavatsky, *Collected Writings*, ed. Boris de Zirkov; 15 vols., including index volume, 1966–1991. Invaluable reminiscences by her companion and co-worker are to be found in Henry Steel Olcott, *Old Diary Leaves*, 6 vols. (1895–1935; reprint, 1941–1975). Mary K. Neff, *Personal Memoirs of H. P. Blavatsky* (1937), an important resource, assembles the subject's life as she related it at various times in her own words, together with some supplemental material. Jean Overton Fuller, *Blavatsky and Her Teachers* (London: East-West Publications, 1988), deals with some of the many biographical problems Blavatsky presents from a sympathetic, Theosophical point of view. A new look at the early years of Theosophy, including fresh insights on the sources

of Blavatsky's writing, can be found in Michael Gomes, *The Dawning of the Theosophical Movement* (1987). The best independent biography is Marion Meade, *Madame Blavatsky* (New York: Putnam, 1980), though it is sometimes speculative and does not do justice to the intellectual dimensions of Blavatsky's work.

4. See H. Murphet, *Hammer on the Mountain: The Life of Henry Steel Olcott* (Wheaton, Ill.: Theosophical Publishing House, 1972). Revised as *Yankee Beacon of Buddhist Light: Life of Col. Henry S. Olcott* (1988).

5. See A. H. Nethercot, *The First Five Lives of Annie Besant* and *The Last Four Lives of Annie Besant* (Chicago: University of Chicago Press, 1960, 1963); and Catherine L. Wessinger, *Annie Besant and Progressive Messianism* (Lewiston, N.Y.: Edwin Mellen Press, 1988).

6. See Emmett A. Greenwalt, *The Point Loma Community in California, 1897–1942: A Theosophical Experiment* (Berkeley: University of California Press, 1955). Revised as *California Utopia, Point Loma: 1897–1942* (San Diego: Point Loma Publications, 1978).

7. Leadbeater long claimed 1847 as his year of birth, and this date is to be found in many sources. However, Gregory Tillett, in his definitive biography, has established that 1854 is correct, and speculates on reasons for his subject's dissimulation on the matter. See Gregory Tillett, *The Elder Brother: A Biography of Charles Webster Leadbeater* (London: Routledge and Kegan Paul, 1982).

8. For Krishnamurti's life see Mary Lutyens, *Krishnamurti: The Years of Awakening* (New York: Farrar, Straus and Giroux, 1975), *Krishnamurti: The Years of Fulfillment* (London: J. Murray, 1983), and *The Life and Death of Krishnamurti* (London: J. Murray, 1990), a one-volume distillation of her previous biographical work on Krishnamurti; and Pupul Jayakar,

Krishnamurti: A Biography (San Francisco: Harper and Row, 1986). Sidney Field, *Krishnamurti: The Reluctant Messiah* (New York: Paragon House, 1989) is an informal memoir of a long friendship. A more controversial memoir which brings out some alleged very human characteristics of the teacher is Radha Rajagopal Sloss, *Lives in the Shadow with J. Krishnamurti* (London: Bloomsbury Press, 1991).

9. See R. Steiner, *Rudolf Steiner, An Autobiography* (Blauvelt, N.Y.: Rudolf Steiner Publications, 1977); and Guenther Wachsmuth, *The Life and Work of Rudolf Steiner* (New York: Whittier Books, 1955).

10. The best source for her life remains her *Unfinished Autobiography* (New York: Lucis Press, 1951).

11. See the "I Am" chapter in Charles S. Braden, *These Also Believe* (New York: Macmillan, 1949), and Robert S. Ellwood, "Making New Religions: The Story of the Mighty 'I AM,'" *History Today* 38 (June 1988). It might be pointed out that "I Am," unlike most wings of the Theosophical movement, makes much of the spiritual role of America and has something of a "rightist" political aura. The same can be said of an apparent emulator of it, the Church Universal and Triumphant of Elizabeth Clare Prophet.

12. Because of its colorful and controversial nature, there is considerable journalistic literature on the Church Universal and Triumphant, but very few if any independent scholarly works to date. The account in J. Gordon Melton, *Encyclopedia of American Religions*, 3rd ed. (Detroit: Gale Research, 1989), 750–52, can be recommended. The church's own basic text is Mark L. Prophet and Elizabeth Clare Prophet, *Climb the Highest Mountain* (Colorado Springs, Colo.: Summit Lighthouse, 1972).

Suggestions for Further Reading

Campbell, Bruce F. *A History of the Theosophical Movement.* Berkeley: University of California Press, 1980.

Mills, Joy. *100 Years of Theosophy: A History of the Theosophical Society in America.* Wheaton, Ill.: Theosophical Publishing House, 1987.

Ryan, Charles J. *H. P. Blavatsky and the Theosophical Movement.* Pasadena: Theosophical University Press, 1975.

32

NEW THOUGHT AND THE HARMONIAL FAMILY
Gail Harley

New Thought in this hemisphere has roots in European and Oriental thinking and has branched out profusely since its beginning. New Thought's philosophical antecedents were contained in the ideas of Emanuel Swedenborg (1688–1772), a noted scientist and inventor, who eventually had to leave his native Sweden to find peace from persecution for his beliefs. Swedenborg postulated that events in the supernatural realm were correlated with phenomena in the finite world (the "As above—so below" principle). Variations of this idea are found in the Native American and Roman Catholic religious traditions. This law of correspondence between the spheres influenced the thought of Ralph Waldo Emerson and the Transcendentalists who rejected Swedenborg's more orthodox approach to sin and guilt. The presupposition of correspondence between the two worlds is widely held in all metaphysical groups today. The Transcendentalists incorporated the value of the sacred texts of the East, a decided departure from normative nineteenth-century religious practice predicated upon Western notions of the Holy.[1]

The mental healing practice of Phineas Parkhurst Quimby (1802–1866) of Belfast, Maine, sparked new ideas regarding the power of the mind. Quimby, a skilled clockmaker, had been exposed to hypnosis. He began to believe that sickness was the result of erroneous thinking and a cure could be effected by changing one's own belief system. He eventually dropped hypnosis as a therapeutic tool and began speaking directly with the patient about linking the individual's spiritual nature with divine spirit. Quimby's work was secular and did not have an overtly religious orientation. He felt that priests and doctors were benefactors of human misery who had nefarious holds on the minds of the people. However, while not being traditionally "religious" he nevertheless developed a deep and abiding spirituality from his healing practice and frequently used religious terminology, identifying healing energy as "The Christ." Among Quimby's clients were Julius and Annetta Dresser, Warren Felt Evans and Mary Baker Eddy, all of whom became vital forces in the growth of metaphysical healing. Quimby's pioneering ventures made unique contributions to the "mind cure" movement which would later evolve into New Thought.[2]

Next to Quimby in importance to the then-embryonic New Thought was Warren Felt Evans (1817–1889), a former Methodist minister who had embraced the teachings of Swedenborg and joined the Swedenborgian Church of the New Jerusalem. In 1863 he was healed by Quimby's methods and as a result became a practitioner of Quimby's system. He wrote prolifically from 1869 onward about spiritual healing methods. Evans stressed that disease is a result of a disturbance in the human spiritual body which adversely affects the functioning of the physical body. Evans employed Quimby's technique of positive affirmation and avoided the use of negative terms. Evans was primarily a writer and like Quimby he founded no church or institution.

After the death of Quimby, Mary Baker Eddy founded the Christian Science Church. According to Catherine Albanese, Eddy's text *Science and Health* (1875) "attracted readers who also read Evans."[3] Many of these readers objected to Eddy's absolute authority over her adherents. Consequently a handful or more innovative thinkers who initially joined Eddy left her ranks. Eddy was accused by Julius and Annetta Dresser of pirating Quimby's healing work and partially creating her church doctrine based upon his healing principles. J. Gordon Melton has examined the original writing of both parties and maintains there is an essential difference in their respective teaching, finding "the major similarity to be in the area of terminology and the attempt to struggle with some of the same questions of religion and health."[4] Polemics concerning Eddy's specific contributions to spiritual healing have raged for one hundred years or more. Part of the early controversy over Eddy's movement seems to have been based on her boldness as a woman in a patriarchal culture to found a new religious tradition and her rejection of conventional medical practice.

While the New Thought and Christian Science movements have been historically related, today they operate along widely divergent avenues. New Thought was founded pragmatically and organizationally by Emma Curtis Hopkins (1849–1925), who had studied with Eddy (1883) and had edited the *Christian Science Journal* in 1884 and 1885. After being excommunicated by Eddy in 1885 (for reasons never disclosed), Hopkins and an assistant, Mary Plunkett, founded the Emma Curtis Hopkins College of Christian Science in 1886.[5] By 1887 there were twenty-one Hopkins associations linked together in a loosely affiliated coast-to-coast network. Hopkins bridged the gap between college and seminary and founded the Christian Science Theological Seminary

in Chicago in 1888.[6] A New Thought publication called *Christian Science,* founded and edited by Ida Nichols, became a key publishing arm. Prior to Hopkins and her organizations there was no clearly developed New Thought movement. Most of the schools or other groups that were operative at this time were lone enterprises limited to single geographical locations. It was her prophetic vision, administrative ability, and commitment to New Thought as a guiding religious principle that gave the movement its direction. For nine years she managed her Theological Seminary and dispatched missionaries to outreach locations throughout the United States.[7] One of her early students, Frances Lord, author of *Christian Science Healing: Its Principles and Practices* (1888) carried the word abroad to England. Mary Plunkett withdrew from Hopkins's ministry in 1888 and became a missionary to New Zealand in 1890. These and other mission journeys made New Thought an American export.

Hopkins was a prodigious writer, publishing in pamphlet form, in New Thought journals, and in the Chicago *Inter-Ocean* newspaper. Her first collected works, beginning with *Class Lessons* (1888) and ending with *High Mysticism* (1923), continue to be read and studied by practitioners today. By the time Hopkins Seminary closed it doors in 1895, New Thought was firmly entrenched and deeply etched on the theological map of America. Hopkins, a charismatic speaker and teacher, taught and ordained the founders of the first generation of New Thought ministers, leaders of a new religion for an upcoming century. She had transformed New Thought from a lay healing movement into a church-oriented movement with ordained clergy.[8] She had graduated over 350 women and some men and had ordained another 111 people as advanced graduates who qualified as ministers. Her graduates included Malinda Cramer and Nona E. Brooks, who began Divine Science in Denver, Colorado; Annie Rix and Charles Militz, who founded Home of Truth on the West Coast, and Charles and Myrtle Fillmore, the co-founders of the Unity School of Christianity in Kansas City, Missouri. Toward the latter part of her life Hopkins (by then a reclusive mystic who only saw students one-on-one) taught a young Ernest Holmes her "newer ways" and he subsequently started Religious Science in Los Angeles, California.

A significant feature that early New Thought shared with several other new American religious groups, such as Spiritualism and Theosophy, was its openness to the leadership of women that had been forbidden in mainstream denominations. Concomitant with this new freedom women assumed pivotal positions as editors, owners, and publishers of early New Thought journals and magazines. It was Hopkins who orchestrated the paradigm shift and decidedly feminist bent of early New Thought. She not only ordained women, empowering them to teach, preach and heal, but went so far as to declare the Holy Spirit, the third person of the Trinity, to be female. Consequently, argues Gary Ward, "the list of women who founded New Thought schools" all over the country "is also staggering."[9] Robert Ellwood intriguingly speculates that "perhaps the spirit of these movements is closer than the Western norm to the feminine psyche.... "[10] Certainly, the pioneering spirit of early New Thought with Hopkins at the helm encouraged women to seek pulpits of power and prestige that had previously been denied them. However, as the movement gained momentum in the twentieth century, males took over many of the leadership roles. Now, New Thought ministries bear more resemblance to the patriarchal power structures of mainline church denominations with men holding the top administrative and ministerial slots and women relegated to lower-level positions.[11]

By the 1890s the confusing and sundry terms for mental healing such as divine healing and mental science were replaced by the term "New Thought." In 1899 in Hartford, Connecticut, proponents of metaphysical religion held a convention that was the forerunner of the International New Thought Alliance (INTA), organized in 1914. It is still active and operational today. An important feature of the INTA has been its ability to allow individualism among its members. The INTA had an in-fancy concurrent with growth explosions in the social and medical sciences and other interdisciplinary areas. Because of the personal freedom allowed members, synthesis has occurred with these other fields strengthening the global influence of New Thought. As a result, New Thought was able to readily assimilate principles of psychosomatic medicine long before the general public could accept such progressive thinking.

The Unity School of Christianity co-founded by the Fillmores in 1886 is the most prominent of New Thought ministries today. Myrtle Fillmore (1845–1931) suffered from tuberculosis and had been slowly healed over a period of two years by affirming the "Truth principle": "I am a child of God, and therefore I do not inherit sickness,"[12] spoken in a lecture by E. B. Weeks in 1886. Statements like this are believed to have restorative or healing power when used daily with the positive power of faith as the underlying dynamic. Consequently, Unity traces its roots to Myrtle's healing process. In 1891, the Fillmores were ordained by Hopkins as Christian Science (New Thought) ministers and their movement officially became known as Unity. The Fillmores never studied with Mary Baker Eddy and did not subscribe to the dogma and authority of Eddy. According to Dell de Chant, "Hopkins was the single greatest personal influence on the Fillmores."[13]

In 1892, Myrtle founded *Wee Wisdom,* the longest-running children's magazine in the United States, published for ninety-eight consecutive years before being phased out in December 1991. In 1894 Unity published *Lessons in Truth,* written by H. Emilie Cady, a homeopathic physician and student of Hopkins. This first book of Unity became a bestseller and the literary foundation for the dissemination of their teachings. It continues to be so today. Charles (1854–1948) published his first book, *Christian Healing,* in 1901 and is credited with writing or co-authoring thirteen books. For decades Myrtle carried on a dedicated correspondence with Unity members throughout the world. The Unity headquarters at 913 Tracy Street in Kansas City was built in 1906, marking the ordination of the Fillmores and seven others as Unity ministers. Up until this time Unity accepted ordinands from other denominations and spiritual groups. In order to regulate unwanted religious practices such as mediumship among ministers, Charles decided to institute a formal training program that solely supported Unity values.

Unity itself is non-denominational, with no creeds or dogmas. The theological emphasis is placed on an indwelling God and everyone is encouraged to find God within. A rapidly changing agenda resulted in an organizational shift and requests from participants facilitated the acquisition of a religious focus for Unity. Early New Thought centers usually had meetings in the afternoon or evening in order not to conflict with participants' existing religious obligations. The Fillmores, in keeping with original New Thought tenets, never intended to compete with mainline denominations and so Unity saw its original mission as that of education. Charles stated,

> Unity is a link in the great education movement inaugurated by Jesus Christ. . . . The truth we teach is not new, neither do we claim special revelations or discovery of new religious principles. Our purpose is to help and teach mankind to use and prove the eternal Truth taught by the Master.[14]

In 1920 land was purchased in Jackson County, Missouri, and became known as Unity Farm. Neither Charles nor Myrtle lived to see the farm evolve into Unity Village in 1953. Myrtle died at the age of eighty-six and Charles died at the age of ninety-three. The leadership of Unity passed to their sons and grandchildren. Today, Connie Fillmore, a great-granddaughter, presides over Unity. From a modest beginning Unity has grown to 521 churches and 215 affiliated study groups. The monthly magazine *Unity* is received by 400,000 persons. The *Daily Word* is one of the most popular inspirational publications of all time, widely subscribed to by individuals of varied religious backgrounds. It has a monthly circulation of 1,595,000 copies including editions in twelve languages, large print, and braille. Silent Unity, a program of prayer initiated by Myrtle in the early days, has grown into a prayer ministry contacted by 2,500,000 people annually.[15]

There is a distinction between the Unity School and the Association of Unity Churches (AUC). While related, the two groups are philosophically and functionally independent. The Unity School, with Connie Fillmore as president, is a center for religious instruction, publications, and prayer. The AUC, an association formed in 1966, has a rotating presidency serving two-year terms and coordinates Unity churches and ministers. There are no formal guidelines for what must be taught at individual centers. According to de Chant, "the first . . . and only doctrine of Unity . . . is spiritual freedom."

Males dominate the current board of trustees (fourteen men to seven women). Males also serve as chair or co-chair of twenty-one of the twenty-nine committees of the AUC. Of the ten largest Unity churches, only the tenth largest has a woman as senior minister.[16] While more than one half of its active ministers are women, the power slots are held by men following the typical paradigm of corporate structures. de Chant concludes that males dominate Unity through the AUC and that Unity has conformed to the paternalistic model of corporate hierarchy.

In 1992 the Unity-Progressive Council was established in Clearwater, Florida. This group is not a member of the Association of Unity Churches (AUC) nor affiliated with the Unity School of Christianity. This new council has established a theological seminary "based on the ideals of the New Thought movement and the Unity Movement specifically."[17] The seminary classes are open to people of all faiths and committed to equalitarian principles. The seminary's motto is *Libertas et Veritas*—Freedom and Truth. This fledgling group intends to prepare its graduates to pursue the highest in spiritual ideals in order to become outstanding leaders not only in religion but in many diverse sectors of society. The Bachelor of Arts program in religious studies cross-lists some courses with the department of religious studies at the

University of South Florida in Tampa. Students can matriculate for these courses at either institution. The Bachelor of Theology program with classes in Clearwater is specifically designed to prepare men and women to serve in the New Thought ministry.

New Thought, by its independent nature, continues to foster innovative developments in the American religious arena. There are many smaller New Thought–type churches that are not affiliated with the better known arteries of New Thought. Most of these Truth teachers and pastors are eclectic in outlook and pick and choose the themes of their ministries from a multiplicity of New Thought ideas, some synthesizing New Thought with New Age or Spiritualist precepts.

Perhaps more important to American culture than the communal forms of New Thought expression is the way its modalities of healing, prosperity, and positive thinking have been carried into sacred and secular spheres of society. Ralph Waldo Trine's *In Tune with the Infinite* has sold over two million copies since it was published in 1897. Norman Vincent Peale (who as a young man read much of the work of New Thought writers such as Ernest Holmes) continued until his recent death to teach and preach in a myriad of forms the *Power of Positive Thinking* that he first published in 1952.[18] Material from Hopkins's text *High Mysticism* was used in the teaching manual for the International Order of St. Luke the Physician, a group dedicated to spiritual healing, started by Dr. John Gayner Banks, an Episcopal priest.[19] New Thought continues to subtly permeate the mainstream culture. What began as an alternative religious tradition of the nineteenth and early twentieth centuries has slowly achieved a measure of integration and acceptance in the wide pluralistic milieu of American religious culture.

Notes

1. According to Sydney Ahlstrom, harmonial religion features ideas about health, prosperity, and spiritual serenity based on the individual's positive affinity with the Universe. *A Religious History of the American People* (New Haven: Yale University Press, 1972), 1019.

2. William James, *The Varieties of Religions Experience* (New York: Penguin Books, 1982), 94.

3. Catherine Albanese, *America: Religions and Religion* 2nd ed. (Belmont, Calif.: Wadsworth Publishing Company, 1992), 270.

4. J. Gordon Melton, *Encyclopedia of American Religions*, 3rd ed. (Detroit: Gale Research Co., 1989), 616.

5. Christian Science was used as a generic term for divine healing by Hopkins and others of the era. She believed no one group or person held the monopoly on Truth. This usage has confused scholars and the general public since that time.

6. Gail Harley, "Emma Curtis Hopkins: 'Forgotten Founder' of New Thought" (Ph.D. diss., Florida State University, 1991).

7. J. Gordon Melton, "New Thought's Hidden History: Emma Curtis Hopkins, Forgotten Founder of New Thought" (paper presented at the American Academy of Religion, Boston, Massachusetts, 1987), 17.

8. Ibid., 14.

9. Gary Ward, "The Feminist Theme of Early New Thought" (paper presented at the American Academy of Religion, Boston, Massachusetts, 1987).

10. Robert Ellwood, *Religious and Spiritual Groups in Modern America* (Englewood Cliffs, N.J.: Prentice-Hall, Inc., 1973), 80.

11. Gary Ward theorizes that when New Thought was a countercultural movement, women held leadership roles. As New Thought became more accepted in the mainstream, men saw the positions as "viable career options" and stepped into them.

12. Charles Braden, *Spirits in Rebellion* (Dallas: Southern Methodist University Press, 1963), 338.

13. Dell de Chant, "Myrtle and Her Daughters: An Observation and Analysis of the Role of Women in the Unity Movement," in *Women*

Outside the Mainstream, ed. Catherine Wessinger (Champaign, Ill.: University of Illinois Press), 1993.

14. Statement found in a publication of Unity School of Christianity, Public Relations Department, Unity Village, Missouri, n.d. For a complete history of Unity see *The Story of Unity* by James Dillet Freeman, rev. ed. (Unity Village, Mo.: Unity Books, 1978).

15. These figures are found in the *Dictionary of Christianity in America* (Downer's Grove, Ill.: Intervarsity Press, 1990) and *Association of Unity Churches, 1989* year book (Lee's Summit, Mo.: Association of Unity Churches, 1989), 212. Statistics for *Daily Word* were supplied on 7 January 1993 by the Public Relations Department of Unity and are for 1991.

16. This is Leddy Hammock, pastor of the Unity Church of Clearwater, Florida, who is also a former editor of Unity books.

17. Unity Progressive, "Catalog for the Inaugural Year 1992–1993," n.d.

18. Braden, *Spirits,* 338.

19. J. Stillson Judah, *The History and Philosophy of the Metaphysical Movements in America.* (Philadelphia: Westminster Press, 1967), 300–301.

Suggestions for Further Reading

Albanese, Catherine. *Nature Religion in America: From the Algonkian Indians to the New Age.* Chicago: University of Chicago Press, 1988.

Freeman, James Dillet. *The Story of Unity.* Unity Village, Mo.: Unity Books, 1978.

Harley, Gail. "Emma Curtis Hopkins: 'Forgotten Founder' of New Thought." Ph.D. diss., Florida State University, 1991.

Judah, J. Stillson. *The History and Philosophy of the Metaphysical Movements in America.* Philadelphia: Westminster Press, 1967.

33

SPIRITUALISM AND CHANNELING
Shawn Michael Trimble

> There are two bodies—the rudiment and the complete, corresponding with the two conditions of the worm and the butterfly. What we call "death," is but the painful metamorphosis. Our present incarnation is progressive, preparatory, temporary.
> —Edgar Allan Poe, "Mesmeric Revelation"

> Why come not spirits from the realms of glory,
> To visit earth as in days of old—
> The times of ancient writ and sacred story?
> Is heaven more distant? or has earth grown cold?
> —Rev. Harbaugh, *Sainted Dead* (quoted in Henry Spicer's *Sights and Sounds*, 1853)

Belief that the living can communicate with the dead is an immeasurably ancient ingredient of human culture. Many primal societies make little or no distinction between the observable physical world and the unobservable world of dead souls and spirit beings; even the roots of the Judeo-Christian tradition bear evidence of belief in divinatory activity.[1] However, Spiritualism as an American religious movement began with events that occurred in upstate New York during 1848. Though the trajectory of this new movement quickly reached a sensational apogee only to suffer a period of equally dramatic decline, Spiritualism endures today as a distinct, if not conspicuous, organized religious phenomenon in America.

Spiritualism in the most general sense is belief in the survival of the self after death, and the ability of humans—especially a select few known as mediums—to establish contact with deceased beings. The phenomenon of Spiritualism has generally existed within the larger tradition of Western Christianity; local Spiritualist congregations are called "churches," the spiritual authority and example of Jesus is usually recognized on some level, and the Bible is often consulted as scripture. However, the elements of traditional Christianity are not central to Spiritualism; emphasis is instead placed upon the revelatory nature of contact with the dead. In Spiritualist churches today, as in the formative years of the movement, the heart of religious practice and belief is the séance, the actual ritual contact with spirit beings performed by a medium.

The first modern séance, to which Spiritualism traces its origin, occurred on 31 March 1848 at Hydesville, New York, when eleven-year-old Kate Fox and her two sisters began to receive intelligible messages in the form of mysterious rapping sounds from an unseen spirit called "Mr. Splitfoot." The young girls functioned as mediums for this disembodied entity who had purportedly been murdered in their cottage some years earlier. Through a code the sisters devised, the spirit would answer questions from observers as to his identity, the nature of the afterlife, and other general matters.[2] The basic form of the Fox sisters' séances would become the general pattern for all other Spiritualist mediums. Though the initial public reaction was for the most part negative, and though the Foxes were censured by their local church, large crowds nonetheless began to arrive at their house in hopes of experiencing contact with the afterlife. The first organized Spiritualist assembly, or circle, as it was called, was formed from this core of early believers. The Foxes' cause was soon championed by Horace Greeley, editor of the *New York Tribune,* and word of the young mediums' activity spread nationally, simultaneously attracting both widespread skepticism and interest. Even such notables as James Fennimore Cooper and Henry Longfellow were drawn to séances held by the teenage mediums.

Though the séances in Hydesville are generally considered the first clear manifestations of Spiritualist activity, the ideological and philosophical groundwork to support the movement was already in place. Perhaps the most obvious influence on Spiritualism's success is the most overlooked: the shamanistic tradition of the Native Americans, which, through missionary accounts and media reports, had become familiar to the American public of the early and mid-nineteenth century.[3] The divinatory practices and beliefs of the shaman helped provide a conceptual frame of reference for the Spiritualist séance. Reciprocally, the theology of Spiritualism was welcomed by many as a means to interpret the otherwise mysterious, but pervasive, shamanistic tradition within the conventional Judeo-Christian paradigm. Spiritualism can thus be seen as both a reaction of traditional Christianity towards shamanism and an adaptation of shamanism to the arrival of Christendom in America. Whatever the nature of shamanism's impact on this movement, its influence is evident in the recurrence of a popular Native American archetypal

spirit known as the "Indian Guide" in Spiritualist circles. The influence of shamanism might also account for the Universalist character of Spiritualist theology; as mediumistic phenomena were not limited to any specific faith, salvation (defined in Spiritualism to loosely refer to the survival of the soul after death) was not exclusive to belief, and therefore not exclusive to Spiritualists.

Two other crucial influences on Spiritualism were the writings of Emanuel Swedenborg and Anton Mesmer, both pioneers in eighteenth-century psychic activity. Swedenborg, a Swedish scientist and metaphysician, wrote extensively of information he claimed to have psychically received from angelic beings, including revelations of the afterlife. Foreshadowing Spiritualism not only in his theory of metaphysics, Swedenborg also reported psychic conversations he held with many deceased notables residing in both heaven and hell. Meanwhile Franz Mesmer, an Austrian scientist, announced his discovery of not only the hypnotic trance, but also "animal magnetism," the latent human ability to manipulate life and energy. Animal magnetism, a popular element in the theology of many nineteenth-century American religious movements, is also evident in Spiritualism in the form of belief in the ability to manipulate and commerce with deceased beings. These two schools of thought were synthesized in the writings of Andrew Jackson Davis, an American Mesmerist who claimed to have psychically encountered the spirit of Swedenborg in the early and mid-1840s. Davis is viewed by many scholars as being the first Spiritualist; they date the origin of the movement at the publication of his 1847 text, *The Principles of Nature,* a full year before the first manifestations at Hydesville.[4] During the 1850s Davis became the foremost spokesman for the Spiritualist movement in America, and his writings were widely used by early devotees.

However, it was the activities of the Fox sisters that caught the attention of America, a nation only one generation removed from its European origins. It was in the context of this new and growing nation, newly freed from the shackles of colonialism, that Spiritualism found its initial success. Spiritualism arose within a vortex of rapid social change and colliding philosophies and paradigms. While new immigrants with diverse beliefs were arriving at an ever-expanding rate, the nation was also expanding geographically, and the frontier was being pushed to the Pacific coast. The nation was in a state of economic flux as well, with industrialization sweeping the country, dividing society into extremes of rich and poor classes. The early nineteenth century was a time of exciting uncertainty in America, and the nation was primed for the introduction of new social and religious models to help bring stability.[5] The independent American citizen and pioneer, having grown accustomed to the individualism and freedom of the new world, looked for answers concerning the fate of his or her soul after death. Rapid social change and the hazards of the frontier only served to make such concerns more immediate. America seemed not only to tolerate new and unorthodox religious movements, but actually to encourage them. Mystic and non-rational sources were increasingly looked to as alternate provenances of knowledge by those who felt themselves alienated by the advances of the Enlightenment. Spiritualism provided not only transcendent revelation, but also the self-verification the skeptical nineteenth-century American individualist wanted.

The activities of the Fox sisters not only captured the attention of the nation, they seemed to prompt an outbreak of similar mediumistic activity across the country.[6] The repertoire of divinatory methods practiced by these early mediums was varied, and included the movement of furniture, the interpretation of mysterious sounds and rappings, trance speaking, automatic writing, gazing into crystals or mirrors, interpretation of unseen images (clairvoyance) or sounds (clairaudience), as well as manifestations of visual phenomena.[7] Despite severe criticism of these practices from many skeptics, the Spiritualist movement quickly won acceptance from a surprisingly large segment of the public. While it is impossible to estimate reliably the actual number of practicing Spiritualists during the movement's heyday, contemporary accounts suggest that the movement was large and well known. A speaker at the 1854 Baltimore Catholic congress suggested that the total Spiritualist population in America totaled over eleven million, and in 1857 it was reported that the majority of residents of Cleveland and western Ohio were Spiritualists.[8] A more reasonable estimate, considering that the total population of the country was still under twenty-five million, is that at the height of the movement in the 1850s there may have been as many as one million individuals who attended Spiritualist meetings on some sort of a regular basis.[9]

Spiritualism spread with astonishing rapidity not only in the Northeast in the area around Hydesville, but in the South and Midwest as well, with centers of activity arising in New Orleans, Chicago, and Cincinnati. By 1849 it had already traversed the continent and Spiritualist circles were being reported in California. For a short while in the late 1840s and early 1850s this newly arrived phenomenon enjoyed an almost faddish appeal; contemporary literature describes how proxy marriages were being performed on behalf of the wishes of deceased spirits (whose intentions were revealed through mediums), and, in place of funerals, special Spiritualist-influenced celebrations were held to commemorate the departure of the soul into a greater realm of knowledge. Even President Lincoln was reported to have consulted with mediums on matters of national policy. Spiritualism enjoyed a brief season of popularity with many of the early-nineteenth-century intellectual utopian communities, such as Ceresco, Hopedale, and New Harmony. The movement exploded on a national level from these initial scattered divinations, utopian associations, and faddish beginnings with greater rapidity than any other movement before or since,[10] evolving eventually into a distinct and organized religious movement.

By 1851 over 150 Spiritualist circles were operating in New York alone. By 1854 at least ten Spiritualist publications were circulating nationally, including the *Boston Spiritual Philosopher* (later known as *Spirit World*) and the *Massachusetts Spiritual Messenger*. Early circles were not doctrinally focused and they attracted members from all quarters of American religious life. Accordingly, early Spiritualist literature avoided detailed sectarian speculation and was almost exclusively Universalist in inclination. The evolution of these early circles into the Spiritualist churches of the twentieth century was prompted by a backlash from traditional Christianity to the initial wave of Spiritualist expansion, and also by the sharp period of decline the movement suffered in the late 1850s.

Because Spiritualism has purported to demonstrate the validity of its theological assertions through activities occurring in séances, which are specific occurrences subject to investigation, the movement has received intense critical scrutiny. Even devout Spiritualists admit a great deal of fraudulent divinatory activity has taken place, which they distinguish from authentic Spiritualist séances. The line between the stage magician and the medium is a thin one, and a number of nineteenth-century magicians, including Harry Houdini, had connections to Spiritualism. For every mediumistic phenomenon, be it spirit rappings or levitation, there exists a stage trick to duplicate the experience. An entire genre of popular literature arose in which skeptics would expose mediums and debunk Spiritualism, and former believers would recant their beliefs and activities. In fact, two of the Fox sisters themselves eventually admitted that the mysterious rapping sounds had been produced by the popping of their toe joints (though one of the sisters later recanted this admission). Other, more sensational accounts detailed elaborate methods of creating photographic illusions of a mysterious psychic substance called "ectoplasm." Though this particular form of divination is rare today, curious, if obviously fraudulent, photographs from the late nineteenth century and early twentieth century depicting "ectoplasmic" hands and structures emerging from the bodies of mediums have been preserved.[11] Exposure of fraudulent mediums

has continually hindered the growth of Spiritualism, and it is probably the ongoing uncovering of fraud, more than anything else, that has kept the movement from enjoying the success in America that it has experienced in Brazil and Europe, where such exposures have not been as common or sensationalistic.

As a particularly critical report on Spiritualism released by Harvard College in 1857 spearheaded the debunking of a great number of fraudulent mediums, a wave of disillusionment overtook the booming movement, and public interest suddenly abated. The advent of the Civil War served to further dampen the original fervor of the movement, and the survival of the movement in the late 1850s and 1860s (a time often referred to by believers as the "period of recantation") seemed questionable. Spiritualism reacted as a movement by centralizing itself in both belief and organizational structure, and the first national Spiritualist convention was held in Chicago in 1864 to address these matters. Later Spiritualist conventions were organized in St. Louis and New York, and by 1869 the first Spiritualist minister, James H. Powell, was ordained in Indiana. Though unsuccessful attempts to form a national Spiritualist organization took place at the first Chicago convention, it was not until 1893 that a stable and enduring organization was formed. The National Spiritualist Association of Churches (NSAC), originally founded by two former Unitarian ministers in Chicago, remains to this day the largest and most representative of the approximately fifty extant national Spiritualist organizations.[12]

Though Spiritualism would never again find the widespread popularity it enjoyed in the 1840s and 1850s, a minor revival occurred in the 1870s, and another in the era between the two World Wars. These resurgences were partially due to the increasing availability of printing facilities. Many of these new Spiritualist publications recorded the transcripts of séances and divinations, and often the entire text was purportedly dictated by a spirit being, including the widely influential *Aquarian Gospel of Jesus the Christ* (transcribed by Levi

H. Dowling), and the more sectarian *Urantia Book* (transcribed by an anonymous medium in the 1930s). These texts were significant in the development of Spiritualism in that they took the divinatory experience out of the immediacy of the séance and extended it into a universal forum. Previously, the primary focus of Spiritualism had been on the recognition of the immortality of the soul as revealed through divination, a belief understood by Spiritualists to be compatible with Christianity and the Bible. However, these new published oracles extended the focus to include elaborate metaphysical speculation and inquiry into unorthodox science and history in ways that were not inclusive of traditional Christian belief. These new texts for the first time presented the Bible with rivals for scriptural authority. Thus, an internal debate arose within Spiritualism over whether the movement could, or should, consider itself "Christian." More conservative Spiritualist groups, of which the NSAC is generally typical, still consider the Bible to be scripturally authoritative, and emphasize that divination is a facet of the practice of true Christianity. However, more liberal groups, now often called "channeling groups," do not consider themselves Christian, and generally have their own scriptures. Representative of channeling groups is the Universal Association of Faithists, an informal group that uses a mediumistically divined text, *Oahspe,* as Scripture. The Faithists understand human souls to be in a state of spiritual evolution, and believe that *Oahspe* provides not only instruction on how to live in this world, but insight on how the soul should progress through an elaborate series of spiritual planes. The text itself details a secret history of the origin of humanity, the story of the long-vanished Pacific utopia called Pan, and reveals other previously hidden scientific, religious, and social beliefs.

Channeling groups are further distinguished from traditional Spiritualism not only by their rejection of traditional Christianity and its Scripture, but also by general belief in reincarnation, a complex of metaphysical hierarchies the soul is believed to travel through, and the belief in the spiritual evolution of the soul. Traditional Spiritualism, on the other hand, usually denies reincarnation, and understands the soul to remain relatively unchanged after death. Therefore, while conservative Spiritualists seek to simply establish contact with dead souls, channelers attempt contact with spiritually evolved beings who have migrated to higher planes of existence. These elaborate metaphysical systems in channeling theology often use symbols and language from the Jewish Kabbala, Hinduism, and Neo-Gnosticism, as well as Christianity, though the use and arrangement of the various elements is unique to each system. It is difficult to generalize about channeling, since it is highly heterogeneous, even more so than the rest of Spiritualism. Many channeling groups are also closely affiliated with Theosophical and UFO-oriented belief systems, while some consider themselves the culmination of all world religions. Nonetheless, most channeling groups generally hold in common an assertion of the need for spiritual transformation of the self, freedom from psychological and social oppression, and a belief in the unlimited power of the human mind.[13] In general, channeling groups tend to avoid dogmatic exclusivism, and instead encompass many religious perspectives under some common mystical aegis.

Channeling has existed as a subgroup since the first years of the Spiritualist movement; as early as the 1850s Scottish medium Daniel Home, a favorite of Spiritualist devotee Arthur Conan Doyle, proclaimed the unlimited and untapped spiritual potential of humankind. Channeling was continued in the twentieth century by such mediums as Edgar Cayce, the famous "sleeping prophet" who channeled information from an "akashic record" purported to hold unlimited knowledge. In recent years channeling has enjoyed an enormous surge in popularity, coinciding with the New Age movement of the 1970s and 1980s. Modern channeling groups, which number in the hundreds, are usually private assemblages, tightly organized around a spiritual entity which is channeled by a single medium, though there are a number of national channeling organizations. Ironically, while channeling groups are traditionally inclusive of other religious systems, there is not much interaction among the different groups themselves. While most Spiritualist groups avoid elaborate eschatological speculation, some modern channeling groups have taken a decidedly apocalyptic tone and see the world as on the verge of cataclysmic ecological, political, and economic change.

Spiritualism remains today a viable, if quiet, alternative in the field of American religions. The typical Spiritualist church service is usually conducted much as worship is in most Protestant churches, with prayer, singing, and some sort of sermon. However, the heart of a Spiritualist service is the séance, in which the pastor or guest medium will present messages received from the spirit world. These communications are usually ritualized in structure, though some churches exercise greater spontaneity, with their séances taking on an almost charismatic ambiance.

As has been noted, there are a number of national Spiritualist organizations today, the NSAC being the largest and oldest. Most Spiritualist denominations,

including the NSAC, have relatively independent and self-governing local churches, although some denominations, such as the Churches of Spiritual Revelation Association and the Spiritualist Episcopal Church, have been more highly structured. The smaller groups tend to keep authority centralized, while the larger organizations leave authority in the hands of the local congregations. Real authority, insofar as the term applies here, is held by the medium and the experience of the séance, however. The Spiritualist organization, be it national or local, operates primarily to provide a framework of fellowship for its members, to disseminate its ideas, and to provide instruction and teaching for its members.

Though Spiritualist organizations generally place little emphasis on proselytizing, membership in them tends to turn over rapidly. The small but steady influx of new members is perhaps a testament more to the enduring human fascination with shamanistic contact with the dead than it is to the often transitory nature of Spiritualism's appeal.

Notes

1. For example, 1 Samuel 28 is commonly cited as a biblical prooftext by Spiritualists.

2. An easily readable yet detailed account of these initial sources can be found in Herbert Jackson, *The Spirit Rappers* (New York: Doubleday, 1972).

3. Geoffrey Nelson, *Spiritualism and Society* (London: Routledge and Kegan Paul, 1969), 41–58.

4. This is a common assertion, expressed by, among others, Robert S. Ellwood in "Occult Movements in America," in *Encyclopedia of the American Religious Experience,* ed. Charles H. Lippy and Peter W. Williams (New York: Scribner's, 1988), 711–22. Spiritualists themselves identify the Hydesville séances as the origin of their movement.

5. Winthrop Hudson, *Religion in America* (New York: Macmillan, 1987), 105–94.

6. For a survey of early Spiritualist figures, including Andrew Jackson Davis, see Frank

Podmore, *Mediums of the Nineteenth Century* (New York: University Books, 1963).

7. Nelson (*Spiritualism and Society,* 29–30) cites a Spiritualist article dating to 1860 in which sixteen different forms of divination are catalogued.

8. Robert S. Ellwood and Harry B. Partin, *Religious and Spiritual Groups in Modern America* (Englewood Cliffs, N.J.: Prentice-Hall, 1988), 55–60.

9. Further confounding attempts to estimate the scale of the early movement is the fact that the first Spiritualists often had little sense of self-distinction from the more traditional forms of Christianity. There was no centralized hierarchy, and briefly in many places Spiritualist thought and practice existed as a subcurrent within traditional Christian churches, just as the charismatic movement does today.

10. Nelson, *Spiritualism and Society,* 68.

11. See Ruth Brandon, *The Spiritualists* (Buffalo: Prometheus, 1984), for example. Brandon also provides an excellent discussion of the methods used by fraudulent mediums.

12. J. Gordon Melton, *Encyclopedia of American Religions,* 4th ed. (Detroit: Gale Research, 1993), provides a catalog of Spiritualist organizations on pp. 695–727.

13. J. Gordon Melton, Jerome Clark, and Aidan A. Kelly, *New Age Encyclopedia* (Detroit: Gale Research, 1990), 97–104.

Suggestions for Further Reading

Brandon, Ruth. *The Spiritualists*. Buffalo: Prometheus, 1984.

Klimo, Jon. *Channeling*. Los Angeles: Jeremy P. Tarcher, 1987.

Nelson, Geoffrey. *Spiritualism and Society*. London: Routledge and Kegan Paul, 1969.

34

NEO-PAGANISM AND WITCHCRAFT

Carol Matthews

Neo-paganism/witchcraft is a spiritual orientation and a variety of ritual practices using reconstructed mythological structures and pre-Christian rites primarily from ancient European and Mediterranean sources. Using a wide variety of techniques, neo-pagans seek to rediscover, reinterpret, and reinvigorate ancient myths, symbols, and deity forms, especially emphasizing goddess figures. Neo-paganism is usually used as an umbrella term that comprehends a wide range of beliefs and practices, including Wicca (witchcraft), druidism, ceremonial magic, and other such things. Popular opinion notwithstanding, most neo-pagans do not repudiate Christianity; on the contrary they point to the elements of Christianity that have been borrowed from pre-Christian practices and borrow widely from many other world religions.

Neo-pagans claim that their beliefs and practices spring from ancient sources. Specifically, most see in goddess worship a rediscovery of folk practices that persisted in rural Europe throughout the Christian era and up to recent times. However, the current neo-pagan revival can only be firmly traced to events and trends in the mid-nineteenth century. One source was the occult revival, which saw the flowering of conspiracy theories involving mysterious fraternities such as Knights Templar, Rosicrucians, and Illuminati, and later the emergence of new mystical religious and ceremonial orders ranging from Theosophy to Spiritualism to the Hermetic Order of the Golden Dawn. Another was romanticism, which in the emerging industrial age nostalgically sought a return to a simple pre-modern life. A third was the rise of modern anthropology, which brought earlier and less "advanced" cultures into the public eye.

Gerald Gardner

One individual was pre-eminently responsible for melding these disparate tendencies into what is now known as neo-paganism. It is possible that modern paganism could have emerged without Gerald Gardner, but without his influence it would have been quite a different phenomenon.[1]

Gardner claimed to have been initiated into magical paganism at a young age by an elderly woman named Old Dorothy. With the assistance of Aleister Crowley and others, Gardner created a set of rituals and a simple interpretation of pre-Christian Celtic worship centered on an image of a great Goddess. The new/old religion he called "Wicca," a word allegedly taken from Old English and meaning "to bend or alter." Practitioners of the religion, called witches, were held to be reawakening ancient powers of pre-Christian deities ignored by the modern world.

Gardner began teaching this religion in Britain during the 1920s. One of his initiates, the brilliant and eccentric Alexander Sanders, developed his own version of Gardner's philosophy. In turn, Sanders's students Janet and Stewart Farrar created yet another style of practice. These three branches of Wicca—Gardnerian, Alexandrian, and Farrarian—are the basis of what is often called "Brit-Trad" (British-Tradition) Wicca. The Brit-Trad "schools" and other variants on the theme began to filter into the United States in the 1960s, just when a new American market for alternative religions was emerging.

Neo-Paganism in the United States

The first generally recognized neo-pagan organization in the United States was founded in 1961 by a young man named Tim Zell. The group called itself the Church of All Worlds, and based its teachings in part on a Robert Heinlein science fiction novel.[2] The church gradually began to incorporate other beliefs and came to see itself as a modern manifestation of an ancient "sensibility" that it was believed many pre-modern peoples shared, that all life on earth is interrelated and interconnected and that the planet is a real living entity. It began to call itself "pagan" in 1967 as an expression of this sensibility. The Church of All Worlds has remained largely distinct from Wicca by maintaining its own rituals and a unique organizational structure and philosophy.

During the 1960s and 1970s neo-paganism in the United States began to take root and develop features that made it distinct from the British and European pagan movements. Philosophers such as Isaac Bonewits developed complex theories of ritual and magic which incorporated computer and technological ideas and language to explain how magic works. Z. Budapest and Starhawk, blending facets of Wicca with other pagan traditions and emerging feminism, created a woman-centered version of the religion

called "Feminist/Dianic Wicca." Individuals who interpreted Gardnerian and Alexandrian traditions in their own fashion created new sects of Wicca, some which have become significant in their own right, e.g., Frostian and Georgian Wicca. During the 1970s other groups began to emerge that were interested in reviving pagan traditions other than those represented by Wicca, such as Asatru (Norse), Hellenic (Greek), and Isis-Osirian (neo-Egyptian). By the 1980s the sheer variety of neo-pagan groups in the United States had become staggering, generating a new genre of books, a growing number of festivals, new computer bulletin boards for networking, and even whole communities for pagans who could afford to purchase land together. The interest in and growth of neo-paganism has continued unabated and today neo-paganism is among the fastest growing new religious movements.[3]

Beliefs and Practices

Despite the central historical position of Gardnerian Wicca, there is no one authority or scripture for all neo-pagans. Neo-pagans borrow quite freely from many religious and philosophical traditions and from each other. This allows for a great deal of personal religious freedom in thought and practice. As a result, the neo-pagan community has been diverse, not centralized. Many neo-pagans "discover" their religion through publications and become "solitary practitioners" rather than members of covens. In the effort to find one another, neo-pagans turn to books, periodicals, computer bulletin board services, and festivals where they can share their beliefs and practices.

As a result of this networking and the influence of Gardnerian Wicca, the following general practices and beliefs have emerged as comprising a "generic" pagan theology and ritual structure. This structure remains loosely true to form even among neo-pagans who do not profess association with Wicca.

1. There is a general tendency to stress the importance of the feminine principle in divinity. Most pagans see this tendency as stemming from the overuse of a male deity in our culture and feel that they are seeking to re-balance this inequity.

2. There are general ethical principles which maintain that whatever one does comes back at some point—a kind of "instant karma," often called the threefold law: whatever you do comes back to you three times over. Connected with this principle is the Wiccan Rede, a general ethical motto that is often cited as the core neo-pagan credo: "An it harm none, do what thou wilt." Closely related to this ethical principle for most pagans is a doctrine of reincarnation that acts both as a means by which the cosmos exacts justice and as a device whereby individual souls spiritually grow and develop.

3. Finally, there is a stress on the need to develop a facility for the working of magic. Magic is to be used for generally constructive and defensive purposes and there is an emphasis, at least in the literature, that one should strive for balance and control of self before working magic.[4]

Most neo-pagans cultivate a healthy sense of humor about their gods and goddesses, stressing the importance of "reverence *and* mirth" in religious practices. Many neo-pagans engage in "discordian" behavior or magic, a practice difficult to describe that frequently emerges during rituals that may be getting too solemn for the sensibilities of some present. It is not uncommon for jokes and silliness to attend the most serious invocations; neo-pagans claim that such antics act as humbling devices designed to remind participants of the divine chaos present in the universe.

Most neo-pagans observe eight high festivals which correspond to the turning points of the agricultural year and the seasons: Yule (Winter Solstice), Imbolg (Candlemas, February 2), Vernal Equinox (March 21), Beltane (May Day, May 1), Midsummer (Summer Solstice), Lammas (August 1), Autumnal Equinox (September 21), and Samhain (Halloween). These are thought to be times of maximum power, when the forces of the land, the ancestors and the goddesses/gods are at their height. Many neo-pagans also observe the phases of the moon with special rituals. A festival is typically observed with a main ritual, in which a sacred place is established by the casting of a circle and the invoking of goddesses/gods and other additional powers that might be considered helpful and which are associated with the season. A rite of the sharing of food and drink usually forms the main portion of the ritual. Although most books describing the festivals recommend the use of cakes (bread) and wine, this author has participated in rites where Kool-Aid, cola, potato chips, and pizza were used as legitimate substitutes. According to neo-pagans, it's the thought and spirit that count, not the literal substance used.

After the ritual there is usually more food and drink shared along with storytelling, songs, and sometimes even short dramas depicting myths both ancient and modern which have been composed for the occasion. There remains a common public perception that neo-pagans also engage in sexual orgies during these rituals. While it is true that neo-pagans are, for the most part, freer in their sexual attitudes and expressions than mainstream Americans, tolerating homosexuality, bisexuality, alternative partnerships, and multiple partners relatively easily, most of these relationships are conducted in private. After attending literally hundreds of rituals, this author has yet to encounter a single orgy. With the current spread of AIDS and other sexually transmitted diseases, neo-pagans have become their own police, freely handing out condoms at festivals and strongly advising safe sex. Responsibility has become a byword.

The most frequent items used in ritual services are the wand, the cup, the pentacle, and the dagger, representing, respectively, the four elements of fire (or air), water, earth and air (or fire). These four elements (tools) also correspond to the will, emotions, body, and intellect of the human being. One uses these elements to "cast a circle," to create a sacred space wherein magic or ritual is to be worked. The powers of the four elements are invoked with the corresponding tools in the four directions: east/air, south/fire, west/water, north/earth. The caster of the circle represents the fifth direction/element, that of spirit. Often the elemental directions are invoked by calling on gods/goddesses, spirits, or angels that are said to rule these elements. Once the circle is cast, and proper purifications have been made, commonly through the use of saltwater and incense, the magical work or ritual may commence.[5]

There is often a confusion in the public's mind about the real function and purpose of magic. While neo-pagans will differ on the precise definition of what they call magic, for most of them, magic or spellwork is a means by which a prayer or petition is acted out in a ritual. It uses props and words to calm and focus the mind in order that the universe/goddess may be made aware of the needs and wants of the practitioner. Most pagans strongly emphasize that while the items used in spells/magic, such as candles, colored cloth, herbs and incense, are facilitators of magic, the real magic lies in one's own focus and intentions. Props are used to help create an atmosphere, and in some instances represent a kind of sacrifice to deities being called upon, as a payment for their attention and concern. Many neo-pagans also keep a record of their rituals and magical workings called a "Book of Secrets/Shadows" in which they keep track of the efficacy of their rites. Neo-pagans regard themselves as practical people who will abandon techniques and rituals which are considered ineffective or negative. Often some form of divination, astrology, tarot, or runework will accompany the ritual as sign or communication from the powers invoked as to the probable outcome of the rite.

The great majority of neo-pagans stress the importance of engaging in magic for only positive or constructive purposes. This general principle does not prevent, however, the odd pagan from occasionally engaging in such practices as "black/destructive magic." If such a person is discovered, he/she is commonly shunned by the community and can be blackballed throughout the networking system. The issue of ethics in magical practice is a topic of continuing debate among neo-pagans who often spend a great deal of time determining whether or not a ritual is well intended prior to a working in order that there may be no confusion among themselves or the powers to be invoked.

According to most neo-pagans, an individual is not "made into a pagan"; rather, one discovers that she/he has been a pagan all along. Typically a person who has been searching for a spiritual practice happens upon neo-paganism through a friend or publication and realizes that there are others who share the same perceptions and feelings about divinity and nature. Neo-pagans do not proselytize openly, and many groups are in fact quite insular, seeking to engender security and intimacy in their magical practice. An individual who wants to become "officially" pagan is often initiated into a particular school of practice by a high priest/priestess or a coven. Self-initiations are also quite legitimate. Some groups maintain a simple degree system based on Gardner's adoption of the spiritual levels practiced by occult lodges. Others simply rotate ritual responsibilities among the membership. Initiation is a ritual of self-sacrifice and commitment that binds an individual to a practice and a set of goddesses/gods that become the protectors of his/her magical and religious practice.

Controversies

Allusion has been made to common public misperception of neo-paganism. Much of the criticism levelled against neo-pagans has come from other marginalized religious groups, notably Christian fundamentalist sects that persistently link neo-pagan practices with "Satanism." These linkages are exacerbated by the tendency of official satanic organizations to blur the distinctions between themselves and neo-pagans, often imitating the practices and language of neo-pagans. Neo-pagans are adamant about the distinctions between themselves and Satanists, pointing out that Satanism tends to focus on "selfish" magic and certain male images of divinity, does not affirm fundamental doctrines of reincarnation and cosmic justice, and bases itself on an affirmation of the Christian doctrine of the duality of good and evil which neo-pagans deny. The most common neo-pagan defense is that they do not believe in Satan and therefore they cannot be said to be worshipping him. For certain Christian fundamentalists, these are superficial protestations, since any faith or practice not corresponding to their own is considered suspect and probably satanic.

Neo-pagans have also come under attack for their generally libertine attitudes toward variant sexual orientations/practices and for their insistence on reclaiming words such as "witch" and "magic" from common negative connotations. Fears of "witchcraft" have led to neo-pagans' losing their jobs, their homes, and their children in some cases; in one instance of which the author is personally aware, a neo-pagan was lynched by a group of fundamentalists who deemed him a danger to the community.[6] In some instances neo-pagan ritual sites on private property have been vandalized and festivals threatened. In 1986 Senator Jesse Helms introduced a bill in Congress that would have prevented already legitimated neo-pagan religious organizations from receiving tax-exempt status, in effect making such bodies not "real" religions in the eyes of the federal government. The measure was killed in committee, but such actions have galvanized the neo-pagan community. There now exist a number of neo-pagan legal networks whose sole purpose is to monitor the activities of government on local, state, and federal levels in order to counter anti–neo-pagan activity with letter-writing campaigns and demonstrations. In addition, there has been a recent movement toward organizing a kind of official clergy that could both serve the neo-pagan community at large and act as representatives of neo-pagan concerns at interfaith gatherings and political hearings. How this would be accomplished is not clear, since the sheer variety of neo-pagan traditions and practices renders any general understanding of the movement inadequate and even inaccurate. Many neo-pagans also feel that the creation of an official clergy would create an atmosphere of dogma, and an authority class within the neo-pagan community that would stifle individuality and creativity. Still, most neo-pagans see a need for solidarity among all the modern pagan traditions in order to meet opposition more effectively. Neo-paganism has found support in some factions of the feminist and environmental movements, with whom the neo-pagan movement has some shared concerns. American neo-paganism is much more politically aggressive than its European counterparts, and, as a result, many neo-pagans often are also members of feminist and environmental groups, using these movements as further legitimation of their rituals and beliefs.

Demographics and Other General Information

The neo-pagan movement has, until recently, been largely a white, urban, middle-class development. During the last decade this trend has continued with some general broadening of the demographic base into rural, working-class and, less frequently, upper-class practitioners. Members of the upper class who are interested in alternative religions tend to become attracted to New Age or Ceremonial Magic spiritualities, since they can afford the complicated tools and the expensive seminars associated with such spiritual paths. Growing movements of Hispanics and African Americans who are rediscovering elements of their own pre-Christian traditions are generally quite distinct from neo-pagans and strongly maintain their independence.

Recent surveys have indicated that over half of all neo-pagans are female, although the gender gap has narrowed considerably in the last five years, and there are substantially more gay and bisexually identified individuals in the neo-pagan population than the national average (25 to 30 percent of the pagan community as compared to 10 to 13 percent overall).[7] The occupations of neo-pagans are a cross-section of middle-class America with everything from teachers, executives, lawyers, laborers, and artists to computer programmers represented. Most neo-pagans, however, reside within that 40 percent of Americans who have attended college, and refer to themselves as voracious readers. Most neo-pagans are up on current affairs and are articulate. Most are as conversant about the federal budget and other public affairs as they are about theories of reincarnation and the latest ritual needs for a healing spell—all within an hour's discourse. In addition, far from being nostalgic nature lovers, most neo-pagans are not anti-technological. Technology is seen as a tool for proper use and management of nature. Pollution and environmental destruction are "bad magic," symptoms of selfish spiritual doctrines. Neo-pagans seem to be particularly entranced with computer technology and recent developments in both physics and biology, which they claim support their views on the flexibility of mind and matter and of divine consciousness residing in all things. A recent development is the use of computers to engage in computer bulletin board long-distance rituals in which different practitioners will dial up and contact each other at an appointed time. They then engage in an ad hoc ritual with each participant adding something to the ritual and then responding via the keyboard as the rite progresses—rather like religious Nintendo.

Pagans in the United States are more politically active than they are in Europe, reflecting the higher level of opposition to neo-paganism in America and the connections between the neo-pagan movement and the feminist and environmental movements.

Summary

Neo-paganism appears to be growing in popularity. Estimates of numbers range from the tens to hundreds of thousands of active participants and individuals sympathetic to the movement. The large festivals, of which there are approximately a half-dozen in the United States every year, and whose numbers are increasing annually, routinely draw five hundred to seven hundred people each. Neo-paganism is counted as one of the most rapidly growing of the new religious movements. A large publishing industry geared specifically to serving the needs and interests of the larger neo-pagan community has already emerged.

Neo-pagans are currently engaged in consolidating and further defining themselves and their political and spiritual agendas. This process will perhaps never be completely implemented as there are many neo-pagans who object to any kind of overall organization of their movement. Still, neo-pagans remain unified and active in the protection of their legal religious rights, and have recently won several concessions from entrenched political opponents. Neo-paganism is alive and continuing to grow in the United States, Europe, and Australia. As neo-pagans themselves put it: "The Goddess is alive and magic is afoot."

Notes

1. Jeffrey Burton Russell, *A History of Witchcraft* (London: Thames and Hudson, 1980), 148–55.

2. The novel was Robert A. Heinlein's *Stranger in a Strange Land* (New York: G. P. Putnam's Sons, 1961; Avon Books, 1962).

3. Margot Adler, *Drawing Down the Moon* (Boston: Beacon Press, 1986), 372–437.

4. Starhawk's view on the working of magic is probably closest to being normative in America. Starhawk, *The Spiral Dance, A Rebirth of the Ancient Religion of the Great Goddess* (San Francisco: Harper and Row, 1979).

5. Starhawk, *The Spiral Dance,* 55–75.

6. Such cases are a regular feature of most neo-pagan periodicals. Example: Gerrie Ordaz, "Lady Liberty Report," *Circle Network News,* no. 45 (Mt. Horeb, Wisc.: Summer 1992): 7.

7. Examples of surveys reflecting these demographics can found in Adler, *Drawing Down the Moon,* 443–65, and, more recently, Carpenter and Fox, "Pagan Spirit Gathering 1991 Tribal Survey Results," *Circle Network News,* no. 45 (Mt. Horeb, Wisc.: Summer 1992): 20.

Suggestions for Further Reading

Adler, Margot. *Drawing Down the Moon.* Boston: Beacon Press, 1986.

Campanelli, Pauline. *Wheel of the Year.* St. Paul: Llewellyn, 1989.

Luhrmann, T. M. *Persuasions of the Witch's Craft.* Cambridge: Harvard University Press, 1989.

Russell, Jeffrey B. *A History of Witchcraft.* London: Thames and Hudson, 1980.

Starhawk. *The Spiral Dance.* San Francisco: Harper and Row, 1979.

35

WHITHER THE NEW AGE?

J. Gordon Melton

In the 1960s the United Kingdom gave birth to a very American social movement. It was metaphysical, immanental, world affirming, and millenarian.[1] Its intellectual roots were in nineteenth-century German idealism but it drew its inspiration more immediately from eschatological hopes that had taken different forms in occult circles, especially in the many groups on the fringes of the realtively conservative and staid Theosophical Society.

The constituency for this movement consisted of the millions of persons open to occult ideas. While the numbers of active members of the several visible occult and metaphysical groups were small, public acceptance of some key occult ideas (reincarnation and astrology, for example) and practices (meditation, most prominently) had quietly mushroomed throughout the twentieth century. Millions had dropped out of churches and synagogues because the established religious institutions were not meeting their spiritual needs. Like many who opted for evangelical Protestantism, these seekers found the traditional religious organizations too bogged down in administrative concerns and secular affairs to nurture the spiritual lives of their members. They saw problems in what they identified as "organized religion" and sought an alternative spirituality, but one that would not take them out of the world. The New Age movement beckoned.

The Long View— Whence the New Age?

Religious history is usually recounted in terms of large denominations; it tends to dismiss the steady current of dissent as a series of trifling outbreaks of heresy and apostasy. In fact, however, by the middle of the eighteenth century powerful dissenting forces were massed against the traditional order. In the salons and cafes of pre-revolutionary France, especially, a working alliance of secularists, political revolutionaries, and occultists emerged, an alliance later vividly portrayed in pictures of the United States' first president in his masonic garb and in the placing of occult symbols on the new country's national seal.[2]

Post-revolutionary governments in France and America allowed many forms of religious dissent even while leaving the older churches in place. England, escaping violent revolution, haltingly made room for dissenters as well. Following different paths, the United States and many western European countries arrived at the same place: in each a powerful Christian community remains, but religious dissent, in bewildering variety, has come into the open as well. The communities of dissent no longer just request space on the cultural fringes, but demand seats on the board of directors.

Possibly the largest of these earlier dissenting movements was Freemasonry, which spread a new gnostic spirituality.[3] Since it was not a "church" and did not openly compete with Christianity, it could spread unopposed to every city and town. Although opposed by the Catholic church and some conservative Protestants, it was generally not seen as a competitor to orthodox Christianity, and many church members and leaders joined. In America, where only 20 to 30 percent of the population were church members in the nineteenth century, masonry functioned as a spiritual home to the religiously unaffiliated. Meanwhile, other movements—Swedenborgianism, magnetism, and Spiritualism, for example, all heavily influenced by the philosophy of Ralph Waldo Emerson—also flourished in the nineteenth century, developing influence far beyond their small core memberships.

Meanwhile, orthodox Christianity was shaken by the early phase of what would later be called modernism. The need to respond to immigration, urbanization, industrialization, new scientific findings in geology and biology, and biblical criticism spawned the most significant theological revolution since the Reformation. Some religious bodies wavered on bedrock doctrines such as the Trinity and the divinity of Jesus, and in the new liberal milieu church membership began to be seen as less than essential to salvation. Churches came more and more to resemble the metaphysical groups.[4]

In some cases modernism and metaphysical religion merged. Christian Science and New Thought appeared in the 1870s and 1880s, respectively, developing their programs around a "practical" application of Emerson's ideas. Both groups enjoyed immediate, enthusiastic popular responses and quickly built national organizations, despite the fact that they were not recognized as Christian by the established churches. Metaphysical books by such authors as Ralph Waldo Trine and Henry Wood became nationwide bestsellers.[5]

For the New Age movement, the most important of these nineteenth-century currents was Theosophy. New Thought and Christian Science were peculiarly American and not spectacularly successful elsewhere, but the Theosophical Society, founded in 1875, spread worldwide in its first generation and spawned many similar groups, some of which would eclipse it in membership.[6]

Alternative Spirituality in the Twentieth Century

By the beginning of the twentieth century several distinct schools of alternative spiritual thought had become well defined. In the 1890s Spiritualism adopted a "church" model, complete with a variety of denominations. New Thought backed away from its initial commitment to a feminist social agenda and focused on a "practical" program of assisting persons seeking healing and trying to find their niches in the new corporate society. As in the case of Spiritualism, several New Thought denominations emerged, among them Unity, Religious Science, and Divine Science. They achieved great popular influence, even though their memberships were never large. Unity, for example, mainly operated a literature ministry, circulating publications far beyond its own adherents. Issued by commercial publishers, writings of leading metaphysical authors Emmet Fox, William Walker Atkinson, Walter Lanyon, Stella Terrill Mann, and others reached millions of readers unaware of the authors' spiritual affiliations.

Two dynamic women, Annie Besant and Katherine Tingley, oversaw a growing Theosophical movement at the turn of the century. Tingley's branch found its focus in the Point Loma community at San Diego, where it built a successful model of the good society. After Tingley's lifetime, unfortunately, the community closed and her group declined. Besant's Theosophical Society saw spectacular growth in the new century, fueled by a burst of messianic millennialism. Convinced of the cosmic role of young Jiddu Krishnamurti, Besant toured the world in the 1920s announcing him as the World Savior. A new age was dawning.

Besant's millennialism did not captivate all Theosophists. Tingley's group rejected it. One movement, the Aquarian Foundation, founded a competing messianism.[7] Occult magician Aleister Crowley announced that a new aeon had already begun in 1904 and should be dominated by his "thelemic" teachings. This wave of millennialism fell in a series of scandals beginning with Krishnamurti's resignation from his exalted status in 1929, but the seed had been sown and the hope of a new age, so much a part of Christian thinking, had a new home in the occult metaphysical world.

One prominent mid-century Theosophist, Alice Bailey, revitalized the movement's millennial hopes. She claimed that Besant had anticipated the new age too soon, that it was really due late in the twentieth century. Theosophy still had time to prepare the world for what was now at hand.[8]

By the 1960s these currents began to converge in England. Spiritualism was firmly entrenched. Theosophy was strong, although divided into many small groups, many only loosely aware of their Theosophical roots. Astrology had made a comeback from near oblivion in the mid-nineteenth century. After World War II religious teachers had immigrated from the mystic East. Influenced by popular interest in consciousness-altering drugs, psychologists turned their attention to the study of religious means of changing consciousness, thus providing new credentials for alternative approaches to the spiritual life. The time was ripe for a new religious movement that could integrate all of these trends.

The New Age

The original New Age movement centered on several fairly simple ideas, notably that of millenarianism. As the twentieth century drew to a close, planet earth would receive new waves of spiritual energy, generally depicted in astrological terms, often as the Aquarian Age. The configuration of the heavens signalled the release of new energies.

A few groups of people began to cultivate these incoming energies. For example, among those who gathered at the Findhorn community near Inverness, Scotland, were some attuned to nature spirits who managed to grow spectacular agricultural produce on relatively barren ground.[9] Ultimate reality, it was held, was not transcendent but *immanent* in life and nature, ordering the world and structuring the environment. Attunement to spiritual law brought happiness; disobeying spiritual laws was the source of all human problems.

Slowly the community of New Age believers grew. Drawing on Theosophical images, they spoke of "spiritual light" and of their own gatherings as points of light. Linked, New Age groups would saturate the world with focused spiritual energy. People and the world itself would be transformed. A New Age would arrive.[10]

The message of the New Age swept through the ranks of the psychically attuned in much the same way that the charismatic movement did at the same time through ranks of evangelical Christians. First articulated in small groups such as the Wrekin Trust in Britain, the New Age quickly reached the continent and North America. The many Theosophical groups readily took up roles in the emerging network of light. By the end of the 1960s an international movement was in place, and travelling evangelists such as Anthony Brooke were planting new centers everywhere.

The early points of light were swamped by the response to the New Age message and somewhat taken aback by the uncontrolled diversification the movement soon manifested. Looking back, we can see that many existing low-profile metaphysical, spiritualist, and occult groups altered their programs and helped set up many new groups. Like Christian revivalists they contrasted their vitality to the dead routines and dreary bureaucracies of older churches. The New Age movement contrasted itself with "organized religion," proclaiming itself neither centrally organized nor a religion, but simply a free-flowing spiritual movement. Although New Age groups gradually took on the functions and provided the services of traditional churches, they adopted the Baptist free-church system as their organizational model—autonomous congregations cooperating to support publishing houses, missionary programs, and other special agencies and activities.

As with the free-church movement, the little overall power that exists in the New Age movement is held primarily by publishers and networkers. New Age theoreticians are almost entirely dependent on the publishing houses and bookstores for reaching their public. Other leaders stand at the nexus of groups and networks, organizing the large New Age conventions and scheduling speakers and workshops.

Much of the success of the New Age movement in the 1980s can be attributed to its establishment of a broad world-affirming program. Traditional occult organizations had tended to renounce worldly action and to focus on individual occult training. In contrast, international relations, health, and the environment topped the New Age social program. Some early New Agers were veterans of the peace movement and promoted its agenda as well. Locked out of formal diplomacy, they worked for peace through contacts with people in countries with which their own governments had less than cordial relationships. They believed that their small efforts would be infused with spiritual energy and directly contribute to global change.

At the same time some physicians with occult interests and others frustrated at the stubborn limitations of modern medicine developed what became known as the holistic health movement. New Agers saw in holistic health a cultural critique similar to the one that metaphysical religion had brought to the churches, and new holistic practitioners found a ready clientele for their new medicine.

Early on the New Agers made common cause with the older environmental movement. The mixing of New Age and traditional environmental ideas became especially easy after the publication of the Gaia Hypothesis, the concept that the earth is best understood as a single living organism. Also closely related to the environmental cause has been the New Age–influenced animal rights movement.

Peace, healing, and environmental restoration mingled readily with spiritual transformation; images of one group became metaphors for another. The New Age movement came to maturity as it offered not just occult training and cultural dissent, but a complete alternative lifestyle.

The Downfall of the New Age

Just as the New Age alternative matured and found a fair degree of acceptance in the general culture it came under attack from both without and within. Outside critics levelled their attacks at the movement's naivete, engaging in ridicule more than argument and focusing especially on Channeling and the use of crystals. Channeling was a new name for what Spiritualists had called mediumship, the claimed ability of certain individuals to contact the world of certain disembodied entities. Some critics dismissed Channeling altogether, but the more effective criticism centered on the successful channels who charged high fees and had become wealthy through the practice. Meanwhile, others attacked the claim that crystals had "scientific" properties that enabled them to store and transmit energy. Crystal promoters were forced to back away from their scientific claims and had to defend the use of crystals entirely on less-attractive spiritual grounds.

While the outside critics were ridiculing the New Age, some of the movement's own leaders began to question its adequacy. Several, including noted New Age theoretician David Spangler, attacked as unrealistic the most central of New Age precepts, the imminent global cultural transformation.[11] As a result, the youthful voices of the 1970s lost their faith that a new age could actually arise in their lifetimes. The internal loss of faith and the stinging external criticisms led many New Age leaders to pronounce the movement's obituary. By the early 1990s fewer persons than previously would identify themselves as New Agers.

Whither the New Age?

The New Age movement may be in decline, but it has not been consigned to the dustbin. Its critics who deemed it a superficial fad, who reduced it all to Channeling and crystals, failed to see that at its heart was a clear, mature religious vision that combined the centuries-old Western metaphysical tradition with new (to the West) Eastern wisdom traditions. The label "New Age" may have lost popularity, but the movement's beliefs and practices remained under new names that, many would argue, actually better describe the community of transformed, spiritually awakened, compassionate, earth-loving persons of which the movement consists. In Los Angeles, for example, the largest New Age–type gathering takes place under the name "whole life."

Other trappings remain as well. The publishers and bookstores are still in business; the number of New Age magazines is stable; the networks still promote a steady diet of lectures and workshops. Annual conventions still attract large crowds, and a fourth to a third of the public still report their adherence to the more popular New Age ideas and practices.

The New Age movement has taken its place in the community of alternative religions. The metaphysical and occult religions have developed a new vocabulary and a new respectability. The New Age holistic, alternative vision of life is prominent in the marketplace of ideas. New Agers may not be able to transform the whole culture, but they stand ready at least to work on their own little parts of the world.

Notes

1. This chapter attempts to synthesize some twenty years of observation of the New Age movement and draws in part on insights from two previously published works: J. Gordon Melton, Jerome Clark, and Aidan A. Kelly, *The New Age Encyclopedia* (Detroit: Gale Research, 1990), and James R. Lewis and J. Gordon Melton, eds., *Perspectives on the New Age* (Albany: State University of New York Press, 1992).

2. See James H. Billington, *Fire in the Minds of Men* (New York: Basic Books, 1980).

3. The gnostic worldview of Freemasonry is well presented in the popular textbook compiled by Albert Pike, *Morals and Dogma of the Ancient and Accepted Scottish Rite of Freemasonry* (Charleston, S.C.: Supreme Council for the Southern Jurisdiction, 1871, plus many later editions).

4. On modernism as a theological movement, see William R. Hutchinson, *The Modernist Impulse in American Protestantism* (Cambridge: Harvard University Press, 1976).

5. On New Thought and related movements see Charles S. Braden, *Spirits in Rebellion* (Dallas: Southern Methodist University Press, 1963).

6. See Bruce F. Campbell, *A History of the Theosophical Movement* (Berkeley: University of California Press, 1980).

7. On the Aquarian Foundation see John Oliphant, *Brother Twelve: The Incredible Story of Canada's False Prophet* (Toronto: McClelland and Stewart, 1991).

8. Alice Bailey's crucial New Age ideas are found in *The Reappearance of the Christ* (New York: Lucis, 1948) and *Discipleship in the New Age* (New York: Lucis, 1944).

9. On the early years of Findhorn see Paul Hawken, *The Magic of Findhorn* (New York: Harper and Row, 1975).

10. Among sources describing the early process of networking and naming the first people to link up is Ralph F. Raymond (Brother Francis), *The Universal Link Concept* (Los Angeles: Universal Link Heart Center, 1968).

11. In 1988 Spangler attempted to redefine the New Age and demythologize its outlook through a series of articles that appeared in a spectrum of New Age periodicals. Among them was "Defining the New Age," *New Realities* (May/June 1988).

Suggestions for Further Reading

Lewis, James R., and J. Gordon Melton, eds. *Perspectives on the New Age*. Albany: State University of New York Press, 1992.

Melton, J. Gordon, Jerome Clark, and Aidan A. Kelly. *The New Age Encyclopedia*. Detroit: Gale Research, 1990.

36

THE ASSOCIATION FOR RESEARCH AND ENLIGHTENMENT: SAVED BY THE NEW AGE

Phillip Lucas

The Association for Research and Enlightenment (ARE), a non-profit corporation founded by supporters of the "sleeping prophet" Edgar Cayce, had already been spreading its hybrid brand of Theosophical Christianity and psychic development for thirty-five years when the youth counterculture exploded on the American scene during the mid-1960s. This explosion was a watershed event for the association. From the mid-1960s to the early 1990s ARE has grown to become an influential promoter of alternative spiritualities in America—particularly the combination of beliefs and practices that scholars have designated as "New Age" spirituality. The story of ARE's successful adaptation to the changes in America's religious ecology during the 1960s and 1970s is a noteworthy example of how a new religious movement that barely survives its founding generation can flourish during a later period of cultural upheaval and renewal.

The association was incorporated in the state of Virginia in 1931 as a research institution dedicated to studying the clairvoyant "readings" given through Cayce (1877–1945). The famed psychic was a native of rural Kentucky who had been reared in the strongly biblicist tradition of the Christian Church. When he was twenty-four, Cayce became disabled by chronic headaches. One day he lapsed into a coma and upon regaining consciousness could barely speak. This condition lasted for a year, during which time Cayce's general health continued to fail. Among those who treated him was a noted New York physician who encouraged Cayce to diagnose his own condition while under self-hypnosis. Cayce was successful in this experiment and, while in hypnotic trance, prescribed a treatment that led to his complete cure.[1]

Soon Cayce was giving "health" readings for people who had heard of his talent and made requests for help via mail or telegram. The young man would put himself into a hypnotic "sleep" and purportedly "view" the body of the petitioner. He would then diagnose the ailment and prescribe a treatment using such folk remedies as herbs, compresses, massage, and castor oil. The many reported cases of successful recovery enhanced Cayce's reputation and made him a nationally known figure.[2]

Cayce's readings began to mention his petitioner's past lives and "karmic" conditions after his meeting with Arthur Lammers, a wealthy Theosophist from Dayton, Ohio, in 1923. From that time on, Cayce delivered both health readings and what he called "life" readings. These life readings mentioned subjects that would become important elements of New Age thought during the 1970s and 1980s, including healing with crystals, the history of the fabled continent of Atlantis, imminent geological and climactic upheavals, and a correlation of esoteric astrology with reincarnation.[3]

Cayce soon attracted the attention of Morton and Edwin Blumenthal, two businessmen who were interested in exploiting his "gift" for oil and mineral exploration. With their help Cayce relocated to Virginia Beach, Virginia, in 1925 and devoted himself exclusively to his clairvoyant work (he had also been a commercial photographer). The Association of National Investigators (ANI) was established in 1927 to promote research into the health readings. The centerpiece of its efforts was an experimental thirty-bedroom hospital built in 1928 to treat patients according to the Cayce remedies. In 1930 ANI also opened Atlantic University, a small liberal arts college whose entire faculty was sympathetic to psychic research.[4]

The Blumenthals sustained devastating financial setbacks at the height of the Depression and both the Cayce Hospital and Atlantic University had to be closed in February 1931. A few weeks later Cayce's most loyal supporters gathered in Virginia Beach with the intention of salvaging the work of ANI. The outcome of this meeting was the incorporation of the Association for Research and Enlightenment as a philanthropic organization dedicated to "psychical research." Between 1931 and 1945 ARE served mainly to facilitate Cayce's clairvoyant readings and to issue a newsletter to members. In 1942 Thomas Sugrue published a popular and a sympathetic biography of Cayce, *There Is a River,* which garnered favorable national attention for the association. The following year a *Coronet* magazine article entitled "Miracle Man of Virginia Beach" brought a flood of new members—most of whom were interested in receiving readings for themselves.[5]

In keeping with Cayce's desire to make his "channelled" information available for medical research, the readings had been recorded verbatim by a trained stenographer from the time of his earliest sessions. By 1945 an archive of almost fifteen thousand transcripts had been assembled— probably the largest record of psychic readings ever obtained from a single source. It was this resource that would soon become the foundation of ARE's work.[6]

The association nearly folded after Cayce's untimely death in January 1945. Most of its two thousand members left when they realized Cayce would no longer be available for readings. Presiding over a membership that had dwindled to three hundred, the ARE's board met in June to decide upon the group's future. Two trustees expressed the view that, with Cayce gone, the association had lost its inspirational center and should dissolve itself. The archive of readings would be given to a university or to the American Society for Psychical Research. The majority, however, rejected this suggestion and voted to continue ARE's program of research and education.[7]

At this point, Hugh Lynn Cayce, Edgar Cayce's eldest son, returned from duty in World War II. The younger Cayce, a trained psychologist, had worked for ARE from its inception, fostering small study groups around the country, hosting a radio show devoted to psychic research, and organizing annual ARE congresses. His goal now, he confided to his friend Harmon H. Bro, was to preserve the Cayce legacy for future generations and to "make the name of Cayce known everywhere."[8]

Hugh Lynn Cayce's strategy was fourfold. First, he initiated a series of winter lectures which took him annually to both coasts, the Midwest, and the South. He spoke of his father's work on radio shows and campuses, in churches and hospitals, and at retreats and conferences. Second, he created the Edgar Cayce Foundation in January 1946 to secure legal guardianship of the readings for the Cayce family. The foundation's main work would be to microfilm and cross-index the readings by subject for research purposes. Third, the younger Cayce sought to put the association on a firmer scientific footing. This was to be accomplished by promoting studies that correlated data from the readings with cutting-edge research in universities and hospitals on such subjects as archaeology, physiotherapy, and parapsychology. Cayce also hired psychologists for his top staff and physicians to start an ARE clinic where the medical readings could be tested. The fourth element in Cayce's strategy was to minimize attacks by fundamentalist Christians by stressing the non-religious nature of the association and by emphasizing the mainstream Christian aspects of the readings. He also curried favor with ministers of Christian denominations by inviting them to lecture at national and regional conferences on topics related to the Cayce material. Finally, Cayce organized the ARE Press, which began to produce books, pamphlets, and other educational materials analyzing the information presented in the readings.[9]

During the 1950s, Hugh Lynn Cayce increased ARE's membership by forming liaisons with groups and movements whose doctrines overlapped with the content of the readings. In groups like Unity, Divine Science, the Rosicrucians, Theosophy, the Arcane School, and Spiritual Frontiers Fellowship, he found people with a ready interest in such ARE teachings as ESP, reincarnation, psychic development, positive thinking, dreams, meditation, astrology, *kundalini* yoga, and ancient cultures. Cayce spoke often before these groups and soon had created a major following for his annual ARE lecture tours—as well as new ARE recruits.[10]

The 1960s marked the association's first decade of significant growth. In the early 1960s there were 2,500 members and 90 study groups nationwide. By 1970 these numbers had increased to 12,000 members and 1,023 study groups, with almost 30 new groups forming every month. The Edgar Cayce Foundation, with an annual operating budget of about twenty thousand dollars, managed to process (for duplication and indexing) nearly every one of the medical and life readings during the decade. The ARE Press steadily expanded its publications list and moved to a new building adjacent to headquarters in 1961. Between 1956 and 1974, it would print nine million books and pamphlets. In 1960, the group had fifteen paid employees at its Virginia Beach headquarters. By 1970 this number had grown to eighty-three.[11]

The bulk of this new growth took place between 1966 and 1970, at the same time the youth counterculture became a nation-wide social phenomenon. ARE developed successful strategies to attract the spiritual seekers within this youth cohort. In the process it shifted demographically from a movement of primarily middle-class, middle-aged adults (60 percent female) who were disaffected from mainstream church life to a much more diverse population that included hippies, teenagers, prisoners, humanistic psychologists, and alternative health practitioners.[12]

These changes in membership were reflected in the workshops, seminars, publications, and new programs that were initiated during this period. In 1963, ARE held what would be the first of its Asilomar Workshop and Camp weeks in Monterey, California, within hailing distance of the Esalen Institute at Big Sur. Unlike the earlier Asilomar meetings, whole families were invited to this workshop and some fifty youths under sixteen participated. These young persons attended sessions on psychic development, holistic medicine, reincarnation, and meditation. Also in 1963 Hugh Lynn Cayce spearheaded the construction of an ARE youth camp on a fifty-acre site in rural southwestern Virginia. By the early 1970s, what had begun as a weeklong wilderness campout for teens had grown to a seven-session camp for children, teens, and families that lasted from mid June to late August. The avowed purpose of the camp was "to offer recreation close to nature for children, youth, and families" so as "to awaken interest in things of a spiritual and a psychic nature." The facility itself grew to include cabins, kitchens, a swimming pool, and a barn.[13]

During the mid-1960s, Hugh Lynn Cayce began lecturing at colleges near Virginia Beach on subjects ranging from reincarnation to ESP research. He then invited interested students to weekend youth programs at ARE headquarters. By 1966 the association was offering research grants to both high school and college students who were interested in using the ARE library to prepare term papers on topics like dreams, clairvoyance, and telepathy. Throughout the next six years, ARE speakers would lecture at colleges and universities throughout the country.[14]

Hugh Lynn Cayce also sought to capitalize on the longstanding ARE theme of "expanded consciousness" when the youth counterculture began its experimentation with hallucinogenic drugs and Eastern mysticism. Prominent examples of his efforts during 1966 included a spring conference in Virginia Beach on "Eastern Thought and the Edgar Cayce Readings," a series of summer lectures at Stanford, Berkeley, and San Jose State on the theme "Expanding Your Awareness," and a fall conference in New York City entitled, "Psychedelic and Meditative Explorations of the Potential of the Human Mind: The Possibilities and Limitations of the Psychedelic Drugs." Several prominent psychologists and researchers including Jean Houston, Stanley Krippner, and Humphrey Osmond (who conducted the famous mescaline experiments with Aldous Huxley and coined the term "psychedelic") were featured speakers at this conference. They became part of a stable of ARE guest lecturers during the late 1960s that included such noted figures as Marcus Bach of Unity, Atlantis researcher Egerton Sykes, nutritionist Adelle Davis, Spiritualist Arthur Ford, psychic investigators Joan Grant, Ruth Montgomery and Hans Holzer, scholars Charles Tart, Walter Pahnke, and George Lamsa, and writer Jess Stearn. Ruth Montgomery's nationally syndicated articles on ARE seminars in 1965 and the phenomenal success of Jess Stearn's 1967 biography, *Edgar Cayce—The Sleeping Prophet,* were watershed events for the association in terms of both book sales and new member recruitment.[15]

The ARE sponsored study groups became the backbone of the association during the late 1960s. They also helped the group become a sophisticated and multi-tiered institution guided at the national level by a board of trustees that in turn oversaw local councils (composed of several study groups in one city) through its regional liaisons.

The study groups used two small books of special Cayce readings (called *A Search for God*) on such topics as prayer, meditation, healing, and faith as the focus of their discussions. Through the group, members had an opportunity to discuss, test, and "make practical" the precepts found in the readings. It was believed that participants created "an actual field of mental and spiritual energy" through their fellowship that accelerated their individual growth.[16]

ARE sought to establish market differentiation for its study groups by emphasizing that they were not encounter or therapy groups and that they did not "advocate the use of drugs or mechanical . . . devices to achieve crash breakthroughs to the unconscious mind." Their work rested on the assumptions that (1) Persons were "in earth" because their "eternal souls" had need of certain experiences; (2) Individuals needed group support to develop spiritually; (3) An overemphasis on ritual and dogma could impede the "spiritual quest"; (4) Group leadership rested on the "Master within" and not some human leader or guru. The study groups managed to avoid the pitfalls of charismatic leadership that plagued many of the era's alternative religious groups because of this egalitarian, inner-directed, and nondogmatic ethos.[17]

The decade of the 1970s saw continuing expansion in membership, study groups, seminars, conferences, and research. By 1981 general membership had more than doubled (from 1970) and stood at 32,000. The number of study groups had reached 1,784 and now extended to Canada, England, Ireland, Australia, Mexico, and New Zealand. The association had 146 paid employees and was sponsoring as many as twenty-four international lectures, workshops, and conferences a month on dream interpretation, holistic healing, prayer, meditation, sex and spirituality, psychic development, and the book of Revelation.[18]

It was during the 1970s that ARE wedded itself to the burgeoning New Age movement and became one of its major promoters. This development was a natural outgrowth of activities and emphases that had long been staples of the association. In fact, ARE should be viewed as a significant predecessor to the entire New Age phenomenon.[19]

The argument is not hard to make. The Cayce readings themselves were "channelled" material purportedly coming from higher spiritual entities. A number of the New Age movement's most prominent channelers, including Kevin Ryerson, Judy Skutch, and Paul Solomon, were either ARE members or had studied the Cayce materials before becoming independent "sources." In addition, the association from its foundation was a forerunner of later New Age efforts to reconcile religious belief and experience with the findings of modern science. This included research into psychic archaeology (Hugh Lynn Cayce took dozens of foreign tours to explore correlations between his father's readings and archaeological research into Atlantis, the Essene community at Qumran, Lemuria, and the Great Pyramid complex at Gizeh), meditation and higher states of consciousness, and predicted catastrophic "earth changes."

ARE was also a forerunner of the New Age's eclectic, pastiche-like approach to spiritual traditions and methods. From its earliest days, the association had promoted such New Age commonplaces as karma, past-life inquiry, *chakras,* the "inner voice," astrology, "group work," and psychic development. During the 1970s it invited Buddhist monks, Native American shamans (among them Shoshoni medicine man Rolling Thunder), and Sufi masters (among them Pir Vilayat Khan) to lead retreats and seminars, and it consistently sought to introduce Eastern yogic practices to its audiences.

Another significant contribution of ARE to the New Age movement was its pioneering research into alternative healing therapies—many of which had been recommended in the Cayce health readings. During the 1960s, the Edgar Cayce Foundation opened osteopathic and chiropractic research divisions and a physiotherapy clinic. It also began sponsoring annual medical symposiums on alternative medicine and recruited over seven hundred medical doctors, osteopaths, and chiropractors who were willing to treat patients according to the Cayce remedies.[20]

Throughout the 1970s the association continued to organize national symposiums on alternative healing methods and to sponsor large-scale research (using vol-

unteer members) on dreams and meditation. The results of this research were uniformly reported in professional journals and newsletters. By 1981, the physiotherapy clinic at Virginia Beach occupied the entire ground floor of the old headquarters building and employed osteopaths, nurses, and massage therapists. During the same year the cooperating doctors' program became the ARE Health Care Professional Program. This health system included M.D.'s, D.O.'s, massage therapists, L.P.T.'s, clinical psychologists, and licensed naturopaths who were committed to helping ARE members benefit from the health concepts found in the Cayce readings.[21]

Evidence of the association's *identification* with the burgeoning New Age phenomenon could be seen in the workshops and conferences it sponsored during the 1970s and early 1980s. As early as June of 1970 it held a conference entitled "Moving into the Aquarian Age" that included a session on "tuning into youth, the New Age, and work." That same summer ARE members organized a "New Age Seminar" in Pennsylvania and participated in the first "New Jersey Tri-Metro New Age Seminar." By the mid 1970s the group was envisioning its study groups as "laboratories of the New Age" and sponsoring large conferences on "Healing in the New Age." This theme continued into the late 1970s and early 1980s. During this period conferences were held on themes ranging from "New Age Partners and the Covenant of Love" to "Creating a New Age Together." The roster of regular speakers at these conferences included such New Age celebrities as Dorothy McLean, Gerald Jampolsky, David Spangler, Sun Bear, Steve Halpern, and Marilyn Ferguson.[22]

Like other New Age–oriented groups whose youthful members were beginning to marry and rear children in the late 1970s, ARE became interested in the establishment of spiritual communities and alternative primary schools. In 1979 it established an information clearinghouse for members interested in forming intentional communities and held a conference on "Spiritual Communities and New Age

Living" that featured Findhorn's Peter Caddy. It also set up an "open standing committee" on children's education in 1978 whose work included an expansion of summer camp activities for young children and the organization of the Cayce material for home-schooling purposes. By 1980 the association had organized a kindergarten along the lines of the Waldorf system, and the following year it sponsored its first annual "Child Development Symposium" in Virginia Beach. The keynote address for the meeting was given by the director of Waldorf's national training institute, Werner Glas.[23]

ARE also expanded as an institution during the 1970s, with its annual operating budget alone increasing from $81,000 in 1969 to $800,000 in 1974 and to $3,916,000 by 1981. New executive staff were hired and new departments opened. The group also organized a board of advisors in the early 1970s that included all regional representatives and chairpersons of the local ARE councils. These members met at annual summer congresses to formulate and submit nonbinding suggestions (on matters of ARE national policy) to the board of trustees. Although the inner circle of Hugh Lynn Cayce and the older trustees continued to hold real authority in the association, these congresses were a significant attempt to include the rank-and-file membership in group administration and policy setting.[24]

In a move that symbolized ARE's growing self-confidence, the board of trustees decided to reactivate the charter of Atlantic University in 1972. For the rest of the decade the school offered intensive summer study sessions on topics ranging from meditation and healing to education and dream interpretation. The attempt was made to coordinate these courses with accredited university programs so that students could receive credits toward their degrees at other institutions. These courses were modestly successful and continued to expand into the early 1980s. The association also initiated an Over the Wall ministry to prisoners in 1972 that by the early 1980s was sending the Cayce material to seventy prison study groups and one thousand "prison pen pals."[25]

Perhaps the most impressive accomplishment during the 1970s was the completion in 1975 of the one-million-dollar Edgar Cayce Memorial Library next to national headquarters in Virginia Beach. This facility became the home of the association's collection of over thirty thousand books on psychic phenomena and spiritual growth and the repository of the readings' transcripts and cross-indexing files. It also provided seminar rooms, study areas, offices, lounges, and an auditorium for the use of conference attendees. By 1981 the facility had been completely paid for with the help of member donations and was receiving over forty-five thousand visitors annually.[26]

The leadership of the association passed gradually from Hugh Lynn Cayce to his son Charles Cayce following the elder Cayce's mild heart attack in 1976. In December of 1978 Charles Cayce became president of ARE and in 1982, following his father's death, the chairman of the Edgar Cayce Foundation. Perhaps because he had been trained as a child psychologist (Ph.D., University of Maryland), the association's new leader has emphasized scientific research and the education of children during his tenure. He has also continued to identify ARE strongly with the New Age movement—particularly in the areas of humanistic psychology and alternative healing.

Shortly after Hugh Lynn Cayce's death, several members of the old ARE guard, including Harmon Bro, attempted to recast Edgar Cayce's image and portray him more as a Christian pastor and folk theologian than as a "master psychic." This effort has proved largely unsuccessful, however, and Edgar Cayce is still viewed at the popular level as a mystic and clairvoyant whose life was a testimony to the hidden powers of the human mind.[27]

During the 1980s and early 1990s, the association has continued to grow as an institution and to expand its range of services. Its 1981 long-range plan included initiatives to (1) communicate the Cayce material through television and film; (2) promote research into the Cayce health concepts in hospitals and major universities; (3) update the documentation and indexing of the readings; (4) organize an office of development that would garner bequests from aged members; (5) further develop Atlantic University.[28]

The association had made significant progress on most of these goals by the early 1990s. The Office of Development was instituted in 1982 and has been actively promoting bequests to ARE in its aging members' wills. Atlantic University now offers a graduate program in Transpersonal Studies, and the Harold J. Reilly School grants a six hundred-hour diploma in massage therapy. The association's catalogue of books, tapes, and video cassettes has become one of the most sophisticated New Age mail-order businesses in the country, advertising over five hundred titles on such subjects as ancient civilizations, astrology, numerology, prosperity, meditation, auras, and healing techniques. An audio-visual department makes tapes of conference lectures for sale to members and for airing on local radio and television stations. The ARE Press continues to add volumes to its Edgar Cayce Library Series, which consists of verbatim excerpts from the readings on various themes. This series provides a continuing focus for ARE study group.[29]

ARE's thorough adoption of modern managerial structures and marketing strategies have helped it achieve a remarkable degree of institutional stability and strength. Over two thousand conferees and forty thousand visitors come to ARE headquarters each year, the number of study groups worldwide is holding steady at seventeen hundred, and membership has reached ninety thousand members—thanks in part to aggressive direct-mail initiatives. The group's strong institutional base in turn has provided the resources that are enabling it to achieve its overall goals: to make the information in the readings accessible to people who might benefit from it, and to tell the story of Edgar Cayce. From its humble beginnings during the Depression, ARE has emerged as one of the country's most successful purveyors of psychism and esotericism as legitimate alternative worldviews.[30]

Notes

1. ARE promotional booklet, "The Edgar Cayce Legacy," 1965, 5; Jeffrey Furst, *Edgar Cayce's Story of Jesus* (New York: Coward-McCann, Inc., 1970), 379–81.

2. Ibid., 381–92; such instances of "travelling clairvoyance" were a common feature of rural nineteenth-century America's hothouse of folk healing practices.

3. Ibid., 24; Hugh Lynn Cayce, *Venture Inward* (New York: Harper and Row, 1964), 29–30.

4. Harmon Bro, "Hugh Lynn Cayce: The Man and His Choices," *ARE Journal* 18 (July 1983): 150; Furst, *Edgar Cayce's Story of Jesus,* 30–31, 390.

5. Ibid., 393–94; J. Gordon Melton, Jerome Clark, and Aidan Kelly, eds., *New Age Encyclopedia* (Detroit: Gale Research, Inc., 1990), 72; H. L. Cayce, *Venture Inward,* 31–32.

6. ARE promotional booklet, "The Edgar Cayce Legacy," 1965, 7.

7. Cheryl Salerno, "A Touch of History—1982," *ARE News* 17 (June 1982): 1–2.

8. Bro, "Hugh Lynn Cayce: The Man and His Choices," 142.

9. Ibid., 149; Cayce, *Venture Inward,* 31–33; ARE promotional booklet, "The Edgar Cayce Legacy," 6.

10. Bro, "Hugh Lynn Cayce: The Man and His Choices," 151–52.

11. "Foundation Announcement," *The Bulletin* 4 (May 1961): 2; ARE promotional booklet, "ARE," 1980, 4; "Study Group Review," *The Bulletin* 5 (October 1962): 2; "Study Group News," *ARE News* 4 (November 1969): 3; "Study Group News," *ARE News* 5 (December 1970): 3; ARE Library "Fact Sheet," 1 January 1975; "ARE Membership Survey Results," *ARE News* 5 (October 1970): 3.

12. Ibid.; Bro, "Hugh Lynn Cayce: The Man and His Choices," 143.

13. ARE promotional booklet, "ARE," 1980, 16; "ARE Camp Director Announced," *ARE News* 9 (April 1974): 2; "New ARE Camp in View," *The Bulletin* 6 (October 1963): 1.

14. "College Students' Week-End," *The Bulletin* 8 (April 1964): 2; "Student Contests at ARE Library," *ARE News* 1 (February 1966): 5.

15. "Virginia Beach Spring Conference," *ARE News* 1 (June 1966): 1; "San Francisco Conference," *ARE News* 1 (July 1966): 2; "New York City Fall Conference," *ARE News* 1 (October 1966): 2.

16. ARE Press, *The Handbook for ARE Study Groups,* rev. ed. (Virginia Beach: ARE Press, 1974), 2–6.

17. Ibid.

18. ARE promotional booklet, "ARE," 1980, 7–16; "Have You Heard?" *ARE News* 16 (September 1981): 1.

19. The New Age movement can best be understood as a postmodern discourse community with no centralized organization or leadership. The movement borrows from a wide array of traditional and modern religious beliefs and practices, but can be said to have four major distinguishing characteristics. First is a belief in an imminent planetary spiritual transformation that will occur at the level of human consciousness. Second is an ethic of self-empowerment and self-healing as a prerequisite to the healing of society. Third is a desire to reconcile religion and science in a higher synthesis that enhances the human condition both spiritually and materially. Finally, the New Age movement evidences a strong eclecticism in its embrace of healing therapies, spiritual practices, and millennial beliefs and encourages its participants to select the combination of these elements that meets their own personal needs. New Agers tend to distrust institutions and favor low-level organization. The movement spreads and communicates through workshops, newsletters, "networking," and national publications such as *New Age Journal* and *East-West Journal*. See Phillip C. Lucas, "The New Age Movement and the Pentecostal/Charismatic Revival: Distinct Yet Parallel Phases of a Fourth Great Awakening?" in *Perspectives on the New Age,* ed. James Lewis and J. Gordon Melton (Albany: State University of New York Press, 1992), 189–211.

20. "A New Development," *ARE News* 2 (February 1967): 1–2; "Physiotherapy Clinic Established at Virginia Beach," *ARE News* 2 (July 1967): 2; "Newly Added Chiropractic Research Division," *ARE News* 3 (April 1968): 1–2; "Membership Message," *ARE News* 6 (January 1971): 3.

21. "Have You Heard?" and "Therapy Department Grows as It Heals," *ARE News* 16 (September 1981): 1; "Research Spreads Enlightenment," *ARE News* 10 (July 1975): 1, 5; Sandra Duggan, "Cooperating Doctors List Grows and Changes Name," *ARE News* 16 (May 1981): 8.

22. "First New Jersey Tri-Metro New Age Seminar," *ARE News* 5 (April 1970): 4; "Art Conference, Youth Conference," *ARE News* 5 (June 1970): 1; "Philadelphia News," *ARE News* 5 (July 1970): 3, 6; "Highlights from the Holiday Youth Conference," *ARE News* 7 (February 1972): 3; "October Field Programs," *ARE News* 14 (September 1979): 6; Marianna Theo, "New Age Healing Techniques," *ARE News* 16 (August 1981): 2; ARE Congress Brochure, June 9–15, 1985.

23. "Notes on Spiritual Communities," *ARE News* 14 (September 1979): 3; "Congress Sharing Group Becomes Child Education Committee," *ARE News* 13 (December 1978): 2–3; "Caring for Children," *ARE News* 15 (September 1980): 6; Robert Witt, "Angel Points the Way for ARE Educators," *ARE News* 17 (January 1982): 8.

24. Public letter to ARE membership, July 1970, from J. Everett Irion, Treasurer; ARE report of board of trustees meeting in Phoenix, Ariz., January 22–23, 1974; Charles T. Cayce, "Highlights from Annual ARE Board of Trustees Meeting," *ARE News* 17 (September 1982): 3.

25. "Atlantic University Finds First Facilities," *ARE News* 7 (July 1972): 1; "Juvenile Outreach Program Launched," *ARE News* 19 (June 1984): 5; "Over the Wall," *ARE News* 14 (December 1979): 5.

26. ARE promotional booklet, "ARE," 1980, 7–16; "Have You Heard?" *ARE News* 16 (September 1981): 1.

27. J. Gordon Melton, interview with author, Santa Barbara, Calif., 29 December 1992.

28. "Office of Development to Make Long-Range Plans a Reality," *ARE News* 16 (October 1981): 1.

29. *ARE Bookstore 1990 Annual Catalogue;* "Director Chosen for Office of Development," *ARE News* 17 (January 1982): 1; Jeff Sherwood, "What's News in Audio-Visual," *ARE News* 16 (May 1981): 3; "ARE Benefits Mankind Through Member's Stewardship," *ARE News* 17 (October 1982): 8.

30. "A Conversation with Charles Thomas Cayce," *The Psychic Guide,* September–November, 1984, 14–18; ARE advertising leaflet sent out to prospective recruits, 1990.

Suggestions for Further Reading

ARE Press, *The Handbook for ARE Study Groups,* rev. ed. Virginia Beach: ARE Press, 1974.

Cayce, Hugh Lynn. *Venture Inward.* New York: Harper and Row, 1964.

Furst, Jeffrey. *Edgar Cayce's Story of Jesus.* New York: Coward-McCann, Inc., 1970.

Puryear, Herbert B. *The Edgar Cayce Primer.* New York: Bantam Books, 1982.

37

ECKANKAR: FROM ANCIENT SCIENCE OF SOUL TRAVEL TO NEW AGE RELIGION

Roger E. Olson

ECKANKAR was "born" (or brought into public view) in 1965. Its founder and formulator was Paul Twitchell ("Paulji"), who proclaimed himself the 971st Living Eck Master—the living oracle of God ("Sugmad")—the "Mahanta" for this age. Twitchell was a dabbler in things mystical and occult, a former Scientologist, initiate of Kirpal Singh of the Ruhani Satsang branch of the Radhasoami tradition of India, and excommunicated staffer of Swami Premananda's Self-Revelation Church of Absolute Monism, an offshoot of the Self-Realization Fellowship.

Sometime around 1960 Twitchell began to formulate the idea of founding his own religion. The exact details of the birth of this new religion in San Diego are difficult to determine as accounts differ widely. Even Twitchell's successor, the present Living ECK Master Harold Klemp, admits that

> Paul loved his privacy. Early in his youth he was involved in a variety of activities, but he made it a point to obscure any facts associated with his life. In so doing, he left a trail so clouded that it's going to take our historians years to piece it together.[1]

Twitchell claimed that he did not borrow ideas from any human source, but experienced his own "God-realization" in 1956 and was initiated by a group of spiritual masters called the "Order of Vairagi Masters" as the Living Eck Master in 1965.

The exact nature of these extraordinary beings is left vague in Twitchell's writings, but they seem comparable to the "Ascended Masters" of Theosophical lore. Twitchell's special master was Rebazar Tarzs, a five-hundred-year-old Tibetan monk, who initiated him and became his spiritual mentor.

Twitchell claimed that ECKANKAR is the oldest and most original religion in the world. All other religions are derivative from it and in some sense inferior to it. Whatever truth is in them belongs to ECKANKAR. According to some careful scholars of Twitchell and ECKANKAR, however, the self-proclaimed Mahanta simply borrowed and reworked the cosmology and spirituality of the venerable Radhasoami tradition of India as mediated to him by Kirpal Singh and the American Radhasoami adept and writer, Dr. Julian Johnson. David Lane's exposé of Twitchell's dependence on these men (and others) is convincing. Lane demonstrates that many of Twitchell's ideas and practices, as well as entire paragraphs and pages of his books, are identical to those of these Radhasoami leaders and interpreters.[2]

Twitchell was not the only new religious founder or leader to be influenced by the Radhasoami tradition. Others include Maharaj Ji, guru of the Divine Light Mission, and Yogi Bhajan, founder of the Healthy, Happy, Holy Organization or "3HO." Like ECKANKAR, these gurus and their American versions of Radhasoami grew in the fertile soil of the counterculture of the 1960s.

The roots of the Radhasoami way are located in both Hinduism and Sikhism; the teachings of its first master, Swami Shiv Dayal, were based in major part on those of Guru Nanak, the founder of Sikhism, while many Radhasoami practices and concepts, including belief in karma and practice of yoga, are classically Hindu.[3] Among the beliefs central to Radhasoami spirituality is that religious experience involves light and sound—seeing divine light, saying or singing divine sounds, and hearing divine words or melodies. The various Radhasoami groups also elevate their spiritual masters to extraordinary spiritual status, viewing them as endowed with divine powers and as not only teaching but embodying ultimate truth.

Several Radhasoami masters, representing various strands of the divergent tradition, have visited or lived in the United States and gathered communities of followers here. Kirpal Singh was the first of them to find a substantial American audience for his message, travelling through the country on a world tour in 1955. He visited again in 1963 and 1972, by which time his organization, known as the Ruhani Satsang, had established dozens of American centers.

Another Radhasoami presence was the previously mentioned Healthy, Happy, Holy Organization of Yogi Bhajan. More consciously Sikh in orientation than most Radhasoami offshoots, 3HO members dress in loose white garments, do not cut their hair, and wear turbans; males, in keeping with Sikh tradition, wear beards and carry daggers. Their geographical spiritual center is the Golden Temple in Amritsar, India, the focal point of traditional Sikhism. On the other hand, 3HO practice centers on Kundalini yoga, the origins of which are in Hinduism. The mantra meditation of the group resembles that of ECKANKAR.[4]

The Radhasoami group that once had the greatest public American presence was the Divine Light Mission. Guru Maharaj Ji inherited from his father, who died when Maharaj Ji was eight, a large following in India. He visited the United States for the first time in 1971 at the age of thirteen; thousands of young spiritual seekers received his message and were initiated into the movement. Initiation, known as "receiving knowledge," involved instruction in hearing divine sounds, seeing divine light, and tasting divine tastes. In 1973 the young movement held a massive festival, called Millennium 1973, at the Houston Astrodome, where premies, as followers were known,[5] expected a world transformation to occur. Although there was some disappointment in the fact that the world continued quite unchanged after the festival, the movement continued to attract large numbers of mainly countercultural followers.

During the 1980s, Maharaj Ji began the slow dissolution of the Divine Light Mission and eventually stepped down as a "Perfect Master." He continued to appear to audiences as Maharaji, a teacher, and established a minimal organization called Elan Vital to receive contributions. He may be reaching more listeners than ever, especially abroad, but his role is that of public speaker, and his religious movement is essentially defunct.[6]

Paul Twitchell remains the most successful and influential translator of the Radhasoami tradition in the American context—even if he disavowed that tradition. For most of Twitchell's tenure as Living ECK Master and president of ECKANKAR, the movement remained relatively small and, for the most part, confined to California. The headquarters was moved from San Diego to Las Vegas. The message of ECKANKAR and its "science of soul travel" was spread through notices in popular esoteric magazines, by word of mouth, and through the spread of Twitchell's books— especially *The Tiger's Fang*, a semi-autobiographical account of Twitchell's initiation by Rebazar Tarzs. Another important book written by Twitchell is *ECKANKAR—The Key to Secret Worlds,* which introduces readers to the ancient art or science of soul travel which Twitchell also called "bilocation." The experience is not so much "astral projection" as consciousness on more than one plane of reality at one time. Yet another publication instrumental in bringing Twitchell and ECKANKAR to public attention was Brad Steiger's hagiography of Twitchell entitled *In My Soul I Am Free*.

ECKANKAR's cosmology, as revealed by Twitchell, paralleled the Radhasoami tradition of India closely. What Twitchell called the "ECK" and the "Light and Sound of God" was described as nearly identical to the *Surat Shabda Mauj* of the Radhasoami Satsang, the "spiritual sound current" and "audible life stream" emanating from the feet of the Supreme Being. According to Twitchell and ECKANKAR, everything is some form of the "ECK Current," and therefore an emanation of Sugmad, their term for the Supreme Being, the Ocean of Light and Love. The human soul is an emanation or spark of Soul Itself—another term for the ECK current. Enlightenment, self-realization, and ultimately God-realization come through hearing the sounds of the Divine Current and seeing its light.

Twitchell's cosmology, also like Radhasoami's, involved a multilayered world of spiritual and material planes of reality with their own vibrations, sounds and lights, guardian spirits, and powers. In fact, a close examination of Twitchell's cosmology will show that it almost exactly replicates that of Kirpal Singh's version of the Radhasoami cosmology—with different terms for everything.[7]

Similarly, Twitchell's spirituality paralleled that of the Radhasoami tradition which is called Surat Shabda Yoga or Surat Shabda Marga. Among other things, it involves the chanting or singing of a mantra under the tutelage and initiation of a God-realized master, a Sant-Sat Guru—a person exactly parallel to ECKANKAR's "Living ECK Master." Twitchell introduced the mantra "HU" which is sung or chanted individually and communally by Eckists to burn off karmic debt and raise their consciousness of Spirit.

To this esoteric, basically gnostic, cosmology Twitchell added the details of the "science of soul travel," although that is not at all alien to the cosmology or spirituality of Radhasomai. Twitchell expounded several kinds of soul travel including soul travel via the dream state and soul-projection via meditation-visualization. The exact source of this teaching and practice other than the so-called "Vairagi Masters" is unclear, although some suggest it may be in Scientology. It is likely that Twitchell developed it out of his early involvement with L. Ron Hubbard.

Just as ECKANKAR was growing, solidifying, and beginning to succeed in the competition of California's 1960s-era new religions, Paul Twitchell died suddenly and without appointing a successor in 1971. According to ECKANKAR, he "translated" or "dropped the body." He is now among the Vairagi Masters doing research in a Temple of Golden Wisdom on the astral plane known as the Temple of Askleposis where he rubs shoulders with such luminaries as Paul the Apostle, Julian Johnson, and Paul Brunton.

A rather obscure lower-level ECKANKAR initiate named Darwin Gross was chosen by the board of ECKANKAR (and by Twitchell's widow Gail Twitchell?) to succeed Twitchell as the 972nd Living ECK Master. Gross assumed the "Rod of Power" and "Mahanta Consciousness" at a worldwide ECKANKAR seminar in Las Vegas on October 22, 1971. His tenure as the Mahanta was marked by growth and great controversy in the movement. Several leading Eckists renounced his leadership and withdrew from ECKANKAR, believing that he was *not* qualified to succeed Twitchell. Gross and Gail Twitchell married shortly after his accession to Mahantaship and then they divorced a few years later. ECKANKAR managed to grow in spite of the controversy and established its worldwide headquarters in Menlo Park, California.

A battle for leadership of ECKANKAR, which can only be described as byzantine, took place between 1981 and 1983. Gross and his lieutenants were ousted by his heir apparent Harold Klemp and Klemp's righthand man Peter Skelskey. The reasons, methods, legality, and legitimacy of the palace coup are matters of debate to this day. The upshot is that Harold Klemp, a rather obscure Eckist until chosen by Gross for leadership and succession in 1981, with the help of Skelskey, now president of

ECKANKAR, gained total control of the organization and all of its corporate subsidiaries (e.g., Illuminated Way Press) and stripped Darwin Gross of his initiations and role as co-Mahanta. Gross became an outcast and plaintiff and defendant in numerous lawsuits over use of ECKANKAR's name, copyrighted terms, books, etc. To this day Gross seems to consider Klemp and Skelskey to be usurpers who have transformed ECKANKAR into another cult.[8]

From ECKANKAR's side, Gross is still considered to have been the 972nd Living ECK Master, but questions about him are deftly turned aside and his picture does not appear in the Temple of ECK or in any publications among the great masters of the past. He is treated as a "non-person." Harold Klemp's second autobiography, *Child in the Wilderness* (1989), barely mentions Gross even though most of Klemp's time in ECKANKAR before becoming the Mahanta was spent under his tutelage.

Under the leadership of Harold Klemp, the 973rd Living ECK Master, ECKANKAR has grown and even flourished at a time when many new religions founded in California in the 1960s have floundered and failed. Although exact membership statistics are not made public, ECKANKAR claims to have "tens of thousands" of members and many more correspondents. In response to a "spiritual vision," Klemp moved the headquarters from Menlo Park, California, to a suburb of Minneapolis, Minnesota, in the late 1980s. A major accomplishment has been the building of the Temple of ECK at a cost of 8.2 million dollars in a former wheatfield on the outskirts of Chanhassen, a southwestern exurb of the Twin Cities. The temple contains a worship center, classrooms, fellowship hall, bookstore, and "chapel" for initiations.

Harold Klemp was born in 1942 and raised on a farm in Wisconsin. His family was Lutheran-Missouri Synod, and he studied for the Lutheran ministry for a time. According to his two autobiographies, *Winds of Change* and *Child in the Wilderness,* he gradually became disillusioned with the theology he was being taught, especially the exclusivity of Christian truth as the only way to heaven. He also began having mystical experiences while in high school and ministerial training school which led him to investigate the psychic and paranormal. For a time after leaving ministerial training, he "dabbled" in Edgar Cayce and Rosicrucianism. The extent of influence these esoteric teachings had on Klemp is difficult to determine, but he refers positively to them in his autobiography *The Wind of Change* and states in another book that before joining ECKANKAR in 1970 he "began a private study that lasted for a number of years through the different aspects of the occult, through different paths such as the Rosicrucians and Edgar Cayce, and through a whole lot of other information."[9] Various allusions to Rosicrucianism throughout his writings show that Klemp continues to consider that teaching to be a legitimate step on the way to the full truth of ECKANKAR for many people.

The reason for stressing this early connection with Rosicrucians and "other occult teachings" and continued sympathy toward them is that Klemp appears to be turning ECKANKAR more and more *away* from its Indian/Radhasoami roots under Twitchell and *toward* the Ancient Wisdom tradition of the West.

Of course this is not a clear-cut difference. Radhasoami scholar Mark Juergensmeyer notes that the Radhasoami cosmology and spirituality are strikingly similar in many ways to gnostic philosophy and that many of the American leaders of this Indian tradition "might easily have been Theosophists or even Rosicrucians, had Radhasoami not been available."[10] There is, then, an affinity between the Radhasoami tradition and the Western esoteric/occult tradition which makes it easy for a new Mahanta like Klemp, steeped in Rosicrucianism, to turn ECKANKAR in that direction.

To argue that ECKANKAR under Twitchell was *not* already influenced by and attractive to people in the Western esoteric tradition (such as Theosophists and Rosicrucians) would be foolish. However, as David Lane has shown, Twitchell's primary inspiration came from Kirpal Singh and Julian Johnson. To state that all

Twitchell really did was change terminology and make that Indian tradition more accessible to Westerners may be an exaggeration (especially in light of the fact that he added the experience of "soul travel"), but there can be no doubt that he stayed very close to its basic concepts. His writings are sprinkled with Sanskrit and pseudo-Sanskrit terms and his "sacred space" was clearly the mythical spiritual realms of the Himalayan mountains. He retained many of the Radhasoami terms and concepts such as "Shabda," which he equated with "the Word" which emanates from God.

Even a cursory reading of Klemp's books reveals a different personality and spiritual emphasis from Twitchell's. For one thing, Klemp *never* mentions the "Shabda" or any other overtly Radhasoami terms. Furthermore, Twitchell was emphatic and exclusivistic about his truth claims. He declared that ECKANKAR and "orthodox religions" were at war! Klemp makes clear that ECKANKAR is the highest and quickest path to God-realization but not the exclusive path. Others, including Christianity, will get one part way to being a "co-worker with God" and are therefore not harmful to Soul. The only thing Klemp seems hostile toward in "orthodox" Christianity is exclusivism. For him, Jesus was a soul traveller and great teacher of wisdom, but not even the Living ECK Master for his time. However, he encourages Christians who want to try his spiritual exercises to chant the name of Jesus or any other name or word meaningful to them. This will bring a *degree* of enlightenment and protection.

The leaders of ECKANKAR acknowledge that Klemp is leading it in new directions, but they stress that this is not inconsistent with Twitchell's teachings. According to Peter Skelskey, president of the religion, ECKANKAR is a dynamic religion which is open to new interpretations as consciousness evolves.

Beyond attempting to soften ECKANKAR's attitude toward traditional religion Klemp seems to be trying to establish or enhance a degree of cultural continuity between ECKANKAR and the dominant religion—Christianity. Klemp's writings and talks are liberally sprinkled with references to Christian mystics and contemplatives such as St. Francis, Brother Lawrence, and Thomas Merton. He quotes the Bible frequently and freely but often without attribution. He encourages Christians to use the spiritual exercises he teaches and warns Eckists against proselytizing. Of course he does not discourage persons of other religions from joining ECKANKAR if they wish. He has even established special classes at the Temple of ECK for those who want to learn about ECKANKAR without any pressure to join. Skelskey states unequivocally that membership in ECKANKAR is not exclusive. One does not have to relinquish association with any other organization in order to join. One can only assume that this is applicable only to the lower levels of initiation—perhaps first and second. Above that one gradually takes on the role and office of ECKANKAR clergy member, which would probably require total loyalty and commitment to ECKANKAR.

This effort at cultural continuity is probably only cosmetic, since Klemp's writings are also filled with references to such Western occult concepts as the Akashic records, Atlantis and Lemuria, the various "bodies" of the human that correspond to the planes of reality (astral, etheric, emotional, causal, mental, etc.), and "spiritual evolution" through spiritual exercises such as chanting "HU." Thus, ECKANKAR is in no danger of becoming a Christian denomination. However, beneath the veneer of accommodation to the prevailing Christian culture, ECKANKAR *is* shifting in a decidedly Western direction. This is more significant in terms of establishing some degree of continuity between ECKANKAR and the dominant culture. When he writes about Twitchell, Klemp identifies him with the (Western) Gnostic tradition in early Christianity. Klemp also relates ECKANKAR very closely with the Ancient Wisdom or mystery schools and brotherhoods which began in Egypt around 3000 B.C. In almost every case where Klemp attempts to describe the historical religious pedigree of present-day ECKANKAR he traces it back through a Western Gnostic–Ancient mystery tradition rather than through an Eastern-Oriental-mystical tradition.

There is a definite de-emphasis on cosmology in Klemp's books and talks which tend rather to be filled with homely homilies with simple spiritual applications about reincarnation, karma, responsibility for one's own choices and actions, being open to opportunities to increase consciousness and sometimes astonishing explanations for human phenomena. For instance, Klemp teaches that children's nightmares are actually memories of their own sufferings and of sufferings they have caused other people in former lives. He offers as proof of reincarnation the answers small children give to the question, what were you when you were big?

Klemp's primary interest is the "spiritual exercises" rather than esoteric knowledge of the universes of Soul. He prefers to communicate esoteric truth through parables, many of which illustrate how ordinary day-to-day activities result in negative karma which needs to be reversed by spiritual exercises such as singing HU. This experiential and pragmatic orientation is another bit of evidence of Klemp's attempt to build bridges, however shaky, between ECKANKAR and the wider American culture.

Klemp's public persona does not fulfill any of the stereotypes of a "cult leader." He is not charismatic, and does not engage in any theatrics or methods of mass hypnosis. In spite of his humble appearance and demeanor, Klemp encourages his followers ("chelas") to think of him as the embodiment of total God-consciousness, the "oracle of God," the vehicle for the unfoldment and upliftment of Soul to God *for Eckists*. To Eckists, he is not only Harold Klemp. In fact, his physical being is considered relatively unimportant, which may explain why his lack of personal charisma and speaking ability do not bother Eckists. To them, he is "Wah Z" on the "inner plane," the "dream master" who appears to them in various dream states often as a tiny blue point of light. They are taught to commune with him and receive guidance from him via these dreams. As Wah Z, Klemp is omnipresent and omniscient.

Chelas write letters to him, but often do not send them. They receive their answers in dreams where Klemp appears (as Wah Z) and speaks to them. Although they are not to worship him, most Eckists keep a picture of him at home and at work and stop twice daily near the picture and sing or chant "HU" for fifteen to twenty minutes. This is to burn off karmic debt, increase God-consciousness, and bring protection, healing, and success in every area of life.

"Soul travel" still plays a very important role in ECKANKAR under Klemp, but more and more it is linked with dreams. That is, whereas ECKANKAR used to purport to teach chelas to project their souls out of the body while fully awake (conscious bilocation), now it focuses on interpreting and manipulating dreams. Classes and correspondence courses teach initiates how to understand their dreams as spiritual journeys and encounters and how to use their dreams to go higher faster in their experiences of soul travel. The highest initiates (such as Peter Skelskey) claim to have travelled via the dream state to monasteries on spiritual planes where they have worked and studied with Vairagi Masters such as Rebazar Tarzs, Gopal Das, Fubbi Quantz, Yaubl Sacabi, and Lai Tsi.

Harold Klemp seems to be reaching out to the myriads of New Agers as potential chelas for ECKANKAR. Besides "The Religion of the Light and Sound of God," ECKANKAR often calls itself "The New Age Religion." Many of its basic concepts and spiritual practices are appealing to New Agers and other American dabblers in things occult and esoteric. Peter Skelskey claims that the New Age movement, like the Radhasoami tradition, is dying if not already dead and that a "remnant" of it will "survive" and join ECKANKAR. Under Klemp ECKANKAR would seem to be positioning itself to receive them. However, Klemp does not condone such common New Age practices as "trance channeling" and past-life regression. These open one up to evil influences of lower planes (Kal Naranjan is ECKANKAR's version of Satan) and hinder one's higher spiritual unfoldment. However, Klemp does teach such practical exercises as spiritual healing, creating one's own reality through visualization techniques, and gaining physical and psychic protection through singing "HU." ECKANKAR's World Wide seminars, always held in October, are heavily advertised and made appealing to anyone interested in nontraditional spiritual paths. They include special music, workshops, lectures, videos, and a late-night party. The great attraction, of course, is the appearance of Harold Klemp, normally a recluse, to speak each night to both ECKists and inquirers.

Several notable changes and new directions bode well for ECKANKAR's future as a well-established "new religion" on the American scene. First, as illustrated above, it is attempting to establish at least cosmetic continuity with part of the dominant culture while maintaining medium tension with that culture. It is working hard to overcome any hint of cultishness by becoming more exoteric—softening its appearance and opening up to outsiders. Klemp's writings, the introductory classes, World Wide seminars, and Temple of ECK are all "user friendly." Outsiders and newcomers are enthusiastically welcomed, their questions answered courteously and competently, and there is nothing of an exotic aura to scare away the person who just walks in off the street. ECKANKAR eagerly seeks favorable publicity and claims to make its basic spiritual teachings and exercises available to all.

According to Skelskey and several prominent members, Eckists are strongly encouraged to be actively involved in their communities outside of ECKANKAR. A major new emphasis from the top down is community service. Eckists are urged to have non-Eckist friends and *not* to spend all their time in ECKANKAR activities. Being a "coworker with God" now includes social involvement for the improvement of whatever community each Eckist lives in. No specifics are given, however. What kind of social and community involvement each Eckist chooses is totally his or her own prerogative. This new emphasis seems to be aimed at overcoming the perception of ECKANKAR as a "cult"—especially in Minnesota where the "religious ecology" is anything but favorable to newly arrived, California-born New Age religions. ECKANKAR is desparately seeking respectability.

On the other hand, it is clear that ECKANKAR wishes to present itself as different from the mainstream of religion and society. It offers experiences and answers *not* available from those sources and disdains any requests or demands for rational explanations or defenses. It is far from falling prey to the perennial temptation of becoming secularized on the road to respectability. Its appeal is strictly to spiritual experience over rational apologetics. When called upon to defend the objective truth of ECKANKAR in the face of its detractors and critics, the leadership simply says, "If ECKANKAR works for you, fine! If not, then we don't care to go out of our way to try to defend or explain ourselves to you."

Notes

1. Harold Klemp, *The Secret Teachings* (Minneapolis: ECKANKAR, 1989), 141.

2. David Christopher Lane, *The Making of a Spiritual Movement: The Untold Story of Paul Twitchell and ECKANKAR* (Del Mar: Del Mar Press, 1990). This "exposé" of ECKANKAR has gone through several revisions and is soon to be revised and published again by Garland Publishing. In it Lane heavily documents Twitchell's early association with Kirpal Singh and argues persuasively that the similarities between ECKANKAR and Kirpal Singh's Ruhani Satsang branch of Radhasoami are more than coincidental.

3. For a synopsis of the emergence of Radhasoami see Mark Juergensmeyer, *Radhasoami Reality: The Logic of a Modern Faith* (Princeton: Princeton University Press, 1991), 3–12.

4. See Alan Tobey, "The Summer Solstice of the Healthy-Happy-Holy Organization," in

The New Religious Consciousness, ed. Charles Y. Glock and Robert N. Bellah (Berkeley: University of California Press, 1976), 5–30.

5. "Premie" means "lover"—i.e., one who loves God, or in this case loves the Guru Maharaj Ji.

6. For details on the pre-dissolution Divine Light Mission, see James V. Downton, *Sacred Journeys: The Conversion of Young Americans to Divine Light Mission* (New York: Columbia University Press, 1979).

7. The present leaders of ECKANKAR admit that its cosmology is nearly identical to Radhasoami cosmology, but argue that this is not because Twitchell borrowed or plagiarized any Radhasoami writings. Rather, they claim, Twitchell had access to the same spiritual sources of truth (e.g., Akashic records) as the gurus of the Indian offshoot of Sikhism.

8. This impression was communicated to the writer by Gross and by his associate Bob Brandt in October, 1992.

9. Harold Klemp, *How to Find God* (Minneapolis: ECKANKAR, 1988), 199.

10. Mark Juergensmeyer, "Radhasoami as a Trans-National Movement," in *Understanding the New Religions* (New York: Seabury Press, 1978), 194.

Suggestions for Further Reading

Juergensmeyer, Mark. *Radhasoami Reality: The Logic of a Modern Faith.* Princeton: Princeton University Press, 1991.

Klemp, Harold. *Child in the Wilderness.* Minneapolis: ECKANKAR, 1989.

———. *The Secret Teachings.* Minneapolis: ECKANKAR, 1989.

Lane, David Christopher. *The Making of a Spiritual Movement: The Untold Story of Paul Twitchell and ECKANKAR.* Del Mar: Del Mar Press, 1990. Soon to be republished by Garland Publishing.

Steiger, Brad. *In My Soul I Am Free.* Minneapolis: ECKANKAR, 1968.

Twitchell, Paul. *ECKANKAR: The Key to Secret Worlds.* Minneapolis: Illuminated Way Publishing Inc., 1969, 1987.

38

THE EVOLUTION OF HIPPIE COMMUNAL SPIRITUALITY: THE FARM AND OTHER HIPPIES WHO DIDN'T GIVE UP

Albert Bates and Timothy Miller

The American hippie culture that achieved its greatest prominence with the summer of love in San Francisco in 1967 was intimately connected with the most prolific flowering of communal living in American history. No one knows exactly how many hippie and hip-oriented communes existed in the 1960s and 1970s, or how many members they had; estimates, however, usually run to some thousands of communal groups, both urban and rural, and tens or hundreds of thousands of participants, including many who lived the life only briefly, sometimes for a summer or less.[1]

In the popular mind the typical hippie commune was an old farmhouse or perhaps several tepees crammed full of dirty, destitute dropouts who changed sexual partners daily and stayed stoned from morning till night, playing loud rock music and subsisting on food stamps or, in the lucky cases, checks from a trust fund. The communards' clothes were ragged but outlandish. They travelled by hitchhiking. The longest coherent sentence any of them could put together was "Oh, wow!"

Like most stereotypes, that one falls far short of reality. Of the communities founded in the late 1960s and early 1970s that championed countercultural values and arose from the hippie idealization of communal living, many were populated by spiritual seekers, variously ex-

ploring Eastern, Native American, Christian, independent mystical, and other paths to enlightenment. Some were composed of environmentalists whose devotion to their cause often had strong spiritual elements. Some hip communes were essentially secular, but they were greatly outnumbered by ones espousing at least a vague spirituality.

Many presume that the communes vanished without a trace as quickly as they supposedly arose.[2] Actually, however, when hippies faded from center stage in the 1970s, more than a few of the communes soldiered on—some for so long that they have now met Rosabeth Moss Kanter's test for communal success by surviving for over twenty-five years.[3] Some kept much of their original vision and form; others changed in various ways to meet new needs and challenges. Moreover, even where communes did close, a survival of the spirit often took place: when a commune died some of its members might go on, educated in the school of hard knocks, to further communal experiences elsewhere. In yet other cases new communes were created—often by a younger generation—to embody ongoing remnants of the hip communal ideal.

Compiling a complete list of surviving hip-era communes (now usually called "intentional communities") would be impossible, but they clearly number in the hundreds. The *Directory of Intentional Communities,* the most authoritative source of such data, includes among its hundreds of listed communities ninety-four that we deem to have been hip at their founding and that still survive in more or less communal form at this writing.[4] In addition, we personally know of enough surviving hip communes not listed in the directory to push the total to over one hundred. And it is probable that many more, probably hundreds more, exist unknown to us.[5] They continue to be diverse in outlook; now as formerly a great majority are based on spiritual or ethical principles of some sort. Communards today range from neo-pagan earth-religionists to spiritual environmentalists to born-again countercultural Jesus freaks to New Agers to devotees of the Eastern religions that became popular during the hip era and with hip constituencies. Thousands of persons, in hundreds of locations, continue to work out their spiritual visions in contemporary communities that are the evolved products of the hippie communes of yore.

Although the communities that have survived the hip era continue to embody some of the diverse ethos of the hippies, some have changed styles and structures in a variety of ways. Lifestyle changes are often prominent: the hippies, for example, advocated the widespread and frequent use of mind-expanding drugs (notably marijuana and LSD), but today incidence of use in most surviving communities is, for a variety of reasons, almost certainly lower than it once was. Similarly the hippies advocated freewheeling sexuality, but the grim reality of AIDS and the responsibilities of family life have tended to curb the if-it-feels-good-do-it impulse. Lifestyles have changed less in the Jesus movement communities, probably the largest subgenre of hip-era communes, where drugs and free sex were typically (but not always) condemned all along; Jesus People USA, for example, today has over five hundred members living communally in Chicago, many of them still looking and acting like Jesus freaks of old.[6]

While some communities continue to hold all things, including money and real estate, in common, many more allow some private property, and an increasingly popular form of landholding is the land trust, in which the community holds title to the land and individual members lease rights to their own dwellings. Even in the halcyon days of hip there never was a single economic pattern in the communes. Albert Bates and Allen Butcher have argued that there are four fundamental social and economic forms found in contemporary communities—collective, cooperative, communal, and diverse—and the last is a catch-all that covers any number of specific local arrangements.[7]

In many communities turnover has declined drastically as the lives of communitarians have become stable. The once common policy of open membership has also vanished as community after community found that free entry let loafers and even hoodlums take over, often to the detriment of the industrious idealists who had made the community work in the first place.[8]

In size, diversity remains the rule; there are evolved hip communes with memberships under a dozen (Sandhill Farm, Missouri, a stable community about twenty years old, has usually had six to twelve members, including children), and several with five hundred or more (Ananda World Brotherhood Village, California, for example). Typically, though, small tends to be beautiful: only a handful of communities with roots in the hip era have as many as fifty members.

To write off the spirituality of some of these experiments as ephemeral pop Aquarianism would be a mistake. Some surviving hippies have codified the experiences of the sixties into a moral code of ongoing relevance to their children, as can be seen in the story of the Farm, which provides an excellent case study of the maturation of a hippie spiritual commune. Founded in Tennessee in 1971, the Farm has changed over time but is very much alive today with much of its original outlook intact.

The roots of the Farm go back to about 1965. Drop City, the first full-blown prototype hip commune, was founded in May of that year near Trinidad, Colorado. In San Francisco the Grateful Dead established a hip outpost in the tony Panhandle district, prankster-author Ken Kesey's acid tests began, and the Diggers emerged as free hip social workers. 1966 saw the Trips Festival and the first laws against LSD. Janis Joplin hitchhiked in from Texas. Lou Gottlieb made his Morning Star Ranch an open-land commune.

1966 also saw a young assistant professor at San Francisco State College schedule classes to talk about the cultural ferment. The classes grew too large for the college halls, so they moved to a church, a theater, and then, in 1969, to the Family Dog, a rock hall. Monday Night Class became a weekly pilgrimage for throngs of hippies from up and down the coast, from high schools and university campuses, from army bases and police academies, from mountain communes and Haight Street crash pads. Thousands came, in various states of consciousness, with love beads and bangles, tambourines and diaphanous gowns, Dr. Strange cloaks and top hats with feathers. The open-ended discussions ventured into hermetic geometry, Masonic-Rosicrucian mysticism, ECKANKAR, and the Rolling Stones, but each opened with a long, silent meditation and closed with a sense of purpose. At the center of this psychedelic crucible the alchemist trying to tie it all together was thirty-one-year-old Stephen Gaskin, known simply to most hippies as "Stephen." Stephen would say,

> Here's the way the class works. It's open doors and it's free and everybody can come in, and the way it's always been is that the questions I like best are the ones that start with "what about" and "what if. . . . " I lead these discussions. I guess I can serve a function as a psychedelic fuse. . . . I have done enough yoga to be able to handle whatever the juice is.[9]

A group of theologians visited one Monday night in 1969 and were impressed by what they saw. They urged Stephen to take his eclectic rap to their colleges and churches. In early 1970, Stephen announced he would adjourn the class and

travel across the country in his remodeled school bus; when he rolled out of San Francisco the following October, twenty or thirty buses full of Monday Night regulars followed him. When the caravan returned, a year later, it numbered sixty buses and dozens of step vans, bread trucks, VW campers, and other reconditioned rolling stock.

The caravan's sense of purpose was strong. Stephen, upon learning that some participants were on welfare, told them to give up their benefits and start working: "We're working and moving the caravan and we're building up the engines and keeping them together and towing buses and accepting new people on top of all that, for no other reason than to go out in the world and say that Spirit is where it's at and that God's love is heavier than violence."[10] The caravan, like the Farm that followed, was open to all—your membership card was your bellybutton. Openness was basic to the hip ethos; the hippies tended to have a naive optimism about human nature, a belief that if one could simply be rescued from the nightmare of American culture and placed in a supportive setting, one would respond in kind and contribute to group harmony. Anyone willing to reject mainstream culture—to drop out, as the argot had it—was welcome.

After months on the road the spiritual wanderers settled down on a piece of land that eventually covered about two thousand acres in southern Tennessee. As word of the experiment spread, more and more visitors came to check it out, and despite repeated attempts to keep the Farm's population under control, it peaked at about fifteen hundred in the early 1980s.

Farm residents, like other hippies, revered sacred drugs. Perhaps hippies were not the first communal druggies; the Shakers, after all, had been major producers of opium. But by the seventies most mood-altering substances except alcohol were illegal, and illegality put a new patina on their use. Stephen Gaskin learned to navigate the LSD ("acid") universe; as he described the journey of his sixth LSD experience, for example,

I started slipping into myself. . . . Then I was looking from over a view of a little creek that was very bright yellow, running down over the rocks. I looked at it, and there were bubbles on it. And suddenly I was one of the bubbles on the creek, running down this little golden river.

I bounced around a few times, and then I popped. My bubble popped, and then I was indistinguishably part of the river. . . . There was no verbal content, no semantic content. That was sort of like a benchmark for me for acid's ego death.[11]

Stephen Gaskin, once a hard-drinking, bar-brawling Marine, took hundreds of such trips, but then spurned LSD, as well as heroin, amphetamines, barbiturates, cocaine, alcohol, tobacco, even coffee. He became deeply convinced that certain substances were spiritually valuable, but that others harmed the body and only numbed the mind.[12] He called his few sanctioned botanical spiritual growth agents "sacraments." The Farm's sacraments—marijuana, peyote, and psilocybin mushrooms—provided access to realms of sight, sound, and perception beyond normal consciousness. They heightened compassion and conferred, at least momentarily, a perceived ability to live harmoniously with others and with nature.

The Farm soon spurned the hippie icon of free love. The standard hip credo was one of total sexual freedom: multiple partners, multilateral relationships, or no commitment at all. Some earlier communes had experimented with unusual sexual mores; the nineteenth-century Oneida Community, for example, had a group marriage involving hundreds of members that lasted for over thirty years. But Stephen Gaskin, who had entered into a four-partner marriage in San Francisco and a six-partner marriage in Tennessee, became an unexpected spokesman for the importance of traditional family values. Those who wished to join the Farm must become fidelitous. "If you're having sex, you're engaged," warned Stephen. "If you're having babies, you're married."

The religious tenets of the Farm gradually evolved from its Sunday morning discussions and came to be known simply as "the agreements." The pre-eminent agreement was "We are all one." Oneness was not limited to the human family, nor was it some abstract sense of Christian love. Farm members believed that matter and energy exist together in a kronon-to-kronon dance of existence and non-existence; that electrical fields co-penetrate; that boundaries between separate individuals quite literally do not exist. As Stephen explained,

Energy . . . what is energy? A lot of things are energy. We are energy. This stuff is energy . . . also this sort of feeling that we have here of being this many people stonedish together . . . is energy. Energy's more specific than that, though—I believe that energy's the Holy Spirit, I believe that it's the body and blood of Jesus, Krishna, Buddha, and anybody along that line. We're a dance of energy, arranged and held in the mind of God.[13]

From this central theme of spiritual unification the Farm's religious tenets followed with reasonably coherent logic: "telepathy is real," "anger and fear are optional," "it doesn't help to turn anyone into meat," "you can change," "how you choose to be makes a difference for everyone."[14] While some saw him as a self-proclaimed prophet, Stephen actually disclaimed any belief in prophecy and argued that each individual had to seek his or her own enlightenment: "I think each one of us has a non-shirkable obligation to figure out the world on our own as best we can. The way we behave as a result of that investigation is our real and practiced Religion."[15]

The hallmark of the Farm's first twenty years was not its communal economy (that lasted only thirteen years for the entire group, although a smaller group of fifty still practices community of goods), its faith in Stephen Gaskin as a leader (which waned even sooner),[16] or even some abiding sense of religiosity (lately Farm members describe themselves as freethinkers and reject religious labels). Instead it was the

Farm's service to others through Farm-based charities such as Plenty, a foundation whose works ranged from Third World development projects to a free ambulance service in the Bronx; the Natural Rights Center, a public-interest law firm; and Rocinante, a communal healthcare facility. From the very beginning the Farm was designed as a catalyst to save the planet that would develop simple and ecologically sustainable methods for cooperative living, by helping to preserve both hippie and native cultures, and by developing low-tech solutions to problems of the global village—from ham-TV, solar cars, and pocket Geiger meters (called "Nukebusters") to ghetto-trained paramedics, free illegal immigrant clinics, and soy ice cream.

A massive depopulation took place in 1983 and 1984 as the Farm experienced a severe economic crunch and abandoned total community of goods; many individuals, faced with earning a living in the larger economy, departed. Today the Farm numbers about two hundred permanent residents who manage some two dozen small businesses, from printing vegetarian cookbooks to making tie-dyed t-shirts. The Farm School is headquarters for the National Coalition of Alternative Community Schools and hosts a summer camp for underprivileged children. Stephen Gaskin is building Rocinante. Looking back on the Farm's first twenty years, Plenty director Peter Schweitzer reflects:

> The values that count are spiritual and universal across all cultures. Discovering these values and universal truths seems to be an individual matter, finally, and it proceeds along myriad paths. I think all of us Farm parents have noticed that our kids have turned out pretty hip. They have strong values and a keen sense of what's fair and decent judgment, especially when we compare them with ourselves at comparable ages. The community we forged for them in the midst of a self-destructive and spiritually bankrupt society was a good incubator. If, as some of us believe, alternative, more cooperative, more spiritually and materially ecological, social configurations are in fact more fun, there's a good reason for hope.[17]

In sum, the hip communal world in which many communes blazed briefly and then folded also produced hundreds of stable communities that continue to press for an alternative to the whitebread American Way of Life. At Twin Oaks (Virginia), East Wind (Missouri), Ganas (New York), and Love Israel (Washington), as well as the Farm, to name only a few typical examples, thousands of persons continue to work out the vision that erupted with the communes of the hippies.

Notes

We want to acknowledge the assistance of Catherine Wessinger, who read and commented perceptively on a draft of this chapter.

1. For estimates of the numbers of hippie communes and their members see Bill Kovach, "Communes Spread as the Young Reject Old Values," *New York Times,* 17 December 1970; Jules Siegel, "West of Eden," *Playboy* 17 (November 1970): 174; Benjamin Zablocki, *The Joyful Community* (Baltimore: Penguin, 1971), 300.

2. Edward K. Spann, for example, while conceding that "small elements of this movement have survived," has argued that "In part because it lacked roots in the past, the communal movement proved to be an ephemeral one that crashed as quickly as it had taken flight." See Spann, *Brotherly Tomorrows: Movements for a Cooperative Society in America, 1820–1920* (New York: Columbia University Press, 1989), 282.

3. Rosabeth Moss Kanter, *Commitment and Community: Communes and Utopias in Sociological Perspective* (Cambridge, Mass.: Harvard University Press, 1972), 245.

4. We define hip-era communes as those founded between 1962 and 1975 and based

on the values typically espoused by the hippies of the late 1960s. There were proto-hip communes active as early as 1962; 1975 is an arbitrary cutoff date (many hip-inspired communes were in fact founded after 1975, so the list could easily be longer). Typical hippie values included such things as peace and love, sexual freedom, drug use, rejection of "establishment" culture, racial and ethnic tolerance, and protection of the environment. While some of the communities have changed their orientation, those we are counting still retain at least a substantial part of their commitment to such values.

For further data, see the *Directory of Intentional Communities: A Guide to Cooperative Living* (Evansville, Ind., and Rutledge, Mo.: Fellowship for Intentional Community and Communities Publications Cooperative, 1992). The directory in this edition lists 365 communities in all (including 26 in Canada and 2 in Mexico); by our definition, 94 of them were hip communes in the United States. That number reflects the deletion of a few listed communities we know to have ceased operation since the *Directory*'s publication.

5. The database on which the *Directory* is based lists 1219 communities in the United States; most of them shun publicity and ask not to be listed in the book. If surviving hip communes are present in that larger communal population at the same rate that they are among the 337 listed U.S. communities, then there are 340 surviving hippie communes in America. But the numbers could be higher still—the *Directory*'s database manager, Geoph Kozeny, notes that the database is incomplete: "My guesstimate is that there are at least ten communities for every one in the database; but who knows? Probably a lot more than that, even" (personal communication, September 23, 1992).

6. For information on Jesus People USA in the 1990s, see Timothy Jones, "Jesus' People," *Christianity Today* (14 September 1992): 20–25.

7. Albert Bates and Allen Butcher, "Options for Incorporation of Intentional Communities," in the *Directory of Intentional Communities*, 98–101.

8. One of many cases in point is Earth People's Park, 592 acres of land established in the early 1970s by a band of hippies that included Wavy Gravy and the Hog Farm commune in the euphoria that followed the Woodstock rock festival. Located in Vermont near the Canadian border, Earth People's Park was declared free land, open to all comers. Eventually, however, a distinctly unenlightened group of occupants showed up: a "wedge of biker-junkies," as Wavy Gravy called them, moved in, started dealing drugs, and commenced to sell the land's extensive timber. Although an effort was undertaken to evict the undesirables, as of the spring of 1991 the situation had not been resolved. See Wavy Gravy (Hugh Romney), *Something Good for a Change: Random Notes on Peace Through Living* (New York: St. Martin's, 1992), 164–71.

9. Stephen Gaskin, *Monday Night Class*, 2nd ed. (San Francisco: Book Publishing Co., 1970), unpaginated.

10. Stephen Gaskin, *The Caravan* (New York: Random House, 1971), unpaginated.

11. Stephen Gaskin, *Amazing Dope Tales* (Summertown, Tenn.: Book Publishing Co., 1980), 19.

12. He abandoned LSD not because it was deleterious to the body or mind-numbing, but because it was dangerous. Said Stephen:

Acid terrified many people. Acid terrified me many times. . . . Tripping well on acid was like being an athlete. It took tremendous amounts of courage. And you had to rely more on your innate character than on how smart you might think you were. Stuff would come on you so fast that you would not be thinking linearly while you were reacting to it . . . you'd be on your reflexes. If you had pretty good habits, you'd tend to rise. If you didn't have good habits, you'd tend not to (*Amazing Dope Tales*, 54–55).

13. *Monday Night Class*, unpaginated.

14. *The Grass Case* (Summertown, Tenn.: Book Publishing Co., 1974), 10–13.

15. Stephen Gaskin, "Weltanschauung" (unpublished, 1992).

16. Martin Holsinger attributes some of the loss of faith in Stephen to the gross errors of judgment he made in what he advocated for the future of the Farm. Specifically, Stephen pushed for progressive farming instead of organic gardening, a community decision that led to near-bankruptcy in the early 1980s. Stephen also advocated abandoning construction trades, the only major source of income besides farming, because they competed with neighbors' livelihoods. See Martin Holsinger, "A House Divided Against Itself" (senior thesis, Goddard College, January 1991), p. 60.

17. Peter Schweitzer, personal communication, 1992.

Suggestions for Further Reading

Directory of Intentional Communities: A Guide to Cooperative Living. Evansville, Ind., and Rutledge, Mo.: Fellowship for Intentional Community and Communities Publications Cooperative, 1992.

Hey Beatnik! This Is the Farm Book. Summertown, Tenn.: The Book Publishing Co., 1974.

Part VII
And Many More. . . .

The categories represented in the six previous sections of this volume attempt to be inclusive, but some alternative religions defy easy insertion into any such typological scheme. Thus the four categories of religions presented here have little in common apart from their separateness from the religious mainstream. They all, however, play important roles in the contemporary alternative religious world and often are focal in ongoing disputes over "cults" and the limits of religious liberty.

Native American new religions represent, in most cases, attempts to define and conserve traditional Indian culture in the face of the European incursion, as well as to help Native Americans cope with the dislocations they have suffered over the last five hundred years. A very different phenomenon is the Church of Scientology, the relatively recent creation of the late science fiction writer L. Ron Hubbard, whose work holds out to members the promise of psychological wellness through technology and mental discipline. Quite different yet are the many and diverse groups concerned in one way or another with unidentified flying objects, contact with alien beings,

and the like; they represent a notable twist on American millennial thinking and provide a new religious perspective on what is going on in the heavens. The survey of religious groupings in this section concludes with Satanism, a movement that actually has few adherents (and ones that are less sinister than they are widely perceived to be) but that is the focus of antagonism entirely out of proportion to its real impact on the culture.

The final chapter of the volume deals with the antagonists of alternative religions, those who believe some or all nonmainstream religions to be harmful to their participants and to society and who sometimes employ extreme—even illegal— means to fight what they regard as a serious social menace. Those who watch the anticult movement have observed that these activists sometimes embody what they decry in those they oppose, following charismatic leaders, extracting large sums of money from supporters, and using deceit, coercion, and scare tactics. They have, in any event, had a substantial impact on the larger culture and have provided a hefty counterweight to any influence the alternative religions have achieved.

39

NEW RELIGIONS AND AMERICAN INDIAN RELIGION

James R. Lewis

Adherents of most religions tend to view themselves as participants in divinely inspired organizations based on unchanging truths. In fact, however, we are always involved in a dynamic process of reinterpreting our traditions in response to changing social conditions. Because these changes are often gradual, the process of reinterpretation and adaption is usually not noticed by those involved in it.

Sometimes, however, reinterpretation and adaptation take place quickly, and we say that a new religion (or a new denomination or sect) has come into being, despite the fact that no truly radical break with tradition has occurred. Christianity and Buddhism were, at the time they were founded, regarded as new religions, despite the fact that both Jesus and Gautama preached doctrines that can be understood as simply modified versions of Judaism and Hinduism, respectively. Similarly, American Indian new religions may be viewed in terms of either their continuities or their discontinuities with prior tradition.

The most radical transformations in Native American religions have come in response to the intrusion of Euroamericans into Indian culture. In some cases leaders of American Indian new religions counseled peace with the invaders; in other cases they counseled violent opposition. Handsome Lake, whose visionary experiences deeply influenced the Iroquois, was a prophet of peace; his revelations legitimated male farming, for example, in a community that had traditionally assigned farming to females. Prior to the Euroamerican invasion men had been hunters and Iroquois religion had been filled with hunting myths and rituals, but Handsome Lake's new religion addressed a changing social and economic situation and provided divine sanction for a new lifestyle.

Tenskwatawa, known as the Shawnee Prophet and one of the most important "War Prophets," taught, on the other hand, that the intruding evil powers must be opposed actively. Together with his brother Tecumseh, Tenskwatawa (literally "The Open Door") forged a pan-Indian alliance opposed to Euroamerican intrusions in the years leading up to the War of 1812. In early 1805 he was a less than successful medicine man for a group of Shawnee in eastern Indiana. In the wake of military defeat and an unfavorable treaty imposed a decade earlier, many of the Midwestern tribes had fallen into a state of social and cultural demoralization. Tenskwatawa, a boastful alcoholic, fully embodied this demoralized state. Then, in the wake of an epidemic, he fell into a comalike state and was believed dead. However, before funeral arrangements could be completed, he was revived, to the amazement of fellow members of his tribe, and began describing revelations he had received during his deathlike trance.

As he related his experience, Tenskwatawa had been permitted to view heaven, "a rich, fertile country, abounding in game, fish, pleasant hunting grounds and fine corn fields." But he had also witnessed sinful Shawnee spirits being tortured according to the degree of their wickedness, with drunkards being forced to swallow molten lead. Overwhelmed by the vision, Tenskwatawa abandoned his old ways. More revelations followed in the succeeding months —revelations that eventually added up to a coherent new vision of religion and society.

Although the new revelation departed from tradition at many points, as by introducing new songs and dances, its central thrust was a nativistic exhortation to fellow tribe members to abandon Euroamerican ways for the lifestyle of earlier generations. Tenskwatawa successfully extended his religion to other tribes, particularly the Kickapoo, Winnebago, Sac, and Miami. New rituals that reflected the Shawnee's contact with Catholicism were developed to facilitate conversions.

The promise of restored greatness was overwhelmingly appealing to the Shawnee. Consequently, the religious leadership of the prophet remained strong until Tenskwatawa's prophecy of victory failed at the battle of Tippecanoe on November 7, 1811. Although from a military viewpoint the battle was indecisive, Tenskwatawa's status at a leader was irreparably damaged. His visionary hope was supplanted by the more secular efforts of his brother Tecumseh to unite the tribes in opposition to Euroamericans.

The pattern of Tenskwatawa's experiences and the transformation of tradition that occurred as a result of his revelation have strong parallels in most Native American new religions for which records have survived. Often, although not always, the new religions incorporated elements of Christianity into their new syntheses. Typically, innovations came about as a result of new revelations to a single prophet. The prophet was often a dissolute individual who exemplified the demoralized state of his people. He also frequently had followed the vocation of shaman and/or healer prior to his visionary experiences.

One of the most famous American Indian religions, the Ghost Dance of 1890, may be instructively compared and contrasted with the new religion of Tenskwatawa. The most widespread Native American millenarian movement of the nineteenth century, the Ghost Dance ("1890" distinguishes the movement from the Ghost Dance of 1870, which may be regarded as its prototype) began among the Paiute of northern Nevada and spread to other tribes—first to other western ones, and later to eastern tribes. Its basic structure, scholars have noted, was taken from the traditional Paiute Round Dance.

The prophet of the Ghost Dance of 1890 was Wovoka (also called Jack Wilson, not to be confused with the peyote prophet John Wilson). In the pattern of many earlier prophets, Wovoka was a healer and shaman who experienced his initial revelation in a vision that occurred when he seemed to fall down dead (in this case, during a solar eclipse). His teachings, which he considered God-given, were, like those of Tenskwatawa and Handsome Lake, strongly ethical. He also announced a revelation envisioning a millennium in which the earth would be renewed, the spirits of the dead return, and death and misery end. The millennium would be preceded by a catastrophe that would destroy Euroamericans and their material culture. Righteous Native Americans would be lifted off the planet and a new earth would be rolled across its surface, burying Euroamericans and unrighteous Native Americans. The catastrophe was to be a divine work, not the product of human military or political activism; therefore Native Americans were instructed to remain peaceful and await the great events.

In the meantime, Wovoka's followers were instructed to perform, periodically, what Euroamericans came to call the Ghost Dance. For the dance men and women painted their bodies to indicate the revelations they had received, and danced in concentric circles. The arms of each dancer rested on the shoulders of both neighbors so that the vibrant rhythm of the dance swayed the worshippers as if they were a single body. The mood created by the dance, which was usually performed at night, induced collective exaltation and trance. Wovoka's original instructions were to practice the dance for five days at a time. Eventually some participants fell into trances during which they received revelations, usually from departed relatives. The performance of the dance would hasten the advent of the new age.

Wovoka's revelation spoke powerfully to his contemporaries, and the dance was taken up by a wide variety of tribes, including Shoshoni, Arapaho, Crow, Cheyenne, Pawnee, Kiowa, Comanche, and Sioux. Relatively stable tribal groups that had adjusted successfully to Euroamerican domination of the continent were less inclined to accept the new teaching. However, the widespread excitement generated by Wovoka's vision declined rapidly in the wake of the Wounded Knee massacre (December 29, 1890), when U.S. troops—mistakenly believing that the new religion was a facade for a violent uprising—massacred a group of peaceful Sioux Ghost Dancers.

Independently of the prophet and the larger movement, however, the Ghost Dance continued. As late as the 1950s it was still being performed by the Shoshonis in something like its original form. Other tribes adapted the Ghost Dance when they revived certain parts of their traditional religions; the Pawnee, for example, reinstituted an abandoned sacred hand game under the influence of the Ghost Dance.

Other nineteenth-century new religions continue to survive as well. Handsome Lake's religion remains alive and well among the Iroquois. The Indian Shakers flourish from California to British Columbia, carrying on the work of the Salish prophet John Slocum, whose visions, beginning in 1881, established a religion offering a new state of grace that produced Pentecostal-like "gifts," including, notably, healing. Meanwhile, the Native American Church has expanded to become the most influential new religion among twentieth-century American Indians.

The Native American Church represents a fusion of Christianity with various local traditional tribal religions. It is best known for its use of peyote in worship. Peyote had been used religiously in Mexico and perhaps southern Texas for centuries; its

spread began with its introduction to the Kiowa and Comanche tribes about 1870, and continued throughout the Plains and surrounding areas in the early decades of the twentieth century. Travelling peyote teachers contributed materially to its spread, prominent among them Quanah Parker, a Comanche chief who attributed his recovery from a serious illness in 1884 to peyote. As Panindian consciousness and a desire to preserve traditional culture have spread in the twentieth century, so has peyote religion, which is easily adapted to local usage.

Peyote contains mescaline, a psychotropic substance whose effects are akin to those of psilocybin and LSD. Peyote users consider the altered consciousness that results from eating peyote to be transcendent religious experience, and peyote itself is regarded as sacred medicine, not a drug, at least insofar as "drug" connotes destructiveness. Nevertheless, Euroamericans have tried to outlaw the use of peyote by declaring it an illegal substance. A complex welter of state and federal laws and court decisions renders the legal status of peyote use murky, although in most of the country the services of the Native American Church are not interfered with by the authorities. In any event, the church has a huge following in Native America and is a source of meaning and symbol of unity for large numbers of American Indians.

A more recent development is the interest of Euroamericans in American Indian religions. While there is a long tradition of romanticizing Native Americans and their spiritual traditions, Euroamericans have rarely been prompted to engage in actual Indian religious practices. This situation changed in the 1960s when certain groups of counterculturists made an effort to adopt what they thought of as "tribal" lifestyles. Particularly noteworthy here is the Bear Tribe, a nontraditional group of young Anglos brought together by founder Sun Bear, an Ojibwa-Chippewa Indian. Sun Bear and others like him have, while claiming to revive authentic Indian traditions, clearly adapted those traditions to the needs of contemporary Euroamericans. Thus Indian spirituality repackaged to appeal to Anglos constitutes yet another new religion.

Although this revival of interest in Indian spirituality began with the 1960s counterculture, it did not become a major phenomenon until the arrival of the New Age movement of the late 1980s. The New Age movement, in some ways a successor to the counterculture, did not turn its attention to Native American religion until the phenomenon that has come to be known as "neoshamanism" became a popular topic within the movement.

Although the term "shaman" has come to be used quite loosely, in the disciplines of anthropology and comparative religion shamanism refers to a fairly specific set of ideas and practices than can be found in many, but not all, world cultures. Characteristically, the shaman is a healer, a psychopomp (someone who guides the souls of the dead to their home in the afterlife), and more generally a mediator between her or his community and the world of spirits (most often animal spirits and the spirits of the forces of nature). For smaller-scale societies, especially hunting and gathering groups, shamans performs all of the functions that doctors, priests, and therapists (and sometimes mystics and artists as well) perform in contemporary Western societies. The religious specialists, sometimes called "medicine men," of traditional American Indian societies are prominent examples of shamans.

New Agers have felt attracted to shamanism for a variety of reasons. A major factor in this attraction is that, while the shaman is a kind of mystic, the shaman's path is a mysticism of attunement to the forces of nature rather than an otherworldly mysticism. Shamans may go to the wilderness to seek visions, but they return to society and to ordinary human life. Also, traditional shamanism's stress on healing is very much in line with the New Age tendency to combine the quest for health, both physical and psychological, with the quest for spirituality. Yet other factors in the attraction are the association of shamanism with mind-altering drugs (including peyote) and with romanticized images of nature.

Many contemporary New Agers have thus come to adopt some of the trappings of American Indian shamanism. The popularity of Native American spirituality has, however, evoked hostility from certain Indian groups. These critics, many associated with the American Indian Movement (AIM), have asserted that New Agers are engaged in a kind of cultural imperialism: whereas the older Euroamerican invaders stole the land, the new invaders are trying to steal the religions of native peoples.

One can come to understand the AIM position by examining the advertisements in New Age magazines through which one can purchase by mail everything from medicine rattles and sacred pipes to a complete "Course in Shamanism" on cassette tapes. Ads also offer "Pilgrimages to Places of Power" as well as innumerable workshops on vision quests, sweat lodges, and the like. The New Age movement has, of course, commercialized other spiritual traditions of the world as well, but few of the world's people feel themselves as directly oppressed and exploited by Euroamericans as do the aboriginal people of this continent. It is not surprising that Native Americans should be hostile to what they believe exploits their culture.

Suggestions for Further Reading

Edmunds, R. David. *The Shawnee Prophet.* Lincoln: University of Nebraska Press, 1983.

Kehoe, Alice Beck. *The Ghost Dance: Ethnohistory and Revitalization.* New York: Holt, Rinehart and Winston, 1989.

Melton, J. Gordon, Jerome Clark, and Aidan A. Kelly. *The New Age Encyclopedia.* Detroit: Gale Research, 1990.

Mooney, James. *The Ghost-Dance Religion and the Sioux Outbreak of 1890.* Chicago: University of Chicago Press, 1965; abridged reprint of 1896 original.

Stewart, Omer Call. *Peyote Religion: A History.* Norman: University of Oklahoma Press, 1987.

40

THE CHURCH OF SCIENTOLOGY: LIGHTNING ROD FOR CULTURAL BOUNDARY CONFLICTS

Mary Farrell Bednarowski

Scientology defies easy definition. Poised on the boundaries of religion, psychology, science, and even magic in the opinion of some of its interpreters, it does not fit readily into any of these categories. In addition the movement has drawn exceedingly hostile criticism from its beginning years. It has frequently responded to its critics in kind with the result that much of the available literature falls into patterns of attack and counterattack. *Time* magazine's 6 May 1991 cover article and Scientology's rejoinder are among the most recent and very public examples.[1]

The histories of new religions in most times and cultures give evidence of rhetoric polarized between the denunciations of critics and the fervent testimonials of members, but the phenomenon is unusually intense and persistent in the case of Scientology. For this reason, any attempt to interpret its place in American religion and culture needs to take this part of its identity into account and to offer interpretations. It is not enough simply to chronicle Scientology's history, worldview, and development.

Scientology has its origins in the writings of L. Ron Hubbard (1911–1986). In fact, one might say that Scientology's worldview and its organization are the products of Hubbard's theological and psychological imagination. Given the contemporary emphasis on religions as human meaning systems and on theology as an imaginative, world-constructing activity, this is not such a negative or startling thing to say as was once the case.[2] Hubbard's foundational book, *Dianetics: The Modern Science of Mental Health,* was published in 1950.[3] Now considered by Scientologists to be part of the early history of the movement, the system it outlines nonetheless contains most of the concepts that remain foundational in the movement, among them *engram, reactive mind, analytical mind, auditing,* and *clear.*

Hubbard described Dianetics as "a science of mind" and claimed for it, among other things, usefulness as "a therapeutic technique with which can be treated all inorganic mental ills and all organic psycho-somatic ills, with assurances of complete cure in unselected cases."[4] He claimed further that the system was built on "definite axioms: statements of natural laws, on the order of those of the physical sciences."[5] At the same time, Hubbard distinguished Dianetics from other therapies or sciences with which he thought it could be confused. In doing so, he gave evidence of what would be ongoing efforts to blend concepts from religion, science, and psychology in his own particular way in combination with a vocabulary distinctive to Scientology. Dianetics, he said,

is *not* psychiatry. It is *not* hypnotism. It is ... defined as what the soul is doing to the body. Dianetics is a system of analysis, control, and development of human thought which also provides techniques for increased ability, rationality, and freedom from the discovered sources of irrational behavior stemming from the mind.[6]

Hubbard's interpretation of how the mind works and what the soul is doing to the body is grounded in the concept of the "engram," his term for unconscious memories of either physical or psychological pain. Engrams are stored in the "reactive mind," primarily a stimulus/response mechanism incapable of analysis. They cannot be described merely as memories, because they function as "inexhaustible sources of power to command the body"[7] and cause people to act in irrational, self-defeating ways. "Auditing" is the process in Scientology by which engrams are brought to consciousness in the "analytical mind." It is the analytical mind that has the capacity to reflect on engrams and to diffuse their power to inhibit rational and productive thinking and behavior—and therefore happiness and success.

Auditing requires the agency of both human auditor and a machine, the Hubbard Electrometer or E-Meter. While the auditor functions as a therapist and has been described in recent years as a pastoral counselor, the E-Meter lends the scientific precision of a machine to the proceedings. Similar to a lie detector, the E-Meter's needle registers emotional reaction to particular words called out by the auditor and thus provides clues to underlying sources of engrams lodged in the reactive mind. The E-Meter, according to advertisements, has increased in power over the years and the latest model is called the Hubbard Professional Mark Super VII E-Meter.

The use of the E-Meter and Scientology's reference to what it has to offer as its "technology" intensifies the emphasis on science and function in the movement. "It works!" is one of Scientology's central affirmations. The most recent publications continue to insist that the technology always works "100% of the time, when it is known and applied without alter-is." Any failures are attributed to staff and organizational er-

rors. Scientology interprets its future as dependent "on having the technology—pure and unadulterated—and seeing that it is applied." To this end there continues to be great emphasis even after his death on Hubbard as the only source of Scientology technology.[8]

When all engrams have been rendered powerless, one achieves the state of "clear," defined in several ways by the *Basic Dictionary of Dianetics and Scientology*: "A being who is unrepressed and self-determined. . . . beings who have been cleared of wrong awareness and useless answers which kept them from living or thinking. . . . One who has become the basic individual through auditing." As a verb, "to clear" means "to release all the physical pain and painful emotion from the life of the individual."[9] In the earlier years of the movement, the powers ascribed to clear included enhanced mental powers, such as perfect memory, healing capacities, and freedom from illness. The claims have been modified over the years, as has the place of clear in the Scientology hierarchy. In addition, several pre-clear levels were added to the system.

Sociologists Rodney Stark and William Sims Bainbridge have suggested that clear has come to function much less as a "state" and much more as "a status in a hierarchical social structure," one which "is being dissolved into a long staircase of statuses leading upward in the stratosphere of OT." They suggest further that Scientology is moving—and will probably have to move further—from offering benefits that might be termed "magical" in nature to results that are less definable and which must be claimed by the particular person rather than bestowed by the movement.[10]

OT, or Operating Thetan, is a more advanced category than clear. The concept came into use in the middle 1950s to accommodate Hubbard's encounter with what he interpreted as engrams from past lives emerging from the auditing process. Its continuing development signalled an expansion of Scientology's cosmos, its understanding of human nature, and its organizational structure. In the worldview of Scientology, the OT is the true human self, "an individual who could operate totally independently of his body whether he had one or didn't have one. He's now himself, he's not dependent on the universe around him."[11]

Hubbard began to elaborate a backdrop sufficiently large for the unfolding of a cosmic drama: the efforts of the OT to escape over a series of lifetimes from the prison of MEST (matter, energy, space, time) and discover its identity as a spirit who inhabits different bodies over billions of years and many lifetimes.[12] In the worldview of Scientology, the thetan is hindered by the physical body in its efforts to be truly itself, and, while Scientology does not go so far as to deny the reality of the body, it considers it a somewhat negligible entity, a tool for the OT, at the bottom of the Scientology hierarchy of body/mind/spirit.

The category of Operating Thetan has provided Scientology with a vehicle for multiplying the number of statuses that an individual can achieve. The levels of OT continue to increase, each bringing with it new powers—some of which at the higher levels have not yet been disclosed. To ascend to these higher levels requires further auditing and the taking of special courses. The courses are offered by the church for a fee. In addition, there are training courses that enable members to become auditors themselves. In this sense, Scientology participates in what Roy Wallis has called an "enrollment economy": "Its economic base is dependent upon the sale of services in the form of auditing and training, books, E-meters and memberships."[13]

The universe of Scientology over which the drama of the OT takes place is composed of eight concentric circles, the Eight Dynamics. It is the task of the Operating Thetan to seek its true identity as spirit across all the Dynamics. The Dynamics begin with the First, the "urge toward existence as one's self," in which full individuality is expressed, through the Eighth, "the urge toward existence as Infinity" or the God Dynamic. In between are the urges toward sexuality and family, groups of individuals, humankind, the animal kingdom, the physical universe, and spirits.[14] Scientology does not elaborate on the

Eighth or God Dynamic and offers several reasons for not providing more detail. One is that little is known about God: "In Scientology we believe that God exists. As to the form in which He exists, we do not yet have dogma. As the Church of Scientology evolves, who can say what might be discovered?"[15] Another is that because the movement is nondenominational, members need to be free to make up their own minds about the nature of God.[16]

If the Eight Dynamics are the arena in which the Operating Thetan finds its true identity, they also comprise the network of relationships in which Scientologists—all of humankind, they would claim—live out their lives. It is the obligation of Scientologists to remain in proper communication with all eight levels of existence, and it is acknowledged that the quality of communication in one person's life may differ from dynamic to dynamic. In other words, there are always areas of life that need work, and it is the function of auditing and the many Scientology courses and publications (on work, study, relationships, marriage, freedom from drugs—hundreds of them) to make this communication possible.

The quality of communication possible at any level of the Eight Dynamics is determined by Scientology ethics and in particular the Table of Conditions—varieties of relationships that may exist between individuals or an individual and a group. Roy Wallis describes them as indicating "the state of grace" of any individual or organization. The common-sense use of these terms is no aid to understanding what the particular terms mean for Scientologists. The conditions of "non-existence" and "danger," for example, indicate lesser states of alienation than "liability." "Normal operation" is not so much the desired state as a neutral state that brings with it neither reward nor punishment.

As an organization Scientology has made use of the Conditions primarily as a means of internal regulation of its technology and its personnel, particularly in regard to their loyalty to Scientology. "Ethics policies," says one publication, "are leveled primarily at making auditing and training honest and flawless."[17] Ethics policies are also used to elaborate on a code of offenses against Scientology that includes giving the movement a bad name in public, perhaps by writing a negative letter to a newspaper or testifying against it in court. Scientology's ethics vocabulary includes offenses by two categories of people: "suppressive persons" (or groups) and "potential trouble sources." The first refers to those who actively try to suppress or damage Scientology, and the second to those who maintain contact with suppressive persons.[18]

In regard to internal regulation and to individuals and groups that Scientology considers hostile to its interests, the application of Scientology ethics and the Conditions intensifies the public perception that Scientology does not take criticism lightly.[19] But there is another dimension to Scientology ethics, a "dailiness," that is not apparent either in the accusations against the movement or in the excessively positive tributes of celebrities in defense of the movement. Scientologists can speak eloquently about how they make use of the various Conditions to analyze relationships and situations in their own personal lives with spouses, friends, children, and various groups. For example, *Marriage Hats* by Mary Sue Hubbard, L. Ron Hubbard's wife, outlines the duties ("hat" is a common term in Scientology for duty or status in the organization) of husbands and wives in terms of the Eight Dynamics.[20] Published in 1974, the advice in the booklet is based on very traditional understandings of gender roles. In a recent interview, a Scientologist who continues to find it useful claimed that she looks upon all the tasks together as those that must be attended to in a marriage; it is up to each couple to determine together who will be responsible for each.

This same Scientologist is now dean of an alternative school, Beacon Heights Academy, in suburban Minneapolis, Minnesota, that opened in the fall of 1992.[21] In early 1993 there were fifteen students enrolled with room for two hundred. Many but not all of the students are children of Scientologists, although the teachers employed at that time were not members of the church. The school does not receive funds from Scientology and does not contribute to the church, but its curriculum and pedagogy are based on L. Ron Hubbard study technology,[22] which includes textbooks. Discipline is administered on the basis of the Table of Conditions, which serves as a resource for interpreting any infraction from late papers or forgotten textbooks to more serious offenses. Parents, according to the dean, are made aware of the use of Hubbard's study technology and Scientology ethics, and emphasis is on the usefulness of the Scientology worldview beyond the organization itself.

Information about the broader uses of Scientology does not seem to have permeated the public perception of Scientology in such a way as to mitigate widespread criticism of the movement. Controversy and constant litigation continue to be a part of its history and identity. At one level, the ongoing hostilities are difficult to interpret. Scientology has been in existence for more than forty years, during which period it has built a worldwide organization. It has moderated its claims for what it can offer through its technology. It has thus far survived the death of its founder, and it continues to expand.

At another level, an examination of Scientology's position on the boundaries of religion, science, and psychology offers some insights into the nature of some of the controversies in which the movement has been involved. Self-described as drawing from all three of these areas of human endeavor, and philosophy as well, Scientology has been claimed by none of them and repudiated, for the most part, by all. Its efforts to interpret and defend itself, whether convincing or not in any particular case, point to issues of definition and cultural assumptions about the very nature of religion—what it can or should offer its members, and, in turn, what it has the right to demand from them.

From its earliest history Scientology's claims that it is a religion have been disputed. While its organization is hierarchical and authoritarian and it has an ordained ministry, the movement seldom makes use of traditional theological language or categories except in a very broad sense and usually to point to parallels with other religious traditions. A widely distributed pamphlet, "What Is Scientology?" answers "Yes!" to the question, "Is Scientology a religion?" "Yes," according to the pamphlet, "in the truest sense of the word, "because, like other religious traditions, it preaches the precept "Love thy neighbor," sees each person as a spiritual being, holds that the spirit survives the death of the body, offers a path to salvation, and points to sin as a deterrent to salvation.[23]

In contrast with many other new religions, Scientology does not accuse the established religious traditions of having incomplete revelations or inadequate theologies. It insists that membership in Scientology is not incompatible with being a Catholic, Protestant, or Jew and goes so far as to encourage dual membership. This stance has not served to prevent its being labeled a "cult" by mainline religions. Nor has its own interpretation of itself as a religion been convincing in the broader culture, if the litigation involving the very question of its religious identity is any indication. Scientology has been involved in endless court cases over its tax-exempt status—sometimes as defendant and sometimes as plaintiff—for most of its history with highly publicized cases in the United States, Australia, Italy, and Canada, and other countries as well.[24]

A further source of concern about Scientology's identity as a religion with a recognizable theology is the contrast between the esoteric material of its creation stories with Scientology's public presentation of itself as "an applied religious philosophy" oriented toward daily human concerns such as communication, relationships, education, and work. Occasionally newspaper accounts mention the existence of Scientology documents that offer advanced students information about the origins of the earth—for example, that seventy-five million years ago it was called Teegeeach and "was among 90 planets ruled by Xemu, who spread his evil by thermonuclear bombs." Xemu destroyed some of the inhabitants of these planets and "implanted seeds of aberrant behavior to affect future generations of mankind."[25] It is often the case that such documents have been confiscated for evidence in court trials. Roy Wallis, a British sociologist, came across similar sources in doing research for *The Road to Total Freedom,* along with directives from L. Ron Hubbard that such materials come under the category of para-Scientology. Hubbard insisted that they are not required belief, and that it is not a good idea to convey them to new inquirers.[26]

Scientologists have objected to the publication of documents that ordinarily would be kept confidential and to which not even all Scientologists have access. They compare them to the Cabala and to sacred and confidential texts from the Vatican. It is, in fact, not unusual in the history of religions that some information is available only to the initiated, and even the outlines of the mythology are not totally unfamiliar to the historian acquainted with ancient gnosticism; but the public response to such revelations takes the form of suspicion that there is much going on in Scientology that is secret, and the stories fuel further the claims that Hubbard's system is the product of his creativity as a science fiction writer rather than a theologian.

In addition to not being theological in obvious ways, Scientology charges money for auditing, for the training required to be an auditor, and for its courses. This practice is unquestioned when it comes to therapy or psychoanalysis, but it is looked at with concern in regard to religion. The closest analogy is to stipends (the amount often left to the discretion of the giver) charged for services such as weddings or funerals in the established traditions and fees for pastoral counseling or spiritual direction. Scientology refers frequently to the services it offers as pastoral counseling, and there have been disagreements between the Tax Court and federal appeals courts as to whether Scientologists can deduct fees as charitable contributions to a religious organization. Other litigation has involved the issue of whether or not Scientologists receive what they pay for in auditing and courses and whether what one receives from a religion is tangible enough to be somehow quantified and evaluated in terms of money. Is Scientology offering a product? A service? Spiritual transformation? And how might the answers to any of these questions affect the interpretation of its standing as a religion?

Yet another source of controversy emerges from some of the social stands Scientology has taken—against the Internal Revenue Service, against Interpol,[27] and against the psychiatric profession, particularly for the use of shock treatments, and drugs such as ritalin, often prescribed for hyperactivity, and Prozac, a new and widely used anti-depressant. Some of Scientology's social outreach programs are related to these stands, while others are not directly connected. There is the Citizens' Commission on Human Rights which cites as its mission the eradicating of psychiatric abuses of human rights. Another is Narconon, a drug rehabilitation center in Chilocco, Oklahoma, and a third is Criminon, a program to deliver Scientology's *The Way to Happiness* course to prison inmates.

Controversial or not, Scientology has survived more than forty years and is likely to remain part of the new religions landscape. As is the case with many new religions, it is difficult to ascertain membership

and even to establish membership criteria. This is especially true of Scientology, since an individual's association might range from taking one course to living out a whole career in the organization. Nonetheless, it is safe to say that Scientology has increased the number of churches, missions, and groups to upwards of seven hundred throughout the world, and it is likely that the movement will continue to expand. Other developments are more difficult to predict, but at least two central questions suggest themselves. Will Scientology have to conform more obviously to the public conception of what a religion should look like? Or will it benefit from the current trend in American culture to separate institutional religion from "spirituality," as is the case in many support groups such as the twelve-step programs? Will Scientology continue to take such an adversarial stance toward its critics? Perhaps the attack/counterattack pattern is part of a kind of synergism between Scientology and its critics and so central a component of L. Ron Hubbard's legacy and the movement's identity that there is little chance of changing it. On the other hand, Scientology might choose to solicit the kind of outside critique that is essential for any religious movements to curb its own excessive traits, whether these are manifested inside or outside the movement.

Notes

1. See Richard Behar, "The Thriving Cult of Greed and Power," *Time* 137, no. 18 (6 May 1991): 50–57; *Facts vs. Fiction: A Correction of Falsehoods Contained in the May 6, 1991 Issue of TIME Magazine* (n.p.: Church of Scientology International [1991]); and *The Story That TIME Couldn't Tell* (n.p.: Church of Scientology International, 1991).

2. See, for example, Peter Berger, *The Sacred Canopy: Elements of a Sociological Theory of Religion* (Garden City, N.Y.: Doubleday and Company, Inc., 1967) and Gordon Kaufman, *The Theological Imagination: Constructing the Concept of God,* rev. ed. (Chico, Calif.: Scholars Press, 1979). For an interesting analysis of some of Hubbard's sources see Harriet Whitehead, "Reasonably Fantastic: Some Perspectives on Scientology, Science Fiction, and the Occult," in *Religious Movements in Contemporary America,* ed. Irving I. Zaretsky and Mark P. Leone (Princeton, N.J.: Princeton University Press, 1974), 547–87.

3. L. Ron Hubbard, *Dianetics: The Modern Science of Mental Health* (Los Angeles: Bridge, 1950, 1978).

4. Ibid., p. 6.

5. Ibid.

6. *Basic Dictionary of Dianetics and Scientology* from the works of L. Ron Hubbard (Los Angeles: Bridge, 1973), n.p.

7. Hubbard, *Dianetics,* 69.

8. *The Scope of Scientology, Auditor's Day, 1991: Announcement of a General Amnesty* (n.p.: Religious Technology Center, 1991), 1.

9. *Basic Dictionary of Dianetics and Scientology.*

10. Rodney Stark and William Sims Bainbridge, "Scientology: To Be Perfectly Clear," in *The Future of Religion: Secularization, Revival and Cult Formation* (Berkeley: University of California Press, 1985), 275. This whole chapter is a helpful interpretation of the development of clear in Scientology with an emphasis on how Scientology has shifted responsibility for claiming clear status to the individual, even though it is the organization that officially confers it.

11. *Basic Dictionary of Dianetics and Scientology.*

12. See L. Ron Hubbard, *Have You Lived Before This Life? A Study of Death and Evidence of Past Lives* (Los Angeles: Church of Scientology of California, 1977). Although Hubbard makes reference to reincarnation in the Introduction as an age-old and widespread belief, in the body of the book he refers to Scientology's concept of past lives as something more simple than the "complex theory" of reincarnation.

13. Roy Wallis, *The Road to Total Freedom: A Sociological Analysis of Scientology* (New York: Columbia University Press, 1977), 157. See particularly chapter 6, "The Scientological Career: From Casual Client to Deployable Agent."

14. L. Ron Hubbard, *Scientology: The Fundamentals of Thought* (Los Angeles: The Church of Scientology of California Publications Organization, 1973), 36–39.

15. *The Background and Ceremonies of the Church of Scientology of California, World Wide* (London: Krisson, 1970), 22.

16. For an elaboration of the more specifically theological aspects of Scientology, see Mary Farrell Bednarowski, *New Religions and the Theological Imagination in America* (Bloomington and Indianapolis: Indiana University Press, 1989).

17. *Scientology: What Is It?* (n.p.: Church of Scientology International, 1985), 13.

18. See L. Ron Hubbard, *Introduction to Scientology Ethics* (Los Angeles: Bridge, 1968), especially the chapter entitled "The Ethics

Code" (pp. 45–68). See also Wallis, *The Road to Total Freedom,* 143–48, for information about penalties attached to the Lower Conditions.

19. See Richard Behar's *Time* article for a lengthy cataloguing of individuals and groups who report harassment by Scientology for various reasons.

20. Mary Sue Hubbard, *Marriage Hats* (Los Angeles: Bridge, 1974).

21. Interview with Cathy Brown, dean of Beacon Heights Academy, Minnetonka, Minnesota, 11 January 1993. Ms. Brown mentioned the Delphian School in Portland, Oregon, a boarding school, as another example of an educational institution that uses L. Ron Hubbard study technology.

22. For a brief elaboration of Scientology study technology, including "word clearing," see the pamphlet "L. Ron Hubbard: The Man and His Work" (no publication data).

23. *Scientology: What Is It?*, 2. See also the question-and-answer section of "The Scientology Catechism," in the large informational volume, *What Is Scientology?* (Los Angeles: The Church of Scientology of California, 1978), 197–206.

24. The volume *What Is Scientology?* provides a chronology of some of the early government actions initiated by the Internal Revenue Service concerning Scientology's designation as a tax-exempt religion and by the Food and Drug Administration in the seizure of E-Meters and literature in 1959 (pp. 154–55). For a discussion of tax-exemption cases from a perspective that is critical of Scientology, see Jerold A. Friedland, "Constitutional Issues in Revoking Religious Tax Exemptions: Church of Scientology of California v. Commissioner [83 T.C. 381]," *University of Florida Law Review* 37 (1985): 565–89.

25. "L. Ron Hubbard Dies," *Minneapolis Star and Tribune,* 28 January 1986, 5A.

26. Wallis, *The Road to Total Freedom,* 106–07.

27. See *Private Group, Public Menace: Interpol, a Police Organization Involved in Criminal Activities* (Los Angeles: Los Angeles Church of Scientology, 1990).

Suggestions for Further Reading

Bednarowski, Mary Farrell. *New Religions and the Theological Imagination in America.* Bloomington: Indiana University Press, 1989.

Hubbard, L. Ron. *Dianetics: The Modern Science of Mental Health.* Los Angeles: Bridge, 1950, 1978.

Stark, Rodney, and William Sims Bainbridge, "Scientology: To Be Perfectly Clear," in *The Future of Religion: Secularization, Revival and Cult Formation.* Ber-keley: University of California Press, 1985.

Wallis, Roy. *The Road to Total Freedom: A Sociological Analysis of Scientology.* New York: Columbia University Press, 1977.

What Is Scientology? Los Angeles: The Church of Scientology of California, 1992.

41

UFO RELIGIOUS MOVEMENTS
Robert S. Ellwood

Few new religious movements of the post–World War II era are more fascinating, or cast a more interesting light on American society, than those associated with UFOs (unidentified flying objects, also called flying saucers). Some observers, to be sure, stoutly rejected the notion that these objects were of religious significance, and held only to scientific investigation of the phenomenon. But, valid as that perspective may be, the religious interpretation of UFOs has tended to overwhelm the scientific in the minds of both aficionados and the general public, and is our present concern. The alleged visitors from outer space quickly took on the role of spaceborne saviors—or else became stock demonic figures. Even when not explicitly intended, the UFO experience easily slipped into the folkloric or mythological characteristics usually associated with supernatural entities. In this respect UFOism acquired attributes of a religion in formation—although it may be added that the formation process never really "jelled" into any substantial liturgical or institutional shape.

The modern UFO movement commenced June 24, 1947, when Kenneth Arnold, a civilian pilot from Boise, Idaho, flying over the Cascades in western Washington in search of a lost Marine C-46 transport, reported seeing nine shiny objects in a chain-like formation speeding by at some 1600 miles per hour. "They flew," Arnold said, "like a saucer would if you skipped it across the water." Seizing on the term "flying saucer," the news media picked up the story, and it was published worldwide. Here began the modern myth of flying saucers and UFOs. Although scholarly commentators compared the apparition to the "foo fighters" of World War II, the mysterious airship widely reported in the America of 1896,[1] and to even earlier accounts of puzzling aerial phenomena from medieval, classical, and Vedic sources, Arnold's account launched a thousand new sightings.

They poured in from around the world, and quickly acquired elaborations. Viewers saw both saucers and cigar-shaped "mother ships"; UFOs caused cars to stall if one swooped too close; in January 1948 an Air Force pilot, Thomas Mantell, died in a plane crash as he was pursuing a UFO over Louisville; in 1952 a fleet of UFOs launched a celebrated radar-traced "invasion" of Washington, D.C. Debunkers, of course, countered the enthusiasm with prosaic explanations, and by the early 1950s UFOs were widely portrayed, at least in the newsmagazines and by editorial cartoonists, with a light touch. But serious believers also tracked the occult aircraft; they saw the enigmatic objects as precursors to what could be the greatest event in human history: contact with an extraterrestrial race. Furthermore, there were prophets—or, in the preferred term, "contactees"—among them who claimed that epochal contact had already been made, and by them.

For the contactees and their believers, UFOs clearly possessed a revelatory significance that can only be termed religious. As we have noted, while UFOs have been the focus of scientific and quasi-scientific investigation, they have also, for some, found a religious role well summed up in Carl Jung's phrase, "technological angels."[2] One may observe a similar schism between "scientific" and "religious" responses to identical phenomena in nineteenth-century Spiritualism. For a religious interpretation of clairvoyance and mediumship one looked to the Spiritualist church and its parallels; for a scientific inspection of the same phenomena, to parapsychology or psychical research. This is one clue that, as we shall argue, nineteenth-century Spiritualism and twentieth-century UFOism belong in the same category.

According to Jung, the UFO visitants have, in a "space age" nurtured on science fiction, played the part once taken by descending gods, angels, saintly apparitions, and heavenly saviors. Mysteriously appearing out of the heavens, they have contacted favored earthlings to deliver messages of warning, hope, or forthcoming apocalypse, and to impart philosophical wisdom. The demonic role is also there, for not all UFO beings are benign. There are accounts of the sinister "Men in Black" who allegedly harass observers of UFOs, and harrowing tales of interstellar abductions and assaults climaxing in bizarre medical procedures or even cosmic rape.

I also put religious UFOism alongside Spiritualism on the grounds that it is essentially a new popular religion of the same type. Both presuppose an order of spiritually significant beings between the human and ultimate reality, with which one can have conversational and disciplic relationships. Whether spirits or space brothers, interaction with them opens up a sense of expanded consciousness and cosmic wonder, quite apart from whatever words are actually communicated. In both there are physical phenomena or "traces" which serve to support belief, but which for real believers are like "signs" in a religious sense, promoting salvific faith, as well as producing anomalies to be investigated scientifically.

For both Spiritualism and UFOism, human commerce with the Others begins with the experience of elect individuals. In both, this privileged exchange soon enough becomes the focus of informal "circles" or even minor institutions, in which messages from the invisible friends are transmitted mediumistically, in trance or through automatic writing. But at the same time, in both, these groups tend to be loose and ephemeral. For interest to be sustained, they need powerful periodic injections of fresh visions or novel messages.

UFOism may have other affinities as well. We must also note links with "Teaching Spiritualism" and Theosophy, discussed elsewhere in this book. Gordon Melton has devised the useful term "Teaching Spiritualism" to refer to mediumship or, in the more recent term, to "channeling," which does not so much emphasize passing on communications from departed relatives and the like as transmitting instruction from highly advanced spiritual teachers.[3] Some of the wise among the extraterrestrials clearly fall into the "Teaching" role, and their wisdom tends toward Theosophical concepts like karma, reincarnation, and spiritual evolution, though sometimes with more of an apocalyptic edge than their older fellow-initiates would have thought fitting. Yet parallels to the universe of Theosophical masters obtain in the concept of an adept who is not simply a god existing by aseity from all eternity, but who has attained high cosmic rank by dint of effort, initiation, and acquired wisdom.

Some commentators have also perceived a remarkable similarity between UFOs and their occupants, and the traditional fairy-folk amply affirmed by generation after generation of European peasants. Jacques Vallee, in *Passage to Magonia*,[4] pointed to striking convergences between the two otherworldly "little men" beliefs: the round saucer traces on the ground like fairy rings, the elven or goblinesque appearance of the alien intruders, the abductions during which ordinary time dissolved as it did for those countrymen of yore taken into a fairy mound, the new/old whispers of "changeling" children and queer half-human pregnancies.

More recently Thomas Bullard, in an article widely considered among the very best treatments of UFOs as a cultural phenomenon, has argued that the social role of UFO belief strongly suggests folkloric parallels, while UFO abduction reports "give rise to an emotional response and coherency of narratives that suggest in strongest terms the impact of an experience"; whether that "experience is subjective or objective" is beyond the power of the folklorist to prove.[5]

The first and most famous of the contactees was George Adamski (1891–1965). A "metaphysical" teacher in the 1930s and by the late 1940s employed by a hamburger stand on the road to the famous Mt. Palomar observatory in southern California, Adamski claimed to have seen squadrons of UFOs after the Arnold sighting. Then, in late 1952, he met a UFO occupant from Venus, Orthon, on the Mojave Desert. This was reported in a popular book, *Flying Saucers Have Landed* (1953), coauthored by the British occult writer Desmond Leslie. In it, and in subsequent books and lectures, Adamski portrayed the extraterrestrials as very much like humans though more beautiful and of a greatly advanced civilization. In a New Zealand lecture, the contactee spoke loftily of Venusian culture and religion (a "science of life" without temples), and their desire to communicate with us, at least "through our minds." "But they say earthmen are so preoccupied with our own thoughts we are unable to receive impressions when they do send them." On Venus, however, religion is conveyed in educational institutions rather than churches, has to do with the power of mind over the body and relationships with the cosmos, and is put into daily rather than weekly practice.[6]

Other celebrated UFO contactees of the fifties offered broadly similar stories, though claiming visits to different planets. Truman Bethurum (1898–1969) also encountered by a flying saucer on the Mojave Desert, though in this case the vehicle was from Clarion, a paradisal world with no war, divorce, or taxes; it was described in *Aboard a Flying Saucer* (1954). Orfeo Angelucci

(1912–?), perhaps the most spiritual of the early contactees, pictured hauntingly beautiful and mystical outer-space worlds in *The Secret of the Saucers* (1955). Daniel Fry (b. 1908), in *The White Sands Incident* (1954), reported a ride in a flying saucer from White Sands, New Mexico, to New York and back, during which time a spaceman named A-Lan explained to him that the visitors were from an ancient earthly civilization that had been destroyed by atomic warfare, and were now contacting their former homeland to warn of the grave danger we were courting with our rediscovery of nuclear power.

Many observers, in fact, proposed that the saucerian mythologies of the early fifties can be understood as antidotes to the tensions of those immediate postwar years of cold war, fervent anticommunism, and the threat of nuclear holocaust, and yet at the same time reflecting some lingering utopianism from the thirties and the wartime dreams. However opportunist most of the professional contactees may have been, the response they garnered could well have been linked to the message they gave. The world, they suggested, can be better, we can overcome poverty and war and understand one another, the dream can be recovered, and there are friends here to help us, friends as up to date as the technological wonders that have brought us to this pass.

An important gathering place of contactees of this type and their following was the Giant Rock Spacecraft Convention, held in the shadow of a huge boulder of that name on the Mojave Desert annually from 1954 to 1977 under the leadership of George Van Tassel (1910–1978), entrepreneur of a small airport and himself a contactee from 1952 on. At their height the conventions drew thousands of people, believers interspersed with a few curiosity-seekers, who camped out, listened to one contactee speak after another, looked for sightings, and exchanged views and literature.

The majority of the fifties contactees were content with structures as vague but benign as their messages; there was little more than books, lectures, and very loose groups of friends and supporters. A few tried for more. Daniel Fry created Understanding, Inc., an organization that, with some sixty chapters in its heyday, served as a platform for many saucer-related speakers. Gabriel Green (b. 1924), who in 1962 received over 171,000 votes in the California Democratic primary for U.S. senator on a radical ban-the-bomb platform, had established the Amalgamated Flying Saucer Clubs of America in 1957. This was an informal but active network during the sixties for the exchange of contactee news and views. Green claimed some contacts himself, and claimed to be a "telepathic channel for the Space Masters and the Great White Brotherhood—the Spiritual Hierarchy of Earth." His expressions suggest the rapidly emerging connection of UFOism with mediumistic Spiritualism and Theosophical language.

That connection was reinforced in several other early UFO groups. Early in the 1950s, the Heralds of the New Age, which originated in New Zealand, sent out literature of the same type. In the United States a young woman of psychic ability, Gloria Lee, established the Cosmon Research Foundation to aid their efforts, and channeled a guide from Jupiter called J. W. In 1962 Lee died after a prolonged fast while waiting in a Washington hotel room for government response to plans for a spaceship she had allegedly received from J. W., but she quickly acquired the status of a martyr in the religious UFO community, and messages from Lee herself were then channeled through the Heralds of the New Age.

Another early UFO group with its own martyr was Christ Brotherhood, Inc., established in 1956 by Wallace C. Halsey, who channeled UFO messages in his sleep of coming world destruction and the gathering of a saved remnant. He disappeared mysteriously in 1963 on a light plane flight from Utah to Nevada. Also Theosophical/apocalyptic was the UFO group now called the Association of Sananda and Sanat Kumara. It was the subject of a famous sociological study, *When Prophecy Fails,*[7] that in turn was probably the inspiration of a delightful novel by Alison Lurie, *Invis-*

ible Friends. The sociological report describes channeled predictions of a global cataclysm from which only a few faithful would be saved by UFOs; when the event failed to happen, it was said to have been alleviated by the faith of the few but fervent believers.

Other mediumistic UFO groups from this period include Mark-Age, founded in 1956 by Charles Boyd Gentzel to channel messages from the spiritual government of the solar system, and Unarius, established in 1954 by Ernest L. Norman. Uranius has continued since his death under his widow, Ruth Norman, who communicates with an Intergalactic Confederation of advanced planets.

Probably the best known group is the Aetherius Society, established in London by George King, who was told in 1955 by the Master Aetherius of Venus to become the "primary terrestrial mental channel" of the Interplanetary Parliament. The Aetherius Society has been heavily engaged in apocalyptic struggles against "black magicians" seeking to enslave earth. Under direction from above, its devotees channel spiritual forces from friendly space ships orbiting our planet toward places of particular need. These activities are typically given military-sounding titles: Operation Bluewater, Operation Karmalight. Like the others just mentioned, Aetherius is very Theosophical in its doctrinal background, and Spiritualistic in its mediumistic modes of operation.

By the 1970s UFO groups emerged that fit the common stereotype of a cult. One of the best examples was HIM (Human Individual Metamorphosis), which appeared in California in 1975. HIM was led by a middle-aged man and woman called Bo and Peep, also known as "The Two," who persuaded followers to give up their possessions and follow them into wilderness camps, where they were to be met by UFOs and carried physically to "the level above human."[8]

A somewhat different note was presented by a UFO group in the 1980s and early 1990s in Ottawa and Russell, Kansas, based on a conservative Christian rather than Theosophical belief system. The tone of the group is suggested by the title of the newsletter, "The Four: A Christian Newsletter of the Tribulation." In essence, the doctrine is that the UFO beings are spiritual guides, including angels and "Cephas" (St. Peter), who will help human beings through prophecy and assistance during the time of the tribulation and the coming the Antichrist. The movement received considerable publicity when one leader, Dr. Scott Corder, had his medical license revoked and another, Marcia Brock, a high school teacher, was dismissed after disappearing for three weeks. It eventuated that she, Corder, Donna Butts, the primary channel of the group, and others had gone on a mysterious mission to Israel.[9]

There was a spiritually negative side of UFOs that also commenced as early as the 1950s. In 1956 the late Gray Barker (1925–1984), then a young UFO enthusiast in West Virginia, published his first book, *They Knew Too Much About Flying Saucers,* a trailblazer in the exploration of demonic counterpoints to saucerian "technological angels."[10] The book centers on the story of Albert K. Bender, of Bridgeport, Connecticut, who until 1953 was director of a UFO club called the International Flying Saucer Bureau. After allegedly discovering the secret of the saucers, Bender received an unpleasant call from three men dressed in black suits who minced no words. Shortly after, Bender terminated the bureau and its publication.

Barker related other appearances of the Men in Black. This fearsome threesome, dressed soberly as undertakers and possessed of an uncanny knowledge of who had seen what, with their odd clockwork gait and mechanical-sounding voices, were now revealed to have phoned or called on a fair number of UFO percipients. In each case they made it very clear that life would not go well for those who knew too much, or worse said or wrote too much, about UFO matters above their competence. These "heavies" of the saucer scene fast became a part of UFO folklore everywhere.[11] Among Barker's alleged "silencing" episodes was one in New Zealand involving John Stuart. Eventually, however, Barker published for Stuart the horrendous account of the rape

of a female associate of his by a cosmic being.[12]

The episodes recounted by Barker and Stuart were among the first signs of a remarkable shift of emphasis spiritual UFOism was to make around the 1970s, from benign to ominous, culminating in the late 1980s spate of works on UFO abductions, "missing time," strange medical examinations, and half-human pregnancies. While not explicitly religious in quite the sense of the fifties-type contactees, these accounts strongly recall parallel narratives in folklore, mythology, and the psychology of religion.

Perhaps the earliest well-known account of this type was the alleged abduction of a twenty-three-year-old Brazilian farmer, Antonio Villas-Boas, in 1957; he reported both medical treatment and sexual intercourse with a beautiful unearthly woman as a captive aboard a UFO. But the case which set the trend was certainly that of Barney and Betty Hill, a New Hampshire couple, in 1961, recorded in a bestselling book by John G. Fuller.[13] This pair was reported abducted in the middle of the night while driving through lonely country, and subjected to a medical examination. Then their memories were erased, only to be later recovered through hypnosis.

Further accounts of "missing time" have been collected by Budd Hopkins and David Jacobs. These experiences have also tended to involve distasteful medical procedures with an emphasis on the reproductive functions and sometimes the disturbing sight of sickly looking human-alien children allegedly partly their own. The reported appearance of the aliens—slight, hairless, pallid, large-eyed—has been fairly consistent.[14]

These accounts were in the same world of experience as those recounted by Whitley Strieber in his bestselling books *Communion* and *Transformation,* in which the prominent novelist retailed allegedly true stories of furtive sightings and meetings in his Catskills vacation home with aliens of similar description, and subsequent recollections of "missing time" experiences involving them from his childhood and youth.[15] But, as the quasi-religious titles suggest, Strieber believed that the aliens he encountered were, despite terrifying aspects of his experience, ultimately benign.

Hopkins and Jacobs are not so sure about the extraterrestrials' intentions; at best, it seems to them, humans may be no more than laboratory animals to our uninvited guests. The same level of anxiety is surely reflected in a growing interest of the 1980s and 1990s in conspiracy theories involving UFOs, government cover-ups, and even secret and sinister relationships between government agencies, aliens, and abductions.[16]

At the same time, other writers, such as Michael Grosso and Kenneth Ring, offered new positive spiritual assessments of UFOs by comparing them to such widely discussed phenomena as apparitions of the Virgin Mary and near-death experiences, all said to herald important transformations of consciousness both individual and worldwide. Ring contends that the UFO abductors may come not from without but from within, but are thereby all the more spiritual in their significance. The presumed aliens come as mirrors to ourselves in an alienated world. Their ashen, emaciated visages reflect ourselves and our children in the soulless, polluted, sterile world we are creating; their brusque, impersonal reproductive experiments throw back to us our own purely instrumental treatment of sex, animals, and other humans; their examinations point toward our own need for self-examination.[17]

UFOs and UFO religions have also produced skeptics. While most seem content to subject it to the light, satirical treatment they believe it richly deserves, a few have gone on to contend UFO belief contains real social dangers. Chief among them have been persons related to the American Humanist Association and the related Committee for the Scientific Investigation of Claims of the Paranormal (CSICOP), its periodical *Skeptical Inquirer*, and the *Skeptics UFO Newsletter*, edited by the most active UFO debunker who is also the CSICOP UFO specialist, Philip J. Klass. While most of the debunking is along the lines of mundane investigations of reported UFO sightings and encounters, Klass and his CSICOP colleagues also have from time to time expressed disquiet at UFOism as religion masquerading as science. They tend to perceive it as dangerous because of its promotion of credulity and of authoritarian, even proto-fascist, truth in charismatic contactee figures; they see the most recent emphasis on abduction scenarios as a no less dangerous valorization of essentially pathological psychological states, which should instead be treated within the framework of a rational worldview.[18]

In summary, the remarkable twentieth-century UFO experience can be seen as reflecting the hopes, dreams, and anxieties of a turbulent era. While not often explicitly religious, UFO experience has certainly employed categories from the worlds of myth and religion to make clear its persuasion that we are not alone, that there are modern entities capable of moving among us of supernatural, or virtually supernatural, power to harm and heal, like unto the demons, angels, and saviors of old.

Notes

1. On "foo fighters" and the 1896 "airship" see Jerome Clark, *The Emergence of a Phenomenon: UFOs from the Beginning through 1959* (Detroit: Apogee Books, 1990), 17–39 and 153–56; David M. Jacobs, *UFO Controversy in America* (Bloomington: Indiana University Press, 1975), 5–34 and 35–36; and, on the "airship," Daniel Cohen, *The Great Airship Mystery: A UFO of the 1890s* (New York: Dodd, Mead, 1981).

2. C. G. Jung, *Flying Saucers: A Modern Myth of Things Seen in the Sky* (New York: Harcourt, Brace and Co., 1959).

3. J. Gordon Melton, *Encyclopedia of American Religions*, vol. 2 (Wilmington, N.C.: McGrath Publishing, 1978), 114–15.

4. Jacques Vallee, *Passage to Magonia: From Folklore to Flying Saucers* (Chicago: Henry Regnery, 1969). See also Keith Thompson, *Angels and Aliens: UFOs and the Mythic Imagination* (Reading, Mass.: Addison-Wesley, 1991).

5. Thomas E. Bullard, "Folkloric Dimensions of the UFO Phenomenon," *Journal of UFO Studies*, New Series, vol. 3 (1991): 1–58.

6. "Mr. Adamski Alights in N.Z.—From Conventional Plane," *Evening Post* (Wellington), January 21, 1959, p. 1. Cited in Robert S. Ellwood, *Islands of the Dawn: The Story of Alternative Spirituality in New Zealand* (Honolulu: University of Hawaii Press, 1993), 86.

7. Leon Festinger, Henry W. Riecken, and Stanley Schachter, *When Prophecy Fails* (New York: Harper and Row, 1956). This book provoked much controversy concerning the ethics of the covert participant-observer role of two of the investigators.

8. Robert W. Balch and David Taylor, "Becoming a Sect: A Story of Social Change in a UFO Cult" (Missoula, Mont.: The authors, 1978). See also Hayden Hewes and Brad Steiger, *UFO Missionaries Extraordinary* (New York: Pocket Books, 1976), with an extensive interview with "The Two."

9. Based on information from papers and newspaper clippings kindly provided by Professor Timothy Miller of the University of Kansas. Undoubtedly the best earlier writer who endeavored to relate UFOs positively to the Bible was Barry Downing, in *The Bible and Flying Saucers* (New York: Lippincott, 1968). On the other hand, some fundamentalist literature has taken a demonic view of the entities.

10. Gray Barker, *They Knew Too Much About Flying Saucers* (New York: University Books, 1956; London: T. Werner Laurie, 1958). It must be noted that Barker was not a particularly careful researcher, quite capable of sensationalizing and "leg-pulling."

11. See also Gray Barker, *M.I.B.: The Secret Terror Among Us* (Jane Lew, W.V.: New Age Press, 1983).

12. John Stuart, *UFO Warning* (Clarksburg, W.V.: Saucerian Books, 1963).

13. John G. Fuller, *The Interrupted Journey* (New York: Dial Press, 1966).

14. Budd Hopkins, *Missing Time* (New York: Richard Marek, 1981); *Intruders* (New York: Random House, 1987). David M. Jacobs, *Secret Life: Firsthand Accounts of UFO Abductions* (New York: Simon Schuster, 1992). See also Raymond E. Fowler, *The Watchers: The Secret Design Behind UFO Abductions* (New York: Bantam Books, 1990); and Thomas E. Bullard, *UFO Abductions: The Measure of a Mystery* (Mount Ranier, Md.: Fund for UFO Research, 1987).

15. Whitley Strieber, *Communion* (New York: William Morrow, 1987); *Transformation* (New York: William Morrow, 1988). See also Ed Conroy, *Report on Communion: An Independent Investigation of and Commentary on Whitley Strieber's "Communion"* (New York: William Morrow, 1989).

16. See, for example, Linda Moulton Howe, *An Alien Harvest* (Little, Colo.: Linda Moulton Howe Productions, 1989); Timothy Good, *Above Top Secret: The Worldwide UFO Cover-up* (New York: William Morrow, 1988), and Lawrence Fawcett and Barry J. Greenwood, *The UFO Coverup* (Englewood Cliffs, N.J.: Prentice-Hall, 1984).

17. See Michael Grosso, *Frontiers of the Soul* (Wheaton, Ill.: Quest Books, 1992); Kenneth Ring, *The Omega Project: Near Death Experiences, UFO Encounters, and Mind at Large* (New York: William Morrow, 1992).

18. See Philip J. Klass, *UFO Abductions: A Dangerous Game* (Buffalo, N.Y.: Prometheus Books, 1989); *UFOs Explained* (New York: Vintage Books, 1974); *UFOs: The Public Deceived* (Buffalo, N.Y.: Prometheus Books, 1983).

Suggestions for Further Reading

Clark, Jerome. *UFOs in the 1980s. The UFO Encyclopedia Vol. I.* Detroit: Apogee Books, 1990.

———. *The Emergence of a Phenomenon: UFOs from the Beginning through 1959. The UFO Encyclopedia.* vol. 2. Detroit: Omnigraphics, 1992.

Curran, Douglas. *In Advance of the Landing: Folk Concepts of Outer Space.* New York: Abbeville Press, 1985.

Jacobs, David M. *The UFO Controversy in America.* Bloomington: Indiana University Press, 1975.

Lewis, James R., ed. *The Gods Have Landed: New Religions from Other Worlds.* Albany: State University of New York Press, 1995.

Melton, J. Gordon. *The Encyclopedia of American Religions.* 3rd ed. Detroit: Gale Research, 1989.

Rasmussen, Richard Michael. *The UFO Literature: A Comprehensive Annotated Bibliography of Works in English.* Jefferson, N.C.: McFarland, 1985.

Story, Ronald D. *The Encyclopedia of UFOs.* New York: Doubleday, 1980.

42

SATANISM AND SATANIC CHURCHES: THE CONTEMPORARY INCARNATIONS

David G. Bromley and Susan G. Ainsley

The 1980s witnessed a wave of fear over devil worship in both North America and Europe. Satanism, however, is not a unitary phenomenon. Satanism in the form of putative rituals that parody Roman Catholic worship can be traced to the inventive minds of fifteenth-century inquisitors bent on stamping out "witchcraft." In fact, there have been few actual satanic groups through history. The 1960s witnessed the emergence of a series of publicly organized, highly visible satanic churches that were one small segment of the counterculture of that period. The satanic cult fears of the 1980s represented a recurrence of the longstanding fears of underground, subversive satanic cults. The public satanic churches have been incorporated into this most recent moral panic. This chapter reviews the history and organization of satanic churches, the current outbreak of satanic subversion fears, and the relationship between them.

The Church of Satan

Anton Szandor LaVey was born Howard Stanton Levy on April 11, 1930, in Chicago.[1] His rebellious nature was clearly in evidence by the age of sixteen when he ran away from home to join the Clyde Beatty Circus. He quickly advanced from cage boy to assistant lion tamer before leaving the circus when he was eighteen to work as a stage hypnotist, mentalist, and organist in a carnival. When the carnival closed in the winter of 1948, he moved to southern California to play burlesque. It was while he was playing the organ at the Mayan Club in Los Angeles that he claims to have had an affair with young Norma Jean Baker, who later became Marilyn Monroe. In 1951 he married his first wife, fifteen-year-old Carole Lansing, and subsequently enrolled at San Francisco's City College as a criminology major in order to evade the Korean War draft. At the same time, he worked for three years as a photographer for the San Francisco City Police Department and furthered his study of the occult. During the early 1960s LaVey met Kenneth Anger, author of *Hollywood Babylon*, who was in San Francisco working on *Invocation of My Demon Brother*, a film that was widely rumored to be a cinematic rendering of the black mass. LaVey and Anger then began informal Friday-night gatherings to discuss occult phenomena, which they called the Magic Circle. These meetings attracted considerable public attention, and, always the showman, LaVey capitalized on this opportunity by selling tickets to the public. At these sessions he would captivate audiences with tales of witches, werewolves, and vampires. The combination of a mysterious house, a coroner's van as a car, and a succession of pets that included a boa constrictor, a black leopard, and a Nubian lion only added to his eccentric image.

The founding of the Church of Satan can be traced to April 30, 1966, when LaVey shaved his head, donned a black robe, pronounced himself the Black Pope and declared that night "Walpurgisnacht." He proclaimed 1966 Year One in the Anno Satanas—the first year of the Satanic Age. Later that same year, he promoted his new beliefs and organization in a topless nightclub called the "Witches Sabbath." The dancers included Susan Atkins (aka Sharon King), who was later to become infamous as a member of the Manson Family.

It was not long before LaVey became something of a national celebrity. In 1967, he received national press coverage by performing a satanic nuptial ceremony in which he wedded socialite Judith Case and ex–Christian Science Monitor journalist John Raymond. In May of that year, he attracted public attention again by baptizing his three-year-old daughter, Zeena, in a satanic ritual. He followed the wedding and baptism in December with satanic last rites for a deceased naval seaman, complete with full color guard. LaVey later served as a consultant and even played the role of the Devil in the film *Rosemary's Baby*. In addition, he attracted a number of celebrities to the Church of Satan, including Sammy Davis Jr., Jayne Mansfield, Barbara McNair, Kennan Wynn, Laurence Harvey, Christopher Lee, and Kim Novak.

The hedonistic philosophy of LaVey's Church of Satan is based on tenets of physical and mental gratification, self-assertion, and anti-establishmentarianism. The philosophy is spelled out in his now-famous Nine Satanic Statements that are found at the beginning of the *Satanic Bible:*

(1) Satan represents indulgence, instead of abstinence! (2) Satan represents vital existence, instead of spiritual pipe dreams! (3) Satan represents undefiled wisdom, instead of hypocritical self-deceit! (4) Satan represents kindness to those who deserve it, instead of love wasted on ingrates! (5) Satan represents vengeance, instead of turning the other cheek! (6) Satan represents responsibility to the responsible, instead of concern for psychic vampires! (7) Satan represents man as just another animal,

sometimes better, more often worse than those that walk on all fours, who because of his divine spiritual and intellectual development has become the most vicious animal of all! (8) Satan represents all of the so-called sins, as they lead to physical or mental gratification! (9) Satan has been the best friend the church has ever had, as he has kept it in business all these years!

Within the Church of Satan, sex is considered natural and encouraged, and is recognized as the biological instinct second only to self-preservation. Drugs are discouraged because they are viewed as escapist and hence as interfering with the realism LaVey preaches. Violence is expressly prohibited, and breaking church rules or state or federal laws constitutes grounds for excommunication.

Local chapters of the Church of Satan are called grottoes; in the mid-1970s grottoes could be found in major cities across the country. Lifetime memberships cost one hundred dollars, and at the height of the church's popularity in the 1970s membership was estimated at five thousand.[2] There are three major categories of ritual in the Church of Satan: *sexual rituals* to fulfill a desire, *compassionate rituals* to help another person, and *destructive rituals* to annoy, anger, or display hatred. Other rituals include *Shibboleth,* to reduce fears by confronting them; *Die Elektrischen Vorspiele,* to charge the ritual chamber with energy; and *Das Tierdrama,* to increase human sensory perception. Worship is based on the belief that humans need ritual, dogma, fantasy, and enchantment.

Temple of Set

In 1969, LaVey met Michael Aquino, who holds a Ph.D. in political science and was at the time a lieutenant in an Army Intelligence unit specializing in psychological warfare.[3] The two met at a lecture that LaVey was giving, and both Aquino and his first wife soon joined the Church of Satan. Aquino was ordained into the priesthood in 1971, and he quickly earned the title of Magister IV, a rank only one level below LaVey himself. Over the next several years the relationship between the two deteriorated. In 1975, Aquino, who at the time was the editor of the Church of Satan's publication, *The Cloven Hoof,* accused LaVey of selling priesthoods. He felt that the church had moved away from its original intent and lost its focus. It was at that juncture that Aquino, Lilith Sinclair (his second wife and the head of the Lilith Grotto in Spottswood, New Jersey), and twenty-eight other church members (including six church leaders), left the Church of Satan to form the Temple of Set.

The Temple of Set is organized into a network of local chapters called "pylons." The total membership of the pylons has never been large; in 1984 the temple claimed a total of five hundred members. Individuals who join the temple pay a fifty-dollar initiation fee and then a twenty-five-dollar annual membership fee. Initiates can progress through the following six degree levels: Setian, Adept, Priest or Priestess of Set, Master of the Temple, Magnus, and Ipsissimus. Above the local pylons is the Council of Nine, which appoints the High Priest of Set and the executive director.

Temple of Set philosophy proclaims that the universe is a nonconscious environment possessed of mechanical consistency. In contrast to the universe, and occasionally violating its laws, is Set. Set is the Egyptian god of night who is actually a metaphysical being, and formerly known under the Hebrew misnomer "Satan." Set has, over a period of a millennia, altered the genetic makeup of humans in order to create a species possessing an enhanced, nonnatural intelligence.[4] Aquino claims to have invoked Set in a ritual on June 21, 1975, and in four hours that night he wrote down their conversation in his book, *The Book of Coming Forth by Night.* According to Aquino, Set ordained him and his Temple of Set to succeed LaVey and the Church of Satan. According to Temple members, Set is not seen as a deity dedicated to evil nor is the temple's theology intended as a refutation of any conventional religion. In fact, the Temple of Set is a rather intellectually oriented religion. For example, Aquino

encourages initiates to study materials from an extensive annotated reading list, which includes topics such as ancient Egypt, ancient and contemporary religions, occultism, psychology, and experimental sciences.

Other Satanic Churches

The Church of Satan and Temple of Set are the largest and most visible of the satanic churches. However, there have been a number of other groups as well. As the following brief review of these groups reveals, they have been both smaller and short lived. As a result, information about most of them is fragmentary. Most formed as reactions to the two major satanic churches, sometimes innovating on their beliefs and practices and sometimes as reactions against them. It is important to note that to the extent deviant practices have been associated with satanic churches, they have occurred largely in these smaller, offshoot groups.

Universal Church of Man was founded by Wayne West, a defrocked Catholic priest from Britain. West was excommunicated from the Church of Satan's Babylon Grotto in Detroit by LaVey in early 1970 for the misuse of fees and for changing rituals to suit his own personal appetite for bondage and homosexuality. The Universal Church of Man's beliefs and rituals were specifically dedicated to fulfilling West's personal fantasies of the flesh, and the organization was very short lived.

Brotherhood of the Ram was founded in Los Angeles in the early 1960s, with a bookstore as its primary axis. The group loosely followed traditional satanic beliefs and practices, including the renouncing of other faiths and pledged devotion to Satan, who was viewed as a god of joy and pleasure. Membership remained concentrated in southern California until the group's demise in the early 1970s.

Our Lady of Endor Coven of the Ophite Cultus Satanas was founded in 1948 by Herbert Arthur Sloane in Toledo, Ohio. Sloane also belonged to the Church of Satan for a short time. Satanas, meaning

"Horned God," is believed to be the messenger who showed Eve that there exists a supreme God above the God who created the cosmos. This God can be reached through Gnosis, or occult knowledge that is humanly attainable. The group had only one coven, which was led by personally by Sloane, and it dissolved soon after his death in the early 1980s.

Thee Satanic Orthodox Church of Nethilum Rite was founded by Terry Taylor and Dr. Evelyn Paglini at the Occult Book Shop in Chicago, Illinois. The group was formalized in 1971 and reached a membership of 538 members in 1973. The church opposed Anton LaVey and the Church of Satan, propounding instead the belief that God was creator of the cosmos and thus Satan was created by God. However, members believe that Satan possesses the greater knowledge and power. This power can be accessed through magic rituals and psychic development that are part of the weekly Saturday-night meetings.

Thee Satanic Church was founded in Chicago in 1974 by Dr. Paglini as a sectarian offshoot of Thee Satanic Orthodox Church of Nethilum Rite. In contrast to the latter, Thee Satanic Church emphasized the occult and de-emphasized Satanism. It published the occult-oriented but not satanic periodical, *Psychic Standard*. The periodical ceased publication and the church dissolved in early 1980 when its founder left Chicago.

Kerk du Satan–Magistralis Grotto and Walpurga Abbey was founded in Etersheim, the Netherlands, by Martin Lamers in 1972. Lamers was a former actor who had assisted in raising funds for the stage production of *Oh! Calcutta!*. In 1976, he moved the Dutch Kerk du Satan to the heart of Amsterdam's red-light district. He obtained two adjacent buildings, one for the Kerk du Satan and the other for the Walpurga Abbey. The abbey was a pub where customers paid a "religious donation" on a per-minute basis to watch "monastic sisters" dance, masturbate, and "perform acts of symbolic communion with Shaitan" for them at "the altar."[5] This combined operation ran afoul of Dutch authorities for claiming both organizations

as tax-exempt churches. Anton LaVey contemplated revoking the Dutch Church of Satan's charter, but instead sent his daughter, Karla, overseas to resolve the situation. Her efforts were unsuccessful, however, and the abbey lost its tax-exempt status.

Church of Satanic Brotherhood was officially founded in March 1973 by former members of Stygian Grotto of the Church of Satan in Dayton, Ohio. Several members of that grotto were charged by Anton LaVey with dealing in stolen property. When LaVey dissolved the Stygian Grotto on February 11, 1973, those former members joined with Wayne West, originally from the Detroit Grotto of the Church of Satan and the founder of the Universal Church of Man, to form the Church of Satanic Brotherhood. With an amended Church of Satan format and an intense hatred of Anton LaVey, the church grew rapidly for a time using its monthly periodical, *The True Grimoire*, for publicity and recruitment. The group was rather disorganized, however, and survived only until early 1974 when one of the founders, John DeHaven, moved to Florida and later during a radio broadcast publicly converted to Christianity.

Ordo Templi Satanas was a splinter group from the Church of Satanic Brotherhood formed in 1974 by Joseph Daniels, one of the founders of the Satanic Brotherhood, and Clifford Amos. Daniels assumed the name of Apollonius, the priest of Hermopolis. Like its parent organization, this group had only a brief lifespan; it did survive long enough to perform a memorial service for John DeHaven after his conversion to Christianity.

Order of the Black Ram and the Shrine of the Little Mother was founded by two members of the Detroit branch of the Church of Satan. The group's theology combined Satanism with the concept of Aryan supremacy. The order was connected through one of its founders to the neo-Nazi National Renaissance Party. For many years James Madole of the National Renaissance Party had sought to establish a union between his organization and LaVey's Church of Satan. LaVey always rejected these overtures. Nonetheless the format of the Order of the Black Ram was structured around LaVey's work, Robert Heinlein's novel *Stranger in a Strange Land,* and neo-paganism.

Temple of Nepthys was founded in 1985 in Novato, California, and is recognized by that state as a non-profit church of the satanic religion. The temple recognizes the Church of Satan as a direct predecessor and close affiliate and details adherence to Anton LaVey's *The Satanic Bible* and *The Compleat Witch.* The philosophy is distinctly "elitist." Temple of Nepthys literature describes the organization as a "liberating magical institution of gifted individuals who are learning how to effectively apply satanic principles for their own success, survival and sexual magnetism."[6] They also assert that their philosophy is not antisocial, but instead is asocial. It is autonomy that permits social interaction, and so ultimately the individuals must retain power over their own lives. The ascending ranks of membership are Satanist I, Satanic Warlock and Witch II, Priest or Priestess of Nepthys III, Magister or Magistra IV, Magnus or Magna V, and Imperial General and High Priestess. Membership in 1990 was estimated at approximately 280, with 90 percent of that number female.

The Process–The Church of the Final Judgement was founded by Robert de Grimston More, an architecture student, and his wife, a former prostitute. In 1963 they founded Compulsions Analysis, which later evolved into the Process Church in 1966. The group subsequently established a commune for the Process Church in Xtul on the Yucatan peninsula in Mexico, with approximately 30 members. The Process is not strictly a satanic church as the theology asserts the existence of four gods—Jehovah, Lucifer, Christ, and Satan. Lucifer is the male god of air, representing sensuousness, liberality, and intellect. Jehovah is the female god of the earth, representing austerity, authoritarianism, and emotion. The group believes that cosmic forces insist on a combination of these two as almost a marriage. Christ exemplifies the male god of waters, standing for the unification of all things; conversely, Satan, the female god of fire, stands for hatred and

the separation of all things.[7] The group believes that at the final judgment, all four deities will be reconciled. Anton LaVey refused any affiliation with the group, referring to them as a bunch of "kooks."[8] The Process disbanded in 1974 when Robert was formally expelled from the group for his continued emphasis on satanic themes. Then later that year, several leaders of the Process Church chose a more orthodox Christian path instead of de Grimston's satanic one, forming the Foundation Faith of God (also called the Foundation Church of the Millennium, and the Foundation Faith of the Millennium).

Satanic Churches and the Satanism Scare

Early in the 1980s a wave of satanic cult subversion fear swept across the United States, and spread to Canada as well as a number of European nations. The satanism scare involved a number of components: beliefs and practices of satanic churches, urban legends, rumor panics, animal mutilation cases, satanic themes in heavy metal rock music, homicide cases, and accusations of ritual abuse of children by satanists. All of these components of satanic activity allegedly are coordinated by a four-tiered satanic cult network.[9] According to this schema, at the lowest level are *dabblers,* primarily adolescents who experiment and play with satanic cultural material. At the next level are *self-styled Satanists,* criminals who appropriate satanic themes in order to rationalize their deviant activities. Above the self-styled Satanists are the *organized Satanists* who belong to various public groups, like the satanic churches. At the apex of this organizational network are *traditional Satanists,* the most diabolic, menacing component of Satanism. Traditional Satanists putatively are organized as an international, secret, hierarchically structured, and tightly organized cult network that is actively engaged in a variety of nefarious activities. These activities include abduction of children, child abuse, commercial production of "kiddie porn,"

sexual abuse and incest, and ritualistic sacrifices of young children that may involve
dismemberment and even cannibalism.
Although it is virtually invisible and im-
penetrable, this cult network is thought to
be extremely large and growing. Both the
number of ritual-sacrifice victims in the
United States, estimated at fifty to sixty
thousand annually, and the rapidly expanding ranks of "ritual abuse survivors"
seeking treatment from therapists suggest
a network of immense scale. Satanic
churches are alleged to be connected to
several elements of organized Satanism. As
the following brief review indicates, there
is no convincing empirical evidence to support these claims and, specifically, there is
no evidence linking satanic churches to the
deviant beliefs and practices attributed to
underground satanic cults.

There have been charges that satanic
churches are *sponsors* of various types of
satanic activity. These churches allegedly
attract antisocial individuals through their
"perverted theologies" that inspire, or at
least rationalize, deviant conduct. As the
preceding description of satanic churches
demonstrated, some of the splinter groups
from the Church of Satan indeed were involved in deviant practices. However, there
is no evidence linking satanic churches
with the central activities attributed to satanic cults—sexual abuse, child molestation, and human sacrifice. And their
theologies and rituals contain no advocacy
of such activities; in fact, animal sacrifice
is specifically prohibited by the Church of
Satan. Further, the satanic churches were
founded only recently and do not constitute the successor groups to a longstanding
satanic tradition. Indeed, if there is a satanic theological tradition it has been created by Christians. As J. Gordon Melton
points out, "The Satanic tradition has been
carried almost totally by the imaginative
literature of non-Satanists, primarily conservative Christians, who describe the practices in vivid detail in the process of
denouncing them."[10]

Urban legends with an "evil corporation" motif have persistently resurfaced in
recent years, and some versions have linked
major corporations to satanic churches.[11]

Two of these narratives assert that the executive leadership of Proctor and Gamble
Corporation and the McDonald's fast food
chain both contribute a substantial proportion of corporate profits to the Church
of Satan. These narratives are a subset of
urban legends that have irresponsible or
malevolent activities by "evil corporations"
as their primary theme. The narratives
have continued to circulate in the United
States despite absence of any empirical vali-
dation.[12]

There has been a virtual epidemic of
rumor-panics across the United States over
the last decade. One of the most prevalent
of these narratives warns of the imminent
abduction of an adolescent in the immediate locale (most often a female, blond, blue
eyed, virgin) for sacrifice in a satanic
ritual.[13] In some regions these abduction
narratives have appeared and reappeared
a number of times, and sometimes outbreaks have persisted over a period of
many months. The spate of child abduction rumor-panics is based on apprehen-
sions similar to those contained in
longstanding "urban legends" with a child
endangerment motif.[14] Public officials have
investigated such reports across the country without discovering any satanic cults
intent on abducting members of the community.

During the last decade there also has
been a surge in reports of suspicious and
unexplained animal deaths. Either a large
number or a succession of animal remains
have been discovered in numerous localities with what appear to be surgically precise incisions and missing organs. This
continuing trail of animal remains has
been attributed to Satanists who are in
search of blood and organs for their rituals.[15] Virtually every investigation of animal mutilation cases has concluded that
unexplained large-animal deaths are the
product of roadkills, hunting, trapping, disease, or poisoning. The "surgically precise"
wounds observed on "mutilated" animal
carcasses are the work of predators and
scavengers.[16]

A variety of adolescent recreational material, particularly heavy metal rock music, has been connected to Satanism. Some

heavy metal rock music is believed to contain deliberately implanted subliminal messages promoting Satanism. However, there is little agreement among investigators that coherent messages even exist.[17] Assuming that such messages could be located, research on subliminal messages finds no significant influence from such messages even if presented in normal rather than reverse order.[18]

In a succession of recent homicide cases perpetrators have linked their offenses to Satanism. In some instances adolescents have killed either parents or peers; other cases have involved adult perpetrators who have killed non-related individuals. In such cases perpetrators have attributed their crimes to participation in satanic cults or experimenting with heavy metal rock music. In several dozen homicide cases Satanism has been offered as a contributing or causal factor in the commission of those crimes. It is clear that perpetrators have confessed to involvement in Satanism to diminish their legal responsibility, have employed satanic themes in order to express alienation from conventional society, and have sought publicity by adding a satanic gloss to their crimes. However, there is no credible evidence either that any of these individuals has been a member of a satanic cult network or that their crimes were committed as elements of organized satanic rituals calling for human sacrifice.

There have been a large number of alleged instances of ritual abuse of children in daycare centers and preschools across the United States. In these cases children have recounted horrific stories of drugging and systematic brainwashing, sexual abuse by adults, pornographic film-making, ritual sacrifice of children, and even cannibalism. However, despite intensive investigation of ritual sites identified by "ritual abuse survivors," not a single sacrifice victim has been discovered whose death can be linked to a satanic ritual.[19] In those instances where daycare centers' staff members have been charged with sexual abuse there has been no evidence linking these individuals to satanic groups of any kind. And while there is virtually no credible empirical evidence of either the existence of an international satanic cult network or of substantial numbers of ritual sacrifice victims, there are numerous instances of disproved claims.[20]

One major daycare center case did involve allegations of a connection between satanic churches and ritual child abuse. The case involved Michael Aquino's Temple of Set.[21] In 1987 an employee of the Presidio Army Base daycare center was charged with twelve counts of child molestation following allegations by children between the ages of two and seven that suggested that as many as sixty children might have been sexually abused. Subsequent medical tests indicated that five of the children were infected with a sexually transmitted disease and fifty-eight children showed evidence of sexual molestation. Statements from the children described cross-dressing by men and women, body painting, robed rituals, and shark feeding. One of the children recognized Aquino on the army base and claimed that the daycare employee had driven her to his home. She correctly identified his home and the existence of a room with black walls. All of the charges against the daycare center employee eventually were dropped, ending the case.

In 1985 there had been allegations of ritual sexual abuse of children at Fort Bragg at the Jubilation Day Care Center. Following the Presidio case, the Army broadened its sexual abuse investigation to surrounding counties after local children reported recognizing Aquino during television coverage of the Presidio case. Ultimately, no charges were filed in the case. Finally, two years after the Presidio case, Ukiah police asked the San Francisco police for assistance in an investigation of a child abuse case similar to the Presidio case. Aquino was questioned in that case as well, but no charges were filed.

Summary and Conclusion

The history of satanic churches is surprisingly brief. They arose in the countercultural decades of the 1960s and 1970s and flourished briefly during those years.

They played to the widespread rebellious-
ness and hedonism of that period. Like
many other communal, human potential,
and New Age groups of the era, their popularity waned as the countercultural period
declined and seekers in the spiritual supermarket discovered alternative paths and
products. Public interest in Satanism was
rejuvenated in the 1980s with the emergence of an international moral panic over
satanic cults. This moral panic postulated
a new form of Satanism and explicitly
linked the satanic churches to this putative satanic conspiracy. Although there is
no credible evidence of a satanic cult conspiracy, and therefore no evidence of related nefarious behavior by satanic
churches, the current moral panic has rejuvenated public concern and reconfigured
conceptions of Satanism.

Notes

1. For information on Anton LaVey and
the Church of Satan see Lawrence Wright,
"Sympathy for the Devil," *Rolling Stone* (5 September 1991): 62–106; and Arthur Lyons,
*Satan Wants You: The Cult of Devil Worship in
America* (New York: The Mysterious Press,
1988), 104–24.

2. Lyons, *Satan Wants You,* 115.

3. For information on Michael Aquino and
the Temple of Set, see Lyons, *Satan Wants
You,* 125–37; Chas Clifton, "The Three Faces
of Satan," *Gnosis Magazine* (Summer 1989):
8–18.

4. J. Gordon Melton, *Encyclopedic Handbook of Cults in America* (New York: Garland
Publishing, 1986), 114.

5. Lyons, *Satan Wants You,* 121.

6. "Temple of Nepthys," unpublished brochure, 1990.

7. William S. Bainbridge, *Satan's Power: A
Deviant Psychotherapy Cult* (Berkeley: University of California Press, 1978), 4–5.

8. Lyons, *Satan Wants You,* 90.

9. See David Bromley, "Satanism: The New
Cult Scare," in *The Satanism Scare,* ed. James
Richardson, Joel Best, and David Bromley
(Hawthorne, N.Y.: Aldine de Gruyter, 1991),
49–74.

10. Melton, *Encyclopedic Handbook of Cults
in America,* 76.

11. Gary Alan Fine, "The Goliath Effect,"
Journal of American Folklore 98 (1985): 63–84.

12. Jean-Noel Kapferer, *Rumors: Uses, In-
terpretations, and Images* (New Brunswick:
Transaction Publishers, 1990); Frederick Koenig,
*Rumor in the Marketplace: The Social Psychol-
ogy of Commercial Hearsay* (Dover: Auburn
House, 1985); Ralph L. Rosnow, *Rumor and
Gossip: The Social Psychology of Hearsay* (New
York: Elsevier Scientific Publishing Co., 1976).

13. Anson Shupe, "The Modern Satanist
Scare in Indiana: A Case Study of an Urban
Legend in the Heartland, U.S.A." (paper pre-
sented at the annual meeting of North Cen-
tral Sociological Association, Dearborn, 1991);
Jeffrey Victor, "A Rumor-Panic About a Dan-
gerous Satanic Cult in Western New York,"
New York Folklore 15 (1989): 23–49.

14. Jan Harold Brunvand, *The Vanishing
Hitchhiker: American Urban Legends and Their
Meanings* (New York: W. W. Norton, 1981).

15. William Ellis, "Death by Folklore:
Ostension, Contemporary Legend, and Murder," *Western Folklore* 48 (1989): 201–20.

16. Leland Cade, "Cattle Mutilations—Are
They for Real?" *Montana Farmer-Stockman* (3
March 1977); James Stewart, "Cattle Mutila-
tions: An Episode of Collective Delusion," *The
Zetetic* 1 (1977): 55–66.

17. Stephen Thorne and Philip Himelstein,
"The Role of Suggestion in the Perception of
Satanic Messages in Rock-And-Roll Recordings," *The Journal of Psychology* 116 (1984):
245–48.

18. John Vokey and J. Don Read, "Subliminal Messages: Between the Devil and the
Media," *American Psychologist* 40 (1985): 1231–
39.

19. Kenneth Lanning, "Satanic, Occult,
Ritualistic Crime: A Law Enforcement Perspective," *The Police Chief* 56 (1989): 62–83.

20. See, for example, Lyons, *Satan Wants
You,* 143–45.

21. For coverage of this episode see "Six of
Seven Molestation Charges Dropped in SF
Day-Care Case," *Sacramento Bee* 2 February
1988; "Satanic Priest Upset at Probe," *Courier
Post* (N.J.) 4 May 1988; "Army Probes Officer
in New Presidio Case," *Orange County Register*
(Calif.) 24 December 1988; "Satanic Priest

Questioned in New Sex Case," *San Jose Mercury-News* 13 May 1989; "Satanist Accused of Child Sex Abuse," *San Francisco Chronicle* 17 May 1989.

Suggestions for Further Reading

Jenkins, Philip. *Intimate Enemies: Moral Panics in Contemporary Great Britain.* Hawthorne, N.Y.: Aldine de Gruyter, 1992.

LaVey, Anton Szandor. *The Satanic Bible.* New York: Avon, 1969.

Lyons, Arthur. *Satan Wants You: The Cult of Devil Worship in America.* New York: Mysterious Press, 1988.

Melton, J. Gordon. "Satanism and the Church of Satan." *Encyclopedic Handbook of Cults in America,* 76–80. New York: Garland, 1986.

Richardson, James, Joel Best, and David Bromley, eds. *The Satanism Scare.* Hawthorne, N.Y.: Aldine de Gruyter, 1991.

43

THE EVOLUTION OF MODERN AMERICAN ANTICULT IDEOLOGY: A CASE STUDY IN FRAME EXTENSION

Anson Shupe and David G. Bromley

New and unusual religions have always had their antagonists and persecutors, and the movements that came into prominence in the United States in the 1960s and 1970s were no exceptions. The latest wave of organized opposition to unorthodox religions, the anticult movement (hereafter ACM), began in 1971 when some families began spontaneously opposing their (typically) adult children's participation in such unconventional religions as the Children of God, the Divine Light Mission, and the Unification Church.[1] Parents and their sympathizers, almost all volunteers, came together in local and regional groups in classic American vigilante tradition after finding that there was little that public officials could or would do to "return" their offspring or shut down the controversial religious movements. Operating on shoestring budgets, various organizations with expressive names such as Citizens Freedom Foundation, Free Minds, Inc., and Love Our Children struggled for resources and public awareness of the "cult menace."

Gradually, following several unsuccessful attempts to create a single centralized national structure, a confederation of the larger regional ACM organizations that had achieved financial stability emerged. At the same time the composition of ACM leadership had shifted. The original grassroots groups had been "Mom and Pop" operations, frequently run out of aggrieved but inexperienced activists' homes and funded exclusively by donations. Along with larger, more solvent organizational structures came professional managers and behavioral science/legal/medical sympathizers to lend the ACM's ideological claims greater credibility.

More importantly, the new leaders of the ACM reshaped the movement's ideology, and it is on that transformation that we will focus here. Ideology is our primary concern in this chapter because, as we have observed before, "the primary issues confronting the ACM relate to its ideology and to its mandate."[2]

Frame Extension in the ACM

Sociologist Erving Goffman defines a "frame" as a schema or discourse of meaning for interpreting actors and situations.[3] Social movement ideologies provide participants with integrated frame sets that include problem definitions, explanations, and goals. Expanding on Goffman's notion of frame, David Snow and his colleagues have noted that social movement development as well as changes in the movement's environment make processes of *frame alignment,* or ideological alteration, an ongoing necessity. One of these processes is *frame extension,* that is, broadening a movement's ideological framework

> so as to encompass interests or points of view that are incidental to its primary objective but of considerable

salience to potential adherents. In effect, the movement is attempting to enlarge its adherent pool by portraying its objectives or activities as attending to or being congruent with the' values and interests of potential adherents.[4]

Frame alignment, particularly extension, characterizes the changes in ACM ideology over the past two decades. It began almost immediately. Initially, families that organized were only concerned about specific groups (i.e., the ones in which their children had enlisted). For instance, the first ACM organization was solely focused on the Children of God, a radical communal sect from the 1960s Jesus movement. Yet other families echoing essentially the same complaints (that their offspring seemed strangely transformed, that the group encouraged members to be alienated from parents and siblings, that their grown children were throwing promising careers and futures away on apocalyptic authoritarian groups, and so forth) brought opponents of the Children of God to the realization that they had common cause with many other persons. Hence a vast array of groups with very different beliefs and backgrounds gradually came to be subsumed under the category of "cult."

Writing of the ACM as it has related to the Hare Krishna movement, David Bromley conceptualizes three stages in the countermovement's development: a formative stage, an expansionist stage, and a professionalization stage.[5] At successive stages the ACM's dominant frames that explain how persons became involved with unconventional religious groups, why they stay, and how they leave have become realigned. This realignment has occurred in large part, we argue, because of how membership and leadership has evolved.

In the formative stage (covering the early to late 1970s) the dominant frame for explaining "cult" participation was a possession metaphor best summarized by the ACM activists themselves as "brainwashing." Mental and physical coercion on the part of cultic leaders was assumed, and deprogrammings (i.e., forcible abduction and then physical restraint during a period of argumentation and verbal haranguing) were thought necessary for any individual successfully to leave the group in question. Deprogrammers typically had no formal credentials in any mental-health field. Some were mercenaries; many were concerned family members or sympathetic ex-"cult" members.

Frame alignment occurred during the expansionist stage (occurring from the late 1970s to the early 1980s) as organizational stability, professional managers, and degreed mental health professionals began assuming a higher profile in the ACM in the roles of speakers, authors, and advisors. A number of conferences and publications, such as the *Cultic Studies Journal,* appeared and were directed at fellow professionals. The crude brainwashing explanation of the formative stage was pushed out by a more sophisticated clinical frame complete with scientific jargon. The "problem" of membership in unconventional religions was medicalized—attributed to mental illness, for example—and the possession metaphor was dropped. The rough, coercive deprogrammings were also largely abandoned in favor of "exit counseling" of disillusioned and embittered ex-group members, a change of tactics that accompanied public education efforts. (Bromley regards the expansionist stage as a transitional phase between the decentralized struggles of the formative stage and the later, more institutionalized ACM.)

The professionalization stage, which we have now entered, has completed trends underway in the previous stage. Much of the conflict over controversial religious movements has been transferred to academic journals and the courts (as both movements and their participants have become increasingly litigious). While state and national legislators have proven generally unresponsive to ACM concerns, inroads have been made professionally. For example, the new ACM activists successfully achieved inclusion in DSM-III (the *Diagnostic and Statistical Manual* used by mental health professional, such as psychiatrists, clinical psychologists, and psychotherapists, in making diagnoses of mental disorders) of special language that covered "cult"-induced disorders. In the revised definition of "atypical dissociative disorder" (a residual category for persons who do not fit any specific dissociative disorder), the symptoms given are

> trance-like states, derealization accompanied by depersonalization, and those more prolonged dissociative states that may occur in persons who have been subjected to periods of prolonged and intensive coercive persuasion (brainwashing, thought reform, and indoctrination while the captive of terrorists or cultists).[6]

The Satanism Scare as ACM Frame Extension

Frame alignment has continued in the form of frame extension to include the ACM's latest discovery of "cult" danger: ritualistic sexual abuse of children by satanic groups. Extension of the "cult" umbrella to include this new concern is actually a response to several trends occurring as the ACM began to become institutionalized during the expansionist stage.

One trend has been the proliferation of social science research with regard to specific unconventional religions, their membership composition, the conversion and commitment processes operating, and even their strategic responses to ACM opposition. The vast preponderance of such studies have had the indirect effect of undermining the ACM's earlier frames concerning how much mental abuse, coercion, and abnormal social pressure routinely occur in these religions.[7] Most ACM research is based on clinical samples of disgruntled or disturbed ex-members, not of fulfilled, functioning religious group members of the type observed by non-ACM researchers who went "into the field" and received much different impressions of life in unconventional religions. As a result, ACM professionals and spokespersons cannot now simply issue sweeping statements about "cults," as activists in the formative stage did, without their instantly becoming test-

able propositions for investigation. It is safe to say that current ACM frames are no more accepted by most behavioral scientists than they were twenty years ago, even if they are now articulated with a more scientific veneer.

A parallel trend has been the "aging" of the memberships of the religious groups in question, their own gradual institutionalization and legitimation as part of North America's religious economy, and the lack of growth in the major controversial groups. As high turnover in membership has declined following the peak period of mobilization in the 1970s, there have been fewer aggrieved parents and fewer angry ex-members, even with repeated widenings of the "cult" definition, to fuel ACM ranks. And the "cult" problem has never occupied an impressive ranking on the average American's list of his or her most pressing concerns and fears. Ironically, the ACM achieved stability in resources and professionalization as the major alleged "cults" started their declines and the "cult" controversy ceased to be of abiding interest in the mass media.

A third trend reveals the danger for a popular movement in loading its frames with jargon and trappings of expertise. The professionals' modification of the brainwashing frame using the complexities of social influence processes inherent in behavioral science and mental health concepts has tended to hurt the ACM's ability to mobilize concern. As David Snow and Robert Benford note about this issue in impeding recruitment mobilization, "to frame any issue in terms that are inaccessible to all but a select few, as is the case with technologically framed issues, is to reduce potential participants to spectators and so make the issue nonparticipatory."[8]

Though perhaps not a premeditated strategy, the ACM's adoption of concerns over Satanism has at least temporarily overcome this problem. Resonating as they do with the American family's ambivalence about two-income families, entrusting children to strangers for child care, and relative unfamiliarity with neighbors and associates due to high geographic mobility, fears about a rising tide of children abused systematically by organized occult and satanic cult groups have to some extent reinvigorated the ACM. Through the Satanism scare (which virtually all social science research has shown to be just that: a form of moral panic created by uncritical media, a cultural fascination with the occult and the pressures of urban life, and spread by mostly unsubstantiated rumors[9]), the ACM has gained renewed attention, a new set of potential constituents, and an immediately useful follow-up to the now-cooled concern over ordinary "cults."

This concern with an alleged satanic underground, operating across state lines and incredibly well organized, fits well with the generic frame in collective behavior David Bromley has termed the "subversion mythology":

> Subversion mythologies are premised on the existence of a conspiracy. They posit a specific danger and a group associated with it, one or more conspirators who have planned and direct the plot, a set of base impulses that motivate the conspiracy leaders, a manipulative process through which the conspirators involve others in their conspiracy, an imminent danger for the entire society, and a remedial agenda that must be followed if catastrophe is to be avoided.[10]

Social movement advantages of promulgating the idea that there are gangs of vicious Satanists operating clandestinely and antisocially include the high visibility of professed apostates (whom the media have seemed only too eager to publicize for their sensationalism) with the accompanying low visibility or relative absence of actual violent Satanists to study. Victims, in other words, predominate while perpetrators are virtually invisible. This paucity of actual Satanists to observe is consistent with the ACM frame that they are so well organized that they can conceal their whereabouts and evidence of their deeds or coopt professionals who would otherwise detect and reveal them. (And, of course, it simultaneously makes research on them that might undermine the current ACM frame difficult at best).

The existence of murderous, ruthless Satanists committing felonies also raises fewer First Amendment concerns for religious liberty among members of the public than those that appeared for groups like the Hare Krishnas and the Unification Church. Yet, by association, this frame tars the other groups the ACM opposes with the "dangerous subversive" label just as the "cult" stereotype lumped them all together. Moreover, the concept of ritual abuse has the appearance of a reliable diagnostic concept in clinical settings, despite its ambiguous meaning. And the Satanism form of frame extension aligns the ACM with a large section of the American public, such as conservative Christians who are most likely to hold an existing belief in a personal devil who makes it his mission to possess souls and wreak havoc in lawful society. During the late 1970s the ACM made intimations about questioning sectarian televangelists like Garner Ted Armstrong and Jerry Falwell. However, the countermovement quickly backed off because of the conservative Christians in its ranks who already possessed their own anticult tradition critical of Jehovah's Witnesses, Christian Scientists, and Mormons (among others) and were perhaps nervous about applying the "cult" label any closer to home. Later, evangelical Christians and charismatics were accused by secular anticultists of being suspect, though such accusations were not without criticism from the Christian branch of the ACM.[11] But the two branches of the ACM—secular and sectarian—did relatively little crossing over into each other's camps as allies.

The Satanism scare frame, however, brings the theological expectations of conservative Christians much closer to the secular ACM. Thus it is much easier for the two wings to pursue a common "enemy." And unlike the family members of Moonies, Krishnas, Rajneeshees, premies, and other youthful "cult members" whose numbers declined by the mid-1980s, the relative absence of any real Satanists will not be such a problem for the ACM. Whereas the countermovement depended on distraught, angry relatives of real "cultists" for its membership rolls during the past two decades, it will not matter for the ACM whether there are actually large numbers of Satanists loose in North America or not. The conservative Christians will still be there to tap as potential constituents, for they have *faith* that there are both a Satan and Satanists, whatever empirical research shows. And those occasional persons who appear from time to time making claims of being former Satanists and/ or their victims will preserve the credibility of the threat for other ACM activists.

In sum, frame alignment has permitted the ACM to adjust its ideology to fit both the realities of the social environment in which its has operated since 1971 and its own organizational development. The addition of Satanism to its list of enemies is therefore no more surprising than the fact that it originally expanded that same list beyond the single group of the Children of God. The ACM is, despite all its claims to being scientific and its denials of antireligious bias, a religiously oriented group operating in a dynamic religious economy. When changes in its leadership and organizations required ideological reorientation during its latest professionalization stage, the necessary corrections were made. Whether new concern over Satanism can sustain the ACM is not known. Certainly the volatile nature of the religious economy suggests the countermovement will someday likely have new subject matter about which to raise concern. It now has the ideology, the organizations, and the career interests of many spokespersons to fuel its energy. And these will not likely soon disappear.

Notes

1. See, in particular, Anson D. Shupe, Jr., and David G. Bromley, *The New Vigilantes: Deprogrammers, Anti-Cultists, and the New Religions* (Beverly Hills, Calif.: Sage, 1980); Anson Shupe, "The Routinization of Conflict in the Modern Cult/ Anticult Controversy," *The Nebraska Humanist* 8 (Fall 1985): 26–39; and David G. Bromley and Anson Shupe, *Strange Gods and Cult Scares* (Boston: Beacon Press, forthcoming).

2. David G. Bromley and Anson Shupe, "The Future of the Anticult Movement," in *The Future of New Religious Movements*, eds. David G. Bromley and Phillip E. Hammond (Macon, Ga.: Mercer University Press, 1987), 230.

3. Erving Goffman, *Frame Analysis* (Cambridge: Harvard University Press, 1974).

4. David A. Snow, E. Burke Rochford, Jr., Steven K. Warden, and Robert D. Benford, "Frame Alignment Processes, Micromobilization, and Movement Participation," *American Sociological Review* 51 (August 1986): 472.

5. David G. Bromley, "Hare Krishna and the Anti-Cult Movement," in *Krishna Consciousness in the West,* eds. David G. Bromley and Larry D. Shinn (Lewisburg, Pa.: Bucknell University Press, 1989), 255–92.

6. Cited in Brock Kilbourne and James T. Richardson, "Anti-Religion Bias in the Diagnostic and Statistical Manual III: The Case of Cults" (paper given at the annual meeting of the Society for the Scientific Study of Religion, Chicago, 1984), 7.

7. See, for two examples, James S. Gordon, "Psychiatry and Krishna Consciousness," in *Krishna Consciousness in the West,* eds. Bromley and Shinn, 238–54; and Marc Galanter, *Cults: Faith, Healing, and Coercion* (New York: Oxford University Press, 1989).

8. David A. Snow and Robert D. Benford, "Ideology, Frame Resonance, and Participant Mobilization," *International Social Movement Research* 1 (Greenwich, Conn.: JAI Press, 1988), 204.

9. See James T. Richardson, Joel Best, and David G. Bromley, eds., *The Satanism Scare* (New York: Aldine de Gruyter, 1991) for an excellent compendium of interdisciplinary articles on the subject.

10. Bromley, "Hare Krishna and the Anti-Cult Movement," 256.

11. For an example of criticism of conservative Christianity as cultic, and thereby dangerous, see Flo Conway and Jim Siegelman, *Snapping: America's Epidemic of Sudden Personality Change* (Philadelphia: J. B. Lippincott, 1978), 44–45; Flo Conway and Jim Siegelman, *Holy Terror* (Garden City, N.Y.: Doubleday, 1982); Lowell D. Streiker, *The Gospel Time Bomb* (Buffalo, N.Y.: Prometheus Books, 1984); and in response to such attacks: Ronald M. Enroth, "Cults and Evangelicals: Labeling and Lumping," *Cultic Studies Journal* 2 no. 2 (1985): 321–25.

Suggestions for Further Reading

Robbins, Thomas. *Cults, Converts and Charisma*. Newbury Park, Calif.: Sage Publications, 1988.

Shupe, Anson, and David G. Bromley. "Social Responses to Cults." In *The Sacred in a Secular Age*, edited by Phillip E. Hammond, 58–72. Berkeley: University of California Press, 1985.

Stark, Rodney, ed. *Religious Movements: Genesis, Exodus, and Numbers*. New York: Paragon House, 1985.

Appendix I

A BIBLIOGRAPHICAL GUIDE TO ALTERNATIVE RELIGIONS

Many alternative religions could not be included among the chapters of this book, given the space constraints inherent in any finite project. Here follows a list of alternative religions including many groups not covered in the preceding chapters, as well as the groups that *are* covered. By consulting the sources listed, the reader can obtain a reasonably comprehensive picture of each group's history, beliefs, and practices. The list is confined to groups currently active in the United States.

For each religious group on this list that is discussed in the main body of this book, the reader is referred to the appropriate chapter for further information and bibliographical references. For each group *not* otherwise mentioned, a brief bibliography is provided. Some of the bibliographical references are abbreviated; they refer, by number, to the works listed in the bibliography at the end of this appendix.

There are thousands of alternative religious groups—yoga centers, unconventional Christian churches, Buddhist meditation societies, and a host of others—active in the United States. They vary widely in size, location, leadership, and degree and kind of divergence from the American religious mainstream. Any list of alternative religious groups, including this one, is thus bound to be selective. Those included here tend to be among the larger, more publicized groups operating in multiple locations. Several of the works listed in the bibliography at the end of this appendix survey many more religions than can be included here.

ADVENTISM

Adventists believe that the Second Coming of Christ is imminent. William Miller gathered thousands of followers for his prediction that the Second Coming would occur in 1843 or 1844; several groups descending from his work survive, including the Seventh-Day Adventists.

See chapter 3.

AETHERIUS SOCIETY

Sir George King's alleged messages from Aetherius, a Venusian, and other Cosmic Masters from other planets are the basis of the Aetherius Society's teachings. Members believe that they are building cooperation between earth dwellers and the Cosmic Forces.

See chapter 41.

ALAMO FOUNDATION

Now formally known as the Music Square Church, the Alamo work began in 1969 when Susan and Tony Alamo (pronounced ah-LAH-mo) started a street ministry in Hollywood. In 1976 the group moved its headquarters to Alma, Arkansas, where it has endured several controversies. The church is Pentecostal and stridently anti-Catholic; members must observe strict behavioral standards.

Robert S. Ellwood, Jr., *One Way: The Jesus Movement and Its Meaning* (Englewood Cliffs, N.J.: Prentice-Hall, 1983), pp. 60–69, 83–85.

Melton (17), 183–88.

AMERICAN MUSLIM MISSION
The American Muslim Mission was one of several factions that emerged from the Nation of Islam following the death of Elijah Muhammad in 1975. Led by Muhammad's son Wallace (later known as Warith) Muhammad, the central organization was dissolved in 1985 and the movement now functions as some 200 independent mosques.

See chapter 26.

AMISH
The Amish are the most conservative of the Anabaptists. They are best known for their strong sense of community and their resistance to modern technology, including motor vehicles and electricity.

See chapter 1.

ANABAPTISTS
Some of the most radical exponents of the Protestant Reformation of the sixteenth century came to be called Anabaptists, or rebaptizers, for their insistence on baptism for adult believers only. The Anabaptists now consist principally of the Mennonites, Amish, and Hutterites.

See chapter 1.

ANANDA MARGA
Ananda Marga ("Path of Bliss"), founded in India in 1955 by Shrii Shrii Anandamurti, combines yoga and meditation with a strong social-reform agenda.

Barker (2), 331–32.

Barker (3), 167–68.

ANTHROPOSOPHY
Rudolf Steiner founded this movement, a derivative of Theosophy, in Germany in 1912.

See chapter 31.

ANTICULT MOVEMENT
A name given to activists seeking to remove members from alternative religions they find objectionable and/or opposing the existence of certain alternative religions at all. The movement's detractors accuse it of having "cult"-like features much like those of the movements it opposes.

See chapter 43.

ARCANE SCHOOL
One of the several branches of Theosophy, the Arcane School was founded by Alice Bailey in 1923.

See chapter 31.

ARICA
Founded in Chile by Oscar Ichazo and brought to the United States by him in 1971, Arica teaches self-integration and ego reduction through a series of disciplined exercises, some taken from various religious and esoteric traditions.

Melton (18), 880–81.

ASSOCIATION FOR RESEARCH AND ENLIGHTENMENT
The ARE is based on the work of the psychic Edgar Cayce. It was founded in 1931.

See chapter 36.

BAHÁ'Í FAITH
The Bahá'í Faith arose in Persia, initially from the work of a forerunner, known as the Báb, or Gate, beginning in 1844, and then, after the Báb's execution in 1850, by Mírzá Husayn 'Alí, who took the name Bahá'u'lláh, meaning the Glory of God. Bahá'í proclaims itself a new world religion teaching human understanding, sexual and racial equality, and world peace.

See chapter 22.

BAWA MUHAIYADDEEN FELLOWSHIP
A group based on the teachings of Bawa Muhaiyaddeen, a Sri Lankan Sufi teacher, the fellowship was founded in 1971 when disciples first brought the teacher to the United States.

See chapter 23.

BEAR TRIBE MEDICINE SOCIETY
Sun Bear, an Ojibwa-Chippewa Indian, founded this organization in 1970 and

1971 to promote a kind of spirituality that draws from traditional Native American shamanic practices as well as various New Age teachings and practices. Most Bear Tribe members are not Native Americans.

See chapter 39.

BLACK JEWS

Various groups of African Americans active since the 1890s have concluded that their proper identity is as Jews and have founded independent synagogues and equivalent groups following Jewish patterns of life and worship but generally not recognized by mainstream Judaism as legitimately Jewish.

See chapter 26.

BLACK MUSLIMS

Various groups of African Americans active since the 1910s have concluded that their proper identity is as Muslims and have founded various independent Islamic groups. The most prominent group, historically, was the Nation of Islam, led for many years by Elijah Muhammad.

See chapters 21 and 26.

BOSTON CHURCH OF CHRIST

The Boston Church of Christ and its affiliated churches in many cities in America and abroad (the larger fellowship was renamed International Churches of Christ in 1993) are derived from the Churches of Christ, the branch of the Campbellite Restoration movement of the nineteenth century perhaps best known for its rejection of instrumental music. The Boston Movement was founded in 1979 by Kip McKean; it stresses heavy involvement of members in church activities and guidance of individual lives through "discipling."

See chapter 13.

BRAHMA KUMARIS WORLD SPIRITUAL UNIVERSITY

Dada Lekhraj founded the Brahma Kumaris movement in India in 1937 as a means of cultivating a spiritual elite that would be able to survive a coming world catastrophe. The movement eventually spread worldwide, establishing a presence in the United States in 1977. The members, a majority of whom are female, practice meditation, are vegetarians, and are encouraged to be celibate.

Lawrence A. Babb, *Redemptive Encounters: Three Modern Styles in the Hindu Tradition* (Berkeley: University of California Press, 1986).

BRANCH DAVIDIANS (SEE DAVIDIAN SEVENTH-DAY ADVENTISTS)

BRETHREN (SEE OLD GERMAN BAPTIST BRETHREN)

BRITISH-ISRAEL

Some residents of various English-speaking countries have concluded that the "lost tribes" of ancient Israel migrated to the British Isles and that nations culturally descended from Britain have inherited the mantle of the chosen people. The largest American group advocating British-Israel ideas has been the Worldwide Church of God.

See chapter 11.

BRUDERHOF

Eberhard Arnold founded a communal Christian group in Germany in 1920. Eventually it modelled its lifestyle after that of the Hutterites. After several migrations the movement established its headquarters in the United States in the 1950s; it has since established several satellite colonies in the United States, Europe, and Africa.

See chapter 1.

BUILDERS OF THE ADYTUM

Paul Foster Case, formerly a member of the Order of the Golden Dawn, founded the Builders of the Adytum in 1920. Never large, the BOTA has followed various paths of traditional occultism, including Kabbalism and Tarot card–reading.

Ellwood and Partin (13), 147–50.

CATHOLIC TRADITIONALISM

At various times, especially following the Second Vatican Council (1962–1966), some conservative Catholics have concluded that their church as a whole has been misled and have started organizations, some within and some outside the church, promoting an earlier form of Catholicism.

See chapter 9.

CHANNELING
A contemporary manifestation of Spiritualism, channeling involves the receiving of messages by mediums ("channels") from persons no longer alive on earth or from other beings or entities.
See chapter 33.

CHILDREN OF GOD
Begun by David Berg (later known as Moses David) in California as a part of the Jesus movement about 1968, the Children of God founded rural communities and became one of the most controversial of Christian movements. The group later called itself the Family of Love, and most recently simply the Family.
See chapter 12.

CHINMOY, SRI
Sri Chinmoy (1931–), a prolific writer and lecturer, is believed by followers to have a state of union with God. His followers are vegetarians, meditate daily, and spread his teachings.
Barker (2), 352–53.
Barker (3), 209–10.

CHRIST THE SAVIOR BROTHERHOOD (SEE HOLY ORDER OF MANS)

CHRISTIAN SCIENCE
Founded by Mary Baker Eddy in the 1870s, Christian Science teaches that the only reality is Mind and that the physical world is an illusion. It is best known for its belief in spiritual healing rather than conventional medicine.
See chapter 5.

CHURCH OF ARMAGEDDON (SEE LOVE ISRAEL)

CHURCH OF GOD AND SAINTS OF CHRIST
This earliest of the black Jewish groups was founded by William S. Crowdy in 1896.
See chapter 26.

CHURCH OF GOD INTERNATIONAL
Garner Ted Armstrong, son of Worldwide Church of God founder Herbert W. Armstrong, was expelled from the Worldwide Church in the 1970s and started his own organization, the Church of God International.
See chapter 11.

CHURCH OF SATAN
The Church of Satan, probably the most prominent of the recent satanic groups, was founded in San Francisco in 1966 by Anton LaVey.
See chapter 42.

CHURCH OF THE NEW JERUSALEM (SEE SWEDENBORGIANISM)

CHURCH OF THE NEW SONG
A religious movement related to a prisoners' rights movement, the Church of the New Song was founded by Harry W. Theriault in 1970 in the federal penitentiary in Atlanta.
Melton (18), 963–64.

CHURCH UNIVERSAL AND TRIUMPHANT
Founded in 1958 by Mark Prophet as the Summit Lighthouse, the Church Universal and Triumphant has been headed since his death by his widow, Elizabeth Clare Prophet. Its roots are in Theosophy.
See chapter 31.

COMMUNITY OF JESUS
In 1970 Cay Andersen and Judy Sorensen, seeking a richer spiritual life through human community and traditional liturgy, founded the Community of Jesus, which has come to encompass hundreds of members in and near its compound on Cape Cod. The group became especially well known for its music, including Gregorian chant.
Leon Howell, "The Controversial Community of Jesus," *Christian Century* (6 April 1983): 307–12.

CULT AWARENESS NETWORK
A group opposed to alternative religions it considers harmful, CAN evolved from several of the anticult groups that rose to prominence in the 1970s.
See chapter 43.

DAVIDIAN SEVENTH-DAY ADVENTISTS

Victor T. Houteff developed a small group of followers within the Seventh-Day Adventist Church in Los Angeles in the early 1930s. The group moved to Waco, Texas, in 1935; during World War II their staunch pacifism caused them to break with the parent SDA body. Houteff died in 1955, and his wife dissolved the group in 1962 following the failure of an eschatological prediction she had issued a few years earlier. Regrouping, several independent Davidian movements emerged soon thereafter; the largest established a headquarters near Exeter, Missouri, and another started a new colony at Waco. Vernon Howell joined the latter group, known as Branch Davidians, in 1984. Soon thereafter he replaced Branch leader George Roden. Howell's theology was highly apocalyptic. In 1990 he changed his name to David Koresh (Hebrew for Cyrus). In 1993 an aborted raid by the Bureau of Alcohol, Tobacco, and Firearms led to a fifty-one-day standoff that culminated in the fiery deaths of over eighty believers.

See chapter 15.

DAWN HORSE FELLOWSHIP (SEE FREE DAIST COMMUNION)

DHIRAVAMSA FOUNDATION (SEE THERAVADA BUDDHISM)

DIANETICS (SEE SCIENTOLOGY)

DISCIPLING (SEE BOSTON CHURCH OF CHRIST)

DIVINE LIGHT MISSION

Guru Maharaj Ji arrived in the United States in 1971 at the age of thirteen and attracted many followers to his program of meditation and communal living. The organization was dissolved in the 1980s, but a less-structured successor, Elan Vital, continues to support Maharaji (as he later preferred to be known) in his worldwide lecturing.

See chapter 37.

DOUKHOBORS

The Doukhobors (the name means "spirit wrestlers") were among several groups seeking deeper mystical experience and simplicity in living that broke off from the Russian Orthodox Church during and after the seventeenth century. In Russia and in Canada they have had a tradition of being radically at odds with the government.

Koozma John Tarasoff, *A Pictorial History of the Doukhobors* (Saskatoon: Modern Press, 1969).

J. F. C. Wright, *Slava Bohu: The Story of the Doukhobors* (New York: Farrar and Rinehart, 1940).

DUNKARDS, DUNKERS (SEE OLD GERMAN BAPTIST BRETHREN)

ECCLESIA GNOSTICA (SEE GNOSTICISM)

ECKANKAR

Derived from the Radhasoami tradition of India as taught by Kirpal Singh, ECKANKAR was founded by Paul Twitchell in 1965.

See chapter 37.

ELAN VITAL (SEE DIVINE LIGHT MISSION)

EMISSARIES OF DIVINE LIGHT

The Emissaries, founded in the 1930s by Lloyd Meeker, operate about a dozen communal sites and other smaller centers worldwide from a headquarters near Loveland, Colorado. The communities function as conference centers and places for New Age therapies and spirituality.

Barker (3), 178.

Dave Thatcher, "100 Mile Lodge—Emissaries of Divine Light." *Communities*, no. 36 (January-February 1979): 39–41.

EST

Werner Erhard (1935–) founded est, Erhard Seminars Training, in 1971. Est is known for its intensive workshops that promote communications skills and self-empowerment. The name of the movement was changed to the Forum in the 1980s.

Barker (3), 170–71.

Ruth A. Tucker, *Another Gospel: Alternative Religions and the New Age Movement* (Grand Rapids: Zondervan, 1989), pp. 367–69.

ETHICAL CULTURE

Felix Adler (1851–1933) founded the Ethical Culture Society in 1876 as an organization dedicated to social reform and ethical living without any specific religious creeds.

Felix Adler, *The Religion of Duty* (New York: McClure, Philips and Co., 1905).

Benny Kraut, *From Reform Judaism to Ethical Culture: The Religious Evolution of Felix Adler* (Cincinnati: Hebrew Union College Press, 1979).

EZRAT NASHIM

This Jewish feminist movement grew out of the Havurah movement (q.v.) in the early 1970s and took shape under the auspices of Conservative Judaism, although its appeal has extended to a broader constituency.

See chapter 10.

FAITH ASSEMBLY

Faith Assembly is located near Wilmot, Indiana. It was founded by Hobart Freeman in about 1966; his teachings require abstinence from all medication and medical means of health care. The church's faith-healing practices have been blamed for over one hundred deaths, including that of Freeman from untreated diabetes in 1984.

Randy Frame, "Indiana Grand Jury Indicts a Faith-Healing Preacher," *Christianity Today,* 23 November 1984.

Chris Lutes, "Leader's Death Gives Rise to Speculation About the Future of His Faith-healing Sect," *Christianity Today,* 18 January 1985.

THE FAMILY (SEE CHILDREN OF GOD)

FAMILY OF LOVE (SEE CHILDREN OF GOD)

THE FARM

In the late 1960s a large group began meeting weekly in an informal class led by hippie philosopher Stephen Gaskin. In 1971 several hundred of them settled near Summertown, Tennessee, where they developed one of the most prominent hip-era communes.

See chapter 38.

FATHER DIVINE'S PEACE MISSION MOVEMENT

Father Divine began developing a communal movement in the New York area about 1919; his followers proclaimed him God in the flesh, and numbered in the thousands at the movement's peak in the 1930s.

See chapter 27.

FLAGELLANTS (SEE PENITENTES)

THE FORUM (SEE EST)

FOUNDATION FAITH OF GOD (PROCESS CHURCH)

In 1963 Robert de Grimston organized the Process Church of the Final Judgement in London; its central theological theme was the reconciliation of Christ and Satan, with an emphasis on Satan. A majority of members withdrew in 1974 and formed a more conventional group now known as the Foundation Faith of God.

See chapter 42.

FREE DAIST COMMUNION

Franklin Jones, an American, founded the Dawn Horse Fellowship (later known as the Free Daist Communion) in 1970 after studying with Swami Muktananda in India. Jones has successively changed his name to Bubba Free John, Da Free John, and finally Heart-Master Da Love Ananda.

Melton (18), 913–14.

FRIENDS

The Religious Society of Friends, or Quakers, was founded in England by George Fox in the seventeenth century. America became an early mission outpost. Friends are traditionally noted for simple living, pacifism, and silent worship.

See chapter 6.

FULL MOON MEDITATION GROUPS

Followers of Alice Bailey and her Arcane School have formed a number of separate Theosophical organizations, including several Full Moon Meditation Groups. Meditation Mount, opened in 1971 near Ojai,

California, is one of the largest centers of Full Moon activity.

See chapter 31.

GHOST DANCE

Recurring several times among various Native American tribes, the Ghost Dance was a pan-Indian movement that prophesied the restoration of traditional Native American culture. The movement's best-known phase was its revival among the Sioux in the late 1880s, which ended with the tragic Wounded Knee massacre in 1890.

See chapter 39.

GNOSTICISM

Gnosticism, or mystical religion, is thousands of years old. Several contemporary organizations seek to continue the Gnostic tradition, among them the Ecclesia Gnostica of Los Angeles, which grew out of the Gnostic Society, founded by James Morgan Pryce in 1928. The Ecclesia Gnostica was initially led by Stephan Hoeller, who became active in Gnosticism in 1959.

Ellwood and Partin (13), 93–97.

Melton (18), 740–41.

GOLDEN DAWN (SEE HERMETIC ORDER OF THE GOLDEN DAWN)

GURDJIEFF

George I. Gurdjieff taught that humans are asleep, not living at their full potential. Awakening can come through spiritual exercises, including "movements," which resemble dancing. Gurdjieff began teaching others around 1917 in Russia; he first visited the United States in 1924.

See chapter 24.

HARE KRISHNAS (SEE INTERNATIONAL SOCIETY FOR KRISHNA CONSCIOUSNESS)

HASIDISM

Hasidism emerged in the eighteenth century in Eastern Europe as an Orthodox movement that embraced mysticism under the leadership of charismatic zaddikim and rebbes. Many migrated to the United States in response to Nazi persecution of Jews; the center of Hasidic population today is Brooklyn.

See chapter 10.

HAVURAH MOVEMENT

Various forms of intimate community define the Havurah movement, which seeks to provide intense programs of Jewish study and fellowship, sometimes in residential or quasi-residential settings. The movement began to emerge in the late 1950s; its first residential commune was established in Somerville, Massachusetts, in 1968.

See chapter 10.

HEALTHY-HAPPY-HOLY ORGANIZATION

Founded in California in 1969 by Yogi Bhajan, 3HO, as it is popularly known, promotes the practice of Kundalini yoga and urges followers to focus on spiritual rather than material concerns in the interest of transforming the world. It considers itself derived primarily from Sikhism, but incorporates elements of other traditions as well.

See chapter 37.

HERMETIC ORDER OF THE GOLDEN DAWN

In 1888 a group of English Masons and Rosicrucians united to form the Hermetic Order of the Golden Dawn. Its interest in elaborate systems of magick soon found followers in the United States as well.

Ellwood and Partin (13), 154–55.

HIMALAYAN INSTITUTE

Swami Rama visited the United States in 1970 to have his powers of bodily control tested by American scientists. He founded the Himalayan Institute the following year; it provides yoga classes and emphasizes holistic health programs.

See chapter 18.

HOLINESS MOVEMENT

Derived largely from the teachings of John Wesley, the founder of Methodism, Holiness Christians believe that one can experience a "second blessing," or cleansing from sin, and thereafter lead a holy, sinless life.

See chapter 2.

HOLY ORDER OF MANS

Earl W. Blighton founded the Holy Order of MANS in 1968 as a Rosicrucian-style Christian mystery school with a highly developed liturgical and ceremonial dimension. The titular acronym had a secret meaning, although it was sometimes explained to outsiders as coming from the Greek words *mysterion, agape, nous,* and *sophia.* In the 1980s the movement dropped its original teachings and liturgical practices, embraced the Eastern Orthodox tradition, and changed its name to Christ the Savior Brotherhood.

See chapter 14.

HUTTERIAN SOCIETY OF BROTHERS (SEE BRUDERHOF)

HUTTERITES

The Hutterites comprise a major wing of the Anabaptist movement whose most distinctive teaching is near-total community of property. They were founded in the late 1520s and migrated repeatedly to escape persecution. In the 1870s they arrived in South Dakota; from there they have branched out into several states and Canadian provinces, establishing hundreds of communal farming colonies.

See chapter 1.

I AM

This branch of Theosophy was founded following Guy Ballard's reports of an encounter with an Ascended Master in 1930. Ballard died in 1939, but the movement continued under the leadership of his widow Edna and others.

See chapter 31.

IDENTITY MOVEMENT

The Identity Movement is nearly synonymous with the British-Israel movement, although "Identity" has lately come to be associated with a millennial and racist element who have in some cases banded together in survivalist communes.

See chapter 11.

INTEGRAL YOGA

Swami Satchidananda founded the Integral Yoga Institute during his first visit to the United States in 1966. In 1979 he and his followers purchased land in Virginia for the creation of Yogaville, a communal spiritual center. Yogaville and Integral Yoga are distinctly ecumenical, emphasizing the universality of spiritual essentials.

See chapter 18.

INTERNATIONAL CHURCHES OF CHRIST (SEE BOSTON CHURCH OF CHRIST)

INTERNATIONAL SOCIETY FOR KRISHNA CONSCIOUSNESS

Swami A. C. Bhaktivedanta arrived in the United States in 1965 as a missionary of Vaishnavite Hinduism. The movement he founded, popularly known as the Hare Krishna movement (after its principal mantra), has been among the most visible and controversial of American alternative religions.

See chapter 19.

JEHOVAH'S WITNESSES

Founded by Charles Russell in the 1870s, the Jehovah's Witnesses survived the failure of their prophecy that the Second Coming of Christ would occur in 1914 to grow into one of the largest alternative religions in the world. Witnesses are known for nonparticipation in public affairs and refusal of blood transfusions, among other things.

See chapter 3.

JESUS MOVEMENT

The Jesus movement emerged as a Christian derivative of the hippies in the late 1960s, most significantly in Los Angeles. The Jesus people (often called "Jesus freaks") combined hippie unconventional clothing, rock music, and communal living with fundamentalist Christian doctrines.

Robert S. Ellwood, Jr., *One Way: The Jesus Movement and Its Meaning* (Englewood Cliffs, N.J.: Prentice-Hall, 1973).

Lowell D. Streiker, *The Jesus Trip: Advent of the Jesus Freaks* (Nashville: Abingdon, 1971).

JESUS PEOPLE U.S.A.

This communal enclave founded by a group of young Christians in 1972 during the heyday of the Jesus movement grew over several years to over five hundred members; based in Chicago, it is one of the nation's largest and most stable Christian communities emulating the first-century church, with several industries and an extensive outreach program.

Timothy Jones, "Jesus' People," *Christianity Today*, 14 September 1992, pp. 20–25.

KERISTA

The roots of Kerista were planted by John Presmont, who took the name Brother Jud, in the 1950s and 1960s; the group was formally established by Presmont and Eve Furchgott ("Even Eve") in 1971. Kerista has been known for its successful computer consulting business and its system of "polyfidelity," a form of group marriage. A schism occurred in 1991 when a majority of members broke with Jud.

"Kerista," *Communities: Journal of Cooperation*, no. 64 (Fall 1984): 19–47.

KRIPALU YOGA

Kripalu Yoga was founded in the 1960s by Yogi Amrit Desai. It teaches a two-stage approach to yoga, beginning with yoga of will and culminating with yoga of surrender.

See chapter 18.

LATTER DAY SAINTS

The Latter Day Saint movement began with the revelations claimed by Joseph Smith, Jr., in the 1820s. He published his new scripture as The Book of Mormon and in 1830 founded a church. The largest successor church, headquartered in Utah, is America's largest alternative religion; there are also over one hundred smaller LDS groups.

See chapter 4.

LAWSONOMY

Alfred W. Lawson (1869–1954), an aircraft pioneer in his early days, became convinced that he had worked out a comprehensive theory of the workings of the universe. He founded a number of organizations, including Lawsonian churches, a few of which survive.

Lyell D. Henry, Jr., *Zig-Zag-and-Swirl: Alfred W. Lawson's Quest for Greatness* (Iowa City: University of Iowa Press, 1991).

LIBERAL CATHOLIC CHURCH

This branch of Theosophy was begun by Charles Leadbeater about 1916; it stresses highly liturgical worship services similar to those of Catholicism, but its ideas are derived from Theosophy.

See chapter 31.

LOCAL CHURCH

The Local Church movement was founded in China by Watchman Nee, who had been converted to Christianity by American missionaries. Its first presence in the United States came in 1952. The church is perhaps best known for its insistence that there is only one "local" church in each city or town and for its practice of "pray reading," praying using phrases from the Bible over and over.

Melton (17), 249–57.

LOVE ISRAEL (CHURCH OF ARMAGEDDON)

Paul Erdmann, who took the name Love Israel, attracted a following during the early days of the Jesus movement in the late 1960s and founded the Church of Armageddon in 1969. Members live a radical Christian communal life; the main center is north of Seattle. All members take the surname Israel.

Melton (18), 605.

MARANATHA CHRISTIAN CHURCHES

Bob Weiner founded the Maranatha movement in 1972 as a student-oriented church. Centers have been set up on a number of campuses; the group engendered controversy in the 1980s for its strict discipline and regulation of members' lives.

Melton (18), 409–10.

MEHER BABA

The followers of Meher Baba (d. 1969) believe that he was an Avatar, or God incarnate. Baba was known for spending his last several decades in silence, communicating with followers nonverbally. Several informal groups of Baba-lovers continue to exist.

Baker (2), 344.
Ellwood and Partin (13), 216–20.
Needleman (20), 75–102.

MENNONITES

The Mennonites are the largest of the general categories of Anabaptists and were named for their early leader Menno Simons. Less radical than the Amish in their separatism from the modern world, they nevertheless were widely persecuted and through extended migrations established a large population in North America. The movement today is comprised of several independent denominations.

See chapter 1.

METROPOLITAN COMMUNITY CHURCH

Troy Perry, a homosexual Pentecostal minister, founded the first Metropolitan Community Church in Los Angeles in 1968 as a church that would affirm the worth and dignity of all persons, including homosexuals. The movement has grown to become the largest of several denominations ministering primarily to homosexuals.

Melton (18), 960–61.

Troy Perry, *The Lord Is My Shepherd and He Knows I'm Gay* (New York: Bantam, 1972).

MOLOKANS

Molokans broke from their parent Doukhobors in the eighteenth century, rejecting what they considered excesses in the Doukhobor leadership, notably the claims of some leaders to be "hereditary Christs." Their pacifism led to their emigration to the United States in the early twentieth century.

John K. Berokoff, *Molokans in America* (Los Angeles: Stockton-Doty, 1969).

Pauline V. Young, *The Pilgrims of Russian-Town* (Chicago: University of Chicago Press, 1932).

MOORISH SCIENCE

This earliest of the African-American Islamic groups was founded in 1913 by Timothy Drew, who took the name Noble Drew Ali, in Newark, New Jersey. The group continues today, although its membership is believed to be small.

See chapters 21 and 26.

MORMONS (SEE LATTER DAY SAINTS)

MOVEMENT OF SPIRITUAL INNER AWARENESS

John-Roger Hinkins was an early member of ECKANKAR who left that movement in 1968 to begin developing MSIA, which was formally launched in 1971. The group's organization, beliefs, and practices are all similar to those of ECKANKAR.

Melton (17), 258–62.

NATION OF ISLAM

The mysterious W. D. Fard began preaching the doctrines of this black racist form of Islam in Detroit in 1930. After Fard's disappearance in 1934, Elijah Muhammad (formerly Elijah Poole) headed the movement for over four decades. Following Muhammad's death the movement split into several factions.

See chapter 21 and 26.

NATIVE AMERICAN CHURCH

The Native American Church has developed a following in many tribes in the twentieth century. Its beliefs and rituals combine Christianity with tribal traditions; the church is best known for its peyote ceremonies.

See chapter 39.

NEO-AMERICAN CHURCH

Psychologist Art Kleps, once associated with LSD advocate Timothy Leary, founded the Neo-American Church in 1964. Psychedelic drugs were the church's sacraments; irreverence and satire were staples in church publications.

Art Kleps, *The Boo Hoo Bible* (San Cristobal, N. Mex.: Toad Press, 1971).

Melton (18), 121.

NEO-PAGANISM

Neo-paganism is a broad term embracing a wide variety of contemporary groups that are usually feminist, environmentalist, and earth-oriented; they typically try to recreate primal religions in a contemporary mode.

See chapter 34.

NEOSHAMANISM (SEE SHAMANISM)

NEW AGE MOVEMENT

Coming to prominence in the early 1970s, and rooted in such nineteenth-century spiritual movements as Theosophy, Spiritualism, and New Thought, New Age groups are diverse schools of thought involving such things as mystical and Eastern spirituality, alternative medical treatments and bodily therapies, and social experiments. The New Age movement at its peak looked forward to a coming massive transformation of the planet; that theme, however, has lately been somewhat muted.

See chapter 35.

NEW THOUGHT

New Thought is an umbrella term for a diverse group of metaphysical religions, typically interested in the powers of the mind, personal growth, and spiritual healing. The movement is rooted in the work of Phineas P. Quimby and other nineteenth-century metaphysical teachers.

See chapter 32.

NICHIREN SHOSHU

One of the "new religions" of Japan that achieved prominence after World War II, Nichiren Shoshu (along with the related Soka Gakkai movement) has made major missionary efforts in the United States.

See chapter 16.

OLD BELIEVERS

Innovations in Russian Orthodoxy under the patriarch Nikon in the seventeenth century led to the rise of an antireform group called the Old Believers. Problems and persecutions in the Soviet Union led to their emigration to North America beginning in 1964; they settled principally in Oregon, Alaska, and Canada.

Melton (18), 56–57.

OLD CATHOLIC CHURCH

The several churches constituting Old Catholicism derive from nineteenth-century schisms within Catholicism, the Old Catholics being the party that rejected certain ecclesiastical innovations, notably papal infallibility. Membes are typically converts who object to ongoing innovations in Catholicism and Anglicanism.

Karl Pruter and J. Gordon Melton, *The Old Catholic Sourcebook* (New York: Garland, 1983).

OLD GERMAN BAPTIST BRETHREN

The Brethren, a pietistic movement founded in Germany in 1708, sometimes known as "Dunkers" or "Dunkards," began to move to North American soon after their founding. Beginning in 1881 a series of schisms established a variety of Brethren churches with differing levels of theological and social conservatism. The Old German Baptist Brethren, or "Old Orders," are among the most conservative.

See chapter 1.

ORDER OF THE GOLDEN DAWN (SEE HERMETIC ORDER OF THE GOLDEN DAWN)

ORDO TEMPLI ORIENTIS (OTO) (SEE THELEMIC MAGICK)

PAGANISM (SEE NEO-PAGANISM)

PEACE MISSION MOVEMENT (SEE FATHER DIVINE)

PENITENTES

Various groups of religious believers engage in ritual physical self-abuse, among other practices, in the interest of demonstrating spiritual dedication. In the United States they are typically found among Hispanic Catholics in a few isolated communities in the Southwest.

Lorayne Ann Horka-Follick, *Los Hermanos Penitentes: A Vestige of Medievalism in Southwestern United States* (Los Angeles: Westernlore Press, 1969).

Marta Weigle, *Brothers of Light, Brothers of Blood: The Penitentes of the Southwest* (Albuquerque: University of New Mexico Press, 1976).

PENTECOSTALISM

Outbreaks of charismatic "gifts," notably speaking in tongues and faith healing, have occurred frequently in the history of Christianity. The specific beginnings of contemporary Pentecostalism as a sustained movement came with the work of Charles F. Parham in Topeka, Kansas, in 1901, and, deriving from Parham's work, the Azusa Street Revival led by William Seymour in Los Angeles in 1906.

See chapter 2.

PEOPLES TEMPLE
Jim Jones began the precursor to the Peoples Temple, a congregation of the Christian Church (Disciples of Christ), in Indianapolis in 1955. The work was moved to California in 1965. Prior to the Jonestown suicides, the church was best known for its interracial character and its political activism.

See chapter 30.

PROCESS CHURCH (SEE FOUNDATION FAITH OF GOD)

QUAKERS (SEE FRIENDS)

RADHASOAMI GROUPS (SEE RUHANI SATSANG, ECKANKAR, DIVINE LIGHT MISSION)

RAELIAN MOVEMENT
Claude Vorilhon, a French race car driver known as Rael to his followers, began to attract followers in 1973 as a result of an alleged encounter with extraterrestrials. The Raelians, who claim a worldwide membership of over twenty thousand, have as a key goal building an embassy in Israel for the Elohim, aliens believed actually to have created the original humans.

Susan Palmer, "Woman as 'Playmate' in the Raelian Movement: Power and Pantagamy in a New Religion," *Syzygy: Journal of Alternative Religion and Culture* 1 (1992): 227–45.

RAJNEESH
Bhagwan Shree Rajneesh (1931–1989), as he was known at the peak of his career, was a philosophy professor in India who gathered a following for his radical views on sex, religion, meditation, and other subjects. A community was founded in Poona, India, in 1974; a large center, Rajneeshpuram, was founded in Oregon in 1981. It was dissolved amid great local controversy a few years later.

Barker (3), 201–205.

Vasant Joshi, *The Enlightened One: The Life and Work of Bhagwan Shree Rajneesh* (San Francisco: Harper and Row, 1982).

RAMAKRISHNA MISSION (SEE VEDANTA)

RASTAFARI
The Rastafari emerged in several separate groups in Jamaica following the coronation of Haile Selassie as emperor of Ethiopia in 1930. They believe in a coming repatriation to Africa of blacks in the Americas, and are well known for growing long, matted hair ("dreadlocks") and for their smoking of ganja (marijuana) as a sacrament.

See chapter 29.

REORGANIZED LATTER-DAY SAINTS (SEE LATTER DAY SAINTS)

RIVER BRETHREN
A popular nickname for the Brethren in Christ, a Mennonite denomination.

See chapter 1.

ROSICRUCIANISM
Rosicrucians claim that their movement is not a religion, but their organizations have been major centers of occultism and esotericism. Generally, Rosicrucianism, which bears some resemblance to Theosophy, teaches that the mind, when properly trained, can help the practitioner achieve his or her most important life goals.

Ellwood and Partin (13), 90–93.

RUHANI SATSANG
Kirpal Singh was one of several Sikh leaders to have developed American followings. His work was in the Sant Mat tradition, which focuses on light and sound as avenues of communion with the divine. Singh laid the foundations for the Ruhani Satsang on his first trip to the United States in 1955. Several separate organizations continue his work today.

See chapter 37.

SANTERÍA
One of several Afro-Caribbean religions, santería is grounded in the Yoruba religion of West Africa and developed in Cuba. It achieved its first major strength in the United States after Fidel Castro's revolution of 1959 inspired waves of emigration from Cuba to the United States.

See chapter 28.

SATANISM

Sensational media reports of "satanic crime" and other reported incidents of Satanism to the contrary, serious practicing Satanists are very few in number. They are organized into a handful of groups, including the Church of Satan and the Temple of Set.

See chapter 42.

SATCHIDANANDA ASHRAM (SEE INTEGRAL YOGA)

SATYA SAI BABA

Although he has never visited the United States, Satya Sai Baba has dozens of centers and study groups here. He is probably best known as a wonderworker who is believed to produce various objects from thin air; otherwise his Hindu teachings are conventional. His followers in India are often involved in relief and charitable work. His American following took shape in the 1970s, following lectures on his work by Indra Devi in Santa Barbara in 1967.

Lawrence A. Babb, *Redemptive Encounters: Three Modern Styles in the Hindu Tradition* (Berkeley: University of California Press, 1986).

Ellwood and Partin (13), 212–15.

SCIENTOLOGY

L. Ron Hubbard published his basic text, *Dianetics,* in 1950, and went on to found the Church of Scientology in 1954. The controversial movement seeks to help followers to overcome psychological and physical inadequacies through counseling and technological devices, enabling them to realize their full potential.

See chapter 40.

SELF-REALIZATION FELLOWSHIP

Paramahansa Yogananda was one of the first Indian swamis to teach in the United States, arriving in 1920. The organization he founded has gone on to become one of the largest Hindu-oriented movements with a predominantly Western membership in America. Its practice is centered on a technique called kriya yoga that is revealed only to properly prepared initiates.

See chapter 17.

SEVENTH-DAY ADVENTISTS (SEE ADVENTISM)

SHAKERS

Ann Lee (1736–1784) became involved in a group of English religious enthusiasts and led the group to America in 1774. She was regarded as Christ in the Second Coming by her followers, who lived celibate lives in orderly communal villages. One village still functions at Sabbathday Lake, Maine.

William M. Kephart and William W. Zellner, *Extraordinary Groups: An Examination of Unconventional Life-Styles* 4th ed. (New York: St. Martin's 1991), chapter four.

Stephen J. Stein, *The Shaker Experience in America* (New Haven: Yale University Press, 1992).

SHAMANISM

Shamans are individuals in traditional societies who are believed to have special access to divine (or at least superhuman) power. They can variously be priests, healers, and political leaders. Certain contemporary groups referred to as neoshamanic try to capture the shaman's sense of power and to recreate traditional shamanic rituals.

See chapter 39.

SHILOH

One of many organizations to emerge from the Jesus movement, Shiloh was organized in 1969 as a network of Christian communes. At its peak it had several thousands of members and over fifty community sites. The group was disbanded amid leadership disputes and tax problems in 1979, although a retreat center at the main campus in Oregon operated for some years after that.

Randy Frame, "Oregon Retreat Center Battles the IRS," *Christianity Today,* 3 October 1986.

James T. Richardson, Mary White Stewart, and Robert B. Simmonds, *Organized Miracles: A Study of a Contemporary, Youth, Communal, Fundamentalistic Organization* (New Brunswick, N.J.: Transaction Books, 1979).

SIDDHA YOGA DHAM

Swami Muktananda first visited the United States and established a Siddha Yoga presence in 1970. The movement focuses heavily on the guru-disciple relationship as essential to inner transformation.

See chapter 18.

SNAKE HANDLERS

In 1909 George W. Hensley came to believe that verses from the gospel of Mark concerning the handling of poisonous snakes and the drinking of poison were commandments to the faithful. He began building a loosely organized group of churches dedicated to such practices throughout Appalachia. Despite many snakebites and deaths, the movement continues in a few locations.

Thomas Burton, *Serpent-Handling Believers* (Knoxville: University of Tennessee Press, 1993).

Weston LaBarre, *They Shall Take Up Serpents: Psychology of the Southern Snake-Handling Cult* (New York: Schocken, 1969).

SOCIETY OF BROTHERS (SEE BRUDERHOF)

SOCIETY OF ST. PIUS X

The largest of several groups of Catholics disgruntled with certain facets of the modernization of the church instituted by the Second Vatican Council, the Society of St. Pius X was founded in the 1970s as a result of the work of Archbishop Marcel Lefebvre, who trained and ordained priests in preconciliar fashion.

See chapter 9.

SOKA GAKKAI (SEE NICHIREN SHOSHU)

SPIRITUAL CHURCHES

During the 1920s several small congregations grew up in New Orleans as a result of the work of Mother Leafy Anderson, a onetime Spiritualist. The Spiritual churches feature a belief system that contains elements of Catholicism, Pentecostalism, Spiritualism, and Voodoo. Worship is animated; women constitute a strong majority of members and ministers. Other similar churches have grown up elsewhere, but are more Protestant than Catholic in flavor.

Hans A. Baer, *The Black Spiritual Movement: A Religious Response to Racism* (Knoxville: University of Tennessee Press, 1984).

David C. Estes, "Ritual Validations of Clergywomen's Authority in the African-American Spiritual Churches of New Orleans," in *Women Outside the Mainstream: Female Leaders in Marginal Religions in America,* ed. Catherine Wessinger (Urbana: University of Illinois Press, 1993).

Claude F. Jacobs and Andrew J. Kaslow, *The Spiritual Churches of New Orleans* (Knoxville: University of Tennessee Press, 1991).

SPIRITUALISM

Spiritualism involves belief in various paranormal phenomena, notably communication with the dead or with other entities not currently humanly alive. Its origins as an ongoing American movement are usually traced to the alleged spirit communications received by Kate and Margaret Fox in 1848 at Hydesville, New York.

See chapter 33.

SRI CHINMOY (SEE CHINMOY, SRI)

STOREFRONT CHURCHES

World War I saw a large migration of African Americans from the South to the urban North. Many of the migrants found the existing black churches unappealing, and created new versions of the informal, spontaneous rural churches of the South. The new congregations (typically Holiness, Pentecostal, or Spiritualist in orientation) often rented storefronts as inexpensive church locations.

Gilbert Osofsky, *Harlem: The Making of a Ghetto: Negro New York, 1890–1930* (New York: Harper and Row, 1971), pp. 144–46.

Allan H. Spear, *Black Chicago: The Making of a Negro Ghetto, 1890–1920* (Chicago: University of Chicago Press, 1967), pp. 174–79.

SUBUD

Muhammad Subuh, usually called "Bapak" by his followers, founded Subud in Indonesia in the 1930s and oversaw its spread worldwide in the 1950s. The movement is best known for the *latihan,* in which assembled members spontaneously let an inner spiritual essence pour out through unrestrained sounds and actions. One major center of interest in Subud has been among students of Gurdjieff.

See chapter 25.

SUFISM
Sufism is the mystical and esoteric branch of Islam whose goal is achievement of divine consciousness. Among the tools used on the long and difficult path to spiritual awakening are certain physical exercises, including the group dances for which Sufis are perhaps best known.

See chapter 23.

SUFISM REORIENTED (SEE MEHER BABA)

SUMMIT LIGHTHOUSE (SEE CHURCH UNIVERSAL AND TRIUMPHANT)

SWEDENBORGIANISM
Emmanuel Swedenborg created a new Christian theology in the eighteenth century that had a mystical and spiritualistic outlook. Some regard him as the earliest exponent of what is now known as New Age thinking. Three Swedenborgian denominations are currently active in the United States.

See chapter 7.

TAOISM
Traditionally said to have been founded by Lao Tzu about twenty-five hundred years ago, Taoism teaches mystical attunement with the way of nature. It came to the United States with Chinese immigrants in the nineteenth century; its first highly visible presence in what is now the United States came with the building of a Taoist-Buddhist temple in Hawaii in 1878.

Melton (18), 209, 983–88.

TEMPLE OF LOVE (SEE YAHWEH BEN YAHWEH)

TEMPLE OF SET
Michael Aquino led a group of dissidents out of the Church of Satan to found the Temple of Set in 1975. The movement regards Set, or Satan, not as an evil figure but as one who embodies and makes available to humans an advanced intelligence.

See chapter 42.

TEMPLE OF THE PEOPLE
What was originally the Syracuse chapter of the Theosophical Society eventually separated itself from the main body and, moving across the country, founded a communal village at Halcyon, California, in 1903. Unlike some other branches of Theosophy, the Temple of the People claims to be in continued contact with the Ascended Masters who through mediumistic communications direct the human practitioners of the movement.

See chapter 31.

THELEMIC MAGICK
Ritual magicians have been active in the United States at least since the nineteenth century. The most famous of them was Aleister Crowley, whose creed, "Do as thou wilt," authorized magic suffused with various sexual practices. Many groups of Thelemic magicians have been active in the twentieth century. The Ordo Templi Orientis, in which Crowley was a leader, has been perhaps the most important of the groups.

J. Gordon Melton, "Thelemic Magick in America," in *Alternatives to American Mainline Churches,* ed. Joseph H. Fichter (New York: Rose of Sharon Press, 1983), pp. 67–87.

THEOSOPHY
Theosophy, which incorporates a variety of mystical and esoteric doctrines and ideas, grew out of American spiritualism in the latter nineteenth century, largely as the product of the fertile mind of Helena P. Blavatsky. The Theosophical Society, the first organization to disseminate widely in the West ideas drawn from Asian religions, was organized in New York in 1875; it has since diverged into several branches.

See chapter 31.

THERAVADA BUDDHISM
Theravada is one of the two principal branches of Buddhism (the other being

Mahayana, represented by the other Buddhist groups listed in this appendix). It is conservative, emphasizing monasticism as the fruitful spiritual path, and has its greatest presence in Southeast Asia and Sri Lanka. Many Theravada groups in the United States are mainly ethnic in constituency; the one with the greatest membership among non-Asians is the Dhiravamsa Foundation (formerly the Vipassana Fellowship).

See chapter 16.

3HO (SEE HEALTHY-HAPPY-HOLY ORGANIZATION)

TIBETAN BUDDHISM

Tibetan Buddhism has entered the United States primarily since the settlement here of several spiritual leaders following the invasion of Tibet by China in 1959. Focused on the concept of compassion, Tibetan Buddhism was a totality of theology, ritual, and social structure.

See chapter 16.

TRANSCENDENTAL MEDITATION

Maharishi Mahesh Yogi was one of many Indian spiritual leaders to take Eastern teachings to the West. His system, which is rooted in Indian religious thought and practice but which his American spokespersons claim is purely secular in nature, involves daily meditation following training and initiation.

See chapter 18.

UFO MOVEMENTS

Many Americans claim to have seen, or even to have ridden in, unidentified flying objects. In several cases they claim to have received religious messages from extraterrestrial beings; several religious movements are based on such messages.

See chapter 41.

UNIFICATION CHURCH

Sun Myung Moon founded the Unification Church in Korea in 1954 following revelations he reported having received earlier in life. He is believed by his followers to be Christ in the Second Coming. The movement is probably best known for its mass marriages, many of them interracial, and its ultraconservative political activism.

See chapter 20.

UNITARIANISM

American Unitarianism began to take shape in New England as a reaction to the stern orthodoxy of the Puritans and their descendants. Especially as a result of the influence of the Transcendentalists in the mid-nineteenth century, the movement has moved increasingly in a liberal and humanistic direction, rejecting any standards of doctrine but retaining a commitment to social activism.

See chapter 8.

UNITED LODGE

One of the Theosophical groups, the United Lodge was founded by Robert Crosbie in 1909 in reaction to doctrinal innovations being introduced in most of the other branches of Theosophy.

See chapter 31.

UNITY SCHOOL OF CHRISTIANITY

Unity is one of the most successful of the many branches of the New Thought movement. It came into being in the late 1880s in Kansas City as the result of the work of Myrtle and Charles Fillmore, who stressed faith healing and positive thinking.

See chapter 32.

UNIVERSAL LIFE CHURCH

Kirby Hensley founded this most successful of the mail-order churches in 1962 at Modesto, California. The ULC ordains, by mail, anyone who asks. Several million persons claim ULC ordination. Many other mail-order churches have been founded along similar lines.

Lewis Ashmore, *The Modesto Messiah: The Famous Mail-Order Minister* (Bakersfield: Universal Press, 1977).

UNIVERSALISM

Universalism emerged from Calvinism in the eighteenth century. Its central premise was that a good God would provide salvation to all and damnation to none. Although Universalism and Unitarianism were originally quite distinct, they converged in the twentieth century and finally merged in 1961.

See chapter 8.

URANTIA

The Urantia Book is a collection of alleged revelations from spiritual beings containing a detailed cosmology and an account of the life and work of Jesus. Readers of the book have formed many study groups and publish several periodicals.

See chapter 33.

VEDANTA MOVEMENT

Swami Vivekananda impressed and delighted many Americans with the open and ecumenical version of Hinduism that he presented at the World's Parliament of Religions in Chicago in 1893. Vivekananda's work in America was expanded by other swamis belonging to the Ramakrishna order who established independent Vedanta societies in major American cities.

See chapter 17.

VINEYARD MINISTRY

Several Bible study groups, originally located within the Calvary Chapel in Costa Mesa, California, began to coalesce into churches in the Los Angeles area in the 1970s and then into the Association of Vineyard Churches. This Pentecostal movement experienced substantial growth in the 1980s.

Melton (18), 365.

VIPASSANA FELLOWSHIP OF AMERICA (SEE THERAVADA BUDDHISM)

VOODOO (SEE VODOU)

VODOU

Vodou (sometimes spelled vaudou, vodun, or voodoo) is one of several new religions that grew up among black slaves in the Americas. Such religions represent a fusion of traditional African religions with other religions, most frequently Catholicism. Vodou has had some following in the United States; its most prominent locus today is the Caribbean, especially Haiti.

See chapter 28.

THE WAY

The Way International was founded by Victor Paul Weirwille as the Vesper Chimes radio ministry in 1942. With a constituency centered on college students, it grew rapidly in the 1970s, although later some decline set in. Opponents attacked the group for its alleged heresies (such as denial of the Trinity) and its demand of strong commitment for members. The movement's headquarters is at New Knoxville, Ohio.

Melton (17), 315–22.

WICCA

Wicca is the branch of neo-paganism that claims to be descended from certain pre-Christian religions of Europe. Like other neo-pagan movements, Wicca has tended to have strong feminist and environmental emphases. Wiccans, or witches, emphatically deny that their religion is evil or that it has any satanic elements in it.

See chapter 34.

WORLDWIDE CHURCH OF GOD

Herbert W. Armstrong founded what is now the Worldwide Church of God in 1933. It has become the largest and most influential of the British-Israel groups in the United States.

See chapter 11.

YAHWEH BEN YAHWEH

Hulon Mitchell, Jr., a former professional football player, founded the Temple of Love in 1978, later taking the name by which his movement is best known, Yahweh ben Yahweh (God, the son of God). His movement now claims thousands of followers and large real estate holdings. For some years the movement has been accused of advocating the killing of whites to avenge oppression of blacks; in 1992 Yahweh was convicted of plotting fourteen murders.

"Yahweh Ben Yahweh," *National and International Religion Report* 6 (21 September 1992): 6.

YOGAVILLE (SEE INTEGRAL YOGA)

YOUNG ISRAEL

Founded in 1912 and now numbering more than one hundred congregations, Young

Israel is a version of Orthodox Judaism designed to respond to both American secularity and perceived problems in Jewish self-presentation. Its members reject old-world clothing styles, for example, but hold fast to such traditions as Sabbath observance, study of the Torah and Talmud, and separation of men and women in synagogues.

See chapter 10.

ZEN BUDDHISM

The Zen school of Buddhism has had its largest following in Japan, although it also exists elsewhere in the Buddhist world. Its central goal is the emptying of the mind through meditation; Zen teaches that only when conventional thinking is laid aside may one experience Enlightenment. American contacts with Japan following World War II had much to do with increased American interest in Zen.

See chapter 16.

Bibliography

Each of these works has useful and reliable information on a variety of alternative religions and/or on issues related to the presence of alternative religions in American society. Numbers in the abbreviated items in the bibliographies for individual religious groups, above, refer to the works listed here:

1. Bach, Marcus. *Strange Sects and Curious Cults.* New York: Dodd, Mead, 1961.

2. Barker, Eileen. *New Religious Movements: A Perspective for Understanding Society,* Lewiston, N.Y.: Edwin Mellen, 1982.

3. Barker, Eileen. *New Religious Movements: A Practical Introduction.* London: Her Majesty's Stationery Office, 1989.

4. Barker, Eileen, ed. *Of Gods and Men: New Religious Movements in the West.* Macon, Ga.: Mercer University Press, 1983.

5. Bednarowski, Mary Farrell. *New Religions and the Theological Imagination in America.* Bloomington: Indiana University Press, 1989.

6. Beit-Hallahmi, Benjamin. *The Illustrated Encyclopedia of Active New Religions, Sects, and Cults.* New York: Rosen Publishing Group, 1993.

7. Braden, Charles S. *These Also Believe: A Study of Modern American Cults and Minority Religious Movements.* New York: Macmillan, 1950.

8. Bromley, David G., and Phillip E. Hammond. *The Future of New Religious Movements.* Macon, Ga.: Mercer University Press, 1987.

9. Bromley, David G., and Anson D. Shupe, Jr. *Strange Gods: The Great American Cult Scare.* Boston: Beacon, 1981.

10. Choquette, Diane. *New Religious Movements in the United States and Canada: A Critical Assessment and Annotated Bibliography.* Westport, Conn.: Greenwood, 1985.

11. Clark, Elmer T. *The Small Sects in America.* Rev. ed. Nashville: Abingdon, 1949.

12. Ellwood, Robert S., Jr. *Alternative Altars: Unconventional and Eastern Spirituality in America.* Chicago: University of Chicago Press, 1979.

13. Ellwood, Robert S., Jr., and Harry B. Partin. *Religious and Spiritual Groups in Modern America.* 2d ed. Englewood Cliffs, N.J.: Prentice Hall, 1988.

14. Kephart, William A., and William W. Zellner. *Extraordinary Groups: An Examination of Unconventional Life-Styles.* 5th ed. New York: St. Martin's, 1994.

15. Kerr, Howard, and Charles L. Crow, eds. *The Occult in America: New Historical Perspectives.* Urbana: University of Illinois Press, 1983.

16. Mead, Frank S., and Samuel S. Hill. *Handbook of Denominations in the United States.* 9th ed. Nashville: Abingdon, 1990.

17. Melton, J. Gordon. *Encyclopedic Handbook of Cults in America.* 2d ed. New York: Garland, 1992.

18. Melton, J. Gordon. *The Encyclopedia of American Religions.* 4th ed. Detroit: Gale Research, 1993.

19. Miller, Timothy, ed. *When Prophets Die: The Postcharismatic Fate of New Religious Movements.* Albany: State University of New York Press, 1991.

20. Needleman, Jacob. *The New Religions.* New York: Doubleday, 1970.

21. Needleman, Jacob, and George Baker, eds. *Understanding the New Religions.* New York: Seabury Press, 1978.

22. Robbins, Thomas. *Cults, Converts, and Charisma: The Sociology of New Religious Movements.* Beverly Hills: Sage Publications, 1988.

23. Robbins, Thomas, and Dick Anthony. *In Gods We Trust: New Patterns of Religious Pluralism.* 2d ed. New Brunswick, N.J.: Transaction, 1990.

24. Saliba, John. *Social Science and the Cults: An Annotated Bibliography.* New York: Garland, 1990.

25. Shepherd, William C. *To Secure the Blessings of Liberty: American Constitutional Law and the New Religious Movements.* New York: Crossroad Publishing and Scholars Press, 1985.

Appendix II

CHRONOLOGY OF ALTERNATIVE RELIGIONS IN AMERICA (AMERICAN FOUNDING DATES PLUS A FEW OTHER MAJOR EVENTS)

1620   Dissenting Puritans begin to arrive in New England

1656   Quakers arrive in Boston and are thrown in jail

1663   Plockhoy's Commonwealth, first post-Native American religious commune in America, founded in Delaware

1683   Mennonite colony founded at Germantown, Pennsylvania

1694   Society of the Woman in the Wilderness, a communal group based on radical Pietism, founded in Pennsylvania

1727   The first Amish arrive in the United States

1732   Ephrata Cloister founded by German Pietists in Lancaster County, Pennsylvania

1766   Thomas Webb preaches America's first Holiness sermon

1774   Shakers arrive in the United States under Ann Lee

1784   James Glen lectures on Swedenborgianism in Philadelphia

1788   Jerusalem community founded by Jemima Wilkinson in Yates County, New York

1790   First national convention of Universalists meets in Philadelphia

1805   Harmony Society established by George Rapp at Harmony, Pennsylvania

1817   Society of Separatists opens communal village at Zoar, Ohio

1825   American Unitarian Association organized

1830   Church of Jesus Christ of Latter-day Saints (Mormons) founded at Palmyra, New York

       Approximate date of the burgeoning of Mesmerism in the United States

       Marie Laveau generally recognized as a voodoo leader in New Orleans

1831   William Miller begins preaching that the world will end "about 1843"; beginning of Adventist movement

1838   Phineas P. Quimby begins to experiment with hypnotism and faith healing, work that eventually led to the New Thought movement

1843   Ebenezer Community founded by the Society of True Inspiration near Buffalo, New York

1844   Assassination of Joseph Smith, Jr., divides Mormons and leads to departure of largest group to Utah

October 22 William Miller's final date for the end of the world; thereafter known as the "Great Disappointment"

Bethel Colony founded in Missouri by William Keil

1846   Bishop Hill Colony founded by dissident Swedish Lutherans in Illinois

1848   Fox sisters hear "rappings"; Spiritualism begins

1851   Mountain Cove community founded by the Spiritualist Thomas Lake Harris

1852   Church of Christ (Temple Lot) begins activity when members reject Mormon polygamy

Celestia Community of Adventists founded in Sullivan County, Pennsylvania

1855   Ebenezer Community moves to Iowa and founds the Amana Colonies

1856   Aurora Colony founded in Oregon as offshoot of Bethel Colony

1860   Seventh-Day Adventists founded by Ellen White

Reorganized Church of Jesus Christ of Latter Day Saints founded under Joseph Smith III

1868   First modern American Rosicrucian group founded by P. B. Randolph

1874   Hutterites begin to arrive in South Dakota

1875   Founding of the Theosophical Society by Helena P. Blavatsky and Henry S. Olcott

Publication of Christian Science textbook, *Science and Health with Key to the Scriptures,* by Mary Baker Eddy

1876   Ethical Culture Society founded in New York by Felix Adler

1878   Taoist temple begun in Honlolulu by Leong Dick Ying

1879   Church of Christ, Scientist, founded by Mary Baker Eddy

First publication of the *Watchtower,* marking the beginning of the Jehovah's Witnesses

1881   First of a series of Brethren schisms establishing the Old German Baptist Brethren, or Dunkards, as a separate denomination

1887   M. M. Eshelman publishes the first American book promoting the British-Israel theory

1888   Order of the Golden Dawn founded by a group of Masons and Rosicrucians

1890   Peak of the Sioux Ghost Dance movement, based on visions of the Indian prophet Wovoka

1891   Unity School of Christianity founded by Myrtle and Charles Fillmore

1892   International Divine Science Federation established by Nona Brooks

Joseph Rene Vilatte consecrated first Old Catholic bishop for the United States

1893   Chicago World's Fair and World Parliament of Religions: Swami Vivekananda's work leads to the founding of the Vedanta movement in America; Soyen Shaku becomes the first Zen monk to visit the U.S.; Dharmapala, a representative from Ceylon, attracts American attention to Buddhism

1894   Bahá'í Faith introduced to the United States by Ibrahim Kheirella

1896   William Saunders Crowdy founds Church of God and Saints of Christ, the first black Jewish group, in Lawrence, Kansas

1897   Theosophical community founded at Point Loma, near San Diego, by Katherine Tingley

1899   Doukhobors begin emigration from Russia to Canada

1901   Pentecostalism begins with the work of Charles F. Parham in Topeka, Kansas

Molokans begin emigration from Russia to the United States

1903 Temple of the People, a branch of the Theosophical movement, founded at Halcyon, California

1906 Azusa Street Revival sparks worldwide spread of Pentecostalism

1909 George W. Hensley begins to organize revivals and churches featuring snake handling

Thelemic Magick and the Ordo Templi Orientis introduced to the United States by Charles Stansfeld Jones

Robert Crosbie founds United Lodge, a branch of Theosophy

1910 Sufism introduced to the United States by Pir Hazrat Inayat Khan

1912 Young Israel founded by a group of young Orthodox Jews in New York

1913 Moorish Science Temple founded by Noble Drew Ali (Timothy Drew) in Newark, New Jersey

1914 Date predicted for end of the world by Jehovah's Witnesses

1914–1918 Migration of rural African Americans to the urban North during World War I leads to the rise of storefront churches

1916 Consecration of Charles W. Leadbeater as Old Catholic bishop leads to the formation of the Liberal Catholic Church

1918 Native American Church incorporated in Oklahoma through the efforts of James Mooney

1919 Father Divine purchases communal home in Sayville, Long Island

1920 Builders of the Adytum founded by Paul Foster Case

Swami Yogananda arrives in the United States; Self-Realization Fellowship eventually emerges from his work

Mother Leafy Anderson begins work in New Orleans that leads to the founding of the Spiritual churches

1923 Arcane School (a derivative of Theosophy) founded by Alice Bailey

1924 George I. Gurdjieff makes his first journey to the United States

1925 Introduction of Anthroposophy to the United States

Charles ("Daddy") Grace founds United House of Prayer for All People

1927 Religious Science movement founded by Ernest Holmes

1928 Gnostic Society founded by James Morgan Pryce

1929 Frank B. Robinson begins advertising campaign that creates the mail-order religion Psychiana

1930 Beginnings of Nation of Islam with teaching of W. D. Fard (or Farrad) in Detroit

Coronation of Haile Selassie as emperor of Ethiopia fosters development of Rastafarianism

1931 Association for Research and Enlightenment founded by Edgar Cayce

Meher Baba makes first trip to the United States

1932 Emissaries of Divine Light founded by Lloyd Meeker

1933 Herbert W. Armstrong founds ministry later known as Radio Church of God, and eventually Worldwide Church of God

1934 Guy and Edna Ballard begin public teaching of I Am concepts

1935 Victor T. Houteff founds the first Davidian Seventh-Day Adventist colony near Waco, Texas

1940 Rebbe Joseph Isaac Schneersohn arrives in New York with the Lubavitcher Hasidim, inaugurating the era of Hasidic growth in America

1942 The Way founded (as "Vesper Chimes") by Victor Paul Weirwille

1944   Des Moines University of Lawsonomy founded by Alfred W. Lawson; its chapel was the first Lawsonian church

1950   First publication of *Dianetics,* the basic textbook for Scientology

1952   Local Church movement established in the United States

1954   Publication of *Witchcraft Today* by Gerald Gardner sparks growth of neo-paganism and witchcraft

1955   *Urantia Book* published for general circulation

      Wings of Deliverance (later Peoples Temple) founded in Indianapolis by Jim Jones

      Kirpal Singh makes first visit to the United States, boosting the work of the newly established Ruhani Satsang

1956   Aetherius Society founded by George King

      Opening of the Islamic Center in Washington makes Islam widely known in the United States for the first time

1958   Summit Lighthouse (later known as the Church Universal and Triumphant) founded by Mark Prophet

1959   Muhammad Subuh ("Bapak") visits the United States; Subud finds its early followers among students of Gurdjieff

      Beginnings of the Unification Church in America with the arrival of Young Oon Kim at the University of Oregon

      Maharishi Mahesh Yogi introduces Transcendental Meditation to the United States

      Cuban revolution ignites outmigration that takes many santería practitioners and leaders to the United States

      Chinese invasion of Tibet causes exiled Tibetan Buddhist leaders to flee to the West

      Stephan Hoeller becomes active in Gnosticism; his work leads to the founding of the Ecclesia Gnostica

1960   Episcopal priest Dennis Barrett announces Pentecostal experiences, inaugurating the charismatic movement

      Masayasu Sadanaga moves to the United States to organize Nichiren Shoshu

      Yogi Amrit Desai moves to the United States to study art; later founds the Kripalu Yoga movement

1961   Unitarians and Universalists merge

1962–1965   Second Vatican Council; Catholic Traditionalists begin to resist church reforms instigated by the council

1962   Universal Life Church founded by Kirby Hensley

1963   Process Church of the Final Judgement founded by Robert de Grimston

      Jane Roberts begins to receive messages from the entity Seth, revitalizing spiritualism in a form that comes to be called "channeling"

1964   Neo-American Church organized by Art Kleps

      Old Believers immigrate into the United States, settling in Oregon and Alaska

      Sri Chinmoy moves to the United States

1965   Beginnings of the International Society for Krishna Consciousness with the arrival of A. C. Swami Bhaktivedanta in the United States

      ECKANKAR founded by Paul Twitchell in San Diego

1966   Church of Satan founded by Anton LaVey

      Swami Satchidananda visits the United States and founds the Integral Yoga Institute

Beginning of charismatic work by Hobart Freeman that leads to the founding of Faith Assembly

1967 Approximate date of the beginning of the Jesus movement in California

Indra Devi's lectures in California launch the organized movement of followers of Satya Sai Baba

1968 Metropolitan Community Church founded by Troy Perry

David Berg begins coffeehouse ministry that becomes the Children of God (later the Family)

Holy Order of MANS founded by Earl Blighton in San Francisco

First Havurah commune established in Somerville, Massachusetts

1969 Healthy-Happy-Holy Organization founded by Yogi Bhajan

Ananda Marga Yoga Society established in the U.S.

Church of Armageddon ("Love Israel Family") founded in Washington state by Paul Erdmann ("Love Israel")

Tarthang Tulku, a Tibetan Buddhist lama, arrives in San Francisco and establishes the Tibetan Nyingma Meditation Center

Shiloh movement of Christian communes organized in Oregon

1970 Bear Tribe initially organized by Sun Bear

Church of the New Song founded at Atlanta federal penitentiary by prisoner Harry W. Theriault

Community of Jesus founded by Cay Andersen and Judy Sorensen in Massachusetts

Free Daist Communion founded by Franklin Jones, later known as Heart-Master Da Love Ananda

New Age movement begins to coalesce as a distinctive religious and philosophical school of thought

Swami Muktananda makes first visit to the United States; his

followers are later organized as Siddha Yoga Dham of America

Swami Rama makes first visit to United States; Himalayan Institute is founded the following year

Chogyam Trungpa, a Tibetan Buddhist lama, arrives in the United States and begins establishing meditation centers

1971 The Farm founded at Summertown, Tennessee

Arica Institute founded by Oscar Ichazo

First deprogramming conducted by Ted Patrick in San Diego

Werner Erhard holds first Erhard Seminars Training (est) sessions in San Francisco

Meditation Mount opened at Ojai, California, as Full Moon Meditation Group center

Kerista organized in San Francisco by John Presmont ("Brother Jud") and Eve Furchgott ("Even Eve")

Guru Maharaj Ji arrives in the United States, founding the American branch of the Divine Light Mission

Bawa Muhaiyaddeen Fellowship founded

1972 Organized anticult groups begin to appear

Ezrat Nashim begins its advocacy of full equality for women in Judaism

Maranatha movement organized by Bob Weiner

Jesus People U.S.A. founded in Chicago

1973 Raelian movement founded by Claude Vorilhon

1974 Citizens' Freedom Foundation, precursor to the Cult Awareness Network, founded as a more broadly focused version of FREECOG (Free Our Children from the Children of God)

1975   Temple of Set founded by Michael Aquino and other dissidents from the Church of Satan

Swami Satchidananda founds order of Sannyasins (monks)

1976   Sun Bear establishes Vision Mountain Center near Spokane as headquarters for the Bear Tribe Medicine Society

Alamo Foundation founds community in Arkansas

1977   Brahma Kumaris World Spiritual University opens first U.S. center

1978   Garner Ted Armstrong founds Church of God International

Mass suicides at Peoples Temple outpost in Jonestown, Guyana

Temple of Love founded by Hulon Mitchell, Jr., later known as Yahweh ben Yahweh

1979   Kip McKean founds Boston Church of Christ movement

1981   Followers of Bhagwan Shree Rajneesh purchase ranch in Oregon that becomes the community of Rajneeshpuram

Church Universal and Triumphant buys Royal Teton Ranch for religious community near Corwin Springs, Montana

1986   Association of Vineyard Churches organized in the Los Angeles area under the leadership of John Wimber

1993   Fiery deaths of some eighty Branch Davidians near Waco, Texas, following fifty-one-day standoff with federal agents

Contributors

Susan Ainsley is a graduate student in sociology and anthropology at Virginia Commonwealth University.

Margaret Hope Bacon is the author of several books, including *The Quiet Rebels: The Story of the Quakers in America.*

George Baker is the co-editor of *Understanding the New Religions* and an independent scholar in Berkeley, California.

Eileen Barker is Professor of Sociology of Religion at the London School of Economics and the author of many books, including *New Religious Movements: A Practical Introduction.*

Albert Bates is an attorney and environmental activist with the Natural Rights Center, the Farm, Summertown, Tennessee.

Mary Farrell Bednarowski is Professor of Religious Studies at the United Theological Seminary of the Twin Cities and author of *New Religions and the Theological Imagination in America,* among other works.

Jerry Bergman is a member of the faculty at Northwest State College and author of *Jehovah's Witnesses and Kindred Groups: A Historical Compendium and Bibliography.*

S. Daniel Breslauer is Professor of Religious Studies at the University of Kansas and the author of many books, including *Covenant and Community in Modern Judaism.*

David G. Bromley is Professor of Sociology at Virginia Commonwealth University and co-editor of *The Satanism Scare.*

Barry Chevannes is Lecturer in Sociology and Social Work at the University of the West Indies.

William Dinges is Associate Professor of Religion and Religious Education at the Catholic University of America.

Walter Driscoll is the author of *Gurdjieff, An Annotated Bibliography* and an independent scholar in Vancouver.

Donald F. Durnbaugh is Carl W. Zeigler Professor of History and Religion at Elizabethtown College, the author of many books and articles, and the editor of *The Brethren Encyclopedia.*

Robert S. Ellwood is Professor of Religion at the University of Southern California and the author of many books and articles, including *Alternative Altars: Unconventional and Eastern Spirituality in America.*

John R. Hall is Professor of Sociology at the University of California, Davis, and the author of *Gone from the Promised Land: Jonestown in American Cultural History.*

Gail Harley is a member of the faculty at the University of South Florida.

Jane Hurst is Professor of Philosophy and Religion at Gallaudet University and the author of *The Nichiren Shoshu and Soka Gakkai in America: The Ethos of a New Religious Movement.*

William L. Ingram is a graduate student in American Studies at the University of Kansas.

Charles Edwin Jones is the author of several books, including *A Guide to the Study of the Holiness Movement* and *A Guide to the Study of the Pentecostal Movement.*

James R. Lewis is Director of the Association of the World Academics for Religious Awareness and the author of many books and articles.

Phillip Lucas is Assistant Professor in the Department of Religion at Stetson University and the author of *The Odyssey of a New Religion: The Holy Order of MANS from New Age to Orthodoxy.*

Carol Matthews is a graduate student in Religious Studies at the University of Kansas.

J. Gordon Melton is Director of the Institute for the Study of American Religion and the author and editor of many books, including *The Encyclopedia of American Religions.*

Timothy Miller is Associate Professor of Religious Studies at the University of Kansas and the editor of *When Prophets Die: The Postcharismatic Fate of New Religious Movements,* among other works.

Joseph M. Murphy is Associate Professor of Theology at Georgetown University and the author of *Santería: An African Religion in America.*

Mason Olds is Professor of Religion and Philosophy at Springfield College, the author of three books and many articles, and editor of the journal *religious humanism.*

Roger E. Olson is Professor of Theology at Bethel College and Seminary.

Russell Paden is a graduate student in Religious Studies at the University of Kansas.

E. Burke Rochford, Jr., is Associate Professor of Sociology and Anthropology at Middlebury College and the author of *Hare Krishna in America.*

Steven L. Shields is the author of several books on the Latter Day Saint movement, a minister in Southern California, and a student in the Graduate School of Religion at Park College.

Anson Shupe is Professor of Sociology at Indiana University–Purdue University at Fort Wayne and the author of many

books and articles, including, with David G. Bromley, *The New Vigilantes: Deprogrammers, Anti-Cultists, and the New Religions.*

Edward D. Silver is a graduate student in Religious Studies at the University of Virginia.

John K. Simmons is Associate Professor of Philosophy and Religious Studies at Western Illinois University.

Robert H. Stockman is an instructor in Religious Studies at DePaul University and Director of the Bahá'í Research Office, as well as the author of *The Bahá'í Faith in America: Origins, 1892–1900.*

Eugene Taylor is Lecturer in Psychiatry at Harvard University.

Gene R. Thursby is Professor of Religious Studies at the University of Florida.

Shawn Michael Trimble is a graduate student in Religious Studies at the University of Kansas.

David E. Van Zandt is Professor of Law at Northwestern University and the author of *Living in the Children of God.*

Gisela Webb is a member of the faculty in Religious Studies at Seton Hall University.

Robert Weisbrot is Professor of History at Colby College and author of *Father Divine and the Struggle for Racial Equality.*

Catherine Wessinger is Associate Professor of Religious Studies at Loyola University, New Orleans, and the author of *Annie Besant and Progressive Messianism.*

INDEX